Sexuality and the Sacred

SECOND EDITION

Sexuality and the Sacred

Sources for Theological Reflection

SECOND EDITION

Edited by

MARVIN M. ELLISON and
KELLY BROWN DOUGLAS

WESTMINSTER
JOHN KNOX PRESS
LOUISVILLE · KENTUCKY

Second edition
Published by Westminster John Knox Press
Louisville, Kentucky

10 11 12 13 14 15 16 17 18 19—10 9 8 7 6 5 4 3 2 1

Except as otherwise indicated, Scripture quotations are from the New Revised Standard Version of the Bible, copyright © 1989 by the Division of Christian Education of the National Council of the Churches of Christ in the U.S.A., and are used by permission.

Other versions cited as identified: KJV, King James Version; NIV, New International Version; RSV, Revised Standard Version.

See acknowledgments, pp. 437–39, for additional permission information.

Book design by Publishers' WorkGroup
Cover design by Eric Walljasper, Minneapolis, MN
Cover illustration: Kupka, Frantisek (1871–1957) © ARS, NY; The Philadelphia Museum of Art/Art Resource, NY

Library of Congress Cataloging-in-Publication Data

Sexuality and the sacred : sources for theological reflection / edited by Marvin M. Ellison and Kelly Brown Douglas. — 2nd ed.
    p. cm.
    Previous ed. edited by James B. Nelson and Sandra P. Longfellow.
    Includes bibliographical references.
    ISBN 978-0-664-23366-2 (alk. paper)
    1. Sex—Religious aspects—Christianity.   I. Ellison, Marvin Mahan.   II. Douglas, Kelly Brown.
    BT708.S4797 2010
    233'.5—dc22

                                                                    2010017844

PRINTED IN THE UNITED STATES OF AMERICA

For
Elizabeth and Bob
and
Rhonda and Averill,
Healers of a Broken World

Contents

Part 2: *Sexuality and Spirituality*

Part 3: *Gender, Race, and Sexual Identities*

List of Contributors

REBECCA T. ALPERT is associate professor in the Departments of Religion and Women's Studies at Temple University. She is the author of *Exploring Judaism: A Reconstructionist Approach* and *Like Bread on the Seder Plate: Jewish Lesbians and the Transformation of Tradition*.

KATIE GENEVA CANNON, Annie Scales Rogers Professor of Christian Ethics at Union Presbyterian Seminary, is the author of *Teaching Preaching: Isaac Rufus Clark and Black Sacred Rhetoric* and *Katie's Canon: Womanism and the Soul of the Black Community*.

PATRICK S. CHENG is assistant professor of historical and systematic theology at the Episcopal Divinity School in Cambridge, Massachusetts. He is currently writing a book tentatively titled *Radical Love: An Introduction to Queer Theology*.

MIGUEL A. DE LA TORRE is professor of social ethics at the Iliff School of Theology and author of *A Lily among the Thorns: Imagining a New Christian Sexuality* and *Out of the Shadows, Into the Light: Christianity and Homosexuality*.

KELLY BROWN DOUGLAS is Elizabeth Connolly Todd Distinguished Professor of Religion at Goucher College in Baltimore. Her books include *The Black Christ*, *Sexuality and the Black Church*, and *What's Faith Got to Do with It? Black Bodies/Christian Souls*.

MARVIN M. ELLISON teaches Christian ethics at Bangor Theological Seminary and co-convenes the Religious Coalition Against Discrimination. He is author of *Erotic Justice: A Liberating Ethic of Sexuality* and *Same-Sex Marriage? A Christian Ethical Analysis*.

CHRISTINE E. GUDORF, professor and chair of the Department of Religious Studies at Florida International University, has published in a number of areas of ethics, especially in sex/gender theory and environmental ethics. Her writings include the second edition of *Boundaries: A Casebook in Environmental Ethics*, coedited with James Huchingson.

W. SCOTT HALDEMAN, associate professor of worship at the Chicago Theological Seminary, is the author of *Towards Liturgies That Reconcile: Race and Ritual among African-American and European-American Protestants*.

BEVERLY WILDUNG HARRISON is Carolyn Beaird Professor Emerita of Christian Ethics, Union Theological Seminary, and author of *Justice in the Making: Feminist Social Ethics*.

CARTER HEYWARD is the Howard Chandler Robbins Professor Emerita of Theology, Episcopal Divinity School, and author of *Touching Our Strength: The Erotic as Power and the Love of God* and *Flying Changes: Horses as Spiritual Teachers*.

DWIGHT N. HOPKINS is professor of theology at the University of Chicago Divinity School and author of *Being Human: Race, Culture, and Religion* and *Shoes That Fit Our Feet: Sources for a Constructive Black Theology*.

MARY E. HUNT is cofounder and codirector of the Women's Alliance for Theology, Ethics and Ritual (WATER) and editor of *A Guide for Women in Religion: Making Your Way from A to Z*.

GRACE M. JANTZEN, deceased, was affiliated with the Centre for Religion, Culture, and Gender, Department of Religions and Theology, University of Manchester, United Kingdom.

YOEL H. KAHN, PhD, is rabbi of Congregation Beth El, Berkeley, California. His writings include *The Three Blessings*, a history of Jewish prayer.

FRANCES KISSLING, for twenty-five years president of Catholics for Choice, is a visiting scholar in the Center for Bioethics at the University of Pennsylvania and a columnist for Salon.com.

KWOK PUI-LAN is William F. Cole Professor of Christian Theology and Spirituality at the Episcopal Divinity School in Cambridge, Massachusetts. She is the author of *Postcolonial Imagination and Feminist Theology* and editor of *Women and Christianity* in four volumes.

KAREN LEBACQZ, Robert Gordon Sproul Professor Emerita of Theological Ethics, Pacific School of Religion, and former bioethicist in residence, Yale University, is coauthor of *Sacred Cells? Why Christians Should Support Stem Cell Research*.

AUDRE LORDE, deceased, was an African American poet, essayist, and activist who lived in New York City and St. Croix, U.S. Virgin Islands.

DANIEL C. MAGUIRE, professor of ethics at Marquette University, is author of *Ethics: A Complete Method for Moral Choice*. He is a past president of the Society of Christian Ethics and president of the Religious Consultation on Population, Reproductive Health, and Ethics.

DALE B. MARTIN is Woolsey Professor of Religious Studies at Yale University and the author of *Sex and the Single Savior: Gender and Sexuality in Biblical Interpretation*.

JAMES B. NELSON, professor emeritus of Christian ethics, United Theological Seminary of the Twin Cities, is author of *Thirst: God and the Alcoholic Experience*. Along with Sandra P. Longfellow, he edited the first edition of *Sexuality and the Sacred* for Westminster John Knox Press.

JUDITH PLASKOW, a Jewish feminist theologian, is professor of religious studies at Manhattan College and past president of the American Academy of Religion. Cofounder and for ten years coeditor of the *Journal of Feminist Studies in Religion*, she is author of *Standing Again at Sinai: Judaism from a Feminist Perspective* and *The Coming of Lilith: Essays on Feminism, Judaism, and Sexual Ethics, 1972–2003*.

CHRISTIAN SCHAREN teaches worship and theology at Luther Seminary in St. Paul. He is currently writing a book titled *Broken Hallelujah: Imagination, Pop Culture, and God*.

LAUREL C. SCHNEIDER is professor of theology, ethics, and culture at Chicago Theological Seminary. Her most recent publications include *Beyond Monotheism: A Theology of Multiplicity* and "Promiscuous Incarnation" in *The Embrace of Eros: Bodies, Desires, and Sexuality in Christianity*.

KEN STONE is academic dean and professor of Bible, culture, and hermeneutics at Chicago Theological Seminary. He is the author of *Practicing Safer Texts: Food, Sex, and Bible in Queer Perspective* and *Sex, Honor, and Power in the Deuteronomistic History* and editor of *Queer Commentary and the Hebrew Bible*.

ELIZABETH STUART, University of Winchester, United Kingdom, is author of ten books and numerous papers on theology and sexuality and pro vice-chancellor of the University of Winchester.

Foreword

When the late Stephanie Egnotovich, superb executive editor at Westminster John Knox Press, contacted me about revising Sandra Longfellow's and my *Sexuality and the Sacred*, I was enormously pleased that our anthology might have new and continuing life. However, other commitments prevented my involvement in the process. To my great delight, two well-published and highly regarded sexual theologians, Marvin M. Ellison and Kelly Brown Douglas, accepted Stephanie's invitation.

The new editors have retained some of the essays that have enduring value. They have also retained some of the seasoned authors from the first volume, but now with fresh essays from them. And they have added some exciting new writers and pieces. A comparison of the tables of contents of the two editions reveals the movement in the field. For example, our original section title "Gender and Orientation" is now "Gender, Race, and Sexual Identities," fittingly more inclusive of sexual and racial realities. Also, the new editors have given needed attention to transgender identities, queer theology, sexual health and bodily integrity, and reproductive ethics and the status of the fetus.

Perhaps the most striking change is the new focus for the final section, "A Test Case for the Church." Fifteen years ago we named that test case "Sexual Orientation," noting that not since the mid-nineteenth century's slavery debates have the churches been consumed by such a heated and divisive issue. Unfortunately, there is still some truth to that observation. It is also true, however, that in the intervening years—in spite of secessionist threats—several major denominations have achieved significant and official movement toward sexual inclusiveness. This volume's new "Test Case" is Marriage Equality. Fittingly so. As of this writing, seven countries and a half dozen U.S. states have now legalized same-sex marriage. While attempts to overturn those actions continue, it is clear that the civil order has moved faster than most religious bodies have dared. It is also clear that much theological and ecclesiastical work remains to be done, and this new section contributes significantly to that task. I am pleased that Marvin Ellison's essay "Marriage in a New Key" is included, for his book of several years ago *Same-sex Marriage? A Christian Ethical Analysis* was groundbreaking.

Returning to the volume as a whole, as in the first edition, Ellison and Douglas make no attempt to include all religious viewpoints. They eschew those long-established parts of the Christian scene that reduce sexuality to genital sex and then treat it as incidental or antithetical to our spirituality. This volume also reflects our earlier conviction that doing sexual theology is different from applying theology to sexuality issues. No longer can we assume that faith has received its truth quite independently of our body experience. No longer can we assume that true religion provides the instruction book that comes with the body appliance, typically saying "Caution! Read Carefully before Operating!" No longer can we assume (as historically male theologians usually have) that the arena of theology is mind and spirit, far different from and removed from the inferior and suspect body. Clearly, no longer can we assume that spirituality is a disembodied state.

Thus, this volume like the first depicts human sexuality as far broader, richer, and more fundamental to our human identities than simply genital sex. It embraces our embodied ways of being in the world, blessed by our Creator and intended to be fully integrated into our spirituality. This volume likewise sees our sexuality as such a source of vulnerability that it is constantly open to distortion, violation, and violence. And the editors fully grasp that sexuality is inevitably social, invariably political, and that the church (for good and ill) is always a sexual community. I celebrate the ways in which this volume continues—with important new insights—the work of incarnationalist, embodied theologies and ethics of sexual justice.

I end with a personal note, hoping to illustrate our continuing need to expand and deepen our sexual theologies into all of the common places of our living and dying. Because of my own circumstances, more than ever before I feel the urgency for dealing with aging persons (whose sexuality is routinely ignored or trivialized by culture, medicine, and church) and persons living with disabilities (an issue rightly addressed in this volume). To these issues I add sexuality and the dying process, a topic seldom addressed.

It is now less than three months since my wife, Wilys Claire, died. She had been my companion, closest friend, and life-giving lover through fifty-six years of marriage. In spite of a lengthy and physically ravaging illness, in spite of increasing and unremitting pain that often surely made her body feel like the enemy, in spite of relentless weight loss, Wilys Claire was to me an utterly beautiful, sensuous, vibrant person to the end. When genital sex became too painful in her last eight months, we continued to share our bodily desires for intimacy in other ways.

Love poetry became an important part of our morning readings, with Pablo Neruda's sonnets our favorites. We cherished bathing each other tenderly in our shared morning showers. The intimacy of evening foot massages and bedtime caressing were anticipated parts of our ritual. All such expressions were living testimonies that our sexuality does not leave us when genital expression becomes impossible. Our sexuality, after all, embraces the whole range of our desires as embodied beings for loving communion. Indeed, such yearnings can be heightened during the dying process.

Before sunrise on Wilys Claire's last morning, I was beside her bed, keeping vigil in the inpatient hospice unit. Unconscious for several days, now her breathing began to change. The nurse came, examined her, and confirmed my suspicion, saying, "It won't be long now." Then the nurse added some of the most gracious and holy words I have ever heard: "Would you like to get in bed with Wilys Claire?" She left and quietly shut the door. For the last thirty minutes of my beloved's life, I was in bed, holding her in close embrace, nestled together, skin touching skin. As her life ebbed, I whispered words of faith, hope, and love—including her favorite phrases from Dame Julian of Norwich: "And all shall be well, all manner of thing shall be well." Our last moments together were a profound embodied intimacy, surely expressing the reaches of this book's title, *Sexuality and the Sacred*. I can only hope that Wilys Claire experienced those moments in some way, at some mysterious subconscious level. I know it was a gift that I will forever treasure.

In faithfulness to the One who has given us our embodied life, we must dare to speak openly and personally of our deepest reunions of body and spirit—in both sickness and in health, in dying as in living. Then we will be able to reflect theologically on their meanings. Such is the unceasing work of sexual theology. I rejoice that this impressive new volume continues and expands the task, and I celebrate this splendid achievement of Marvin Ellison and Kelly Brown Douglas.

James B. Nelson
October 2009

Introduction

This collection of nearly three dozen essays, written by some Jewish but for the most part Christian theologians, offers good news about sexuality and spirituality. We agree wholeheartedly with how the editors of the first edition put this matter: "First, sexuality is a far more comprehensive matter, broader, richer, and more fundamental to our human existence than simply genital sex. And second, our sexuality is intended by God to be neither incidental to nor detrimental to our spirituality, but rather a fully integrated and basic dimension of that spirituality."[1] *Sexuality*, "the physiological and emotional grounding of our capacities to love," is intimately connected with *spirituality*, "the response of our whole being to what we perceive as the sacred in our midst."[2] A denominational study titled "Keeping Body and Soul Together: Sexuality, Spirituality, and Social Justice" expresses the conviction this way: "No affirmation [is] more important than our belief that the God of Abraham and Sarah is a gracious God, *delighting in our sexuality* and calling us to wholeness in community."[3]

Alas, however, this sex-positive view has not prevailed in the history of Christendom. Protestant theologian John Cobb correctly points out that, in a post-Freudian era, "most Christians acknowledge that humans are sexual beings and that the desire for sexual contact with others is natural and inevitable."[4] Meanwhile, fierce debate continues over whether sexual expression should be limited to heterosexual (and procreative) marriage and how the church should respond to sexually active single persons, including gay, lesbian, and bisexual persons. Too often transgender persons are not even on the ecclesiastical radar. Dealing with these matters is complicated by the fact that the dominant Christian tradition reflects a long-standing negativity toward sexuality, reinforced over the centuries by two interlocking dualisms. The body-spirit or spiritualistic dualism elevates the superior spirit over the inferior body, which must be disciplined and kept under control. A male-female or gender dualism reflects a patriarchal hierarchy of value, status, and power in which good order requires male control of women's lives, including their procreative power. Under the influence of these twin dualisms, Christianity has never fully debunked the troubling notion that sex is unclean and should be avoided or, at least, restricted as a necessary evil.

In a culture strongly influenced by Christian norms about sex, women, and the body, sex is, as cultural theorist Gayle Rubin observes, "presumed guilty until proven innocent." It is cast perennially as a "problem" to be treated with suspicion and "burdened with an excess of significance."[5] That's the bad news. The good news is that a seismic earthquake, an extensive process of critical reflection and renewal, is currently underway within Christianity and other traditions, seeking nothing less than to reverse the sex-negative and patriarchal legacy that distorts sexuality and inhibits spiritual vitality for so many. There is nothing modest in this theological agenda!

The essays that follow reflect this process of theological critique and reconstruction in moving toward theologies and life practices that are sex-positive, women-friendly, and gay-affirming. Theologically, their prevailing sentiment resonates deeply with the central affirmation of the Religious Declaration on Sexual Morality, Justice, and Healing: "Our faith traditions celebrate the goodness of creation, including our bodies and our sexuality. We sin when this sacred gift is abused or exploited. However, the great promise of our traditions is love, healing, and restored relationships."[6] Our colleague Daniel Maguire sums up the challenge and the promise of this project by speaking of religious traditions as "symbolic powerhouses" that are at the same time "flawed classics" in need of ongoing moral scrutiny. We hope that the theological scholarship represented in this volume will help communal efforts to reclaim the "renewable moral energies" of our traditions, not only for the healing of women and men, but also for "the healing of the religions themselves."[7]

This vision toward healing has informed our selection of essays for this volume. We were presented with a vast richness of essays from which to select, a richness that speaks to the movement being made toward a more sex-positive, body-positive theology. Although this volume reflects only a sampling of the work underway, we hope it adequately reflects the diversity of voices, methodologies, and visions that is moving this conversation along. In all but the final section (on marriage equality), we have retained at least one article from the first edition in order to show the continuity as well as the shifts taking place in the conversation regarding spirituality and sexuality. Without the significant deconstructive and visionary work reflected in the earlier edition, this renewed conversation—and hence this second edition—would not be possible.

"Part 1: Methods and Sources" opens the conversation by noting that the meanings of human sexuality are always shaped by history and context and influenced by questions of power and authority. Who has the right to reflect theologically about these matters, and what are the appropriate sources to draw on for theological and ethical insight?

"Part 2: Sexuality and Spirituality" examines the tensions between these two dimensions of human existence along with strategies to connect them in life-affirming and creative ways. Along the way the authors address the power and place of the erotic in personal and public life, the struggle to honor the sexuality of Jesus, and the wisdom of rethinking sin and grace in relation to sexuality and sexual difference.

"Part 3: Gender, Race, and Sexual Identities" opens with an appreciative inquiry into emerging social-scientific paradigms about human psychosexual development that challenge the conventional binary gender construct, raise questions about the fixed character of sexual identities, and make room for greater sexual diversity and fluidity. This section also explores the intersections of race, racism, and sexuality by drawing especially on feminist and womanist scholarship.

"Part 4: Rethinking Sexual Ethics" maps out the contours of a sex-positive and explicitly justice-centered ethical framework by paying attention to some of the personal and social-political meanings of human sexuality. Any contemporary ethic of sexuality will be required to deal adequately with single persons as well as partners; with public policy as well as personal decision making; and with shifting patterns of regulation, including the regulation of marriage by church and state.

"Part 5: Sexual Health and Bodily Integrity" focuses on several themes within the broad rubric of sexual health and well-being by addressing sexuality and disabilities, religious responses to the HIV/AIDS pandemic, and debates over procreative freedom and the morality of abortion.

"Part 6: Marriage Equality: A Test Case for the Church" offers theological and ethical reflection on extending the freedom to marry, religiously and civilly, to same-sex couples. In the first edition of this book, this section identified "sexual orientation" as the test case, and homosexuality was spoken of as "the most divisive and yet potentially most liberating issue for today's churches."[8] A sign that the conversation has shifted, even matured, is how the debate has moved beyond the "rightness" of same-sex eroticism to considerations of how best to respect and support same-sex partnerships and families. At the same time, it is fair to say that the debate over same-sex marriage remains highly contentious, in part because it concerns same-sex intimacy and in part because it concerns marriage, an institution about which the church has historically had, at best, a deep ambivalence. Addressing same-sex marriage as a case study is a fitting way to draw together insights about sexuality and spirituality, ethical integrity and justice making, and social and religious change—insights that permeate this volume's essays.

As editors, we are grateful for this opportunity to update a collection that has been widely used in seminaries and religious studies programs, as well as in congregations. Our thanks go especially to Jim Nelson for his gracious encouragement to revise an anthology that he first put together with such care and quality; to the late Stephanie Egnotovich at Westminster John Knox Press for her enthusiasm for the project; to Jana Riess for pitching in midstream and seeing us through to completion; and to Erika Lundbom, production wizard extraordinaire. Goucher College and Bangor Theological Seminary provided much-needed financial support.

All of us agree that a second edition is greatly needed because religious discourse about sexuality, spirituality, and ethics continues to evolve and expand and because over the course of the past fifteen years new issues have emerged and old issues have taken different shape. Above all, there is now available a remarkably rich and diverse array of feminist and womanist scholarship, as well as more published writings by LGBTQ theologians and ethicists. When the discerning/speaking/writing *theologizing* subject changes, so inevitably does the theological discourse.

With gratitude and high expectations that "there is yet more truth and light to break forth," we close by quoting, once again, our colleagues Jim Nelson and Sandra Longfellow from their introduction to the first edition. With them we acknowledge that "we live in an exciting and perplexing time regarding Christian perceptions of sexuality," and with them and our distinguished authors in this second edition, "we wish the reader a good journey in wrestling with the meanings of God's good gift."[9]

Marvin M. Ellison
Kelly Brown Douglas

NOTES

1. James B. Nelson and Sandra P. Longfellow, "Introduction," *Sexuality and the Sacred: Sources for Theological Reflection* (Louisville, KY: Westminster/John Knox Press, 1994), xiv.

2. Ibid.

3. *Presbyterians and Human Sexuality 1991* (Louisville, KY: Office of the General Assembly, Presbyterian Church (U.S.A.), 1991), 7, with emphasis added.

4. John B. Cobb Jr., *Matters of Life and Death* (Louisville, KY: Westminster/John Knox Press, 1991), 94.

5. Gayle S. Rubin, "Thinking Sex: Notes for a Radical Theory of the Politics of Sexuality," in *The Lesbian and Gay Studies Reader*, ed. Henry Abelove, Michele Aina Barale, and David M. Halperin (New York: Routledge, 1993), 11.

6. Religious Declaration on Sexual Morality, Justice, and Healing; accessed at the Web site of the Religious Institute at www.religiousinstitute.org on March 2, 2010.

7. Daniel C. Maguire, "Introduction: The Religiously Induced Illness of Women's Subordination and Its Cure," in *Violence against Women in Contemporary World Religion: Roots and Cures*, ed. Daniel C. Maguire and Sa'diyya Shaikh (Cleveland: Pilgrim Press, 2007), 2.

8. Nelson and Longfellow, "Introduction," xvi.

9. Ibid., xvii.

PART 1

Methods and Sources

Carter Heyward
Judith Plaskow
Christian Scharen
Kelly Brown Douglas

Introduction
to Part 1

For this opening section, the editors of the first edition posed two questions: "What does our sexuality mean?" and "From whence come those meanings?" Although a debate continues to this day between essentialists (those who hold that sexual meaning is more biologically derived) and social constructionists (those who adopt a more contextualized approach to sexuality), the following essays support the view that sexual meanings are historically shaped, influenced by social power, and open to significant modification, thereby providing the possibility for fresh theological responses toward sexuality, the body, and sexual identities.

From various vantage points, our authors engage two major tasks: exploring the sources and sites of authority that have traditionally governed understandings of sexuality, and reconfiguring those sources and views of authority in order to develop more body-positive theologies. Although they share a constructionist approach when it comes to sexuality, their reasons for "changing the subject" are shaped by their particular social, historical, ecclesiastical, and sexually gendered realities. These realities also influence the sources they engage and their understandings of authority. What follows, then, is a rich conversation that suggests diverse methodological paradigms for transforming theological and ethical sexual narratives.

In her essay "Notes on Historical Grounding: Beyond Sexual Essentialism," Carter Heyward enters the conversation by recounting the story of Grant, a theological student whose spiritual journey alienated him from his sexuality. This story exemplifies Heyward's methodological assumption that "our sexual relations, indeed our sexual feelings, have been shaped by historical forces—the same contingencies, tensions, politics, movements, and social concerns that have shaped our cultures, value systems, and daily lives." These forces have created

3

sexual relations that abuse power. For Heyward, sexuality is about "power in relation" and "how people historically have or have not embodied our capacities for mutually empowering relationships." A "revolutionary transformation" is called for, she contends, not simply of sexual attitudes, but also of sexual relations.

Judith Plaskow in "Setting the Problem, Laying the Ground" points to the need to "hear the silences" insofar as tradition has relegated women to a "terrain of silence." As in other traditions, the Jewish tradition defines women by and in relation to men. Women's experiences and voices do not "decide the questions with which Jewish sources [and traditions] deal." Plaskow further explains that "women are part of the Jewish tradition without its sources and structures reflecting [women's] experiences." "Women are Jews," Plaskow says, "but we do not define Jewishness. . . . The central Jewish categories of Torah, Israel, and God all are constructed from male perspectives." Even when women are present within Jewish sources, they are still silenced for again their presence is predicated on "male purposes, designs, and desires." As Plaskow contends, the "terrain of silence" must be broken. In an effort to do this, she proposes a methodology that "hears the silences" of Jewish women and assumes "women's full humanity."

Christian Scharen enters the conversation by speaking the truth of his own history. In "Experiencing the Body: Sexuality and Conflict in American Lutheranism," he shares influential experiences from his own life that moved him from "condemning homosexuality" to "celebrating gay people as God's good creation." While he recognizes the way other sources—such as Scripture, church teachings, and reason—impact moral judgments, he maintains the primacy of experience, both "our unconscious experience," which shapes our "taken-for-granted knowledge," and "our conscious experiences," which challenge this knowledge and "ultimately revise some aspect of our sense of 'how things really are.'" A change in a person's moral judgments, Scharen asserts, requires that individuals recognize the experiences that have shaped their judgments and that they remain open to experiences that can change those judgments.

In "Black and Blues: God-Talk/Body-Talk for the Black Church," Kelly Brown Douglas explores an unexamined theological source in the black faith tradition: the blues. She enters the conversation by asserting that something is "going all wrong" in the black church. Identifying the controversy concerning LGBT rights as a "kairos" time for the black church, Douglas asserts that what is going wrong in the black church is its inability to accept "blues bodies." Blues are bodies of those who embrace what it means to be "embodied" beings and thus people who affirm and celebrate their sensual/sexual selves. Because of their positive regard for their own sexual bodies, "blues bodies" are routinely marginalized, if not demonized, within the black church's tradition. Given the current debate concerning LGBT issues, Douglas suggests that LGBT bodies represent the blues bodies currently "targeted" within the black church community. She proposes that only with a blues methodology can the black church overcome this body-denouncing tradition and subsequently maintain its black and Christian identity.

These diverse essays confirm the need for a more body-positive/sex-positive theological ethic. Most important, they also affirm that such a theological ethic is possible, even within faith traditions that have been most unforgiving when it comes to matters of sexuality. In this regard, they set the stage well for what is to follow in this volume.

1
Notes on Historical Grounding: Beyond Sexual Essentialism

CARTER HEYWARD

Our history is inseparably part of our nature, our social structures are inseparably part of our biology.

Joan L. Griscom[1]

From my "Holiness" Christian background, complete with sexual taboos, I discovered and hid in puberty the pleasure of masturbation, a delicious bathtime/bedtime thrill. Fantasies and pictures of Marilyn Monroe were hidden too, and I was constantly convicting myself of the sinfulness of my nightly obsession.

I began dating after I left my parsonage home for college. I thrilled at the first touch of a woman's thigh. I fell in love repeatedly and ached for intimacy. But at my religious college, my few serial loves considered sexual exploring ("feeling them up") to be prurient—and spiritual exploring was unheard of. I was rejected by a woman (to whom I had proposed marriage) because of my "weird" ideas—like seeing nothing wrong with sex as long as she didn't get pregnant.

After a stint in the factory, as a graduate student in philosophy at a midwestern university, I blossomed. I saw movies, drank beer, smoked pot, and fell in love twice again. I discovered sexual intimacy with each of these women, and they marveled at the wonder with which I touched their bodies. Yet, despite my devotion, each left me.

For the next seven years, I explored a number of liaisons, sharing sexual intimacy in most but finding no lasting spiritual connection. Beginning to practice Buddhist prayer, I enlarged my agenda from only desires for sexual intimacy to attention to the others' depths of concern. . . .

6

Sexual relationships became fewer. In 1982, after six years of Buddhist fellowship, I was expelled by my fellow Buddhists for theological questioning, and I became socially isolated.

Grant,
theological student

Our sexual relations, indeed our sexual feelings, have been shaped by historical forces—the same contingencies, tensions, politics, movements, and social concerns that have shaped our cultures, value systems, and daily lives.

In *The Handmaid's Tale,* Canadian Margaret Atwood portrays with chilling, imaginative insight the centrality of sexual control in the new Christian fundamentalist nation of Gilead, formerly the United States: White women are forced to breed and are forbidden to have sex except with the Commanders, the white men who own them. Gaymen and lesbians are summarily executed. Black people are ghettoized in Detroit. These are the very forces about which social anthropologist Gayle Rubin speaks: "The right has been spectacularly successful in tapping [the] pools of erotophobia in its accession to state power."[2]

Good social history is written not just from the perspective of "the winners." It teaches us about the connections between the control of women's bodies for procreation; the suppression of homosexuality; the economic system and conditions of a particular place and time; the virulence of such forces as racism and anti-Semitism; and the exercise of social control by institutional custodians of such normative "virtues" as spiritual growth, mental health, and physical well-being.

It would be small solace for us to imagine that we are nearing the end of a period of blatant political reaction against sexual and gender justice in the United States. Even if this were superficially the case, the radicality of the injustice in our power relations goes deeper than any one political party or heyday of the religious right. The problems in our sexual and gender relations are historical, they are critical, and they connect us all.

A historical reading of sexuality is a reading about power in relation, specifically about how people historically have or have not embodied our capacities for mutually empowering relationships. The study of sexuality is also an exploration of how the exercise of power-over (power-as-control by kings, customs, corporations, gods, and so forth) has shaped our capacities and incapacities to act mutually.[3]

We use and abuse power in relationships. We also are used and abused in relationships. Our capacity to act as cocreative subjects in the dynamics of mutually empowering relations is affected, and determined in some cases, by how we have been objectified and acted upon in our significant relationships. An example of the connection between how we are treated and how we treat others and ourselves is the large extent to which abusive adults have been battered and abused as children.

The late French structuralist Michel Foucault (and, with him, radical British social historian Jeffrey Weeks and feminist liberation theologians in the United States such as Sharon Welch and Beverly Harrison) insisted that no experience of power, sexual or other, is intrinsic to a person or to a relationship, but rather that our experiences of power-in-relation are socially constructed. Sexuality is socially constructed. . . .

For example, few people in Euroamerican culture are strangers to feelings of sadomasochism in our social relations, including our sexual relationships, regardless of how we may act. Ours is a society fastened in dynamics of control and subjugation. None can escape the psychosexual or spiritual fallout of such a system.[4]

In an appreciative but unapologetic critique of such sexologists as Havelock Ellis, Jeffrey Weeks charges, "Possibly the most potent of their legacies is what is now generally known as 'sexual essentialism.'" Weeks is referring to "ways of thinking which reduce a phenomenon to a presupposed essence—the 'specific being,' 'what a thing is,' 'nature, character, substance, absolute being'—which seeks to explain *complex* forms by means of an identifying inner force or truth."[5]

A historical reading of sexuality will move us beyond sexual essentialism as explanation of anything, including either homosexuality or heterosexuality. If we accept a relational, historical matrix as our origin, the womb of who we are becoming, we will not fall into believing that either our identities or our relational possibilities are fixed and unchanging. This is because relationality—the basis of historical agency—presupposes relativity: All of us, and all of everything, is relative to everything else—changing, becoming, living, and dying in relation.

There can be nothing static in a personal identity or relationship formed in such a matrix. There is no such thing as a homosexual or a heterosexual if by this we mean to denote a fixed essence, an essential identity.[6] There are rather homosexual and heterosexual people—people who *act* homosexually or heterosexually.

Relationality relativizes our essence. We are only who we are becoming in relation to one another. Self-knowledge is steeped in awareness of movement and change.

Because history involves change and movement, understanding our sexualities involves knowing in what ways our sexualities are changing and in being open to changing understandings of our sexualities as we continue to learn about our bodyselves. Not only are we not living in the nineteenth century, we are not living in the 1950s or 1960s in terms of how we may experience nutrition, sexual activity, pregnancy, disease, and other bodyself phenomena. Understanding our sexualities historically involves understanding ourselves as people whose sexualities are in flux.

A historical rather than an essentialist perspective on sexuality involves framing our sexual ethics around issues of what we *do* rather than of what we *are*: What we do as hetero/homosexual persons—how we act in relation to lovers and friends—is the stuff of sexual ethics, rather than whether it is right or wrong to *be* heterosexual or homosexual.

A historical reading of sexuality may make living as lesbians and gaymen more difficult, because we cannot plead for acceptance on the basis of being something we can't help and therefore of needing special sets of rights and understanding because we are homosexuals who didn't choose to be who we are. When we are clear with ourselves and others that our sexual identities are not "essential" but rather are being shaped by many factors, including our own "permission," the difficulties we may incur politically will be offset by our own shared sense of the relational power born among us as we call each other forth and help shape each other's identities.

We no longer have to wage our campaigns for "rights" on the basis of being homosexuals who can't help it because it's just the way we are. Rather, whether we are heterosexual or homosexual, we expect our society to offer basic conditions of human worth and self-respect to *all* people, regardless of sexual preference.

A historical reading of our sexualities that is rooted in our assumption of responsibility for what we do demands responsible engagement from others. It is easy enough for many Christian liberals to "love" gaymen, lesbians, divorced women and men, single parents, people with AIDS. It is harder, but more honest and of deeper social value, for us to engage one another's lives in a spirit of mutual respect and discovery. And what better definition of love?

A historical perspective on sexuality is important also because such a view enables us to envision and perhaps experience our own possibilities as sexual persons beyond the constraints of any particular failure in historical imagination—whether the failure be religious, psychological, economic, or cultural.

Dorothee Soelle writes of *Phantasie*, a creative mix of intuition and imagination that enables us to participate in shaping the future even as we are grounded in the present.[7] Our *Phantasie* helps us experience and understand sexuality as an open, changing, relational dynamic. Our sexual future is not set or predetermined. We are involved in shaping our own dreams.

A historical reading of sexuality moves us beyond sexual essentialism toward understanding ourselves radically as persons-in-relation. We move through *phantasie* toward questions that we would miss altogether unless we were thinking historically, such as Jeffrey Weeks's question about when heterosexual behavior became an ideology—when it began to develop into "compulsive heterosexuality" or "heterosexism." No one knows the answer to this question; but it is interesting and it could become a locus of historical inquiry further into connections between sex, women, and political control.[8]

The Christian church plays the central formative role in limiting and thwarting our sexual *phantasie*, or sexual imagination. Most historians, sexologists, and others who are interested in how sexual practices and attitudes have developed historically seem to agree that in the realm of sexual attitudes, Western history and Christian history are so closely linked as to be in effect indistinguishable.[9] That is to say, the Christian church has been the chief architect of an attitude toward sexuality during the last seventeen-hundred years of European and Euroamerican history—an obsessive, proscriptive attitude, in contrast to how large numbers of people, Christians and others, have actually lived our lives as sexual persons.

The church's antisexual preoccupation dates from early in the church's history. The Council of Elvira (Spain), at which for the first time an explicitly antisexual code was made law for western Christians, was held in 309 CE. This was on the eve of the Constantinian settlement, in which the church formally made its peace with the state and in so doing lost a major element of its identity: its role as a body of resistance to oppressive power relations.

Historical theologian Samuel Laeuchli writes of the Council of Elvira:

> In the turmoil of a decaying empire the Christian Church attempted to find its communal identity; in the crisis that had come about at the twilight of antiquity, the Christian elite [bishops and presbyters] sought to carve out a clerical image. Both of these struggles rose to the surface whenever the synod of Elvira dealt with matters of sexuality. By establishing sexual codes the synod meant to define the particular character of Christian life; by setting sexual taboos, the synod meant to create the image of an ascetic clerical leadership. . . . [These texts] were of far reaching import for the history of Christianity. Few ancient texts provide such evidences and opportunity to examine the purpose behind the Christian elite's antisexual drive as do these canons.[10]

Laeuchli goes on to suggest five reasons why the church's elite became preoccupied with sexual control of the clergy and, to a lesser extent, the laity. First, the need to carve out a new identity for Christians as the old identity (of contending against the state) faded into oblivion. Second, the determination on the part of the clergy to establish themselves as powerful in a new sociopolitical context in which Christian laity would be looking to Roman leadership as locus of power. Third, the overwhelming emotional and physical demands of becoming part of the Roman world in its expansive, urbane environment. Fourth, the disquieting urbanization of Christians who, as increasing numbers became city dwellers, lost their tribal and rural ties. And finally, the breaking apart of religious mythology, both pagan and Christian, as the claims of each relativized the other. Laeuchli writes,

> It is no coincidence that the second-century movement which so desperately tried to recover the mythological canopy, namely Gnosticism, picked Genesis 3, the idea of a fall, as the starting point for its remythologication in which sexual copulation belongs to heaven, as an abstract cosmic event beyond human reach. Nor is it a coincidence that the philosophical parallel to Gnosticism, middle Platonism . . . , declared body and matter as evil. When man began to lose his secure place in the mythic-cosmic structure which he had hewn for himself, he was thrown into crisis. Perhaps he lost his place because he became urban, and thus conscious of man's universal predicament. No matter what caused this crisis, the bishops and presbyters of Elvira, as the leaders of an exclusive religion, offered an alternative which reckoned with the sexual dilemma of their age.[11]

Ideas, or philosophical possibilities, are seeded in social realities—political, economic, and so on. In periods of social unrest, theologians historically have idealized the human condition by spiritualizing it. At Elvira, this spiritualization took the shape of calling men (it was addressed to males by males) to rise spiritually above their sexual bodies.

Laeuchli's primary thesis is that the church's ordained leadership tightened the sexual reins of the church during a period of confusion and chaos. It was the only control they had. Moreover,

> the decisions of Elvira show . . . a crisis in male identity. In the image of manhood which these canons presuppose, the woman as a sexual being was excluded. Where such sexual dualism was predicated, man no longer defined himself in relation to woman . . . or expressed the conflict creatively; instead, he defined himself in separation from the woman.[12]

Laeuchli notes that the Christian church still operates on the basis of this same antisexual dualism, which is, in effect, an antifemale dualism.[13] From the second century on, the church had portrayed sex as something pertaining to women and as evil, "the devil's gateway."[14] This attitude, for the first time, is canonized at the dawn of the era in which the church's social, political, and economic power is inaugurated.

The Elvira synod illustrates that a historical perspective on sexuality in western societies involves understanding the antisexual and antifemale (as well as anti-Semitic) character of Christian teachings as a means of maintaining control in what was experienced as a chaotic social milieu, much like our own historical period.[15]

Understanding sexuality historically involves making connections between the social control of sexuality and the social control of women. Not only in Christian history but moreover in western history (in which social control has been dominated by the church), the connection between women and sex has been so close as to be synonymous.

"The place of women in this chaotic world" is one of toil and trouble, scapegoating and violence, hatred and trivialization, poverty and despair.[16] Economically, under global structures of late capitalism, women are kept in poverty.[17] It is the way profit is maximized. Women's bodies are kept in the service of heterosexist patriarchy—as wives, whores, fantasy objects, and as a vast, deep pool of cheap labor.

We cannot comprehend the meaning of sexuality from a historical perspective without viewing its place in the context of power relations between genders. In particular, we must understand sexism, the oppression of women in which men are expected to play their manly roles—on top of women, enforcing the rules by which patriarchal, androcentric society is naturally and rightly ordered.

Behind the hostile slogan that "what a lesbian needs is a good fuck" is the less individualistic and more honest threat that what the society needs, in order to be well ordered, is for men to make women "enjoy" being dominated, held down, and screwed.

A historical reading of sexuality will teach us that sexual performance is often less a matter of enjoyment or pleasure—especially for women—than of necessity. Weeks writes of the modern movement for sexual liberation in the United States and Europe:

> The sexual liberation of women was developing in a dual context: of male definitions of sexual need and pleasure, and of capitalist organisation of the labour market and of consumption (including consumption of sex in all of its many, frequently pornographic varieties). The junction of the two (male definitions of sexual need and capitalist organization of labor) came through the material reality of family life. The economic position of most women—lower pay, fewer job opportunities—still ensures that marriage is seen as a gateway to financial as well as social security and position. And increasingly during this century, sex or at least sexual allure has emerged as a guarantee for attaining status and security. We pay homage to an ideology of voluntarism in relation to marriage; the reality is often of an iron determinism, especially for women: economic, cultural, moral *and sexual*.[18]

For many women much of the time and some women all of the time, sex is not fun, it is not pleasurable, and yet it is what we are here to do—provide it for men. A historical understanding of sexuality demands that this reality be recognized.

Although Western societies historically have been patriarchal and, on the whole, erotophobic, at no historical period have the links between sexual, gender, and economic control been more pernicious than today. Advanced capitalism literally feeds off of men's control of women's bodyselves, including the production of pornography, prostitution, rape, and other forms of sexual exploitation. Sex pays; and, in a culture of power-over social relations, coercive sex—involving pain and humiliation—pays best.

As a window into viewing our power in relation, a historical understanding of sexuality might help us begin to envision sex as erotic—the "life force" of the later Freud.[19] In his early writings, Freud linked sex and death. He never got fully away from this, but he did begin to move away from his own theory. Building on the later Freud, Herbert Marcuse speaks of the "eroticization of the entire personality."[20] In so doing, he prefigures Audre Lorde's articulation of the erotic as the source of our creativity, the wellspring of our joy, the energy of our poems, music, lovemaking, dancing, meditation, friendships, and meaningful work.[21]

History, including the stories of our own lives and those of our forebears in relation, can teach us something about the erotic as creative power. The testimonies are there. Theologically, we are speaking of our power in right relation; from a Christian perspective, the power of God.

Understanding sexuality historically might enable us also to experience sexual pleasure as good, morally right, without need of justification. Viewed through the traditional Christian lens, this perception is scandalous—that our sensual, sexual pleasure is good, in and of itself, not merely as means to a good end.

In doing sexual ethics, we can refuse to play a defensive role. We do not need to justify pleasure. Let us rather have to justify pain—try to understand in what ways pain and suffering may be unavoidable, and sometimes necessary, in our lives. If we are to live with our feet on the ground, in touch with reality, we must help one another accept the fact that we who are Christian are heirs to a body-despising, woman-fearing, sexually repressive religious tradition. If we are to continue as members of the church, we must challenge and transform it at the root. What is required is more than simply a "reformation." I am speaking of revolutionary transformation. Nothing less will do.[22]

Beverly Harrison, Dorothee Soelle, Margaret Huff, Janet Surrey, and other feminist liberation theologians and relational psychologists do not accept the concept of a personal "self" or "identity" apart from the relational matrix in which it is shaped. Theologically and ethically, our questions must include what it means for any of us to know her sexual "identity" in the relational praxis of transformation.

Language and change are a difficult fit. Words seem static, not fluid, which is why adjectives and transitive verbs tend to serve us better than nouns and intransitive verbs. And yet we must speak words as best we can. At no time has the urgency been more acute than today for us to share honest words about our bodyselves.

Our silence will not protect us.[23] Our best protection is to speak the truths of our lives insofar as we can, with one another's presence and help, and cultivate carefully together those truths we cannot yet speak, truths that may be still very unformed and young. We are shaping history with our words. Either we speak as best we can or our power in relation will slip away like a thief in the night.

NOTES

1. Joan L. Griscom, "On Healing the Nature/History Split," in *Women's Conscious-ness/Women's Conscience*, edited by Barbara H. Andolsen, Christine E. Gudorf, Mary D. Pellauer (San Francisco: Harper & Row, 1985), 97.

2. Quoted in Jeffrey Weeks, *Sexuality and Its Discontents: Meanings, Myths and Modern Sexualities* (London: Routledge & Kegan Paul, 1985), 44.

In his *History of Sexuality*, Michel Foucault asks how power has become a factor in sexuality. His understanding of the sexual relation is one in which relations of power are immanent to it. Sexuality is one of the "specific domains formed by relations of power." Rather than acting out of a mutually empowering relation, Foucault accepts that "disequilibriums" are embedded in the sexual relation. Further, a competitive, aim-oriented power relation gives power to some ("men, adults, parents, doctors") and denies it to others ("women, adolescents, children, patients"). Michel Foucault, *History of Sexuality*, vol. 1 (New York: Vintage, 1978), 94–95, 99.

3. The body is a site for historical molding and transformation because sex, far from being resistant to social ordering, seems peculiarly susceptible to it. We know that sex is a

vehicle for the expression of a variety of social experiences: of morality, duty, work, habit, tension release, friendship, romance, love, protection, pleasure, utility, power, and sexual difference. Its very plasticity is the source of its historical significance. Sexual behavior would transparently not be possible without physiological sources, but physiology does not supply motives, passion, object choice, or identity. These come from "somewhere else," the domains of social relations and psychic conflict. If this is correct, the body can no longer be seen as a biological given which emits its own meaning. It must be understood instead as an ensemble of potentialities which are given meaning only in society. Weeks, *Sexuality and Its Discontents*, 122–23. See also Mario Mieli, *Homosexuality and Liberation: Elements of a Gay Critique*, trans. David Fernbach (London: Gay Men's Press, 1980).

4. Weeks, *Sexuality and Its Discontents*, 8.

5. Ibid.

6. Ibid. Jeffrey Weeks challenges the idea of a "pre-given essence of sexuality." Weeks understands sexuality to be open, fluid, and flowing, influenced by changing elements in the culture. Sexuality is moved and shaped by a variety of circumstances. A "fixed identity," one that is static and eternal, inhibits this "flow of different forces and influences." Weeks, *Sexuality and Its Discontents*, 121–22. See also Mieli, *Homosexuality and Liberation*; and Beverly Wildung Harrison, "Misogyny and Homophobia: The Unexplored Connections," in *Making the Connections: Essays in Feminist Social Ethics*, ed. Carol S. Robb (Boston: Beacon Press, 1985).

7. Dorothee Soelle writes, "In German, *phantasie* has a potentially far more positive value than the word "fantasy" has in English. Its meaning includes the dimensions of imagination, inspiration, inventiveness, flexibility, freedom and creativity." Dorothee Soelle, *Beyond Mere Obedience: Reflections on a Christian Ethic for the Future*, trans. Lawrence W. Denef (Minneapolis: Augsburg Publishing House, 1970), 10.

8. Further resources that discuss sex, women, and political control are Harrison, "Sexuality and Social Policy," in *Making the Connections*, 83–114; Weeks, "The 'Sexual Revolution' Revisited," in *Sexuality and Its Discontents*, 15–32; and Sheila Briggs, "Sexual Justice and the Righteousness of God," in *Sex and God: Some Varieties of Women's Experience*, ed. Linda Hurcombe (New York: Routledge & Kegan Paul, 1987), 251–77.

9. In the early Christian church, sexual dualism intensified to the point that sexuality was hyper-regulated and made permissible only through pure and exclusive love. Samuel Laeuchli writes that it was a conflict won over by "a tipping of the scale so against sexuality that sexuality becomes synonymous with evil. The sexual act becomes abhorrent and people either flee into deserts or write books on the perfection of virginity." Samuel Laeuchli, *Power and Sexuality: The Emergence of Canon Law at the Synod of Elvira* (Philadelphia: Temple University Press, 1972), 103.

Elaine Pagels discusses the struggle within the church in the first three centuries for control over people. Pagels notes that sexuality is one distinct area of people's lives that the church can regulate, thus regulating their theology and social lives. See Elaine Pagels, *The Gnostic Gospels* (New York: Vintage Books, 1981).

10. Laeuchli, *Power and Sexuality*, 88.

11. Ibid., 112–13.

12. Ibid., 104.

13. Laeuchli notes that the church is still not willing to open the explosive, yet crucial, issue of sexuality (114). The Council of Elvira's refusal to confront the issue of sexuality perpetuates its hierarchical, ecclesiastical authority when dealing with contemporary matters of the modern world. The church's refusal to face its antisexual stance keeps it from confronting relational and interactive issues around sexuality. Laeuchli, *Power and Sexuality*, 122–23.

14. Tertullian, quoted in Mary Daly, *The Church and the Second Sex* (New York: Harper & Row, 1968), 45.

15. Examples of canons that expose the antifemale, antisexual, and anti-Semitic characteristic of teachings include the following: Number 72: "If a widow has intercourse with a man and later marries him, she shall be reconciled to communion after a period of five years, having completed the required penance; if she marries another man, having left the first, she shall not be given communion even at the end." Number 78: "If one of the faithful who is married commits adultery with a Jewish or pagan woman, he shall be cut off, but if someone else exposes him, he can share Sunday communion after five years, having completed the required penance." Laeuchli, *Power and Sexuality*, 134–35.

16. Haunani-Kay Trask, *Eros and Power: The Promise of Feminist Theory* (Philadelphia: University of Pennsylvania Press, 1986), 56.

17. For more on women and poverty, see Caroline Allison, "It's like Holding the Key to Your Own Jail," in *Women in Namibia* (Geneva: World Council of Churches, 1986); Beverly Bryan, Stella Dadzie, and Suzanne Soate, *The Heart of the Race: Black Women's Lives in Britain* (London: Virago, 1985); Victoria Byerly, *Hard Times Cotton Mill Girls: Personal Histories of Womanhood and Poverty in the South* (Ithaca, N.Y.: ILRPress, 1986); Zilla R. Eisenstein, *Feminism and Sexual Equality: Crisis in Liberal America* (New York: Monthly Review Press, 1984), particularly 114–38; Harrison, *Making the Connections*; Karin Stallord, et al., *Poverty in the American Dream: Women and Children First* (Boston: South End Press, 1983); Soon-Hwa Sun, "Women, Work and Theology in Korea," *Journal of Feminist Studies in Religion* 3, no. 2 (fall 1987): 125–35; Rosa Dominga Trapasso, "The Feminization of Poverty," *Latinamerica Press* (May 31, 1984): 5.

18. Weeks, *Sexuality and Its Discontents*, 26–27.

19. In his later writings, Sigmund Freud began to see the "sexual instincts" as the "true life-instincts." He began to understand the sexual instincts as an energy that "preserved life itself." This was a major affirmation not only of the life-instinct in human nature, but the life-affirming instinct of sexuality. Sigmund Freud, *Beyond the Pleasure Principle: The Pioneer Study of the Death Instinct in Man*, trans. James Strachey (New York: Bantam Books, 1959), 74–75, 79.

This was a major shift for Freud, who had earlier considered the sexual instinct to be a death-instinct. The distinction in his theory came about as Freud began to hypothesize on the "ego-instincts," pressured for death, and the "sexual instincts pressured . . . toward a prolongation of life." Ibid., 78.

20. Herbert Marcuse, *Eros and Civilization: A Philosophical Inquiry into Freud* (Boston: Beacon Press, 1955), 201.

21. See Audre Lorde, "Uses of the Erotic: The Erotic as Power," in *Sister Outsider: Essays and Speeches* (Trumansburg, N.Y.: Crossing Press, 1984), 53–59.

22. Mary Daly and Sarah Bentley Doely were two of the first women to recognize that it was not merely changing male god language or ordaining women into the priesthood that was needed for human liberation. They understood that these issues were symptoms exposing the need for vast structural changes within the church. See Mary Daly, *The Church and the Second Sex*; and Sarah Bentley Doely, *Women's Liberation and the Church* (New York: Association Press, 1970).

Radical Christian feminists are continuing to explore and expand on the ideas put forth in the above-mentioned texts. See, e.g., Elisabeth Schüssler Fiorenza, *In Memory of Her* (New York: Crossroad-Seabury Press, 1983); Rosemary Radford Ruether, *Sexism and God-Talk: Toward a Feminist Theology* (Boston: Beacon Press, 1983); and Harrison, *Making the Connections*.

23. Lorde, "The Transformation of Silence into Language," *Sister Outsider*, 41.

2

Setting the Problem,
Laying the Ground

JUDITH PLASKOW

The need for a feminist Judaism begins with hearing silence. It begins with noting the absence of women's history and experiences as shaping forces in the Jewish tradition. Half of Jews have been women, but men have been defined as normative Jews, while women's voices and experiences are largely invisible in the record of Jewish belief and experience that has come down to us. Women have lived Jewish history and carried its burdens, but women's perceptions and questions have not given form to scripture, shaped the direction of Jewish law, or found expression in liturgy. Confronting this silence raises disturbing questions and stirs the impulse toward far-reaching change. What in the tradition is ours? What can we claim that has not also wounded us? What would have been different had the great silence been filled?

Hearing silence is not easy. A silence so vast tends to fade into the natural order; it is easy to identify with reality. To ourselves, women are not Other. We take the Jewish tradition as it has been passed down to us, as ours to appropriate or ignore. Over time, we learn to insert ourselves into silences.[1] Speaking about Abraham, telling of the great events at Sinai, we do not look for ourselves in the narratives but assume our presence, peopling the gaps in the text with women's shadowy forms. It is far easier to read ourselves into male stories than to ask how the foundational stories within which we live have been distorted by our absence. Yet it is not possible to speak into silence, to recover our history or reclaim our power to name without first confronting the extent of exclusion of women's experience. Silence can become an invitation to experiment and explore—but only after we have examined its terrain and begun to face its implications.

This chapter has two purposes: to chart the domain of silence that lies at the root of Jewish feminism and to take up the methodological presuppositions that inform my thinking. While it is not my primary intention in this book to set out an indictment of Judaism as a patriarchal tradition, criticism is an ongoing and essential part of the Jewish feminist project. Not only is criticism a precondition for imagining a transformed Judaism; without a clear critique of Judaism that precedes and accompanies reconstruction, the process of reconstruction easily can be misconstrued as a form of apologetics. In exploring the territory of silence and describing my methodology, I mean to prevent this misunderstanding by clarifying the stance and intent that underlie my constructive thinking.

EXPLORING THE TERRAIN OF SILENCE

In her classic work *The Second Sex,* Simone de Beauvoir argues that men have established an absolute human type—the male—against which women are measured as Other. Otherness, she says, is a pervasive and generally fluid category of human thought; I perceive and am perceived as Other depending on a particular situation. In the case of males and females, however, Otherness is not reciprocal: men are always the definers, women the defined.[2] While women's self-experience is an experience of selfhood, it is not women's experience that is enshrined in language or that has shaped our cultural forms. As women appear in male texts, they are not the subjects and molders of their own experiences but the objects of male purposes, designs, and desires. Women do not name reality, but rather are named as part of a reality that is male-constructed. Where women are Other, they can be present and silent simultaneously; for the language and thought-forms of culture do not express their meanings.

De Beauvoir's analysis provides a key to women's silence within Judaism, for, like women in many cultures, Jewish women have been projected as Other. Named by a male community that perceives itself as normative, women are part of the Jewish tradition without its sources and structures reflecting our experience. Women are Jews, but we do not define Jewishness. We live, work, and struggle, but our experiences are not recorded, and what is recorded formulates our experiences in male terms. The central Jewish categories of Torah, Israel, and God all are constructed from male perspectives. Torah is revelation as men perceived it, the story of Israel told from their standpoint, the law unfolded according to their needs. Israel is the male collectivity, the children of a Jacob who had a daughter, but whose sons became the twelve tribes.[3] God is named in the male image, a father and warrior much like his male offspring, who confirms and sanctifies the silence of his daughters. Exploring these categories, we explore the parameters of women's silence.[4]

In Torah, Jewish teaching, women are not absent, but they are cast in stories told by men. As characters in narrative, women may be vividly characterized, as objects of legislation, singled out for attention. But women's presence in Torah does not negate their silence, for women do not decide the questions with which Jewish sources deal. When the law treats of women, it is often because their "abnormality" demands it. If women are central to plot, the plots are not about them. Women's interests and intentions must be unearthed from texts with other purposes, for both law and narrative serve to obscure them.

The most striking examples of women's silence come from texts in which women are most central, for there the normative character of maleness is especially jarring. In the family narratives of Genesis, for example, women figure prominently. The matriarchs of Genesis are all strong women. As independent personalities, fiercely concerned for their children, they often seem to have an intuitive knowledge of God's plans for their sons. Indeed, it appears from the stories of Sarah and Rebekah that they understand God better than their husbands. God defends Sarah when she casts out Hagar, telling Abraham to obey his wife (Gen. 21:12).[5] Rebekah, knowing it is God's intent, helps deceive Isaac into accepting Jacob as his heir (Gen. 25:23; 27:5–17). Yet despite their intuitions, and despite their wiliness and resourcefulness, it is not the women who receive the covenant or who pass on its lineage. The establishment of patrilineal descent and the patriarchal family takes precedence over the matriarch's stories.[6] Their relationship to God, in some way presupposed by the text, remains an undigested element in the narrative. What was the full theophany to Rebekah, and how is it related to the covenant with Isaac? The writer does not tell us; it is not sufficiently important. And so the covenant remains the covenant with Isaac, while Rebekah's experience floats at the margin of the story.

The establishment of patrilineal descent and patriarchal control, a subtext in Genesis, is an important theme in the legislation associated with Sinai. Here again, women figure prominently, but only as objects of male concerns. The laws pertaining to women place them firmly under the control of first fathers, then husbands, so that men can have male heirs they know are theirs. Legislation concerning adultery (Deut. 22:22, also Num. 5:11–31) and virginity (Deut. 22:13–21) speaks of women, but only to control female sexuality to male advantage. The crime of adultery is sleeping with another man's wife, and a man can bring his wife to trial even on suspicion of adultery, a right that is not reciprocal. Sleeping with a betrothed virgin constitutes adultery. A man who sleeps with a virgin who is not betrothed must simply marry her. A girl whose lack of virginity shames her father on her wedding night can be stoned to death for harlotry. A virgin who is raped must marry her assailant. The subject of these laws is women, but the interest behind them is the purity of the male line.

The process of projecting and defining women as objects of male concerns is expressed most fully not in the Bible, however, but in the Mishnah, an important second-century legal code. Part of the Mishnah's Order of Women (one of its six divisions) develops laws discussed in the Torah concerning certain problematic aspects of female sexuality. The subject of the division is the transfer of women—the regulation of women who are in states of transition, whose uncertain status threatens the stasis of the community. The woman who is about to enter into a marriage or who has just left one requires close attention. The law must regularize her irregularity, facilitate her transition to the normal state of wife and motherhood, at which point she no longer poses a problem.[7] But it is not even the contents of the order, male-defined as they are, that trumpet most loudly women's silence. In a system in which a division of Men would be unthinkable nonsense, the fact of a division Women is sufficient evidence of who names the world, who defines whom, in "normative" Jewish sources.

Thus Torah—"Jewish" sources, "Jewish" teaching—puts itself forward as Jewish teaching but speaks in the voice of only half the Jewish people. This scandal is compounded by another: The omission is neither mourned nor regretted; it is not even noticed. True, the rabbis were aware of the harshness of certain laws pertaining to women and sought to mitigate their effects. They tried to find ways to force a recalcitrant husband to divorce his wife, for example. But the framework that necessitated such mitigations went unquestioned. Women's Otherness was left intact. The Jewish passion for justice did not extend to Jewish women. As Cynthia Ozick puts it, one great "Thou shalt not"—"Thou shalt not lessen the humanity of women"—is missing from the Torah.[8]

For this great omission, there is no historical redress. Indeed, where one might expect redress, the problem is compounded. The prophets, those great champions of justice, couch their pleas for justice in the language of patriarchal marriage. Israel in her youth is a devoted bride, subordinate and obedient to her husband/God (for example, Jer. 2:2). Idolatrous Israel is a harlot and adulteress, a faithless woman whoring after false gods (for example, Hos. 2; 3). Transferring the hierarchy of male and female to God and his people, the prophets enshrine in metaphor the legal subordination of women.[9] Those who might have named and challenged women's marginalization thus ignore and extend it.

The prophetic metaphors mark an end and a beginning. They confront us with the injustice of Torah; they link that injustice to other central Jewish ideas. If exploring Torah means exploring a terrain of women's silence, this is no less true of the categories of Israel or God.

Israel, the bride, the harlot, the people that is female (that is, subordinate) in relation to God is nonetheless male in communal self-perception. The covenant community is the community of the circumcised (Gen. 17:10), the community defined as male heads of household. Women are named through a filter of male experience: that is the essence of their silence. But women's experiences are not recorded or taken seriously because women are not perceived as normative Jews. They are part of but do not define the community of Israel.

The same evidence that speaks to women's silence in the tradition, to the partiality of Torah, also reflects an understanding of Israel as a community of males. In the narratives of Genesis, for example, the covenant moves from father to son, from Abraham to Isaac to Jacob to Joseph. The matriarchs' relation to their husbands' God is sometimes assumed, sometimes passed over, but the women do not constitute the covenant people. Women's relation to the community is also ambiguous and unclear in biblical legislation. The law is couched in male grammatical forms, and its content too presupposes a male nation. "You shall not covet your neighbor's wife" (Ex. 20:17). Probably we cannot deduce from this verse that women are free to covet! Yet the injunction assumes that women's obedience is owed to fathers and husbands, who are the primary group addressed.

The silence of women goes deeper, however, than who defines Torah or Israel. It also finds its way into language about God. Our language about divinity is first of all male language; it is selective and partial. The God who supposedly transcends sexuality, who is presumably one and whole, comes to us through language that is incomplete and narrow. The images we use to describe God, the qualities we attribute to God, draw on male pronouns and experience and convey a sense of power and authority that is clearly male. The God at the surface of Jewish consciousness is a God with a voice of thunder, a God who as lord and king rules his people and leads them into battle, a God who forgives like a father when we turn to him. The female images that exist in the Bible and (particularly the mystical) tradition form an underground stream that occasionally reminds us of the inadequacy of our imagery without transforming its overwhelmingly male nature.

This male imagery is comforting and familiar—comforting because familiar—but it is an integral part of a system that consigns women to the margins. Since the experience of God cannot be directly conveyed in language, imagery for God is a vehicle that suggests what is actually impossible to describe. Religious experiences are expressed in a vocabulary drawn from the significant and valuable in a particular culture. To speak of God is to speak of what we most value. In attributing certain qualities to God, we both attempt to point to God and offer God's qualities to be emulated and admired. To say that God is just, for example, is to say both that God acts justly and that God demands justice. Justice belongs to God but is also ours to pursue. Similarly with maleness, to image God as male is to value the quality and those who have it. It is to define God in the image of the normative community and to bless men—but not women—with a central attribute of God.

But our images of God are not simply male images; they are images of a certain kind. The prophetic metaphors for the relation between God and Israel are metaphors borrowed from the patriarchal family—images of dominance softened by affection. God as husband and father of Israel demands obedience and monogamous love. He repays faithfulness with mercy and loving-kindness, but punishes waywardness, just as the wayward daughter can be stoned at her father's door (Deut. 22:21). When these family images are combined with political images of king and warrior, they reinforce a particular model of power and dominance. God is the power over us, the One out there over against us, the sovereign warrior with righteousness on his side. Family and political models of dominance and submission are recapitulated and rendered plausible by the dominance and submission of God and Israel. The silence and submission of women becomes part of a greater pattern that makes it appear fitting and right.

What emerges then is a "fit," a tragic coherence between the role of women in Jewish life, and law, teaching, and symbols. Women's experiences have not been recorded or shaped the contours of Jewish teaching because women do not define the normative community; but of course, women remain Other when we are always seen through the filter of male interpretation without ever speaking for ourselves. The maleness of God calls for the silence of women as shapers of the holy, but our silence in turn enforces our Otherness and a communal sense of the "rightness" of the male image of God. Moreover, if God is male, and we are in God's image, how can maleness not be the norm of Jewish humanity? If maleness is normative, how can women not be Other? And if women are Other, how can we not speak of God in a language of Otherness and dominance, a language drawn from male experience?

Confronting these interconnections is not easy. But it is only as we hear women's silence as part of the texture of Jewish existence that we can place our specific disabilities in the context in which they belong. Women's exclusion from public religious life, women's powerlessness in marriage and divorce are not accidental; nor are they individual problems. They are pieces of a system in which men have defined the interests and the rules, including the rules concerning women. Manipulating the system to change certain rules—even excision of many of them—will not of itself restore women's voices or women's power of naming. On the contrary, without awareness of the broader context of women's silence, attempts to redress concrete grievances may perpetuate the system of which they are part. Thus, as feminists demand that women be allowed to lead public prayer, the issue of language is often set aside. Traditional modes of liturgical expression are assumed to be adequate; the only issue is who has access to them. But women's leadership in synagogue ritual then leaves untouched the deeper contradictions between formal equality and the fundamental symbols of the service, contradictions that can be addressed only through the transformation of religious language. Similarly, attempts to solve particular legal (halakhic) problems often assume the continued centrality and religious meaningfulness of *halakhah* (law). But halakhah is part of the system that women did not have a hand in creating. How can we presume that if women add our voices to tradition, law will be our medium of expression and repair? To settle on halakhah as the source of justice for women is to foreclose the question of women's experience when it has scarcely begun to be raised.

Clearly, the implications of Jewish feminism reach beyond the goal of equality to transform the bases of Jewish life. Feminism demands a new understanding of Torah, Israel, and God. It demands an understanding of Torah that begins by acknowledging the injustice of Torah and then goes on to create a Torah that is whole. The silence of women reverberates through the tradition, distorting the shape of narrative and skewing the content of the law. Only the deliberate recovery of women's hidden voices, the unearthing and invention of women's Torah, can give us Jewish teachings that are the product of the whole Jewish people and that reflect more fully its experiences of God.

Feminism demands an understanding of Israel that includes the whole of Israel and thus allows women to speak and name our experience for ourselves. It demands we replace a normative male voice with a chorus of divergent voices, describing Jewish reality in different accents and tones. Feminism impels us to rethink issues of community and diversity, to explore the ways in which one people can acknowledge and celebrate the varied experiences of its members. What would it mean for women as women to be equal participants in the Jewish community? How can we talk about difference without creating Others?

Feminism demands new ways of talking about God that reflect and grow out of the redefinition of Jewish humanity. The exclusively male naming of God supported and was rendered meaningful by a cultural and religious situation that is passing away. The emergence of women allows and necessitates that the long-suppressed femaleness of God be recovered and explored and reintegrated into the Godhead. But feminism presses us beyond the issue of gender to examine the nature of the God with male names. How can we move beyond images of domination to a God present in community rather than over it? How can we forge a God-language that expresses women's experience?

METHODOLOGICAL UNDERPINNINGS

Although I intend to devote the rest of this book [*Standing Again at Sinai*] to exploring the implications of feminism for the transformation of Jewish life, I must touch first on another foundational aspect of my feminist reconstruction of Judaism. My basic critique of Judaism as a male-defined religion rests on a number of assumptions concerning texts, sources, experience, and authority, assumptions that inform my efforts at construction as much as they do my critique. My perspective as a Jewish feminist is shaped not singly by the personal experiences I delineated in the introduction [to my book], but also by a series of theological and methodological presuppositions that are influenced by my experiences but cannot be reduced to them. These presuppositions are as essential to my argument as my understanding of Judaism as a patriarchal tradition.

WOMEN'S EXPERIENCE

"Women's experience" is an important and problematic phrase I mention repeatedly in the preceding pages. At several points in discussing women's silence, I turn to this term to name an element missing in Jewish sources and Jewish communal life. The phrase is sufficiently obvious to be overlooked, and at the same time fraught with significant difficulty. It conceals a number of problems and comprehends a major methodological decision.

On one level, the term "women's experience" is quite straightforward. I mean it to refer to the daily, lived substance of women's lives, the conscious events, thoughts, and feelings that constitute women's reality. To say that women's experience is not part of the Jewish tradition is to say that we do not know the world as women have perceived it. We do not have women's account of Jewish history in its large and small moments, filtered through women's perceptions and set in a framework of their making.

On this definition, "women's experience" is not an essence or abstraction. It does not refer to some innate capacity of women, some eternally female mode of being that is different from male being. If women's experience is distinct from men's—and I believe it is—the reasons are primarily historical and social. The different socialization of men and women, present in different ways in every culture, nurtures divergent capacities and divergent experiences of the world. But also, insofar as women are projected as Other, women's experience is doubled in a peculiar way. Knowing she is just herself, a woman must nonetheless deal with the imposition of Otherness. She must forever measure herself against a standard that comes from outside. If she would act against prevailing stereotypes, she must do so being aware of their existence, and this adds an extra burden to whatever she undertakes.[10] Like the Jew, who is always a Jew in the eyes of the world, a woman is assessed in terms of her particularity. The social and historical situation of the Other is not the same as the situation of one who takes identity for granted.

If "women's experience" is primarily a product of culture rather than of some innate female nature, however, then it is also not unitary or clearly definable. The problem with the phrase "women's experience" is that it implies uniformity where—even if we restrict ourselves to Jewish women—there is great diversity. One can delineate certain common elements to women's situation: shared biological experiences, common imposition of Otherness, exclusion from the encoding of cultural meanings. But women have appropriated, interpreted, and responded to these elements very differently, both as individuals and as members of different (Jewish) cultures. It is too easy for one dominant group—in this case, the North American Ashkenazi Jew—to define women's experience for all women, forgetting that even Jewish women's experience is a great tapestry of many designs and colors. Since no woman's work can ever include the whole tapestry, each must remember she speaks from one corner, the phrase "women's experience" qualified by a string of modifiers that specify voice.

Yet despite the real danger of defining it monolithically, the phrase "women's experience" can hardly be avoided. It is indispensable both for signifying a terrain of silence—no group of Jewish women has had the privilege of defining Jewish reality—and for signaling an important methodological choice. In a system in which women have been projected as Other, there is no way within the rules of the system to restore women to full personhood. The conviction that women are fully human is a critical and disruptive principle that comes from outside. Commitment to "women's experience" marks precisely an *a priori* commitment to women's humanity. It is the fundamental feminist methodological move. Without the presupposition of women's full humanity, there is no bridge from the male Jewish tradition to a feminist Judaism. All one can do is manipulate the rules of the system to alleviate women's disabilities, without altering the assumptions from which those disabilities arise. To commit oneself to recovering women's experiences within Judaism, on the other hand, is to say that women as well as men define Jewish humanity and that there is no

Judaism—there is only male Judaism—without the insights of both. This is the starting point for a feminist Judaism, and it represents a basic realignment of the feminist's relationship to tradition.

SUSPICION AND REMEMBRANCE

If insistence on the full humanity of women represents a deliberate and important break with Jewish tradition, it clearly has important implications for the feminist's relationship to Jewish sources. Insofar as Jewish sources assume women's Otherness, are they simply evidence for women's oppression? Do they have anything of value to teach Jewish women? How does one sort out the oppressive from the nonoppressive elements in Jewish sources? How does one decide that a certain fundamental presupposition—like the presupposition of woman's Otherness—must be disavowed? These questions are part of the critical issue of authority that commitment to women's experience raises. Since this is an issue with many ramifications, it needs to be approached deliberately and from several sides.

Attitude toward sources is one dimension of the issue of authority. In discussing the deep-rooted sexism of the Jewish tradition, I use the Tanakh (Hebrew Scriptures) to demonstrate women's silence in Jewish writings. In doing so, I presuppose a dual and paradoxical relationship to the biblical text. I take for granted my critical freedom in relation to the Bible; but I also take for granted my connection to it, the value of examining its viewpoint and concerns. I pronounce the Bible patriarchal; but in taking the time to explore it, I claim it as a text that matters to me. This double relation is not unthinking. It stems from my belief that the Jewish feminist must embrace with equal passion (at least) two different attitudes to Jewish sources. These are described by Elisabeth Schüssler Fiorenza, who in developing feminist principles of interpretation for the study of the New Testament, distinguishes between a "hermeneutics of suspicion" and a "hermeneutics of remembrance," both of which must inform a feminist appropriation of religious texts.[11]

A hermeneutics of suspicion "takes as its starting point the assumption that biblical texts and their interpretations are androcentric and serve patriarchal functions."[12] Since both the Tanakh and rabbinic literature come from male-dominated societies and are attributed to male authors, they need to be examined for androcentric assumptions and content, and for their attention, or lack of it, to women's experiences and concerns. While mainstream sources may have much to say to women, they cannot be accepted uncritically.[13] All too often, they serve to consolidate or reinforce patriarchal values or to inculcate models of power that are destructive or oppressive.

Moreover, it is not just a few obviously patriarchal texts that must be subjected to critical examination and judgment. Feminists cannot assume that any traditional source is entirely free from sexism. Some years ago, referring to Phyllis Trible's project of "depatriarchalizing" the Bible, Mary Daly quipped that a depatriarchalized Bible would make a nice pamphlet.[14] While the comment is clever, it could have gone further: a depatriarchalized text would not exist. Biblical insights are formulated in a patriarchal culture and expressed in patriarchal terms. The husk and the kernel interpenetrate; each can be named, but they cannot be divided. Thus the fact that the prophets expressed their concern for justice in the language of patriarchal marriage does not make that concern trivial or unreal. But it does mean that, in different contexts, the very same texts can be liberating or oppressive. To ignore this fact—to talk about justice without reference to the patriarchal metaphors in which justice is described—is to leave the oppressive aspects of texts to do their work in the world.

At the same time Jewish sources must be viewed with mistrust, they are, however, the sources we have. If suspicion is one side of the feminist's relationship to tradition, the other side is remembrance. Jewish sources have formed us for good and for ill, and they remain our strongest links with the Jewish historical experience. Since, in Schüssler Fiorenza's words, "the enslavement of a people becomes total when their history is destroyed and solidarity with the dead is made impossible," feminists must appropriate Jewish sources not simply as witnesses to women's oppression but as testimonies "of liberation and religious agency." A "hermeneutics of remembrance" insists that the same sources that are regarded with suspicion can also be used to reconstruct Jewish women's history. Just as no source, however neutral or liberating it may seem, is exempt from feminist scrutiny, so even the most androcentric text can provide valuable information about Jewish women's past.[15] Biblical legislation concerning menstruation, for example, can serve as the basis for reconstructing women's understanding of menstruation taboos. Prophetic injunctions against idolatry can furnish clues concerning women's participation in polytheistic traditions.[16] Read with new questions and critical freedom, traditional sources can yield "subversive memories" of past struggles for liberation within and against patriarchy, memories that link contemporary women to a transformative history.[17]

CRITICAL METHOD AND
RELIGIOUS UNITY

The distinction "suspicion/remembrance" suggests a dual attitude toward Jewish texts that is central to a feminist critical appropriation of Jewish sources. Other aspects of the problem of authority and textual interpretation plague modern readers more generally and thus enter into feminist interpretation without emerging specifically from feminist concerns. Modern scientific criticism, for example, has left many people with a divided relationship to religious texts different from the division "suspicion/remembrance." The same religious sources that claim to give overarching significance to life, and that may indeed provide frameworks of meaning, are simultaneously seen as human creations, culture-bound expressions of past religious values. The distinction "critical method/

religious unity" points to a second tension in attitudes toward religious texts, a tension not unique to feminism but with which feminists must grapple.

On the one side, modern scientific thought and historical scholarship have eroded the sacred authority of traditional sources. Religious texts, they tell us, are not a transcript of divine revelation but the work of human beings living in particular social and historical contexts and responding to historical and cultural needs. The same critical tools, literary and historical, that one would bring to reading any text are appropriate to religious sources. We cannot understand either "biblical attitudes" toward women or women's roles in "the biblical period," for example, without taking into account that biblical texts span a thousand years of history and come from very different cultures. We should not expect that the roles of women in the period of early Israelite settlement would be the same as women's roles under the monarchy or in the postexilic period. Similarly, a rabbinic midrash on a biblical text reflects the questions and concerns of the rabbinic period. It does not give us the meaning of the Tanakh for biblical times. Thus, in my earlier discussion of the narratives of Genesis as an instance of women's silence, I did not consider the ways later midrash takes up and elaborates the themes of the stories, sometimes, shifting their emphasis or meaning. That is not relevant to the changing biblical silence concerning women, which can be examined in its own right.

But while religious texts can be broken down literarily and historically, as received tradition, they come to us whole. One may divide and analyze for purposes of criticism or historical reconstruction. The religious meaning of a work, however, may lie in its historical impossibilities, the tensions of the final editing, or the rhythm of the narrative heard as a totality.[18] Scholars may debate, for instance, whether there was an Exodus from Egypt, what proportion of the future Israelite community dwelt in Egypt, and how the Exodus narrative became part of Jewish experience. Whatever they decide, however, the Exodus story, as a story, is constitutive for Jewish self-understanding. As such, it has a claim on contemporary Jews, who must wrestle with its meaning. An analogous point can be made for rabbinic midrash. Midrash may not tell us what the Bible meant in its own time, but it often tells us how particular narratives are comprehended by the Jewish community, and therefore how certain texts have shaped communal values. It may therefore be appropriate sometimes to consider the midrashic meaning of a text as if it were its true meaning, for it may be through the midrash that a text is read and known.

Suspicion/remembrance and critical method/religious unity are aspects of textual appropriation that, on first consideration, may appear to correspond. Critical methods are appropriate to suspicion, for they allow us to see sources in their patriarchal contexts; while to remember our history, we seem to need texts whole. In fact, however, the categories are interwoven. Critical methods are necessary both in analyzing androcentric texts and in historical reconstruction. They can help us recover both the patriarchal setting of our sources and the religious possibilities the sources conceal. Similarly, a text may be considered as a unity or in the light of later interpretation both in order to scrutinize its sexism and in order to get at its religious meaning. Traditional stories may be mediated to us through androcentric midrash, but midrash can also unveil in a text religious import that would otherwise go unseen.

A complex view of texts, then, can be part of any reading. Indeed, a multi-layered consciousness can be difficult to avoid. The modern reader may find it hard to look for religious meaning without a critical view of sources intruding in the background.[19] This divided awareness is both burdensome and liberating. A critical reading can yield results that are disturbing to religious faith, but it can also free texts for deeper appropriation. To approach texts critically is not to dismiss them. On the contrary, it can be part of what it means to take sources seriously as a modern person. When we understand the meaning of a religious text in and for its time, we are freer to take the text and apply it to our own time. Seeing how particular sources answered the religious needs of some people in the period in which they were written allows us to look at contemporary needs and to interpret for today. Thus awareness of how midrash dealt with rabbinic questions might lead us to write midrash that deals with women's questions. Awareness of women's silence in the narratives of Genesis might lead us to restore women's voices, connecting to the text in fresh ways.

AUTHORITY

To use Jewish texts as a basis for historical reconstruction and to take them seriously as literary units is nonetheless different from investing them with final authority. Particularly since neither the intent nor direction of feminist reconstruction is derived from Jewish sources, the issue of the authority of these sources for feminist thought needs to be pressed further. How do a "hermeneutics of suspicion" and the use of critical methods accord with the authority of traditional texts? In the process of interpretation, where does authority finally reside? While this question intersects with a number of issues to be considered in other chapters, it is too central to any project of religious transformation to be treated only piecemeal. It will be necessary to anticipate some later discussion, therefore, to take it up in this context.

Modernity has brought increasing awareness of both the global diversity of religious beliefs and practices and the cultural location and historical development of individual religious traditions. This awareness has undermined the authority of traditional religions and weakened their claims to universality or to eternal truth. Feminists have participated in confronting the breakdown of old authority structures, and have responded to the problem of authority in several different ways. While some religious feminists have used the weakening authority of the Western traditions to criticize and move outside them entirely, others have sought within their traditions authority structures consonant with their beliefs. A number of Christian feminists, for example, have sought to find a "real (that is, nonsexist) Paul" or a feminist Jesus who can function as models for Christians today.[20] This nonsexist strand of the tradition is identified with "true" Christianity, while sexist Christianity is false and must change. Other feminist thinkers have acknowledged the basic androcentrism of biblical thinking, but have found within Scripture minority themes that submit the Bible to self-criticism. Some have focused on the prophetic tradition—not necessarily as a set of texts, but as an ongoing process of criticizing the status quo. Others have pointed to the equality of the original creation or to the presence of female God-language throughout the Bible.[21] While such themes are not statistically the norm, they may function as normative in that they provide a scriptural basis for feminist faith.

The problem with attempting to ground feminist (or any contemporary) conviction in Scripture, however, is that it denies or disguises the authority of the reader. When one element of a text is declared true or normative, where does authority actually lie? Do biblical texts themselves provide a sure basis for judging between their conflicting perspectives? The contrary uses to which the Bible has been put suggest that the needs and values of a community of readers are as much a source of norms as the texts themselves. Different communities have different stakes in maintaining and defending the authority of the Bible, but the selection of particular texts or passages as central or normative can seldom be justified on purely textual grounds.

If it is not the Bible itself that tells us which parts are authoritative, authority must rest in some outside source. In our individualistic American culture, this source is often identified as the individual, who picks and chooses among texts according to "personal preference." If we do not have the divine word, ostensibly we are left with only our own words, words that are changeable and subject to sway.[22] From a feminist perspective, however, human choices are not reducible to God/text or whim. Human beings are fundamentally communal; our individuality is a product of community, and our choices are shaped by our being with others.[23] Scripture itself is a product of community. It may be revelatory or communicate lasting values, but revelation is communally received and molded. Revelation is the experience of a reality that transcends language, that cannot be captured or possessed in words. The communal experiences of God's presence and power that lie at the origins of Jewish existence were crystallized by certain sensitive individuals, and recreated in language to be stored in memory. Language bears witness to revelation. It allows the possibility that, centuries after the original event, one may find reverberating in a text the extraordinary experience in which it was formed.[24]

But language bears witness to the enduring in words that are limited. Not only must it suggest rather than chronicle the revelatory experience, it does so within the cultural framework that language itself inscribes. Revelation may surprise us and destroy our preconceptions, but it must compete with language already in place. The Bible emerged in a context in which patriarchal modes of social organization were being consolidated and justified. The record of revelation is for the most part assimilated to this task and never decisively breaks with it.[25] As we have seen, women's revelatory experiences are largely omitted from the sources; narratives are framed from an androcentric perspective; the law enforces women's subordination in the patriarchal family. Insofar as biblical texts silence women and serve to oppress them, they must be criticized as "revealing" patriarchy.

The authority that grounds this criticism, however, is not individual experience or some private intuition. It is rather the experience of particular communities struggling for religious transformation.[26] For example, the community that is my central authority is the Jewish feminist community, for it is in this community my identity finds fullest expression. But beyond it lie the *havurah* and broader feminist communities, the wider Jewish community, and the communities of all those working for religious and political change. Just as Jews of the past experienced God and interpreted their experiences in communal contexts that shaped what they saw and heard, so we also read their words and experience God in communities—communities in continuity with, but different from, theirs. It is the contemporary feminist community that has taught me to value and attend to women's experience. It is this community that has taught me that Jewish sources have been partial and oppressive, occasionally ugly and simply wrong.

It is true that through and behind the androcentrism of Jewish teaching may lie profound and important insights and frameworks of meaning. Jewish sources have a claim on me to be read and heard and taken seriously. But the claim is not final. I am responsible first to the Jewish feminist community and its struggle to create a Judaism that includes all Jews. To say that this community is my central source of authority is not to deny the range of ideas or disagreements within it, or the other communities of which I am part. It is simply to say that I have been formed in important ways by Jewish feminism; without it I could not see the things that I see. It is to say that my most important experiences of God have come through this community, and that it has given me the language with which to express them. To name this community my authority is to call it the primary community to which I am accountable. It is to claim that its vision enhances life beyond itself—that it can enhance Jewish life and life on this planet.

To locate authority in particular communities of interpreters is admittedly to make a circular appeal. Yet it is also to acknowledge what has always been the case: that in deciding what is authoritative in sacred texts, deciding communities take authority to themselves. When the rabbis said that rabbinic modes of interpretation were given at Sinai, they were claiming authority for their own community—just as other groups had before them, just as feminists do today.

A WORD ABOUT THEOLOGY

In the last several pages, I have addressed certain of my theological presuppositions, but not my reasons for writing a theology. Yet it may seem that if my goal is a feminist Judaism, feminist theology is a peculiar place to begin.

Theology, after all, has had only a limited role in Jewish religious life.[27] Reflection on God, the mission of Israel, the nature of human life has more often been confined to the interstices of rabbinic discussions or dealt with midrashically than considered independently in works on such subjects. While there is a history of Jewish philosophy from Philo to the present, philosophy is generally left to a marginal few with the interest in and inclination to such things. The main energy of Jewish intellectual life has gone into the elaboration of the law, and it is observance of the law, rather than adherence to theological principles, that marks one a religious Jew. Law takes precedence over beliefs and feelings, which are expected to flow from action rather than to ground it.

But if the law maintains its primacy in Jewish self-understanding, theology affects Jewish practice in important, unseen ways. Indeed, there is a mutually reinforcing relationship between Jewish theology and Jewish religious practice and institutions. Patriarchal theology, while it cannot of itself give rise to patriarchal structures, supports patriarchy as a religious and legal system. When Torah is thought of as divinely revealed in its present form, the subordination of women is granted the seal of divine approval. When God is conceived of as male, as a king ruling over his universe, male rule in society seems appropriate and right. The correlate of this relationship between patriarchal theology and religious structures is that feminist theology may help to undermine patriarchal institutions, and at least will no longer support them. When Torah embraces the experience of women and men as full members of the Jewish people, it will no longer be possible to base women's subordination on appeals to the divine will. When we think of God as male/female friend and lover, or as the ground and source of being, new images of human relating will be fostered in our imaginations, and we will not be able consciously or unconsciously to appeal to metaphors for God to justify male social domination.

So long as theology is dismissed as unimportant, the sexism built into certain basic Jewish ideas is aided and abetted by the neglect of theology. It is difficult to confront the structural implications of God's maleness, for example, if the community is not really interested in thinking about God anyway. The issue of the gender of God can always be jettisoned on the grounds that theology is trivial, at the same time old images continue to work their effects. Only when the basic categories of Jewish thought are reconstructed in the light of women's silence will unexamined theological assumptions cease to operate at women's expense.

The fact that theology surreptitiously affects many aspects of Jewish practice may make theology relevant even to secular Jewish feminists. Jewish literature and communal life, radicalism and ethnic identity are governed by a host of presuppositions concerning which Jews are normative, what constitutes Jewish values, the proper ways to order community, and the proper tasks of life. Many of these presuppositions have infiltrated from the theological sphere but remain doubly hidden when religion as well as theology is rejected. Theological analysis, because it lays bare some of the assumptions that operate unnamed in secular

Jewish movements, can provide secular feminists with more power to transform these assumptions.

But there is another reason why theology is important. When a religious system has become established and its structures self-perpetuating, it often loses contact with the experiences at its root. Rabbis need not stand at Sinai with the first generation to make legal decisions. They must read the works of their predecessors and follow the appropriate rules. Moreover, insofar as Jewish identity is based on orthopraxis, there is no necessary relation between practice and religious experience; practice is self-justifying: it makes one a Jew. But for those who would transform the tradition, the situation is different: Reform always begins in conviction and vision. Jewish feminism, like all reform movements, is rooted in deeply felt experience and a powerful image of religious change. Wherever the individual feminist locates her active interests—in liturgy, theology, midrash, law—she acts out of commitment to an animating vision that has important repercussions for community life and practice. My central reason for writing a Jewish feminist theology, then, is to articulate one version of this vision and to foster its growth. If feminist theologies help to reanimate the connection between practice and belief in the Jewish world more generally, they will have made another important contribution to Jewish religious life.

NOTES

1. Carol P. Christ, "Spiritual Quest and Women's Experience," in *Womanspirit Rising: A Feminist Reader in Religion*, edited by Carol P. Christ and Judith Plaskow (San Francisco: Harper & Row, 1979), 229.

2. Simone de Beauvoir, *The Second Sex*, translated by H. M. Parshley (New York: Bantam Books, 1961), xv–xvii.

3. Dina's birth is mentioned in Gen. 30:21; her story is found in Gen. 34. In naming their anthology of Jewish feminist writing *The Tribe of Dina: A Jewish Woman's Anthology* (1986; reprint ed., Boston: Beacon Press, 1989), Melanie Kaye/Kantrowitz and Irena Klepfisz restore Dina to her rightful place.

4. The following discussion is based on my article, "The Right Question is Theological," in *On Being a Jewish Feminist: A Reader*, edited by Susannah Heschel (New York: Schocken Books, 1983), 223–33.

5. The fact that God takes Sarah's side does not alter the problematic nature of the relationship between Sarah and Hagar, which has been explored especially powerfully by black women. See, for example, Delores Williams, "Womanist Theological Perspectives on the Hagar-Sarah Story" (paper delivered at Princeton University, May 17, 1988).

6. See Savina Teubal, *Sarah the Priestess: The First Matriarch of Genesis* (Athens, OH: Swallow Press, 1984) and "Sarah and Hagar: Power in Ritual" (paper delivered at the 1985 Annual Meeting of the American Academy of Religion).

7. Jacob Neusner, *A History of the Mishnaic Law of Women*, 5 vols (Leiden: E. J. Brill, 1980), 5:13f., 271f.

8. Cynthia Ozick, "Notes Toward Finding the Right Question," in *Lilith* 6 (1979): 19–29; reprinted in Heschel, *On Being a Jewish Feminist*, 120–51; quotation, 149.

9. See T. Drorah Setel, "Prophets and Pornography: Female Sexual Imagery in

Hosea," in *Feminist Interpretation of the Bible*, edited by Letty M. Russell (Philadelphia: Westminster Press, 1985), 86–95.

10. De Beauvoir, *The Second Sex*, 641–42. See Judith Plaskow, *Sex, Sin, and Grace: Women's Experience and the Theologies of Reinhold Niebuhr and Paul Tillich* (Washington, D.C.: University Press of America, 1980), chapter 1, for an extended discussion of "women's experience" and its relation to prevailing cultural role definitions.

11. Elisabeth Schüssler Fiorenza, *Bread Not Stone: The Challenge of Feminist Biblical Interpretation* (Boston: Beacon Press, 1984), 15ff.

12. *Ibid.*, 15. "Androcentric" and "androcentrism" refer to the assumption that maleness is constitutive of humanity. See Rita Gross, "Androcentrism and Androgyny in the Methodology of the History of Religions," in *Beyond Androcentrism: New Essays on Women and Religion*, edited by Rita Gross (Missoula, MT: Scholars Press, 1977), 7–21.

13. See my "The Jewish Feminist: Conflict in Identities," in *The Jewish Woman: New Perspectives*, edited by Elizabeth Koltun (New York: Schocken Books, 1976), 4.

14. Mary Daly, "Post-Christian Theology: Some Connections Between Idolatry and Methodolatry, Between Deicide and Methodicide" (address given at the Annual Meeting of the American Academy of Religion, 1973); for a more general reference see the paper of the same name in Joan Arnold Romero, *Women and Religion: 1973 Proceedings* (Tallahassee, FL: American Academy of Religion, 1973), 33. For Phyllis Trible's discussion of depatriarchalizing, see her *God and the Rhetoric of Sexuality* (Philadelphia: Fortress Press, 1978).

15. Schüssler Fiorenza, *Bread Not Stone*, 19–20.

16. See T. Drorah Setel, "Power and Pollution: The Ritual Purity/Impurity System in the Hebrew Bible" (paper delivered at the Annual Meeting of the American Academy of Religion, 1982); Merlin Stone, *When God Was a Woman* (New York: Dial Press, 1976), chapter 8.

17. Schüssler Fiorenza, *Bread Not Stone*, 19–20. The phrase in quotation marks is Johann Baptist Metz's.

18. See, for example, Richard Elliot Friedman, *Who Wrote the Bible?* (New York: Summit Books, 1987), chapter 14.

19. Emil Fackenheim calls this divided consciousness that characterizes modern faith "immediacy after reflection" (*God's Presence in History: Jewish Affirmations and Philosophical Reflections* [New York: New York University Press, 1970], 47–49), while Paul Tillich talks about "broken myths" (*Dynamics of Faith* [New York: Harper & Row, 1957], 50–51).

20. In editing *The Woman's Bible* (1898; reprint ed., Seattle: Coalition Taskforce on Women and Religion, 1974), Elizabeth Cady Stanton took advantage of the advent of biblical criticism to radically question biblical authority from a feminist perspective. Today the whole women's spirituality movement takes place outside the authority structures of Judaism or Christianity. See Charlene Spretnak, ed., *The Politics of Women's Spirituality: Essays on the Rise of Spiritual Power within the Feminist Movement* (Garden City, NY: Anchor Books/Doubleday, 1982) for a range of examples. For a Christian response to the problem of authority, see Robin Scroggs, "Paul and the Eschatological Woman," *Journal of the American Academy of Religion* 40 (September 1972): 283–303, and Scroggs, "Paul and the Eschatological Woman: Revisited" and Elaine Pagels, "Paul and Women: A Response to Recent Discussion," *JAAR* 42 (September 1974): 532–49 for a small sample of the debate on Paul. Leonard Swidler was the first to propose the "Jesus was a feminist" argument which has been reiterated innumerable times; see "Jesus Was a Feminist," *Catholic World* 212 (January 1971): 177–83.

21. On the prophetic tradition, see Rosemary Ruether, *Sexism and God-Talk: Toward a Feminist Theology* (Boston: Beacon Press: 1983), 22–27 and "Feminist Interpretation: A Method of Correlation," in Russell, *Feminist Interpretation*, 118–22. On the themes

of equality in creation and female God-language, see Trible, *God and the Rhetoric of Sexuality*. Russell's book provides a general overview of feminist hermeneutics, as does Adela Yarbro Collins, ed., *Feminist Perspectives on Biblical Scholarship* (Chico, CA: Scholars Press, 1985). Jewish feminist hermeneutics is in the earliest stages of development.

22. For example, at a major symposium on "Cultural and Religious Relativism," held at the 92nd Street YM-YWHA, January–February 1986, the issue of authority was presented as a conflict between communal imperatives rooted in divine sanction and individual choice. Martha Ackelsberg helped me to see and criticize this dichotomy.

23. See Judith Plaskow, *Standing Again at Sinai: Judaism from a Feminist Perspective* (San Francisco: Harper & Row, 1990), 76–81, chap. 3, for a fuller discussion of this point.

24. Martin Buber ("The Man of Today and the Jewish Bible," in *On the Bible* [New York: Schocken Books, 1968], 1–13 and *Moses: The Revelation and the Covenant* [New York: Harper & Row, 1958]) and H. Richard Niebuhr (*The Meaning of Revelation* [New York: The Macmillan Company, 1941]) are the two theologians who have most influenced my view of revelation.

25. See Norman K. Gottwald, *The Tribes of Yahweh* (Maryknoll, NY: Orbis Books, 1979), 685; "Yahweh's asexuality was apparently not invoked to challenge or shatter male dominance in the Israelite society as a whole in the decisive way, for example, that class dominance was challenged and shattered by Yahweh's liberating action."

26. In this, I agree with Elisabeth Schüssler Fiorenza, *In Memory of Her. A Feminist Theological Reconstruction of Christian Origins* (New York: Crossroad, 1983), 29, 32 and *Bread Not Stone*, 3.

27. Both Louis Jacobs (*A Jewish Theology* [West Orange, NJ: Behrman House, 1973], 10–12) and Michael Wyschogrod (*The Body of Faith: Judaism as Corporeal Election* [San Francisco: Harper & Row, 1983], xiii) begin their Jewish theologies by addressing this point.

3

Experiencing the Body: Sexuality and Conflict in American Lutheranism

CHRISTIAN SCHAREN

Some issues that most vex the Christian church today I address in this article.[1] Sexuality, and particularly homosexuality, as terms in debate really point to larger collections of issues that have and are still causing untold strife in denominations and many local churches. The hot-button issues come to mind, such as should the church bless same-sex unions? Should the church ordain gay and lesbian pastors if they are in committed relationships? More fundamentally, what shall the church say about the moral status of gay partnerships and gay sex? And beyond these, what shall we say about the increasing numbers of young adults who live together before marriage? What of a society where even those newlyweds who go to church have a 50% chance of filing for divorce before their twentieth anniversary? What of violence against women? Pornography? Prostitution? Sex tourism? I could go on and on, sadly. While I will not pretend to be a neutral observer to these questions, my primary object in this article is not to sell you on my point of view or even the "Christian point of view" on any particular question. Rather, I want to examine with some care what a "point of view" entails. I'll focus on the meaning of a "point of view" by thinking through the ways experience informs moral discernment. In doing so, I attend to the multiple ways "experience" influences one's point of view, and the role "experience" plays in changing one's mind.

My aim is really quite simple and can be summed up in a guiding thesis, a thesis that I will slowly unpack through three related points.

Christian moral discernment depends on four sources—Scripture, tradition, reason, and experience—and recognizing the priority of experience aids the success of such discernment in community.

My method in defending this thesis is the following. First, I will discuss the powerful story of the Honorable Dan Ponder and his role in passing hate crimes legislation in the Georgia legislature. His story witnesses to the ways the stories of our lives powerfully shape who we are. Second, I turn to my own story of moving from a place of condemnation of homosexuality as sin to a place of embracing gay and lesbian people as a grace in my life and as God's good creation. In telling this story, I will examine more analytically the use of four sources in moral discernment and judgment: Scripture, the Christian tradition, reason, and experience. I will both show how these four sources interact and what I mean by focusing on the priority of experience, especially when one changes deeply held convictions. Third and last, shifting from my own experience to the experience of the denomination in which I serve, the Evangelical Lutheran Church in America (ELCA), I conclude with reflections on the role of experience in the corporate body of the church as it debates changes on same-sex unions and ordination.

DAN PONDER: TWO KINDS
OF EXPERIENCES

Former Georgia State Representative Dan Ponder, Jr. was in the last days of his term in the legislature. A white Republican from an ultra-conservative south Georgia district, Ponder was known as a consensus builder behind the scenes rather than a fiery orator. Yet as it became clear that a hate crime bill under debate was headed for defeat, being accused by conservatives as creating special protections for a special "class" of people, Ponder rose to speak. He took his place in the well and began, voice trembling: "I am probably the last person, the most unlikely person that you would expect to be speaking from the well about Hate Crimes Legislation."

He shared how he had grown up as the son of a prosperous peanut farming family, raised in a conservative Baptist church. His town was so conservative that, he recalled, when his third-grade classmates learned that President Kennedy had been shot, they erupted in cheers. He attended a large, mostly white Southern university and was president of the largest all-white fraternity there. He confided that nine of his great-great-great grandfathers fought for the Confederacy. He did not have one single ancestor who lived north of the Mason-Dixon Line going back to the revolutionary war. "Although I'm not proud of it," he noted, "not one, but several of those ancestors actually owned slaves."

"So," Ponder continued, "you would guess just by listening to my background that I'm going to stand up here and talk against hate crime legislation. But you see, that's the problem when you start stereotyping people by who they are and where they come from, because I totally, totally support this bill."

He then began to systematically recount his various experiences of discrimination. His sister married a Catholic and while his Baptist church refused to host the wedding, his [brother-in-law's] priest refused to officiate as well. Another sister married a Jew, a difference of religion that has split the family for 25 years. And although 6 of his 100 fraternity brothers are now openly gay, the "lasting bond of brotherhood" that they pledged themselves to during those years has not stopped these brothers from being ostracized.

Suddenly, Rep. Ponder turned to the main reason for his speech. He pleaded for the attention of the assembly, and launched in to a painful public confession of his own act of discrimination. I'll tell the story in Ponder's words:

> There was one woman in my life that made a huge difference and her name was Mary Ward. She began working for my family before I was born. She was a young black woman whose own grandmother raised my mother. Mary, or May-Mar as I called her, came every morning before I was awake to cook breakfast so it would be on the table. She cooked our lunch. She washed our clothes.
>
> But she was much more than that. She read books to me. When I was playing Little League, she would go out and catch ball with me. She was never, ever afraid to discipline me or spank me. She expected the absolute best out of me, perhaps, and I'm sure, even more than she did her own children. She would even travel with my family when we would go to our house in Florida during the summer, just as her own grandmother had done.
>
> One day, when I was about 12 or 13, I was leaving for school. As I was walking out the door she turned to kiss me goodbye. And for some reason, I turned my head. She stopped me and she looked into my eyes with a look that absolutely burns in my memory right now and she said, "You didn't kiss me because I am black." At that instant, I knew she was right. I denied it. I made some lame excuse about it. But I was forced at that age to confront a small dark part of myself. I don't even know where it came from. This lady, who was devoting her whole life to me and my brother and sister, who loved me unconditionally, who had changed my diapers and fed me, and who was truly my second mother, somehow wasn't worthy of a goodbye kiss simply because of the color of her skin.
>
> I have lived with the shame and memory of my betrayal of Mary Ward's love for me. I pledged to myself then and I re-pledged to myself the day I buried her that never, ever again would I look in the mirror and know that I had kept silent, and let hate or prejudice or indifference negatively impact a person's life . . . even if I didn't know them.

By the time Rep. Ponder finished his speech, fellow lawmakers were stunned and silent. Some openly cried in their seats. He received two standing ovations and it took 45 minutes for him to get back to his seat. And the law passed overwhelmingly, making Georgia the 43rd state in the Union to pass such legislation.[2]

As remarkable as this story is, its effectiveness resulted not from its unique character, even though it was quite personal. Rather, the story found its power in the fact that so many of his fellow white Republican legislators were shaped by similar stories, and guarded similar dark secrets. We are all strongly shaped by the culture of our childhood, by the stories we learn at home and in church and at school. Those stories combined in quite unconscious ways to lead young Dan Ponder to the point of an unthinking rejection of Mary Ward's kiss. He might not have given it much thought had she not forced the issue and caused him to make conscious the reason for his rejection. That one moment, likely spoken out of Mary Ward's great pain and sadness, placed in his mind a creative and ultimately redemptive conflict between the assumptions of his culture of white Southern privilege and the assumptions of a Christian love which shows no partiality.

I want to highlight two modes of experience at work in this story.[3] First, the unconscious formative power of experience that shapes who we are. It is not so much that we tell stories, but that our stories tell us. They are the water we swim in, the air we breathe. We are schooled from the earliest age to know if the world is trustworthy and full of possibility or to be feared as a place of hurt and pain. We learn markers of distinction that tell us what is expected of "people like us," with implicit or explicit markers of distinction for those who do not meet our standard. These formative experiences are powerful largely because they are assumed, and taught by example. They are passed on as beliefs, manners, customs, and they mark our body as much as our mind and spirit. Dan Ponder began with a description of this type of experience and concluded that on the basis of the evidence about the stories that live in him, of Confederate soldiers and slave owners, his colleagues in the legislature expected him to speak against the hate crimes legislation.

Yet, there is *a second type of experience*, at once more time-specific and conscious yet no less powerful in its effects. These are the experiences that change us because we are confronted with a compelling story we've not heard before. These experiences usually create conflict and set in motion a process of change whose outcome is never determined in advance, but is nonetheless driven by the memory of certain people and things that happened to us at a particular moment in life. Dan Ponder describes this sort of experience in his story about rejecting Mary Ward's kiss that morning when he was leaving for school. Her look and her words of truth came as a jolting event that set him off-balance and shook his taken-for-granted view of the world. He did not respond well at the time, for as he recalls, he denied the truth and made up a lame excuse for his behavior. Yet he had been confronted with the truth and as he lived with that new experience, he began to see differently. He saw the prejudice and hate all around him. He was a part of causing it. And he began to see that his new story required him to rethink his assumptions and to act differently than he had before.

If you, kind reader, pause for a moment and reflect for a few minutes about what Dan Ponder's story evoked in you, I'll wager that it sparked a memory of your own experiences with discrimination. Maybe it sparked a memory of a time when you changed your mind about something. Before I turn to a more analytical and more confessional section, I want you, also, to understand how utterly real and powerful are our experiences, especially those formative of our very being.

CHRISTIAN MORAL DISCERNMENT: FOUR SOURCES AND THE PRIORITY OF EXPERIENCE

I've asked you to call to mind your own experiences. Now I'll share mine. My grandfather, who is a Missouri-Synod Lutheran pastor, baptized me and I grew up in a small city in Southwest Montana where big boys like me played football from the 6th grade on. With a conservative religious background and the tough-guy ethic of the football locker room, I never heard anything that would lead me to see that being gay was good. We harassed "geeks" and "sissies," calling them "gay-boys" in our attempts to humiliate them. Yet I, too, got my taste of that same harassment because I was fat and had "breasts" and because I played in the band, which made me categorically suspect from the perspective of the "real guys" on the football team. So I lifted weights and went to the right parties and tried my best to get into trouble so that I'd fall on the right side of the divide between the tough guys and the wimps. In the tough halls of junior high and high school, "love of neighbor" too often translates into "love of those like me."

During those high school years, I became attracted to the highly individualistic gospel of positive thinking, for instance, as promoted by Norman Vincent Peale. I thought that mainly Jesus was interested in me being successful in life, and if I were good, and worked hard, I would gain what I wanted with His blessing. This mode of life fit right in with my early experience in college. I played football on a team saturated by positive-thinking Christianity. I went to classes, had fun, lifted weights, and generally waited for God to make everything turn out splendid. Out of this background, my second year in college, I wrote a response paper in a course on Christian Ethics. This paper asked my response to the case of an otherwise highly gifted and well-trained young man who wished to be ordained into the ministry but was openly gay. To me, it was an open and shut case. One called to the ordained ministry is called to be a model of the Christian life and promises to hold up a standard of "holy living" in the midst of the church. I quoted the standard bible texts condemning homosexuality. I think I mentioned proof-texts from Leviticus and Romans. And on that basis, I concluded that despite his high qualifications, he should not be ordained.

My argument in that college paper is a common perspective held by many Christians today. Marc Kolden, Professor of Systematic Theology and Academic Dean at Luther Seminary, argues much the same line in the theological journal *Dialog*.[4] Yet I wrote this out of my experience, my taken-for-granted view of the world, never having (knowingly) met a gay or lesbian person, let alone befriended or loved one. That changed the year after college. I spent the year serving in the Lutheran Volunteer Corps. I worked in a Franciscan ministry to the homeless. Brother Delvin (not his real name), one of the friars I worked with, who with his fellow friars taught me about the true meaning of dignity and love for the poor and outcast, was gay. He welcomed me into their community, and all the friars, as far as I could see, were faithful Christians by virtue of their total commitment to serve the ones without clothing, without food, and without shelter. During that same year, at the local Lutheran church I attended, the pastor and minister of music learned of my desire to go to seminary. They conspired together to begin my seminary education on the spot, helping me learn the assisting minister role and offering me my first experience preaching.

Fred (also not his real name), the music minister, was openly gay. I took vocal lessons from him and met some of his circle of gay friends.

In that year, I got to know and respect and love two men whom I learned were gay. Both were in ministry professionally, but neither was ordained as a priest or pastor. So, technically my argument against gay ordination did not apply. Still, my joy in them as men, and my experience of their lives of committed service in the church grated against the easy condemnation I'd worked out in my college paper. Thus I began a long and searching process of rethinking my assumptions.

I hope it is clear that present in this story of my life are the same two elements of experience I highlighted in Dan Ponder's story. First, I highlight my formative experience of "the way things are" in childhood that predisposed me to judge homosexuality negatively. And second, the critical experience during my LVC year as I came to know gay people for the first time. I have since become close to many gay and lesbian people, some of whom are pastors and some who are not. And I have come to view homosexuality positively, and I celebrate gay people as God's good creation, subject to sin like we all are, but not simply by virtue of their desires for partnership and love from those of the same sex. How did such a change occur in my moral evaluation of homosexuality? And what does this say about the role of experience in moral discernment and debate more generally?

Let me make some methodological comments about ethical reflection, and then fold these back into a discussion of how I changed my mind on this issue. It is commonly held that there are four components for making Christian ethical decisions. While not necessarily how everyday people make judgments, when the church as a community of moral deliberation pauses to deliberate we turn to four sources to aid us.[5] The four are Holy Scripture, the teachings and tradition of the church catholic, the findings of reason as expressed in academic disciplines of, say, biology or psychology, and finally our everyday experience. You might picture a group floating down a river on a raft, and each source represents one corner of the raft. Tipping the raft one way or another will influence the outcome of one's moral discernment.

While many disagreements over the proper balance of these four sources exist in the scholarly literature, I wish to point out that experience is never simply just one among the four sources. Rather, it infuses all the others, as a sort of founding source or means of knowing. So, for example, Holy Scripture records people's experience and reception of God and God's revelation in Jesus Christ; the church's traditions represent the collective experiences of God's pilgrim people over time; and it is now common to assume scholarly work to be influenced by the experiences of the scholar her- or himself. In addition, our experiences deeply influence how we interpret the data drawn from sources: how and what we draw from Scripture, tradition, and the secular disciplines. But I am already arguing for the priority of experience among the sources, and before I move to that, I'd like to note another prominent view.

In an article on sexuality in ministry, Steven Ullestad, Bishop of the North-eastern Iowa Synod, offers a traditionally Lutheran view on moral discernment and change drawing on these four sources.[6] He argues that the primary source is Holy Scripture. He cautions that interpretation must be done in community, rather than individually. By doing so, the body must come to some consensus about the witness of Scripture rather than simply one person saying, "But to me, Scripture says this!" Second, he turns to reason. He suggests that the church has changed its view that the earth is flat, and has changed its guidelines regarding divorce, not only through study of scripture but through the sciences and academic study. Change must be reasonably supported, in addition to fitting with an accepted interpretation of Scripture. Bishop Ullestad then places experience and tradition next to one another, as if they are a balance of powers. Individual experience sometimes must protest injustices, as Luther did, but the tradition helps discern the truth of individual experience—is it of God, or simply misguided desire? We can listen to the voices of the church catholic to find a broader view as a balance to our own sense of God's will.

With this model for using the four sources in moral discernment, Bishop Ullestad rejects the ordination of gay and lesbian pastors. He argues that in order to persuade him and the majority of his synod's congregations, an argument must move beyond stories of gay and lesbian experience to ground these stories in Holy Scripture. In his own words, the Bishop notes that changing the church's moral evaluation of homosexuality, and thus its ordination standards, "must communicate a profound respect for the inspired Word of God that is the source and norm for our lives."[7] Further, he argues, such an argument for change must grapple with the fact that the wisdom of the church catholic shows a vast majority does not favor changing the rules regarding gay ordination.

Typical of those who do not support gay and lesbian ordination and blessing of same-sex unions, Bishop Ullestad tips his raft toward the Scripture and tradition corners. When one looks at the arguments of those who do support gay and lesbian ordination and blessing of same-sex unions, you will not be surprised to see the raft tipping towards the reason and experience corners. Yet, as helpful as it is, in one respect the raft metaphor is misleading.

Here is where I make my own case for moral discernment and change on moral views. Proper moral discernment requires attention to all the sources, but I believe that we ignore at our peril what James Gustafson has called "the priority of human experience."[8] How is this so? Let me pick up my story again and see if I can make all this ethical methodology more concrete and clear. First, experience is prior because it is our experiences that we try to understand by use of the sources. In college, I was faced with the question whether my church should ordain gay and lesbian people who are either in a relationship or were open to it. I turned to Scripture for texts that dealt with homosexuality, found they confirmed my experience of negative cultural views about homosexuality, and made a negative judgment. I didn't bother to look into the views of Scripture scholars, historians or scientists.

But, after befriending gay and lesbian people, seeing their powerful callings to work for God in the church, and yet seeing the church reject their leadership and their relationships solely on the basis of their identity as gay or lesbian, I found myself thrown back onto the sources for another look.[9] I'll briefly venture some comments here about the steps I took. Already disposed to find in favor of a new position, yet unwilling to simply disregard Scripture and the tradition altogether, I tackled the traditional texts of condemnation first.

Scripture, it turns out, does not speak so clearly as I thought. As I read the careful work of bible scholars, I began to see that it is indeed a complex matter to discern what biblical references to same-sex relationships refer to, and then to make the leap to say if those negative judgments can be extended to what we understand today as a relatively given and stable gay or lesbian identity. Yet, despite my doubts, I came to grips with the fact that the bible, especially the text in Romans 1, views homoerotic behavior negatively. Then, I was faced with what to do with that fact.

I began to ask about other examples of texts that are largely disregarded today, and could this also fall in that category? I began to ask myself if I must accept at face value everything that the bible says. Do I think women should speak in church? Do I believe that slavery is acceptable and one should simply be obedient in one's given station in life? On both counts, I answered no. This, then, led me to ask about broader themes in Scripture and I took hold of texts regarding the covenant between God and Israel, between God and the church. Such texts are traditional scriptural texts for marriage, an institution that in the Christian view is not finally defined by which body parts fit together but by the commitment of love and life-long fidelity of one person to another.

In a similar way, I tackled our tradition. It, like Scripture, has little to say about homosexuality, and when it does comment, until very recently it is very unfavorable. Yet, I asked myself, has the church always been right? Has it not changed its mind regarding certain issues including the struggle in the New Testament church over inclusion of Gentile believers, and quite recently, the ordination of women (still a live question for various churches)? Does not, I asked myself, the church worship a *living Lord*, who through the Spirit's movement does new thing in the church? Such changes generally do not come from the institutional hierarchy. Rather, the Spirit seems most to find openings for change at the margins of society, at the margins of the church. So I looked to see and found many local congregations carrying out vital mission to and with gay and lesbian Christians. Some even called gay and lesbian pastors. And I said to myself, if this is of God, this ferment will grow and it will take hold. If it is not, then it will die away (the logic of the wise Rabbi Gamaliel, speaking of the followers of Jesus: see Acts 5:33–42). But insofar as I am able, I thought, I will find resources in our common tradition to support a new vision.

I found a good partner in this work in the person of Martin Luther. Luther did a similar thing, although the case was different in important ways. In his pastoral work and church leadership, he saw men and women suffering miserably under vows of celibacy because, while they in fact lived together in a common-law marriage, the priest could not take the woman as his wife and remain a priest. With this experience vexing him, he studied Scripture, asking about marriage, about sexuality, and about the vows God requires of those who serve in ministry. While he held the utmost respect for Scripture and certain of the Fathers of the church, Luther was no simple literalist. Luther counseled:

> one must deal openly with the scriptures. From the very beginning the word has come to us in various ways. It is not enough to simply look and see whether this is God's word, whether God's word has said it; rather we must look and see to whom it has been spoken, whether it fits us. That makes all the difference between night and day.[10]

Furthermore, he warned that the early church Fathers "often speak as a result of an emotion and of a particular mood which we do not have and cannot have, since we do not have similar situations."[11] As a result, he took on the work of fresh theological thinking and biblical interpretation in response to the experience of his day.

As with Luther, I am suggesting that our experiences are prior in the sense that we are driven to study by what we have experienced in the world. Our taken-for-granted moral understandings are challenged in some way, and we are forced to try to make sense of the conflict between what we thought right and a new possibility. Yet, experience, as Luther suggests, is also prior in the sense that we must look to see if the witness of Scripture, or tradition, or the sciences makes sense to us. In short, we won't be convinced by evidence that doesn't fit our frameworks of understanding. These two senses of the priority of experience match up with the two senses of experience I pointed out earlier: our unconscious experience that shapes and forms our view of "how things really are" and our conscious experiences in particular moments that challenge and ultimately revise some aspect of our sense of "how things really are."

I'm basically describing a process of conversion that entails three stages, in which a radically new experience dislodges our taken-for-granted way of understanding and causes us to work out a new understanding, resolving the tension into a new taken-for-granted view. How we experience the challenge to our deeply held understanding, and how we go about resolving that challenge, will be widely divergent. At times, experience leads to a reversal of our former position. Yet, it may lead to a retrenchment behind the traditional view. No matter the outcome of one's process of moral discernment and change, understanding the "priority of experience" as central to *all* our moral views enables us to see that it is not only naive to expect very different people to agree, but to expect an easy, quick, or painless change of mind.

At the very least, understanding the way in which experience both shapes our settled opinions and has a key place in our changing moral understanding gives us a realistic starting place in conversation with others. Dialogue will go nowhere if we only trade back and forth with our settled opinions, without inquiring into the assumptions and formative experiences that are the roots of such taken-for-granted moral views, on issues of sexuality or any other. That means that we do best when we are in a relationship over time with those who may disagree so that the conversation is just that, and not slinging slogans.

BUILDING UP OR BREAKING DOWN:
SLOGANS, RIGHTS, AND DISSENT

I've now landed in the middle of my third point about the role of experience in change. I've already hinted at this earlier so I'll be brief and clear here. Over the last decade, the language of "culture wars" has entered our public debate.[12] One option for dealing with conflict over difficult moral issues is most clearly evidenced in the abortion debate. Activists on either side use words as weapons, trading slogans on placards and bumper stickers. They don't live together, let alone talk together over time, pausing each week to pray and sing and break bread at the table of the Lord. Such a black and white debate mostly serves the interests of the media who like a simple story between two clear opponents. As we all know, good sound bites and bloody fights sell papers and garner high viewer ratings. But woe is the church if we choose this way. Change will come, but not change that builds the body up.

Another problematic option for dealing with conflict over difficult moral issues is captured in all the talk in the public arena about "rights." This is tied to the culture wars debate, but is a separate issue regarding entitlement and our peculiar American definition of liberty. The motto of the state of Vermont sums up this liberal tradition of so-called negative liberty: "don't tread on me." Liberal individualism has had positive fruits, including the right to dissent itself, but the logic of claiming rights can foster a nation of client-citizens who depend on others for recognition.[13] Such logic has influenced the gay rights movement, both in society and in the church. Somehow, because one experiences oneself as oppressed, one has a right to legal protection and restitution. But this is not the language and logic of the church. God does not have clients, and does not guarantee rights. We are all sinners before God's gracious and merciful judgment. As Luther put it on his deathbed, "we are all beggars." Organizing to fight for the right to baptism or the right to ordination will lead away from true change because it pushes the whole issue into the realm of legislation and institutional provision for the needs of those dependent on centralized power.

So, if fighting culture wars and demanding individual rights won't aid change that builds the body up, what can be a source of hope for those who, like me, wish and work for change on an individual and a church-wide level? How does change happen? In one sense, my argument as a whole describes the role of experience in changing deeply held moral views. But thus far, I've focused on the individual level and not the corporate level. Let me tell one more story that helps make the leap from individual to corporate, and offers an example of what

I think holds the most promise for change that will place great pressures on the church, but not in the end break it down, but rather build it up.

In a number of public forums Paul Egertson, the former ELCA bishop of the Southern California West Synod, recounts the process of change he and his wife, Shirley, went through after their eldest son told them he was gay.[14] A painful process, to be sure, but in retrospect one in which they see God's creative grace. Thus, they tell the story drawing on the motif of the seven days of creation. On the first symbolic day of their creation, they reported a strong desire to deny what their son told them. They responded with a knee-jerk rejection of homosexuality based on their understanding of Scripture and common sense. But, as they grappled with the tension between their taken-for-granted experience and the new challenge of their son's news, they moved to a sixth day of creation in which they celebrate his homosexuality. They see his minority sexual orientation as "variety in nature" rather that "contrary to nature," and find delight in God's wide and diverse creation.

Like Dan Ponder and his experience with Mary Ward, like my experience in the Lutheran Volunteer Corps, Bishop Egertson faced the crisis situation where one's assumptions about moral virtue and vice are strongly challenged by a new experience. This sort of story-telling, this telling of the truth, may become the catalyst for change. Yet, I still am primarily talking about an individual level of change. Equally important, but dependent on the changed individuals for its power, is corporate change. Here, the point is not slinging slogans like the culture warriors, nor demanding access on the basis of a right to full membership like the liberal activists.

Rather, I think that faithful dissent, guided by conscience and shared with a community of believers, offers a more realistic chance. Growing numbers of congregations, including my former congregation in Atlanta, are simply and quietly calling qualified openly gay or lesbian candidates. This is accepted in the church technically, but in fact is not widely known.[15] By doing it, these congregations make the point that our current rules do not preclude openly gay and lesbian clergy from the ordained ministry. Rather, the ELCA requires of its gay and lesbian pastors chastity in singleness, with no option of a romantic relationship that leads to a lifetime commitment. This is widely noted to be an ironic stance for a church that stood against vows of celibacy at its founding. And, furthermore, an ill-conceived rule that disrespects the real and rare true gift of celibacy lived by monks and nuns and priests in our sister Catholic and Orthodox churches.

In an additional step beyond "playing by the rules," clergy and laity are joining together to ordain and install qualified gay or lesbian candidates who have met all the other requirements for ordination except that they are in committed relationships. This took place with dramatic effect on April 28, 2001 at St. Paul-Reformation, an ELCA congregation in St. Paul, Minnesota. Bishop Egertson was one of four former or current Lutheran Bishops present to participate in the ordination and to stand with Anita C. Hill, the candidate who was ordained and installed. While it cost Bishop Egertson his job, he nonetheless felt compelled to act on his convictions. In defending his actions, he gives hints at what loyal dissent might involve:

> St. Paul/Reformation Lutheran Church has voted to move forward outside the bounds of constitutional partnership in the ELCA. They do so only after one of the longest periods of intentional ministry with and to gay and lesbian people of any congregation in this church. They do so with a candidate as qualified by spiritual gifts, academic preparation, and experience in ministry as any Ordinand in this church. They do so after exhausting every reasonable avenue of recourse available within the polity of this church. This is no act of defiant congregationalism, but an act of conscience-driven faithfulness to their ministry of the Gospel.[16]

While this event has a long history and many complicated details, the fact I wish to bring to the fore is its character as an act not of slogan warfare, nor liberal protest for rights, but loyal dissent, ecclesial disobedience done in fear and trembling but with faith that such action will serve as one more powerful catalyst experience, calling the church to the work of rethinking its taken-for-granted views and policies.[17] St. Paul-Reformation has engaged in mission work to gay and lesbian Christians for more than 18 years, making it one of a handful of lead churches in the ELCA on this front. Once we stop and listen to this congregation's story, and the experiences that have brought them this far on the way, we should not be surprised by their actions at all and we might even be changed by the hearing.

NOTES

1. Thanks to the good people of St. Mark's Lutheran Church, Spokane, Washington (especially the Rev. Beth Jarrett and the Diversity Committee) for hosting and responding to an early version of this work. Thanks also to the folks at the 2002 Lutherans in Diaspora Conference (a gathering of East Coast Lutheran seminarians attending non-Lutheran seminaries) for similar duty. Both were a joy.

2. Dan Ponder, "Remarks on SB 390 Hate Crimes Legislation," Georgia State Legislature, Thursday, March 16, 2000. For more on this remarkable story, see John Blake, "Unlikely Crusader," *The Atlanta Constitution*, 16 March 2001. The whole text of the speech is available many places on the web, including www.stophate.us/ponder-speech.htm.

3. In thinking this way about the formative power of experience and about change, I'm drawing on the work of Ann Swidler (*Talk of Love: How Culture Matters* [University of Chicago, 2001]), in which she expands her very influential article, "Culture in Action: Symbols and Strategies," *American Sociological Review* 51 (April 1986): 273–286.

4. Marc Kolden, "No" (in response to editorial question, "Can Pastors be Openly Gay or Lesbian") in *Dialog* 40 (Spring 2001):19–20.

5. The best analysis of the ELCA as a community of moral deliberation is Per Anderson, "Deliberation, Holism, and Responsibility: Moral Life in the ELCA," *Journal of Lutheran Ethics* 1 (September 2001).

6. Steven Ullestad, "No" (response to editorial question, "Can Pastors be Openly Gay or Lesbian?") in *Dialog* 40 (Spring 2001): 9–11.

7. Ullestad, "No," 11.

8. James Gustafson, *Ethics from a Theocentric Perspective, Volume One: Theology and Ethics* (Chicago: University of Chicago, 1981), 115ff.

9. It is exactly at this point that my understanding of experience pushes back on such critics as the recent "Pastoral Statement of Conviction and Concern" resulting from a Fall 2002 Conference on Christian Sexuality sponsored by the American Lutheran Publicity Bureau. Under point three in their statement, they argue that they "are troubled by the process that has been used in recent studies on human sexuality within the ELCA. The conversations on this issue thus far have largely focused on personal experience and the sharing of anecdotes, rather than on the teaching of Holy Scripture and the theological and confessional witness of the church. We call the church to recognize that personal experience is not a reliable interpretive key to the Word of God." What I argue here is that experience a) always shapes our reading of "normative" sources including Scripture and tradition, and b) at times causes us to reassess our settled opinion of the "normative" sources in relation to the issue at hand—in this case the moral status of same-sex sexual relationships.

10. Martin Luther, "How Christians Should Regard Moses," in Timothy Lull, ed., *Martin Luther's Basic Theological Writings* (Minneapolis: Fortress Press, 1989), 145.

11. Martin Luther, "Lectures on Genesis 1–5," George V. Schick, trans., *Luther's Works, American Edition,* Jaroslav Pelikan and Helmut T. Lehmann, eds. (St. Louis: Concordia Publishing House, 1957), 61.

12. Of course, the basic book here is James Davidson Hunter, *Culture Wars* (New York: Basic Books, 1992). Yet very interesting subsequent testing of his thesis has shown that the polarization is mainly among activists whose antics the media favor. As a general trend across various social issues, decreased polarization seems to be the case. See Paul DiMaggio, Paul Evans and Bethany Bryson, "Have Americans' Social Attitudes Become More Polarized?" *American Journal of Sociology* 102 (1996): 690–755.

13. Michael Walzer is most influential on my thinking here, and he works on this idea in any number of places. For a beginning, see his influential article, "The Idea of Civil Society: A Path to Social Reconstruction," *Dissent* 38 (1991): 293–304.

14. For one source, see Paul Wennes Egertson, "One Family's Story," 24–30, in Walter Wink, ed., *Homosexuality and the Christian Faith: Questions of Conscience for the Churches* (Minneapolis: Fortress Press, 1999).

15. In point of fact, the question posed by the editor of a major Lutheran theology journal, "Can pastors be openly gay or lesbian" (see footnote 4 above) makes my case. Technically, one can indeed be openly gay or lesbian and be acceptable. The issue, in the language of the document *Vision and Expectations,* is that "Ordained ministers who are homosexual in their self-understanding are expected to abstain from homosexual sexual relationships." See *Vision and Expectations: Ordained Ministers in the Evangelical Lutheran Church in America* (Chicago: Office of the Secretary of the ELCA, 1990), 13.

16. Letter of (then) Bishop Paul Egertson to (then) ELCA Presiding Bishop H. George Anderson, dated March 29, 2001, and circulated by email.

17. The language of loyal dissent today is claimed by people across a wide spectrum of issues and positions, from my use here, to leaders in the Word Alone movement who protest recent ecumenical partnership with the Episcopal Church, to advocates of dialogue on tough social issues who use the term to call dissenters to faithfulness to the Church even if the majority favors another view. I find Michael Walzer most thoughtful on issues of dissent and obligation in political terms. See, for example, *Obligations: Essays on Disobedience, War, and Citizenship* (Cambridge: Harvard University Press, 1970). Yet, more careful work needs to be done on the issue of polity, ecclesiology, and dissent in the Lutheran tradition. As Conrad Bergendoff noted now almost 50 years ago in his Knubel-Miller lectures on The Doctrine of the Church, Lutherans in the United

States have dealt with incredible diversity in their patterns of church organization and theological and historical justifications for them. See Conrad Bergendoff, *The Doctrine of the Church in American Lutheranism* (Philadelphia: Muhlenberg Press, 1956). A contemporary starting place would be Edward LeRoy Long's treatment of Lutherans as "connective congregationalists" in his *Patterns of Polity: Varieties of Church Governance* (Cleveland: The Pilgrim Press, 2001), 103–117.

4

Black and Blues: God-Talk/Body-Talk for the Black Church

KELLY BROWN DOUGLAS

Ooh, there's something going all wrong;
Ooh, ooh there's something going all wrong;
The way I'm thinking, I know I can't last long.

Ma Rainey[1]

"There's something going all wrong" in the black church. This essay will attempt to discern what is going wrong in this church through examining its responses to sexuality by using a "blues" methodology. Before doing so, however, two things must be clarified: the meaning of the black church and the significance of sexuality to black church identity.

There is no single entity that can be pointed to as the black church. The black church is a diverse grouping of churches that reflects the rich complexity of the black community itself. It is defined by both its historical and social-cultural significance. Historically, the black church emerged as a fundamental part of black people's resistance to white racial oppression, particularly slavery. This church continues to play a central role in the black struggle for life and freedom. Socially and culturally, the black church has been one of the most significant influences upon black values. It shapes black people's notions of what is morally acceptable or unacceptable. The black church is also a critical resource for black well-being, whether physical, emotional, or spiritual. The black church's significance to black life is undeniable.[2] That there is something going wrong within it is, therefore, of vital concern.

What is going wrong in the black church? The black church's attitudes toward issues of sexuality help us to answer this question.

Black churches consistently garner headlines for what many consider to be backward if not unjust views toward sexuality, particularly homoerotic expressions of sexuality. Black clergy have been vocal in their reluctance to support

LGBT efforts to gain legal "protections" for their bodies.[3] For example, 70 percent of black voters in California supported Proposition 8 in 2008. Proposition 8 was a ballot initiative and constitutional amendment to the California Constitution, which restricts marriage to heterosexual couples. Black clergy came out strongly in support of the measure. Moreover, by failing to act in the HIV/AIDS crisis and making misguided statements about HIV/AIDS as a "gay" disease, black clergy publicly marginalized many LGBT people and blamed them for the AIDS epidemic. They have been just as die-hard in their refusal to recognize issues concerning LGBT equality as civil rights matters. Some in the black church community have gone so far as to accuse the LGBT community of hijacking the term "civil rights" as a ploy to gain black community support. Without question, there is an outspoken and influential tendency within the black church community to regard the LGBT body as sinful, not worthy of the rights and respect given non-LGBT bodies.

It is not coincidental that sexuality would provide a window into what might be going wrong within the black church. Sexuality is about more than sex. As aptly defined by ethicist James Nelson, while sexuality is certainly not the whole of who humans are, it is basic to being human. It involves how women and men relate to their own bodies and to the bodies of others. Sexuality is what propels human beings into relationships with themselves, one another, and even with God. Nelson puts it best when he says that sexuality is a "sign, a symbol, and a means of our call to communication and communion."[4]

Given the primacy of sexuality to the ways in which humans see themselves and interact with others, it follows that reactions to hot-button questions might involve more than simply the particular issue at hand. Such is the case for the black church when it comes to LGBT sexuality. Black church "discomfort" with the LGBT body points to black church anxiety with human bodies in general, whether they are LGBT or not. So, to return to our opening question—What is going all wrong in the black church?—the answer is that the black church cannot accommodate what we call here a "blues" body.

THE BLUES AND THE BLUES BODY

There is no tradition more suitable for understanding the relationship between the black church and blues bodies than that of the blues itself. While it is important not to fetishize or romanticize the blues as if they are pure reflections of black life and culture, they do capture a profound side of black living that other forms of black expressive culture do not. In so doing, they provide an informal yet precise perspective concerning the relationship between the black church and blues bodies and hence the depth of the wrong in the black church. An appreciation for the nature of the blues body helps us to understand the significance of the blues to the black church. Before we undertake the question of the blues as lament, let us explore three aspects of the blues body: it is non-bourgeois, sensuous, and rejected.

A Non-bourgeois Body

One day every week, I prop myself at my front door.
One day every week, I prop myself at my front door,
And the police force couldn't move me 'fore that mail man blow.

'Twas a little white paper Uncle Sam had done addressed to me.
'Twas a little white paper Uncle Sam had done addressed to me.
It meant one more week, one more week of sweet prosperity.

After four long years, Uncle Sam done put me on the shelf.
After four long years, Uncle Sam done put me on the shelf.
'Cause that little pink slip means you got to go for yourself.

Ida Cox[5]

Blues is more than a music form; it is a story of black living. The blues emerged from black people who existed on the edges of life. These were sharecropping, migrating, hand-to-mouth, poor black people. Their bodies provided the manual labor for the white plantation and farm economy. The blues tells personal yet shared stories of the common realities of poor black existence. Blues stories are of the everyday hardships, disappointments, sorrows, loves, and desires of plain black women and men. These are stories of black women and men "propped" at the front door, waiting for government checks. They are stories of black lives put at risk when the pink slip comes to tell them that their government check will be no more. As Ida Cox sang, "Uncle Sam done put [them] on the shelf," and somehow they must find a way to "go for [themselves]." This brings us to the meaning of the blues body.

Blues bodies are non-bourgeois bodies. They are the bodies of the black underclass. They provide the necessary hand-dirtying work to keep a white economy going, yet they have virtually no access to the benefits of that economy. The life conditions of blues bodies offer no middle-class, bourgeois illusions. These bodies suffer not simply because they are black, but also because they are poor. They exemplify the notion of "racialized" poverty, that is, that blackness and poverty are intertwined realities. Yet while the blues body seeks a better life, it is not impressed by black bourgeois compromises with white middle-class culture or captivated by white middle-class values.

While the bodies of those on the underside of black life are readily identified as blues bodies, and hence blues people, it is crucial to understand that what it means to be a blues body is not fixed by class privilege or social status. In other words, the fact that one may be educationally and socially middle class does not mean that one cannot be a blues body. Blues bodies, and hence blues people, reflect not simply a social condition of status, but also a choice about one's identity and accountability. Blues people are those black bodies who are accountable to blues realities, who identify not with "white mainstream" norms and values, but with the experiences, values, and struggles that characterize the realities of blues people and blues existence. In short, a black middle-class body does not have to become a bourgeois body. A black middle-class body can be a blues body.[6]

A Sensuous Body

Seem like the whole world's wrong since my man's been gone.
I need a little sugar in my bowl,
I need a little hot dog in my roll.

Bessie Smith[7]

Blues is often depicted as a highly sexualized if not lewd music form. To be sure, sexual themes are prevalent within blues, especially those sung by women.[8] Blues women sing, seemingly without shame or restraint, about their sexual needs, desires, and preferences. It is clear what Bessie Smith is clamoring for when she sings that her man is gone and she needs "a little sugar in [her] bowl" and "hot dog in [her] roll." Yet as titillating as blues can be, to become preoccupied with its suggestive lyrics is to miss the underlying meaning. Blues' sexiness points to its essential sensuous character.

Blues is in touch with the feelings of blues bodies. Blues does not begin with ideas in the head, but with the experiences of the body. Blues does not intellectualize those experiences; rather, it passionately expresses them. Blues listens to the call of the body and responds by conveying what the body is communicating, making visible that which is invisible. Through lyrics, music, and performance, blues boldly utters what the body feels. Blues lets loose its feelings of pain, sorrow, loneliness, and desire as well as joy, happiness, solitude, pleasure, and satisfaction. The feelings of blues bodies resound through the rhythms and inflections of blues. Blues speaks to the listener, becoming virtually a "mirror" as it reflects previously unarticulated feelings.[9] In this way blues is sensuous music because it is animated by the feelings of blues bodies, including sexual feelings.

The blues body, therefore, is not ashamed of itself. Blues bodies are of black people who are not embarrassed by their bodies and what their bodies feel. They celebrate the individuality of their bodies in terms of size, color, shape, and other bodily characteristics. It follows then that blues bodies stand in stubborn opposition to a culture that is ashamed of or disapproves of the body and all of its needs.

A Rejected Body

Everybody cryin' mercy, tell me what mercy means.
Everybody cryin' mercy, tell me what mercy means.
If it means feeling good, Lord, have mercy on me.

Ma Rainey[10]

The black church has typically regarded the blues as the "devil's music." It is clearly the explicit sexuality of the blues that earned it this demonic label. To the black church, inasmuch as the blues is sensuous in nature, it speaks the language of the devil and is not welcome. Blues-singing men and women are, therefore, as unwelcome in the church as the blues they sing—at least as long as they continue to sing the blues.

Considering the black church's disregard for blues, the message for blues bodies is clear. Simply put, the relationship between the blues bodies and the black church typifies the relationship between blues and the black church. Neither is offered much mercy. Both are judged and rejected. While the reasons for this rejection will be explored more fully later, it is important to note for now that as long as the black church cannot accept blues, it will be unable to accommodate blues bodies. And thus, it is only in finding a way to appreciate blues that the black church will be able to accept blues bodies, and perhaps safeguard its own blackness.

THE BLUES: A SIGNIFYING LAMENT

Lord, one old sister by the name of Sister Green
Jumped up and done a shimmy you ain't never seen.
Sing 'em, sing 'em, sing them blues, let me convert your soul.

Bessie Smith[11]

One of the gifts the blues has to offer the black church community is its tradition of signifying lament. Lament is prominent within the biblical tradition, to which the black church holds itself accountable. The ability to lament was essential to the Israelites' journey from an enslaved people to a free people. Lament allowed them to "rend their hearts" and to recognize the ways in which they had betrayed their own faith tradition. Lament was both a "pastoral activity" and a "prophetic activity."[12] It was pastoral as it provided a means for the Israelites to give voice to their suffering. It was prophetic in that it allowed them not simply to name the crisis they were facing, but also to recognize any responsibility they may have had in producing or sustaining the named crisis. With such recognition, they were then equipped to discern the power they had to end the crisis. In short, among the many positive aspects of the lament, it most notably served the Israelites as a vehicle for self-critique and accountability.

The blues echoes the biblical tradition of lament. Blues is both a pastoral and prophetic activity. Like the Israelite laments, it allows black women and men to identify particular crises that beset the community and recognize their role in perpetuating those crises. More to the point of this essay, when functioning as lament, blues confronts the black church about its behavior in a manner reflective of its biblically based faith, and then challenges this church to transform its behavior in a way consistent with that faith.

As *signifying* lament—a lament that affirms an identity of playful resistance in the face of an oppressive and dehumanizing reality—blues provides shrewd insight into the black church's culture and practices. A signifying lament is one that allows an otherwise powerless people to speak the truth about life and their own oppression in a coded way that hides the real message from those for whom it was not intended. One can see this in Bessie Smith's rendition of "Preachin' the Blues." The title of this song itself provides a signifying play upon the relationship between the blues and the black church. That one could actually preach the blues places them in a context in which they are not wanted: the church. This signifying title foreshadows what is to come in the song.

Using lyrics ripe with sexual innuendo, Smith sings about Sister Green. In the black church culture, the "sisters" are those women who are routinely considered the most holy, sanctified, saved ones. In many instances, they are held in high esteem as models of virtue and salvation. They are also known to cast a scornful and harsh eye on the unsaved. For Bessie Smith to suggest that Sister Green is "shimmying" to the blues is to signify upon this high and mighty black-church culture. Smith does this specifically by mocking the instance in many black churches when the choir's soul-stirring rendition of a particular church hymn or spiritual can lead one of the sisters in the church to "get happy," jump up and "shout," or engage in a "Holy Dance." This dance supposedly demonstrates the sister's salvation and how touched she is by the Holy Spirit.

Playing upon this dramatic display of salvation, Smith portrays Sister Green jumping up to the blues. Resonating to the message of the blues, she cannot help but jump up and shout/shimmy. It is as if the blues touches her in a place that even her saved state cannot erase. The blues speaks deeply to who she is in a way that perhaps the church does not. Through the blues, she is put back in touch with her body.

Though other signifying messages certainly lurk in "Preachin' the Blues," one is clear: Smith is signifying upon a church culture that draws a judgmental line between the saved and the unsaved. In singing about Sister Green, Smith suggests that in spite of how "holy" Sister Green may be, she still has a "blues body" that calls out to be satisfied. Thus, try as the black church might to keep the blues out of its holy space, blues resides in the bodies of those in the pews, even in the most sanctified of people. Smith, therefore, reveals the black church's naive view of the saved and the hypocrisy of its scorn for the blues and blues-singing people. Through a blues lament, Bessie Smith draws attention to the black church's misguided rejection of blues bodies.[13]

The final signifying irony of Smith's blues is found in its intuitive astuteness. The very fact that Smith is able to sing about Sister Green shows her profound wisdom concerning the ways of the black church. The implication of such a song is that Smith, who as a blues-singing woman is scorned by the black church, undoubtedly knows this church better than it knows itself. To be sure, she knows the Sister Greens of the church better than the church women know the Bessie Smiths of the blues.

"Preachin' the Blues" is just one example of the many signifying laments found in the blues. The blues provides numerous signifying laments that offer intuitively astute commentary on various aspects of the black church's culture and life. It is, however, through the blues' signifying laments on sexuality that we are able to discern the magnitude of what is going wrong between the black church and blues bodies and how to fix this urgent problem.

THE BLACK CHURCH AND THE BLUES BODY

I'm a one-hour mama, so no one-minute papa
Ain't the kind of man for me.
Set your alarm clock, papa, one hour, that's proper.
I may want love for one hour.
Then decide to make it two.
Takes an hour 'fore I get started,
Maybe three 'fore I'm through.
I'm a one-hour mama, so no one-minute papa
Ain't the kind of man for me.

                                                Ida Cox[14]

They said I do it, ain't nobody caught me.
Sure got to prove it on me.
Went out last night with a crowd of my friends.
They must've been women, 'cause I don't like no men.

                                                Ma Rainey[15]

As pointed out earlier, blues women sang unapologetically about their intimate sexuality. They sang about their sexual needs and preferences, as in Ida Cox making clear that she is a "one-hour mama" who does not want a "one-minute papa." They also sang matter-of-factly about their homoerotic appetite, as in Ma Rainey also making clear that she "don't like no men." While these women sang about the most personal aspects of their lives, they did not do so unreflectively or simply to provide lurid entertainment. Rather, they sang and performed with seemingly thoughtful signifying intent. Through sexualized lyrics and sexually charged performances, blues women signified upon a time-honored way of thinking within black culture—especially the black church's distortion of black people's relationships to black bodies, even their own bodies, and its failure to recognize the power in black people's identities as sexual beings. Essentially, these very blues, which again the black church finds offensive, engage in a signifying lament that reveals a perceptive awareness of the many narratives that render black people sexually impotent and threaten their power over their own bodies. Let us look briefly at narratives about black sexuality and how blacks have historically responded, looking to understand what is going wrong in the black church.

Intersecting *Sexual* Narratives

The dominant white cultural narrative about black sexuality depicts black people as hypersexual beasts. It portrays black men and women as driven by the unrelenting urges of their genitalia, their libidos out of control and insatiable. This white cultural stereotype relegates black people to a constant lustful state,[16] a narrative that reinforces white privilege and justifies white violence against black bodies.

Such a depiction clearly renders black people as little more than beasts, driven—like other beastly creatures—by their baser instincts and bodily desires. Because of this, black people are assumed to have no capacity for rational thinking. Their bodily desires simply overwhelm their rational faculties. Inasmuch as black men and women are supposedly governed by their hypersexual nature, they are at best inferior to whites (who are governed by reason) and at worst subhuman, for it is presumably the ability to reason that separates the beastly animal from the human animal.

In addition to being considered nonrational, the white cultural narrative deems black people as dangerous since they are controlled by their insatiable sexual appetites. Black men are branded as predatory bucks and black women as promiscuous seductresses. Essentially, according to the stereotyping narrative of white racist culture, blackness is synonymous with abnormal hypersexualized behavior.[17]

Such sexualized stereotyping is typical of cultural narratives that function to sustain oppressive power. The French philosopher Michel Foucault explains that discourses of power invariably attack the sexuality of whatever people the regime wishes to subjugate. To manipulate a group's sexuality, therefore, is to have power over that group's reproductive capacity as well as their capacity for positive relationships.[18] To reiterate a point established earlier, sexuality is integral to one's ability to be in relationship with one's body-self, others, and even God. In this regard, the sexualized stereotyping of black people serves not only to question their very humanness, but also to disrupt their web of relationships, both human and divine.

The black community has not remained passive to white culture's sexualized narrative. It has produced its own narratives to counteract the presumption that black people are hypersexual. The first is a social-cultural narrative that urges black people to conform to a "hyperproper" standard of sexual conduct. This standard is, for all intents and purposes, as aggressive in its attempt to *de*sexualize black men and women as white culture is in its attempts to sexualize them. What it means to be "proper" is based upon what is acceptable according to the standards of mainstream white society. Thus, whatever is ostensibly unacceptable according to white sexual standards is absolutely intolerable for the black community.[19] Given the heteronormative and patriarchal nature of white society, this standard of acceptability is not only white-biased, but also heterosexist and sexist. Thus, homoeroticism is considered improper, as well as any expression of female sexuality that is independent of male participation. This means that lesbian and gay persons are to abstain from sexual intimacy altogether and that "decent" (i.e., middle-class, married, white) women are to engage in sexual activity only when initiated by men and only for reproductive purposes.

This heterosexual, male-defined white standard of sexual conduct has been influential within the black community. Most notably, it is seen in black middle-class aspirations to be accepted within white mainstream society. It ostensibly becomes the task of the black middle class to display a "hyperproper" sexuality and to encourage the black working class to do the same. Those black persons who do not are seen as uncouth and as fulfilling the white cultural stereotype. In addition, they are considered a threat to the black middle class's acceptance into white society. For, while the black middle class is a part of the black minority, it enjoys certain white majority privileges that it is determined to protect. This is typically a more-educated class and one that does enjoy certain social acceptance within white society. The black middle class, in this regard, is W. E. B. DuBois's "talented tenth." Unfortunately, this more privileged class of black people too often harbors a patronizing mentality that lies behind their efforts to "civilize" the recalcitrant black bodies. If their civilizing efforts fail, then the black "uncouth" are marginalized or rejected.

This particular dynamic of the hyperproper sexual narrative and its elitist implications has played out in various black middle-class organizations, movements, social clubs, and even historical black colleges and universities. Generally speaking, various middle-class black organizations, while sincerely committed to black well-being, have modeled standards of "white acceptability" and have too often been infused with a determination to protect a privileged status in white society. Unfortunately, the black church has also been a part of this elitist dynamic. It too has produced a narrative to govern black sexuality with similar rejecting implications for nonconforming black bodies. The black church narrative is perhaps more troubling because it claims sacred authenticity. It is, in other words, a "holy" narrative—a phenomenon that has a long legacy.

During the eighteenth century, a significant population of black women and men were converted to an evangelical Protestant tradition during widespread religious revivals. Black churches most influenced by this tradition tend to affirm the assertions of the apostle Paul that one should "make no provision for flesh," but if one must engage in sexual behavior, "it is better to marry than to burn."[20] This Pauline, evangelical sexual ethic is based on an influential Western philosophical tradition, a Platonist tradition, which places the body and soul in an antagonistic, oppositional relationship. Christianity inherited from Plato the notion of the soul as the seat of salvation, relegating the body to an inferior position as the source of sin. Desires of the body are, therefore, to be overcome at all cost, especially sexual desires—the ultimate temptations of the devil. Christianity developed a sexual ethic in which procreative engagement was viewed as tolerably good; nonprocreative engagement became intolerably sinful.[21]

Thus the black church inherited a body-negating sexual ethic and has employed it as the religious counterpart to the black community's social-cultural sexual narrative. It provides a sacred cover for the black community's standard of hyperproper sexuality, making violation of this hyperproper sexual standard not simply a social breach, but also a sin against God. Ironically, the black narratives of hyperproper sexual standards validate the same white cultural narrative they attempt to contest. They do so in two ways. First, they affirm the nonsensuous norm of white culture. As suggested earlier, white culture views the body as a source of danger to one's humanity, since it is the seat of sexuality. And as long as the body is seen as dangerous and incidental to human existence, then one can attack it with self-righteous indignation.

Second, these black narratives also affirm the white cultural narrative by implicitly validating the white cultural stereotype of black people as a hyper-sexualized beast. In accepting this stereotype, they attempt to get black people to squelch their bodily desires and sexual proclivities, as if black people must pay attention to these aspects of themselves in a way that others do not. Admittedly, black men and women are rightly "hyperaware" of their conduct, sexual or otherwise, given the price that they have too often paid for displaying what white racist society considers offensive conduct. In this regard, these hyperproper narratives can be viewed as a "Faustian" pact that the black community has made with the white community in order to survive. These narratives have no doubt prevented black people from engaging in behaviors that might actually end their very lives. Nevertheless, as helpful they may appear, they do not challenge the very thing that makes them necessary in the first place: the sexualized stereotype. The hyperproper narratives merely attempt to mask the stereotypic behavior with "proper" behavior. They do not deny the authority of the original white stereotype. As such, they may actually serve the purposes of white culture far better than they protect the well-being of black people. From this we see that the narrative of hyperproper sexuality and demonizing of the body are constraining and confining narratives. They alienate black people from their bodies and seize control of black sexuality by limiting the ways in which their sexuality may be expressed. In this respect, these black narratives have become as oppressive to certain bodies within the black community as white cultural narratives have been to all black bodies. This leads us to the heart of what is going wrong in the black church—on which the blues provide signifying lament.

A Blues Class of People

In the final analysis, the black church's sanctioning of a hyperproper standard of sexuality makes it virtually impossible for it to accept, let alone be a sanctuary of support and empowerment for, blues bodies—which, as earlier described, are invariably sensuous bodies.

This is nothing new, and is inherently tied up with classism. Throughout history the black church has rejected various black people because of their refusal or inability to comply with its nonsensuous hyperproper standard of acceptability. Black churches, therefore, became more of a place of judgment for certain black peoples than a place of refuge.[22] It is in recognizing this tendency within the black church that a disturbing aspect of the black church's tradition becomes crystal clear: almost as intrinsic to the black church as its "black" identity is a "bourgeois" tendency. That is, in its no-doubt sincere efforts to advance the life of the people—thus making them more acceptable to white society— it has fostered a "bourgeois" culture. Bourgeois, in this regard, indicates an adherence to values and standards of acceptability according to the dominant cultural group—in this instance white society.[23]

It cannot be emphasized enough that this narrative takes on such profound meaning because of the centrality of sexuality to human dynamics. As we have seen, sexuality is a key and irreplaceable component of what it means to be human, and to diminish the sexuality of an entire group of people is to do violence to that people. Bourgeois culture inexorably creates a blues class of people who are rejected by the dominant narrative, who don't fit in. This is true of the black church, which has spawned a movement of those who do not comply in one way or the other and at any given time to the hyperproper sexual narrative of the church.

In striking ways, the black church sexualizes those persons it finds unacceptable just as white culture sexualizes black people. The black church seizes an effective tool of oppressing power, the sexuality of those it opposes, and maligns it. In short, the blues class is a hypersexualized class of people defined in the black church by their intimate sexual behavior. For instance, women are seen as sexual temptations to the men of the church, just as they are viewed by white culture as temptresses to white men. Therefore, within various black churches women are expected to "cover" their sexuality by placing cloths over their legs. At the same time, they are often blamed for the sexual transgressions of "holy" men, and even for the domestic violence these "holy" men may perpetrate against their female bodies. Likewise, gay and lesbian persons are hypersexualized. To be gay or lesbian is to be promiscuous. They are viewed as persons controlled by an abnormal, homoerotic libido. They are thus expected to remain celibate. While they may not be able to do anything about who they are (gay and lesbian in orientation), they are expected to renounce the sin of homoerotic engagement.

Whether we're talking about women, gays, or lesbians, blues bodies are not respected. Consequently, the issues that affect their bodies, such as domestic violence or HIV/AIDS, are given scant if any attention within the black church. They are issues that have certainly not been priorities within the black church, and that thus have not been effectively addressed and are too often perceived as the harsh consequences of "sinful" body behavior. In the end, it is because the black church narrative conforms to the nonsensuous norm of the white cultural narrative that the black church finds itself fostering a blues class, and thus, not only disrespecting but also rejecting various black bodies and subsequently ignoring the suffering imposed upon those bodies. This brings us to the seriousness of what is going wrong in the black church.

It is about more than LGBT sexuality, even as it is precisely about the LGBT body. The LGBT body is a vibrant reminder to the black church of what it has striven to overcome and all that it is trying to escape. It is as if the LGBT body itself is a "demonic" temptation. To support LGBT issues would in effect mean to not simply make a compromise with bodily sin, but perhaps also to make a "pact with the devil."[24] At the least, such issues are frequently viewed as a trap by white society to once again link black people with abnormal, beastly sexuality. Hence, black church leaders oftentimes proclaim such issues as white issues, not pertaining to the black community, as if to turn the tables on white people— linking *them* to abnormal sexuality while disassociating their black selves from it. The body-denying narrative of hyperproper sexuality has become so embedded within the black church that it all but defines contemporary black-church culture. It assures the palpable reality of a bourgeois "mentality." And most seriously, it shapes black church responses to various social justice issues. Inasmuch as the issues at stake concern blues bodies, then they are issues about which the black church will at best provide an ambivalent response and at worst ignore or contest.

In this regard, the hyperproper sexual narrative results in a church that is at times manifestly bourgeois, classist, sexist, and heterosexist. And perhaps most troubling, it is a church that sometimes ignores the pain and suffering of black bodies. It is unquestionably a narrative that frequently overwhelms the black church's black identity. The end result is that the black church is unreliably black, and untrustworthy when it comes to protecting and advocating for the well-being of all black bodies. As long as the black church harbors narratives that fuel a bourgeois culture and sustain a blues class of people, it is not black. In fact, it is effectively an advocate of the very white cultural norms that sexualize and reject black bodies.

It is the "right" time, therefore, for the black church to adopt a new narrative. This narrative must be one that is true to the best of the black church—that is, when the black church has been at its "radicalized" best (true to its roots, as will be clarified in the final section below). This requires a new narrative that must benefit all black bodies and actually contest the white cultural sexualizing narrative of black people. It is in the signifying lament of blues that the possibility of such a new narrative comes into focus. Let us now return to the blues as signifying lament.

SAVED BY THE BLUES:
A CROSSROADS WORLDVIEW

I went down to the crossroads, fell down on my knees.
I went down to the crossroads, fell down on my knees,
Asked the Lord above, "Have mercy now, save poor Bob if you please."

Robert Johnson[25]

The notion of "crossroads" has played an important part in blues lore. At a crossroads in Mississippi, Robert Johnson presumably struck a deal with the devil. Lore has it that for the price of his soul, the devil gave him the gift of guitar playing. Within black folklore, the crossroads is an ominous place, a site of ghosts and other such spirits. Most significantly, it is the place where the devil hangs out. This crossroads mythology traces back to African mythology about the gods. The crossroads is where the prominent god, Esu, resides. Esu is a trickster god, acting sometimes for good, sometimes for bad; he is also the messenger god, interpreting the messages of the Great High God. In this way the crossroads suggests a worldview that is instructive for decoding the signifying lament of the blues.

The crossroads is a place where various realities intersect, interact, and influence each other. A crossroads worldview is one, therefore, that denies rigid, antagonistic boundaries, even when two dimensions of existence may seem to be intrinsically oppositional—such as sacred and secular dimensions of life. Instead, a crossroads paradigm suggests that the "truth" of life is found in appreciating the inherent dialectic nature of human existence, and thus forging a "harmony" between these dialectics of living. The meaning of this will become clear as we examine the signifying lament of blues in relation to sexuality. As we do this, it is worth noting that understanding the significance of the crossroads in black culture enables us to decode blues signifying meaning. Let us now return to the sexualized blues to see how this is the case.

As pointed out earlier, blues women sang without inhibition about their sexual appetites and preferences. Just as Bessie Smith clamored for a "hot dog" in her roll, she also confessed that she couldn't "get enough" of "papa'[s] thing." Likewise, Ida Cox let it be known that she was a "one-hour mama" who did not want a "one-minute papa." The black church has interpreted such declarations of sensual sexuality as affirming the sexualized stereotype that the church and community have so desperately tried to escape.

But again, to see the blues women as fulfilling and affirming the sexualized white cultural stereotypes of blackness misses the subtlety of what they were doing. For instead of reinforcing the stereotype, they were actually subverting it. The fact that they sang so fervently and so often about sexual and sensual matters should be construed as a form of "signifying" protest against the sexualized stereotype of blackness. Indeed, unlike the black social and religious hyperproper narratives, the blues women did not avoid the white cultural stereotypes of black people. They confronted them head-on by repeating them. In so doing, they provided a different approach to dealing with them, turning the stereotype on its head. They refused to be confounded by the sexualized stereotypes of black people or even restrained by the black church's and community's hyperproper response to those stereotypes. And so, while black sexual narratives contest the white stereotype by projecting a hyperproper sexual norm, blues women dealt with this stereotype by not granting it any authority. They did not validate it. They transcended the white sexualized caricatures of blackness and crafted a new black identity, denying the white cultural narrative any claims over their sexual selves.

Furthermore, through their lyrics blues women did not adopt the nonsensuous norm upon which the white cultural narrative was based. By making love and desire the key for decoding the signifying message, they contested the notion that erotic sexuality is an impediment to life. Instead, they advanced sexuality as the tool for grasping life's truths. As various blues singers boldly declared what blues bodies crave, they proclaimed the necessity of being in touch with the needs of one's body. They moved "sensuality and sexuality out of the private and into the public sphere."[26] As they did so, they moved sex from a place of shame to a place of ultimacy. They essentially grasped the nature of sexuality itself. As blues women foregrounded sexuality, they affirmed its centrality to human existence.

Moreover, by flaunting their sexual taste and preferences, blues women were not only protesting against white cultural hypersexualization of them, but also against the very systems and structures that such sexualization serves—the very ones that would seek to deny them freedom. One of the fundamental tasks of cultural narratives of power is to seize control of a people's sexuality, which has been the case for black men and women since slavery. The lack of freedom has meant the lack of sexual agency, or the inability to determine how to express one's sexuality and to choose one's sexual partners. By taking back their sexuality, blues women stripped oppressive power of one of its most crucial weapons.[27]

As these women sang of their taste and preferences, they also challenged a heteroerotic norm. They sang about their homoerotic desires as freely and openly as they sang of their relationships with men. In so doing, they recognized and valued the fluidity of human sexuality. They did not project a sharp distinction between different ways of sexual expressions. They made clear that they sometimes preferred the love of women and sometimes the love of men. Each was fulfilling and an acceptable way to love. Neither was considered better or more holy than the other.

Just as the sexualized blues lyrics signified upon the sexualized stereotypes of white cultural narratives, so too did they provide a signifying lament on the black church's sanctified hyperproper sexual narrative. In so doing, they were doing more than disrespecting black church piety, if they were doing that at all. They were merely rescuing sexuality from its "taboo" space in the black church.

It is here that we can begin to understand the theological depth of blues signifying lament. An appreciation of the aforementioned crossroads worldview helps us with this understanding. Blues signifying lament puts forth a crossroads approach to sexuality—and hence to navigating life. As blues women sing of sexuality, they refuse simple either/or choices. They instead navigate the dialectic of what it means to be a human, to have a body and a soul. They suggest not an oppositional relationship between the two, but a harmonious one. For as seen earlier in Bessie Smith's "Preachin' the Blues," the sanctified soul resides in a sexual body. Moreover, the blues body can be a saved body. The "sacred" and "secular" are all a part of one reality. They are intersecting, interacting crossroads of human existence.

To hold the body and soul together, recognizing the intrinsic crossroad nature of being human, actually maintains the integrity of the black religious tradition itself. This is a tradition rooted in an African religious heritage in which all life is considered sacred, including the body and sexuality. This tradition does not foster rigid splits between the divine and the human. There is, simply put, no notion of "secularity."[28] There is no taboo, inherently demonized space of human living.

It is no doubt an appreciation of this African worldview that made it possible for the enslaved crafters of the black religious tradition to grasp the meaning of the Christian God. This was a god who entered history in the embodied presence of Jesus. This embodied God was not divided against itself; rather, as Christians profess, this God was "fully divine and fully human."

Emerging from the blues, therefore, is a "crossroads theology." Such a theology is by definition a sensual theology, incarnational and playful. It not only takes the body seriously but also recognizes that all human relationships are embodied interactions. In order for women and men to encounter themselves, one another, and God, they must do so in their bodies, not apart from their bodies. Women and men cannot avoid the gendered, sexual nature of their bodies. The sensuous nature of a crossroads theology rebuffs efforts to overcome the body at the same time that it challenges people to embrace the body in an affirming manner. A crossroads theology ultimately recognizes the value and rich possibilities of embodied life. It is in this way that a crossroads theology is also incarnational, affirming the intrinsic sacred quality of the human body.

The black church can learn from what God did incarnationally in the person of Jesus. In taking a human body, Jesus as Christ literally makes clear the sacred relevance of the human body at the same time that it signals the very significance of the body to all interactions. Through his very body, Jesus touches lepers, reaches out to women, and heals other rejected bodies. In so doing, Jesus affirms the sacredness of these particular human bodies, thus providing an opportunity for these rejected bodies to acknowledge their divine worth while also opening up new life possibilities.

In short, Jesus' ministry to human bodies makes real the very meaning of who he is as God incarnate. That he is God incarnate reflects the crossroads of a human/divine meeting both ontologically and existentially. Both aspects of being were essential to what it meant for Jesus to be the presence of God in human history, and most especially in black lives. It was because of God's embodied presence in Jesus that the enslaved could testify that God took care of their every need.

The black religious tradition, shaped in slavery and informed by an African religious narrative, recognized that God's embodiment was critical to any understanding of God's meaning in black lives. This tradition makes clear that it is only through their bodies that humans can reach out to God and that God can reach out to them. When true to its slave heritage, the black religious tradition affirms the theological meaning of the incarnation itself: that the body is vital to the human/divine connection. It cannot be emphasized enough that the body is a tool for salvation, not an impediment. This is what a crossroads theology makes clear. One thing is sure: a faith tradition that demonizes the body certainly cannot comprehend the embodied, incarnational reality of the Christian God.

A crossroads theology is also "playful." Within the black faith tradition, various forms of play have often been rejected and characterized as sinful. It is as if a playful body is considered breeding ground for the devil's activity. Yet play has been crucial to a black culture of resistance. Through play, black people have been able to transcend the limits of their oppression and affirm their indispensable humanity.

In play one gets lost in time. Play virtually becomes a space where eternal time enters into finite reality. Hence, the finite constraints of an oppressive life are broken by the eternal reality of joyful life. Furthermore, through play one's very humanness is affirmed. For instance, the fact that the enslaved could engage in play—could laugh and have fun—suggested that they were more than beasts of labor. They were people with creative imagination, who could indeed think beyond the given circumstances of life.[29]

Since it defies time and contests dehumanizing assumptions, play is a subversive activity and thereby a divine activity. It turns evil realities on their head, revealing the delusional character of evil itself. Play can reveal that evil has no real status, no stable existence. Its only power is that which humans give it.[30] With the evil reality of imposed labor meant to validate their beastly existence, the enslaved turned to play and thereby declared their humanity. What the master might have assumed to be a happy-go-lucky slave—hence fulfilling a stereotype of the "happy darky"—was actually a masterfully inventive mind, foiling the dehumanizing designs of slavery itself. Inasmuch as play subverts oppression, divests evil of its power, and affirms the humanity and sanctity of human bodies, then it is nothing less than a "holy" activity.

It is no wonder, then, that play was so much a part of Jesus' very ministry. Through the playfulness of parables, Jesus subverted the power of evil. The climax of Jesus' playfulness can be seen in the resurrection itself. As if engaging in a game of "Now you see me, now you don't," Jesus revealed the impotence and utter powerlessness of human claims to power. In defying death itself, Jesus showed the very futility of life-negating, dehumanizing power and thus the transitory character of evil constructs.

In this way blues should be seen as sacred/holy activity. To reiterate an earlier point, as signifying play, it indeed turns evil on its head. Inasmuch as bluesmen enter into the world of the blues at the crossroads, they enter into divine discourse, projecting in their blues a crossroads theology. If blues lore has it that Robert Johnson and others made a pact with the devil at the crossroads, then perhaps the black church has made a bedeviling pact by *not* stepping into the crossroads. It is as if the black church has made a pact with white Protestantism, thus trading its sensuous African religious heritage for a chance to be accepted within mainstream nonsensuous white society. Worse yet, it has betrayed its incarnational faith tradition.

The blues reflects a crossroads perspective that refuses to make either/or choices. Blues reflects this even in its refusal to reject the people the black church so frequently rejects. Blues does not make choices between the "saved" and "unsaved," choosing instead to recognize the sacredness of all black people.[31] Most important, it recognizes two dimensions of what it means to be saved and how those two dimensions interact with one another. Essentially, for blues bodies, both the body and the soul need to be saved. It is no wonder then that in the juke joints, where blues is performed, a blues class of people experience "mercy." The juke joints do what the black church does not do: provide sanctuary for blues bodies. They make the body feel good. In this way the juke joint becomes the church. The juke joint is a place where the needs and desires of the body are tended to, and the blues is where the demands of the body are vindicated. What this indicates once again is the necessity for black life of maintaining a dialectic harmony between the church and blues. The challenge to the black church is to be for blues bodies both "church" and "juke joint," speaking to the soul and body.

Returning to "Preachin' the Blues," Smith sings in this song, "I will learn you something if you listen to this song. I ain't here to try to save your soul. Just want to teach you how to save your jelly roll." She concludes the song by singing, "Sing 'em, sing 'em, sing them blues, let me convert your soul." True to what it means to be a signifying lament, "Preachin' the Blues" reveals to the black church a way to right the wrong within it. For what is going wrong is not about the black church's ability to save souls, but its effectiveness in saving "jelly rolls," that is, the sexual black body. The way to right this wrong is clear: the black church must lament. It must appreciate the blues. For it is surely not until the black church is able to accept the blues as sacred discourse that it will be able to accept blues bodies. Put simply, if the black church is to be a liberating, sustaining, and life-affirming agent for all black bodies, regardless of how those bodies are gendered or sexually oriented, then the church must be black and blue.

NOTES

1. Ma Rainey "Mystery Record," Guy Early and Thomas Dorsey, 1924 remastered JSP Records 2007.

2. In a 2002 study of the black church, Anthony Pinn noted the black church's continued significance even for those who had once abandoned the church. He noted the black educated and middle class return to the church for support in their struggles against racism. Pinn suggests that despite an apparent decline in the black church attendance, it remains the "strength" of the black community. See Pinn, *The Black Church in the Post-Civil Rights Era* (Maryknoll, NY: Orbis Books, 2002).

3. See, for instance, Michael Paulson, "Black Clergy Rejection Stirs Gay Marriage Backers," *The Boston Globe* (February 10, 2004), www.boston.com/news/local/articles/2004/02/10/black_clergy_rejection_stirs_gay_marriage_backers.

4. James B. Nelson, *Embodiment: An Approach to Sexuality and Christian Theology* (Minneapolis: Augsburg Publishing House, 1978), 117–18.

5. Ida Cox, *Pink Slip Blues*, Document Records, vol. 5, 31 October to 29 December 1940.

6. In this regard I do not accept what appears to be a pessimistic and fixed view of

the black middle class offered by Leroi Jones (later known as Amari Baraka). He seems to equate middle-class status with a "slave mentality" and an inexorable "orientation towards white mainstream values and culture." For him, the black middle class cannot be "blues people." See his argument in *Blues People: The Negro Experience in White America and the Music That Developed from It* (New York: Morrow Quill Paperbacks, 1963).

7. Bessie Smith, "Need a Little Sugar in My Bowl," 1927, *The Essential Bessie Smith* remastered, Columbia Legacy.

8. Blues women will be the central focus of this blues exploration. This is the case because the black female body personifies the multiple interacting forms of oppression that impinge upon black bodies, i.e., racism, sexism, classism, and heterosexism.

9. Charles Keil provides a similar analysis of the significance of the blues as he offers perceptive insight regarding the role of the "bluesman and the black preacher." See this in *Urban Blues* (Chicago: University of Chicago Press, 1966), esp. chaps. 6–7.

10. Ma Rainey, "Blues the World Forgot—Part 2," *Ma Rainey: Complete Recorded Works in Chronological Order, Vol. 4: 1926–1927*, Document Records DOCD-5584.

11. Bessie Smith, *Preachin' the Blues*, 1927.

12. This analysis of laments draws upon Emilie Townes's chapter "The Formfulness of Communal Lament," in *Breaking the Fine Rain of Death: African American Health Issues and a Womanist Ethics of Care* (New York: Continuum Publishing Co., 1998).

13. Angela Davis provides similar insight into Smith's rendition of "Preachin' the Blues" in *Blues Legacies and Black Feminism* (New York: Pantheon, 1998).

14. Ida Cox, "One Hour Mama," Document Records DOCD-5651, vol. 5, 31 October 1939–December 1940.

15. Ma Rainey, "Prove It to Me Blues," 1928.

16. When I speak of white culture, I am specifically referencing a culture that nurtures white racism and is undergirded by a white supremacist ideology. This is a culture that devalues that which is nonwhite and thus serves as a safeguard for white, patriarchal hegemony. See a fuller discussion of this in *Sexuality and the Black Church*, esp. 13–18.

17. A fuller discussion of this narrative can be found in Kelly Brown Douglas, *Sexuality and the Black Church: A Womanist Perspective* (Maryknoll, NY: Orbis Books, 1999).

18. Michel Foucault, *The History of Sexuality: An Introduction*, vol. 1, trans. Robert Hurley (New York: Vintage Books, 1990).

19. For fuller discussion of this social-cultural narrative, see *Sexuality and the Black Church*.

20. See Rom. 13:14; 1 Cor. 7:9 KJV.

21. See an in-depth discussion of this tradition in Kelly Brown Douglas, *What's Faith Got to Do with It? Black Bodies/White Souls* (Maryknoll, NY: Orbis Books, 2006).

22. One such time was during the period of the Great Migrations when the northern black churches were unable to easily accommodate the black southern migrants. Northern black churches often tried to impose a form of worship upon these migrants that was less emotional and more reflective of white worshiping styles. This period gave rise to other movements within the black community and saw the founding of various black religious traditions that spoke to spiritual and worship needs of the southern migrants. For a very fine and thorough analysis of the northern black church in relation to the Great Migration, see Milton Sernett, *Bound for the Promised Land: African American Religion and the Great Migration* (Durham, NC: Duke University Press, 1997). For more on this period in terms of the developments within the black church, see Gayraud S. Wilmore, *Black Religion and Black Radicalism: An Interpretation of the Religious History of African Americans*, 3rd ed. (Maryknoll, NY: Orbis Books, 1998).

23. To be black and middle class does not automatically render one bourgeois. Adherence to a bourgeois culture in this regard reflects a choice one makes concerning how to relate to mainstream white society as well as to blues people.

24. In *Blues Legacies and Black Feminism,* Angela Davis speaks of how the black church views blues singing women as having made a "pact with the devil."

25. Robert Johnson, *Crossroad Blues,* 1936.

26. Hazel Carby, *Cultures in Babylon: Black Britain and African America* (London/New York: Verso, 1999), 18. Carby argues as well that blues women "had no respect for sexual taboos." Daphne Duval Harrison in *Black Pearls* (New Brunswick, NJ: Rutgers University Press, 1988), 100, similarly argues that through their songs blues women assert their power and "project a new image of themselves."

27. Angela Davis provides a very compelling analysis of the relationship between sexual agency and freedom in *Blues Legacies and Black Feminism.*

28. See Peter Paris, *The Spirituality of African Peoples: The Search for a Common Moral Discourse* (Minneapolis: Fortress Press, 1995).

29. In his book *Down Up and Under: Slave Religion and Black Theology* (Minneapolis: Fortress Press, 2000), Dwight Hopkins talks about play as integral to the enslaved's creation of their humanity.

30. One prominent example of how the enslaved turned labor into play is seen in the rituals and games the enslaved engaged in during cornshucking (cornhusking). The "play" of cornshucking is vividly depicted in Sherley Anne Williams's novel, *Dessa Rose* (New York: W. Morrow, 1986).

31. Bluesman Henry Townsend offers a sharp critique of the black church as he recognizes its rejection of blues people by proclaiming that "the church should take in everyone." Quoted in Paul Oliver, *Conversations with the Blues* (New York: Horizon Press, 1965), 181.

PART 2

Sexuality and Spirituality

Audre Lorde
Katie Geneva Cannon
James B. Nelson
Patrick S. Cheng
Kwok Pui-lan

Introduction
to Part 2

While a tension between sexuality and spirituality is pervasive within the Christian tradition, there is a larger truth to grasp: both sexuality and spirituality reflect the human capacity—and embodied desire—for intimate connection. While sexuality is about the overall potential for human relationships, spirituality points to a particular human relational potential. Spirituality refers to the human capacity to connect with the divine. It signals the promise for a human/divine connection. It is, in fact, the "means and ways" in which humans relate to that which they consider divine.

There is a natural overlap between sexuality and spirituality. Both signal the relational quality of being human. Both indicate humans' ability to reach beyond themselves toward others in loving ways. Inasmuch as sexuality provides the foundation for our ability to reach out, it is inextricably linked to spirituality. Without our sexuality, spiritual connections would not be possible. If human beings are called by God to be in relationship with God (our spirituality), then sexuality is a gift from God that helps make that relationship possible.

There is, however, a prevailing Christian tradition that does not see it that way.

Unduly influenced by classical Western body-denouncing philosophies, Christianity has fostered a theological perspective that views sexuality and spirituality as antagonistic dimensions of being human. Influenced by the Greco-Roman world of which they were a part, early Christian thinkers and apologists integrated into their theologies the most prominent philosophies of their day. In so doing, they established within mainstream Christian thought a body-devaluing perspective that disavows the goodness of human sexuality. In this view, the body is condemned as a source of sin. The locus of that sin is human passion. The most threatening of all passions is sexual pleasure. It has the most sinful potential for alienating humans from God and impeding their salvation. Therefore, the body is to be overcome. And most urgently, sexual pleasure is to be avoided at all cost.

What are the consequences of such body-negating theology? Its proponents condemn erotic sexual engagement unless it has procreative intent. The only "good sex" is procreative sex, and that must take place within the bonds of heterosexual marriage. With such a view of the body and sex, sexuality is considered a curse, not a blessing. Sexuality and spirituality are no longer complementary, inextricably connected dimensions of being human. Instead, they are seen as opposing, conflicting forces. Unfortunately, this notion of the relationship between sexuality and spirituality still persists within the Christian tradition. In fact, it dominates public discourse, disrupting individuals' ability to affirm who they are as both sexual and spiritual beings.

The good news is that a theological/ethical tradition is being forged that reclaims the body as a part of God's good creation and attempts to restore more mutually enhancing connections between sexuality and spirituality. The essays in this section are a part of this tradition. In various ways, these essays speak of how the split between sexuality and spirituality has affected certain human bodies. They then suggest, in creative ways, a theological/ethical road toward a Christian perspective that maintains the sacredness of sexuality and affirms the indispensable link between sexuality and spirituality.

This section opens with Audre Lorde's "The Uses of Erotic: The Erotic as Power." Though Lorde does not identify herself as a part of a particular religious tradition or even as a theological thinker, this essay is widely used by theological/ethical thinkers (including many in this volume) in their efforts to move beyond erotophobic Christian traditions. In this influential essay, Lorde identifies the erotic as an unrecognized source of power. She defines it as "our deepest and non-rational knowledge," that which puts us in touch with the depth of our feelings and generates our deepest satisfaction. As such, the erotic is one of the most powerful dimensions of human existence, and Lorde urges us to claim our erotic power. She says that claiming the erotic is most crucial for it allows humans to connect with themselves and others in more complete ways. She further explains that claiming and experiencing our erotic selves compels us to aspire for other equally affirming experiences. Because the erotic is so powerful, Lorde acknowledges that Western patriarchal traditions have targeted women in nurturing within them a fear and distrust of their erotic power. Lorde, therefore, challenges women in particular to get in touch with their erotic power and to assert it, resisting the systems that alienate them from their sexual/erotic selves.

In her essay, "Sexing Black Women: Liberation from the Prisonhouse of Anatomical Authority," Katie Cannon recognizes that Lorde's call for women to claim the erotic is most urgent for black church women. Recognizing how the black church has integrated within its faith tradition a body-denying/sex-fearing theology, Cannon laments that black churchwomen have endured almost unbearable suffering as a result. "Black churchwomen live in the midst of two competing sexual realities," she observes. One reality claims sex as a "positive blessing for procreative purposes" while the other views sex as a "curse that lays claim to bodily pleasure, contaminating the mind." These competing realities, Cannon notes, have caused "far too many [black churchwomen] to struggle [with how to reconcile] two fundamental pillars of their identity—spirituality and sexuality." The history of sexualized denigration and violent abuse that black women have had to endure only exacerbates their struggle and complicates their ability to value their erotically sexual selves. Therefore, Cannon asserts that it is "a moral imperative" to liberate these women. She highlights womanist ethical approaches that explore black women's stories of sexual tyranny and oppression in an attempt to find "hidden meanings" in black women's "complicated survival strategies." For Cannon, these "hidden meanings" that womanists unearth indeed provide the resources for a sexually liberating ethic.

In his "Where Are We? Seven Sinful Problems and Seven Virtuous Possibilities," James B. Nelson redefines sin as it relates to the relationship between Christians and their sexuality: It is the split between sexuality and spirituality that reflects a sinful reality, not the embrace of sexuality as a positive. Nelson argues that the "sexual distortions" predominating within Jewish and Christian traditions are "perversions" of the traditions' own central teachings and that, moreover, reclaiming a more authentic tradition about sexuality is the path to sexual healing. With this underlying assumption, Nelson delineates "seven deadly sins through which the Jewish and Christian traditions have contributed to our sexual alienation," including "spiritualistic dualism" (the separation of the body and spirit, sexuality and spirituality). He also specifies "seven virtues" as "positive resources," which counter the seven sins. In the end, Nelson says that "while Christianity and Judaism have often confounded good sexuality education and social policies," what is more authentic to these faith traditions is that which nurtures "sexual health, sexual responsibility, and sexual justice, and . . . more adequate body theologies."

Patrick S. Cheng also argues that an antisexual, erotophobic tradition betrays the core of the Christian tradition in his "Rethinking Sin and Grace for LGBT People Today." Emphasizing the way in which the split between sexuality and spirituality has damaged the lives of Asian LGBT women and men, Cheng puts forth four christological models that contest this split and again values human sexuality. Each of these models is predicated on a reconception of sin and grace. Cheng starts with the grace of Jesus in discerning christological models that preserve the integrity of sexuality and foster sexual wholeness: the Erotic Christ, the Out Christ, the Transgressive Christ, and the Hybrid Christ. In the end, Cheng provides creative ways for us to think about Christology and about sin and grace that will permit LGBT persons and others to affirm both their sexual and spiritual selves.

One of the issues that inevitably emerges in any discussion of Christianity and sexuality involves the sexuality of Jesus. Postcolonial and feminist theologian

Kwok Pui-lan addresses "Touching the Taboo: On the Sexuality of Jesus" by asking, "Why is the sexuality of Jesus shrouded in a thick cloud of mystery, forbidden even in the realm of imagination?" After delineating theories of religious taboo, she suggests that the silencing around Jesus' sexuality creates a "surplus of meaning," and by the very treatment of this topic as forbidden, "the Christian church has exerted enormous power over believers' sexual life in intimating what they are supposed to do or not do to their bodies." In particular, Kwok is interested in investigating what this silence may disclose about the intersection of Jesus' gender, sexuality, and race, especially in terms of the nineteenth-century quest for the historical Jesus and its construction not only of European ideals of sexuality but also its distortion of the non-European Other. "My intention," she explains, "is to interrupt a discourse on the sexuality of Jesus defined largely by the imagination of white scholars, which tends to isolate sexuality from social, racial, and cultural dimensions."

Once again, the good news of these essays is that diverse theological and ethical thinkers are working to restore a life-affirming relationship between sexuality and spirituality.

5

Uses of the Erotic:
The Erotic as Power

AUDRE LORDE

There are many kinds of power, used and unused, acknowledged or otherwise. The erotic is a resource within each of us that lies in a deeply female and spiritual plane, firmly rooted in the power of our unexpressed or unrecognized feeling. In order to perpetuate itself, every oppression must corrupt or distort those various sources of power within the culture of the oppressed that can provide energy for change. For women, this has meant a suppression of the erotic as a considered source of power and information within our lives.

We have been taught to suspect this resource, vilified, abused, and devalued within western society. On one hand the superficially erotic has been encouraged as a sign of female inferiority—on the other hand women have been made to suffer and to feel both contemptible and suspect by virtue of its existence.

It is a short step from there to the false belief that only by the suppression of the erotic within our lives and consciousness can women be truly strong. But that strength is illusory, for it is fashioned within the context of male models of power.

As women, we have come to distrust that power which rises from our deepest and non-rational knowledge. We have been warned against it all our lives by the male world, which values this depth of feeling enough to keep women around in order to exercise it in the service of men, but which fears this same depth too much to examine the possibilities of it within themselves. So women are maintained at a distant/inferior position to be psychically milked, much the same way ants maintain colonies of aphids to provide a life-giving substance for their masters.

But the erotic offers a well of replenishing and provocative force to the woman who does not fear its revelation, nor succumb to the belief that sensation is enough.

why do men deny these powers? Because they are ultimately more powerful than force / physical strength...

The erotic has often been misnamed by men and used against women. It has been made into the confused, the trivial, the psychotic, the plasticized sensation. For this reason, we have often turned away from the exploration and consideration of the erotic as a source of power and information, confusing it with its opposite, the pornographic. But pornography is a direct denial of the power of the erotic, for it represents the suppression of true feeling. Pornography emphasizes sensation without feeling.

The erotic is a measure between the beginnings of our sense of self, and the chaos of our strongest feelings. It is an internal sense of satisfaction to which, once we have experienced it, we know we can aspire. For once having experienced the fullness of this depth of feeling and recognizing its power, in honor and self-respect we can require no less of ourselves. . . .

This internal requirement toward excellence which we learn from the erotic must not be misconstrued as demanding the impossible from ourselves nor from others. Such a demand incapacitates everyone in the process, for the erotic is not a question only of what we do. It is a question of how acutely and fully we can feel in the doing. For once we know the extent to which we are capable of feeling that sense of satisfaction and fullness and completion, we can then observe which of our various life endeavours bring us closest to that fullness.

The aim of each thing which we do is to make our lives and the lives of our children more possible and more rich. Within the celebration of the erotic in all our endeavours, my work becomes a conscious decision—a longed-for bed which I enter gratefully and from which I rise up empowered.

Of course, women so empowered are dangerous. So we are taught to separate the erotic demand from most vital areas of our lives other than sex. And the lack of concern for the erotic root and satisfactions of our work is felt in our disaffection from so much of what we do. For instance, how often do we truly love our work?

The principal horror of any system which defines the good in terms of profit rather than in terms of human need, or which defines human need to the exclusion of the psychic and emotional components of that need—the principal horror of such a system is that it robs our work of its erotic value, its erotic power and life appeal and fulfillment. Such a system reduces work to a travesty of necessities, a duty by which we earn bread or oblivion for ourselves and those we love. But this is tantamount to blinding a painter and then telling her to improve her work, and to enjoy the act of painting. It is not only next to impossible, it is also profoundly cruel.

As women, we need to examine the ways in which our world can be truly different. I am speaking here of the necessity for reassessing the very quality of all the aspects of our lives and of our work.

The very word "erotic" comes from the Greek word *eros*, the personification of love in all its aspects—born of Chaos, and personifying creative power and harmony. When I speak of the erotic, then, I speak of it as an assertion of the life-force of women; of that creative energy empowered, the knowledge and use of which we are now reclaiming in our language, our history, our dancing, our loving, our work, our lives.

There are frequent attempts to equate pornography and eroticism, two diametrically opposed uses of the sexual. Because of these attempts, it has become fashionable to separate the spiritual (psychic and emotional) away from the political, to see them as contradictory or antithetical. "What do you mean, a poetic revolutionary, a meditating gun-runner?" In the same way, we have attempted to separate the spiritual and the erotic, reducing the spiritual thereby to a world of flattened affect—a world of the ascetic who aspires to feel nothing. But nothing is farther from the truth. For the ascetic position is one of the highest fear, the gravest immobility. The severe abstinence of the ascetic becomes the ruling obsession. And it is one, not of self-discipline, but of self-abnegation.

The dichotomy between the spiritual and the political is also false, resulting from an incomplete attention to our erotic knowledge. For the bridge which connects them is formed by the erotic—the sensual—those physical, emotional, and psychic expressions of what is deepest and strongest and richest within each of us, being shared: the passions of love, in its deepest meanings.

The considered phrase, "It feels right to me," acknowledges the strength of the erotic into a true knowledge, for what that means and feels is the first and most powerful guiding light towards any understanding. And understanding is a handmaiden which can only wait upon, or clarify, that knowledge, deeply born. The erotic is the nurturer or nursemaid of all our deepest knowledge.

The erotic functions for me in several ways, and the first is in the power which comes from sharing deeply any pursuit with another person. The sharing of joy, whether physical, emotional, psychic or intellectual, forms a bridge between the sharers which can be the basis for understanding much of what is not shared between them, and lessens the threat of their difference.

Another important way in which the erotic connection functions is the open and fearless underlining of my capacity for joy. In the way my body stretches to music and opens into response, hearkening to its deepest rhythms, so every level upon which I sense also opens to the erotically satisfying experience, whether it is dancing, building a bookcase, writing a poem, examining an idea.

That self-connection shared is a measure of the joy which I know myself to be capable of feeling, a reminder of my capacity for feeling. And that deep and irreplaceable knowledge of my capacity for joy comes to demand from all of my life that it be lived within the knowledge that such satisfaction is possible, and does not have to be called marriage, nor god, nor an afterlife.

This is one reason why the erotic is so feared, and so often relegated to the bedroom alone, when it is recognized at all. For once we begin to feel deeply all the aspects of our lives, we begin to demand from ourselves and from our lives' pursuits that they feel in accordance with that joy which we know ourselves to be capable of. Our erotic knowledge empowers us, becomes a lens through which we scrutinize all aspects of our existence, forcing ourselves to evaluate those aspects honestly in terms of their relative meaning within our lives. And this is a grave responsibility, projected from within each of us, not to settle for the convenient, the shoddy, the conventionally expected, nor the merely safe.

During World War II, we bought sealed plastic packets of white, uncolored margarine, with a tiny, intense pellet of yellow coloring perched like a topaz just inside the clear skin of the bag. We would leave the margarine out for a while to soften, and then we would pinch the little pellet to break it inside the bag, releasing the rich yellowness into the soft pale mass of margarine. Then taking it carefully between our fingers, we would knead it gently back and forth, over and over, until the color had spread throughout the whole pound bag of margarine, leaving it thoroughly colored.

I find the erotic such a kernel within myself. When released from its intense and constrained pellet, it flows through and colors my life with a kind of energy that heightens and sensitizes and strengthens all my experience.

We have been raised to fear the yes within ourselves, our deepest cravings. For the demands of our released expectations lead us inevitably into actions which will help bring our lives into accordance with our needs, our knowledge, our desires. And the fear of our deepest cravings keeps them suspect, keeps us docile and loyal and obedient, and leads us to settle for or accept many facets of our oppression as women.

When we live outside ourselves, and by that I mean on external directives only, rather than from our internal knowledge and needs, when we live away from those erotic guides from within our selves, then our lives are limited by external and alien forms, and we conform to the needs of a structure that is not based on human need, let alone an individual's. But when we begin to live from within outward, in touch with the power of the erotic within ourselves, and allowing that power to inform and illuminate our actions upon the world around us, then we begin to be responsible to ourselves in the deepest sense. For as we begin to recognize our deepest feelings, we begin to give up, of necessity, being satisfied with suffering, and self-negation, and with the numbness which so often seems like their only alternative in our society. Our acts against oppression become integral with self, motivated and empowered from within.

In touch with the erotic, I become less willing to accept powerlessness, or those other supplied states of being which are not native to me, such as resignation, despair, self-effacement, depression, self-denial.

And yes, there is a hierarchy. There is a difference between painting a back fence and writing a poem, but only one of quantity. And there is, for me, no difference between writing a good poem and moving into sunlight against the body of a woman I love.

This brings me to the last consideration of the erotic. To share the power of each other's feelings is different from using another's feelings as we would use a Kleenex. And when we look the other way from our experience, erotic or otherwise, we use rather than share the feelings of those others who participate in the experience with us. And use without consent of the used is abuse.

In order to be utilized, our erotic feelings must be recognized. The need for sharing deep feeling is a human need. But within the european-american tradition, this need is satisfied by certain proscribed erotic comings together, and these occasions are almost always characterized by a simultaneous looking away, a pretense of calling them something else, whether a religion, a fit, mob violence, or even playing doctor. And this misnaming of the need and the deed give rise to that distortion which results in pornography and obscenity—the abuse of feeling.

When we look away from the importance of the erotic in the development and sustenance of our power, or when we look away from ourselves as we satisfy our erotic needs in concert with others, we use each other as objects of satisfaction rather than share our joy in the satisfying, rather than make connection with our similarities and our differences. To refuse to be conscious of what we are feeling at any time, however comfortable that might seem, is to deny a large part of the experience, and to allow ourselves to be reduced to the pornographic, the abused, and the absurd.

The erotic cannot be felt secondhand. As a Black Lesbian Feminist, I have a particular feeling, knowledge, and understanding for those sisters with whom I have danced hard, played, or even fought. This deep participation has often been the forerunner for joint concerted actions not possible before.

But this erotic charge is not easily shared by women who continue to operate under an exclusively european-american, male tradition. I know it was not available to me when I was trying to adapt my consciousness to this mode of living and sensation.

Only now, I find more and more woman-identified women brave enough to risk sharing the erotic's electrical charge without having to look away, and without distorting the enormously powerful and creative nature of that exchange. Recognizing the power of the erotic within our lives can give us the energy to pursue genuine change within our world, rather than merely settling for a shift of characters in the same weary drama.

For not only do we touch our most profoundly creative source, but we do that which is female and self-affirming in the face of a racist, patriarchal, and anti-erotic society.

6

Sexing Black Women: Liberation from the Prisonhouse of Anatomical Authority

KATIE GENEVA CANNON

The vast majority of Black churchwomen live in the midst of two competing sexual realities.[1] Either sex is a positive blessing for procreative purposes only, or sex is a negative curse that lays claim to bodily pleasure, contaminating the mind. This moralizing hegemonic construct of irreconcilable opposites insists that normal sexual activity should only occur between female and male inside of reproductive contexts. Given the specificity of the African American ecclesial backdrop,[2] the very talk about the pleasures of genital-sexual eroticism[3] locks women between rigidly disembodied hetero/homo binaries. Far too many African American women struggle, says Susan Newman, with the deep division between the two fundamental pillars of their identity—spirituality and sexuality.

> The church tells them that to live "holy and sanctified" lives that they must give up sexual activity outside the institution of marriage, and yet their bodies and souls cry out for a way to express and fulfill their natural passion.[4]

In her assessment of this type of antisensual ambivalence, Beverly W. Harrison writes:

> The religious dictum that the only moral expression of sexuality is that which is at least open to the possibility of procreation has been a source of many women's inability to achieve a self-defining role in relation to their bodies. Many women have been denied their own needs for bodily pleasuring at the cost of being "good" women. Conversely, when women have been sexually active or self-initiating, society has defined them as "whores" or "deviants."[5]

Perceived through the lens of hetero-patriarchal imagination, Black women's bodies have been degraded, demeaned, demonized—locked into an oppressive gaze of beauty created in opposition to us.[6] So, in a collective struggle to counter more than four hundred years of dehumanizing, racist stereotypes of the

78

Black-body-as-ugly, while simultaneously being an object-of-sexual-desire, the Black Church tends to confine sexual ethics to abstract, Puritanical condemnations.[7] The underpinning of anti-body dualism, compounded by chattel slavery and racial segregation, signify Black bodies, female and male, as inferior, mere performers of brute drudgery; white male bodies as unmarked, normative, full humanity, signifying superior individuality; while white female bodies represent the apex of "genteel" femininity, the prized possession in a privileged masculinist culture.

Therefore, in order to inscript our skin that is "too dark," our hair that is "too nappy," our facial features that are "too broad," and our buttocks that are "too wide" as definitive loci of positive human beingness, Black churchwomen are taught that we must suppress the sexual aspect of our humanity, by reinforcing norms and practices that proclaim procreational sex as a gift from God and relational/recreational sex as the devil's handiwork. Harrison goes on to say that "we are conditioned by religious and philosophical orthodoxy, or the official doctrines of the elites, to view the body and bodily needs as 'lower,' 'animal' modalities of existence that have to be tamed or in some way overcome and transcended by a higher and loftier power that is 'really' rational and spiritual."[8]

Living between the razor-blade tensions of heteronormativity and hypersexuality, Evelyn Brooks Higginbotham contends that the politics of respectability caused some women to promote the ill-fitting Victorian cult of true womanhood as the proper way to eradicate distorted images of the sexually immoral Black woman.[9] Darlene Clarke Hines agrees that by embracing the socially conservative, circumscribed notions of super-morality, as a defensive survivalist strategy, Black women hoped to put an end to negative stereotypes, garnering greater social respectability for all African Americans.[10]

This deferential, Victorian strategy of lady-like super-morality results in churchwomen assuming the supplicant-position, renouncing their own erotic pleasures in the name of procreation, and, in turn, engaging in sexual activities as part of their wifely duty; quieting the needs of husbands, while laboriously compressing, depressing, repressing their own desires. Beverly Harrison observes that "many of us are at our moral worst in our closest relationships, we frequently use sexual exchange, or its withholding, as a weapon to wound, punish or reward . . . . Why do we, in fact, usually 'hurt the ones we love'"?[11] We must ask what norms of justice can church members appropriate in erotic practices when intimate relationships, which supposedly facilitate domestic tranquility, require many women to accept unfulfilling sex lives as dependant appendages. One of the more detailed descriptions of the considerable cost of sex-role counterproductivity in the Black community goes like this:

> I know a woman who lives in Harlem who has reared her biological children and her husband's illegitimate children in poverty, suffered his mistress under her roof, had to ask for money to buy sanitary napkins, been sent out to work when he needed money, been forced to quit when it looked as if she was saving some money for herself on the side, been forced to steal from the house money to buy

a bottle of toilet water from the Avon Lady. She has endured indignities beyond measure; beyond sadness, beyond bitterness and redress. Now this much abused, long-suffering lady is said to be crazy.[12]

In sharp contrast to a firmly fixed life of domesticated resignation, other women pay homage to an excessive lifestyle of self-abnegation, misusing and abusing their bodies in cruel, exploitative and wasteful ways, because their capacity for sensual-sexual pleasure operates as an end unto itself. In the Introduction to her recently published book, *Longing to Tell: Black Women Talk about Sexuality and Intimacy*, Tricia Rose sums up the dilemma of "living as we do in a culture both fearful of the body and of sex and, at the same time, nearly preoccupied with these concerns,"[13] in this way:

> Black women's sexual lives are pinned between the powerful uses of distorted myths about black sexuality to fuel racist, demeaning stories about black men and women and the sexuality myths used to maintain the subordination of women as a whole.[14]

Individually and collectively, far too many African American Christian women restrict their sexual agency, by binding them with all kinds of biblical cords and ecclesiastical strings, in order to counter the age-old, pervasive stereotypes of being either sexually insatiable wenches—virile, promiscuous, and lusty, or fat, jolly, neutered mammies. Within this value-laden matrix of moral interpretations, that moves back and forth between past and present, churchwomen feel overwhelmed by contradicting socialization, and in turn they deny the gift of sexuality. As Blanche Richardson, the editor of *Best Black Women's Erotica*, explains:

> As women, so many of us are deprived of a healthy respect of and connection to our sexuality. For some, it is shrouded in so much shame, by so many convoluted messages, that we actually become detached from our sexual identities. We like sex, but we can't talk about it. We engage in sex, but we are, at times, afraid to enjoy it. When we do enjoy the act, and our partners, we are often subjected to ridicule and heartbreak. It can get confusing and tiring. How something so good, can be bad for you? How can something that feels so good, cause so much pain?[15]

Lest we forget, there are significant resemblances as well as differences oscillating between the sexed-body imprisonment of men-identified women and women-identified-women. If the statistical ratios regarding the variance of sexual orientation among members of the dominant society also ring true in the African American context, then this spectrum of sexual equation indicates that at least one out of every ten Black women is a woman-identified-woman.[16] The basic assessment is that lesbians in the Black Church community are confined to a mode of closeted exclusion that can be compared to isolation in solitary confinement.

Evelyn Hammonds suggests that the operating assumption is that Black lesbian women hide the truth of their lives because their desire for women is considered deviant sexuality existing within an already preexisting deviant sexuality.[17] Moreover, Renee L. Hill speaks disapprovingly of how the subordination of lesbian women as "other" licensed their invisibility.

> Her otherness has been such a powerful source of fear that she has had to be made invisible, her liberation and well being made non-issues. But in looking directly into the eyes of the "other" and by listening to her voice, womanists may find the tools to re-examine and do away with not only lesbian stereotypes, but also other negative images of Black women (the "Mammy," the "whore," and the baby maker for example). . . . In listening to the lesbian voice womanists, heterosexual and lesbian, can learn the importance of self-naming.[18]

To begin with, powerbrokers in the Black Church, all too often, subject women to a litany of verbal abuse, known as lezzy-baiting. To a large degree, anti-lesbian hysteria consists of assaultive speech, wherein the word lesbian is used as a weapon, as a defiant verbal punch, teetering on the edge of physical violence, in order to terrorize women who refuse to acquiesce to the so-called supremacy of the mama-papa, missionary position as the solo, dominant pattern for love making.

Second, bulldagger-phobia is deployed so as to indoctrinate African American women to eschew any allegiance except to men, because a straight-laced, male gaze is the all-important prize that supposedly legitimizes women's existence.[19] In order to understand the death-dealing insinuations operative in this scare tactic, we have to begin from the premise that bulldagger-phobia is an unfounded aversion to female homosexualities, wherein imaginary anatomical body parts are grafted onto the genitalia of women who desire and engage in same-sexual lovemaking activity, because the arrogant presumption is that some form of the male penis is essential for sexual gratification. In *Outlaw Culture*, bell hooks explains that patriarchal pornography has always appropriated and exploited homoeroticism, while simultaneously fanning the flames of homophobia, by consistently reinforcing the stereotypical notion that gay folks are predators, eager to feast upon the innocent.[20] In essence, pervasive, overt lezzy-baiting and anxiety inducing bulldagger-phobia exacerbate the lockdown of genital-sexual eroticism for women of faith.

Renita Weems's essay, "Just Friends," captures a vivid portrait of a common dynamic that often reaches obsessional fervor whenever the story of Sodom and Gomorrah is discussed in Bible classes. On this occasion a deacon argued vehemently against homosexuality on the grounds that it is not natural. In turn, in an effort to demystify the rights and wrongs of natural sex acts, Weems poses the following questions to parishioners:

> . . . Will you also want to legislate what type of sex between consenting adult men and women is natural? Must it be one woman and one man, or can it be one woman and two men? The man on top or the woman on top? The Sixty-Nine position or the elusive Venus Butterfly? Vaginal only, or will you permit oral sex, too? Must there be love for sex to be normal? Or is the presence of a marriage certificate enough?[21]

When we consider the warped theological teachings that threaten the with-drawal of male approval and economic support under the auspices of sexual abnormality, and the jack-leg preaching that vilifies and condemns Christian lesbians to eternal damnation, we must stay mindful that there are increasing numbers of Black churchwomen who refuse to remain docilely confined inside the walls of compulsory heterosexism. Most significantly, the fact is that due to the persisting legacies of slavery, including racial segregation and its pernicious regimes, the African American church community has not been able to liber-ate lovemaking from this dichotomous entrapment of normalized procreative economy in order talk about "good sex"[22] for Black women.

Keith Boykin claims that much of the homophobia and heterosexism mani-fested in the Black Church community has nothing to do with prejudiced fear and irrational hatred of those who sexually love members of their own gender, but these uncharitable attitudes are merely survival strategies for African Ameri-can people living in a white supremacist society.[23] However, my data reveal that women who love other women, sexually and/or non-sexually, face a greater risk of physical violence even in the churchhouse, because too often the climate of worship is one of warlike hostility.

Audre Lorde combines her intimate knowledge of African American culture with existential evidence as a lesbian-woman-mother-activist-poet in order to disentangle the social environment in which this rule of terror reigns:

> The black lesbian has come under increasing attack from both black men and heterosexual women. In the same way that the existence of the self-defined black woman is no threat to the self-defined black man, the black lesbian is an emotional threat only to those black women who are unsure of, or unable to, express their feelings of kinship and love for other black women, in any meaningful way. For so long, we have been encouraged to view each other with suspicion, as eternal competitors, or as the visible face of our own self-rejection.[24]

However, in taking survivalist cues from Jewelle L. Gomez and Barbara Smith, in order to move in the direction of right-relating in the household of faith, women-identified-women must deal not only with external manifestations of disembodiment, but must also attend to internalized distortions. Smith con-tends that being homophobic is not a healthy state for people to be in. Gomez points out that she thinks that it is despicable and a desecration that spiritual beliefs are perverted and used against Black gay people. "Anyone who under-stands what the spirit of Christianity is supposed to be would never use it against gays."[25] Both Gomez and Smith argue in favor of the intellectual, political, and moral character of lesbian women:

> The black lesbian must re-create our home, unadulterated, unsanitized, specific and not isolated from the generations that have nurtured us . . . so that we, who have been lost in the shadows of the past, can be revealed and appreciated for the powerful legacy that we bear.[26]

As a consequence, the significant contributions of Christian lesbians to the Black

Church community will no longer be ignored, marginalized, and excluded from the larger tapestry of theological discourse. As heterosexual, lesbian, bisexual women, Audre Lorde argues that we are raised to fear the yes within ourselves, to run from our deepest yearnings. In turn, Church traditions keep the vast majority of women living in a dichotomous state of binary opposites, a mind-body split of conflicted fluctuation. And yet, Lorde maintains that within each of us, there are reservoirs of erotic power that know no boundaries.[27]

In this essay, "Sexing Black Women," the generosity of my students' interrogation regarding the multiplicity of sexual identities and subjective experiences provide me with data relevant to the erotic desires and embodied beauty of Black femaleness. In order to liberate Black women's bodies from the ideological prisonhouse of male supremacist power, students enrolled in Resources for a Constructive Ethics, a course that focuses on Black women's literature as an ethical source for justice-making moral agency, navigate the complex terrain of racialized sexuality. A graduate student puts it this way: "All of us must take personal risks associated with growth and change if we are going to be our best erotic selves. Be forewarned, the risks of embodiment can range from being considered crazy, to being ridiculed, to actually experiencing physical hurt and harm."[28]

Undaunted by historical constructions of propriety and perversion,[29] Womanist ethicists must make available to the contemporary church community counter-hegemonic strategies that debunk and unmask normalizing structures of compulsive heterosexual acceptability. In other words, the Black women's literary tradition acknowledges the discomfort with our bodies in a world where white supremacy associates black bodies with hyper-sexuality and licentiousness, and yet, such discomfort no longer justifies the church's lack of attention to sexuality as a good gift from a gracious God. The objective of this study is to introduce the problem of genital-sexual eroticism in the lived-world experiences of African American women and establish a continuity between our movement from slavery to freedom, so that the Black Church community can begin to envision an ethics of "erotic justice"[30] for African American women in the twenty-first century that embraces the well being of us all.

INVISIBLE VISIBILITY IN SLAVERY

In attempting to grasp the relation between African American Christian women and the pleasures of genital-sexual eroticism, Womanists begin our analyses writing about women's experiences of New World slavery. Either we assess the usable truth in Black women's narratives that tell stories of rape, battering, compulsory childbearing, medical butchering, sex-motivated murder, forced prostitution, and physical mutilation as verifiable data with lasting cultural meaning and enduring social consequences;[31] or, we reconstruct bits and pieces of fragmented reflections that expose "the attendant invisibility of black women as the unvoiced, unseen, everything that is not white."[32]

In her novel, *Free Enterprise*, Michelle Cliff[33] contends that as women of African descent we carry within us the haunting presence of our ancestors who empower us to act in the present. Cliff's narrative strategy is predicated on the notion that if our lips, hips, skin color, and bone structure are passed on from our foreparents, then why, why not memory? "In resuscitating the lives of the dead," writes Jenny Sharpe, "by raising the painful memory of slavery,"[34] we make visible not only the sexual abuse that was done to Black woman, but according to Deborah E. McDowell, female-gendered subjectivity in slave novels dramatize "what they did with what was done to them."[35]

While helping us rethink a liberating balancing act between what was done to us sexually and what we can do with those memories, a graduate student says that the twists and tweaks of moral logic used by powerbrokers, professing to be Christians, result in contradictory messages. In *Incidents in the Life of a Slave Girl* by Harriet Jacobs, the enslaved African supposedly has no soul, just an inferior body that enslavers can do with as they pleased. White-skin privilege indicates "transparent skin," a so-called inner self symbolizing reason, while Black-skin is labeled as an inscrutable, blank page.

Overall, sorrow was the lot of Black women who were at the mercy of white men's lascivious desires and sexual violence. Either as soulless bodies or bodiless souls, women bore the constant torture of never knowing when their children would be torn from them.[36] Linda Brent could not tend to her daughter at all once she was assigned major housekeeping duties on the plantation. Even someone with a lighter workload, like her grandmother, was forced to stop nursing her own baby to take care of the white baby's needs.

For most enslaved women, children—instead of being a joyful blessing—were used as hostages. The constant threats from slaveholders, both spoken and unspoken, meant that if Black women did not do what white men wanted, they were whipped, had food withheld from them, or their children were sold down the river. Everywhere the enslaved woman turned, with few exceptions, she was controlled by institutionalized patterns of rape.[37] Several students wrestled with the questions, "how can we heal from hurting memories that we carry in our bodies when we only see God's back? How can God guide us in acts of self survival, when God always walks in front of us, never turning or looking back to see whether or not we are able to follow?"

Slavocracy was the rude transformation of African people into marketable chattel.[38] Enslaved women were answerable with their bodies to the sexual casualness of "stock breeding" with Black men and to the sexual whims and advances of white men. Being slave and female, the Black woman survived wanton misuse and abuse.

> The systems of slavery and caste encouraged white and black males sexually and socially to exploit black women. Thinking of profits or believing in the inferiority of Afro-Americans, some slave masters encouraged or ignored black male advances to black females, regarding the mating of slaves much in the same way they did their livestock.[39]

Virtually all the slave narratives as well as slave novels contain accounts of the high incidence of rape and sexual coercion.[40] White men, by virtue of their economic position, had unlimited access to Black women's bodies. Sexual victimization of Black women was accepted as inevitable almost as soon as African women were introduced into America. At the crux of the ideology that African American women are an inferior species was the belief that Black women, unlike white women, craved sex inordinately.

La Frances Rodgers-Rose in *The Black Woman* describes the sexual exploitation of the Black slave woman in this manner:

> The Black woman had to withstand the sexual abuse of the white master, his sons and the overseer. A young woman was not safe. Before reaching maturity, many a Black woman had suffered the sexual advances of the white male. If she refused to succumb to his advances, she was beaten and in some cases tortured to death.[41]

Womanist ethics requires that we excavate the rich trove of oral testimonies, recovering lost stories of freed women and their descendents in order to craft stories that reveal hidden meanings of complicated survival strategies. In order to challenge white supremacist narratives that present slavery as benign, tranquil, and benevolent, wherein Black females are stereotyped as docile, servile automatons, Black women novelists uncover lingering memories of painful degradation.[42]

The body politic of auction-block visibility makes every woman of African descent a member of the collective social-self. At slave auctions, Black people were stripped naked, exposed to public view, and humiliated with pokes, probes, and crude physical examinations. Often traders made slaves run, leap, and perform acts of agility to demonstrate their value as chattel.[43] It is virtually impossible to discuss the enslaved Black woman's sexual-self as solo-singleness, apart from the collective, corporeal scarredness of communal realities.

Conditions of slavocracy forced women into an embattled status; both objects-of-exploitation (those who are violated by others), and agents-of-exploitation (those who are forced to do the reproductive work, producing those who will be violated). For instance, as "brood-sow" the Black woman

> was forced to give birth as often as once a year. Her body was misused, and quite often she was old before her time. Not only was she forced to have children rapidly, but she was given very little time to regain her own strength and only two weeks to care for her children. After that time, the slave woman had to return to work.[44]

Jacqueline Jones' article, "My Mother Was Much of a Woman: Black Women, Work, and the Family Under Slavery," describes the Black woman as reproducer-producer in this way:

> One North Carolina slave woman, the mother of fifteen children, used to carry her youngest with her to the field each day and "when it get hungry she just slip it around in front and feed it and go right on picking and hoeing . . . ," symbolizing in one deft motion the equal significance of the productive and reproductive functions to her owner.[45]

Neither pregnant women nor new mothers were exempt from hard labor. The slave narratives of Moses Gandy include the stories of women who were reproducer-producers and the pain they endured because they were unable to nurse their infants regularly.

> On the estate I am speaking of, those women who had sucking children suffered much from their breasts becoming full of milk, the infant being left at home. They therefore could not keep up with the other hands: I have seen the overseer beat them with raw hide, so that the blood and milk flow mingled from their breasts.[46]

Black bondswomen were supposedly impervious to the onslaught of sado-masochistic torture and the pervasive experiences of sexual brutality. Thomas Thistlewood, who assumed the duties of overseer in 1751 on a Jamaican sugar estate, called Egypt, meticulously records in his diary the date, time, and place—the cane field, the curing house, the boiling house, the parlor—of his 1,774 separate sexual acts with 109 different enslaved women during a 13-year period. Jenny Sharpe goes on to say that if the slave women complied, Thistlewood gave them a small sum of money; if they resisted, he raped them.[47]

As a "work-ox" the Black woman was subjected to hard, steady, often-strenuous labor. Slave women worked as common laborers in mines extracting coal, lead, and gold, as well as in pine forests, turpentine, tar, pitch, and rosin plantations. From sunup to sundown Black women either worked alongside enslaved males in the cotton, tobacco, rice, and sugarcane fields or catered as a domestic, from before dawn to late at night, to the demands made by the mistress and other members of the enslaver's family. This compulsory labor forced Black women into anomalous marginal positions in relation to the evolving ideology of femininity. Angela Y. Davis contends, "Where work was concerned, strength and productivity under the threat of the whip outweighed consideration of sex."[48]

INVISIBLE VISIBILITY IN FREEDOM

The second aspect of Womanist analyses related to African American Christian women and the pleasures of genital-sexual eroticism describes the various ways that Black women sustain dignity in the most inhumane of circumstances. The Civil War, from 1861 to 1865, destroyed the institution of chattel slavery. Emancipation removed the legal and political slave status from approximately four million African Americans in the United States, which meant that, in principle, Blacks own their embodied selves and their labor for the first time.

During the post-emancipation period, racism and male supremacy continued to intersect patriarchal and capitalist structures in definitive ways. Black women, young and old, were basically freedwomen on their own. Perhaps deserted or perhaps never married, hundreds of thousands of Black women walked from plantation to plantation searching for lost and stolen children. Due to the more than 38,000 deaths of Black soldiers who fought in, serviced, and led guerrilla actions for the Union Army and Navy during the Civil War and the estimated 5,000 Black men killed during the 10 years following the war, large numbers of African American women found themselves widowed. Hordes of ex-slaves fled as aimless refugees when the Union Military Armies penetrated the South. Other women were fortunate enough to cross the greatest chasm one can imagine, from slavery to freedom, with their families intact. Whether a Black woman began her career as a free woman, as an autonomous family supporter or as a copartner with her spouse, the African American woman began her life of freedom with no vote, no protection, and no equity of any sort.

The Black woman continued to experience the traditional White-Black, master-servant relationship via the sharecropping system that replaced slavery. The relationship of power dynamics remained much as it had before the war. The standardized land-tenure contract was structured so as to maintain the hegemony of the antebellum slave-owning aristocracy. As a result of the crop lien laws passed in 1865, African American people were financially unable or not allowed to purchase land. The Black woman and her family's legal emancipation trapped them in grossly unequal poverty cycle of debt peonage. Every year the white landowners and commissary merchants provided Black sharecroppers with high rates of interest for credit in order to purchase seeds, tools, food, fuel, and other necessities. At the end of the harvest season, the sharecroppers were compelled to accept a settlement of their share of the crop minus charges according to the landlord's rendition of the farm accounts.

Even with newly won civil rights, the economic opportunities for African Americans tottered between dependency and despair. A full complement of Black people soon found themselves legally bound to labor for payment on trumped-up charges that accrued in excessive amounts from year to year. This type of perpetual indebtedness resulted in involuntary servitude for an overwhelming majority of African American families.

The patterns of exploitation of the African American woman as reproducer-producer were only shaken by the Civil War. By no means were they destroyed. Throughout the nineteenth and early twentieth century, Black women were severely restricted to the most unskilled, poorly paid, menial jobs. Virtually no Black woman held a job beyond those of field hand or domestic servant. Farming land, keeping house, bearing and rearing children continued to dominate all aspects of the Black woman's life. This systematic exclusion and routinized oppression of Black females from other areas of employment served as confirmations for the continuation of the servile status of Black women.

It is estimated that three out of every four farmhands were Black females put to work at a very young age, between six and eight. Black women sharecroppers who worked the land, with or without husbands, chopped, hoed, planted, plowed, primed, and picked crops as well as completed those tasks usually defined as within the male domain such as the care and feeding of livestock. The urgency of trying to survive as sharecroppers demanded every hand—female and male—from the youngest to the oldest.

The theme of sexual objectification inherent in the domestic servitude of the Black woman continued to permeate her life. Bereft of formal education and advanced skills, the Black woman as a domestic worker was usually at the white employer's mercy. Her employment arrangements had few, if any, demands that white people were obligated to meet. In lieu of salary she was often paid with used clothing, discarded household items, and leftover food. The low and no pay, precariousness of job security and irregular work hours caused many domestic workers to situate their families in the backyards of white households. Sexual harassment became the lineal descendant of the institutionalization of rape, of Black women under slavery. As a vestige of slavery, white male heads of households assumed the sexual accessibility of the Black female domestic worker.

African Americans believed that education made one less susceptible to the indignities and proscriptions of an oppressive white South. From the outset, the education of the Black woman differed from her white counterpart, in that Black women were taught that their education was not an ornament, meant to "uplift" her alone, but that formal education prepared her for a life of service in the "uplifting" of the entire community. Thus, teaching, nursing, and social work represented the pinnacle of professional achievement for the Black woman.

The accelerated movement of African Americans out of the South, to northern and western cities, that began in 1910 and gained momentum after each of the world wars, impinged on the Black woman's moral situation in very definite ways. Tens of thousands of African American females were members of the mass exodus seeking social democracy and economic opportunities. Black females soon found that their situation as women was much more difficult than that of migrant men.

Economic necessity dictated that most Black women who migrated to northern urban centers find work immediately. As a wife and mother, the Black migrant woman was responsible for transmitting the culture, customs, and values of the African American community to her children. At the same time that she was trying to organize family life according to her traditional roles, the male-dominated industrial society required that she serve as a catalyst in the transition process from the rural South to the urban North. Her own unfamiliarity and adaptation difficulties had to be repressed because she was responsible for making a home in crowded, substandard housing, finding inner-city schools that propagated literacy for her children while earning enough income to cover the most elementary needs. Many landlords refused housing to Black women with children. They preferred to provide room and board at excessive rates to single Black men who were thought to be at the height of their wealth-producing capacity.

In order to survive themselves and to provide for their families, African American women once again found only drudge work available to them. Black men worked as porters, janitors, chauffeurs, window cleaners, elevator operators, and as menial laborers in industry, while Black women were restricted to domestic jobs that northern white women scorned or considered demeaning.

Racist and male supremacist constraints forced Black women into a status of live-in domestic servants, wherein Black women tried to earn a living as cooks, cleaners, washerwomen, and wet nurses under very hard and exhausting conditions. Barbara Ransby assesses the overall situation in this way:

> Although poor black women were sexually exploited as women, there was no magical, raceless, classless sisterhood between them and the white female employers, who were just as eager to exploit them for their muscle as their husbands were to use them for their sexual services. The economic rigors of the depression had intensified all forms of oppression, pushing black women from the lower rungs of the wage labor force back to day work and even into occasional prostitution.[49]

World Wars I and II brought about the most visible changes in the Black woman's moral situation. As a result of widespread racial animosity of white factory employers and employees, African Americans found scant acceptance in northern communities. Small numbers of Black women were allowed inside of the industrial manufacturing system but were confined to the most tedious, strenuous, and degrading occupations. White manufacturers alleged that undeniable hostility by white labor and the lack of separate entrances, doorways, drinking water buckets and cups, pay windows, and lavatories forced them to exclude Black women from skilled jobs and craft positions. In conjunction with racist stereotypes of Black women's lewdness and immorality that emanated from sexual exploitation of enslaved persons by white masters, northern Black women were subjected to discrimination and pettiness of all kinds. Hazel V. Carby makes the point this way:

> The need to police and discipline the behavior of black women in cities, however, was not only a premise of white agencies and institutions but also a perception of black institutions and organizations, and the black middle class. The moral panic about the urban presence of apparently uncontrolled black women was symptomatic of and referenced aspects of the more general crises of social displacement and dislocation that were caused by migration. . . . Thus, the migrating black woman could be variously situated as a threat to the progress of the race; as a threat to the establishment of a respectable urban black middle class; as a threat to congenial black and white middle-class relations; and as a threat to the formation of black masculinity in an urban environment.[50]

During the 1950s postwar period, a number of African American women became heads of households. Marital instability, low remarriage rates and an increase in out-of-wedlock births resulted in large numbers of Black women becoming dependent on the social welfare system. The persistent obstacles of poverty, sexual apartheid, and white supremacy continue to enslave the Black woman and her family to hunger, disease, and the highest rate of unemployment since the Korean and Vietnam wars. Education, housing, and other necessities which were gained during the mid-1970s and early 1980s are deteriorating faster now than ever before. This overarching sociocultural context renders visibility to Black women's invisible legacy of hard work, perseverance, and tenacity as we spell out new standards for intimate relations that embody mutuality.

CONCLUSION

Liberating Black churchwomen who live in the midst of two competing sexual realities is a moral imperative. The unjust, oppressive dualism that either sex is a positive blessing for procreative purposes only or sex is a negative curse that lays claim to bodily pleasure, contaminating the mind, must be eradicated. More choices and greater understanding regarding genital-sexual eroticism as a gift from God is the way we must go. To be sure, the issue is not procreative choice for some and no choice for others, but, under the mandate of Christian social solidarity, we must create conditions in which choices of bodily integrity are consistent with our understanding of right-relating that affirms equal discipleship in the household of God.

I believe wholeheartedly that it is time for African American churchwomen who believe in the healing power of sexual touch, to engage in dialogue about the various dimensions of human intimacy. Those of us who see the constraints of anatomical authority as death-dealing, must initiate critical conversations with women, men, and children throughout the Black Church community, so that together we can examine and remove impediments to erotic justice.

The impediments to giving and receiving pleasure are legions, especially among those of us whose ecclesial histories bear witness to our embodiment being rendered hyper/in/visible. Therefore, it is time for clergywomen in particular to speak out, to articulate nothing short of a revolutionary agenda that enables Black females to resist enforced sex role socialization. There is no such thing as neutral, color-blank, value-free space. In these troubled times, acquiescence, indifference, and conformity to oppressive value systems are out of order. As Audre Lorde insists in her remarkable wisdom, "Our silence will not save us."

NOTES

1. Major credit is due to my bestest friend, the Reverend Angelin Jones Simmons, for her prophetic accuracy in naming this essay.

2. Kelly Brown Douglas, *Sexuality and the Black Church: A Womanist Perspective* (Maryknoll, NY: Orbis Books, 1999); and Samuel K. Roberts, *African American Christian Ethics* (Cleveland: Pilgrim Press, 2001) provide historical frameworks for analyzing religious conventions that substantiate antisexual bias in African American Christianity.

3. For a fuller discussion of sexual eroticism from Black women's perspective, see Gail Elizabeth Wyatt, *Stolen Women: Reclaiming Our Sexuality, Taking Back Our Lives* (New York: John Wiley & Sons, 1997); Miriam Decosta-Willis, Roseann P. Bell, and Reginald Martin, eds. *Erotique Noire: Black Erotica* (New York: Doubleday, 1992); Maxine Leeds Craig, *Ain't I a Beauty Queen? Black Women, Beauty and the Politics of Race* (New York: Oxford University Press, 2002); Hortense Spillers, "Interstices: A Small Drama of Words," in *Pleasure and Danger: Exploring Female Sexuality*, ed. Carole S. Vance (New York: Routledge, 1984).

4. Susan Newman, *Oh God! A Black Woman's Guide to Sex and Spirituality* (New York: Old World/Ballantine Books, 2002). See also Hilda Hutchison, *What Your Mother Never*

Told You About S. E. X. (New York: Putnam, 2002) and Dorothy Roberts, *Killing the Black Body: Race, Reproduction and the Meaning of Liberty* (New York: Pantheon, 1997).

5. Beverly W. Harrison, "Sexuality and Social Policy," in *Making the Connections: Essays in Feminist Social Ethics*, ed. Carol S. Robb (Boston: Beacon Pr., 1985), 87. My indebtedness to Beverly W. Harrison and Audre Lorde for their theoretical sensibilities to the erotic as a source for embodied creativity, which guide this essay, should be obvious to all who know their work.

6. Farah J. Griffin, "Textual Healing: Claiming Black Women's Bodies, the Erotic and Resistance in Contemporary Novels of Slavery." *Callaloo* 19, no. 2 (1996): 519–36; Scholars who devote special attention to this topic are Brenda Dixon Gottchild, *The Black Dancing Body: A Geography from Coon to Cool* (New York: Palgrave Macmillan, 2003); Deborah Willis and Carla Williams, *The Black Female Body: A Photographic History* (Philadelphia: Temple University Press, 2002); Sander Gillman, "Black Bodies, White Bodies: Toward an Iconography of Female Sexuality in Late Nineteenth-Century Art, Medicine, and Literature," in *"Race," Writing, and Difference*, ed. Henry L. Gates, Jr., (Chicago: University of Chicago Press, 1985), 223–61; Michael Bennett and Vanessa D. Dickerson, eds. *Recovering the Black Female Body: Self-Representation by African American Women* (New Brunswick: Rutgers University Press, 2001).

7. Cornel West, "Black Sexuality: The Taboo Subject," in *Race Matters* (Boston: Beacon Pr., 1993), 81–91.

8. Harrison, op. cit., 135–36.

9. Evelyn Brooks Higginbotham, "African American Women's History and the Metalanguage of Race," *Signs* 17:2 (1992): 251–74. One of the best available discussions of the sexual virtues of Black churchwomen is Higginbotham's *Righteous Discontent: The Women's Movement in the Black Baptist Church, 1880–1920* (Cambridge: Harvard University Press, 1993). See also E. Frances White, *Dark Continent of Our Bodies: Black Feminism and the Politics of Respectability* (Philadelphia: Temple University Press, 2001).

10. Darlene Clarke Hines, "Rape and the Inner Lives of Black Female Sexuality in the Middle West: Preliminary Thoughts on the Culture of Dissemblance," *Signs* 14.4 (1989): 915–20. A very important study, which disentangles this history in specific details, is Kathleen Thompson and Hilary MacAustin, eds. *The Face of Our Past: Images of Black Women from Colonial America to the Present* (Bloomington: University of Indiana Press, 1999).

11. Harrison, op. cit., 150. Also, Carter Heyward, *Our Passion for Justice: Images of Power, Sexuality, and Liberation* (New York: Pilgrim Press, 1984).

12. Barbara Walker's article in *Redbook* (March 1976): 33; see especially Carolyn M. West, ed. *Violence in the Lives of Black Women: Battered, Black and Blue* (New York: Haworth Press, 2002); Traci West, *Wounds of the Spirit: Black Women, Violence and Resistance Ethics* (New York: New York University Press, 1999).

13. *Presbyterians and Human Sexuality 1991* (Louisville: Office of the General Assembly, Presbyterian Church (USA) 1991), 1. Recognition of human sexuality as a contestable issue is receiving attention in the works of Christian ethicists James B. Nelson, *Embodiment: An Approach to Sexuality and Christian Theology* (Minn: Augsburg, 1978) and Susan E. Davies and Eleanor Haney, eds. *Redefining Sexual Ethics* (Cleveland: Pilgrim Pr., 1991); and in anthologies such as, *Sexuality and the Sacred*, ed. James B. Nelson and Sandra P. Longfellow (Louisville: Westminster John Knox Pr., 1994) and Delroy Constantine-Simms, ed. *The Greatest Taboo: Homosexuality in Black Communities* (Los Angeles: Alyson Books, 2000).

14. Tricia Rose, *Longing to Tell: Black Women Talk About Sexuality and Intimacy* (New York: Farrar, Straus and Giroux, 2003), 5.

15. Blanche Richardson, *Best Black Women's Erotica* (San Francisco: Cleis Press, 2001).

16. For excellent interdisciplinary critiques of sexuality, read Bryan Strong, Christine Devault, Barbara Werner Sayad, and William L. Yarber, eds. *Human Sexuality: Diversity in Contemporary America* (Mountain View, CA: Mayfield Publishers, 1997); Kathleen Kennedy and Sharon Ullman, eds. *Sexual Borderland: Constructing an American Sexual Past* (Columbus: Ohio State University Press, 2003); Eugene Kennedy, *The Unhealed Wound: The Church and Human Sexuality* (New York: St. Martin's Press, 2001).

17. Evelyn Hammonds, "Black (W)holes and the Geometry of Black Female Sexuality," in *Differences* 6 (1994): 125–45. See also Leanne McCall Tigert, *Coming Through the Fire: Surviving the Trauma of Homophobia* (Cleveland: United Church Press, 1999); Cheryl Clarke, *Living as a Lesbian* (Ithaca, NY: Firebrand, 1986); Anita Cornwell, *Black Lesbian in America* (Minneapolis: Naiad Press, 1983); and S. E. Wieringa and E. Blackwood, eds. *Female Desire: Same Sex Relations and Transgender Practices Across Cultures* (New York: Columbia University Press, 1999).

18. Renee L. Hill, "Who Are We for Each Other: Sexism, Sexuality and Womanist Theology," in *Black Theology: A Documentary History, Vol. II: 1980–1992* ed. James H. Cone and Gayraud S. Wilmore (Maryknoll, NY: Orbis Books, 1993), 350. See also Lisa C. Moore, ed. *Does Your Mama Know? An Anthology of Black Lesbian Coming Out Stories* (Decatur: Red Bone Press, 1997); Catherine E. McKinley and L. Joyce DeLaney, eds. *Afrekete: An Anthology of Black Lesbian Writing* (New York: Anchor Books, 1995).

19. Audre Lorde, "Scratching the Surface: Some Notes on Barriers to Women and Loving," *The Black Scholar* (April 1978), 34.

20. bell hooks, *Outlaw Culture: Resisting Representations* (New York: Routledge, 1994), 15.

21. Renita J. Weems, "Just Friends," in *Que(e)rying Religion: A Critical Anthology*, ed. Gary David Comstock and Susan E. Henking (New York: Continuum, 1997), 353. See Irene Monroe's monthly religion column online, *Queer Take*, for *The Witness Magazine* (www.thewitness.org); Roderick A. Ferguson, *Aberrations in Black: Toward a Queer of Color Critique* (Minneapolis: University of Minn. Press, 2003); and G. Winston James, ed. *Voices Rising: An Anthology of Black Lesbian, Gay, Bisexual and Transgender Writing* (New York: Other Countries Press, 2002).

22. By using the phrase "good sex" I join the conversation of the international, interreligious feminist scholars whose anthology, *Good Sex: Feminist Perspectives from the World's Religions* ed. Patricia Beattie Jung, Mary E. Hunt, and Radhika Balakrishnan (New Brunswick: Rutgers University Press, 2001) is evoking sexual justice discussions in theoethic classrooms.

23. Keith Boykin, *One More River to Cross: Black and Gay in America* (New York: Anchor Books/Doubleday, 1996), 167. To understand open and affirming congregations, see Gary David Comstock, *A Whosoever Church: Welcoming Lesbians and Gay Men into African American Congregations* (Louisville: Westminster John Knox Press, 2001).

24. Audre Lorde, "Scratching the Surface," 31–35. Also Lorde's *Zami: A New Spelling of My Name* (Freedom, CA: Crossing Press, 1982).

25. Jewelle L. Gomez and Barbara Smith, "Taking the Home Out of Homophobia: Black Lesbian Health," in *The Black Women's Health Book: Speaking for Ourselves*, ed. Evelyn C. White (Seattle: Seal Press, 1990) 198–213. Barbara Smith, *The Truth that Never Hurts: Writings on Race, Gender and Freedom* (New Brunswick: Rutgers University Press, 1998).

26. Jewelle Gomez, "A Cultural Legacy Denied and Discovered: Black Lesbians in Fiction by Women," in *Home Girls: A Black Feminist Anthology*, ed. Barbara Smith (New York: Kitchen Table Press, 1983), 110–23.

27. Audre Lorde, *Sister Outsider: Essays and Speeches* (Trumansburg, New York: Crossing Press, 1984).

28. I thank the students who allow me to quote from their work.

29. Marcia Y. Riggs, *Plenty Good Room: Women Versus Male Power in the Black Church* (Cleveland, Ohio: Pilgrim Press, 2003); and Marita Golden, ed. *Wild Women Don't Wear No Blues: Black Women Writers on Love, Men and Sex* (New York: Anchor Books, 1994) are important sources in transforming African American women's self-understanding regarding bodily integrity.

30. A comprehensive understanding of this concept is elaborated in Marvin Ellison, *Erotic Justice: A Liberating Ethic of Sexuality* (Louisville: Westminster John Knox Press, 1996).

31. My notion of embodied-memories-as-reincarnation is dependent on the work of Toni Morrison, *Beloved* (New York: Knopf, 1987); Charlotte Pierce-Baker, *Surviving the Silence: Black Women's Stories of Rape* (New York: W. W. Norton, 1998); Patricia Hill Collins, *Black Sexual Politics: African Americans, Gender, and the New Racism* (New York: Routledge, 2004).

32. Evelyn Hammonds, op. cit., 132.

33. Michelle Cliff, *Free Enterprise: A Novel* (New York: Penguin Books, 1993).

34. Jenny Sharpe, *Ghost of Slavery: A Literary Archaeology of Black Women's Lives* (Minneapolis: University of Minnesota Press, 2003), xi.

35. Deborah E. McDowell, "Witnessing Slavery after Freedom—Dessa Rose," in *Slavery and the Literary Imagination*, ed. Deborah E. McDowell and Arnold Rampersad (Baltimore: Johns Hopkins University Press, 1989), 146.

36. Among novelists who deal with this theme, read Lorene Cary, *The Price of a Child* (New York: Vintage, 1995); Gayl Jones, *Corregidora* (New York: Random House, 1975; rpt. Boston: Beacon, 1990).

37. Of special importance, read Margaret Walker, *Jubilee* (Boston: Houghton Mifflin, 1966; rpt. New York: Mariner Books, 1999); Sherley A. Williams, *Dessa Rose* (New York: W. Morrow, 1986; rpt. New York: Quill, 1999); Hilda Gurley-Highgate, *Sapphire's Grave* (New York: Doubleday, 2003); Austin Clark, *The Polished Hoe* (New York: Amistad, 2002); Ishmael Reid, *Flight to Canada* (New York: Scribner, 1998).

38. Katie G. Cannon, "The Black Woman's Moral Situation, 1619–1900," in *Black Womanist Ethics* (Atlanta: Scholars Press, 1988), 31–57.

39. W. Augustus Low, ed., and Virgil A. Clift, asst. ed., *Encyclopedia of Black America* (New York: McGraw Hill Book Co., 1981), 862.

40. See especially Harriet Jacobs, *Incidents in the Life of A Slave Girl, Written by Herself* (1861; rpt. New York: Penguin, 1987); and Beryl Gilroy, *Stedman and Joanna—A Love in Bondage* (New York: Vintage, 1991).

41. La Frances Rodgers-Rose, ed., *The Black Woman* (Beverly Hills, CA: Sage Publications, 1980), 20.

42. For examples, see J. California Cooper, *The Wake of the Wind* (New York: Doubleday, 1998); Octavia Butler, *Kindred* (New York: Doubleday, 1979; rpt. Boston: Beacon Press, 1988); and Caryl Phillips, *Cambridge* (New York: Knopf, 1992).

43. Katie G. Cannon, "Surviving the Blight," in *Katie's Canon: Womanism and the Soul of the Black Community* (New York: Continuum, 1995), 27–37. See Walter Johnson, *Soul to Soul: Life Inside the Antebellum Slave Market* (Cambridge: Harvard University Press, 2000).

44. Johnson, "Soul to Soul," 8.

45. Jacqueline Jones, "My Mother was Much of a Woman: Black Women, Work, and the Family Under Slavery," *Feminist Studies* 8 (Summer 1982): 238.

46. Moses Grandy, in E. Franklin Frazier, *The Negro Family in the United States* (Chicago: University of Chicago Press, 1939), chap. IV.

47. Cited by Jenny Sharpe, *Ghost of Slavery: A Literary Archaeology of Black Women's Lives* (Minneapolis: University of Minnesota Press, 2003), 63, based on Thistlewood's sexual practices in Hilary Beckles, *Centering Women: Gender Discourses in Caribbean*

Slave Society (Princeton: Marcus Weiner, 1999) 38–58. Such atrocities are clearly depicted in Eddie Donoghue, *Black Women/White Men: The Sexual Exploitation of Female Slaves in the West Indies* (Trenton: Africa World Press, 2002).

48. Angela Y. Davis, *Women, Race and Class* (New York: Random House, 1981), 6.

49. Barbara Ransby, *Ella Baker & the Black Freedom Movement: A Radical Democratic Vision* (Chapel Hill: University of North Carolina Press, 2003) 76–77.

50. Hazel V. Carby, "Policing the Black Woman's Body in an Urban Context," in *Critical Inquiry* (Summer 1992): 738–55. See also, Frances A. Kellor, "Southern Colored Girls in the North: The Problem of Their Protection." *Charities* (March 18, 1905): 584–85.

7

Where Are We?
Seven Sinful Problems
and Seven Virtuous
Possibilities

JAMES B. NELSON

It is commonly observed that religion is a very ambiguous human enterprise. The creative power of religion is great, for the divine presence is, indeed, often mediated with life-giving power through religious patterns of doctrine, morals, worship, and spirituality. The religious enterprise is also one of the most dangerous of all human enterprises, since it is always tempted to claim ultimate sanction for its humanly constructed beliefs and practices. This ambiguous mix of the creative and the destructive in religion is particularly evident when it comes to religious dealings with human sexuality. That is because the dynamisms of human sexuality give it particular power for both good and ill. Thus, throughout history most religions have given unusual attention to this dimension of human life, have attempted to control it, and often have shown considerable fear of it.

Early in Christian history two lists arose: the seven deadly sins and the seven virtues.[1] The original contents of those early lists are not my concern at this point. I simply want to name seven deadly sins through which the Jewish and Christian traditions have contributed to our sexual alienation, countered by seven virtues or positive resources which these same traditions offer to nurture our sexual wholeness. I am assuming two things. First, the sexual distortions in these traditions have largely resulted from perversions of their own central teachings. Through reclaiming that which is more authentic to the core of these faiths, there may be sexual healing. Second, each of these seven sins betrays profound suspicions of the human body. The body, especially in its sexual dimensions, often evokes anxieties about mortality, loss of control, contamination, uncleanness, personal inadequacy, and a host of other fears. Thus, we sorely need body theologies that will illuminate our experience, and that is a concern of these chapters.

SPIRITUALISTIC DUALISM
OR THE BODYSELF UNITY?

Spiritualistic dualism is the first deadly sin. With its counterpart, sexist or patriarchal dualism, spiritualistic dualism underlies and gives shaping power to all the other sins of the list. Any dualism is the radical breaking apart of two elements that essentially belong together, a rupture which sees the two coexisting in uneasy truce or in open warfare.

Though quite foreign to Jewish scriptures and practice, spiritualistic dualism was grounded in Hellenistic Greco-Roman culture and had a profound impact on the early Christian church. Continuing with power to the present, it sees life composed of two antagonistic elements: spirit, which is good and eternal, and flesh or matter, which is temporal, corruptible, and corrupting. The sexual aspects of the body are the particular locus of sin. With this perspective, escape from the snares of bodily life through the spirit's control is central to the religious life.

There is, however, a countervailing virtue in both Judaism and Christianity, one much more authentic to the roots of each faith. In Judaism it is a strong belief in the goodness of creation and with it an anthropology that proclaims the unity and goodness of the human bodyself. The Hebrew scriptures show little reticence about human bodies and their varied functions. Neither do they divide the person into parts or locate the core of personhood in some disembodied spirit. They take for granted the created goodness of sexuality, and at times display lyrical celebrations of the delights of robust, fleshly love.

Christianity also expresses this antidualistic virtue by affirming creation as good, and it adds to this its particular emphasis on divine incarnation. Incarnation proclaims that the most basic and decisive experience of God comes not in abstract doctrine or mystical otherworldly experiences, but in flesh. True, the faith's ongoing struggle with dualism has been evident in its marked discomfort over taking incarnation radically. Both Christian doctrine and practical piety have largely confined the incarnation of God to one, and only one, human figure, Jesus of Nazareth. Further, persisting body denial has made most Christians suspect Jesus' full humanity through silence about or actual denial of his sexuality.

There is another possibility, however implausible it may seem to some: without denigrating the significance of God's revelation in Jesus, incarnation might yet be understood more inclusively. Then the fleshly experience of each of us becomes vitally important to our experience of God. Then the fully physical, sweating, lubricating, menstruating, ejaculating, urinating, defecating bodies that we are—in sickness and in health—are the central vehicles of God's embodiment in our experience.

Nevertheless, Christian suspicions of the body and its pleasures continue. The sexual purity campaigns did not end with the Victorian era. But the authentic core of both religious traditions affirm the unity of spirit and body, mind and matter, spirituality and sexuality. The creation-affirming Jewish faith and the incarnational Christian faith attest to the goodness of the bodyself with all its rich sexuality as part of God's invitation into our full humanness and loving communion.

PATRIARCHAL DUALISM
OR HUMAN EQUALITY?

The second deadly sin is sexist or patriarchal dualism. The systematic and systemic subordination of women is the counterpart of spiritualistic dualism, for men typically have defined themselves as essentially spirit or mind, and men have defined women as essentially body and emotion. The logic, of course, is that the higher reality must dominate and control the lower.

Patriarchal dualism pervades Jewish and Christian scriptures and their cultures as well. In Christianity, however, it has taken particular twists that powerfully join the male control of women to body denial. For example, classic understandings of the crucifixion and the atonement have given many Christians throughout the ages the sense that suffering is the necessary path to salvation. At the same time, Christian theology has often denigrated sensual pleasure, suggesting that deprivation and pain are mandatory if eternal joy is to be found. But women's suffering has particularly been encouraged, for in patriarchy it is they and not males who essentially represent the evil (the fleshly body) that needs redemption.[2] That sexist dualism is a deadly sin dangerous to the health and well-being of women needs no elaboration. That it is also enormously destructive for males, even while men continue to exercise dominant social power and privilege, needs to be recognized as well.

The good news, the countervailing virtue in these religious traditions, is the affirmation of human equality. In one of his better moments the apostle Paul wrote, "There is no longer Jew or Greek, there is no longer slave or free, there is no longer male and female; for all of you are one in Christ Jesus" (Gal. 3:28). The second great wave of feminism in our society, occurring in the latter third of the current century, has produced real gains in gender justice and inclusiveness—few would doubt this. That Jewish and Christian communities have far to go is also beyond question. Continuing resistance to women's religious leadership and ongoing religious justifications for male control of women's bodies are but two of many sad illustrations possible.

Nevertheless, gender equality is a truer expression of our common religious heritage. Sexism is the religious perversion. At the same time, the continuing power of sexist dualism displays a deep fear of the body, and sexism declares that the body is central to woman's being in a way that is not true for the man. All the issues about our bodies are enormously complicated by the interplay of these two faces of dualism, as are all the major moral issues of our day. Not only are the more obvious issues of body rejection, sexism, homophobia, and heterosexism rooted in dualistic dynamics, but so also are crucial dynamics of social violence, militarism, racism, economic oppression, and ecological abuse (about which I shall say more later).

HETEROSEXISM AND HOMOPHOBIA,
OR GAY AND LESBIAN AFFIRMATION?

The third deadly sin is heterosexism (socially enforced compulsory hetero-sexuality) and its companion phenomenon homophobia (the irrational fear of same-sex feelings and expression). Tragically, this sin has pervaded both Jewish and Christian histories. Yet, it cannot be justified by careful biblical interpretation. The Bible does not even deal with homosexuality as a psychosexual orientation. Such understandings did not arise until the latter part of the nineteenth century. While scriptures do condemn certain homosexual acts, they appear to do so because of the lust, rape, idolatry, violation of religious purity obligations, or the pederasty expressed in those acts in specific contexts. We find no explicit biblical guidance on same-sex genital expression in relationships of mutual respect and love. On the other hand, the Bible pointedly celebrates instances of same-sex emotional intimacy, a fact often overlooked by fearful proof-texters.

The dynamics of homophobia are numerous and complex. Frequently they are deeply rooted in misogyny, in the fear of and contempt for the "failed male," in the fear of one's own bisexual capacities, in general erotophobia (the fear of sexuality itself), and in the alienation from one's own body and hence the desperate envy of anyone who appears to be more sexual than oneself.

The good news—the virtue—is that Jews and Christians have significant resources for dealing with these things. The same religious convictions that resist the spiritualistic and sexist dualisms also undercut heterosexism and homophobia. Central to each faith is God's radical affirmation of every person, each unique bodyself. Further, when we experience that grace that pervades the heart of biblical faith, there grows a sense of personal security that releases us from the anxious need to punish those who seem sexually different from ourselves. Then the issue becomes not sexual orientation as such, but rather whether, whatever our orientation, we can express our sexuality in life-giving ways.

That both faith communions are making some progress on issues of sexual orientation seems evident from a number of indications. That this subject is still the most divisive one for many congregations and judicatories is also evident— witness the passionate and often rancorous debate over lesbian and gay ordinations. In all of this one fact seems clear: fear of the body is a central dynamic in the resistance to equality in sexual orientation.

SELF-REJECTION
OR SELF-LOVE?

The fourth deadly sin contributing to sexual dis-ease is guilt over self-love. Christian theologies and pieties have had a more difficult time with this than have Jewish. Dominant Christian interpretations all too frequently have understood self-love as equivalent to egocentrism, selfishness, and narcissism, and hence incompatible with the religious life. A sharp disjunction has been drawn between agape (selfless, self-giving love believed normative for the faithful) and eros (the desire for fulfillment).

When suspicion about self-love is combined with a suspicion of the body and of sexual feelings, the stage is set for sexual dis-ease. Masturbation is a case in point. To be sure, this subject is no longer inflamed by passions akin to those of the nineteenth-century sexual purity reformers. Sylvester Graham's "graham crackers" and John Kellogg's cornflakes are no longer persuasive as bland diets to prevent the solitary vice, though this was their original purpose. Yet, masturbation is still an obvious arena of guilt, simply because giving oneself sexual pleasure seems to be sheer self-centeredness. Self-love, in its larger sense, has had a bad press, particularly in Christianity. And when self-love is denigrated, authentic intimacy with a sexual partner is made more problematic, for true intimacy always is rooted in the solid sense of identity and self-worth of each of the partners.

The good news is that self-love is not a deadly sin. Both Hebrew and Christian scriptures bid us to love our neighbors as ourselves, not instead of ourselves. Both religious traditions at their best know that love is indivisible and non-quantifiable. It is not true that the more love we save for ourselves the less we have for others. Authentic self-love is not a grasping selfishness—which actually betrays the lack of self-love. Rather, it is a deep self-acceptance, which comes through the affirmation of one's own graciously given worth and creaturely fineness, our "warts and all."

Furthermore, genuine self-love personalizes the experience of one's own body. "My body is me, and I am worthful." When this is our experience, we are less inclined to exploit others sexually or, for that matter, to exploit ourselves. Genuine self-love is essential to our experience of fullest sexual pleasure as well as to an inner-directed sense of sexual responsibility for ourselves and toward others. When we are deeply self-affirming we lose the desire to control others, sexually or otherwise.

Better theological work in recent decades has brought corrections in earlier simplistic condemnations of self-love. Such theological shifts undoubtedly have been undergirded by a growing psychological sophistication within religious communities. Even more important, Christian and Jewish feminists, gay men, and lesbians have shown how dominant males have made the virtue of self-denial a means of controlling those whose sexuality was different from theirs.

Nevertheless, the battle about self-love is far from over, particularly in its sexual expressions. While theological treatises are beginning to give sexual pleasure some justification, most congregations would still be embarrassed by its open endorsement except, perhaps, in a discreet hint spoken during a wedding service. The affirmation of masturbation as a positive good for persons of all ages, partnered or unpartnered, is rarely found in religious writings and even more rarely mentioned aloud in synagogue or church. The sexual and body aspects of self-love surely are not the only dimensions, but they are barometers that remind us how our problems with genuine self-love appear intricately intertwined with our continuing bodily denial.

LEGALISTIC ETHICS
OR LOVE ETHICS?

The fifth deadly sin is a legalistic sexual ethic. Many adherents of both Christian and Jewish faiths have fallen into more legalism about sexual morality than about any other arena of human behavior. Legalism is the attempt to apply precise rules and objective standards to whole classes of actions without regard to their unique contexts or the meanings those acts have to particular persons. Masturbation, homosexual expression, and nonmarital heterosexual intercourse are frequent targets for religio-moral absolutes. So also, however, are numerous issues related to reproduction: contraception, abortion, and various new reproductive technologies such as in vitro fertilization.

The virtue that speaks to the deadly sin of legalism is love. Our bodyselves are intended to express the language of love. Our sexuality is God's way of calling us into communion with others through our need to reach out, to touch, to embrace—emotionally, intellectually, and physically. Since we have been created with the desire for communion, the positive moral claim upon us is that we become in fact what essentially we are: lovers, in the richest and deepest sense of that good word. A sexual ethic grounded in love need not be devoid of clear values and sturdy guidelines. Indeed, such norms are vitally important. The morality of sexual expression, however, cannot adequately be measured by the physiological contours of certain types of acts. For example, religious legalism typically has condemned genital sex outside of heterosexual marriage and has blessed sex within marriage. Such a morality consequently has prevented us from blessing the loving unions of same-sex couples or finding ways to affirm committed heterosexual relationships short of legal marriage. At the same time, that morality (even if unwittingly) has given moral justification for unloving and exploitive sex within marriages by insisting that the rightness of sex is measured not fundamentally by the quality of the relationship but by its external form.

The alternative to sexual legalism is not laxity and license, but an ethic grounded in the centrality of love. Such an ethic is based on the conviction that human sexuality finds its intended and most profound expression in the kind of love that enriches the humanity of persons and expresses faithfulness to God. Such an ethic cannot guarantee freedom from mistakes in the sexual life, but it aims to serve and not to inhibit the maturation and human "becoming" of sexual persons.

Perhaps more than ever, many Christians and Jews are now open to a nonlegalistic approach to sexual ethics. But sexual legalism is not a thing of the past. The unbending stringency of Orthodox Judaism, the official Roman Catholic retreat from Vatican II sexuality teachings, and the strident moralisms of fundamentalist Protestants are still with us. What we seldom recognize, however, is that religious legalism is much more commonly applied to sexuality and body issues than to any other area of human morality. Many people who customarily operate with more flexible and contextually applied rules in other areas of life are wedded to exceptionless absolutes when it comes to sex. That should not surprise us. The body is still a great source of anxiety, and we typically want desperately to control that which we fear.

more @ stake

SEXLESS SPIRITUALITY
OR SEXUAL SPIRITUALITY?

The sixth deadly sin of which our religious traditions are often guilty is a sexless image of spirituality. This has been a bane of Christianity more than of Judaism, for the church more than the synagogue has been influenced by the Neoplatonic split between spirit and body. In its more extreme forms, such a view perceived true spirituality as sexless, celibacy as meritorious, and bodily mortification and pain as conducive to spiritual purification. In the early centuries of the church, the pressures of the last imperial persecutions brought a new wave of anti-body thought, and an ethic of sexual renunciation took hold in the teachings of the church fathers. Thus, Origen spoke of two distinct creations, the spiritual and the material, one higher and one lower. Acting on his beliefs, Origen actually castrated himself "for the kingdom of God." Similarly, Jerome could say, "Blessed is the man who dashes his genitals against the stone." Tertullian typically connected antisex, anti-body perceptions with a misogynist, anti-woman bias. Speaking to women in one of his sermons, he proclaimed, "The sentence of God on this sex of yours lives on even in our times. . . . You are the one who first plucked the fruit of the forbidden tree; you are the first who deserted the divine law."[3]

While these negative extremes were not the whole story, even in that early period, they dramatically illustrate a significant current that has influenced the Christian sexual story and, unfortunately, still has its hold. In our more recent history it has been "sexual Victorianism." (H. L. Mencken was wrong in his quip about the Puritans. They were not really the ones tortured by the haunting fear that others somewhere else might be enjoying themselves. That was the Victorians—and many others since that time.)

Good news comes in the recognition that a sensuous, body-embracing, sexual spirituality is more authentic to both Jewish and Christian heritages. We are beginning to see that repressed sexuality "keeps the gods at bay" and does not bode well for the fullest, healthiest spirituality. We are beginning to recognize that the kind of erotic and bodily hungers celebrated in the Song of Solomon are human sharings in the passionate longings of God, the divine One who is shamelessly the earth's Lover.

The seventeenth-century Puritan bard John Milton expressed this "delicious Paradise" in his depiction of Adam and Eve beyond the Fall:

> half her swelling breast
> Naked met his under the flowing gold
> Of her loose tresses hid
> . . . .

Thus these two
Imparadised in one another's arms
The happier Eden, shall enjoy their fill
Of bliss on bliss.[4]

Similarly, incarnational theologians are reclaiming the sacramental possibilities of body experience. Thus Evgenii Lampert described the promise of sexual intercourse:

It is the mystery of a sudden merging and union into a single indivisible being of flesh and spirit, of heaven and earth, of human and divine love. The divine spirit touches human flesh . . . in the burning moment of erotic ecstasy. We are witnessing to a true sacrament: the Spirit of God invades the cosmic element, without ceasing to be Spirit, and the flesh widens into the transcendence of the Spirit, without ceasing to be flesh.[5]

PRIVATIZED SEXUALITY OR PERSONAL AND PUBLIC SEXUALITY?

The seventh deadly sin of our religions has been the privatization of sexuality. My word play is intentional. Sexuality has been religiously consigned to the nonpublic world and narrowed to a genital matter—"the privates." To that extent, the public, institutional, and justice dimensions of human sexuality have often been neglected.

Yet one of the ironies of American history is that the nineteenth-century "sexual purity movements" most determined to push sex back into the confines and privacy of the marital bed frequently heightened its visibility and made sex a matter of more public discussion. Thus, early in the twentieth century even Anthony Comstock's war on obscenity unwittingly served Margaret Sanger's movement for birth control.[6]

"The personal is public." This familiar feminist affirmation is also a conviction of the Jewish and Christian religious traditions at their best. Sexuality issues are inevitably political, and the most deeply personal is at the same time connected with the social. Yet, there are different ways of understanding this. The radical religious right wing of Christianity exemplifies one. Clearly, sexuality issues are at the core of its public agenda: opposition to gender equality, sex education, abortion, homosexuality, pornography, the Equal Rights Amendment, and family planning, on the one hand, and support of those programs that would strengthen "the traditional family," on the other. Yet, for all its public emphasis on sexuality, the radical right exhibits a thinly veiled fear of it. The two familiar dualisms shape its agenda: patriarchy's hierarchical ordering of the sexes and spiritualism's denigration of the body. The message becomes clear. The right wing's current public sexual agenda is to get sexuality out of the public and back into the private sphere once again. And the private sphere is that of the male-controlled "traditional family."

There is a different way of seeing sexuality as a public issue. It is to recognize that the sharp distinction between private and public is a dualism directly growing out of the sexual dualisms. It is to see that sexual politics is inevitable, for politics (as Aristotle taught us) is the art of creating community, and human sexuality at its core deals with those intimate relationships that shape the larger communities of life. Thus, the bedroom cannot be confined to the bedroom. Justice issues for the sexually oppressed, sexual abuse, reproductive choice, population control, exploitation in commercialized sex, adequate sexuality education—these, among others, are now obviously public issues. Yet, we are only beginning to understand that there are important sexual dimensions to other vast social issues that previously we had not recognized. Social violence is a case in point. Whether it is crime on the city streets, or the arms race, or economic oppression, or the assumptions behind our foreign policies in Vietnam, Central America, or the Persian Gulf, such violence has important sexual dimensions.

To be sure, violence is complex in both causes and manifestations. No single explanation is adequate. But the sexual dimensions of social violence are present, and we have usually overlooked them. What, for example, of the competitiveness, the cult of winning, the armoring of emotions, the tendency to dichotomize reality into either-ors, the abstraction from bodily concreteness, the exaggerated fear of death manifested in a morbid fascination with death? All of these feed social violence, and all of these are deeply related to sexual distortions. Perhaps we are late in recognizing the sexuality embedded in these matters because of our continuing penchant for dualisms. Body anxiety still bids us to keep sex private, or to try to return it to the realm of the private, but it will not be so contained.

So, the seven (or more) deadly sexual sins are still very much with us. Nevertheless, they are neither the last nor the truest word about our religious traditions. I repeat my thesis: While Christianity and Judaism have often confounded good sexuality education and social policies, they have done so through the perversions and distortions of their own central teachings. What is more authentic to the core of both faiths can become the renewed wellspring for sexual health, sexual responsibility, and sexual justice, and for more adequate body theologies.

NOTES

1. See also James B. Nelson, "Religious Dimensions of Sexual Health," in *Readings in Primary Prevention of Psychopathology: Basic Concepts,* ed. Justin M. Joffe et al. (Hanover, N.H.: University Press of New England, 1984).

2. See Joanne Carlson Brown and Carole R. Bohn, eds., *Christianity, Patriarchy, and Abuse: A Feminist Critique* (New York: Pilgrim Press, 1989).

3. Helpful documentations of these teachings of the church fathers can be found in Frank Bottomley, *Attitudes to the Body in Western Christendom* (London: Lepus Books, 1979), chs. 4–6; and in Raymond J. Lawrence, Jr., *The Poisoning of Eros* (New York: Augustine Moore Press, 1989), ch. 3.

4. John Milton, *Paradise Lost*, ed. Scott Elledge (New York: W.W. Norton & Co., 1975), Book IV, 91.

5. Evgenii Lampert, *The Divine Realm* (London: Faber & Faber, 1944), 97f.

6. See John D'Emilio and Estelle B. Freedman, *Intimate Matters: A History of Sexuality in America* (New York: Harper & Row, 1988), ch. 10.

8

Rethinking Sin
and Grace
for LGBT People Today

PATRICK S. CHENG

Sin is a difficult issue for many, if not most, lesbian, gay, bisexual, and transgender (LGBT or queer) people of faith. It is the primary reason why LGBT people are denied full participation in the life of the church, including the denial of sacraments and rites such as marriage and ordination, and denied many secular rights such as civil marriage and anti-discrimination laws. Sin also torments LGBT people starting from a young age. We are taught very early on that same-sex acts are sinful, and we will be condemned to eternal punishment in hell if we fail to repent and abstain from such acts.

As a result, many LGBT people are unable to understand what grace—the unmerited gift of what God has done for us in Jesus Christ—is all about. If a central part of our identity, the ability to experience embodied love and pleasure with another human being, is understood as intrinsically sinful and in need of repentance and abstinence, then why should we care about God's grace? In fact, what kind of sadistic God would create people one way and then insist that they change who they are in order to attain salvation? It is not surprising, then, that many LGBT people have turned away from the church and organized religion.

Even for those of us who remain in the church, sin and grace are difficult topics to discuss and often avoided by LGBT pastors and theologians. The lack of discourse about sin and grace in ecclesial and theological contexts is highly problematic because it has led to a devaluing of christology and the role of Jesus Christ in the economy of salvation. In other words, if there is no sin, then there is no need for grace or redemption in the form of God's breaking into the world in the person of Jesus Christ. Thus, many LGBT people of faith see Jesus Christ as a great prophet or teacher, but not as truly God or the Word made flesh. As such, christological discourse—including incarnation, atonement, and eschatology—has been weakened in the LGBT faith community.

This essay will argue that the traditional condemnation of sexual acts between people of the same sex (same-sex acts) is based upon a legal model of sin and grace that is fundamentally flawed. Instead, this essay proposes a christological model of sin and grace based upon Karl Barth's work in volume 4 of his *Church Dogmatics*. Rather than defining sin in terms of specific acts or omissions, Barth defines sin as that which opposes the grace of what God has done for us in Jesus Christ. In other words, according to Barth, the traditional legal model of sin has it backward! Rather than starting with an autonomous definition of sin, we must start with the grace of Jesus Christ and understand sin as anything opposed to the grace of what God has done for us in Jesus Christ.

In addition to arguing for a christological understanding of sin and grace, this essay will also use examples from the LGBT Asian American experience to illustrate how sin and grace are present in the lives of LGBT Asian Americans today.[1] One of the reasons for citing these examples is to give voice to a perspective that has not been widely acknowledged in either LGBT or Asian American theologies.[2] These examples also illustrate how the christological model of sin and grace might speak to the experiences of various groups within the LGBT community.

THE TRADITIONAL LEGAL MODEL OF SIN AND GRACE

The church traditionally has talked about sin and grace in legal terms. Same-sex acts are understood as sinful because they violate biblical law, natural law, and/or other divine prohibitions against such acts. To sin is to violate God's laws or commands, just as Adam and Eve committed the first sin by disobeying God and eating from the tree of the knowledge of good and evil in the garden of Eden.

By contrast, grace is traditionally understood as God's forgiveness (that is, justification) of those who have committed sins and then repented for such violations of God's laws. God's grace is truly a gift because there is nothing that humans alone can do to repair the breached relationship between God and the sinner. Grace is also understood as a gift that allows the sinner to refrain from future violations of God's laws (that is, sanctification).

As noted above, same-sex acts traditionally have been viewed as violations of both biblical and natural law. Although only a handful of biblical passages discuss same-sex acts (Gen. 19:5; Lev. 18:22 and 20:13; Rom. 1:24–25; 1 Cor. 6:9; 1 Tim. 1:10), they have been cited time and time again to "prove" the sinfulness of such acts. Furthermore, the Roman Catholic Church has also relied upon natural law to argue that human sexuality must always be expressed in the context of procreation, and any delinking of sexual pleasure and procreation is a violation of God's law.[3]

By contrast, grace under the traditional legal model is understood as God's forgiveness of those who have engaged in same-sex acts (that is, justification), as well as God's assistance in helping such people to abstain from such prohibited acts in the future (that is, sanctification). In other words, to accept God's grace is to refrain from having any nonprocreative sex, including same-sex acts.

There are a number of problems with this traditional legal model of sin and grace. First, this model detracts from a central message of the New Testament, which is justification by grace alone. By characterizing sin as the violation of God's eternal laws, the focus inevitably shifts to who may or may not be violating such laws. This in turn leads to an obsession with groups thought to be sinners (for example, LGBT people), as opposed to a focus on God's unmerited grace, which is actually the only thing that can help any of us to overcome the bondage of original sin.

Second, the traditional legal model results in an obsession with defining precisely what the rules for right and wrong behavior are. Specifically, this takes the form of endless argumentation and proof-texting over what the Bible "actually" says about same-sex acts. What does the word "know" mean in the Sodom and Gomorrah narrative in Genesis 19:5? What does it mean for a man to lie with another male "as with a woman" in Leviticus 18:22 and 20:13? Was the prohibition against same-sex acts in Romans 1:24-25 really about idolatry? What about the words used to describe people who engage in same-sex acts in 1 Corinthians 6:9 or 1 Timothy 1:10?

A great deal of ink has been spilled over the last few decades over interpreting a handful of "texts of terror" for LGBT people. Although I believe in the importance of biblical exegesis, a narrow focus on what God prohibits or allows in scripture takes away from the larger framework of original sin and the theological significance of Jesus Christ in salvation history. The Bible becomes simply a book of rules as opposed to the revelation of God's relationship with—and love for—humanity as the Word made flesh.

THE CHRISTOLOGICAL MODEL
OF SIN AND GRACE

This essay proposes, as an alternative to the traditional legal model, a christological model of sin and grace. Such a model is based upon the approach used by Karl Barth. Although Barth would likely reject the use of experience, including LGBT experience, as a source for theology, I believe that the christological model is a more appropriate way of thinking about sin and grace for LGBT people today.

For Barth, the starting point for thinking about sin and grace is Jesus Christ. Barth contends that it is impossible to start with a definition of sin that has its own independent ontological status (which is what the traditional legal model attempts to do). Sin is nothingness; it is a privation of good as opposed to being part of God's created order. As such, Barth views any attempt to establish an independent doctrine of sin to be a sin in itself![4]

Instead, Barth understands sin as whatever is opposed to the grace of what God has done for humanity in Jesus Christ. Sin is defined in terms of one's relationship to Jesus Christ. It cannot be reduced to a laundry list of commandments to obey. Not only is this approach more comprehensive than the traditional legal model; it is also more flexible in terms of taking into account the diverse contexts in which humans exist.

Barth sets forth three christological models of sin and grace. The first model relates to sin as pride and grace as condescension. To the extent that Jesus Christ is the grace of God's coming down from heaven for our salvation (condescension), then sin is defined as humanity's urge to raise itself up above God (pride).[5] Liberation theologians have characterized this sin as the economic and political subjugation of the marginalized.[6]

The second model relates to sin as sloth and grace as exaltation. To the extent that Jesus Christ represents the grace of God's lifting up of humanity in the victory of the resurrection (exaltation), then sin is humanity's refusal to rise to the level of what God has called us to be (sloth).[7] Feminist and womanist theologians have characterized this as the sin of hiding or the negation of the self.[8]

The third and final model relates to sin as falsehood and grace as true witness. To the extent that Jesus Christ represents the grace of God's fullest revelation of Godself to humanity (true witness), then sin is humanity's refusal to recognize the truth of that revelation (falsehood).[9] Certain contemporary theologians have characterized this as the sin of refusing to recognize the truth of the Christian message in an increasingly secularized world.[10]

Building upon Barth's work, the remainder of this essay describes four christological models of sin and grace that arise out of the experiences of LGBT people. The models use the experiences of LGBT Asian Americans to illustrate how sin and grace manifest themselves within a specific social context. It is my hope that these models can lead to a more thoughtful discussion—as opposed to silence or avoidance—about what sin and grace mean to LGBT people today.

MODEL ONE: THE EROTIC CHRIST

The first christological model of sin and grace for LGBT people is the Erotic Christ. According to Audre Lorde, the Black feminist lesbian writer, the erotic is about relationality and desire for the other. It is the power that arises out of "sharing deeply" with another person. The erotic is to "share our joy in the satisfying" of the other rather than simply using other people as "objects of satisfaction."[11]

The Erotic Christ arises out of the reality that Jesus Christ, as the Word made flesh, is the very embodiment of God's deepest desires for us. Jesus Christ came down from heaven not for his own self-gratification, but rather for us and for our salvation. In the Gospels, Jesus repeatedly shows his love and desire for all those who come into contact with him, including physical touch. He uses touch as a way to cure people of disease and disabilities, as well as to bring them back to life. He washes the feet of his disciples and even allows the Beloved Disciple to lie close to his breast at the Last Supper.[12]

Conversely, Jesus is touched physically by many of the people who come into contact with him. He is touched by a bleeding woman who hopes that his powers can heal her. He is bathed in expensive ointment by the woman at Bethany. After his resurrection, Jesus allows Thomas to place his finger in the mark of the nails and also to place his hand in his side.[13] All of these physical interactions are manifestations of God's love for us—and our reciprocal love for God—through the Erotic Christ.

Carter Heyward, the lesbian theologian and Episcopal priest, has written about the Erotic Christ in the context of the "radically mutual character" of Jesus Christ's life, death, and resurrection. For Heyward, the significance of Jesus Christ lies not only in the ways in which he touched others (both physically and otherwise), but also in the ways in which he was "healed, liberated, and transformed" by those whom he encountered. This power in mutual relation is not something that exists solely within the trinitarian relationship between God, Jesus Christ, or the Holy Spirit. Rather, this power is present in all of us who have ever "loved, held, yearned, lost."[14]

SIN AS SELF-GRATIFICATION

So what is sin and grace in light of the Erotic Christ? If the Erotic Christ is understood as God's deepest desire to be in relationship with us, then sin as what opposes the Erotic Christ can be understood as self-gratification or the complete lack of mutuality or concern for the needs and desires, sexual or otherwise, of one's partner.

For many LGBT people, sin in the context of the Erotic Christ takes the form of sexual practices in which one's partner is treated as merely an object of gratification or something less than a full person (for example, sex arising out of addiction). Many gay men, particularly those who struggle with sex addiction, have engaged in anonymous, unsafe, and/or drug-fueled hookups in which self-gratification is the primary if not only concern. The sex addict's partner or partners are reduced to objects for stimulation and not seen as human beings in themselves.

A number of LGBT Asian Americans have written about the sin of self-gratification, particularly as a way to lessen the pain of self-hatred and low self-esteem. Guy Nakatani, a gay Japanese-American man who was diagnosed with full-blown AIDS at the age of twenty, first began having sex with other men at age fifteen to escape the trauma of being Asian and gay in high school. For Nakatani, "more was better," and because his first priority was "filling up the void," his "needs completely overwhelmed any judgment" and he was "never concerned about anybody else."[15] This is the sin of self-gratification at work: using one's partner as an object for stimulation and not as a fellow human being.

GRACE AS MUTUALITY

By contrast, grace in the context of the Erotic Christ is mutuality or the awareness of being-in-relationship with the other. As Lorde describes it, grace can take the form of something as simple as "sharing deeply any pursuit with another person" such as dancing.[16] For Heyward, the grace of the Erotic Christ necessarily takes the form of "justice-love" and sharing in "the earth and the resources vital to our survival and happiness as people and creatures."[17] Grace is understanding that we are all connected deeply to each other. As such, we must do more than just engaging in one-on-one interactions with others. Rather, grace requires a commitment to changing how we see and interact with the world.[18]

Many LGBT Asian Americans experience the grace of mutuality when they come together with other LGBT Asian Americans socially, politically, or sexually. For example, Yoko Yoshikawa, a Japanese American lesbian activist, writes about the joy of seeing a gay Asian American man with a jacket that read "San Francisco-Born Gay Man of Korean Descent" at a protest of the racist depiction of Asians in the Broadway musical *Miss Saigon*. Yoshikawa felt a deep connection with that man because of their shared experiences as LGBT Asian Americans.[19]

MODEL TWO: THE OUT CHRIST

The second christological model of sin and grace for LGBT people is the Out Christ. The Out Christ arises out of the reality that God reveals Godself most fully in the person of Jesus Christ. In other words, God "comes out of the closet" in the person of Jesus Christ. It is only through the incarnation, ministry, crucifixion, and resurrection of Jesus Christ that we understand the true nature of God and God's solidarity with the marginalized and oppressed. Indeed, the notion of the Out Christ as the revelation of God is supported by Jesus Christ's description as the logos, or Word of God.[20]

Chris Glaser, the gay theologian and Metropolitan Community Church minister, has written about the Out Christ in his *Coming Out as Sacrament*. In that book, Glaser describes Jesus Christ as nothing less than God's very own coming out to humanity: "The story of the New Testament is that God comes out of the closet of heaven and out of the religious system of the time to reveal Godself in the person of Jesus the Christ."[21]

For Glaser, God reveals God's solidarity with the marginalized and oppressed of the world in Jesus Christ. God comes out as an infant who is born in the midst of the filth of a stable in "a strange town and in a land and culture dominated by a foreign power, the Roman Empire." God also comes out in the ministry of Jesus, who "defends women and eunuchs and those of mixed race (Samaritans) and responds to other races (the Roman centurion, the Syrophoenician woman)." In the crucifixion, God comes out by extending "an inclusive paradise to a crucified criminal." And finally, in the resurrection, God comes out as one who "lives despite human violence, a true survivor of human abuse and victimization."[22]

SIN AS THE CLOSET

If the Out Christ is understood as the One through whom God most fully reveals Godself to humanity, then sin—as what opposes the Out Christ—can be understood as the closet or the refusal to reveal oneself fully to one's families, friends, coworkers, and other loved ones. Not only does the closet prevent a person from truly connecting with others; it also has a corrosive effect on her self-esteem and well-being to the extent that she is constantly forced to keep her life as a secret from others.

Many LGBT Asian Americans have written about experiencing the sin of the closet. For them, coming out to families and friends is particularly difficult, particularly due to unique cultural issues, such as theological fundamentalism, cultural patriarchy, and immigrant anxieties.[23] Rich Kiamco, a gay Filipino man in New York City, wrote about his experiences of coming out to his parents. His father reacted by saying that they would "cure" him of his homosexuality, and his mother reacted by giving him a Bible and telling him that she would pray for him.[24] LGBT Asian Americans also experience an ethnic closet by trying to hide their minority status within the broader white community. David Lee, a Chinese American gay man, writes about dyeing his hair orange-blond in college in order to separate himself from that "class of laughable Asians."[25]

GRACE AS COMING OUT

By contrast, grace in the context of the Out Christ can be understood as the courage to come out of the closet or sharing one's sexual orientation and/or gender identity with others. For LGBT people, the process of coming out can only be understood as grace or an unmerited gift on the part of God. There is no one correct pattern or single path to coming out. Some people come out very early in life; others wait until much later. For some people, it is a slow and private process; for others, it is a fast and public announcement.

Regardless of how one ultimately comes out, the act of coming out reflects the very nature of a God who is also constantly coming out and revealing God-self to us in the Out Christ. Coming out is a gift accompanied by other gifts, such as self-love, the love for others, and the overcoming of shame and internalized homophobia.[26] The grace of coming out is not something that can be "willed" or "earned"; it can only happen as an act of grace from God.

Many LGBT Asian Americans have written about the grace of coming out, particularly in terms of strengthening relationships with their families and loved ones. Wei Ming Dariotis, a bisexual young woman of mixed Chinese and

European descent, writes about how her coming out ultimately has brought her closer to her mother. Her coming out has also taught her mother to make the connections between homophobia and racism, which are two "oppressions that support each other."[27] Thus, coming out has been a gift for not only Wei Ming, but also for her mother.

MODEL THREE:
THE TRANSGRESSIVE CHRIST

The third christological model of sin and grace for LGBT people is the Transgressive Christ. The Transgressive Christ arises out of the reality that Jesus Christ was crucified by the religious and political authorities of his day for refusing to conform to their standards of behavior. Indeed, Jesus is constantly seen in the Gospels as transgressing the commonly accepted religious and legal boundaries of his day. In a world obsessed by purity codes, he touches those who are unclean, including lepers, bleeding women, and the differently abled. He eats and drinks with outcasts such as tax collectors and sinners.[28]

Jesus also challenges the religious authorities with respect to their teachings (such as healing on the Sabbath, and the grounds for divorce). He rejects his biological family, and he is rejected by his hometown. Many of his parables are about those who are on the margins of society, such as Samaritans.[29] As such, the Transgressive Christ can be understood as God's solidarity with the suffering of LGBT people and others who refuse to conform to the rules of the principalities and powers of this world.

Robert Goss, the gay former Jesuit priest and current Metropolitan Community Church minister, writes about the Transgressive Christ in his book on LGBT Christology, *Jesus Acted Up*.[30] In that book, which was an angry theological response to the silence and inaction of both civil society and the church with respect to the HIV/AIDS crisis, Goss argues that Jesus Christ is a model for "transgressive practice" with respect to advocating for sexual justice.

Specifically, Goss compared Jesus' actions in driving out the animal merchants and overturning the tables of the money changers in the temple[31] to the ACT UP/New York protest in St. Patrick's Cathedral during the height of the HIV/AIDS crisis, in which a protester crumbled up a consecrated host instead of eating it. For Goss, both actions "violated sacred space, transgressed sacred ritual, and offended sensibilities." Yet, according to Goss, both acts exhibited a "profound reverence for the sacred based on God's justice-doing."[32]

SIN AS CONFORMITY

If the Transgressive Christ is understood as the One who is tortured and executed for daring to break society's rules, then sin as what opposes the Transgressive Christ can be understood as mindless or blind conformity with the rules of the ruling majority. The sin of conformity is something that occurs within all groups, including the LGBT community. For example, it is easy for gay men to get caught up in the white, middle-class gay male "scene," in which superficial standards of beauty, body types, and material possessions are the primary measures of a person's worth.

There is also the destructive behavior of "mainstream" lesbians and gay men who look the other way or fail to speak up with respect to the sufferings of other people on the margins, LGBT or otherwise, whether it be issues of racism, social and economic injustice, or hostility towards marginalized elements (such as transgender and bisexual people) within the LGBT community itself. In fact, the sin of conformity can easily lead to mob violence against an innocent scapegoat or even the genocide of entire groups.

Many LGBT Asian Americans have experienced the sin of conformity with respect to the broader white LGBT community. Justin Chin, a gay Chinese American performance artist, has made fun of how many gay Asian "Castro boys" fall into four archetypes: the superficial party boy, the submissive boyfriend, the angry activist, and the moody artist.[33] LGBT Asian Americans have also experienced the sin of conformity by refusing to challenge the standards of beauty as portrayed in the white LGBT media. As long as LGBT Asian Americans measure and judge themselves by standards that are imposed by others, they will never be able to love themselves for who they are.

GRACE AS DEVIANCE

By contrast, grace in the context of the Transgressive Christ can be understood as deviance or the willingness to transgress social, legal, and religious boundaries and norms. As in the case of coming out, one's ability to challenge such boundaries and norms is not something that can be "willed" or "earned," but is rather a gift of grace from God. Although there is always the very real risk of crucifixion for challenging societal norms, there is also the promise of resurrection on the other side in terms of being true to one's own God-given sexual orientation and gender identity.

Many LGBT Asian Americans have written about the grace of deviance in their lives. Kaui, a transgender woman of Hawaiian, Chinese, Filipino, and Samoan descent, has described trans people as the gift of grace to the world: "We're actually angels. We were sent down to earth to soak up all of man's [sic] sins. I was sent up to earth to make people laugh and happy, to give them counseling that they need."[34] Van Darkholme, a gay Asian erotic artist and leatherman who produces and stars in kink and fetish videos, has written about how much he loves and enjoys what he is doing, despite the fact that it may seem deviant to others.[35] And Lani Ka'ahumanu, a mixed-race and bisexual poet from Hawaii, has written about the grace of her deviance: "I am a proud, visible and vocal, mixed-race multicultural woman. I claim it all and have no shame for it is the truth." According to Ka'ahumanu: "Assimilation is a lie. It is spiritual erasure."[36]

MODEL FOUR: THE HYBRID CHRIST

The fourth and final christological model of sin and grace for LGBT people is the Hybrid Christ. Hybridity is a concept from postcolonial theory that describes the mixture of two things that leads to the creation of a third "hybrid" thing.[37] For example, the experience of being a racial minority or an immigrant within the United States can be described in terms of hybridity. In the case of Asian Americans, they are neither purely "Asian" because they live in the United States, nor are they purely "American" because they are of Asian descent. Rather, they are a third "hybrid" or "in-between" thing, which ultimately challenges the binary and hierarchical nature of the original two categories of "Asian" (outsider) and "American" (insider).

For me, the Hybrid Christ arises out of the theological understanding that Jesus Christ is simultaneously divine and human in nature. He is neither purely one nor the other. In the words of the Athanasian Creed, Jesus Christ is simultaneously both "God and human," and yet he is "not two, but one Christ."[38] As such, he is the ultimate hybrid being. This hybrid nature is reflected in the double consciousness that is experienced by many racial minorities in the United States, such as Asian Americans, African Americans, Latino/as, Native Americans, and others.

Marcella Althaus-Reid, the late bisexual theologian from the University of Edinburgh, wrote about the Hybrid Christ in her book *Indecent Theology*. Specifically, Althaus-Reid wrote about the "Bi/Christ," in which the bisexual Jesus challenges the "heterosexual patterns of thought" of hierarchical and binary categories. Just as the bisexual person challenges the heterosexual binaries of "male/female" and "straight/gay," the "Bi/Christ" challenges the either/or way of thinking with respect to theology (for example, by deconstructing "poor" and "rich" as mutually exclusive categories in liberation theology) and therefore can be understood as the Hybrid Christ.[39]

Thus, a theology of the Hybrid Christ recognizes that Jesus Christ exists simultaneously in both the human and divine worlds. This can be seen most clearly in the postresurrection narratives. As a resurrected person with a human body, Jesus Christ is "in-both" worlds (that is, both human and divine), and yet he is also "in-between" both worlds (that is, neither purely human nor purely divine).[40] Although this can be a painful experience, metaphorically speaking, Jesus Christ has no place to lay down his head.[41] His hybridity is what ultimately allows him to build a bridge between the human and divine.

SIN AS SINGULARITY

If the Hybrid Christ is defined as the One who is simultaneously both human and divine, then sin—what opposes the Hybrid Christ—is singularity or the failure to recognize the reality of existing in multiple worlds. For example, sin is failing to recognize the complex reality of multiple identities within a single person, which in turn silences many experiences of those individuals who exist at the intersections of race, gender, sexual orientation, age, and other categories. As postcolonial theorists have pointed out, this kind of singularity (for example, defining the "gay" community solely in terms of sexual orientation and not taking race into account) results in the creation of a number of "others" who are never fully part of the larger community and thus feel like perpetual outsiders (for example, LGBT people of color).

Eric Wat, a Chinese American gay man, has written about experiencing the sin of singularity in the form of being rejected by both the straight Asian American community and the white LGBT community. Because of the one-dimensional nature of singularity, Wat's racial identity as an Asian American is erased within the predominantly white LGBT world, whereas his sexual identity as a gay man is erased within the predominantly straight Asian American world. For Wat, LGBT Asian Americans are "nobody's children," and they are "forever left in the middle of the road, unacceptable to those at either side of the street."[42]

GRACE AS HYBRIDITY

By contrast, grace in the context of the Hybrid Christ can be understood as hybridity or existing in the interstitial or "in-beyond" space between two or more intersecting worlds. In an essay entitled "Disrupted/Disruptive Moments," Black lesbian theologian Renée Hill has written about how her theological reflection has been shaped by her existence at the "intersections, in-between places, and borderlands" of her identities of race, gender, and sexual orientation. Hill's own experience of this hybridity as an "African American lesbian, Christian, theologian, and worker for justice" has convinced her of the need to create new "multireligious and multidialogical" processes for doing theologies and to embrace "questions, disruptions, and moments of ambiguity and uncertainty."[43]

Like Hill, LGBT Asian Americans have written about the grace of hybridity. For example, Wat writes that, instead of being caught in the middle of the race/sexuality divide, "gay Asian men must find that third side of the street where we can grow, find our voices, learn about ourselves, and educate others about who we are, so that eventually we can join them at both sides of the street."[44] Ann Yuri Uyeda, a queer Asian American activist, writes about her "overwhelming" experiences in being in a room of nearly 200 queer Asian American women for the first time: "[We were] Asian and Pacific Islander. And queer. All at once. And all together."[45] Indeed, the very fact that theological writings by LGBT Asian Americans such as Eric Law, Jeanette Lee, Leng Lim, and myself have been emerging in recent years,[46] as well as writings by allies such as Kwok Pui-Lan,[47] can be attributed to the grace of hybridity.

CONCLUSION

LGBT Christians must continue to wrestle deeply with the theological doctrines of sin and grace. Because LGBT people have been hurt by the traditional legal model of sin and grace, I believe that these doctrines should be rethought in christological terms such as the Erotic Christ, the Out Christ, the Transgressive Christ, and the Hybrid Christ. My hope is that a christological model of sin and grace will allow LGBT people of faith to enter into a more-meaningful theological dialogue among ourselves, as well as with the broader theological community as we enter into the third millennium of the Christian tradition.

NOTES

1. For writings about the LGBT Asian American experience, see Quang Bao and Hanya Yanagihara, eds., *Take Out: Queer Writing from Asian Pacific America* (New York: Asian American Writers' Workshop, 2000); Song Cho, ed., *Rice: Explorations into Gay Asian Culture and Politics* (Toronto: Queer Press, 1998); David L. Eng and Alice Y. Hom, eds., *Q&A: Queer in Asian America* (Philadelphia: Temple University Press, 1998); Kevin K. Kumashiro, ed., *Restoried Selves: Autobiographies of Queer Asian-Pacific-American Activists* (New York: Harrington Park Press, 2004); Russell Leong, ed., *Asian American Sexualities: Dimensions of the Gay and Lesbian Experience* (New York: Routledge, 1996); Sharon Lim-Hing, ed., *The Very Inside: An Anthology of Writing by Asian and Pacific Islander Lesbian and Bisexual Women* (Toronto: Sister Vision Press, 1994); and Gina Masequesmay and Sean Metzger, eds., *Embodying Asian/American Sexualities* (Lanham, MD: Lexington Books, 2009).

2. For theological reflections on the LGBT Asian American experience, see Patrick S. Cheng, "Multiplicity and Judges 19: Constructing a Queer Asian Pacific American Biblical Hermeneutic," *Semeia* 90/91 (2002): 119–33; Patrick S. Cheng, "Reclaiming Our Traditions, Rituals, and Spaces: Spirituality and the Queer Asian Pacific American Experience," *Spiritus* 6, no. 2 (2006): 234–40; Patrick S. Cheng, "Roundtable Discussion: Same-Sex Marriage," *Journal of Feminist Studies in Religion* 20, no. 2 (2004): 103–7; Michael Kim, "Out and About: Coming of Age in a Straight White World," in *Asian American X: An Intersection of 21st Century Asian American Voices*, ed. Arar Han and John Hsu (Ann Arbor: University of Michigan Press, 2004), 139–48; Eric H. F. Law, "A Spirituality of Creative Marginality," in *Que(e)rying Religion: A Critical Anthology*, ed. Gary David Comstock and Susan E. Henking (New York: Continuum, 1997), 343–46; Jeanette Mei Gim Lee, "Queerly a Good Friday," in Kumashiro, *Restoried Selves*, 81–86; Leng Leroy Lim, "'The Bible Tells Me to Hate Myself': The Crisis in Asian American Spiritual Leadership," *Semeia* 90/91 (2002): 315–22; Leng Leroy Lim, "Webs of Betrayal, Webs of Blessings," in Eng and Hom, *Q&A*, 323–34.

3. Mark Jordan has argued that the idea of "sodomy" was invented precisely because of ecclesial anxieties about delinking pure sexual pleasure from procreation. See Mark D. Jordan, *The Invention of Sodomy in Christian Theology* (Chicago: University of Chicago Press, 1997).

4. Karl Barth, *Church Dogmatics*, ed. G. W. Bromiley and T. F. Torrance, trans. G. W. Bromiley (Edinburgh: T&T Clark, 1956), IV/1:139–42.

5. Barth, *Church Dogmatics*, IV/1:142–43.

6. Gustavo Gutiérrez, *A Theology of Liberation: History, Politics, and Salvation*, trans.

and ed. Caridad Ina and John Eagleson, 15th anniversary ed. (Maryknoll, NY: Orbis Books, 1988), 103; James H. Cone, *A Black Theology of Liberation*, 20th anniversary ed. (Maryknoll, NY: Orbis Books, 1990), 106–9.

7. Barth, *Church Dogmatics*, IV/1:143.

8. Valerie Saiving Goldstein, "The Human Situation: A Feminine View," *Journal of Religion* 40, no. 2 (1960): 108; Judith Plaskow, *Sex, Sin, and Grace: Women's Experience and the Theologies of Reinhold Niebuhr and Paul Tillich* (Washington, DC: University Press of America, 1980), 3; Delores S. Williams, "A Womanist Perspective on Sin," in *A Troubling in My Soul: Womanist Perspectives on Evil and Suffering*, ed. Emilie M. Townes (Maryknoll, NY: Orbis Books, 1993), 147.

9. Barth, *Church Dogmatics*, IV/1:143–44.

10. Joseph Ratzinger and Jürgen Habermas, *The Dialectics of Secularization: On Reason and Religion*, ed. Florian Schuller, trans. Brian McNeil (San Francisco: Ignatius Press, 2006), 55–56.

11. Audre Lorde, "Uses of the Erotic: The Erotic as Power," in *Sexuality and the Sacred: Sources for Theological Reflection*, ed. Marvin M. Ellison and Kelly Brown Douglas (Louisville, KY: Westminster John Knox Press, 2010), 75, 77.

12. Matt. 9:29, Mark 7:31–37 (healing); Mark 5:35–43, Luke 7:11–17 (raising the dead); John 13:1–20 (footwashing); John 13:23 (Beloved Disciple).

13. Mark 5:28–34 (bleeding woman); Mark 14:3–6 (ointment); John 20:24–29 (Thomas).

14. Carter Heyward, *Saving Jesus from Those Who Are Right: Rethinking What It Means to Be Christian* (Minneapolis: Fortress Press, 1999), 74. See also Carter Heyward, *Touching Our Strength: The Erotic as Power and the Love of God* (New York: HarperSanFrancisco, 1989).

15. Molly Fumia, *Honor Thy Children: One Family's Journey to Wholeness* (Berkeley, CA: Conari Press, 1997), 231–35.

16. Lorde, "Uses of the Erotic," 75.

17. Heyward, *Saving Jesus*, 71.

18. For a discussion about the ethics of eroticism, see Marvin M. Ellison, *Erotic Justice: A Liberation Ethic of Sexuality* (Louisville, KY: Westminster John Knox Press, 1996).

19. Yoko Yoshikawa, "The Heat Is on Miss Saigon Coalition: Organizing across Race and Sexuality," in Eng and Hom, *Q&A*, 55.

20. John 1:1.

21. Chris Glaser, *Coming Out as Sacrament* (Louisville, KY: Westminster John Knox Press, 1998), 85.

22. Ibid., 82–84.

23. Eunai Shrake, "Homosexuality and Korean Immigrant Protestant Churches," in Masequesmay and Metzger, *Embodying Asian/American Sexualities*, 147.

24. Richard Kiamco, "Powershowgirl: Unaccessorized," in Bao and Yanagihara, *Take Out*, 113.

25. David C. Lee, "All-American Asian," in Kumashiro, *Restoried Selves*, 74–75.

26. Gershen Kaufman and Lev Raphael, *Coming Out of Shame: Transforming Gay and Lesbian Lives* (New York: Doubleday, 1996); John J. McNeill, *Taking a Chance on God: Liberating Theology for Gays, Lesbians, and Their Lovers, Families, and Friends* (Boston: Beacon Press, 1996), 54–74 ("Lifting the Burden of Guilt, Shame, and Self-Hate").

27. Wei Ming Dariotis, "On Becoming a Bi Bi Grrl," in Kumashiro, *Restoried Selves*, 46.

28. Matt. 8:1–4; Luke 17:11–19 (lepers); Matt. 9:18–26; Mark 5:21–43 (bleeding women); Mark 7:31–37 (differently abled); Matt. 9:9–13 (tax collectors and sinners).

29. Mark 3:1–6 (Sabbath); Mark 10:2–12 (marriage and divorce); Mark 3:31–35

(rejection of family); Matt. 13:53–58 (rejection by hometown); Luke 10:29–37 (the good Samaritan).

30. Robert E. Goss, *Jesus Acted Up: A Gay and Lesbian Manifesto* (New York: HarperCollins, 1993).

31. Matt. 21:12–13; Mark 11:15–17; Luke 19:45–46; John 2:14–22.

32. Goss, *Jesus Acted Up*, 149–50.

33. Justin Chin, *Attack of the Man-Eating Lotus Blossoms* (San Francisco: Suspect Thoughts Press, 2005), 62–65.

34. "Kaui," in Andrew Matzner, *'O Au No Keia: Voices from Hawaii's Mahu and Transgender Communities* (Bloomington, IN: Xlibris Corporation, 2001), 112–13.

35. Van Darkholme, blog entry posted February 5, 2007, http://www.vandarkholme .com/journal/ 07journalfeb.html (accessed June 27, 2010).

36. See Lani Ka'ahumanu, "Hapa Haole Wahine," in Lim-Hing, *The Very Inside*, 451–52.

37. In postcolonial theory, hybridity refers to the "creation of new transcultural forms within the contact zone produced by colonization." In other words, the interaction between the colonizer and the colonized gives rise to a "third space" that destabilizes such categories and "makes the claim to a hierarchical 'purity' of cultures untenable." See Bill Ashcroft, Gareth Griffiths, and Helen Tiffin, *Post-Colonial Studies: The Key Concepts* (London: Routledge, 2000), 118.

38. *Symbolum Quicunque* ¶34, in Philip Schaff, *Creeds of Christendom*, 6th ed. (Grand Rapids: Baker Books, 2007), 2:69 ("*Qui licet Deus sit et homo; non duo tamen, sed unus est Christus.*").

39. Marcella Althaus-Reid, *Indecent Theology: Theological Perversions in Sex, Gender and Politics* (London: Routledge, 2000), 114–16.

40. For an Asian American theological reflection on the hybrid nature of Jesus Christ, see Jung Young Lee, *Marginality: The Key to Multicultural Theology* (Minneapolis, MN: Fortress Press, 1995), 85.

41. Matt. 8:20.

42. See Eric Wat, "Preserving the Paradox: Stories From a Gay-Loh," in Leong, *Asian American Sexualities*, 78.

43. See Renée Leslie Hill, "Disrupted/Disruptive Movements: Black Theology and Black Power 1969/1999," in *Black Faith and Public Talk: Critical Essays on James H. Cone's Black Theology and Black Power*, ed. Dwight N. Hopkins (Maryknoll, NY: Orbis Books, 1999), 138, 147–48. For more about sexuality and the black church, see Kelly Brown Douglas, *Sexuality and the Black Church: A Womanist Perspective* (Maryknoll, NY: Orbis Books, 1999).

44. Wat, "Preserving the Paradox," 80.

45. Ann Yuri Uyeda, "All at Once, All Together: One Asian American Lesbian's Account of the 1989 Asian Pacific Lesbian Network Retreat," in Lim-Hing, *The Very Inside*, 121.

46. See sources cited in note 2.

47. Kwok Pui-lan, "Asian and Asian American Churches," in *Homosexuality and Religion: An Encyclopedia*, ed. Jeffrey S. Siker (Westport, CT: Greenwood Press, 2007), 59–62; Kwok Pui-lan, *Postcolonial Imagination and Feminist Theology* (Louisville, KY: Westminster John Knox Press, 2005), 100–121.

9

Touching the Taboo:
On the Sexuality of Jesus

KWOK PUI-LAN

Ta-boo *also* ta-bu [Tongan *tabu*] (1777) 1: forbidden to profane use or contact because of supposedly dangerous supernatural powers; 2 a. banned on grounds of morality or taste b. banned on constituting a risk.

Webster's Ninth New Collegiate Dictionary

For us the meaning of taboo branches into two opposite directions. On the one hand it means to us sacred, consecrated; but on the other hand it means uncanny, dangerous, forbidden, and unclean.

Sigmund Freud[1]

Christianity's greatest taboo [is] Christ's sexuality.

Leo Steinberg[2]

Was Jesus a celibate, an asexual person? Was he gay or heterosexual? Did he have sexual needs or desires? What kind of sexual relations might he have had with Mary Magdalene and the prostitutes who trusted him as their friend? And who was his beloved disciple in John's Gospel? After more than two centuries of historical and interdisciplinary quests about what Jesus actually said and did, why do we know so little about the people with whom Jesus may have gone to bed? Did he sleep at all? Where did he sleep? Was he always by himself, alone? Why is the sexuality of Jesus shrouded in a thick cloud of mystery, forbidden even in the realm of imagination? If the scholars are interested in what Jesus ate, shouldn't they be more curious about the sexual life of Jesus?

The sexuality of Jesus is a highly tabooed subject in the Christian church and in the academy. How did this become a highly charged topic, such that merely touching on it becomes profane, dangerous, and risky? Do we assume that decent, respectable, and objective scholars should never broach the subject? And should God-fearing and churchgoing folks not be interested at all?

RELIGIOUS TABOO AND
THE SURPLUS OF MEANING

The word "taboo" entered the English language from Captain James Cooke's account of his third and last voyage to the islands of the Pacific. In 1777, he reached Tonga, or the Friendly Islands, and learned the Tongan word "tabu," which meant something forbidden.[3] Other travelers soon found out that similar ideas could be found in the Polynesian religious systems, signifying sacred objects, places, rituals, persons, or something expressing a "connection with the gods." For example, William Ellis of the London Missionary Society wrote in his *Polynesian Researches* published in 1829:

> The idols, temples, persons, and names of the king, and members of the reigning family; the persons of the priests, canoes belonging to the gods; houses, clothes, and mats of the king and priests; and the heads of men who were the devotees of any particular idol were always *tabu*, or sacred. The flesh of hogs, fowls, turtle, and several others kinds of fish, coconuts, and almost everything offered in sacrifice, were *tabu* to the use of the gods and the men.[4]

In 1888, James George Frazer wrote a short article on the system of taboo in the *Encyclopedia Britannica*, and he and other scholars used the term frequently in the study of "primitive" religion and magic. The word "taboo" exerted a fascinating grip on the religious imagination of the West, for it provided a vocabulary or a force field to talk about the risk, boundary, terror, and dread of the "sacred" as well as longing, desire, fascination, and possible transgression. In fact, the discussion of "taboo" with its various shades of meanings has initiated some of the most innovative and groundbreaking contributions in the study of religion. Émile Durkheim, in the early twentieth century, turned to the Australian Aborigines to show that the sacred/profane duality corresponds to the universal distinction formulated by every culture between taboo and transgression, the individual and the collective, and euphoria and dysphoria. His study of the so-called "elementary" forms of religious life (1912) aims to present a sociological theory of religion.[5] Rejecting the older definitions of religion as beliefs in the supernatural or divine, Durkheim stresses that religion is an observable phenomenon and a social fact, arising out of the nature of social life itself. In his analysis of totemism as the most primitive religious form, he argues that the totemic animal or plant, which is considered sacred or taboo, is in fact the clan itself divinized. Religion, as the repository of the group's collective sentiments and values, functions to maintain its solidarity and continuity.

In a sharp contrast to Durkheim, Sigmund Freud traced the origin of religion to a taboo located not in society, but in the psyche—the unconsciousness derived from the desire to murder the father and possess the mother. In *Totem and Taboo* (1913), Freud amasses a wide range of religious data from the

Aborigines, the Melanesians, the Battas of Sumatra, and various tribes in Africa to show that the psychic life of these "savages" has close parallels to the infantile period of child development. He proposes the provocative thesis that the totemic system and its exogamous stipulations are related to the incest dread of the primitive people. The incest dread is "a subtle infantile trait and is in striking agreement with the psychic life of the neurotic."[6] While the mature person has freed himself from these incestuous desires, the neurotic has not been able to break free from the psychic infantilism. Later, in *The Future of an Illusion* (1927), Freud develops the idea that religion is based on the helplessness of children and the need for protection to allay fears and dangers of life. Religion is portrayed as a collective neurosis in which the father is projected and sublimated in the father-image of God.[7]

Several decades later, British anthropologist Mary Douglas presented yet another theory on taboo through the perspectives of purity and pollution. Defilement and pollution, she argued, is based on society's classification of order and disorder, as well as external and internal boundaries. The rituals of purity and impurity both create and display the symbolic patterns of meaning of society and foster unity in experience of the group. Since the publication of her influential text *Purity and Danger: An Analysis of Concepts of Pollution and Taboo* (1966), biblical scholars and students of early Christianity have used its insights to study identity formation as well as the religious practices and prohibitions of the early Christian communities.[8]

As we have seen, the deployment of the term "taboo" allows these authors to present different theories or schema to understand religion and its relation to social life, the human psyche, the creation of meaning, and the erection of boundaries. I apply some of their insights to analyze possible frames of meaning for the greatest taboo in Christianity: the sexuality of Jesus. I am interested not so much in what the silence suppresses, but in what such silence enables—the surplus of meaning that is created and constructed. By treating this topic as a taboo, the Christian church has exerted enormous power over believers' sexual life in intimating what they are supposed to do or not do to their bodies.

Many theologians who have written on the taboo surrounding the sexuality of Jesus point to the historic church's ambivalent attitude regarding human sexuality and a church hierarchy that is deeply homophobic. Robert Goss, for example, has written:

> Early Christianity understood Jesus as remaining unmarried, and he became a model of celibacy for elite Christians and more recently a model of compulsory heterosexuality for contemporary fundamentalist Christians. Jesus has remained a symbol of asexuality for Christian sexual puritans. For nearly two millennia, elite Christians kept Jesus and sexuality totally apart from each other in order to maintain their purity agenda. Sexual puritans have surrounded human sexuality with prohibitions, regulations, and restrictions. The denial of human sexuality within spirituality is damaging to the human spirit because it alienates Christians from their own sexual selves and from their own bodies.[9]

That Jesus must be seen as asexual, unmarried, and celibate is a direct result of an erotophobic church maintained for a long time by a celibate, male, and dominating clerical hierarchy. They have projected onto Jesus their values and ideals as a means to control behavior and maintain their sacred status. Almost like the Aborigines' totem system, the asexual Jesus functions to perpetuate the social values of these elite males.

While we may not agree with Freud's bold psychoanalytical interpretation of totemism, his highly imaginative proposal points to the significance of imagination and fantasy in constructing what the society or group holds as taboo. Freud regards the danger and prohibition surrounding the sacred totem as primitive people's way to express what is unspeakable and unimaginable: incestuous desire and dread. In the case of Jesus, suggestions that Jesus might have any kind of sexual relation have been met with disbelief, disgust, and even strong protest. In Nikos Kazantzakis's book and the subsequent movie, the last temptation of Jesus is portrayed as the carnal desire of a thirty-something man and his wish to have children and a family. The spiritual vocation of Jesus and his desire for love and domestic life are seen as constantly in conflict with one another. The movie met with scorn and protest because the erotic desire of Jesus was considered off-limits, belonging to the realm of the unimaginable. Even the milder proposal by William Phipps that Jesus as a rabbi was most likely married according to the social customs of his time irritated a broad spectrum of people, and the author received personally threatening letters. Phipps learned the hard lesson that "religion becomes explosive when mixed with sex, for the responses were related less to the historical than to the hysterical."[10] It can be expected that the iconoclastic suggestion that Jesus might have been gay in plays like *Corpus Christi* would be condemned as blasphemous, outrageous, and transgressive. Why is it that Jesus cannot be imagined either as heterosexual or gay, or as someone who is sexual? What does this have to say about a Christian tradition, as Richard Rambuss describes poignantly, that finds "Jesus' exposed and macerated body to be paradoxically both a sight of horror, shame, and defilement *and* a vision of astonishing, even erotic beauty?"[11]

Mary Douglas's treatment of pollution and taboo invites us to look at the sexuality of Jesus through the cultural-anthropological lenses of meaning making, classification systems, and the delineation of external and internal boundaries. Applying queer theory, which questions precisely the rigid and binary constructions of gender and sexuality, gay and lesbian theologians have offered new images and symbols of Jesus. In *Jesus Acted Up*, Robert Goss argues that Jesus is the queer Christ, who is God's embodied solidarity, with justice and love for oppressed gay and lesbian outsiders.[12] British theologian Elizabeth Stuart presents the model of friendship as a way to reimagine Jesus' life and ministry: "One could say that the essence of Jesus' ministry was simply befriending—the formation of mutual, equal, loving, accepting and transforming relationships."[13]

Prompted by queer studies and the turn to the body in postmodern discourse, the sexual body of Jesus is not off-limits anymore. Jesus on the cross, at once tortured and bruised, yet an icon for devotion and fascination, has attracted the attention of scholars from diverse disciplines. In a hilarious article, Stephen Moore traces the discussion of the physique of Jesus in the early church fathers: Jesus was not tall and not handsome, according to the image provided by Isaiah. Moore satirically compares this image of Jesus to the rather attractive and appealing faces of Jesus on some contemporary book covers.[14] In his highly inventive and disturbing book *God's Gym*, Moore furnishes data about the tortured body and the resurrected body of Jesus and the bodies of Yahweh, with graphic illustrations of physical pain and visions of bodybuilding and the perfectibility of male bodies.[15]

Recent scholarship has also focused on the sexual body of Jesus as featured in the devotional literature of medieval monastics and English poets. For example, Mark S. Burrows studies the erotic and sensual sermons on the Song of Songs by Bernard of Clairvaux as resources for constructing an erotic Christology. Preaching to his fellow monks, Bernard deployed a deeply passionate and sexually explicit language to describe kissing and touching the feet and body of Jesus as a "tender lover."[16] Among the Protestants, as Richard Rambuss has shown, seventeenth-century English poets and writers such as John Donne, George Herbert, Richard Crashaw, and Thomas Traherne displayed a kind of "closet devotions," by which he means courting a desirable and beautiful Savior and expressing oneself in a homodevotional manner (male God and male devotee).[17]

While I find the above discussion of the sexuality of Jesus and homoerotic devotion to Jesus fascinating and helpful to the development of a healthy and inclusive Christian sexual theology, my plotting of the "surplus of meaning" of the untouchable taboo of Jesus' sexuality follows a different path. My focus will be on the following questions:

(1) If the historical quest for Jesus aims at recovering the "historical" man, not a mythical savior, how does that historical consciousness alter or change our way of looking at the sexuality of Jesus?

(2) What does the silence on the sexuality of Jesus tell us about the intersection between Jesus' gender, sexuality, and race? I have found relatively little discussion of Jesus' race either in the feminist debate on the masculinity of the Savior or in the gay and lesbian recovery of homoerotic religious relationships.

(3) What does the sexuality of Jesus as depicted by the nineteenth-century historical quest tell us about the construction of sexuality of Europe at the time?

My intention is to interrupt a discourse on the sexuality of Jesus defined largely by the imagination of white scholars, which tends to isolate sexuality from social, racial, and cultural dimensions. I begin with an analysis of Jesus within the larger sociocultural matrix of the body politics of European bourgeois society.

JESUS AND BOURGEOIS BODY POLITICS

Serious talk about sexuality is inevitably about society.

Thomas Laqueur[18]

To contemplate Jesus' sexuality, we have to "think through the body," to borrow a phrase by feminist critic Jane Gallop.[19] In the case of Jesus, we have to think through the social, cultural, and religious configurations that mark a masculine-sexed Jewish body in the modern period. The discussion of the body of Jesus invariably brings us to the fertile and richly textured nexus of the emerging discourse of sexual difference from the late eighteenth century, the use of racial stereotypes in social and political theories, and the colonial discourse of European or Aryan superiority. As Mary Douglas has rightly observed, "The human body is always treated as an image of society and that there can be no natural way of considering the body that does not involve at the same time a social dimension."[20] I would argue that the silence around Jesus' body and sexuality points to the anxiety about the external and internal boundaries of the bourgeois body over race, gender, and sexuality. The body of Jesus—as the incarnate flesh of God—brings into sharp relief the demarcations between the sacred and the profane, power and danger, margins and boundaries reproduced by a bourgeois society that was undergoing rapid changes, when at the same time some of the foundations of its religious belief were severely challenged.

Since theologians in the nineteenth century were preoccupied with the quest for the historical Jesus, we might assume that they would provide a lot of data about Jesus as a Jewish person. The historical quest was supposed to separate the myths and legends about Jesus from his real life through a critical scrutiny of the Gospels. The fact that Jesus was a Jew would require these scholars to pay attention to the Jewish environment in the nascent period of Christianity and to the Jewish scholarship of that particular period. But the opposite seemed to be the case, as there was a steady avoidance of Jesus' Jewish background among biblical scholars and theologians from the mid-nineteenth century onward. Susannah Heschel has called this disturbing and ironic phenomenon "the Protestant flight from the historical Jesus."[21] Instead of a fully embodied Jewish Jesus, the liberal theologians presented a universal Christ centered on his unique religious consciousness. What Jane Gallop observes as the wrong turn of the male European philosophical tradition is equally applicable to the theological tradition: "Rather than treat the body as a site of knowledge, a medium for thought, the more classic philosophical project has tried to render it transparent and get beyond it, to dominate it by reducing it to the mind's idealizing categories."[22]

In the early part of the nineteenth century, F. C. Bauer and the Tübingen School had attended to Jesus' Jewish background in order to delineate the relationship between Judaism and Christianity and the dynamic struggle between Jewish and gentile Christianity. Although Judaism was invariably cast in a negative, nationalistic, and conservative light, these scholars at least took into serious consideration that Christianity developed out of Judaism. Since the 1860s, however, Heschel argues that various reconstructions of Jesus' life had moved the spotlight away from his Jewish milieu more toward his consciousness of a unique relationship with God as the basis of a generalized, liberal moral teaching. She cites as evidence the third edition of *Life of Jesus* by D. F. Strauss (1864), *Life of Jesus* by Ernest Renan (1863), and the far-reaching influence of Albrecht Ritschl's liberal theology.

Heschel offers several reasons for this flight from the Jewish Jesus. First, these theologians harbored old and stereotypically negative perceptions of Judaism, and they wanted to proclaim that Christianity was a new religion created and inaugurated by Jesus. At the same time, their historical studies were largely based on the works of Christian scholars, for they were also quite ignorant of Jewish scholarship on the Second Temple period and the work of Abraham Geiger on the internal struggles among the Jewish community in Jesus' time. Second, these theologians followed the lead of liberal theologian Friedrich Schleiermacher, who championed the position that Jesus was the founder of a new religion and developed a unique and extraordinary religious consciousness. His Jewish cultural and religious environment had to be deemphasized in order to foreground the ingenuity and creativity of the genius or hero Jesus. For Strauss, Jesus was a unique, highly distinguished person, who felt himself one with his heavenly Father and by means of his exalted character exerted a decisive influence on humanity.

The third and the most significant reason for our discussion is that these scholars, notably Ernest Renan, introduced racial categories to the study of Jesus to demonstrate the superiority of the Indo-Europeans over the Semites. Renan suggested that Jesus' conception of divinity and his relation to God as father and son was "his grand act of originality; there was nothing here in common with his race."[23] Renan also insisted that when Jesus adopted the Jewish maxims of the synagogue in his teachings, Jesus imbued them with a superior spirit and clearly saw the insufficiency of the Mosaic law.[24] In the debate of racial politics of the second half of the nineteenth century, Renan tried hard to show that Christianity had gotten rid of the vestiges of Judaism and was the Aryan religion par excellence. Such a de-Judaization process in the study of the inception of Christianity, Heschel notes, leads to the dehistoricization of Jesus, the tendency toward anti-Semitism, and the subsequent argument that Jesus was in fact an Aryan who fought against Judaism.[25] The beliefs in the superiority of the Aryan race and Christianity as the highest form of religion helped to justify Europe's domination and colonization of the majority of the world's peoples.

While the Jewish identity of Jesus had to be suppressed in order to fit into the racial politics of the bourgeois order, what about his masculine sex? We will see that the race and gender of Jesus intersected in the European imagination or fantasy of a Jewish male body. In *The Making of the Modern Body*, the contributors have shown that at the end of the eighteenth century, there emerged in Europe a new interpretation of the body and the relation between the two sexes along with intense debates about the sexual differences between the male and the female. Cultural historian Thomas Laqueur argues that since the Greek period, the female had been treated as a replica of the male in the one-sexed hierarchical model of human anatomy and physiology. Women were seen as having the same sexual organs as men, except these organs were inside rather than outside because women were believed to have less heat in their bodies than men. But this traditional view could no longer be sustained during the time of the Enlightenment, when philosophers argued for human equality and dignity for everyone, and not just for one sex. The liberal thinkers thus had to come up with new interpretations of the body. Laqueur writes:

> Liberalism postulates a body that, if not sexless, is nevertheless undifferentiated in its desires, interests, or capacity to reason. In striking contrast to the old teleology of the body as male, liberal theory begins with a neuter body, sexed but without gender, and of no consequence to cultural discourse. The body is regarded simply as the bearer of the rational subject, which itself constitutes the person.[26]

Although nineteenth-century theologians clearly presumed Jesus to be male, and although the image of a genius-hero derived from aesthetics and art better suited ideals of the masculine at the time, there had not been much interest in the sexed body of Jesus. While quest after quest has undertaken the *religious* or messianic consciousness of Jesus, there has been no concomitant quest for the *sexual* consciousness of Jesus. The internal relation of Jesus to his Father was seen as having little to do with his bodily needs or functions.

But the liberal presupposition of a sexless body tells only half the story, for such a theory does not explain the real world of male domination over women, of sexual division of labor, and of different sexual desire and passion. In physiology, anatomy, and philosophical discourses, the hierarchical model, which construed the female body as lesser, gradually gave way to a biology of the incommensurability of the two sexes, with intensified discussions of sexual difference, prompted in part by the first wave of the feminist movement in Europe.[27] The tortuous debate on sexual difference reflected the changing body politics of society, with the demand for the redrawing of the boundaries between the public and private roles of women, access to education and job opportunities, and the redistribution of power and privileges.

The rhetoric of sexual difference was much related to the rhetoric of race, as both were presumably based on biological or anatomical distinctions. Just as women are differentiated from men by their reproductive organs and biological functions, Jews are distinguished by a practice inscribed on the body—infant male circumcision. Sander L. Gilman argues that in the anti-Semitic climate in Europe at the turn of the twentieth century, circumcision was unconsciously equated with castration, and Jewish manhood was thought to be less than masculine: "The mutilation of the penis was a feminizing act."[28] Anti-Semitism projected onto the Jewish body the powerlessness of the Jews as analogous to the powerlessness of the female—at a time when both Jews and women were gaining more power in the society of Western Europe. For Freud, the diseased body of the Jews—the sexuality of the Jew associated with circumcision or castration—created a kind of anxiety, if not neurosis, in the Aryan, who feared that he would become a Jew himself.[29] Thus an interesting triad was created: the fearful and anxious Aryan male, the castrated female, and the circumcised Jewish male. If women without a penis are considered somewhat inferior to men, the Jews with their penis circumcised are also seen as less than masculine. Daniel Boyarin notes that there is still a widespread assumption that being Jewish in Western culture renders a boy effeminate, who may be labeled a sissy or a Jewish male femme. The feminization of the Jewish male and the belief in Jewish male passivity have also been associated with queerness in a homophobic European environment.[30]

Thus, I would suggest that the flight from the historical Jesus might have been caused not only by his Jewishness, as Heschel has convincingly demonstrated, but also by anxiety with his masculine body. The Jewish sexed body of Jesus serves as an uneasy marker both of racial and ethnic difference and of the tension in the construction of masculinity and femininity. It would seem much safer and prudent to theologize about Jesus' inner religious consciousness as generic human than to touch the volatile, unstable, and dangerous sexed body of a Jew. To borrow Freud's terminology, the anxiety of white men over their own sexuality and masculinity in maintaining purity and control of the bourgeois body had to be suppressed and sublimated in the universalistic representation of Christ. It was this universal Christ, abstract and separated from his particular Jewish context, who was proclaimed by missionaries and colonial officials as the savior of all peoples, at the name of whom every knee should bow. In the next section, I discuss how an asexual description of Jesus and his teaching justified the moral superiority of the European bourgeoisie and colonization.

ASEXUAL JESUS AND COLONIZATION

> For a long time, the story goes, we supported a Victorian regime, and we continue to be dominated by it. Thus the image of imperial prude is emblazoned on our restrained, mute, and hypocritical sexuality. . . . Sexuality was carefully confined; it moved into the home. . . . On the subject of sex, silence became the rule.
>
> Michel Foucault[31]

Foucault begins his influential text *The History of Sexuality* with a discussion of the imperial prude. This is the only reference to the fact of the empire in his entire book. He then goes on to argue that such an image of the prude is a misguided reading of nineteenth-century sexuality because beneath the veneer of a repressive and policed Victorian bourgeois sexuality, there was incitement to produce discourses about sex: in the confessions to the clergy in the church, the hysterization of women's bodies, the pedagogic advice on children's sexuality, the socialization of procreative life, and the psychiatrization of perverse pleasure. But as Ann Laura Stoler has pointed out, Foucault's fascinating "history" is biased and one-sided because he confines himself to the discourses taking place in the metropolitan West and leaves out completely the implications of empire-building in shaping "modern western sexuality."[32] Her critical engagement with Foucault's text leads to two important contentions. First, Europe's modern discourses on sexuality, just as cultural, political, and economic assertions, cannot be charted in or limited to Europe alone. Much of Europe's history has taken place outside Europe, which is critical to understanding Europe's self-definition. Second, the discourse on sexuality was much imbued with racial obsession, the technologies of power policing the bourgeois self, and the boundaries of the "civilized" European nations. She writes:

> Bourgeois identities in both metropole and colony emerge tacitly and emphatically coded by race. Discourses of sexuality do more than define the distinctions of the bourgeois self; in identifying marginal members of the body politic, they have mapped the moral parameters of the European nations.[33]

Applying Stoler's insights to our discussion, I argue that Foucault has overlooked one critical site of bourgeois discourse on sexuality: the sexuality of the natives or the colonized. In order to bolster the moral superiority and sexual purity of the European bourgeoisie, peoples of foreign lands were often portrayed as promiscuous, lustful, and polygamous in medical, missionary, and anthropological literature. Anthropologists have furnished much data about the strange courtship and marriage customs among the so-called primitive peoples. British sexologist and eugenicist Havelock Ellis and others found that there was a widespread natural instinct toward homosexual relationship among the "lower races."[34] At the same time, missionaries were busily debating whether polygamy should be allowed in Christian churches. How did the nineteenth-century discourse on sexuality, imbued with racial obsessions and polemics, influence scholars' construction of the sexuality of Jesus, who was seen as the moral teacher and the embodiment of human ideals in liberal thought?

Renan begins his *Life of Jesus* by placing Jesus in the history of the world in a kind of evolutionary framework. He says that humans distinguish themselves from the animals by being religious. He traces the beliefs in sorcerers in Oceania to the degeneration of the "hideous scenes of butchery" in the ancient religion of Mexico. The African peoples did not go beyond fetishism and the belief of material objects and their supernatural powers. Although the civilizations of China, Babylonia, and Egypt represented some progress, their contributions to human civilization were not important. For him, the religions of Babylonia and Syria never "disengaged themselves from a substratum of strange sensuality," and these religions continued to be "schools of immorality" and "only threw into the world millions of amulets and charms."[35] Although Renan does not explicitly discuss the sexuality of the natives, the sexual overtones in his condemnation of the world's other religions cannot be mistaken. Renan then goes on to contrast these religions with the soul, faith, liberty, sincerity, and devotion of Christianity, which emerged out of the two races—the Aryans and the Semites—with the Aryans finally superseding the Semites.

With such a highly charged racial and sexual rhetoric, Renan's "Jesus" fits the projected image of a self-controlled, restrained, and morally superior bourgeois gentleman. In Renan's description, "an infinite charm was exhaled from his person," and he showed an amiable character. There was a common spirit felt among his followers, and the brotherhood of men, as sons of God, was seen as having moral consequences. Jesus demanded perfection, beyond the duties of the Mosaic law, and espoused the Christian virtues of "humility, pardon, charity, abnegation, and self-denial."[36] He preached about loving and forgiving one's enemies, being merciful, giving alms, doing good works, and showing kindness and charity to others. With such refined and sweet qualities, Jesus was celebrated and loved by many around him. But Renan says that Jesus never allowed human affection to interfere with his ministry and calling.

In one particularly telling passage that touches on Jesus' sexuality, Renan writes:

> Jesus never married. All his power of loving expended itself on what he considered his heavenly vocation. The extremely delicate sentiment which one observes in his manner towards women did not interfere with the exclusive devotion he cherished for his idea. Like Francis d'Assisi and Francis de Sales, he treated as sisters the women who threw themselves into the same work as he did; he had his Saint Clare, and his Françoise de Chantal. However, it is probable that they loved himself better than his work; he was certainly more beloved than loving. As happens frequently in the case of very lofty natures, his tenderness of heart transformed itself into an infinite sweetness, a vague poetry, a universal charm.[37]

Renan's Jesus sublimated his sexual desire to pursue his real vocation. Even his relations with the women of doubtful character, though free and intimate, were of an entirely moral nature and a means to carry out the will of the Father. Jesus evolved a religious ethic based not on outward behavior, but on the purification of the individual human heart. He was contented with praying, meditating, and maintaining a close relation with God. The Jesus that is inscribed on the pages of *Life of Jesus* is not value-neutral or scientifically reconstructed from the Gospels, but is heavily imbued with the bourgeois values and morality of Renan's high French culture.

While Renan's best-selling *Life of Jesus* attracted a large audience, Ritschl's liberal understanding of Christology cast a long shadow on German theology. Karl Barth charged liberal Protestant thought in general and Ritschl in particular as "the very epitome of the national-liberal German bourgeois of the age of Bismarck."[38] Ritschl believed that Jesus was the founder of the perfect religion, in contrast to all other religions. He regarded Judaism as politically nationalistic and Buddhism as a kind of cosmology which does not balance the ethical and religious aspects of faith. These non-Christian religions are secondary and incomplete, for the life of Jesus provides the source for the knowledge of God:

Christianity, then, is the monotheistic, completely spiritual and ethical religion, which, based on the life of its Author as Redeemer and as Founder of the Kingdom of God, consists in the freedom of the children of God, involves the impulse to conduct from the motive of love, aims at the moral organization of mankind, and grounds blessedness on the relationship of sonship to God, as well as on the Kingdom of God.[39]

Ritschl sought to combine the historical critical study of the New Testament with his dogmatic theological interests to present the Christian faith intelligibly within the context of nineteenth-century German thought. His Jesus is a moral exemplar, who embodies the highest ideals of human life. Christians should strive for Christian perfection, which corresponds to the example set by Jesus himself. In his instruction on Christian life, Ritschl commends the virtues of obedience to God, humility, patience, fidelity to one's vocation, self-control and conscientiousness, and love of one's neighbor.[40] Such a morally superior, diligent, and self-denying Jesus met the ideals of the German bourgeoisie, who were playing an important role in the expanding power of Prussia, a political move that Ritschl supported.

Ritschl devoted much of his last decade to studying the history of pietism and included an interesting comparison of Catholic piety with Protestant piety under the influences of Lutheranism and Calvinism. He had a lengthy and detailed exposition of Bernard's sermons on the Song of Songs, which he said epitomized the Catholic approach. He noted Bernard's use of erotic language, such as kissing the Lord's feet, hands, and mouth, to describe the union between Christ and the individual soul. Bernard described the love for God as sensuous, passionate, and powerful. Just as Luther disapproved of Bernard's interpretation of the Song of Songs, Ritschl wrote that this perspective on the love of Christ was from the very beginning alien to Protestant piety. He said that this kind of mystical union might be expected of monks who did not have to face the temptations of the secular world, but Protestant Christians had to conduct their everyday life through their trust in God and in the redemption of their sin and guilt. Thus, for Ritschl, Catholic piety allowed for more "sentimental pathos" and "sentimental desire" for the unity of the spirit with Christ, while Protestant piety, influenced by Lutheran and Calvinism, tended to be more austere and ascetic because of a different understanding of grace. He wrote: "The certainty of reconciliation as it is expressed in trust in God is the necessary presupposition of sanctification for the protestant Christian, whereas for the Catholics the enjoyment of redemption in tender intercourse with the redeemer is a possible appendage to their sanctification."[41]

In Britain, the theological climate was quite different from that on the European continent; British theologians had not produced texts as influential about the life of Jesus as had Renan, Strauss, and Schweitzer. But this does not mean that they were not concerned about the historical-critical study of the Bible. In fact, one of the dominant concerns in Anglican theology at the turn of the twentieth century was the Incarnation, as theologians tried to harmonize the

Christ of dogma with the picture of Jesus presented by the historical study of Scriptures. John Robert Seeley was credited with producing the first English book on the life of Jesus, *Ecce Homo: A Survey of the Life and Work of Jesus Christ*, published in 1865. Seeley had the model of the British Empire in mind when he talked about the kingdom of God and the ministry of Jesus. Emphasizing the royalty of Jesus, he argued that Jesus was the founder and legislator of a new theocracy, a new Christian Commonwealth. Through obedience to his laws and teachings, his followers can become subjects or citizens of the Christian republic.[42] Although this Christian Commonwealth is universal and open to all, Seeley believed that human beings are not all equal and gifted. He upheld the authority of the father over the child, the husband over the wife, and the master over the slave. He also justified British colonial rule in India by arguing that the Indians were not capable of ruling themselves and would revert to instability and anarchy if the British left.[43]

Writing less than a decade after the British suppression of the formidable Indian national struggle in 1857, Seeley portrayed Jesus as an enlightened king; Jesus had royal pretensions and power, yet used them with patience and restraint. Seeley wrote: "For the noblest and most amiable thing that can be seen is power mixed with gentleness, the reposing, self-restraining attitude of strength."[44] Jesus was also full of sympathy and appreciation, and his combination of greatness and self-sacrifice had great appeal to his followers. Jesus did not win them over by power and might, but through moral example, benevolence, and the relief of their suffering. Just as the British did not conquer India, as Seeley would argue, but ruled over the Indians because of the Brits' alleged innate superiority, he argued that "in Christ's monarchy no force was used, though all power was at command; the obedience of his servants became in the end, though not till after his departure, absolutely unqualified."[45]

Seeley discussed the pursuit of pleasure and bodily gratification in Jesus' legislation for the new kingdom. He said the sensualist would make bodily comfort and pleasure his goal for life while forgetting that he also possesses the soul. The Stoics and the ascetics, on the other hand, seek discipline and coercion of the body. Seeley argued that Jesus did not deprecate the life of the body since he had healed the sick, attended weddings and banquets, and sometimes been accused, along with his disciples, of indulgent behaviors. Yet Jesus directed followers' attention to seek the kingdom of God first and not in worldly pursuits. Temperance and moderation are necessary to safeguard against what Seeley called sensualism and excessive pursuit of pleasure.[46]

At the end of the nineteenth century, Anglican theologians were preoccupied with the issue of Incarnation, prompted partly because of the theories of evolution and partly because of the critical study of the Bible. Commenting on that particular era of Anglican theology, Arthur Michael Ramsey remarks: "The Incarnation was the centre of a theological scheme concerning nature and man, in which Christ is both the climax of nature and history and the supernatural restorer of mankind."[47] Charles Gore's Bampton Lectures, published as *The*

Incarnation of the Son of God in 1891, laid down some of the basic questions that were explored over the next several decades. Gore was concerned with the question, How could the fully human Jesus be the incarnated Son of God? Gore went to great lengths to defend the full humanity of Jesus and dismissed any form of docetism: "He passed through all stages of a human development, willing with a human will, perceiving with human perceptions, feeling with human feelings."[48] Defending passionately the doctrine of Christ's two natures, Gore maintained that God the divine Creator humbled himself to take the form of the creaturely life of humanity.

Gore and his contemporary theologians were more interested, however, in the preconsciousness of Jesus in their kenotic theory of incarnation than in the embodiment of a fully enfleshed Jesus. The debate focused on the idealistic discussion of whether Jesus had to give up his divine knowledge and consciousness when he assumed the personality and nature of a human being. Gore insisted that Jesus is fully human with human consciousness, the perfect exemplar of what humankind should be: "We contemplate Jesus Christ, the Son of man, in the sinlessness, the perfection, the breath of His manhood, and in Him we find the justification of our highest hopes for man."[49] Jesus' sinlessness was seen in his exercise of moral freedom over temptations, which include lust of the flesh, worldliness, and pride. Jesus is the perfect example for sinners, for he overcomes "the tyranny of passions, the disorder of faculties, the inward taint and weakness."[50] Once again, the body, desire, and passion were seen as obstacles and hindrances that needed to be suppressed in order to become a perfect human.

As I have shown, the taboo of Jesus' sexuality in the nineteenth-century quest of the historical Jesus served not only to discipline individual sexual behavior, but also to maintain racial boundaries and cultural imperialism to facilitate the expansion of Europe. Jesus' sexed body provided a provocative site for the inscription and projection of powerful myths about sexuality, race, gender, and colonial desire. By emphasizing the humanity of Jesus and touting the superiority of Christianity as an ethical religion, the nineteenth-century bourgeoisie linked human perfection to the "cultivation of the self." In contrast to the sexualized natives and the lower classes, Jesus was seen as exemplifying bourgeois ideals: controlling his passions, managing his desires, and sublimating his bodily needs. Such ethical demands guaranteed the hygiene, purity, and health of the bourgeois body.

While I appreciate the efforts of gay, lesbian, and queer theologians in breaking the taboo about the sexuality of Jesus, I have argued that the control of the body and sexuality must be consistently placed in its larger social, economic, and political contexts. For me, a transgressive re-imagining of the sexuality of Jesus calls for the simultaneous emancipation of multiple Others: the sexual Other, the Racial and Ethnic Other, and the Religious Other. This can only be done through a vigorous analysis of how Christianity's most powerful symbol—Jesus—has been deployed to provide religious sanction for heteronormativity, capitalism, and colonialism in the past and new forms of oppression in the present.

NOTES

1. Sigmund Freud, *Totem and Taboo: Resemblances between the Psychic Lives of Savages and Neurotics* (New York: Vintage Books, 1960), 26.

2. Leo Steinberg, *The Sexuality of Christ in Renaissance Art and in Modern Oblivion*, 2nd ed. (Chicago: University of Chicago Press, 1996), 219.

3. Hutton Webster, *Taboo: A Sociological Study* (Stanford: Stanford University Press, 1942), 3.

4. As quoted in ibid., 5.

5. Émile Durkheim, *The Elementary Forms of Religious Life*, trans. Joseph Ward Swain (Glencoe, IL: Free Press, 1954).

6. Freud, *Totem and Taboo*, 24.

7. Sigmund Freud, *The Future of an Illusion* (New York: H. Liveright, 1928).

8. Mary Douglas, *Purity and Danger: An Analysis of Concepts of Pollution and Taboo* (New York: Fredrick A. Praeger, 1966).

9. Robert E. Goss, "Christian Homodevotion to Jesus," in his *Queering Christ: Beyond Jesus Acted Up* (Cleveland: Pilgrim Press, 2002), 113.

10. William E. Phipps, *The Sexuality of Jesus* (Cleveland: Pilgrim Press, 1996), 2.

11. Richard Rambuss, *Closet Devotions* (Durham, NC: Duke University Press, 1998), 25.

12. Robert Goss, *Jesus Acted Up: A Gay and Lesbian Manifesto* (San Francisco: HarperSanFrancisco, 1994), 77–78.

13. Elizabeth Stuart, *Just Good Friends: Towards a Lesbian and Gay Theology of Relationships* (New York: Mowbray, 1995), 168.

14. Stephen D. Moore, "Ugly Thoughts: On the Face and Physique of the Historical Jesus," in *Biblical Studies/Cultural Studies*, ed. J. Cheryl Exum and Stephen D. Moore (Sheffield: Sheffield Academic Press, 1998), 376–99.

15. Stephen D. Moore, *God's Gym: Divine Male Bodies of the Bible* (New York: Routledge, 1996).

16. Mark S. Burrows, "Foundations for an Erotic Christology: Bernard of Clairvaux on Jesus as 'Tender Lover,'" *Anglican Theological Review* 83, no. 4 (1998): 477–93.

17. Rambuss, *Closet Devotions*, 13.

18. Thomas Laqueur, "Orgasm, Generation, and the Politics of Reproductive Biology," in *The Making of the Modern Body: Sexuality and Society in the Nineteenth Century*, ed. Catherine Gallagher and Thomas Laqueur (Berkeley: University of California Press, 1987), 4.

19. Jane Gallop, *Thinking through the Body* (New York: Columbia University Press, 1988).

20. Mary Douglas, *Natural Symbols: Explorations in Cosmology* (New York: Pantheon Books, 1970), 70.

21. Susannah Heschel, *Abraham Geiger and the Jewish Jesus* (Chicago: University of Chicago Press, 1998), 127–61.

22. Gallop, *Thinking through the Body*, 3–4.

23. Ernest Renan, *Life of Jesus* (New York: Peter Eckler Publishing Co., 1925), 115.

24. Ibid., 117–19.

25. Heschel, *Abraham Geiger*, 125.

26. Laqueur, "Orgasm," 19.

27. Ibid., 19–35.

28. Sander L. Gilman, *Freud, Race, and Gender* (Princeton, NJ: Princeton University Press, 1993), 85.

29. Ibid., 82–83.

30. Daniel Boyarin, *Unheroic Conduct: The Rise of Heterosexuality and the Invention of the Jewish Man* (Berkeley: University of California Press, 1997), 212–13.

31. Michel Foucault, *The History of Sexuality*, vol. 1, *An Introduction*, trans. Robert Hurley (New York: Vintage, 1978), 3.

32. Ann Laura Stoler, *Race and the Education of Desire: Foucault's History of Sexuality and the Colonial Order of Things* (Durham, NC: Duke University Press, 1995), 13–14.

33. Ibid., 7.

34. Havelock Ellis and John Addington Symonds, *Sexual Inversion* (1897; repr., New York: Arno Press, 1975), 4.

35. Renan, *Life of Jesus*, 67–68.

36. Ibid., 118.

37. Ibid., 112.

38. Karl Barth, *Protestant Thought: From Rousseau to Ritschl* (New York: Harper & Row, 1959), 392.

39. Albrecht Ritschl, *The Christian Doctrine of Justification and Reconciliation* (Clifton, NJ: Reference Book Publisher, 1966), 3:13; as quoted in Gerald W. McCulloh, *Christ's Person and Life-Work in the Theology of Albrecht Ritschl with Special Attention to Munus Triplex* (Lanham, MD: University Press of America, 1990), 34.

40. Albrecht Ritschl, "Instruction in the Christian Religion," in *Three Essays*, trans. Philip Hefner (Philadelphia: Fortress, 1972), 240–54.

41. Albrecht Ritschl, "'Prolegomena' to the History of Pietism," in *Three Essays*, 105.

42. J. R. Seeley, *Ecce Homo: Life and Work of Jesus Christ* (1865; repr., New York: E. P. Dutton, 1908), 56–57.

43. J. R. Seeley, *The Expansion of England* (Boston: Little, Brown & Co., 1905), 226–27.

44. Seeley, *Ecce Homo*, 37.

45. Ibid., 86.

46. Ibid., 94–95.

47. Arthur Michael Ramsey, *An Era in Anglican Theology: From Gore to Temple* (New York: Charles Scribner's Sons, 1960), 18.

48. Charles Gore, *The Incarnation of the Son of God* (New York: Charles Scribner's Sons, 1891), 176.

49. Ibid., 185.

50. Ibid., 240; see also 179–80.

PART 3

Gender, Race, and Sexual Identities

Christine E. Gudorf
Beverly Wildung Harrison
    and Carter Heyward
Mary E. Hunt
Laurel C. Schneider
Dwight N. Hopkins
Miguel A. De La Torre

Introduction
to Part 3

As the editors of this book's first edition rightly pointed out, "The sexual issues now dividing religious communities the most are clearly those related to gender and to sexual orientation." Because in this society, gender, race, and class are primary conduits for distributing benefits and burdens, is it any surprise that a very great deal is made, for example, of gender? After all, the first question asked at birth is, is it a boy or girl? Furthermore, the gender of a person's "love object" choice is used to determine his or her "normalcy," his or her (at least outward) conformity to normative heterosexuality.

Our aim in Part 3 remains, as in the first edition, not "to present all sides of the current debates," but rather to select "representative voices who speak for the transformation of sexual oppressions." After all, we develop our sexualities only within institutions and systems, never independently of society or history. Therefore, we cannot grasp sexuality's purpose and meaning by biology alone. A historical, contextualized approach is needed to analyze sexuality within social power relations.

This social-historical approach recognizes, first, that sexuality is not a static thing, but rather a dynamic process, constantly being reshaped and reassigned value and meaning in the midst of conflicting social interests. Second, sexuality has a history, some of which is oppressive. Because sexuality is a social, cultural, and political issue and not only a personal concern, a social ethic is needed to examine how social structures and belief systems affect sexualities for good or ill. Third, transformations have occurred in social practice and meaning about sex, gender, and social power, but these shifts take time, require social as well as personal struggle, and are not accomplished simply at will.

To address the cultural crisis of sexuality and promote justice as right relation in our congregations and communities, we must identify the right problem and define the problem rightly. Toward this end, we propose *changing the subject* in two respects. First, we recommend changing *what* we're talking about, the topic of conversation. We need to get past the misplaced preoccupation with sexual orientation and, in particular, homosexuality in order to refocus attention on sexual oppression: the pervasive patterns of sexualized violence and of race, gender, sexual, and economic injustice. Simply put, the problem in this culture is not homosexuality, but heterosexism and the devaluing of same-gender loving people.

Second, we suggest changing the *subject* who speaks and is listened to. What is shaking the foundations in diverse religious traditions is a power shift as the overlapping groups of women, people of color, and LGBT persons claim their right to be the subjects of their own lives. Fresh insight emerges, morally speaking, only as people are no longer positioned as objects of other people's discourse (as if alien creatures or abstractions) and when, instead, they become self-defining subjects, real persons with whom to engage in dialogue. The change agenda is for women along with gay and nongay people of all colors to acknowledge and encourage each other to share what they have come to know, often at great risk, about resisting oppression, enhancing human dignity, and revitalizing community.

Christine Gudorf's "The Erosion of Sexual Dimorphism" analyzes the postmodern shift toward a more complex, fluid, and multidimensional interpretive framework that maps out a diversity of human sexual identities. Gudorf challenges the naturalist assumptions that humans are neatly divided into two distinct categories, male and female, and that individuals' biological sex determines their gender identification (masculine or feminine), social role, and erotic attraction. "The erosion of sexual dimorphism today," Gudorf explains, "is challenging traditional religious teachings on sex, which are based on sacred texts that assume human sexual dimorphism." After reviewing the scientific literature that undermines confidence in a strict gender binary and arguing that "dimorphism is only a paradigm for interpreting sexuality," Gudorf addresses how recognition of a multiplicity of human sexualities—and specifically how making space for gay, lesbian, bisexual, and transgender sexual identities within our frameworks—might challenge religious communities to rethink everything from marriage and family to leadership eligibility and images of the Divine. Her essay ends with suggestions for how religious traditions might structure their approaches to welcome "a more polymorphous concept of sexuality today."

In "Pain and Pleasure: Avoiding the Confusions of Christian Tradition in Feminist Theory," Beverly Wildung Harrison and Carter Heyward argue that it would be naive to presume that women's sexualities are "untouched by the disordered power dynamics of patriarchal eroticism." Sexual expression and erotic desire, while rooted in psyche and physiology, are also shaped by cultural dynamics. In other words, "sexuality and eroticism have a history," some of which is oppressive. For this reason, many women recognize how "sex is often experienced as a dynamic of conquest and surrender rather than as power in mutual relation." As Christian feminist theologians, they probe how eroticism and injustice are linked and investigate "the role of Christianity in developing and sustaining a social (not only sexual) relation—a sadomasochistic relation—in which pleasure is available chiefly through pain." Their hope is not only to disentangle reasons why women under patriarchy are encouraged to "accept, even enjoy, our powerlessness" (as well as why so few heterosexually oriented men seem "turned on" by strong, self-reliant women), but more urgently, to help reclaim the positive role of eroticism in human well-being and "recover a respectful appreciation of the centrality of pleasure to human fulfillment."

In "Lovingly Lesbian: Toward a Feminist Theology of Friendship," Mary E. Hunt begins by asserting that lesbian feminism must be understood contextually, and "that context is both patriarchal and heterosexist." Because in a patriarchal culture women are defined not only by their gender, but also by their sexual and other kinds of relationships with men, Hunt proposes to redefine as lesbian any woman who loves herself as a woman and also loves other women as friends. "This renewed definition of lesbian [also] comes from a particular social context," the three social movements of the so-called sexual revolution, the women's movement, and the lesbian/gay movement. In agreeing with Charlotte Bunch's analysis that the institution and ideology of heterosexuality has been the lynchpin of male gender supremacy, Hunt argues that "the point is not that every woman act in a particular way, but that every woman be freed from the constraints that patriarchal heterosexism places upon her," so that all women are free to structure their lives in self-respecting and community-building ways. Finally, she proposes, "it is not sexuality per se but friendship which determines what the quality of life can be," including intimate connection with God as friend.

Theologian Laurel C. Schneider takes on the provocative question, "What if it is a choice?" in her essay subtitled "Some Implications of the Homosexuality Debates for Theology." In recounting the story of a friend who identifies as lesbian, but falls in love with and enters into intimate partnership with a man, Schneider considers that the idea of homosexuality as a choice is alarming only because of the ammunition it appears to give to those who will fight all the harder to coerce gays and lesbians to *un-choose* their loves and lives. What if sexual identity is not as stable and "naturally" settled as often presumed, but even more important, what if identity itself is not "really the question that we should be trying to resolve in our public theological discourses," especially in light of the theological affirmation that we are made in God's image? Where choice legitimately enters in, Schneider contends, may be far less about identity per se and far more about our ethical and political choices, for example, how we conduct our lives in the midst of social diversities and what we choose to *do in community* with one another. What if, she surmises, the real choice about which we bear accountability is not about our natures, but about our moral freedom? Wouldn't a more politically relevant and theologically astute question have us ask, "What if God simply wants us to be alive and to love without ceasing?"

In "The Construction of the Black Male Body," theologian Dwight Hopkins argues that "the American Black male body, individual and corporate, is defined by eroticism and religion." This has played out in a culturally constructed drama, a "triangle of desire," which pits black men and white men in an adversarial contest over control of and access to women's lives and women's bodies. The bad news is that black men are caricatured as the sexualized beast, and "somehow," as Hopkins contends, "Black men have become a primary cathartic scapegoat for the evils committed by maleness at large." The good news is that black men are renaming themselves and claiming an alternative mode of masculinity that honors a healthy, nonexploitative eroticism and expresses an empowering religious tenacity that seeks liberation-survival for all. As Hopkins puts the matter, "Love of the Spirit in oneself provides the condition for self body-love and male-male, male-female body love (sexually and non-sexually)."

In "Beyond Machismo: A Cuban Case Study," liberation ethicist Miguel De La Torre, while identifying as a "recovering *macho*," moves quickly beyond any rhetoric of blame in order to analyze the sociohistorical construction of machismo at the intersection of sexist, heterosexist, racist, ethnocentric, and class oppressions. "Too often," he suggests, "we who are Hispanic ethicists tend to identify the oppressive structures of the dominant Eurocentric culture while overlooking repression conducted within our own community." In seeking to correct that oversight, De La Torre analyzes the machismo paradigm as a means to explicate intra-Hispanic oppression. By analyzing how the personal is also political within the history of colonized Cuba, he clarifies how "in defining what it means to be a *macho* by emphasizing the differences with our Others [Amerindians, Africans, Asians, women, and the poor], one reflects, established power relations exist which give meaning to those differences."

With this essay we shift from a cultural critique of sexuality in relation to race, gender, and class to consider the contours of an ethical eroticism, the character of our sexualities-in-relation, and the ongoing project of rethinking sexual ethics.

10

The Erosion of Sexual Dimorphism: Challenges to Religion and Religious Ethics

CHRISTINE E. GUDORF

At the heart of modernity has been a perceived dichotomy between humanity and the rest of nature in which humanity has been largely understood as dynamic, active, and progressive and nature has been understood as more or less static raw material to be shaped by humans in the creation of culture. This has been an especially strong motif in North America, where the land was interpreted by Europeans as "virgin" and "un-inhabited," waiting to be cleared, plowed, and ultimately civilized by modern humans. By late modernity, the nature/culture dichotomy had changed as the human body and human nature itself became objects of human attention and manipulation and as evolutionary theory insisted on the relationship between humans and the rest of nature. The modern distinction between nature and culture did not erode so much as it became more nuanced and less unidirectional. Instead of approaching nature as simply static raw material to be manipulated, humans today treat "nature" both as an array of simple building blocks to be manipulated and as the model for how to manipulate the elements of the world. For example, genetic research still presents itself in modernist terms that stress human intelligence as entailing domination of nonrational creation, as an attempt to improve on nature. But genetic research also presents itself as based on and justified by the model of genetic transformation that exists within nature itself.[1] This dual self-presentation by genetic research is postmodernist in that it makes no pretense at logical consistency but is founded on pragmatic communications considerations. Capitalist notions of nature as raw material that acquires value only through transformation in production exert great power in our society;[2] at the same time, older concepts of nature as somehow sacred, primordial, and exemplary have been revivified by the environmental crisis. Both ideas can be and are effectively used to justify present social practices. Nature is thus dually constructed as both static and dynamic, as both nonrational and eminently rational, as both raw material without animus and archetype of creative scientific activity.

The human body, at one level clearly a part of nature, is understood in even more complicated terms than the rest of nature. Throughout modernity the human body was, like the rest of nature, reified as object and made the subject of research (biology) and treatment (medicine). As a part of nature, the body was a given; the human task with regard to the body was to decipher the laws that govern it so as to be able to preserve the original or intended design (e.g., health).

POSTMODERN SEXUALITY: MORE CONTESTED BUT LESS DEFINITIVE

The prominence of sexuality has been one of the most obvious aspects of the late modern-early postmodern period. Controversies over gender roles and genital-sexual behavior have been repeatedly spotlighted. But a deeper look at the last 150 years shows a great many more developments around sexuality. These developments together have kept sexuality a prominent, because contested, area of human life at the same time that, as we shall see, sexuality has been becoming less and less predictive both of individual identity and of sexual roles.

At the heart of the postmodern approach to sexuality—and the body and nature in general—is the dissolution of the categories of nature and culture that have structured our thought until now. Our understanding of how change takes place, causation, the role of human will, the animal world, the plant world, machines, and the biosphere as a whole is newly chaotic. Machines and animals have joined humans as sign interpreters today. Historians of science such as Donna Haraway force us to realize the inadequacy of our categories by pointing out that in today's cancer research we have created transgenic mammals such as OncoMouse.[3] These animals are not inert laboratory supplies, nor is it simply sentimental to object to such understandings of them. Mice are chosen as lab research subjects not only because they are small, cheap, and easy to maintain but also because they share a mammalian evolutionary history with human beings. OncoMouse was created subject to breast cancer in order to further that link. Once we recognize these links between Onco-Mouse and humans, how can we retain traditional understandings of technoscience with their sharp distinctions between active researcher and passive research subject, human intelligence and nonhuman matter, rational science and nonrational nature?

In the following essay, I will not tackle the huge subject of nature within the shift from modern to postmodern but will instead limit myself to tracing the implications for western religions of the postmodern shift from human sexual dimorphism to human sexual polymorphism. Like Haraway in her treatment of the larger subject, I cannot claim to have seen the far distant shore toward which humans are, or should be, moving. It does seem to me that in sexuality, unlike the larger field of technoscience that Haraway studies, there is more room for optimism because a great many changes in theory, law, research structure, and medical/psychological practice in sexuality over the last forty years have begun at the grassroots. Haraway's goal is a more democratic science. Sexuality, because it involves not only science but issues of personal identity and relationship as well, may be more accessible to grassroots influence than other areas of science more easily controlled by elites.

At the same time, this greater openness to sexual diversity from the grassroots has been made possible because of the late modern splintering of the concept of human sexuality into a multitude of fragments: (religious and governmental) elites only began losing direct control of sexuality when it became more diffused and less powerful. This diffusion of sexuality then allowed it to become ever more subject to commercialization both directly (pornography, prostitution, medicine, and pharmaceuticals) and indirectly (objectification of human sexuality in advertising).

SEXUALITY AS DIMORPHIC

Sexual dimorphism has been a general assumption throughout human history, though that assumption had sometimes been weak compared with the strong form that sexual dimorphism took in western history. Sylvia Marcos, for example, speaking of the Mesoamerican universe, writes: "The feminine-masculine dual unity was fundamental to the creation of the cosmos, its (re)-generation, and sustenance. The fusion of feminine and masculine in one bi-polar principle is a recurring feature of Mesoamerican thinking."[4] Human societies often operated not only with a concept of humans divided into males and females but also with a category or categories of exceptions, usually described in terms of some combination of maleness and femaleness. It was assumed that humans were "naturally" divided into two sexes, male and female, and that the fact of maleness or femaleness determined individual gender—masculinity or femininity—as well as social role. Certainly this assumption is reflected in the most ancient sacred texts—the Vedas,[5] the Hebrew Torah,[6] the Confucian classics,[7] the "Chuang Tzu,"[8] Buddhism's Pali Canon,[9] the New Testament,[10] the Quran[11]—which all use either male or female terms (e.g., man, woman, boy, girl, husband, wife) to distinguish human beings and in moral and legal sections assume that maleness or femaleness determines social role and the sex of the object of sexual desire. Sexual dimorphism seems more rigid in western than in eastern religions, in which, among other factors, the transformation in an individual's sex through successively reincarnated lives serves to relativize sex to some extent. Here I will restrict my treatment of the erosion of sexual dimorphism on religious communities to the western religious traditions of Judaism, Christianity, and Islam. The divine being in the West has been gendered in one virtually consistent manner (masculine),[12] which is unlike the case in eastern religions such as Hinduism, Shinto, and Mahayana Buddhism, which have both male and female deities. Insofar as we know, the human sources of the sacred texts in all three western religions were male: some of these texts even assume male audiences (e.g., Deut. 3:19, Quran 4:29).

Dimorphism is present in the Hebrew Scriptures from the very first book in two ways. The creation story in Genesis clearly states that God created humanity in the image and likeness of God, "male and female he created them" (Gen. 1:27). The text states that both human males and human females are made in the image of God; the failure to mention other types of humans, or to attribute likeness to God to other forms of life, suggests sexual dimorphism. In the second creation story in Genesis, the dimorphic message becomes even stronger, for God first makes a human figure; then, seeking a fit companion for the human, makes a series of other animals; and at last gives up on animals and makes a companion for the human from his own rib (Gen. 2:18–22). At the end of this process the first human calls himself man and his companion woman, and it is stated, "Therefore a man leaves his father and his mother and cleaves to his wife, and they shall become one flesh" (Gen. 2:23–24). The Quran does not include a specific creation story but refers to a roughly similar origin (4:1) that accords with its knowledge of other Jewish/Christian stories and characters and its sense of shared origin (as People of the Book, descendants of Ibrahim).

Sexual dimorphism is not merely understood as part of original creation as depicted in sacred texts. Throughout all three sets of sacred texts, Jewish, Christian, and Muslim, males and females are distinguished from each other again and again in terms of social function, worth, and relation to each other and to God, that is, in terms of religious norms. All three sets of texts dictate different sets of religious and moral, social and domestic norms for those dimorphically divided into men and women. There are, of course, some differences among Christianity, Judaism, and Islam here. Judaism is perhaps, as the oldest of the traditions, certainly in terms of sacred texts, the most sexually differentiated tradition. Beginning with male circumcision as the mark of the covenant, through the provisions of the Mosaic Law and the Talmud, men and women are expected to fulfill different functions because they are understood to be differently constituted and intended.

In Christianity there is less differentiation between the sexes in religious terms: there are no religious obligations of men that are not also binding on women. Yet, by the second century, leadership in Christianity came to increasingly require maleness (I Tim. 3:1–7); as the church gave up on the imminence of the Second Coming, women were pushed back into patriarchal roles in family and society.[13] I Tim. 2:15 says, "Yet woman will be saved through bearing children, if she continues in faith and love and holiness"; thus, not only do women become subject to the sexually undifferentiated demands imposed by Jesus' teaching on all followers, but their salvation also requires compliance with sexually differentiated cultural demands, in this case, for motherhood. This is ironic given Jesus' teaching about those who are eunuchs for the Kingdom of Heaven (Mt. 19:12), his disavowal of blessings on his own mother because of her motherhood (Lk. 11:27–28), and the preference of Paul (and most of the subsequent tradition) for the unmarried, even virgin, state for believers (I Cor. 7:8).

In Islam it is well recognized that both the Quranic treatment of women and the actions and sayings of Muhammad with regard to women show a deliberate and conscious attempt to raise the welfare and status of women in Arab society through new religious legislation. That legislation, based in both Quran and the *hadith* of Muhammad, banned (female) infanticide (males were seldom killed), limited the number of a man's wives, gave women control of their own property, urged the education of daughters as well as sons, and gave daughters inheritance rights.[14] But this legislation not only elevated the status of women in society; it also made the categories of male and female opposite and complementary and thus incorporated dimorphic assumptions into all specific legislation on social and domestic roles and behaviors that has made continuing reforms in new situations difficult.

While at least weak versions of sexual dimorphism seem to be found in virtually every corner of the world, most societies also recognized the existence of exceptions, of individuals who did not "fit" in every way this dimorphic pattern. Different societies have understood these exceptions in varied ways and to various extents. Children born with ambiguous genitalia (or other abnormalities) were killed in some societies; similarly, in some societies older individuals evidencing same-sex desire, or twins, or left-handed children were also sometimes eliminated as mistakes in nature.[15] Other societies might tolerate the presence of one or more of these differences but interpret them—as with other more disabling differences such as blindness, deafness, or crippled limbs—as evidence of parental sin or of the sin of the individual him- or herself (John 9:1–14). Still other societies interpreted such difference as a divine sign intended for the whole tribe, as either a warning or a blessing.

Some societies that tolerated exceptions to the dimorphic sexual pattern even created special social roles, which brought honor and leadership responsibilities to affected persons. These special roles include those of the (castrated) *hijras* of India (Nanda); the Sworn Virgins of Albania, expert (female) hunters and woodsmen sworn to celibacy who were not considered women but "virgins";[16] shamans of Siberian communities who were often called by possessing spirits during vision quests and healing trances into reluctantly entered gender changes[17] that even led to same-sex marriages in a society that absolutely forbade homosexuality;[18] and various two-spirit roles among many of the Native American tribes, including the Mojave[19] and the Zuni.[20] Societies that allowed for nonmale, nonfemale persons to function within the society's lifeways, however, recognized this path as restricted to a small number of persons, explained this identity role by special realignment of the categories of maleness and femaleness,[21] and designated specific ceremonies for recognizing such persons and assigning group functions to them.

Some societies have had a name for a biological phenomenon recently referred to as the "5-alpha reductase deficiency," which produces genetically normal males whose male genitalia fail to develop both in the womb and in childhood until puberty. They are commonly assigned as females at birth and reared as girls until male genitalia begin to develop at puberty. This condition has been reported in approximately a dozen countries, first in the Dominican Republic. Herdt studied it among the Sambia of New Guinea, who can often recognize the condition at birth and call it *kwolu-aatmwol* or "turning into a man." In the Dominican Republic the condition was known as *guevedoche* or "penis at twelve." Though Herdt interprets this cultural recognition of the condition as recognition of a third sex, this seems debatable, for by his own account the males affected are pressured to abandon femaleness and adopt maleness at puberty but are not usually accepted as fully male. That is, they are not generally allowed to complete the process of ritual initiation into manhood, and most "moved to distant towns where they could pass as men."[22] The "5-alpha reductase deficiency" may fit somewhat better into a category of culturally recognized exceptions to dimorphism than into a third sex category.

The existence of exceptions who do not fit either the male or the female pattern does not itself necessarily undermine an assumption of sexual dimorphism. This is, of course, the way that paradigms work. A paradigm is a concept used to interpret a body of data. A given concept is accepted as the paradigm because it accounts for the vast majority of data—but seldom all the data—better than any alternative interpretive concept. A particular paradigm reigns until the amount of data that it does not interpret increases and another concept is proposed that seems to account for more of the data than the previous paradigm does.[23] In the early postmodern age we are seeing the waning of sexual dimorphism as the prevailing paradigm for interpreting human sexuality as the evidence of exceptions continues to mount, as well as the rise of a body of related, potential new postmodern sexual paradigms.[24]

The erosion of sexual dimorphism as the reigning paradigm for interpreting human sexuality has been difficult for religions in a number of different ways. Thus far it has been especially difficult for Christianity, for the erosion is both best reflected in popular lifestyles and most widely known within the historically Christian developed West. Until the second half of the nineteenth century, sexuality in western society was a dimorphic concept understood to govern virtually all of human life: identity, role/function, behavior, and attitudes.

The erosion of sexual dimorphism today is challenging traditional religious teachings on sex, which are based on sacred texts that assume human sexual dimorphism. Religious commentary and interpretation of Hebrew Scriptures, the New Testament, and the Quran, for example, can hardly avoid reflecting the understanding prevalent at the times of these texts' composition that sex determines one's personal traits and abilities, one's appropriate social and familial roles (including power and worth), and the object of one's sexual desire.

At another level the erosion of sexual dimorphism has challenged the institutional structures of religions, as we have seen in controversies over the exclusion of women Muslims from being judges in postrevolution Iran or more recently from being trained as imams in Turkey,[25] priests in the Catholic Church, or rabbis in Orthodox Judaism, not to mention the battles over membership and leadership for gays and lesbians in Protestant denominations.[26] At yet another level, the moral authority of religions, most directly the moral authority of their teaching on sexual behavior, is challenged when the imperatives of that sexual teaching appear to be based on mistaken data. This is what is at stake, for example, when individuals who cannot clearly be defined as either male or female claim, in the face of religious insistence that sex is only legitimate in marriage between a male and a female, the religiously recognized right (and sometimes, as in Judaism, the duty) to marry and procreate.

THE LIMITS OF REVISIONISM TO SAVE SEXUAL DIMORPHISM

The strong form of sexual dimorphism that prevailed in the early modern West understood virtually every aspect of sexuality (nature, role, desire, and identity) as biologically fixed and determined by the dimorphic division into male and female. The process of erosion in the sexual dimorphism paradigm began with the emerging distinction between sex and gender. Liberal feminism lobbed one of the first volleys in those debates. Liberal feminism arose in the United States in the mid-nineteenth century among middle-class white women who challenged a number of prevailing ideological assumptions about women as well as a number of legal and other institutional arrangements based on those assumptions.

Every aspect of the campaign waged by middle-class white women for equal rights in the late nineteenth century contested the prevalent assumption that biological sex determined social role and sexual identity. They insisted that individual societies constructed sex roles and reared men and women into sexual identities based on the society's interpretation of the meaning of biological sex. Many of these women's rights activists took up roles and behaviors that had previously been limited to males. For example, the Blackwell sisters, Elizabeth, Emily, and Anna, became doctors and an international journalist; Antoinette Brown Blackwell became the first ordained American woman minister; the indefatigable campaigner Susan B. Anthony was arrested for casting a ballot before women could legally vote;[27] and, on a less serious note, Amelia Bloomer abandoned skirts in favor of baggy pants she designed for women. By the 1920s and 1930s there were well-known women doctors, athletes, lawyers, and pilots, as well as significant numbers of women with graduate degrees teaching in colleges and universities and even women in government office, none of whom fully conformed to traditional U.S. concepts of feminine gender but all of whom were recognized as female.

This multiplication of exceptions to the understanding that maleness and femaleness were not only different but opposite natures that constituted persons capable of living out only one very clear and specific gender role received some academic support in the late nineteenth and early twentieth century when a new type of academic who studied other cultures arose. Gradually, anthropological work, which relatively quickly included the work of women scholars such as Margaret Mead[28] and Ruth Benedict,[29] began to disseminate very different cultural accounts of gender that began to erode western assumptions that maleness and femaleness were understood in similar ways—or should be understood in western terms at all—throughout the world. Lewis Henry Morgan's anthropological research[30] was influential, for example, in grounding the theories of Frederick Engels in *The Origin of the Family, Private Property and the State*.[31] Engels proposes that pairing marriage developed from group marriage (and made women into serfs) under the impetus of the shift from matrilineality to patrilineality because men wanted to ensure that their property passed to their children. He suggests that in societies that had not experienced property accumulation, or had done so only recently, this shift from group to pairing marriage was not yet complete.[32]

Morgan's study of a number of North American tribes demonstrates not only the differences between native and European constructions of gender (in which the very fact of the differences suggests that gender is a social construction) but also differences among tribal constructions of gender. As more and more different treatments of gender in societies became known, it became easier to accept that biological maleness or femaleness does not unilaterally determine one's gender traits and roles but, rather, one's particular social culture interprets maleness and femaleness, creating its own variety of feminine and masculine norms. Thus, sex and gender were separated, with sex understood as a biological given and gender as socially constructed.

By the mid-twentieth century sex research began putting the next nail in the coffin of dimorphism. Beginning with the work of Alfred Kinsey yet another aspect came to be separated from what had been a unitary and all-inclusive category of sex. This time it was sexual orientation that was broken out of the concept of sex. Kinsey's research proposed that, instead of the dominant heterosexist model in which biological maleness dictates sexual attraction to females and vice versa for femaleness, there is, in fact, a spectrum of human sexual orientation from exclusively heterosexual at one end to exclusively homosexual at the other.[33] Kinsey's proposal cut at sexual dimorphism in two ways. First, it separates sex from sexual orientation, thus weakening the inherited dimorphic division of sexual beings and behavior, and, second, it resists dimorphism altogether in its classification of orientation in favor of an unlimited number of types of orientation on a spectrum.

The rejection of the dimorphic model for orientation had severe repercussions within religion because it was a clear rejection of the dichotomous virtue/ sin model with which western religions had approached heterosexuality/

homosexuality. Kinsey in effect challenged the religious view in Judaism, Christianity, and Islam that heterosexism is integral to God's plan of creation and therefore "natural" and that homosexual acts are deliberately chosen acts of perversion: sin. Instead, homosexual acts are seen as reflecting patterns of homosexual desire, which themselves call into question the existence of heterosexuality as constant in human identity. The Kinsey spectrum became more and more accepted in the medical/psychological research field as studies of homosexuality multiplied. Those studies have shifted away from the act-centered approach of the earlier religious sin/virtue approach,[34] and they instead have interpreted sexual orientation as a relatively stable aspect of individual personalities that does not necessarily differentiate individuals in terms of carrying out social, personal, occupational, or familial responsibilities.[35]

THE BIOLOGICAL CASE
AGAINST DIMORPHISM

Biological research in the late twentieth century added a new and, for many, unexpected voice to the crowd challenging human sexual dimorphism. Biologists pointed out that in terms of sex chromosomes there are, in fact, more than two human patterns. Humans exist not only in the predominant XX and XY forms but also in XXX, XXY, XYY, XO, and occasional XXXX forms.[36] All forms other than XX and XY were originally interpreted, given the dimorphic paradigm, as aberrations or mistakes in nature. But by the 1970s, in light of all the other challenges to a dimorphic model of sex, this biological information began to be viewed in a new light.

The sheer numbers of persons with these more uncommon chromosomal patterns are daunting. The most common of these unusual patterns, Klinefelter's Syndrome (XXY) and Turner's Syndrome (XO), occur once in every 700 males and once in every 2,500 females, respectively;[37] XYY and XXX are somewhat more rare, and XXXX is very rare. But in the earth's population today the number of persons with only Turner's or Klinefelter's Syndrome, without even adding the other less common patterns, is over 5.5 million—as large as the population of Finland or El Salvador or twice as big as that of Uruguay.

These less common chromosomal patterns are only the tip of the biological challenge to sexual dimorphism. In addition, there are hormonal irregularities that change the way that chromosomal sex is embodied in humans. The two most common hormonal irregularities affecting genitalia and sexual identity are andrenogenital syndrome and androgen insensitivity syndrome. In andrenogenital syndrome an XX fetus is exposed to high levels of androgen, the male hormone, either from external sources or from its own hormonal system,[38] so that its external genitalia are masculinized. In androgen insensitivity syndrome an XY fetus, and the child he or she becomes, is chemically unable to absorb the testosterone produced by his or her body, so that the body responds only to its low levels of female hormones and develops feminine external genitalia, even

breasts at puberty, but has no internal reproductive organs other than unde-
scended testes producing testosterone that the body cannot use.

In these uncommon chromosomal and hormonal patterns the dimorphic
paradigm is hard-pressed to indicate who is male and who is female. The vast
majority of people in the world today, and virtually all peoples in the past, have
diagnosed maleness and femaleness based on external genitalia at birth. External genitalia were never totally adequate to the diagnostic task because of the
existence of hermaphrodites, a very rare phenomenon, and, more commonly,
pseudohermaphrodites (often persons with andrenogenital or androgen insensitivity syndrome). In the twentieth century developed societies have attempted
to diagnose sex by using chromosomal sex, but, as we have seen, chromosomal
sex does not eliminate ambiguities either.

In fact, biologists today tell us that there are six different biological factors
that together make up one's sex, each of which has a spectrum with poles at
either end. For many people these six different factors do not line up in any consistent "male" or "female" pattern. The six biological factors are chromosomal
sex, hormonal sex, sex of the external genitalia, sex of the internal reproductive
organs, gonadal sex, and sex of the brain.[39] These are obviously interrelated,
though not always in the same way in all persons. For example, the brain normally gets its "maleness" or "femaleness" from the predominant hormones cir-
culating in the blood, just as hormones can make the external genitalia develop
without correspondence to chromosomal sex.

Not only do these six biological factors of sex not always agree, but human
societies have no single method of prioritizing them. Sometimes we recognize
the sex indicated by the external genitalia, sometimes we use the sex indicated
by the chromosomes, and sometimes we create new genitalia that do not correspond to chromosomal sex. For example, when ambiguous genitalia are discovered at birth, drug and surgical interventions serve to conform the genitalia
with the chromosomal sex. But the discovery of children born with ambiguous
genitalia who have been reared in a chromosomally incorrect sex has for decades
in the United States and Europe led to surgical intervention to make the external genitalia of the child accord with the gender identity the child has developed
and not with the chromosomal sex. (This is because gender identity, at least
where consistent with the sex of the brain, has seemed to be irreversible.) The
case is similar for transsexuals, adults who undergo a process of transforming
themselves from one gender to the other, culminating in a surgical transformation to the other sex: surgical and drug interventions transform the body of the
patient from accordance with chromosomal sex to accordance with the patient's
self-identified sex.

Yet another group in our society that challenges any neat assignment of all
people into the dimorphic division of male and female is trans-gendered persons. These are persons who accept the sex of their bodies in a biological sense.
Those who have a penis and testes want a penis and testes, and those who
have a uterus and vagina want a uterus and vagina. But they do not accept the

roles that are socially assigned to those bodies. Some persons who have biologically "fathered" children want to "mother" their children dressed as traditional feminine women, speaking and acting as women and carrying out more or less traditional women's roles. Some of these transgendered persons have remained married to their spouses of the other sex; their children have two mothers or two fathers who happen to be of different physiological types.

Clearly, then, in terms of both the data on human sexuality today and the choices that are made by human societies about sex, it is no longer correct to distinguish sex and gender by saying that sex refers to our biological givenness as male or female and gender refers to the traits and roles that a particular society and individuals construct for male and female persons. Today we should recognize that both sex and gender are socially constructed categories; both sex and gender must be interpreted.

To say that sex and gender are socially constructed should not be interpreted to mean that humans, and certainly not individuals, are in complete control of the process. While it is true that even with regard to sex, humans do decide which among a variety of factors will count to determine sex, humans do have constraints on how we will think about sex. There are obviously some biological processes we do not completely control. Social construction of sex and gender signals that our individual and communal choices are aspects, along with biological, social, political, economic, and many other factors, that shape our sexual reality.

Thus, in our society sex, at both a biological and a psychological level, not to mention the level of genital sexual activity, has become much more complex than the dimorphic model ever allowed. Many conservative Jews, Christians, and Muslims respond that this is just the degenerate late modern West; what can one expect? But the challenge to dimorphism is not at all limited to the West or to modern societies.

Dimorphism is only a paradigm for interpreting sexuality. No paradigm completely explains all the data, and sexual dimorphism never completely explained human experience of sexuality, as we have seen with hermaphroditism, which has always been known. But a successful paradigm explains the vast majority of the data in any given area. Sexual dimorphism has been the major paradigm for interpreting human sexuality, but different human communities have always had different ways of interpreting those cases that did not fit the dimorphic paradigm. As mentioned above, societies have had different levels of tolerance for those who differ in some way from the dimorphic norms. But in a variety of societies in which the general dimorphic character of sex was preserved, exceptions were recognized, accepted, and even assigned special social roles. These roles have been described as third gender or third sex roles, as anthropologist of sexuality Gilbert Herdt explains:

> Through the long course of generations and with sufficient historical time, the necessary presence of individuals who desire to be different and serve in third-gender and third-sex roles enables us to understand how a community might provide for these alternative sexual lifeways. For the third gender, as in the case of

women who dress in men's clothes, we are dealing with biologically normative individuals who only change their role. That is, they learn the knowledge and social performance of the other gender. However, in the case of third-sexes, we are dealing with individuals who are biologically hermaphroditic or who make themselves that way through cultural means, such as castration. Examples of third sexes are the famed sexual eunuchs of the Byzantine Empire or classical Arabia; the Hijiras of India, who are either biologically hermaphroditic at birth or undergo a castration rite in late adolescence; and the modern transsexual.[40]

Herdt describes the geography of historic third sex and third gender roles as including the New World, insular Southeast Asia, and a sparse but wide-ranging area of distribution in Africa. He attributes our primary knowledge of these roles to the two-spirit person (formerly called *berdache*) among North American natives, the cross-dressing women of Europe from the fourteenth to the early twentieth centuries, and Polynesian forms of gender transformation. In all of these, the culture in question not only constructed a role for the person but also elaborated a mythology and social ritual that supported the development of the person taking on the role. For example, Herdt cites the Mojave initiation of two-spirit people at age ten and the Navajo fertility magic controlled by the two-spirit person.[41] Recruitment into this role might come through personal feelings of being different, a vision quest, the desires of one's family, or the decisions of religious groups. Studies by Blackwood and by Williams have found the two-spirit role widespread and well accepted in more than 100 North American native tribes. In all of these tribes men took on the role, while in about one-third women also took on the two-spirit role.

Eunuchs have been a part of western history until very recently. In the Byzantine Christian Empire (James), in the Ottoman Empire (Marmon), and in the Vienna and Sistine Choirs until the nineteenth centuries,[42] eunuchs were recognized, often honored, and usually self-recruited because of the social rewards in the role.

One reason for the building pressure on the concept of sexual dimorphism today is enhanced communications that has produced an explosion of information about human cultures. We are now confronted with the variety of ways that different cultures have "explained away" the sexual facts and experiences that could not be subsumed under dimorphism. The exceptions to, and denials of, the dimorphic paradigm begin to multiply, take on growing significance, and ultimately bring the paradigm itself into question. There can be no doubt that this is happening all over the world,[43] but it is most explicit in the postmodern West. Youth culture in the West since the 1960s has had a strong and growing unisex emphasis; today many men and women socialized in the sixties continue this emphasis even into late middle age. Having rejected the dimorphic division that exaggerated the differences between men and women by making them dress and behave very differently, many western men now wear long hair and ponytails, just as some women have burr haircuts. Among music and film stars and models these trends are even more dominant. Much of women's clothing, and virtually all women's casual wear including shoes, is indistinguishable from men's, just as more men are carrying bags (purses) and wearing jewelry. More and more offices, hospitals, and public institutions of all types have unisex restrooms both in the United States and Europe. Calvin Klein began introducing unisex fragrances in the early nineties, and diaper suppliers have begun a trend toward unisex diapers.[44]

All of these trends in dress reflect a century and a half of gradual unisex trends in education and job training, which themselves followed employment trends initiated in, and developing gradually since, the Industrial Revolution. While women took on many kinds of industrial labor alongside men and have gradually taken on more and more mechanized work, more equal access to the top echelons of professional work did not follow until recently. Recent labor studies show that women in the United States only began to pursue those professional programs necessary to achieve the top rungs of professional work around 1970, as a result of access to contraception.[45] The incremental nature of the unisex trend has disguised it, permitting attention to focus on a few pieces of the trend at any one time: at one moment, male nurses and airline servers; at another, female police and firefighters; and at yet another, unisex toilets. Individually none has seemed revolutionary.

Nevertheless, while some members of our society, and certainly critics of the West, dismiss unisexuality as simply a passing fad in clothing, video, and music, there is at least one group in our society that is unambiguous in its rejection of sexual dimorphism, and that is the Intersexuality Society of North America. This society is largely constituted by those who were sexually reassigned as children (most often by surgery) and is strongly opposed to all forms of sexual reassignment for children or adults with ambiguous sexuality. Members argue that, instead of reassignment in order to fit the norms of sexual dimorphism, children should be taught to accept and appreciate themselves as sexual beings regardless of the sexual configuration of their bodies. There is, they insist, no basis for privileging the "male" or "female" body and viewing all other naturally occurring bodies as defective bodies that should be mutilated in order to conform to the chosen norms.[46]

Men and women who enter the same field of labor increasingly have the same education, training, and employment. In leisure and recreation women have moved into sports from peewee to professional levels. Men are agitating for child custody in divorce cases, and growing though still small numbers of men are now househusbands with wives who are principal breadwinners. Perhaps even more telling, the number of persons who have lived for significant portions of their lives as members of one sex/gender and then changed to another is growing; the number of those who have changed sexual orientation is much larger still. And while sexual activity does not appear to have lost any of its place in human life in postmodernity, the role of sex in stratifying society and determining personal identity has certainly changed and become yet another area of life open to choice.

RELIGION AND THE EROSION
OF SEXUAL DIMORPHISM

In terms of sacred texts, the erosion of sexual dimorphism presents some western religions with a serious dilemma. Because their sacred texts present humanity as sexually dimorphic, if human sexuality is not dimorphic, then those groups who understand their sacred texts to be both divinely authored and final—among them Sunni Islam, Orthodox Judaism, and much of Evangelical Protestantism—have a problem. For this reason, these religious bodies are strongly tempted to define sexual dimorphism not as a paradigm for interpreting sexuality but as the divinely revealed foundation of human sexuality found in scriptures. In the face of research on sexual orientation or transsexuality, their spokespersons have therefore tended to insist that instances of the erosion of sexual dimorphism are due not to any inadequacy in the concept but, rather, to human infidelity to the divine will. Escaping captivity to this outmoded paradigm is not impossible, but it requires some theological creativity and will certainly not happen in the immediate future.

Discomfort with the erosion of sexual dimorphism will not be confined to very conservative religious communities. Queries to rabbis, pastors, and imams concerning these issues evoke a broad spectrum of responses, one of the most common of which is that none of these "problems" is present within their communities. Even religious bodies that understand sacred texts as divinely inspired but mediated through fallible human beings (Catholicism, Reform Judaism, liberal Protestantism, and various modernist currents in Islam) do not relish having to explain away yet another "mistake" in the texts.

Human sexual dimorphism, however, figures not just in creation stories or basic assumptions about the nature of the divine within sacred texts and theologies; it has also been foundational for the moral and religious rules and commandments of religions. There are at least three areas, in addition to issues around myths in sacred texts, that present a serious challenge to western religious traditions: (1) marriage/sexual morality legislation, (2) gendered traditions of holiness, and (3) legislation on sex and religious leadership/office. All three of these areas are contested and have been for some decades. Until recently that contestation has been largely understood to come from within the dimorphic paradigm: men wanting to marry men, and women, women; women questioning religious norms requiring women to be subordinate (meek, obedient, etc.); and women wanting to be rabbis, priests, ministers, judges, and imams like men are. When these same challenges are grounded outside the sexual dimorphic model of sex, they become much more destabilizing, for what is at stake is not (merely!) the justice of the religious norms and regulation but their very intelligibility.

For instance, in marriage legislation, should a religion recognize or perform a marriage for a woman and her transsexual fiancé (who is chromosomally female) or for a man and his chromosomally male fiancée who suffered a circumcision accident at birth and was surgically reassigned and raised as a girl from six months? Or how about the transgendered person—a couple, chromosomally and anatomically male and female, both present themselves as women who want to bear and rear children as joint mothers? How does one interpret the (dimorphic) regulations in these situations? Who is male, and who is female? In the recent past, these were questions answered by science in the developed world; before the late modern period, and still in most of the world, these have been questions answered by observation of external genitalia. Certainly today few religions want—or should want—responsibility for definitively interpreting sexuality.

New work roles and domestic roles for men and women clearly impact religious norms of holiness. Contemporary middle-class women have been formed by long periods of educational and other training side by side with men and have gone on to equal employment with men in positions of responsibility and authority in many cities of the world. They have become competent and self-confident managers and leaders who share authority and decision making with others every day. They cannot become different people in their spiritual or domestic lives so as to be capable of rendering obedience, humility, or the self-effacement that religious traditions have deemed necessary modesty in women. All over the world educated, professional women come to expect that same affirmation in their domestic lives that they receive in their work lives: to be partners of their husbands, not subordinates (Eph. 5:22–24, Quran 4:38); to be consulted and involved in joint decision making, not called to obedience; to have an equal sharing of the burden involved in running a home and raising children; and to have a right to equal consideration by their spouses. The Christian idea that women's salvation comes through childbearing (I Tim. 2:15) and obedience (Eph. 5:22) while their spouses' salvation comes from living out neighborly love in all the tasks and roles of their larger lives is less and less acceptable, as is the Islamic idea that men are in charge of women, who must be obedient or risk punishment (Quran 4:34).

In the same way, late modern western societies have allowed a public space for gay and lesbian persons and communities that is, despite the serious remaining threats that plague it, much safer and better supported than any in recent western history. As the number of self-identified gay, lesbian, bisexual, transgendered, transsexual, and intersexed persons who are successful both in their chosen fields of work and in constructing supportive social circles increases, its increase encourages other gay, lesbian, bisexual, transgendered, transsexual, and intersexed persons to make claims for equality on society and on religions. They claim the right to be obliged by the same moral rules and expectations applied to all other citizens and believers, and they reject any attempt at differential treatment that is not based in their own self-identity.

In short, late modern experience in the developed world is that all human beings have certain universal obligations to our society based on social need, ability and skill levels, and relations with others. We all have obligations to preserve God's creation; to contribute to just and effective government and economy; and to see that children, the elderly, and the disabled are safe, educated, respected as individuals, and involved in their society so far as is possible for them. How we do each of these will differ according to a number of factors—but for most of us sexual identity, gender identity, and sexual orientation no longer either excuse us from any of these or specially oblige us to them. Sexual identity, gender identity, and sexual orientation have less and less to say in defining our moral obligations and less and less relevance to our habits of virtue and our salvation status. Thus, we see in many areas of Islam a movement of women, who traditionally attended mosques much less than men, to now attend mosques in greater numbers and more frequently. In Christianity women have taken on many roles in public ministry that were formerly reserved to men, in liturgy, administration, and education, as well as in ordained ministry. In Judaism there is a similar growing insistence among women that women should not be excused from the bulk of the commandments because, as Judith Plaskow points out, full membership requires being bound by the full range of the commandments.[47] To be exempt is to be outside. Increased ritual participation and increased knowledge of the tradition both follow from understanding women's religious responsibilities as being similar to men's. It is not surprising, then, that in all three major religions of the West religious and moral virtue is becoming less and less sex differentiated.

In the same way, the multiplicity of sexualities has serious implications for the sex of leaders in religious communities. Many Protestant Christian denominations have significant numbers of ordained women. The Catholic Church in the last decade or so has tended to defend its exclusion of women from ordination by claiming that the issue cannot be discussed because the Church does not have the authority to change this practice; it has not focused so much on biblical and theological arguments as the original declaration did in 1976.[48] At the same time, though, the Catholic Church, pressed by the global shortage of priests, has been moving more and more of those nonsacramental ministerial tasks traditionally done by priests into the hands of laypersons, including women. Reform and Conservative Jewish synagogues have created bat mitzvahs for girls to parallel bar mitzvahs for boys to celebrate their full membership in the worshiping community, and middle-aged and elderly women have completed the preparation and undergone this initiation not available to them earlier.

In Islam (and among Jews and Christians as well) there has been in recent decades increased emphasis on the religious education of females not only among children but also for adult women and even at higher levels of the university and institute, from Egypt through Iran and Indonesia.[49] There are growing numbers of Muslim women in both the West and Muslim countries today who are well trained in Islamic studies and are debating the *shari'a* on women in print and orally in universities, in public, and in policy-making venues.[50] Scholars such as Riffat Hassan use the Quran and hadith to demonstrate an Islamic foundation for human rights and insist that women have been subjugated not by

Islamic revelation but by biased interpretations and institutions. Hadith regarding Muhammad's insistence on the education of girls have offered support for the shift toward female education,[51] despite the fact that such hadith were not interpreted in the past to demand for girls formal schooling in general, much less equal or the same schooling as males.

As males and females become similarly educated both in secular education and in their faith, the selection process for religious leaders will become inevitably more inclusive of admirable traits from traditional models of both males and females. Thus far this has been most apparent within Protestantism, where it has become commonplace both within churches and on radio and TV talk shows to hear references to traditional feminine traits (sympathy, support, empathy, sensitivity, patience) that are required of ministers in addition to more intellectual or authoritative qualities useful in preaching that used to be considered masculine but are becoming more neutral. To the extent that many Reform Jewish congregations have adopted a model of ministry closer to the Protestant model than to more traditional Jewish models of rabbi as scholar and judge (though the direction of change among Reform congregations now seems to be back toward the tradition), it has been easiest for women rabbis to be validated and succeed in Reform. There has been significant advance for women's leadership, however, among Conservatives as well, and there are large associations of Orthodox feminists too, though there is less integration of female leadership within Orthodox congregations.

Among Catholics the identification of priesthood with the sacraments has made priesthood more resistant to rational demands for equality, for sacraments invoke nonrational power and mystery in a way that word-based ministry does not. Ironically, feminism's grounding of its claim to equality in modern understandings of rationality has not advanced its case within Catholic theology, for the central sacramental function of priesthood is not understood as "rational" (though neither is it understood as contrary to rationality).

POSTMODERN DIRECTIONS
FOR SEX AND RELIGION

Given the shift toward a more polymorphous concept of sexuality today, how should religious communities structure their approaches to sexuality? Here are some initial suggestions:

1. *Religious communities should resist defining sexuality.* While traditional western religions all assumed sexual dimorphism, Moses, Jesus, and Muhammad and the legions of theologians, scholars, and judges who followed them all managed to avoid defining sexuality. For religions to define nonreligious concepts is not only to act outside their area of expertise and therefore to expose themselves to attack, it is also to take unnecessary risks with their authority among the faithful. Concepts are both interdependent and fluid. There is no way to issue "ultimate" definitions; what we mean by nature, culture, male, female, homosexual,

and heterosexual, among many other terms, is in transition, and new concepts ("transgendered," "third sex") that alter the meanings of existing concepts are constantly arising. There is nothing morally problematic with this dynamism.

2. *Religious communities should decenter sexuality.* Sexuality was not a focal part of the teachings of Moses, Jesus, or Muhammad. There is no reason that it should be the primary litmus test for all other decisions in religious bodies. Disputes about sexuality should neither paralyze ministry nor determine policy in other areas. The bottom line here is that religious education, legislation, and ritual should focus on the dignity, value, and obligations of human persons to each other irrespective of those persons' sexual identities. For example, if pregnancy is deemed to require special legal protections, then give that protection to whoever is pregnant instead of trying to define femaleness with reference to pregnancy and privileging all females. The young should be protected from predatory sexuality regardless of the sex/gender/orientation of the predator.

3. *Religious communities should historicize sexuality.* Religions at this particular point in history seem paralyzed around sexuality, unable to move beyond the modernity paradigm, as if modernity had been the universal and eternal form of human life. But all three western religions under discussion have made numerous adjustments to different understandings of sexuality and different models of marriage and family throughout history. Moreover, all three have existed over large geographical areas in times when travel and communication difficulties made communities much more cut off from each other, encouraging differential development. Recovery of the diversity regarding sexuality that has existed within past religious communities could be a tremendous help in allowing present communities to think creatively.

4. *Protect the weak without disempowering them.* All religious communities understand themselves as called to protect the weak. YHWH heard the distressed cries of the enslaved Hebrews and came to their aid because of their weakness and need. Moses and Muhammad both laid down divine law in which protection of the weak—the poor, widows, and orphans and strangers—is a consistent concern, and Jesus exemplified a similar concern for the weak. But sometimes the shape that protection of the weak has taken—varieties of paternalism, for example—has perpetuated weakness and vulnerability. Women have been perhaps the most obvious recipients of such protection by religions.

Whenever possible, the weak must be protected without perpetuating their weakness and rendering them permanently in need of protection. In the area of sexuality, religions have frequently understood sex as the sexual use of the weak by the powerful, sexual virtue as characterized by ignorance, and sexual knowledge as something dangerous from which the weak should be protected. But real protection of the weak in sexuality requires that religions support lifelong, age-appropriate sexual education. The elevated rate of teen suicide among gays and lesbians in the United States can be addressed by access to supportive information about sexual orientation, its varieties and development. People will not—and cannot—act in their own defense against child sexual abuse, sexual harassment, rape, domestic battery, pregnancy, or infection by sexually transmitted diseases without full and complete information, and that information must include the accumulating data not accommodated by the paradigm of sexual dimorphism.

In addition to lifelong, age-appropriate sex education, protection of the weak involves the creation of a basic social ethic, widely recognized and observed, that clearly outlines how persons are to be treated by other persons in sexual as well as other types of relationships. For example, honest disclosure is an imperative that could apply in a number of areas of life, from business to sexuality. If one is selling a car in certain states today, one is legally barred from changing the odometer reading and is required to supply full information about service work and accidents. In sexuality honest disclosure requires that persons infected with HIV or other sexually transmitted diseases disclose that information to potential sexual partners, including spouses, as well as information such as one's sexual history, one's ability or interest in having children, and one's level of interest in a committed relationship. In the last analysis, protecting the weak involves strengthening all through fuller sexual education, more facile communication about sex, and shared sexual expectations.

CONCLUSION

Polymorphous sexuality greatly increases the freedom that individuals exercise in terms of both sexual identity and sexual behavior, but that very freedom also exacts certain costs. Specifically, polymorphous sexuality means that we may be attracted to a person only to find out that the person does not have a body sexed in the way we thought, or may have a body sexed the way we thought but not the sexual identity we thought would accompany that body, or may have a body sexed the way we thought and the sexual identity we thought would accompany it but not be interested in the sexual acts that we are interested in. Polymorphous sexuality calls into question our most basic language about sexuality; it forces us to ask whether our children are either boys or girls and how we differentiate these boys and girls from each other and from other options.

Compared with sexual dimorphism, polymorphism is complex. Whereas under a sexual paradigm of dimorphism our sexual expectations for self and others were based on narrow dualisms that included character stereotypes, a paradigm of polymorphous sexuality gives us much less guidance in constructing/ analyzing/envisioning our own sexual identity, much less help in discovering/ understanding/naming objects of our sexual desire. We have yet to see how humans will adapt to the challenges of finding their way in a sexually polymorphous world, though one could predict that there will be social and even evolutionary advantage in becoming as open and flexible as possible in one's sexual preferences. It is difficult to avoid the conclusion that the multiplication in sexual possibilities in the shift from dimorphous to polymorphous sexuality, combined with decreased conceptual clarity about sexuality, will continue to encourage a greater reliance on experience and experimentation. For example, open polymorphous sexuality makes us question whether perhaps human sexual identity is a never settled question, task, and option. Is the future to be filled with parents and grandparents, as well as children and young adults, who change their genitalia, their sexual roles, or their sexual orientation as frequently as people today change their clothing or hair color? Regardless of how much religious communities are troubled by such a turn, if they are to have a chance at preventing it, they must offer an alternative means for interpreting and coping with the complexities of polymorphous sexuality and not merely close their eyes to the reality of the shift from dimorphism to polymorphism.

NOTES

1. Donna J. Haraway, *Modest_Witness@Second_Millennium. FemaleManc_Meets_ OncoMouse™: Feminism Meets Technoscience* (New York: Routledge, 1997), chapters 1 and 4.

2. Marxism, the historical rival to the theory of capitalism, essentially shared the view of capitalism that raw nature was without value until transformed, but it attributed the new value to the human labor invested in the transformation process.

3. Donna J. Haraway, *Modest_Witness@Second_Millennium*, chapter 2.

4. Sylvia Marcos, ed., "Embodied Religious Thought: Gender Categories in Mesoamerica," in *Gender/Bodies/Religions*, 93–114 (Cuernavaca, Mexico: ALER Publications, 2000), p. 95.

5. In the *Rig Veda* for example, see 1.179, "Sex and the Yogin," and 10.159, "A Clever Woman," both of which deal with women who have triumphed, one over a scholar husband whom she seduces from his meditation, and the other over both rival wives and her husband, who now obeys her. Both the gods and the humans in the *Rig Veda* have male or female identity and are further designated as husbands and wives, sons or daughters (James Fieser and John Powers, eds., *Scriptures of the World's Religions* [Boston: McGraw-Hill, 1998], p. 14).

6. In Genesis, the first book of the Torah, God is said to have created humans: "So God created humankind in his image, in the image of God he created them; male and female he created them" (1:27). From that point on the text treats all humans as either male or female and establishes legal and moral status based on gender.

7. In the classics of Confucianism, the three basic concepts are relationship, hierarchy, and harmony, all of which were interrelated. For Confucius, the essential building blocks of reality are nonbeing and ultimate being, and from these came yin and yang, respectively the female and male principles. It is the interaction of these two principles that brings about all else, including human beings. The family is a relationship of male and female persons, hierarchically ordered toward harmony and serving as a model for all of society. See the selection on the family from the *I Ching* (Serenity Young, ed., *An Anthology of Sacred Texts by and about Women* [New York: Crossroad, 1993], pp. 346–47) or the selections from the *Book of Songs* (Ibid., 347–49) on a bride serving her husband's ancestors, a dynasty that begins with a woman, and how differently a girl is to be raised from a boy in the same house. Selections from the *Book of Rites* put dimorphic sexuality at center stage, dealing with how men and women should deal with each other and how boy children and girl children should be educated (Ibid., 350–53).

8. In the Taoist *Biographies of Spirit Immortals*, the adepts are clearly distinguished

as either males or females. And in "Chuang Tzu," chapter 3, there are husbands and wives, mothers and fathers, men and women, boys and girls (William T. De Bary, *Sources of Chinese Tradition*, vol. 1 [New York: Columbia University Press, 1949], pp. 73–75). One of the more famous sections (chapter 18) tells of Chuang Tzu's mourning for his wife and why he stopped (Young, *Anthology of Sacred Texts*, p. 381).

9. The Pali Canon is full of references to humanity as two sexed. For example, in the *Digha-nikaya* 1.4–10, the asceticism of the Buddha is detailed in a long list of descriptives, including "He abstains from accepting women or girls, male or female slaves, sheep or goats, birds or pigs, elephants or cows, horses or mares, fields or property" (Fieser and Powers, *Scriptures of the World's Religions*, pp. 85–86). Division of humans into two sexes is assumed, and as a number of texts make clear, in the organization of the Buddhist community, the sangha, this division became important, though it certainly has no ultimate importance in Buddhism. The *Vinaya-pitaka II* tells of the intercession of Ananda for Mahapajapati, aunt and foster mother of the Buddha, who wanted to be ordained a nun in the sangha, and the special conditions under which Buddha agreed that she and other women could be ordained (Edward Conze, J. B. Horner, David Snellgrove, and Arthur Waley, eds., *Buddhist Texts through the Ages* [New York: Harper Torchbooks, 1991], pp. 23–26).

10. In the Gospels humans are repeatedly designated both by the narration and by Jesus himself as men or women, husbands or wives; in many of the epistles separate roles and codes of conduct are sometimes described for men and women, for example, 1 Cor. 11 on husbands as the heads of wives—men are to pray without head coverings, and women, with head coverings. Furthermore, like the Hebrew Scriptures, the New Testament strongly discourages any blurring of heterocentric sexual dimorphism, as in Romans 1.

11. In the Quran, sura 4 is largely devoted to the topic of women and lays out the Quranic distinctions between men and women in terms of marriage law, inheritance, divorce, child custody, the education of male and female children, the rules regarding concubinage, adultery, and incest. Like Judaism and early Christianity, Islam has displayed a relatively strong and uncompromising sexual dimorphism.

12. The only Islamic references to Allah as feminine are, so far as I know, found in Sufi (mystical) writings not in *shari'a* texts. There are, however, a few indirect scriptural references to the god of the Hebrew Scriptures and New Testament as feminine (Elizabeth A. Johnson, *She Who Is: The Mystery of God in Feminist Theological Discourse* [New York: Crossroad, 1993], ch. 5). In Christianity, as in Islam, it has been the mystics who have been most likely to experience God as feminine. Scholars speculate that this was not true for Israel because during its formative period Israel saw itself surrounded by and tempted to fertility rituals associated with female divine figures; thus, the maleness of Israel's god became a primary symbol of the religion's integrity.

13. See Elaine Pagels, *The Gnostic Gospels* (New York: Random House, 1981) and Elisabeth Schüssler Fiorenza, *In Memory of Her: A Feminist Theological Reconstruction of Christian Origins* (New York: Crossroad, 1984).

14. Karen Armstrong, *Muhammad: A Biography of the Prophet* (San Francisco: HarperCollins, 1992), pp. 190–91.

15. Vernon Reynolds and Ralph Tanner, *The Social Ecology of Religion* (New York: Oxford University Press, 1995), pp. 91–92.

16. Gilbert Herdt, *Same Sex, Different Cultures* (Boulder: Westview Press, 1997), p. 106.

17. Vladimir Basilov, "Chosen by the Spirits," in *Shamanic Worlds*, 3–48, Ed. by M. M. Balzer (London: North Castle Press, 1997), p. 38.

18. Gilbert Herdt, *Same Sex, Different Cultures,* pp. 107–108.

19. *Ibid.*, 90–98.

20. See Will Roscoe, *The Zuni Man-Woman* (Albuquerque: University of New Mexico Press, 1991).

21. Gilbert Herdt prefers to see these small numbers of persons as constituting a third gender; this fits the postmodern paradigm of multiplicity in distinction to the dichotomy common to modernity. Yet his explanations in terms of specific peoples fit equally well the dimorphic pattern. For example, he cites the Inuit, who understand persons as having been members of the other (dimorphic) sex in past lives and understand ritually inducted shamans as exceptions to dimorphism, being neither fully male nor fully female but a combination of both. Thus, the Inuit fit the dimorphic pattern with perhaps a greater range of exceptions (Gilbert Herdt, *Same Sex, Different Cultures*, pp. 10–11).

22. Gilbert Herdt, *Same Sex, Different Cultures*, p. 48.

23. See Thomas Kuhn, *The Structure of Scientific Revolutions* (Chicago: University of Chicago Press, 1962).

24. Chromosomal definitions of maleness and femaleness constituted one new sexual paradigm when they were proposed. Kinsey's spectrum of sexual orientation, which separates sex from sexual orientation, represented another paradigm shift. More recently feminist theorists and others have examined individual identity formation as a socially constructed process in which conventional concepts largely understood as dichotomous (sex, race/ethnicity, and class, among others) interact. Judith Butler (*Gender Trouble: Feminism and the Subversion of Identity* [New York: Routledge, 1990]) has provoked other theorists to reexamine identity formation—including what it could mean to identify oneself as a woman—as an ongoing sociopsychological process. Identity, which Butler says is performatively constituted ("Contingent Foundations," in *Feminist Connections* by Seyla Benhabib, Judith Butler, Drucilla Cornell, and Nancy Fraser [New York: Routledge, 1995]), is never complete but, rather, always in formation and thus open to significant transformation and redefinition. These discussions (Seyla Benhabib, *Situating the Self: Gender Community and Postmodernism in Contemporary Ethics* [New York: Routledge, 1992]; Benhabib et al, *Feminist Connections*; Young, *Anthology of Sacred Texts*) followed a period of frequent attacks from African American, postcolonialist, and Third World feminists regarding the failure of middle-class, white, Anglo feminists to separate other binary categories (race/ethnicity, class, nationality) from sex in their analysis of male/female relations. The various but related proposals for a new identity paradigm that have developed share a tendency to reject dimorphism in favor of polymorphism at many different levels of identity formation.

25. Ziba Mir-Hosseini, "Stretching the Limits: A Feminist Reading of the Shari'a in Post-Khomeini Iran" In *Feminism and Islam*, 285–320, Ed. by Mai Yamani (New York: New York University Press, 1996), p. 292.

26. Kathy Rudy, *Sex and the Church* (Boston: Beacon Press, 1997), ch. 5.

27. Alice Rossi, *The Feminist Papers* (New York: Bantam, 1973), pp. 323–56, 378–95.

28. See Margaret Mead, *Coming of Age in Samoa* (New York: Morrow, 1961); *Sex and Temperament in Three Primitive Societies* (New York: Morrow, 1963); and *Anthropologists and What They Do* (New York: F. Watts, 1965).

29. See Ruth Benedict, *Patterns of Culture*. 2d ed. (Boston: Houghton Mifflin, 1948) and *The Chrysanthemum and the Sword: Patterns of Japanese Culture* (Rutland, VT: C. E. Tuttle, 1954).

30. Lewis Henry Morgan, *Ancient Society, or Researches in the Lines of Human Progress from Savagery to Barbarism to Civilization* (New York: Macmillan, 1877).

31. Frederick Engels, *The Origin of the Family, Private Property, and the State* (New York: International New World Publishers, 1972 [1884]), pp. 110–22.

32. *Ibid.*

33. See Alfred Kinsey, W. Pomerey, and C. Martin, *Sexual Behavior in the Human Male* (St. Louis: Saunders, 1948).

34. In an act-centered approach to sexual ethics the focus is on the structure of the particular act viewed in isolation from personality, relationships, moral habits, and circumstances. Persons are assumed to be heterosexual, but some, overcome by temptation to perverse evil, decide to choose a homosexual act in a given moment.

35. Evelyn Hooker's groundbreaking research has demonstrated that experts could not discern the psychological tests, personal histories, or psychological evaluations of homosexuals from those of heterosexuals, thus challenging the designation of homosexuality as a psychopathology.

36. William H. Masters, Virginia E. Johnson, and Robert C. Kolodny, *Human Sexuality.* 4th ed. (San Francisco: HarperCollins, 1992), pp. 184–85.

37. Janell Carroll and Paul Root Wolpe, *Sexuality and Gender in Society* (San Francisco: HarperCollins, 1996), p. 76.

38. The most common occurrence of external exposure was in the female fetuses of pregnant women prone to miscarriage who were given an androgen-based drug to inhibit miscarriage during the 1960s. Some of these female fetuses were found to have ambiguous genitalia; many were found to have masculinized behavior as children—they preferred rougher outdoor play and boys' toys to girls' toys, had higher energy levels and less ability to sit still, and were less interested in motherhood and more interested in male occupations when asked about their futures. Moreover, virtually all these girls' families had been unaware that the medication contained androgen (John Money and Anke Earhardt, *Man and Woman, Boy and Girl* [Baltimore: Johns Hopkins University Press, 1972]).

39. Robert Crooks and Karla Baur, *Our Sexuality.* 6th ed. (Pacific Grove, CA: Brooks-Cole, 1996), pp. 43–48.

40. Gilbert Herdt, *Same Sex, Different Cultures,* p. 89.

41. *Ibid.,* 90.

42. *Ibid.,* 104.

43. In much of the world this debate is further complicated by secular postcolonialist charges that cultural imperialism by the West imposed western models of sex, including rigid sexual dimorphism and sexism, on other peoples; religious postcolonialists often charge that it is sexual dimorphism that is truly native to particular peoples and that the degenerate polymorphous forms are western impositions. For an excellent treatment of the complexities of this argument, see Lila Abu-Lughod, *Remaking Women: Feminism and Modernity in the Middle East* (Princeton: Princeton University Press, 1998).

44. David Teather, "A Question of Gender: Calvin Klein Started It All with His New Fragrance CK One" in *Marketing,* 30 November 1995, p. 30.

45. See Claudia Goldin and Lawrence Katz,"The Power of the Pill: Oral Contraceptives and Women's Career and Marriage Decisions," National Bureau of Economic Research Working Paper #7517, 2000. Available at http://www.nber.org/papers/w7527.

46. See Karen Lebacqz, "Difference or Defect? Intersexuality and the Politics of Difference" in *The Annual of the Society of Christian Ethics* 17 (1997): 213–229.

47. Judith Plaskow, "The Wife/Sister Stories: Dilemmas of a Jewish Feminist" in *Speaking of Faith*, 119–31, ed. by Diana Eck and Devaki Jain (Philadelphia: New Society Press, 1987), pp. 125–26.

48. The original document is the "Declaration on the Question of the Admission of Women to the Ministerial Priesthood" by the Congregation for the Doctrine of the Faith in 1976 (Leonard Swindler and Arlene Swindler, *Women Priests* [New York: Crossroad, 1977]). On 30 May 1994 John Paul II issued an apostolic letter, "Ordinario

sacerdotalis," which recaps the arguments of the 1976 document and, in order to stop the ongoing debate, declares that the Church has no power to ordain women. In November 1995 the Congregation for the Doctrine of the Faith added in its "Response to Dubium" that the teaching of John Paul II that the Church has no power to ordain women is to be understood as part of the deposit of faith binding on all Catholics and is therefore not open to debate.

49. Following the Iranian revolution, women were excluded from a great many areas of education at the university, including (shari'a) law. But through the organization of Iranian Muslim feminists in the last few decades, almost all of these areas of study have been reopened to women. Though women are still barred from being judges in Iran, they have been added as formal advisers to judges and are considered essential to the legal process in many areas of (family) law.

50. See Lila Abu-Lughod, *Remaking Women: Feminism and Modernity in the Middle East* (Princeton: Princeton University Press, 1998) and Mai Yamani, ed., *Feminism and Islam: Legal and Literary Perspectives* (New York: New York University Press, 1996).

51. It is interesting, however, to examine the origins and purposes of many of these female education projects. Khaled Fahmy, for example, writes of the early-nineteenth-century origins of the School for Midwives in the medical school in Cairo. Policies of Pasha Mehmed Ali of Egypt had created an epidemic of syphilis and exacerbated the spread of smallpox by his massive enlargement of the Egyptian army through conscription, the subsequent packing of large numbers of recruits into training schools and barracks, and the movement of that army from one locale to another. Male doctors could, within Islam, deal with the soldiers themselves but not with either the female relatives of the soldiers or with the many thousands of commercial sex workers the enlargement of the army occasioned. Once the corps of women doctors were trained, they were used not only to combat the epidemics but as police agents of the pasha—for example, in ensuring that midwives reported all births to the government so that conscription would not miss unreported births as in the previous period. The pasha's other purpose in founding the School for Midwives was to prove to European visitors that he was enlightened and civilized, able to bring modernity and science to Egypt—and should be supported in his bid to obtain from the Ottomans hereditary rights to rule in Egypt. It would be difficult to demonstrate that this or many similar education projects for women were primarily aimed at improving the lives of women (Khaled Fahmy, "Women, Medicine and Power in Nineteenth Century Egypt," in R*emaking Women: Feminism and Modernity in the Middle East*, ed. Lila Abu-Lughod [Princeton: Princeton University Press, 1998]).

11

Pain and Pleasure: Avoiding the Confusions of Christian Tradition in Feminist Theory

BEVERLY WILDUNG HARRISON AND CARTER HEYWARD

As political repression accelerates in the United States, feminists must sharpen their critiques of the cultural, social, religious, and economic roots of women's oppression. It is imperative, moreover, that in this reactionary climate feminist theorists admit the complexity of the reconstructive perspectives they are attempting to forge. Theories that oversimplify the constructive feminist agenda or challenge the troubling dualisms of patriarchal culture in an overly reactive way merely feed the divisiveness among women that political repression seeks to sow.

Contemporary feminist politics and theory, liberal and radical, converge in the face of pervasive violence against women and mounting efforts to foreclose the already limited options that women have regarding reproductive choice and health care. But in discussions about pornography, or about what constitutes an optimal conception of women's eroticism, consensus among feminists gives way to acrimony, and our politics tend to become a battleground of conflicting normative theories and strategies.[1] In matters of sex, more than in any other political arena, feminists are inclined simply to superimpose their individual preferences or senses of morality upon others. In this way, the feminist insistence that "the personal is political" (and, conversely, that the political always yields personal, concrete meaning) ironically receives skewed, negative confirmation rather than constructive expression. That the personal is political is a social fact, and our personal preferences and sensibilities always are steeped in a more complex social dialectic. These personal preferences acquire moral meaning in relation to the well-being of a larger social-cultural order. As it is, among contemporary feminists, wherever eros, sex, and sexuality are envisioned differently, conflicting personal agendas jockey competitively to become the "right" answer to the public question of which strategies and policies actually contribute to the liberation of women.

While we agree with Mariana Valverde that "the debate on sexuality has not been one of the success stories of the women's movement,"[2] we also acknowledge the oft-repeated claim that, from a historical point of view, the greatest breakthrough of contemporary feminist theory is precisely this securing of the cultural and intellectual space to forge a genuine female "discourse on sexuality."[3] Conflict over sexuality should not obscure this gain. The burgeoning feminist literature on sexuality, including discussions of pornography and sadomasochistic practice among women, has brought sex out of the closet into the realm of public discourse and has sharpened reflection among feminists on their values. On all sides of these contemporary debates, feminists agree that relational dynamics of domination and submission, images and acts that ritualize violence, make widespread contributions to the sexual pleasure of men—and women—in our society.[4] In other words, it is beyond dispute that many women find sexual pleasure in patterns of erotic domination and submission, whether these images lurk largely in the realm of women's sexual fantasies or are acted out in women's sex lives.

We are grateful for the work of the many secular feminists who have been unwilling to let specific questions of eros and sex go unexplored, a failing, as we see it, of many religious feminists. This essay is an attempt by two religious feminists to integrate and expand insights from this discussion of women's eroticism and genital pleasure. We share with many secular feminists a conviction that feminist theory must incorporate a profound positive evaluation of the vitality of the erotic in women's lives. We understand eros to be body-centered energy channeled through longing and desire. With Audre Lorde we affirm eroticism as essential to our well-being and believe it to be the source of creative personal power and, as such, essential to creativity.[5] In our work, we have attempted to show how eros also is central to an adequate feminist theory not only of politics but of religious and moral experience.[6] We also share the suspicion, now widely voiced in feminist literature, that resistance to pervasive pornographic manipulation is tempting some feminists to embrace a subtle prudery or a new antisexual moralism.[7] That women now must seek sexual fulfillment in a context where "pleasure and danger"[8] are intertwined seems to us obvious. The threat of violence and the objectification of women's bodies create genuine barriers to women's realization of the erotic, but the way forward is not to adopt prematurely a feminist theory of women's sexuality that portrays women's sexual needs simplistically, as if our desires were homogeneous or untouched by the disordered power dynamics of patriarchal eroticism.

Feminist theorists whose insights contribute most to the emerging discourse on sexuality are those who have been most attentive to the sociohistorical shifts in patterns of eroticism, recognizing that forms of sexual expression and erotic desire, while rooted in physio-psychic potential, are shaped by complex cultural dynamics—recognizing, that is, that sexuality and eroticism have a history. This history of sexuality is embedded in social structures of patterned power relations such as institutionalized heterosexism, racism, and cultural imperialism.[9]

To explore how senses of personal power and eroticism have been linked historically in heterosexist patriarchy is to begin also to see that the self-other relation which elicits strong erotic desire frequently is one of domination and submission. As such, sex is often experienced as a dynamic of conquest and surrender rather than as power in mutual relation.[10]

In such "eroticization of domination," sexual desire is linked with either self-oblivion or self-assertion. It would be ahistorical and naive to imagine that anyone's eroticism in this culture could be untouched by this dynamic.[11] Feminists such as Valverde and Linda Gordon insist that the "eroticization of equality" must be understood as a historical project of feminism. They acknowledge, however, that this project is necessarily long term,[12] so securely fastened in our society, and our psyches, is the felt need for a sexual mediation of relational power to confirm our superiority or subjection in relation to others, whether for a moment or a lifetime.

To probe the linkage of erotic desire and inequality so characteristic of patriarchal culture we need to focus on the subtle connection between relational dynamics of domination and submission and erotic experiences of pain and pleasure. We realize that this connection—between experiences of relational power or powerlessness and of sexual pleasure enhanced by pain—might be approached critically from a number of directions (e.g., natural or social science; art, literature, or film; comparative studies of religion or culture), as well as with different focuses (e.g., gender relations, sexual customs, ascetic traditions). As feminist ethicists and theologians who are Christian, we approach this issue with a critical interest in the role of Christianity in developing and sustaining a social (not only sexual) relation—a sadomasochistic relation—in which pleasure is available chiefly through pain. We are committed, moreover, to participation in the reconstruction of theological and moral theory which is both socially responsible, contributing to the creation of justice for all, and deeply affirmative of erotic pleasure as a source of moral good.

We will now examine some Christian theological roots of the equation of pain with pleasure and also suggest ways in which the legacy of liberal individualism, the dominant ideological underpinning of Western society, tempts feminists to reformulate the dilemmas of female eroticism in a way that perpetuates rather than challenges this theologically legitimated confusion. We shall conclude with images showing how erotic relationships might contribute to fully socialized, self- and other-empowering relations.

PAIN AS PLEASURE:
CHRISTIAN FOUNDATIONS

Christian orthodoxy (culminating for the Western church in Augustine) eschewed the notion of a radical dualism in which Creator and Creation exist in a posture of unmitigated opposition. Orthodox Christian dualism, by comparison to more radically dualistic religious systems eventually deemed heretical, has been more experientially complex, more dialectical in the relation between cosmologically "higher" and "lower" realities.[13]

Still, the primary architect of the identification of pain with pleasure in Western culture has been the Christian church with its basically dualistic anthropology. On the basis of Neoplatonic cosmology, early church fathers explained their religious experience as essentially that of breaking tension between such oppositional realities as spirit and flesh, male and female, light and dark, good and evil.[14] The role of religion in general, Christian religion in particular, was thus to mitigate the opposition by enabling the two forces to "co-operate" rather than to compete for the headship of society as well as the human soul. Such opposites as spirit and flesh, male and female, could be cooperative only insofar as the higher was in control of the lower—and as the lower accepted its place as a weaker reality, both naturally and morally subordinate in relation to the higher. Whether by will or force, the resolution of tension between potentially competitive cosmic forces was to become a test of Christian faith: a faithful Christian woman, for example, would accept her role gladly as man's helper and a faithful Christian man would accept his role cheerfully as head of the household. Patristic theological discourse bears written testimony to social relations of domination and subjugation in which "the fathers" of the family (both civil and ecclesial households)[15] believed that they should be in charge of women, children, slaves, and all other creatures—and in control, moreover, of their own "lower" selves: flesh, body, passions, and eroticism.

Because in this system good Christian men—and through men's authority, women as well—must deny the enjoyment of flesh, females, darkness, evil, and the sensuality associated with these negativities, early Christian anthropology required that pain—the deprivation of sensual pleasure—be accepted as an important element in attaining the joy of salvation. We cannot trace here the long process by which this dualistic asceticism in which the exercise of faith involved attempts to transcend the sensual pleasures of human being—hunger for food, warmth, and touch—became in time not only acceptable as a dimension of Christian spirituality, but moreover normative for it: to be Christian was to accept or even to seek pain.

This establishment of antisensual pain as a foundation of Christian faith is a complex story informed by diverse historical processes. For example, the extended sociopolitical repression, torture, and martyrdom that some Christians endured and that threatened others in the Roman Empire in the middle of the third and during the early fourth centuries contributed to the spiritualizing of deprivation and suffering. But it is one thing to accept suffering for the sake of a moral or religious good when confronting unjust power, and another to perceive suffering as itself an intrinsic moral or religious value, the point to which much institutional Christianity came after the collapse of the Roman Imperium.

The earlier anti-material, anti-body, anti-woman dualisms of Neoplatonic patriarchal Christianity laid the groundwork for this romanticization of suffering but the full flowering of masochism in the Christian ethic can be best measured by the increase, over time, of a sex-phobic and sex-preoccupied focus within the Christian ethic.[16] Historian Samuel Laeuchli has traced one strand of the story of this move from a Christian spiritual discipline focused at least in part on resistance to the Roman state to one morbidly preoccupied with the control of human sexuality.[17] Laeuchli acknowledges that this development had deep roots in early dualistic patristic theory about spirit and flesh and in the developing church's transparent fear of women.[18] Not insignificantly for feminist theory, Laeuchli also connects this impulse to sexual control and the rapid development of centralized ecclesiastical hierarchy within Western Christianity. We can only speculate as to how such dynamics of pain and pleasure took hold of Christian experience such that the suffering associated with sensual self-denial became essential to Christian spiritual and moral life, and thereby a source of spiritual satisfaction. Without pain, pleasure was immoral; whereas by pain, with pain, and through pain, pleasure became a happy consequence of the Christian pilgrimage.

This spiritual paradigm of Christian pain as virtue and as pleasure was also developed theologically: The Christian drama of salvation has been staged historically as a transaction between an almighty God and a powerless humanity. As the lower relational entity, humanity has been cast as a "fallen" partner, able to be "saved" or "redeemed" into right relation only insofar as human beings know ourselves to be unworthy of anything but punishment from God. Into our unworthy lives comes Jesus, the Christ, to bear our sins and to submit, on our behalf, to the Father God's Will. Thus, standing in for us (as only the elder obedient Son is worthy to do in this patriarchal schema), Jesus is humiliated and killed, becoming thereby a perfect sacrifice to the Father. As the classical portrait of the punitive character of this divine-human transaction, Anselm of Canterbury's doctrine of the atonement (1093–1109) probably represents the sadomasochism of Christian teaching at its most transparent.

But there is a subtler sadomasochistic hue to Christianity, an effect also of the litany of dualistic oppositions such as those between earth and heaven, flesh and spirit, and present and future. The patriarchal Christian story is basically one of a fierce war between good and evil forces in the cosmos, from the farthest outreaches of the universe to the individual's soul. In this praxis of opposition, Christians have believed that, in fact, God—the supreme force for good— already has won the war. This faith has reflected the Christian experience on two different levels of meaning in their lives: God's victory is on a spiritual level whereas the numerous incessant battles which constitute the war are material as well. Christians have believed that the spiritual power of the resurrection has overcome human history and thus the pain of the cross, so real in "this world," has been vanquished by the power of God in the "other world" above or beyond us. We may catch glimpses even now of the spiritual world through faith that embodied life as we know it is not all there is.

But for most people on the earth embodied pain is much of all there is—the pain of poverty, oppression, alienation, loss and, from a liberation perspective, the pain incurred in struggling against injustice and oppression. In Christian theology, eternal joy may have the upper hand and the spiritual victory, but daily pain and sorrow play the more visceral, sensual roles in shaping the lives of most women, men, and children on earth. This split sensibility between what is experienced and what is yearned for provides, for many Christians, a foundation for their faith. This faith in turn functions as a state of mind, a cosmology, and as a way of interpreting daily events and historical movement.

In this dualistic praxis that is not peculiar to Christianity, yet which takes a distinctive shape in Christian theology, pain in the present and hope for the future together form a bridge between earth and heaven, human and divine life, estrangement and unity, conflict and resolution. Pain and hope thereby constitute the link for most Christians between such immediate sensual experiences as hunger and loneliness and such "delayed gratification" as food and intimacy. This tension, existential and political, personal and historical, provides an eschatological backdrop against which sadomasochism is acted out as the most typically "Christian" of all social relations: We learn to experience the deprivation of pleasure—the pain of being hurt, hungry, or rejected; of feeling weak, stupid, bad in the immediate present—as a moment filled with intense anticipation of pleasure that is yet to come. In short, Christians learn theologically to equate the anticipation of pleasure with pleasure itself. This disembodied sensibility, in which pleasure is fundamentally a state of mind, is steeped in the eschatological promise that the realm of the divine—a spiritual arena of unity, joy and ecstasy—is, for Christians, here but not quite here; now but not quite yet.

The covert popularity among Christians of pain-filled sexual (and other social) relations can be explained in part by this politic of pain and hope that is so basic to classical Christian practice and theory and that is as forceful and erotic a politic in the lives of women as of men. This difficult social relation is rooted most deeply, we submit, in the pain of alienation generated historically by political and religious structures of domination and control. Such structures as male gender superiority and white racial supremacy have shaped to an extent the relational dynamics and erotic feelings of all members of all institutions and societies that are themselves established on these foundations of domination and control. Thus do all Christians, as well as many others, bear scars of sadomasochistic relations.

Beyond a common experience as dreamers of an eschatological relief and pleasure, Christian men and women have a very different political and sexual history, a point that, thanks to feminist religious scholarship, is finally widely acknowledged today.[19] The differences between them are nowhere more apparent than in the ways in which Christian sadomasochism is actually embodied by the sons of the Father, on the one hand, and his daughters on the other.

Consider the sons: Unless reconstructed along the lines of a feminist liberation hermeneutic, or of a radical womanism, Christianity—even in its most liberal dress—remains quintessentially a religion about men controlling men's bodies, men's women, men's children, and men's other property. This fundamental male-male relation is imaged as that between father and son. The father is willful and benevolent, loving and just, one who desires—but does not always receive—obedience from his sons, in which case the sons can be punished justly. (Apologists for the sexism of Christianity are apt to insist that the "sons" include the "daughters." To the extent that the daughters fall for such patriarchal "inclusion," we can read ourselves into this drama of disobedience and discipline.)

The explicit sadomasochistic dynamics of classical Christianity do not often receive voice in "modern" Christian theologies. Even so, they live on in the sexual fantasies of many Christian men and are frequently expressed in closeted homosexual eroticism so much denied and so widely practiced among Christian males. This is especially true among those men drawn to traditional Catholic liturgical spirituality—perhaps because this spirituality offers such dramatic opportunity to dress up, role play, and act out a very sensual relation between men. In a much more literal way than at the altar, the "meat-rack" is often the arena for enacting the justice of the father who must whip his sons, humiliate them, and require them to beg for his mercy. The sons' pain is merely in proportion to what they deserve for the sin of their disobedience which, in the dualistic praxis we have described above, includes their experiences of sexual passion. The sadistic father will feel pleasure in disciplining his sons "for their own good." Masochistic sons will enjoy the discipline because it will set them into right relation with their father, whose love they seek.

But did not Jesus suffer and die in their stead? Why is there this violence between father and son if the ransom for the wages of sin has been exacted already? Perhaps it is the guilt of the younger sons in relation to the innocent Jesus? Or their catholic desire for participation? Or simply their need for hands-on experience? Most of these sons believe that with Jesus they too must be beaten and broken in order to satisfy their almighty father. Becoming Christ-like—good sons, submissive to the father's will—is accomplished repeatedly and ritualistically through a pain which the sons experience as the love of God and as such a source of deep satisfaction and pleasure. In this erotic fantasy, the father is turned on by his absolute power over another.

A theology of scourged buttocks and torn anuses, and the accompanying violence, can nevertheless be understood as a yearning, a reaction, of Christian men against the dualistic character of the divine-human relation in which no son except Jesus has immediate access to the Father; nor for that matter does the Father have intimate relations with his human sons. The sadomasochistic sexual relation between Christian "fathers" and "sons" might be comprehended as a father-son transaction in which is expressed their mutual desire for immediate and intimate relation.[20]

To be sure, not all Christian men are driven to enact this sadomasochistic imaging of divine-human relations. But we believe that Christianity has intensely eroticized male-male transactions of subordination and dominance, obedience and defiance. In the face of this we interpret much male fear of sexuality as a defense against these desires and interpret the lure of celibacy within Christianity as a fragile defense against them.

Since the Protestant Reformation, which reestablished "compulsory heterosexuality," male sexual transactions with women have frequently been interpreted as "duty"—a "burden" to be assumed by spiritual and intellectual superiors toward inferiors. We perceive the continuing split in male eroticism, in which sex and intimacy are rarely associated, as historically conditioned by these dynamics of gender inequality. Men who are "turned on" to women are rarely turned on by strong, self-reliant women or women who make demands for full integrated relationship. The objectification of women as "sex objects" is sustained primarily by the split in men's lives—between sex and intimacy, friendship and eroticism, man and man, and man's sense of "spirit" and his own body. "Woman" has become historically a convenient scapegoat for men's lack of sexual and spiritual integration.[21]

Consider now the daughters of God. However harshly men may be dealt with by God in the sadomasochistic imagination, the raison d'être behind the discipline they receive is to make them worthy to share in the father's inheritance, his power and dominion over his kingdom. Patriarchal daughters by contrast are not heirs at all but rather are their brothers' helpers on the way toward men's appropriation of the power of God. As the sons are redeemed by their obedience to God, so too are the daughters redeemed by their obedience to the sons.

Patriarchal heterosexism is founded less upon deep male heterosexual desire than upon men's use of women's bodies as a means of public social control. In this situation, women have no body rights, no moral claim to our bodies as self-possessed. In Christianity, woman is equated with flesh, body, but Christian women have no integrity of embodied selfhood; no authoritative voice in determining where we put our bodies/ourselves, with whom we share our bodies/ourselves, where we put our embodied energies, time, and talents. Women in Christianity are meant to live for others. The inability of so many women even to imagine that they should be well-treated in a relationship with a man or that they deserve physical and emotional pleasure is conditioned by the demand that we have our being for others.

Women's bodies, sensual and hungry, are on the one hand needy impediments to the sacrifices expected of us. On the other hand, our bodies are all we have, all we are, and as such are our best and only hope. If Christian women are to be liberated, it will be through the aegis of our sensual, hungry, needy bodyselves, which we learn are dangerous, dirty, and bad—and, at the same time, the source of our power. Such body alienation is then reinforced by the pervasive threat of rape, sexual harassment, and other widespread forms of bodily exploitation. Thus do we learn to live in radical ambivalence toward our bodies/ourselves. The very womanly flesh we learn to despise is the source of our redemption—from material and spiritual bondage, from self-loathing and from our contempt for women in general. As feminists attempt to show, the possibility of women's liberation is seeded in women's self-respect, a revolutionary act because it embodies a challenge to fundamental assumptions about womanhood which have been espoused both by the church and by Western societies for two millennia.

While feminists speak often with passion and good reason about women's self-respect, being woman-identified, taking women seriously, we should not underestimate the force—and devastating effects—of misogyny in patriarchal heterosexist Christianity and in those cultures shaped largely by it. It is far easier to embrace feminist ideology in our public work than to live radically in a strong love for our bodies/ourselves, or with love and advocacy for our sisters.

While we acknowledge the sexual sadomasochism acted out among Christian women as well as men, we believe that sexual sadomasochism is, as we have suggested, a sexual politic of male-male relations—even when the participants include females. All women in patriarchy are, to a degree, male-identified. To that extent, we are likely to enjoy sadomasochistic relations, sexual and other.[22] The shape of sadomasochism among women, however, is probably less genitally sexual than among men. More often, female sadomasochism is more generally sensual, more a matter of women's body-integrity.[23] For this reason a more clearly female embodiment of sadomasochism originates not in our desire to control others but in an ambivalence toward our bodies. This is reflected in bodily obsessions such as fear of aging, fixation on cosmetic beauty, and eating disorders which have grown to epidemic proportions in our time and culture.[24]

Eating disorders provide an especially poignant illustration of sadomasochism among women because they embody, literally and vividly, the confusion of pain and pleasure. Whether an eating disorder takes the form of anorexia nervosa (self-starvation), bulimia (gorging oneself with food and then purging oneself of it), or compulsive overeating, its source is pain—social, political, and emotional pain—and its consequences are a short-lived pleasure which becomes pain and which continues the cycle of self-destructive behavior. The eating disorder signals a woman's resistance to the role imposed upon her body/herself by her religion or culture.[25] It represents, moreover, a woman's ambivalence toward her body/herself. An anorexic woman, for example, wants to be thin since thinness is a virtue, and a pleasure, in men's eyes (and, thereby, her own). She is willing to starve herself, literally to death if need be, to become thin enough to enjoy herself. Another woman, who is bulimic, takes pleasure in eating—and wants to be thin. She experiences tension between pleasing herself with food and pleasing men (and, thereby, herself) with a trim figure. This tension generates a pattern of compulsive eating finally more painful than pleasurable, to be followed by compulsive elimination of the food. For the bulimic the pleasure of eating has become painful, and the pain of induced vomiting becomes a relief and a pleasure. Rather than make public challenge to institutions that teach misogyny, or embody this protest in her work and relationships (perhaps more common today), the woman internalizes the misogyny and punishes herself for daring to dream of her own liberation. From a psychoanalytic perspective, the daughter has internalized the father and, as such, acts sadistically toward herself—and toward her mother. The heart of the problem, the woman's masochism, far from being "natural," is the psychosocial result of the patriarchal aim to help women accept, even enjoy, our powerlessness in relation to men and the pain we necessarily will incur if we attempt to alter this relation.

The dynamics of Christian heterosexist sadomasochism, sketched only in bold relief here, are no longer explicitly emphasized in the theologies of liberal Christianity, that is, in those Christian communities that do not contend against the modern scientific world view. Here Christian asceticism has given way to a qualified embrace of the value of the created world. The blatant antisensuality bias of the highest forms of patristic and medieval spirituality has been replaced by the more dialectical dualism characteristic of the early church. Liberal Christians affirm embodied sensuality when it is expressed in heterosexual monogamous marriage, perceiving that interpersonal intimacy and love redeem sex; they have transmitted eros to a spiritual plane.[26] Christian women, in particular, learn an erotic patterning in which eros is affirmed if and when it is expressed in "love" relations with men. The modern female disposition to "fall madly in love," to be "swept away" in order to justify sexual desire, surely has its roots in this liberal shift.[27]

In our view, the Christian theological liberal response to the need for a more adequate theory of eros is unsatisfactory. Some theological liberalism, for instance, rejects sadomasochistic imagery of divine mediation by qualifying or repudiating the Anselmnian doctrine of atonement.[28] While stressing the ethical character of divine and human interaction, this theological posture nonetheless maintains a bias toward the spiritual, thereby perpetuating a subtle devaluation of both material and female existence.[29] Here the doctrine of the inferiority of women is replaced by a complementarity doctrine in which women (good women, those who express their sexuality in lifelong committed heterosexual relations) are in fact more spiritual, less carnal, than men. This teaching, which continues to tempt Christian feminism and postchristian theory to adopt a dualistic doctrine of female erotic supremacy in which women are more spiritual than men, serves to reduce the pressure for a theological reconstruction of the terms of divine-human interaction predicated by Christian patriarchal imagination. It also frequently leads Christian or formerly Christian feminist theorists to evade the full religious and ethical impact of the secular feminist struggle to place women's sexuality at the heart of a feminist liberation theory.

FEMINIST RESPONSE TO PATRIARCHAL
CHRISTIAN MASOCHISM

Even so, most postchristian and Christian liberation feminists have positioned themselves in opposition to the basic masochistic assumptions about women's spirituality generated by orthodox patriarchal Christianity. Insofar as religious feminists acknowledge embodied pleasure as fundamentally life-enhancing, we join many secular feminist theorists and, with them, affirm a post-Enlightenment,

Pain ⟶ Pleasure   pleasure ⟶ personal power

modern stance against the antisexual obsession of Christian metaphysics. In our view, a dramatic recovery of a world-affirming, sex-affirming perspective could not have occurred without the rupture that post-Enlightenment modernity created between dominant Christian ecclesiastical culture and a secular, world- and human-experience-centered way of interpreting the world. Though many interpreters have recognized that the basic cultural shift stemming from the Enlightenment led to a recovery of this-worldly interest, few have observed the fact that the shift characteristic of this transition is one in which concrete, worldly pleasure is positively embraced. In some post-Enlightenment theory it is even predicated as "the highest good."[30] One need not endorse a full-scale hedonistic psychology or the monistic value theory that it entails in order to acknowledge the critical character of this shift for human well-being.

The long struggle required to recover a respectful appreciation of the centrality of pleasure to human fulfillment and the essential role of eros and sex in human well-being would never have occurred if the political and theological control exercised by patriarchal Christianity had not been displaced. Yet we submit that it is one thing to break the ecclesiastical monopoly on the definition of the relation of spiritual pleasure and physical pain, and another to disentangle, at the level of personal erotic experience, a clear difference between what hurts and what gives pleasure. Physiologically, the line between pain and pleasure is at times a fine one. It is not surprising that human beings learn a psychological preference for an eroticism that is tinged, if not with pain, with tension that is close to pain. We suspect, however, that the widespread cultural entanglement of violence and sex reflects a blurred distinction between pain and pleasure in many people's experience, and moreover that few people experience tension-free relationships as erotic.

It is the clear intent of most feminist theorists to affirm pleasure and the importance of seeking its enhancement as a path to deeper personal power. Were the modern post-Enlightenment embrace of the erotic its only legacy, feminist reconstruction could proceed with an agenda of affirming women's eroticism without contradiction. But Enlightenment tradition, with its gradual affirmation of embodiment, nevertheless maintained a strong continuity with Christian patriarchal interpretation of the meaning of personal power in relationship. In fact, modern liberal theory, with its uncritical commitment to capitalism, exacerbated the patriarchal imaging of self-other relations as nonmutual. The individualism of the Enlightenment became, increasingly, a conception of social relations in which power-in-relation, if not antagonistic, is at least competitive such that either self or other must prevail. In this schema, personal power and personal fulfillment are envisaged as the realization of "autonomy," understood as "self-possession" or as freedom from dependency.[31]

The basic philosophical and political tenets of so-called free societies are suffused with such assumptions. Feminists too have been schooled by life as well as books in a highly individualized and possessive understanding of personal power: an ability to generate action, a capacity to effect. Our power, we see clearly, includes our feelings which can serve to catapult us into commitment or action. We must not forget that in the West (especially in the United States), our senses of personal power (including our feelings), our sexualities (how we use this power), and our eroticism (our specifically sexual feelings) always are mediated to a degree by these deities of individualism and possession. A feminist reconstruction of sexual theory must acknowledge that the continuing confusion between pain and pleasure that besets patriarchal Christianity cannot be disentangled without also challenging the bias that personal pleasure consists primarily in the realization of independence. Both patriarchal Christianity's hierarchical social relations, characterized by domination and submission (however benignly exercised), and a feminist commitment to a woman's self-possession (rather than her being possessed by others) continue to reflect a dualistic apprehension of embodied power and thus an erotic split.

The effect of the split between top and bottom and between male and female (patriarchal distinctions), and between belonging to oneself and belonging to others (a liberal dichotomy sustained in much feminism) is to associate the erotic with ongoing tension. Patriarchy has conditioned us to feel, as erotic, the tension between top and bottom, male and female, self and other. While most feminists have rejected flatly the hierarchical- and gender-based dualisms, individual feminists often remain captive to the need for relational tension.[32] Even some of the most subtle feminist theory has not yet adequately repudiated the association of eroticism with the split between self and other that is endemic to the patriarchal view of reality. In other words, if we are likely to be "turned on" in patriarchal praxis by being on top or on bottom, giver or receiver, in traditional male or female roles, we may still, in feminist praxis, be "turned on" by a sense of being either self-possessed or belonging to another. In the context of this dualistic eroticism, for a woman to feel that she belongs both to herself and to another is rare. To do so involves breaking the tension generated by the split between oneself and others. To those shaped by the power relations of patriarchal culture (all of us), the loss of such tension is experienced unavoidably as the diminishment or elimination of erotic power. Few are able to find their way, in this dualistic praxis, to full eroticization in mutuality.[33]

This may suggest why so many people (feminists and others) find it hard to sustain high levels of sexual excitement in the context of friendship.[34] It suggests also that the erotic split is the ground upon which we learn to feel as pleasurable or sexually stimulating that which in fact is the source of much pain to us: our alienation from one another, as people who have difficulty feeling power by sharing it. To put it another way, it is rare in this culture to experience power when shared as genuine power because we are inured to perceiving as powerful anything that does not have a zero-sum quantity, that does not appear "over against" us or someone else. As we have already insisted, the identification of eros with the tension created by power disparity cannot be transcended until we repudiate the legacies of patriarchal social relations at root, rejecting the way patriarchy images self-other relationship. . . .

PLEASURE AND TRANSCENDENCE

Transcendence, the wellspring of religious intuition and spiritual resource-fulness, is the power to cross over from self to other.[35] It is the act of making connections to one another, to the rest of creation, and, from a monotheistic religious perspective, to the source of our creative power in relation. Transcendence is also the resource of the desire to overcome structures of alienation such as heterosexism, sexism, racism, and class exploitation that impede even our best efforts to love our neighbors or ourselves very well. If sex is experienced as enhancing a shared sense of power, it is an avenue to transcendence, to deepening our relations with the world.

If self-other dynamics are fated to bear the mark of tension between self- and other-possession, then good sex can be at best an occasional, even accidental, striking of delicate balance. But experiences of good sex, however rare, precisely lack this quality of balance. The pleasure of sex is in its capacity to enhance sensuality; the full-body orgasm feels good because it increases a sense of well-being, of integrated bodily integrity. The pleasure in making love comes from experiencing one's own sensuous empowerment while being present to that of one's lover. Good sex involves a simultaneous enhancement of one's own and one's lover's well-being. Good sex does not involve simply one partner giving and the other receiving, one empowering and the other being empowered. The causes and effects of good sex are more complex, more dialectical, more interesting, and more difficult to categorize on the basis of separate roles or functions.

Insofar as sex is merely a balancing act, a matter of reducing tension, it is an alienated act which, while it may embody a desire to transcend alienated power in relation, can do no more than momentarily resolve it. Experienced simply as an exchange of power or as a means of resolving emotional and physical friction in our relational lives, sex cannot move us beyond the zero-sum experience of personal power in which one person's gain is another's loss. As long as this remains our primary experience of sexual activity or desire, we are likely to be titillated by fantasies of being taken, ravished, or raped by those who hold power over us. Conversely, and less frequently among women in the dominant culture in the United States, our erotic images may be fueled by a desire to take, ravish, or rape those whom we wish to have power over or experience as powerless. We have tried to show that this sexual dynamic is a disturbing, often violent, embodiment of a broader social relation, and that this social relation lays bare the core of sadomasochism: the embodied, sensual appropriation of absolute power, or abject powerlessness, in relation to others. Our dominant culture and theological systems continue to legitimate this zero-sum power arrangement in which giving or enduring pain signifies good sex or good behavior. Whether we personally view this situation through moralistic, deterministic, hedonistic, or playful lenses, none of us as individuals, or as sex partners, can simply rise above the sadomasochism that deforms our common life.

We can re-vision, however, our life together in such a way that we participate in sparking a sexual phantasie that presses beyond sadomasochism. We borrow Dorothee Soelle's term to denote a reality that is more than simply "fantasy." Phantasie is generated by the collective power of human beings actively to "imagine" a present-future and, in so doing, to begin to create it among ourselves.[36] In our sexual phantasie, sex is fueled by the realization of ourselves as subjects of our own lives and as partners in the realization of common pleasures. In this sexual relating, which is political and spiritual as well, we realize our power as we are touched, delighted, and moved by others and experience them as subjects of their own lives rather than of ours. We discover that our pleasure is not largely in exchanging power or reducing tension but rather in realizing together the power that we have in relation to one another. Indeed, as [Jessica] Benjamin would suggest, erotic pleasure may always be enhanced to some degree by the tension between self and other. But our sexual phantasie is that the strongest and most durable pleasure has little to do with tension reduction between people who possess unequal quantities of power. It is rather a matter of relational celebration between people who realize sensually—in our bodies—that genuine personal power belongs to either only insofar as it belongs to both and who know deeply that sharing common goods, such as pleasure and self-esteem, generates more rather than less power and pleasure for all.

NOTES

1. Carol Vance, ed., *Pleasure and Danger: Exploring Female Sexuality* (Boston: Routledge & Kegan Paul, 1984); Ellen Willis, "Feminism, Moralism and Pornography," in *Powers of Desire: The Politics of Sexuality*, ed. Ann Snitow, Christine Stansell, and Sharon Thompson (New York: Monthly Review Press, 1983), 460–68; Varda Burstyn, ed., *Women against Censorship* (Toronto: Douglas & McIntyre, 1984); Robin Linden, Darlene Pagano, et al., *Against Sadomasochism* (Oakland: Frog in the Well Press, 1982); Laura Lederer, ed., *Take Back the Night: Women on Pornography* (New York: William Morrow & Co., 1986); Andrea Dworkin, *Pornography: Men Possessing Women* (New York: A Perigee Book, 1979); *Coming to Power*, 2d ed., Samois Collective, a lesbian feminist S/M organization (Boston: Alyson Publications, 1982); "Sex Issue," *Heresies* 12, 3, no. 4 (1981); Haunani-Kay Trask, *Eros and Power: The Promise of Feminist Theory* (Philadelphia: University of Pennsylvania Press, 1986).

2. Mariana Valverde, *Sex, Power and Pleasure* (Toronto: Women's Press, 1985), 14.

3. Ibid., 9–46. See also Linda Gordon, *Woman's Body, Woman's Right: A Social History of Birth Control in America* (New York: Viking-Penguin, 1976); Adrienne Rich, *On Lies, Secrets and Silence: Selected Prose 1966–1978* (New York: W. W. Norton, 1979), 185–94, 199–202. For reviews of the development of literature on women's sexuality in the United States, see Introduction, in Snitow et al., eds., *Powers of Desire*.

4. Vance, ed., *Pleasure and Danger*; Linden et al., *Against Sadomasochism*; Samois Collective, *Coming to Power*; Snitow et al., eds., *Powers of Desire*; Valverde, *Sex, Power and Pleasure*; "Sex Issue," *Heresies*.

5. Audre Lorde, "Uses of the Erotic: The Erotic as Power," in *Sister Outsider* (Trumansburg, N.Y.: Crossing Press, 1984), 53–59.

6. Carter Heyward, *Our Passion for Justice: Images of Power, Sexuality and Liberation*

(New York: Pilgrim Press, 1984); Beverly W. Harrison, *Making the Connections: Essays in Feminist Social Ethics*, ed. Carol Robb (Boston: Beacon Press, 1985), 3–21, 81–173; idem, "Human Sexuality and Mutuality," in *Christian Feminism: Visions of Humanity*, ed. Judith J. Weidman (New York: Harper & Row, 1984), 141–57.

7. See the following essays in Vance, ed., *Pleasure and Danger*: Vance, "Towards a Politics of Sexuality," 1–27; Linda Gordon and Ellen Carol Dubois, "Seeking Ecstasy on the Battlefield: Danger and Pleasure in Nineteenth-century Thought," 31–49; and Alice Echols, "The Taming of the Id: Feminist Sexual Politics, 1968–1983," 50–72. See also Willis, "Feminism, Moralism, and Pornography," in Snitow et al., eds. *Powers of Desire*, 460–68.

8. From Vance, ed., *Pleasure and Danger*.

9. See Cherrie Moraga and Gloria Anzaldua, eds., *This Bridge Called My Back: Writings by Radical Women of Color* (Watertown, Mass.: Persephone Press, 1981); Cherrie Moraga, *Loving in the War Years* (Boston: South End Press, 1983); Rennie Simpson, "The Afro-American Female: The Historical Context of the Construction of Sexual Identity," in Snitow et al., eds., *Powers of Desire*, 229–35; Jacquelyn Dowd Hall, "The Mind That Burns in Each Body: Women, Rape, and Racial Violence," in Snitow et al., eds., *Powers of Desire*, 328–50; Barbara Omalade, "Hearts of Darkness," in Snitow et al., eds., *Powers of Desire*, 350–67; Bonnie Thornton Dill, "On the Hem of Life: Race, Class and the Prospects for Sisterhood," in *Class, Race and Sex: The Dynamics of Control*, ed. Amy Swerdlow and Hanna Lessinger (Boston: G. K Hall, 1983), 173–88; Paula Giddings, *When and Where I Enter: The Impact of Black Women on Race and Sex in America* (New York: William Morrow, 1984), 84–94, 299–357; Bell Hooks, *Feminist Theory: From Margin to Center* (Boston: South End Press, 1984); Adrienne Rich, "Compulsory Heterosexuality and Lesbian Existence," in Snitow et al., eds., *Powers of Desire*, 177–205; and Joanna Ryan, "Psychoanalysis and Women Loving Women," in Sue Cartledge and Joanna Ryan, *Sex and Love: New Thoughts on Old Contradictions* (London: Women's Press, 1985), 196–209. See works by Linda Gordon, Mariana Valverde, and Carol Vance already cited; and Ellen Ross and Rayna Rapp, "Sex and Society: A Research Note from Social History and Anthropology," in Vance, ed., *Pleasure and Danger*. See also Rosalind Pollack Petchesky, *Abortion and Woman's Choice: The State, Sexuality, and Reproductive Freedom* (New York: Longmans, Green & Co., 1984); Beverly Wildung Harrison, *Our Right to Choose: Toward a New Ethic of Abortion* (Boston: Beacon Press, 1983); Rayna Rapp and Ellen Ross, "The Twenties' Backlash: Compulsory Heterosexuality, the Consumer Family, and the Waning of Feminism," in Swerdlow and Lessinger, eds., *Class, Race and Sex*, 93–107.

A few male writers provide extremely helpful historical-structural reinterpretation of the history of eroticism and confirm dynamics discussed here. E.g., Marco Mieli, *Homosexuality and Liberation: Elements of a Gay Critique* (London: Gay Men's Press, 1977). Mieli interprets male homosexual desire as universal and male heterosexual attraction to women as "split off," a form of hostility. He argues that so-called "heterosexual male sexuality" is always suffused with homosexuality. A British historian whose works are also important is Jeffrey Weeks, *Coming Out: Homosexual Politics in Britain from the 19th Century to the Present* (London: Quartet, 1977); idem, *Sex, Politics and Society: The Regulation of Sexuality Since 1800* (London: Longmans, Green & Co., 1981); and idem, *Sexuality and Its Discontents: Meanings, Myths and Modern Sexuality* (London: Routledge & Kegan Paul, 1985).

10. On mutual relation, see Carter Heyward, *The Redemption of God: A Theology of Mutual Relation* (Lanham, Md.: University Press of America, 1982); and idem, *Our Passion For Justice*, 83–93, 116–31. See also Harrison, "Human Sexuality and Mutuality," in Weidman, ed., *Christian Feminism*, 141–57.

11. Popular studies of women's sexual fantasies make clear that fantasies of seduction

and domination are widespread and that even the repression of such sexual imagery may be understood as a response to domination.

12. Gordon, *Woman's Body: Woman's Right*; Valverde, *Sex, Power and Pleasure*.

13. Margaret Miles has argued for this dialectical viewpoint in her study of Augustinian theology; see her *Fullness of Life: Historical Foundations for a New Asceticism* (Philadelphia: Westminister Press, 1981).

14. J. N. D. Kelley, *Early Christian Doctrine*, 2d ed. (New York: Harper & Brothers, 1960), 15–17, 127–37, 163–88, 459–79. Once the Neoplatonic dualism is presupposed, the dichotomy worked its way into Christian christological discussions. This discussion can be traced in Richard A. Norris, *The Christological Controversy* (Philadelphia: Fortress Press, 1980).

15. Elisabeth Schüssler Fiorenza has carefully reconstructed the repatriarchalizing process that occurred in early Christianity through the household codes; see her *In Memory of Her: A Feminist Theological Reconstruction of Christian Origins* (New York: Crossroad, 1983), esp. chap. 7.

16. John Boswell, *Christianity, Social Tolerance and Homosexuality: Gay People in Western Europe from the Beginning of the Christian Era to the Fourteenth Century* (Chicago: University of Chicago Press, 1980); and Bernadette J. Brooten, "Paul's View on the Nature of Women and Female Homoeroticism," in *Immaculate and Powerful*, ed. Clarissa Atkinson, Constance H. Buchanan, and Margaret A. Miles (Boston: Beacon Press, 1985), 61–87.

17. Samuel Laeuchli, *Power and Sexuality: The Emergence of Canon Law at The Synod of Elvira* (Philadelphia: Temple University Press, 1972), 56–113; Anne L. Barstow, *Married Priests and the Reforming Papacy: The Eleventh Century Debates* (Lewiston, N.Y.: Edwin Mellen Press, 1982); and Harrison, *Our Right to Choose*, 119–53.

18. Laeuchli, *Power and Sexuality*, 57–72, 102–13.

19. A few examples of this massive feminist research are: Rosemary Radford Ruether, *New Woman/New Earth: Sexist Ideologies and Human Liberation* (New York: Seabury Press, 1975); Schüssler Fiorenza, *In Memory of Her*; and idem, *Bread Not Stone: The Challenge of Feminist Biblical Interpretation* (Boston: Beacon Press, 1984); Phyllis Trible, *Texts of Terror: Literary-Feminist Readings of Biblical Narratives* (Philadelphia: Fortress Press, 1984); Rosemary Radford Ruether and Eleanor McLaughlin, eds., *Women of Spirit: Female Leadership in the Jewish and Christian Traditions* (New York: Simon & Schuster, 1979); Atkinson, Buchanan, and Miles, eds., *Immaculate and Powerful*; and Elizabeth A. Clark, *Jerome, Chrysostom, and Friends: Essays and Translations* (Lewiston, N.Y.: Edwin Mellen Press, 1979).

20. The theological significance of immediate relation is illumined in Heyward, *Redemption of God*, 2–9, and chap. 2. Heyward's discussion of "mutual relation" is indebted to the work of Jewish theologian Martin Buber. This work is also critical for understanding feminist theological claims that the effect of Christian dualism was to denigrate the human.

21. The tendency of men to separate "sex" and "intimacy" is widely acknowledged in the literature on sexuality. What is less frequently acknowledged is that this split reflects the social reality of sexist society: that men are to "desire" women sexually but are encouraged to locate equality in friendship—with men like themselves. Integration of sexual desire and intimate friendship remains a difficult task for men. We believe that Mieli's analysis, *Homosexuality and Liberation*, explains not only why homoeroticism suffuses male sexuality but why so much male eroticism toward women depends upon women conforming to male tastes regarding proper femininity.

22. Samois Collective, *Coming to Power*. We note, in women's defense of sadomasochism, the characteristic claim that it is a way to come into one's power. Our uneasiness with this defense rests not in the fact that ritualized sadomasochism is too sexual but

that its proponents tend to equate coming to power with personal autonomy. As we will argue below, such an equation incorporates a conception of power and relationship that extends the traditions of patriarchal social theory.

23. The importance of the Boston Women's Health Collective, *The New Our Bodies, Ourselves* (New York: Simon & Schuster, 1984) rests precisely in its stress on teaching bodily integrity to women. As such, it deserves the accolade "the bible" of the women's movement.

24. Susie Orbach, *Fat Is a Feminist Issue* (New York: Berkley Publisher, 1982); and idem, *Hunger Strike: The Anorexic's Struggle for Survival as a Metaphor for Our Age* (New York: W. W. Norton, 1986). See also Kim Chernin, *The Obsession: Reflections on the Tyranny of Slenderness* (New York: Harper & Row, 1982); and idem, *The Hungry Self: Women, Eating and Identity* (New York: Harper & Row, 1985).

25. The role of Christianity in anorexia is illumined in Leadoff M. Bell, *Holy Anorexia* (Chicago: University of Chicago Press, 1985). Orbach has illumined this thesis of female protest in her works.

26. Christian sexual ethics cannot fully transcend this spiritualizing tendency until or unless that ethic officially ceases to privilege lifelong marital sexuality as "the" proper normative form of sexuality. For a philosophical analysis of this problem see Dorothea Krook, *Three Traditions of Moral Thought* (Cambridge: Cambridge University Press, 1959), 333–47. A Christian ethic cannot celebrate sexuality as per se good because sex is only good when it functions to support other values—procreation, or, in liberal theology, "unitative" or "communicative" values. Even the most progressive Christian reinterpretations of sexuality tend to extend this spiritualizing tendency. When, for example, sexuality is affirmed because of its unitative and integrative functions, it is assumed that what sexual longing involved is the desire for merging with another. See Anthony Kosnick et al., *Human Sexuality: New Directions in American Catholic Thought* (New York: Paulist Press, 1977), 48–52. Charles Davis, a progressive who purports to affirm bodily sexuality in an unqualified way, nevertheless insists, "One yearns for the other as for a lost part of oneself, with a longing to merge oneself and one's life with the other into a single person and a single life," *Body as Spirit: The Nature of Religious Feeling* (New York: Seabury Press, 1976), 134. A Protestant example of the tendency to spiritualize love and evade sexuality is Frederick Sontag, *Love Beyond Pain: Mysticism Within Christianity* (New York: Paulist Press, 1977), 59ff.

27. It is interesting that there is a spate of recent bestsellers dealing with women's difficulties with heterosexual love and/or sexual relations. See Carol Cassell, *Swept Away: Why Women Confuse Love and Sex . . . And How They Can Have Both* (New York: Bantam Books, 1983); Robin Norwood, *Women Who Love Too Much* (New York: Pocket Books, 1986); Connell Cowan and Melvyn Kinder, *Smart Women: Foolish Choices* (New York: Crown Publisher, 1985); Christine Dowling, *The Cinderella Complex: Women's Hidden Fear of Independence* (New York: Summit Books, 1981). While several of these books are indeed helpful to women in disentangling their lives from destructive relationships with men, the latter two blame the victim and discourage women's relational expectations. What is more important to acknowledge is the destructiveness of male socialization that encourages fear of dependency. We also need a more rigorous critical perspective on female socialization in relation to the institution of compulsory heterosexuality than these works provide. See, e.g., Michelle Barrett and Mary MacIntosh, *The Anti-Social Family* (London: Verso Press, 1982).

28. Daniel Day Williams, *What Modern Day Theologians Are Saying*, rev. ed. (New York: Harper & Brothers, 1959), 135–37.

29. Harrison, *Our Right to Choose*, 67–90.

30. The classic formulation of pleasure as the central, and except for immunity from pain, the only, good is Jeremy Bentham's hedonistic utilitarianism. See Jeremy Bentham

and John Stuart Mill, *The Utilitarians* (Garden City, NY: Doubleday & Co., 1961), 100–125.

31. For an excellent analysis of the way male socialization conditions preoccupation with self-possession, see John R. Wikse, *About Possession: The Self as Private Property* (University Park, Pa.: Pennsylvania State University Press, 1977).

32. This is probably the real source of the "difficulties" women have with sexual and intimacy relations discussed in the recent popular literature cited in n. 27. What troubles us is a tendency in feminist theory to encourage female independence, predicated upon a male model, rather than mutual relation as the simultaneous realization of self-possession and other-dependence.

33. The recognition that the experience of eroticized mutuality is so rare is one of the many insights that commends Mariana Valverde's analysis; see *Sex, Power and Pleasure*.

34. This theme of the eroticization of friendship is helpfully explored by Mary Hunt in *Fierce Tenderness: Toward a Feminist Theology of Friendship* (New York: Harper & Row, 1986).

35. Heyward, *Our Passion For Justice*, 243–47.

36. Dorothee Soelle, *Beyond Mere Obedience* (Minneapolis: Augsburg Press, 1970), 62–67.

12

Lovingly Lesbian: Toward a Feminist Theology of Friendship

MARY E. HUNT

What is lesbian feminism? Where did it come from and why won't it go away? Why use the word *lesbian*? Can't women just be friends? Why isn't there a new word for it? These are the kind of first-level questions which need to be answered in order to move on to creative analysis.

The theopolitical reality of lesbian feminism is that it can only be understood in a particular social context. That context is both patriarchal and heterosexist. By patriarchal, I mean that the entire social fabric is so imbued with the normativity of male experience that female experience is excluded. This means that schools, churches, businesses, governments, etc., are arranged according to male principles of competition, aggression, and production to the extent that so-called female characteristics of cooperation, agreeability, and process are negated. Patriarchy expresses itself in sexism in the culture, and has been responded to in some initial ways by what is known as feminism. Feminism is the insight into the historical and contemporary oppression of women, and at the same time a movement dedicated to strategies for overcoming it. Major work has been done on sexism from a theological perspective by Sheila Collins, Mary Daly, Rosemary Ruether, and others, and from a theoretical angle by Charlotte Bunch, Susan Griffin, Adrienne Rich, and company. More recently however, we have come to understand that this same patriarchal context is heterosexist as well.

The insight into heterosexism is just beginning to be explored logically by a generation of scholars who have benefited from the work which has been done on sexism. Heterosexism means that normative value is given to heterosexual experience to the extent that legal and acceptable expression of homosexual experience is excluded. As in patriarchy, there is no claim that heterosexual experience as such (like maleness as such) is bad. Rather, its normativity to the exclusion of homosexuality (just as the exclusion of women) makes it oppressive. When all social relationships and social institutions are arranged according to heterosexist principles, i.e., male-female dating and marriages, child rearing in heterosexual families, and the presumption that all are heterosexual until proven otherwise, it is nearly impossible for healthy, good, and natural homosexual relationships to flourish. That they do is some proof of grace.

Women whose experiences do not conform to this model realize early on that the context in which definitions are born is patriarchal and heterosexist. They realize that all women are defined not only according to their gender but according to their sexual relationships with men as well. The litany is something like the following: married women sleep with men, divorced and widowed women used to, separated women might again, single women would like to, lesbian women do not, and nuns, well, they are not even supposed to talk about it. Thus the "normal" (Webster's) definition for a lesbian in this context is "a female homosexual," the word itself coming from "the reputed homosexual band associated with Sappho of Lesbos." Here it is clear that even a lesbian in heterosexist patriarchy is defined in male terms, that is, as homosexual who does not happen to be male. Even the word chosen for such women is defined in terms of male fantasies about Sappho's friends.

So it goes, but the confusions are even helpful for understanding what a lesbian is not. A lesbian is not defined by her sexual partner any more than she is defined by those with whom she does not sleep. This is to fall into the patriarchal trap of defining women according to sexuality, which only serves to divide us. What we need is to be united in order that our strength will free all of us. A lesbian is an outlaw in patriarchy. But she is the herald of the good news that patriarchy is in its decline. A lesbian is a woman who in the face of heterosexist patriarchal messages not to love women—the others, the outsiders, the despised—indeed not to love herself as woman, in fact does both. She loves other women as friends, that radical relationship of laying down one's life that has always been valued in Christianity. And by loving other women she comes to that authentic self-love which is, in the words of novelist Doris Grumbach, "It was the very opposite of narcissism—it was metamorphosis."[1] To be a lesbian is to take relationships with women radically seriously, opening oneself to befriend and be befriended, so that by loving, something new may be born. When all women are free to have this experience, then, and only then, can we say that any women are free.

This renewed definition of lesbian comes from a particular social context. Three social movements paved its way. They are: the so-called sexual revolution, the women's movement and the lesbian/gay movement. I will treat each one briefly so that we may see the backdrop for this new definition. Agreeing with these movements is not important, but being aware of them as forming part of our history in the evolution of a postpatriarchal, postheterosexist culture, is.

First is the sexual revolution, perhaps the most dubious of all three. This was the much heralded and mercifully short-lived revolt against puritanical ways in the sixties. It was made popular through such slogans as "Free Love," "Abortion on Demand," "Make Love Not War," etc. The very expressions themselves give away the patriarchal nature of this movement. For men it meant license for sex wherever and whenever with whomever, taking away from women the "nice girls don't" excuse. For women it meant the need for more birth control, more abortions, and ultimately less freedom to really choose. Heterosexual activity in and of itself was seen as revolutionary, for still inexplicable reasons. But if anything positive did come out of this rather virulent period it was the fact that people finally began to talk more freely about sexuality. This was no small matter when we reflect that even to the present day, discussion of sexuality is taboo in some circles, including most of theology.

The second and far more significant social movement to have an impact on the definition of lesbian was the women's movement. This movement recognized the class nature of women's oppression in the historical and contemporary scenes. At the same time it began to use women's experience as the starting point for developing strategies to overcome oppression of all types. In consciousness-raising groups women not only mentioned sexuality but took it as a major focus, seeing it as the mirror which reflected all of women's treatment in the society. The woman who was oppressed in bed, who was raped or beaten, whose husband or lover did not use birth control, the woman who was called frigid, the postmenopausal woman, all of these are various facets of the same woman, namely, the oppressed woman in patriarchy.

Lesbians were told to keep their voices down during the early years of the women's movement. Betty Friedan and others (who later, happily, repented publicly) referred to lesbians as the "lavender menace," and made it clear that lesbians could cost all women their rights if lesbians insisted upon theirs. So, dutifully the dykes closed their mouths, remained invisible, and worked on birth control, abortion rights, child care, etc., for what amounted to straight women's liberation. It was only with the lesbian/straight split in the women's movement (1970–71) that feminists began to understand the politics of lesbianism. As Charlotte Bunch indicated, "lesbian feminist politics is a political critique of the institution and ideology of heterosexuality as a primary cornerstone of male supremacy."[2] Until this cornerstone is removed, the structures of patriarchy will stand firm.

The point is not that every woman act in a particular way, but that every woman be freed from the constraints that patriarchal heterosexism places upon her. Then and only then can women make real choices about relationships with particular people, not excluding a whole class of people (women) from the beginning. This same dynamic of instant exclusion of whole classes of people is operative in racism, in classism, in discrimination toward the differently able, those from Third World countries, etc. It is this dynamic that lesbian feminists seek to change in its many manifestations.

The third major social movement which set the stage for present thinking about lesbianism is the lesbian/gay movement itself. When gays first fought back against police at the Stonewall bar on New York's Christopher Street in 1969, they opened a new era for homosexuals. No longer were same-sex relationships simply the stuff of back rooms and Mafia-run bars. Homosexuals were persons with dignity and (eventually) legal rights equal to all others. The movement was primarily male in that the leadership, focus, and values were basically derived from male experience. But women, even women who were not feminists, could see their rights as well. And everyone was finally able to see the lives and contributions of lesbians and gay men throughout history, who could now be celebrated by the gay community.

Feminists quickly became aware that being part of the gay community was important but no panacea. *Gay* had become another false generic like man, referring to both male and female homosexuals. This symbolized the values of the movement as well, which were focused on making male homosexual expression valid, and little else. Feminists could not stop our analysis with the sexual, but always understood our sexuality within the complex constellation of racism, classism, sexism, etc. The "natural alliance" between lesbian feminists and gay men was not so natural after all. This is not to say that there are not some obvious and important links, but it is to say that very different emphases have been made from the two perspectives.

Gay males, for example, have emphasized their sexual lives as the locus of their liberation. But since *gay* is not a generic word we can conclude that the lesbian emphasis is quite different and not to be homogenized. Lesbian feminists have not defined ourselves according to sexuality, although that has been important. Rather, we have defined ourselves according to certain relational commitments to other women, or what I am calling female friendship. The nature of our relationships with regard to the specifically sexual aspect is quite simply no one else's business. This is not to say that lesbian feminists are in the closet about our sexuality, nor that we advocate continuing the hidden relational lives of our foresisters with the women they loved. Far from it. Rather, the goal from a lesbian feminist perspective is that persons eventually be allowed to love whom they will without current heterosexist gender restraints.

To achieve such a goal, we are reclaiming the word *lesbian* for what it has always meant, namely, women loving women without fixating on the presence or absence of genital activity to define it. What we are talking about is the basic feminist truism that the personal is political. This is important to distinguish from the private, which has never been claimed to be political. Concretely, that I take my relationships with women seriously is an important personal choice in patriarchy which has clear political implications. But that my friend and/or sexual partner is Susie and not Debby is private, therefore not political, though it is of course both public information in a certain way and something which we choose to share among our families and friends. This distinction is important because it allows lesbian feminists to have private lives like everyone else. We can live without having our sexuality politicized beyond what relationships can handle. At the same time, we can make claims about the political nature of loving women within a patriarchal, heterosexist culture without those claims being tied to one or another relationship. In short, sexuality is not privatized, but neither are specific relationships publicized, at least not beyond the usual small circle of friends who know, support, and critique any human relationships.

This analysis must be seen in the light of contemporary women's studies and what we might call lesbian feminist theory. Adrienne Rich has suggested that the cost of heterosexism has been so high as to erase the lives and loves of many lesbians from history.[3] The threat of lesbianism has served to divide women, alienating them and making them fearful of one another. The ultimate epithet for any woman, regardless of her sexual preference, is *lesbian*. To diffuse this, Rich has suggested the notion of the lesbian continuum, placing all women somewhere on the continuum. This would include married women who take their relationships with women friends seriously on the one hand, and women who live together in primary affective relationships on the other, and everyone in between.

Rich's analysis suggests that when all women can embrace and celebrate the lesbian in them the distinctions between "who is" and "who is not" will finally fall away. It has been suggested that perhaps letting all women onto the continuum might degrade or de-emphasize the value and dignity of those relationships which are on the latter end of the spectrum, those which would traditionally be defined as lesbian anyway. However, it is clear that such a wholesale identification of women as lesbians is not about to happen, though for those few who do so identify there will undoubtedly be a warm welcome. The idea, rather, is that all women take seriously their friendships with women, and the only word which we have to indicate this revolutionary reality is *lesbian*. Thus, it is at our peril that we back off of the word. To do so is to deny the powerful women's reality which has gone before us and probably to short-circuit what is ahead. I feel for women who say that they agree with the concept—frightening as it is for many of them to think of the implications of taking relationships with women seriously—but only wish we could employ another word, please. As yet there is no word, so I simply remind them that there was a time not so long ago when the word woman had distinctly sexual overtones. All females were described as "girls" and "ladies." How quickly language and concepts change together. The point is that no one knows all of the implications of integrating sexuality into women's friendships. But we do know that the important thing is not that they necessarily do it, but that they do it lovingly and responsibly.

This is why we insist on reclaiming the word *lesbian*, wrenching it from its patriarchal context, à la Mary Daly, and giving it a content worthy of the lives of some great women friends throughout history. Inviting all women to share its richness, it is important that *lesbian* not be forced to carry the symbolic freight of sexuality for all women. Instead, we can insist on our self-identification as friends in a culture which tells all of us to keep our distance from one another. Thus *lesbian* takes on a new meaning. It becomes paradigmatic of all types of friendships in a culture which provides precious few structures for women and men, men and men, women and women to relate to each other as friends without the corruption of such unions with partial, distorted notions of heterosexism.

Throughout the country and in fact in many places in the world a women's community is emerging. This community is made up of women who understand and value the necessity of women's friendships for our collective survival. Here, female friendships can flourish in places and spaces where they go unquestioned in themselves and are subsequently evaluated according to the persons involved. Music, art, poetry, drama, dance, etc., can be shared in the women's community without the annoyance of male objectifiers or the more subtle drain of liberal male hangers-on. The community is dynamic and shows its resourcefulness by great mobility and simple comfort. It is, however, almost completely white and middle class, something which limits its value, although women of color are beginning to make their voices heard as well in contributions which promise new life for all of us.[4] The women's community, however, is a tiny fraction of a percentage of the general culture where women's lives and friendships are trivialized unto death.

However, lesbian feminism and the women's community are having a significant impact in the culture if reports in popular news magazines can be taken seriously. For example, it seems that lesbians on campus are more visible than ever before, and that their visibility is both political as well as personal. They are not simply part of the larger male gay movement. They evidence instead a clear awareness of how relationships with women offer them more depth and possibilities for growth. There are even reports of some straight women wondering about themselves, whether they are whole persons or if indeed there is something wrong with them. While I have some sympathy for their confusion, I encourage their line of thinking. It points to what lesbian feminists are saying, namely, that loving other women, thus being free to love oneself, is good for every woman's health. This is nearly impossible under patriarchal, heterosexist influences.

Just as quickly as this insight into what we call woman identification out of lesbian feminism comes to consciousness, Hollywood and Madison Avenue are right there to counteract it. We can expect a spate of films of the *Personal Best* caliber which will capitalize on and trivialize women's friendships. These films play on male fears and fantasies about what the world would really be like if women loved women. Of course the results are predictably shallow, neurotic, one-dimensional, stereotypic, sexually focused relationships. These simply do not ring true about most lesbian feminist friendships, where it is not an instant attraction due to a compatibly toned body, but an attraction born of friendship with a sister in the struggle, and perhaps a sister in the snuggle too! These are the life-giving friendships which grace women even in a patriarchal, heterosexist culture, and which give some hope and role models for the next generation.

Lesbian feminist friendships are known to us through a variety of sources. I look at my own experience and smile to think how blessed I have been with a very particular friendship, but also with a constellation of friendships which participate to one degree or another in the richness which is lesbian feminism. I look at my friends' experiences and the quality of relationships we share. It is astonishing how in the midst of our culture any women's friendships can flourish. But they do and we cultivate them like out-of-season flowers because we know all of the forces which mitigate against them.

We have other sources on women's friendships now. Finally the literature is coming to the fore. We have the formidable collection *Surpassing the Love of Men*, which details literary loves over the past centuries,[5] and few have missed the adventures of Molly Bolt, who made *Rubyfruit Jungle* the first feminist best seller.[6] This was a far cry from *The Well of Loneliness*, which convinced a whole generation that love between women had to be role-defined and tragic.[7] We learn about women's friendships from women's music, that growing group of compositions for, by, and about women. Meg Christian's "Ode to a Gym Teacher," sometimes referred to as the lesbian national anthem, provides a satirical look at the desperate search for role models prior to feminism. There are also the tender, powerful love songs of Holly Near and Chris Williamson, as well as the bawdy tunes of Teresa Trull, all celebrating the fact that women do love women. And there are the haunting melodies of Sweet Honey in the Rock, assuring us that "Every woman who ever loved a woman you ought to stand up and call her name."[8]

All of these give us clues to women's friendships, clues earlier generations simply did not have. The clues are as varied as the friendships. But there are some general lines of agreement. Women are not to be possessed but to be shared. Friendship means support through the difficulties. Making love with a woman can be a delightful experience. Many women have loved women. These kinds of cultural affirmations allow women to see that their experiences are not unique, that the most natural feelings in the world have been distorted by patriarchy. This does not mean that solving the riddles of patriarchy will result in hassle-free relationships. But it does mean that the challenge of loving well is tough enough without having a whole layer of cultural negativity to make it even tougher.

These sources show that something new is struggling to be born in women's friendships. Perhaps it is that the cynicism and exploitation which mask love in straight society are finally being overcome. The mockery which has been made of love in patriarchy, the pain and prerequisites which prevent people from embracing one another in a deep, life-giving way are being put to rest. This is a major contribution to Christian culture, one which can model for relationships of all kinds the way into the future. No other contemporary source, neither the churches nor the gay male movement, nor even the straight women's movement, is making such a self-conscious effort to improve the quality of love.

Classical male qualities of friendship include such characteristics as care, responsibility, respect, and knowledge, according to such writers as Eric Fromm, etc. But for lesbian feminists it seems that some other characteristics come to the fore. The first of these is *mutuality*, that quality of a mature friendship when giving and taking are possible between equals, when one can truly complement the other not from role expectations but because of gifts. It is a rare, if existent, heterosexual relationship which is truly mutual. This is because in a heterosexist, patriarchal world women and men cannot be equal. This is the nature of patriarchy. Thus a friendship which is characterized by mutuality is possible only when a man and a woman live in contradiction with the prevailing culture. Living in this state of contradiction, conscious of all of its pressures, is usually more than most such friendships can take. However, friendships between women, on the other hand, can have this quality by their very nature. There can be an honest assessment of the strengths and liabilities of each one, and some sharing accordingly to each one's ability and each one's needs can be actualized. Then roles can be tossed aside and new possibilities emerge. Hence it is friendships between women which model mutuality for everyone.

A second characteristic of a woman-woman friendship is *community*. It seems that there is some urge in women to broaden, nurture and enlarge a friendship so that it will always exist in a network of relationships. This urge toward community is exactly the opposite of what happens in a male-female relationship in patriarchy when the urge to possess, to close off, and to protect seem[s] to overpower even the most communally oriented of couples. Conversely, in women's friendship there seems to be a desire not to close off relationships but to join them with other similar friendships and create a kind of community. This may simply be a survival mechanism, a response to the fact that in patriarchy friendships between women are dangerous and need all of the support they can muster. But I like to think of it as a programmatic commitment on the part of women to give friendship a communal dimension. It seems also to guarantee a much healthier life-style, where neurotic minuets will be minimized and where groups in which ups and downs, holidays and tragedies may be shared will be the norm.

We are only beginning to structure friendships in this communal way. As noted above, it will be some time before those already in communities will be able to come out about the friendships which exist among them. But I submit that when both of these processes get under way, when communities are built intentionally on friendships and when communities make explicit their friendships, then the richness and power of women's friendships to transform the culture will really be felt. This kind of community building based on friendship will be the stuff of the ecclesia of women to which theologians refer when talking about the impact of feminism on the churches.[9] I support this move and only hope that the lessons of friendship and community building which will result from it can be broadened to include all members of the ecclesia.

A third aspect of women's friendships is a direct dealing with sexuality and the consequences of doing so, namely, *honesty*. This is perhaps the single greatest contribution of lesbians to all women, in that lesbians have urged upon all women an honest and forthright dealing with sexual dynamics which exist between them. It seems that up until very recently women functioned toward one another as if out of a completely heterosexist mind-set. Sexual dynamics were something one had to confront with men, always and everywhere, but friendships with women were cultivated without such complications. I have even heard straight women say that they do not confront sexuality with women because their experience with men is that when sex is no longer a part of the relationship the relationship itself is gone. They claim they do not want to risk this with their women friends, whose friendships are too important to them. The implications for their relationships with men are frightening. However, we have learned more recently that all mature, adult relationships have some kind of sexual component. We have found that it is better to face and deal with such dynamics than to let them stand in the way of quality relating.

This is not easy, given our socialization. But the rewards are many. What lesbian feminists have learned is that acknowledging and facing honestly the fact that in some friendships, for reasons which remain altogether mysterious, there may exist between two women sexual energy which calls for resolution. If the friendship is to flourish, this resolution is imperative. Otherwise, there is great risk of thwarting an otherwise good friendship.

Dealing directly with sexuality in any situation is simply a question of honesty. Failure to do so means introducing distrust into the relationship, distrust which will usually manifest itself in other aspects as well as the sexual one. What it means to be lesbian in a nonpatriarchal, nonheterosexist age is to take the risk which comes with acknowledging sexual energy and resolving it. The experience of many women is that not every friendship leads to the expression of sexuality. This is a myth created by the media to sell everything from liquor to paper towels. But it is equally women's experience that some kind of attraction often needs to be named, simply named. But in those cases where sexual dynamics do come into play there will often need to be some exploration between friends, which more often than not will result in a mutual decision that sexual expression will not enhance and might detract from the friendship. This is simply because we find that sexuality involves so much time and energy and emotion, participates on so many symbolic levels which for women are usually well integrated into the entire personality fabric (unlike men, who seem to have greater ease at distancing their sex life from the rest of their personalities), that we do not have the resources for too many such relationships in a lifetime, and rarely for more than one at a time.

In those few and cherished friendships in which the integration of sexuality is desired by both friends there is a symbolic signaling of a deepening of friendship and commitment. This is never a decision taken lightly. But it is one which involves the friends in each other's lives in ways that demand responsibility, ongoingness, nurture, etc. We are only beginning to see how such relationships, when encouraged and celebrated by families and friends, will transform the relational life of the church.

Of course, the fact that women do not have to worry about birth control in their sexual explorations is no small incentive for greater honesty with women.

Imagine if this same depth of honesty could be realized between women and men. Imagine the improved quality of friendships and even marriages which might result if the dynamics of dishonesty, which are so often set up at the sexual level and played out at every other level in relationships, were not in play.

Another characteristic of women's friendship is their *nonexclusivity*. Of course we can all think immediately of exclusive, clingy relationships between women which make the most possessive male-female relationships seem positively open. But contemporary lesbian feminist friendships simply are not that way. On the mixed side these were the result of male property orientation toward women, and on the female-female side a kind of shutting out of the world from that one little peaceful relational spot which women had found. Now we are creating a women's community in the broader culture so as to create the space that women's friendships need. The formation of solid bonds between and among women over generations and national boundaries is another attempt at creating womanspace adequate to the expansive nature of growing friendships. Thus friendships can be open and inviting, letting in the light of other friendships and sharing the goodness without fear of loss or trivialization. This invites women not to relational or sexual promiscuity but to the creation of friendships in a communal context which will in the long run mean added strength and richness for each one. The implications of this model for the entire church remain to be spelled out, but it seems clear that opening the space for women will only lead to greater openness for women and men, as well as for men with men.

Another characteristic of female friendship is *flexibility*. Flexibility means the freedom to express oneself and grow with others in a variety of ways. It means letting go of the old role models which lesbians and gay men picked up from the only (heterosexual) model which existed. It means having to come up with new categories through which to explain and nurture friendships, because the ones we have are simply inadequate. Are Susie and Cathy lovers? Well, Susie and Cathy are friends. Why do you need to know more, so that you can discriminate? This is the kind of response which comes when the categories are no longer adequate.

We are learning to be flexible about our loving. We are learning that we do not necessarily have to live in the twos of the nuclear family. We are learning that we can have intense, romantic friends but still live in the wider community or in fact even alone if that seems best. We are learning to develop the communities and networks of communities which multiply our options and spread out the energy of friendship where it is so badly needed.

Finally, female friendships are remarkable in their *other-directedness*, the extent to which they point beyond themselves to something larger, something more beautiful, something more inclusive, some might even say something divine. This is something which male-female relationships in a patriarchal, heterosexist culture strive to attain but never reach. The reasons for this are historical in that female friendships have been forced outward, forced to understand and relate to the culture in order to survive. On the other hand the usual heterosexual relationship, which all too often is not even a friendship underneath it all, is focused in on itself, trying to reach some norm which patriarchy has established as the most effective way of stifling growth. Hence it is women's friendships which hold the key to transcendence, because they must transcend what is in order to be at all. This is a burden for women, but one which promises to make all things new if only women can survive long enough.

I have suggested that women's friendships are mutual, community seeking, honest about sexuality, nonexclusive, flexible, and other-directed. These qualities, it seems to me, have tremendous potential not simply for relationships among women, though that potential has yet to be explored, but for the whole church. It is these characteristics which will transform our culture and create the preconditions for the possibility of the reign of God. I am not arguing that all women's friendships participate in these qualities as yet. That is wishful thinking. Rather, by naming them I hope to make it so, or at least bring to consciousness what might be possible in women's lives so that our contribution to the whole church can be forthcoming.

A theology adequate to this kind of friendship model is much more promising than the theology of sexuality which some of us have hinted at in the past. It is more adequate because it acknowledges that it is not sexuality per se but friendship which determines what the quality of life can be. In patriarchy it is certainly the sexuality dimension which makes the difference. But after patriarchy it is the entire relationship which makes the difference.

New constructive theologies are recognized as such by their saying something new about the fundamental theological categories God, humanity, and the world. This is done in a systematic way when some new insight, experience, or concept is used to illumine these basics. Friendship, it seems to me, is in its postpatriarchal, postheterosexist potential an insight, experience, and concept able to carry us to new heights in theology. Although I will save a full exploration of this possibility for a later essay when we have had more time to live into the idea, I offer now a few hints toward such a theology. To do so I will make certain Christian presuppositions which can be summarized by the normativity of love and justice as the essence of revelation. And of course since this constructive theology attempts to be systematic, the three concepts, God, humanity, and world, are each interdependent. They will be explored according to the six characteristics proposed for female friendships in hope that the specific new content about friendship can be brought to bear.

We begin by exploring who God is, what language and characteristics we can use for meaningful talk about God. The model of friendship, while not in and of itself adequate to exhaust the reality of God, is surprisingly helpful. No longer are we left with Father, Lord, Ruler, and King, nor even with Spirit and Mother Hen, which are often trotted out to balance the gender. But now we have the androgynous, unfettered notion of God as friend to add to the list.

Two of the characteristics gleaned from female friendships which are useful for understanding God as friend are mutuality and the urge toward community.

Mutuality is suggested by process theologians who are concerned with how God is affected by humankind, and obviously vice versa. Mutuality is that quality of the otherness of God which is really God's oneness with us. To characterize otherness as mutuality is to say that God can only be understood in human terms, but that the very understanding is affected by our belief in God. In short, mutuality means that our relationship with God, like all friendships, is freely chosen on both sides (unlike family or government images like Father and Lord, in which the relationships are not necessarily intentional and gratuitous). More needs to be explored, of course, but it is clear that God as friend opens up a new paradigm for our understanding.

A second characteristic of female friendships, the urge toward community, is an essential aspect of the Christian God. The idea of the reign of God, the omega point, the gathering of all that is into a harmonious community, these are all Christian ways of talking about the God-human cooperation which will result in salvation. Jesus is the force in Christianity, the friend whose relationship with us is manifested by our being part of the Christian community. This membership is evidenced by the work of love and justice. This is not the pietistic "what a friend we have in Jesus." Rather it is the experience of being part of a historical group of friends. Jesus' friendships, especially the example of his particular friendship with the beloved disciple (John 13:23, 21:7, etc.) as well as with his immediate community of women and men, are a model for contemporary Christian life. This is the community which derives its identity from the laying down of life for friends. Again, much remains to be explored, but we can conclude that the missionary urge which springs from Christianity is in fact to go and make friends in all nations.

Likewise the theological concept of humanity can be understood anew using friendship as the defining model. We have been developing what humanity will look like in postpatriarchal, postheterosexist age, and we have looked at characteristics of female friendships. Focusing on two more of these, honesty and nonexclusivity, gives us a way to see the friendship model operating on the macro as well as the micro level.

The honesty which begins with direct dealing on sexuality questions in a relationship is the same habit of honesty which is needed for a renewed human family. It is the honesty which invites people to see our common heritage rather than stressing the accidental differences like age, race, nationality, sexual preference, physical handicap, etc. It is in the most optimistic of moments this honesty which could lead nations to face the nuclear threat and act like friends for once. It is a dream of course, but why not when options are limited?

Nonexclusivity as a characteristic of female friendship is helpful for imagining a renewed humanity. This could mean an end to preserving national boundaries at all costs while at the same time inviting international cooperation. Nothing would be seen as exclusively mine. Rather, things and people and ideas would be seen as here for the sharing not for the taking; they would be seen realistically as part of what is given to be enjoyed and given back. Nothing and no one would be seen as object or property, only as participating in a kind of cosmic subjectivity which encompasses all of creation. Needless to say, we are some distance from such values. But they give us goals against which to measure our collective progress as well as something toward which to aspire. This is, after all, the task of theology: to develop ethics and strategies to bring us closer to our goals.

Finally, the third theological basic, world, can be reunderstood in the light of a friendship model. World is a great abstraction, almost too great for meaningful discussion. But understood in terms of the earth and all nonhuman life, it is easy to see how flexibility and other-direction, characteristics of female friendships, are helpful lenses through which to examine it.

Flexibility means the freedom to develop a new relationship to the earth. In a nuclear age it means scaling down our grandiose notion of humanity and letting it come into line with the more modest role that was meant for us in creation. Likewise it means changing our attitudes toward the earth, understanding that our very future is tied up with our practices of ecology.

Other-directedness too helps us to see how the world is really oriented not for our pleasure but for our collective future. The pleasure of a few cannot be allowed to determine the future of everyone, or what will surely be no future at all at the rate we are going. This need for balance is critical over against the contemporary nuclear myopia, and it may be this insistence on balance which saves us from ourselves. To whom or to what we ought to be directed is not clear. But what is clear is that an orientation beyond what we know is the hallmark of faith, faith in a friendly future.

This treatment of lesbian feminist friendships and the beginnings of a theological sketch are an attempt to clarify some basic concepts, most of which have been previously misunderstood. Clarification is but a first step toward embracing the new, risking the friendship itself. It is that risk which will open the way for an enrichment of the God-human-world friendship in which we are all invited to participate.

NOTES

1. Doris Grumbach, *Chamber Music* (New York: Fawcett, 1979), 203.

2. Charlotte Bunch, *Lesbianism and the Women's Movement*, ed. Nancy Myron and Charlotte Bunch (Baltimore: Diana Press, 1975), 10.

3. Adrienne Rich, "Compulsory Heterosexuality and Lesbian Existence," *Signs: Journal of Women in Culture and Society* 5, no. 4 (Summer 1980): 631–60.

4. The best example of this emerging contribution is a collection entitled *This Bridge Called My Back: Writings by Radical Women of Color*, ed. Cherrie Moraga and Gloria Anzaldua (Watertown, Mass.: Persephone Press, 1981).

5. Lillian Faderman, *Surpassing the Love of Men: Love Between Women from the Renaissance to the Present* (New York: William Morrow & Co., 1981).

6. Rita Mae Brown, *Rubyfruit Jungle* (Plainfield, Vt.: Daughters, 1973).

7. Radclyffe Hall, *The Well of Loneliness* (New York: Simon & Schuster, 1974). Original publication: Covici-Friede edition, 1928.

8. Lyrics from the popular song "Every Woman" by Bernice Johnson Reagon, recorded by Sweet Honey in the Rock on their album *B'lieve I'll Run On . . . See What the End's Gonna Be*, Redwood Records, Ukiah, California, 1978.

9. Elisabeth Schüssler Fiorenza, "Gather Together in My Name . . . Toward a Christian Feminist Spirituality," in *Women Moving Church*, ed. Diann Neu and Maria Riley (Washington, D.C.: Center of Concern, 1982), 11; reprinted as the epilogue to Elisabeth Schüssler Fiorenza's *In Memory of Her: A Feminist Theological Reconstruction of Early Christian Origins* (New York: Crossroad, 1983).

13

What If It Is a Choice?
Some Implications
of the Homosexuality Debates
for Theology*

LAUREL C. SCHNEIDER

I have a good friend from graduate school days whom I'll call Camille. She is a lesbian. We all love her for her kindness, her intelligence, her humor and, yes, her devastating good looks. She went through several significant relationships during the years that I've known her since Harvard. I heard her stories about these women, walked with her through the ups and downs of those relationships, and in general did for Cam what we lesbians tend to do for each other, even over thousands of miles. We generally turn to lesbian friends, rather than family or straight friends, primarily because we don't have to explain the basics to one another. We share language, and experiences, and yes, often exes. . . . In other words, we are a community without streets or ethnic histories. But we generally will do anything for each other. So imagine my reaction when, last summer, Camille told me that she was dating a man. It's not that this was the first time I've ever encountered this. Indeed, before she came out, Cam had dated men. But with other women—well, it always seemed easier to come up with reasons for the apparent defection—internalized homophobia (a reality, we all nod, for all of us), confusion (yep, she was never really a lesbian), desire for children without homophobia on the playground (how sad). But Camille . . . , she's a lesbian's lesbian. And her "defection" couldn't be out of some attempt to go back into the closet—at least I don't believe so. She agonized over her attraction and love for this man, and seemed grateful to me for my lack of judgment and my encouragement, simply, to live life.

Now, those of us who love her have had to admit: This may not be a phase. When she visited me a few months ago, we had breakfast and she said that she wants to be with him for the rest of her life, that they both want this. She's

*This chapter is excerpted from a public talk delivered at Chicago Theological Seminary in 2000.

highly intelligent. She seems aware of the ironies of her choice, of the mantle of privilege she is drawing over herself. I still smile and tell her I'm happy for her, but I worry that my hugs may be a trifle less warm in spite of myself. I *want* her to be happy. I don't want her to do without the love she so richly deserves. I do wonder about this choice she has made however—I can't help myself—and the deep privileges it carries. Will she remember what it is like to be out here where we are? Alone, with *everything* working against us being whole in relationship? I wonder. But the surprises didn't end there. I asked her, with some trepidation, what she now considers herself to *be*. The day before, I'd heard her say something to others about her preference for queer identities. Did she mean herself? I asked. What does she call herself now?

She didn't hesitate. "Oh, I'm a lesbian of course," she answered. Of course? I was confused. How do you mean, lesbian? I stammered. It's just how she feels, she said. "Todd aside, nothing has changed" (how do you put Todd aside, I wonder?). Does she intend to have female lovers? No. She intends to be—wants to be—monogamous. And bisexual doesn't get at it? No, bisexual is not her self-understanding, lesbian is. She knew I was struggling, trying to understand, and perhaps she could see in my eyes the growing suspicion that she may want to continue to think of herself as lesbian just so that she can have her cake and eat it too, so to speak. She can have the man she loves but not lose that particular connection we have had *specifically as lesbians* in a basically non-lesbian world. I was trying to keep my suspicion at bay—I don't want to think that *I'm* a lesbian just because it gives me membership in an exclusive, albeit strange, club. I've been judged and found wanting too many times by the insiders of too many clubs to start behaving as if I'm in one.

"Maybe this will change after a few years," she conceded. "Maybe I'll start thinking of myself as bisexual, or even straight." She looked lonely when she said that. Could she choose to be bisexual, or even straight? Did she choose to be a lesbian to begin with? *What if it is a choice?* And what difference does that make, not only for us as intimate friends, but also for the very understandings of identity and community that motivate and give substance to our theological work?

This is how I began preparing for this talk—thinking about the question of whether sexual identity *is* a choice, something we can choose and also unchoose, and what impact that possibility has on public religious discourse and theological thinking about homosexuality. I do want to say some things about that, but I also want to take the question further. In fact, I want to ask whether sexual identity is really the question that we should be trying to resolve in our public theological discourses. When we allow ourselves to get hooked into trying to answer the question what gay, lesbian, bisexual, transgendered, and even straight really are in God's plan, have we been diverted into an endlessly turning eddy, arguing about a fundamentally unresolvable, and possibly irrelevant question?

I want to challenge us tonight to think a little bit about the theological and political implications of thinking about the "it" in "What if it is a choice" as something other than a presumably stable identity included in the usual list of lesbian, gay, bisexual, transgendered, and straight, not to mention the unusual list of heterosexual transvestites, pansexuals, and so forth. Do we have the courage to entertain the theological possibility that stability of identity is quite irrelevant, *particularly when we understand ourselves to be made in God's image?* I do not begin to presume that all of you here share my presupposition that same-sex eroticism and sexuality are both good and valuable in God's sight. I do, however, maintain that presupposition for my own theological work, and so am challenged to think through what it means for theology, not just in terms of practical theology, but in terms of philosophical principles of divinity as well.

Instead, I am asking tonight whether the choice here refers not to sexual *identity* per se, which may be something we can't pin down, but rather to choices concerning our life together—our political choices, for example, on behalf of creation in all of *its* promiscuous sexuality? What if these are our choices, not the question of some identity hewn into solid form? So you can see, I want to put the question that entitles this talk into a different framework, one that relates who we are as lesbian, gay, bisexual, transgendered or straight to much larger theological questions of divine freedom and human will.

And I will get to that. But first, let me say a few things about sexual identity, because that is where our current public discourse is mired. Assuming that sexual identity does exist (whether in classical ontological terms, or in social-ontological terms, or, as is most easily argued, in purely historical terms), what if my being a lesbian is indeed a choice rather than a stable, given "nature" designed, and so presumably intended by God? The question here is whether sexual identity is a constitutive and substantive part of my being or something I can create through performance. When I came out, was it a discovery—a dis-covering—of a pre-existent lesbian self that had been covered over and obscured by hetero-normative socialization? Or did I make, or remake, myself? Is lesbian something I choose to be in the personal act of loving particular women? Do I fall somewhere, in some identifiable and stable way, on the Kinsey scale, for example?

I know why those of us engaged in contemporary religious debates tend to resist entertaining the possibility that sexual identity could be a matter of choice and change—for one thing, it disrupts a whole gender cosmology founded on such stability, and for another thing, that is not how many of us interpret our experience. But what is the real truth here? By way of illustration of the problem, let me tell the following anti-coming out story about myself: At 13, walking down the Jr. High halls behind Jenna Kilpatrick (she rode horses, she was fine), I realized with devastating horror that I felt the most powerful and graphic sexual attraction for her. Now, to be fair, I also fantasized in those years about the two Jameses from television—Kirk and West that is (both of whom I realize today would have made excellent dykes had they been women!).

In any case, the thing that horrified me in that hallway (I remember the precise location) was that I could not mistake what I felt about Ellen, and that it was completely unbidden. I did an about-turn, skipped whatever class I was supposed to attend, and spent the next hour locked in a stall in the girls' bathroom beating myself physically until I was bruised, crying, and chanting "sick, sick, sick, sick." I left that bathroom so aggressively heterosexual that, well, perhaps I was . . . for the next 10 years anyway. When I tell that story today, I usually end with a laugh—I was so aggressively heterosexual that I guaranteed I'd come out eventually.

So, is this a story about an essential lesbianism beaten into long and painful submission by a very strong-willed girl, or is it a story of choice that, while violent, has nothing to do with the vagaries and complexities of physical desire? We avoid the possibility that "it" is a choice because that is precisely what many of the religious right folks are claiming, on the assumption that God created humans, ontological male and female He created them, and heterosexual He created them, amen and that any other "orientation" is a choice against that nature. It is, of course, on this assumption of nature that such things as ex-gay ministries have come into being.

It is not that the argument from nature is wrong—I am in no position to lay claim either way—but those who invoke it seldom realize that natural law theory is a relatively late addition to Christian thought. Although natural law theory can be traced to the decidedly pagan Aristotle, it was Thomas Aquinas in the medieval synthesis who interpreted natural law *into* Christian theology, giving to Christians this most powerful and enduring juridical tool for separating the sheep from the goats, so to speak. God created, called creation Good, and so determined that anything that can be shown to be naturally occurring is therefore intended by God for the good of creation. Of course, by the same logic, anything that can be shown to be unnatural is neither good nor worthy of tolerance. Aquinas eliminated Aristotle's very Greek sense of the tragic by disallowing natural evil and thereby making natural law a basis for Christian ethics and a self-referencing demonstration of God's absolute goodness. Thomas could not know that he was actually providing future gay-by-nature activists a bit of ground on which to claim their natural goodness. . . .

In any case, I want to suggest that the argument from nature *is not essential* to Christian theology, and I also want to suggest that it ultimately gets us into an endless, self-referencing loop of coercive sameness. It may be curtailing our ability to think most deeply about human diversity *and* most theologically about divine freedom and human will (those who are paying attention will note that I did not say divine will and human freedom here!). I believe that arguments from nature, while politically effective to a point, are fundamentally shortsighted, defensive and oppositional, and they necessitate the very policing of identity that we are protesting to begin with. The master's tools, in other words, may not dismantle the master's house in this case. Identity, as I may have discovered in the girls' bathroom at 13, may be a fundamentally malleable and coercive thing.

Nevertheless we have, for the most part, accepted the religious right's framing of this argument in terms of divinely ordered nature over against human free will to disrupt it. If they are marshalling Christian homophobia against us on the basis of a theology of creation, it is difficult to defend our *choices* to be gay, lesbian, bisexual, or transgendered against those traditions when choice is the very thing that accounts for the existence of evil in the Christian tradition. If there were clear warrants in biblical and church traditions that supported sexual diversity, the question of supporting choice in sexual identity would be less problematic. But such warrants are so slim it is fair to call them non-existent, and so religious folks who see their homosexuality as a good thing have little traditional ground on which to stand to support a non-straight identity, *particularly* if it is a choice.

So it has seemed much more effective to accept the terms of the debate as framed by the religious right, and to counter their claims of our deviance from nature with the counter-claim that we are gay, lesbian, or bisexual *by nature*. This is easier than taking on the entire theological premise that, when in doubt, human choices that are clearly consistent with biblical, doctrinal, and church tradition stand a much better chance of being good while those that counteract those traditions are more likely to be evil. In other words, by claiming that I was *created* this way, my lesbianism becomes a part of God's will and the homophobia of the tradition is an error—based on *nature* as God's blueprint for the good. God, according to this kind of theological deferral, does not create evil but only allows us the capacity to *choose* it over the good. Uh oh. And there's that "choose" word again—so we can *choose* evil. And, as I've said, on what religious grounds can I claim—against the world's religions—that I am not choosing evil when I choose a woman? Just the fact that I want her? Not persuasive, since even I know that I'm capable of wanting things I shouldn't have. You see the problem.

So arguing that God made me a lesbian gives me the benefit of being able to tell my opponents and their armies of pastoral counselors that to dissuade us of our gayness would be to defy God's will for us. But the only problem is that we do not know if gay-by-nature (or straight-by-nature, for that matter) is indeed the case! I for one am unwilling to relegate my pre-coming out relationships with a few good men to the trash heap of error—even though it was with enormous relief and a profound sense of rightness that I did eventually come out. I refuse what would be the gay-by-nature theological conclusion that, after beating myself up at 13, I lived in sin for years because I would not acknowledge my "real" lesbianism. The *choice* at hand there, in that bathroom, was not an identity, but, as Alice Walker might say, a set of choices about how I would—or would not—love myself and others, regardless.

And according to some of our gay, lesbian, and bisexual friends, gay-by-nature does not seem to be the case for them. How do we stand in solidarity with these brothers and sisters and provide theological ground on which they can stand even as the fur is flying around them between religious friends and foes?

How does our defensive premise of identity from nature help them? Do we just leave them to the wolves? I think not. Yet locking ourselves into having to find an unchallengeable answer to the question of nature pushes us toward

natur as arg as defensive

making a choice that only weakens all of us—it pushes us to adopt a reflexively defensive stance in which I define my identity one way, and you define your identity another way, and we find ourselves defining *each other* in oppositional ways—defining each other right out of the circle of real companionship. No, I think that we have to find stronger theological ground on which to stand, ground that is neither determined by homophobic attempts to naturalize heterosexuality *or* homosexuality, nor attempts at self-protection that undermine our particularity and diversity.

What I'm suggesting is something really more queer than it is lesbian, gay, bisexual, or straight. I find it just as confusing to think about choosing to be a lesbian as I do about not choosing to be one. And in fact, the point is not *my* choice or lack of choice either way. The point is that identity is really a communal designation, never an individual one. I am white, middle-class, lesbian, academic, etc. etc. —*in community* where those labels designate sameness with others of the same designations, and difference from others who share different designations. All of those labels are meaningless individually apart from that. So whether I *am* a lesbian or *choose* to be one seems relevant only in terms of what I ultimately *do* with being one. *How* does being lesbian make me a better, more whole person working toward a better, more honest world? Does it give me strength to love others more deeply and courageously? If the designation helps me with that—and in my case it does—so much the better. But that is a different kind of choice—it changes the framework of the debate.

Identity is therefore not what the theologian should be considering first here. Please don't mistake me. I agree with Sharon Welch that ideas have the *effect* of truth, and so questions of identity matter because others think that they are true—people are killed (and kill themselves) because of the perceived truth of identity, and benefit or lose in legal systems, in religious systems, and so forth because of the perceived truth of identities. Yes, labels and constructed identities matter. But they are not Truth. And to return briefly to Aristotle, Truth with a capital "T" can be assumed to *exist*, but cannot be presumed to be *known*. In this case, who needs to know it anyway? The danger of the question of identity as some kind of truth with a capital "T" is that it can substitute or take precedence over more ultimately crucial questions such as the one Dietrich Bonhoeffer asked: "how is the coming generation to live?"

Theologians like myself need to be concerned with more than the perceived truth of identities if we are to really help lesbians, gay men, bisexuals, and transgendered persons find a place to stand that recognizes us, but does not imprison us. We need to be concerned that *our* arguments—when they invoke divinity for any purpose—are persuasive on theological grounds that are not so synonymous with our own political beliefs and values that God cannot constitute a challenge to *us* but only to *them,* the oppressors. In other words, I want my arguments about God's relationship to us to be both consistent and to constitute a persistent challenge that is equivalent across political differences. I must insist that God be God, not just my God.

This means that when I invoke divinity in my discussion of human sexuality I need to ask if I am invoking a notion of the divine that reflects what I really truly believe about God regardless of my current particular commitments and investments, or whether I am constructing a concept of God that is subordinate to those beliefs and investments. Do I, for example, *need* God to have created me lesbian and you straight so that I don't have to navigate the rapids of continual renegotiation of our being together, and consequently do I then *really* believe that God makes identities and seals them indefeasibly into the fabric of our being? And if I do, how do I square *this* understanding of God with my hope for fundamental transformation of human community? How do I know that God has not willed us to be the nasty, brutish, and violent folk we so often prove ourselves to be even when given every opportunity to be otherwise?

The choice at hand, it seems to me, is far more deeply a *set* of choices that have more to do with *how* we live our lives as gay, lesbian, bisexual, straight, and less to do with whether we *are* lesbian, gay, bisexual, or straight. This is not a naïve deferral of the implications of identity. I am not advocating the kind of simplistic and falsely privileged position that actress Anne Heche made famous in her interview on Oprah when she stated blithely that she was neither lesbian nor straight nor bi—she just loved Ellen, that's all. She came subsequently to rethink that statement, not only because she incurred the wrath of so many lesbians for whom that designation has meant life or death (meaning that it *does* matter, sometimes for life and sometimes for death) but because she came to experience the force of prejudice and violence, joy, freedom and community, that accompany lesbian "choices" *as such*. She didn't come *out* so much as she came *into* a community with a history of heroism, sacrifice, suffering and achievement that so astounded her that she wrote a movie about it.

So I am not advocating that we stop talking about lesbian, gay, bisexual or even straight identities—I have suggested instead that the question of resolving the volitionality of that identity is a dead end in our current religious debates, one that serves to distract us from the more pressing—and maybe more radical—questions of how then we are to live in relation to what we really believe about God's freedom and intentionality for each one of us. I am asking a more political question about our daily choices and our institutional commitments in a homophobic world rather than that which aligns us together or apart. We choose moment by moment to stand aside or to stand with, to bear witness to divine freedom in our associations, and in our actions—or not. So I am asking a more queer question about choice that leaves the question of identity fundamentally unresolvable in much the same way that Jesus seemed to be quite queer when it came to love. . . .

I have argued elsewhere that contemporary gay and lesbian constructive christologies may be beginning to elaborate a queer Jesus although not yet a truly queer theology.[1] Jesus was certainly queer in his practice of a politics of radical kindness and openness—he did not limit his own intercourse with "identities" such as adulteress, tax collector, leper, rich, unclean, child, foreigner, and divorcee and so "queered" love itself. I am not intentionally de-sexualizing the discussion here. Jesus did love freely and queerly in his disregard for regulatory identities, and it is clear that a certain politics and social dynamic flowed from that queer love.

So, in conclusion, what if God simply wants us to be alive and to love without ceasing? That is a political choice. And isn't *that* the real choice—or set of choices—always before me? If that is a choice, then the implications for theology have as much to do with elucidating the ways that we can better love one another queerly—past the distinction of whether Camille is still a lesbian or not—because she is who God created her to be—an ever changing being, wondrously made. I make political choices every day about my love for women— *every* day I have to come out or not—as you too have to make political decisions every day about your loves. How we do that together, it seems to me, is the choice that makes the difference.

NOTE

1. Laurel Schneider, "Homosexuality, Queer Theory, and Christian Theology" in *Religious Studies Review*, Vol. 26, No. 1, Jan. 2000.

14

The Construction
of the Black Male Body:
Eroticism and Religion

DWIGHT N. HOPKINS

Like the pounding blows of a steam hammer, devastating images of the African American male body repeatedly hit the U.S. public's psychic during the end of the 1990s. Recurring themes of sexual lust akin to religious fervor acted as foundational planks in this construction of what it means to be a Black man in America. Yet the stereotypical blueprinting of the African American male identity actually began to intensify at the close of the 1980s, specifically in the 1988 presidential campaign. Indeed, we will see that the American Black male body, individual and corporate, is defined by eroticism and religion.[1]

TRIANGLE OF DESIRE

The 1988 presidential elections pitted the Republican George Bush against the Democrat Michael Dukakis. Hoping to ensure a victory in the Fall elections, Bush drew on a tried and true formula from the U.S. cultural matrix and psychological reflex. In a vicious attack media advertisement, which proved quite successful, Bush drew heavily on then Massachusetts Governor Dukakis's apparent record of being soft on crime. The state of Massachusetts, under the governor's leadership, had released African American Willie Horton, who, during his furlough, was convicted of raping a white woman. With this lurid case, Bush launched a national crusade to discredit Dukakis as a wimp regarding law and order. The image of Bush, the white patriarch, defending the sanctity and purity of the innocent, American white female citizen from the rapacious copulating appetite of the out-of-control, Black brute criminal saturated the air waves. If not the decisive nail in the proverbial coffin of Dukakis's failed bid for the White House, this compelling story line of sex, sanctity, and race at least added to Bush's victory in November.[2]

The following year, a pregnant white Bostonian female, Carol Stuart, died from a gunshot blast. Her baby expired also after a Caesarean section. White male Charles Stuart, the husband, claimed that this double homicide as well as his gunshot wound had been inflicted by an overpowering Black man. The state authorities apprehended at least three African American men in the process of discovering which Black male in Massachusetts had committed such a heinous crime—the violation of innocent, white female motherhood in America.

> Somewhere along the line the narrative failed and Charles Stuart committed suicide. Shortly thereafter, it became clear that he had concocted the ploy in order to kill his wife. Charles had rehearsed the events with his brother, who met the car shortly after the shooting to take away Carol's pocketbook, which also contained Charles's gun. At the end is the corpse of the white family as social construction, the feared result of violation from the "nigger rapist."[3]

These two sensationalized strategies of Bush and Stuart symbolized an ongoing U.S. legacy of the primal archetype drama: white male and Black male protagonists moving through scenes of violence of the Black sexual body, religious-like obligation to defend [the] white female body, and intervention of the white male body, all foregrounded by the erotic. "A common structure, a triangle of desire, unites these cases on a paradigmatic level with the death of Emmet Till. Although each is a variation, the triangle positions Black men and white men as adversaries in a contest over the body of women."[4]

THRESHOLD OF THE
TWENTY-FIRST CENTURY

The 1990s exemplified the triangular dynamic with even more force, often clouded over with intimations of erotic pleasure at the expense of Black bodies. For instance, after falsely arresting him, New York City police raped Abner Louima, a Black man, by driving the handle of a toilet plunger up his anus. And [in] what could be considered an ecstatic climax of orgiastic violence, New York City police executed Amodou Diallo, a Black man, with nineteen shots because they feared that this dark male body threatened their safety. (Diallo was actually reaching for his wallet.) The Federal Bureau of Investigation captured on tape District of Columbia Mayor Marion Barry in a hotel room with nonprescription drugs and a woman who was not his wife. The surveillance video suggested that the mayor planned to move in sexually on the woman after consuming the illegal substance. Michael Jackson endured strip-searching and examination of his pubic hair by state authorities who implied that he had sexually molested a child. A group of white male, citizens of Texas lynched James Byrd, Jr., a Black man, by dragging his body from the back of a moving vehicle through the street. Byrd lost his penis in the ordeal. The U.S. Senate's confirmation hearings of Clarence Thomas to the U.S. Supreme Court exhibited white men judging the fate of a Black man in the midst of sexual predator accusations and high-tech lynching charges. (And who will ever forget the television framing of direct shots of Judge Thomas with a white wife on one side and a white male patron senator on the other?)[5] Rap star Tupac Shakur was accused of participating in a gang rape of a female.[6] A jury acquitted O. J. Simpson of murdering blond, blue-eyed Nicole Simpson while doubts persisted about his guilt and prior sexual and emotional domestic violence complaints.[7] Los Angeles police officers repeatedly dealt near-lethal blows on Rodney King's Black body because they sensed he might over power them with brute (erotic?) strength. (King had two prior arrests for domestic abuse.)[8] In fact, one of the terrorist-like officers referred to King as "Gorillas in the Midst." And the judicial courts convicted boxing heavyweight champion Mike Tyson of date rape and two counts of "deviant sexual conduct."[9]

Despite disparate instances and differing scenarios in the above narratives, what we want to argue is that the "triangle of desire" serves as the overarching backdrop for Black men's American identity in U.S. culture and mentality. Moreover, the *ménage a trois* signifies the intertwining of eroticism and religion in the construction of the Black male body. The United States' obsession with eroticism of the Black corporeal identity is akin to if not actually a religion, revealed in Christianity and the wider U.S. culture.[10]

A SEXUALIZED BEAST BODY

Conceptually, the Black male body has been constituted from several sources. The Frenchman Rene Descartes' theoretical reflections on the mind and body separation helped lay the seeds for and, thereby, influenced greatly the eighteenth century European Enlightenment's understanding of a material and immaterial split in what it means to be a human being. In a word, the mind, symbolized by whites in Europe, strove for loftier goals in the human situation, while the body, embodied in Blacks and other darker peoples of the globe, longed for expressions of the carnal. The body's traits mean "passion, biology, the inside, otherness, inertness, unchanging, statis, matter—a more primitive way of being. To the mind is attributed reason, the self, the same, action, movement and intelligence, a more developed way of being or not being."[11] In Descartes' *Discourse on Method* (1637, and furthered elaborated on in his *Meditations*, 1641), the mind is pure thought, the body mere materiality. The mind can affect the body. The body can only be acted upon by the mind. In this sense, the body becomes an object and a mechanical instrument—a machine.[12] Particularly for Black folk, in this anthropological model, Black body results from external factors and lacks power to think, decide, impact history, or forge a spirituality on its own. The Black body is deficient by nature and creation. The white mind is pure intellect, decision making, or a proactive anthropology. The Black body succumbs to fate; the white mind indulges in freedom.[13] The white mind exhibits rational, calm deliberation. The Black male body, in particular, thrives on raw, animal eroticism.

Descartes' structures of thought have dangerous implications for African American Christians. Despite the sensuousness of play found in Black church worship, most Black Christians attempt, at all costs, to drive the funkiness of the Black body out of its domain. Rarely is the erotic mentioned and, in instances of sex-talk, it becomes prohibition: don't have sex before marriage, don't cheat on one's wife, don't have homosexual sex, don't let sex be your driving force in life, don't look at women's bodies, God sees what you're doing in the bedroom, and so forth.

> We continue to live in Cartesian captivity: the mind-body split thought up by philosopher Descartes flourishes in Black theologies of sexuality. Except it is translated as the split between body and soul. Black Christians have taken sexual refuge in the sort of rigid segregation they sought to escape in the social realm—the body and soul in worship are kept one place, the body and soul in heat are kept somewhere else.[14]

The irony is African American Christians have opposed white Christian racists on grounds that they continue to pit a gospel of spiritual liberation against a gospel of material freedom for Black folk. For example, African American believers oppose white supremacists for telling Blacks to have faith in a theology of "you can have the world, just give me Jesus" while, in the really real world, when Blacks turn toward heaven, whites control earth. Yet, Black Christians then unite with the same theological structures of thought regarding the body-soul bifurcation. Conceptually, the split between body and soul or body and mind fervently preached in too many Black churches implies double trouble for Black believers. First, the church fails to craft a positive theology of eroticism for the Black body (especially the male identity), which helps to drive many Black men away from Christian institutions. Second, the notion of the split perpetuates further the dangerous myth that a theology separating mind and body reinforces religious claims that Black people are "body" people. They embody carnal tastes, nasty sex, and lustful libido. So, Blacks who advocate this split are actually affirming theories about their own bestiality and lasciviousness.

An additional conceptual piece in how religion and eroticism contribute to the making of the Black male body is a prudish theology. Such a religious way of thinking springs from two reactionary ways of believing—self-denial Puritanism and conservative Victorianism. To be pure entails restricting the mind from thinking about body eroticism and, above all, a guilt whipping to prevent engaging in such activities. A Victorian, in this instance, upholds high culture and advanced civilization, both of which contrast radically with the sexual consumption of the peasant masses.

> In sharp contrast to the heat of most Black worship experiences, there emerged almost immediately in Black churches a conservative theology of sexuality. In part, this theology reflected the traditional teachings of white Christianity. Out of moral necessity, however, Black Christians exaggerated white Christianity's version of "p.c."—Puritan Correctness. Later, many Black Christians adopted white Christianity's Victorian repression to rebut the myth of Black sexuality being out of control.[15]

A theology of antagonistic dualism and a theology of prudishism, in the realms of eroticism and religion, undergird the construction of the Black male body. The material and immaterial separation arises from Descartes' narrow, personal experiences. The Victorian accent overcompensates for white Christians' negative depiction of Blacks. The Puritan thrust derives from a European legacy and the biblical Paul.[16]

Finally the idea of the male Black as Beast haunts the triangular interplay of African American male body on (white) female body defended by white male (authority) body. This prominent notion seeks to seduce us in various disguises. But, perhaps in the popular imagination, an old television commercial of National Basketball Association star Patrick Ewing propagandizes a most sensational pornographic portrayal. In this television advertisement, Ewing, then with the New York Knicks, is seen scaling the New York City Empire State Building, itself thrust into the heavens as an emblematic phallus. A blaring echo of King Kong movies is hammered into the viewer's conscious and subconscious mind. With dark skin, flaring nostrils, close-cropped hair, and broad lips, the prostituting portrayal of Ewing strikes a similar pose of the sexual bestiality of the Kong freak. In the King Kong movies, one has an overpowering gorilla from the wilds of Africa brought into civilized New York City; and of the eight to ten million inhabitants, he stalks a blond, blue eyed white female to hold in the palm of his gigantic hand. Could a Black male thing so big actually physically love a white woman without crushing and splitting her open? And, following the predominant American cultural script, it is powerful white men who perceive their sacred crusade to destroy this ugly, Black man-monkey.[17]

Moreover, this religious-like fervor against the erotic Black beast forces the most egregious acts of all American males onto the Black man's body. It is "an established fact that our culture links manhood to terror and power, and that Black men are frequently imaged as the ultimate in hypermasculinity. . . . The cops who beat Rodney King and the jury who acquitted King's assailants openly admitted that the size, shape, and color of his body automatically made him a threat to the officer's safety."[18] Somehow Black men have become a primary cathartic scapegoat for the evils committed by maleness at large.

BENEFITS OF SCAPEGOATING

Scapegoating inevitably entails a sustained and systematic elaboration of an ultimate lie—ultimate in the sense of life and death meaning in particular. To maintain singular focus on African American males as the ultimate center of all American male perversion, one has to comprehensively dress up falsehood with the air of scientific objectivity. But, such scientism or commonsense beliefs evade the true notion of erotic insecurity of the dominant male community in the U.S. For, it "is still true, alas, that to be an American Negro male is also to be a kind of walking phallic symbol: which means that one pays, in one's personality, for the sexual insecurities of others."[19] The dominating culture prosecutes and

perpetrates insecurities on Black others because of the white tradition's simultaneous fear and fascination, dislike and desire. Yet the push-pull of apparent
polar opposites masks a fundamental cornerstone of erotic phobia about the
Black other's potential prowess in contrast to a white legacy of self-perceived
impotency. There is "probably no greater (no more misleading) body of sexual
myths in the world today than those which have proliferated around the figure
of the American Negro. This means that he is penalized for the guilty imagination of the white people who invest him with their hates and longings, and is the
principal target of their sexual paranoia."[20]

Imaginative scapegoating, therefore, draws together a comprehensive Black-
ening of the other in order to paint a narrative portrait of commonsense metaphor and scientific image. Colorful metaphor conjures up a collation of complex
caricatures—sexually aggressive, violent, animalistic. And vibrant image offers
visual frames and memorable pictures—primal brute, kinetic sensuality, superhuman genitalia. Is this eroticism (that is, the addiction of focusing on Black
male, perverse body) and religiosity (that is, an ultimate life and death fixation)
in mainstream construction of the Black body simply about penis size envy and,
hence, the notorious need to protect white womanhood?[21]

Perhaps. But the triangle of desire (i.e., Black male body–woman body–white
male body) is, as indicated previously, what too many white men fathom and
deploy for definite self-serving goals. "With respect to rape, for example, and as
the white feminist Andrea Dworkin has observed, white men often employ and
invoke the image of the Black male rapist to obscure, deny, or excuse their own
participation in this crime."[22] As a result, part of the Black man's burden is to
carry a disproportionate load of the legacy of white men's evil sexual acts against
white and Black women. To be a male rapist in America translates into being an
African American man.

However metaphor and image must have sanction from a more powerful
institution in order to convince the broad populace and have transcendent
longevity. Enter the state apparatus—which even today is still controlled by a
minority of U.S. citizens: powerful white men in executive, judicial, and legislative branches. The U.S. state apparatus originates the concept of Black men
raping white women. This idea is not spontaneous. "It does not come from
the people, who knew better, who thought nothing of intermarriage until they
were penalized for it: this idea comes from the architects of the American state."
Similarly the state fosters and manipulates the notion of Black bodies as labor
commodities for capitalism. "The idea of Black persons as property, for example,
does not come from the mob. It is not a spontaneous idea."[23]

And the (white) state functions in collusion with, if not at the behest of, the
small minority of white families who monopolize the majority of the wealth in
the U.S.[24] To provide free (under slavery) and cheap (until today) Black labor
for white profit and further accumulation of wealth, the state works with the
wealthy to evangelize the American public that Black citizens are sensuous commodities. Toward this end, the white republic treated Black folk as less than

human and then justified the treatment by grooming the public's mind that Blacks were, in fact, less than human.

For instance: the thirteen colonies' and the U.S. government's support of slavery; the 3/5ths clause in the U.S. Constitution; the government's providing land for white citizens in the Western "frontier"; the federal administration's backing of segregation well into the 1960s; federal, state, and local officials providing pro-wealthy financial policies with a negative impact on the poor comprised disproportionately of African Americans; the state's removal of Black people from their land or housing to make way for wealthy developers, and the state's collaboration with the wealthy elite to divide and conquer Blacks and other minority citizens[25]—all indicate that the humanity of Black folk (and brown, red and yellow peoples) represents a low priority in America. The subordination of African Americans "was not an act of God, it was not done by well-meaning people muddling into something which they didn't understand. It was a deliberate policy hammered into place in order to make money from Black flesh."[26] Furthermore, one could argue persuasively today that the inordinate amount of virile Black men in prison in the twenty-first century results from a deliberate collaboration between monopoly capitalist-related prison industries and local, state, and federal governments. Someone is making billions of dollars from the incarcerated labor of Black male bodies.

ECHOES OF THE PAST

The religious concept of sexualized Black beast body (cemented in a theology of antagonistic dualism and a theology of prudishism) did not fall from the sky. A historical legacy has birthed it with white, European Christianity as a prime architect. "The church officially reinforced this entanglement of aesthetics, carnality, and negativity of Blackness at the fifth-century Council of Toledo."[27] White religious men decided that Satan was a monster with a huge penis. Three centuries later, one finds a naked black Devil painted in Europe. Given this genealogy of their Christian European ancestors, it is not totally surprising that when European ethnic groups came to the U.S. and changed their identity into "white" people (against Blacks),[28] white Christianity and the broader U.S. civic religion (that is, white monopolization as a god-complex) enslaved Africans and African Americans.[29] Indeed, white "anxiety about alleged erotic allure of Blacks exploded in America as early as 1662, when the British colony of Virginia passed a law that forbade sexual relations between Black male slaves and white women." The white male rulers of the Virginia colony cited biblical warrant as justification.[30]

During the British colonial (1607–1776) and U.S. slavery (1619–1865) periods, white Christians instituted the castration of the Black male body for at least two reasons. One rationale asserted the necessity of subduing "spirited" Black men accused of raping white women. Another suggested a form of freaky voyeurism among segments of the dominant white population. Castration, here, was "linked to carnal curiosity about the Black male's phallus," a perversion going back to ancient Greek and Roman civilizations.[31]

The Reconstruction era (1865–1877) saw the relative success of former enslaved Blacks stretching into government, civic, and business areas, domains of exclusive monopoly of privileged white men. As a result, lynching of Black men became the order of the day. White Christian terrorists orchestrated beatings and hangings in the Black community. "The closer the black man got to the ballot box, one observer noted, the more he looked like a rapist."[32] Lynching during post-Reconstruction, Jim Crow America became as common as "mom's apple pie." On one Sunday afternoon (the day of Jesus Christ), April 23, 1899, over two thousand white folk congregated and frolicked to witness the lynching of the Black male, Sam Hose. Like the overwhelming amount of cases, no evidence was produced. After chaining Mr. Hose to a tree, "they cut off his ears, fingers, and genitals, and skinned his face. While some in the crowd plunged knives into the victim's flesh. . . ." Jubilant participants removed his liver and heart while others broke up his bones. The festive crowd of Christians fought over these precious souvenirs. Crucified on resurrection Sunday, Hose's dying body deteriorated near an adjacent sign declaring "We Must Protect Our Southern Women."[33]

Throughout the South and Midwest, lynching persisted well into the twentieth century. It became a religious ritual signified by both its Sunday occurrences but also by a sense of (white) ethical duty to engage in an American pastime. White terrorists often held prayer services prior to hangings. Christian fathers and mothers brought their girls and boys along with picnic baskets. Some chartered trains to attend the affair of entertainment. Newspaper reporters flooded the scene and ordinary citizens flashed their Kodak cameras. Industrious white men made instant postcards on the spot with white citizens taking pictures beside Black men's castrated bodies, and then having these scenes developed into postcards to send to friends and relatives. White bankers, lawyers, merchants, and landed gentry occupied prime seats.

Yet the accused African American man rarely had had sex with a white woman. As a true motivation, wealthy white men, backed by those who followed them, sought accumulation of more wealth under capitalism. A leading (1916) South Carolina newspaper wrote: Black property "ownership always makes the Negro more assertive, more independent, and the cracker can't stand it."[34]

BLACK CREATIVITY IN EROTICISM AND RELIGION

Despite lethal blows in the construction of the Black male body, African American men built creatively the scaffolding for their own self identity. Theirs was a comprehensive crafting of healthy eroticism and positive religiosity in the manufacturing of individual and collective body. In contrast, the larger architecture of American civil religion equated carnality and bestiality with Black manhood. Black men, on the other hand, even with all their own shortcomings, laid the foundations of transcendent meaning within immanent manifestations. In a word, religion took on an ebony body. And this body displayed, acted out, and embraced eroticism. For our purposes of asserting the proactive posture of Black male body construction, the expressions of eroticism and religion follow.

> "Eroticism": The powerful life force within us from which spring desire and creativity and our deepest knowledge of the universe. The life force that flows like an inscrutable tide through all things, linking man to woman, man to man, woman to woman, bird to flower, and flesh to spirit. Our ancestors taught us this in their songs of love, their myths of creation, their celebrations of birth, and their rituals of initiation. Desire. Pleasure. Wholeness.[35]

Eroticism speaks to Black men's identity flooded with a life force in their very bodies. Here, eroticism distances itself from the dominating culture's and oppressive religion's planks in the building of the Black male body. Yes, eroticism includes sex; yet it surpasses sex by situating it within a fluid and broader framework. Eroticism works itself from the inside out. The inside consists of a transcendent life force, an integrated spirituality clinging sensuously to flesh. The flow of the force of life is communal and interactive among human, animal, and plant life, as well as the natural elements. It recognizes its cornerstone as the holy legacy of Black ancestors. Consequently, eroticism is history, knowledge, desire, pleasure, wholeness, and creativity.

And religion means orientation—"orientation in the ultimate sense, that is, how one comes to terms with the ultimate significance of one's place in the world. The Christian faith provided a language for the meaning of religion, but not all the religious meanings of the Black communities were encompassed by the Christian forms of religion." How does the Black male body construct itself to come to terms with the ultimate (that is, the holy, the sacred) in its being, its consciousness, its feelings, and its doing? How does it come from within and overflow itself in experience, rhythms, behaviors, styles, motivations, and intentions?[36] That which is ultimate (in terms of life and death—meaning the sacred) resides in embodiment. It is life force. Religion, therefore, is erotic.

For example, Jesus Christ, in Black Christianity, is body revelation of sacred life force. "Jesus Christ clearly signifies that God loves us not in spite of or apart from our bodies, but that God loves us in our bodies as uniquely embodied creatures."[37] Simultaneously, the blues moan and groan out another revelation of sacred life force. In the blues, physicality and spirituality exist as a dynamic quilting of the life force among Black folk. The folk perceive a powerful "spiritual function of the human body." The sacred and the secular, the divine and human coalesce. "For black people the body is sacred, and they know how to use it in the expression of love."[38]

And so, Black men redesigned the definitions of eroticism and religion to create their own plumb line in Black male body construction. Specifically, a set of building blocks in the positive self forging of the Black male body can be seen in an African American man's reworking of Alice Walker's notion of "womanism."[39] Learning from how Black women have renamed themselves, African American men are renaming a new mode of masculinity.

1. From High John the Conqueror: A mode of masculinity for Black men who are committed to the liberation and survival whole of Black people. Inspired by a trickster figure in African American folklore also known as Jack who is the human analogue of Br'er Rabbit. As a slave, John is a redemptive, transgressive, and resourceful figure who achieves advantages over "Old Massa" through motherwit, laughter, and song. He lives in the slaves' quarters of plantations and in the conjure root that bears his name.

2. Also: A man of courage who routinely "beats the unbeatable." A man who laughs at himself and also understands the many uses of laughter. As the hope-bringer, a man who's been "down so long that down don't bother" him. Unflappable. Responsible, as in: "Takes care of business" or "On the case." Traditionally capable, as in: "able to make a way out of no way and can hit a straight lick with a crooked stick." A man of strength possessing confidence and a durable constitution, as in: "Ain't no hammer in dis lan strikes like mine." Admirable and honorable, as in: "You de man." (Opposite of trifling, jive, half-stepping, irresponsible, player, not serious.)

3. In his youth: mannish. From the Black folk expression of elders to male children: "You acting mannish," i.e., like a man. Often referring to bodacious, defiant, willful, and risky behavior, as in: "He's smelling himself" or "You trying to be grown." Evincing a premature interest in adult activities and privileges.

4. Loves the Spirit. Loves men (sexually and/or nonsexually) and the society of men. Loves women (sexually and/or nonsexually) and the society of women. Loves children. Loves his ancestors. Loves difference. Loves creativity, song, and dance. Loves the beautiful/ugly. Loved by others: as in, "My main man" or "Show me some love." Loves movement: as in, "Gotta highball thru some country." Loves himself. Irregardless.

5. Free, as in "I ain't worried about that." Spunky. Crazy but got good sense. Regular. Committed to coalitions, but capable of independent action. Nonviolent, but capable of self-defense. Persevering and enduring, as in "Keep a-inchin' along lak a po' inch worm." A man who flourishes in the "Be class," as in: "Be here when the ruthless man comes and be here when he is gone." Cool.

6. "A bottom fish," as in values knowledge, truth, and wisdom. Values process and improvisation. Values collective work and solitude. Values dialogue, listening, and harmony. Values tenderness. Values the strength in feelings and tears. Values freedom and its responsibilities. Values justice. Values peace.

7. A mode of masculinity for Black men who are committed to the abolition of emasculating forms of masculinity; a mode of masculinity for Black men who are committed to the abolition of racism, sexism, homophobia, and other ideological traps.[40]

I would argue that this new mode of Black masculinity is constituted by at least healthy eroticism and empowering religion. We remember that eroticism is pleasurable life force internal to the body; this force draws on history, knowledge, desire, pleasure, wholeness, and creativity. And religion is orientation toward the ultimate in one's life and death. Thus, erotic religion or religious erotic of the Black male body concerns the ultimate living in the body and a spirituality clinging to every dimension of the flesh.

Part 1 of the above definition lifts up the Black male identity as pro-liberation and survival whole of all Black people. The Black male body transcends itself, first of all, by being dedicated to the entire community. This allegiance equals a religious commitment or ultimate faith in the sense of one's life and death calling to be there for the entire extended family and not mainly focus on the individualism of the self. Commitment, faith, and ultimate suggest that part of being an African American male is to put one's Black body on the line for others. The internal life force inspiring this liberation-survival commitment consists of definite attributes; that is, redemption, transgression, and resourcefulness. Moreover, a flesh life force of being present for other bodies enables the new mode of Black masculinity to practice both survival (i.e., to make do within negative structures) and liberation (i.e., to transform radically entire systems and establish new ones).

To follow the life force within toward liberation and survival, furthermore, necessitates courage, part 2 of the definition. Any Black male in America called to put his body on the line against nonintentional (i.e., liberal) and intentional (i.e., conservative) white supremacy is either insane or courageous. By being there, in crisis and out of crisis, the visibly present Black male body helps to engender hope, responsibility, strength, confidence, admiration, and honor.[41]

Part 3 honors the younger generation of Black males. "Mannish" is a term bantered about between father figures and male youth. By seemingly criticizing precocious manhood, the elder male is actually teaching the young about what he is up against when the youth thinks, acts, and has faith like a man. In other words, the older figure is training the younger how to come to terms with the calling of the life force within his Black male body, the spirituality clinging to the throbbing of his flesh. The boy needs to properly comprehend the implications of the sacred legacy of a man's erotic body, especially when "he's smelling himself."[42]

One of the most challenging aspects of the life force–flesh dynamic, for the grooming of young Black males, is confusion about, volatility of, and ambiguity about love. For the flesh to endure the pleasures of a healthy eroticism, it must first embrace the Spirit. This is the ultimate life force already present in the erotic Black body. Love of the Spirit in oneself provides the condition for self body-love and male-male, male-female body love (sexually and non-sexually). It enhances love of the ancestors (i.e., the living dead), the unborn (i.e., those spirits preparing to enter the realm of body flesh), and the children (i.e., the embodiment of ancestral inheritance). The ultimate Spirit love, put differently, fosters a universal love of all humans, plants, animals, and the natural elements. As a foundational plank, Black men must love religiously their own erotic body, "irregardless."[43]

A spirit filled body produces an outward love that sees and treats one's lover as a full independent human being. Referring to Black men in hetero-erotic relations, we perceive deep and broad love in the following:

The strength of a man isn't in the deep tone of his voice. It's in the gentle words he whispers. The strength of a man isn't in the weight he can lift. It's in the burdens he can carry. The strength of a man isn't in how hard he hits. It's in how tender he touches. The strength of a man isn't in how many women he's loved. It's in how true he can be to one woman.[44]

Building a sacred erotic Black male body with this perspective facilitates an understanding that love precedes sex. Sex, here, is the culmination of an ongoing sensuous body interchange of talking, reliability, and the unsolicited surprise. In a monogamous commitment, foreplay starts with the hug and kiss good-bye as one leaves the home in the morning. "Which was followed up by taking out the trash and dropping her clothes off at the cleaners. The foreplay was continued by the phone call in the middle of the day to see how her day was going, to removing the dinner plates from the kitchen table, and helping the children with their homework." A love of commitment to one's partner and allegiance to the Spirit will naturally lead to Black bodies in spiritualized eroticism of the flesh.[45] This is what it really means for the Black male body to hit the right spot.

Parts 5 and 6 help us to understand that freedom comes from the inside out. In this manner, the Black male body is never a slave. He might be enslaved, but still remain free within. Consequently, external chains of slavery don't determine the inner life force of the eroticized body. So he can "be here when the ruthless man comes and be here when he is gone." With this sense of what's in his body, a Black man is free to leave options open from nonviolence to self-defense, from joint work to independent action. And the practice of the "bottom fish" prompts the ethics of dialectical values. That is to say, freedom on the inside allows for a both-and embracing of seemingly polar opposites in the man's thought, talk, and walk.

Finally part 7 instructs us about the abolition of emasculating structures of Black masculinity. To build a Black male body, one has to also repair fundamental fault lines in Black masculine identity. The struggle against white supremacy cannot succeed if Black men (here we mean heterosexual male) construct walls of hierarchy against and exclusion of others who endure similar barriers of oppression in their body lives. The fight against the power of racism and for healthy individual and collective masculine healing will succeed when the humanity of one individual depends on aiding the humanity of others.

"Reading men in the context of race is thus a dialectical intervention: an attempt to understand men at the (construction) site of specific power relations, each relation mediating the reproduction and transformation of another."[46] The new Black male identity helps in the empowerment and health of working-class people, African American women, and Black lesbians and gays. While all African American men endure the sinister, subtle, and shocking cases of white supremacy, Black middle and upper income, heterosexual male bodies occupy a status of privilege vis-a-vis the working class, the poor, women, and lesbians and gays.[47]

And so the Spirit grounded in flesh is a location of different power dynamics. A foundational question is whether the new mode of Black masculinity fosters an equalization of resources and rights among African Americans as well as between the whole of Black people and the dominating society. If we answer "yes," we enlarge our own definitions of who we are and, consequently, destroy emasculating structures. Therefore to struggle for the other as well as the self opens the door to a new type of theology—that is, critical self-reflection on how Spirit dwells in flesh. In other words, the construction of the Black male body with a positive religion and healthy eroticism requires surveying the implications of a theology of eroticism. "We must recover the erotic use of our bodies from the distortions of white racism and the traps of Black exploitation. We must liberate ourselves to embrace the Christian bliss of our Black bodies." And we can quickly add that so-called secular Black spirituality (seen in the creative genius of Marvin Gaye, Prince, Howlin' Wolf, and Lightnin' Hopkins) has already succumbed to the seductive possibilities of the Black male body in music and song.[48] Actually the Saturday night Black love of "oh, yes, baby, I'm yours, baby . . ." is not too far from the Sunday morning church irruptions of "oh, yes, Jesus, I'm yours, Jesus. . . ." As long as the body focuses on the sacred life force within, both nighttime and daytime forms of erotic release point to a proactive self-love and self-empowerment.

NOTES

1. For an insightful thesis on the global Black body, refer to Radhika Mohanram, *Black Body: Women, Colonialism, and Space* (Minneapolis, MN: University of Minnesota Press, 1999), chapters 1–2.

2. See Robert Hood's *Begrimed and Black: Christian Traditions on Blacks and Blackness* (Minneapolis, MN: Fortress Press, 1997), xi.

3. George P. Cunningham, "Body Politics: Race, Gender, and the Captive Body," in *Representing Black Men,* ed. Marcellus Blount and George P. Cunningham (New York: Routledge, 1996), 148.

4. Ibid., 134–35. Emmet Till, a 14-year-old Black boy from Chicago visiting relatives in the Delta of Mississippi, was lynched in 1955 by two local white men because they explicitly stated they needed to protect Southern white womanhood from Black male sexual predators. Examine Stephen J. Whitfield, *A Death in the Delta: The Story of Emmet Till* (New York: Free Press, 1988), and "Eyes On the Prize: America's Civil Rights Years 1954–1965. 'Awakenings (1954–56)' Series 1 Volume 1."

5. See an excellent analysis of the implications of the Thomas-Hill hearings in Marcia Y. Riggs's *Plenty Good Room: Women Versus Male Power in the Black Church* (Cleveland, OH: Pilgrim Press, 2003), 54–55.

6. Devon W. Carbado, "The Construction of O. J. Simpson as a Racial Victim," in *Black Men on Race, Gender, and Sexuality,* ed. Devon W. Carbado (New York: New York University Press, 1999), 159.

7. Ibid., 172. Toni Morrison deepens this conversation in her edited work, *Racing Justice, En-gendering Power: Essays on Anita Hill, Clarence Thomas, and the Construction of Social Reality* (New York: Pantheon Books, 1992).

8. Carbado, op. cit., 159.

9. Examine Michael Awkward's "'You're Turning Me On': The Boxer, the Beauty Queen, and the Rituals of Gender," in Carbado, op. cit., 129.

10. On the notion of American civic or civil religion, Leroy S. Rouner offers a compelling analysis. For my purposes, I would add race-wealth-gender to his discussion. Compare Leroy S. Rouner, "What Is an American?" in *The Key Reporter/The American Scholar* (www.pbk.org/pubs/keyreporter/spring99/rounder.htm).

11. Mohanram, op. cit., 199.

12. Observe Dalia Judovitz's *The Culture of the Body: Genealogies of Modernity* (Ann Arbor, MI: The University of Michigan Press, 2001), 68–69.

13. See Lewis R. Gordon, *Bad Faith and AntiBlack Racism* (Amherst, NY: Humanity Books, 1999), 101.

14. Michael Eric Dyson, "When You Divide Body and Soul, Problems Multiply: The Black Church and Sex," in *TRAPS: African American Men on Gender and Sexuality*, ed. Rudolph P. Byrd and Beverly Guy-Sheftall (Bloomington, IN: Indiana University Press, 2001), 316–317.

15. Ibid., 313.

16. Though Paul was not among Jesus' twelve disciples and never met Jesus on earth, Paul occupies much more of the Christian Scriptures than Jesus' words. Hence Paul's theology carries a great deal of weight for Black Christians. Furthermore, he believed that Jesus' return to earth was rather imminent and the main thing was to prepare one's soul for the second coming of the Redeemer. So Paul is not known for embracing a positive theology of the body.

17. For other constructions of the Black male body in the U.S. popular culture, refer to Phillip Brian Harper, *Are We Not Men? Masculine Anxiety and the Problem of African-American Identity* (New York: Oxford University Press, 1996).

18. Robin D. G. Kelley, "Confessions of a Nice Negro, or Why I Shaved My Head," in *Speak My Name: Black Men on Masculinity and the American Dream*, ed. Don Belton (Boston, MA: Beacon Press, 1995), 15.

19. James Baldwin, *Price of the Ticket: Collected Non-fiction 1948–1985* (New York: St. Martin's Press, 1985), 290.

20. Ibid., 273.

21. In his *Constructing the Black Masculine: Identity and Ideality in African American Men's Literature and Culture* (Durham, NC: Duke University Press, 2002), 32, Maurice O. Wallace argues that "Black men come to embody the inverse picture necessary for the positive self-portrait of white identity." This picture is what he calls an "ideograph for the American propensity to see Black men half-blindly as a blank/Black page onto which the identity theme of American whiteness, with its distinguishing terrors and longings, imprints itself as onto a photographic negative."

22. Ishmael Reed, "Buck Passing: The Media, Black Men, O. J., and the Million Man March," in Carbado, op. cit., 46.

23. Baldwin, op. cit., xix.

24. Regarding the white wealthy minority that control the U.S. and their impact on Black America, refer to Robert L. Allen, *Black Awakening in Capitalist America: An Analytic History* (Garden City, NY: Doubleday & Company, 1969); Manning Marable, *How Capitalism Underdeveloped Black America* (Boston, MA: South End Press, 1983); David Rockefeller, *Memoirs* (New York: Random House, 2002); Nelson W. Aldrich, Jr., *Old Money* (New York: Vintage Books, 1989); Michael Parenti, *Democracy for the Few* (New York: St. Martin's Press, 1977); G. William Domhoff, *Who Rules America Now?* (Englewood Cliffs, NJ: Prentice-Hall, Inc., 1983); Richard C. Edwards, Michael Reich, and Thomas E. Weisskopf, eds. *The Capitalist System* (Englewood Cliffs, NJ: Prentice-Hall, Inc., 1972); David N. Smith, *Who Rules the Universities?* (New York: Monthly Review Press, 1974); Frances Fox Piven & Richard A. Cloward, *The New Class War*

(New York: Pantheon Books, 1982); and Felix Greene, *The Enemy: What Every American Should Know About Imperialism* (New York: Vintage Books, 1971).

25. Review Derrick Bell, "The Sexual Diversion: The Black Man/Black Woman Debate in Context," in Carbado, ed., op. cit., 239.

26. Ibid., 328–29.

27. Robert E. Hood, *Begrimed and Black: Christian Traditions of Blacks and Blackness* (Minneapolis, MN: Fortress Press, 1994), 89.

28. There exists a beginning but vibrant intellectual tradition on the study of how European ethnic and tribal groups became "white" once they left their ancestors' continent and came to the land of the Native Americans (e.g., now the United States). For instance, see Thomas K. Nakayama and Judith N. Martin, eds. *Whiteness: The Communication of Social Identity* (Thousand Oaks, CA: Sage Publications, 1999); Joel Kovel, *White Racism: A Psychohistory* (New York: Columbia University Press, 1984); Birgit Brander Rasmussen, Eric Klineberg, Irene J. Nexica, and Matt Wray, eds. *The Making and Unmaking of Whiteness* (Durham, NC: Duke University Press, 2001); Richard Delgado and Jean Stefanici, eds. *Critical White Studies: Looking Behind the Mirror* (Philadelphia, PA: Temple University Press, 1997); Mike Hill, ed. *Whiteness: A Critical Reader* (New York: New York University Press, 1997); Matthew Frye Jacobson, *Whiteness of a Different Color: European Immigrants and the Alchemy of Race* (Cambridge, MA: Harvard University Press, 1998); and Theodore W. Allen, *The Invention of the White Race: Racial Oppression and Social Control, volume one* (New York: Verso, 1994).

29. See Dwight N. Hopkins, *Down, Up & Over: Slave Religion and Black Theology* (Minneapolis, MN: Fortress Press, 1999).

30. Hood, op. cit., x.

31. Ibid., 150–51.

32. Leon F. Witwack, "Hellhounds," in *Without Sanctuary: Lynching Photographs in America* (no editor cited) (Santa Fe, NM: Twin Palms Publishers, 2000), 30.

33. Ibid., 9–10.

34. Ibid., 28. Also examine Don Belton, "Introduction," in *Speak My Name: Black Men on Masculinity and the American Dream,* ed. Don Belton (Boston, MA: Beacon Press, 1995), 2.

35. Miriam DeCosta-Willis, "Introduction," in *Erotique Noire: Black Erotica,* ed. Miriam DeCosta-Willis, Reginald Martin, and Roseann P. Bell (New York: Anchor Books, 1992), xxix.

36. Charles H. Long, *Significations* (Philadelphia, PA: Fortress Press, 1986), 7.

37. Kelly Brown Douglas, *Sexuality and the Black Church: A Womanist Perspective* (Maryknoll, NY: Orbis Books, 1999), 123.

38. James H. Cone, *The Spirituals and the Blues* (New York: The Seabury Press, 1972), 128.

39. Alice Walker, *In Search of Our Mothers' Gardens: Womanist Prose* (New York: Harcourt Brace Jovanovich, 1983), xi–xii.

40. Rudolph P. Byrd, "Prologue. The Tradition of John: A Mode of Black Masculinity," in *TRAPS,* 1–2.

41. On the notions of staying, being there, and setting examples, see James Baldwin, *The Evidence of Things Not Seen* (New York: Henry Holt and Co., 1995), 20–21; Arthur Flowers, "Rickydoc: The Black Man as Hero," in Belton, ed., op. cit., 263; and Randall Kenan, "Mr. Brown and the Sweet Science," in Belton, ed., 66.

42. Compare Dennis A. Williams, "A Mighty Good Man," in *Speak My Name* where he describes the reflections of a younger man on the older and young Black male interchange: "I can only now begin to appreciate how much effort and genius that requires—to guide without commands, to correct without rebuke, to set limits without saying no," 84–85.

43. This type of love, I believe, would encourage more Black men to stay in church and relish the company of their wives and, in the process, reaffirm their wives' authority. See Dennis A. Williams, "A Mighty Good Man," in *Speak My Name*, 24–25.

44. Sadie B. Gandy, "Blessed Boys!," in *What Keeps Me Standing: Letters from Black Grandmothers on Peace, Hope, and Inspiration*, ed. Denis Kimbro (New York: Doubleday, 2003), 181.

45. Elder Sharon T. Jones, "The Love We've Lost" in ibid., 205.

46. Michael Uebel, "Men in Color," in *Race and the Subject of Masculinities*, ed. Harry Stecopoulos and Michael Uebel (Durham, NC: Duke University Press, 1997), 2.

47. Examine Marlon T. Riggs, "Black Macho Revisited: Reflections of a SNAP! Queen," in Carbado, 308; and Devon W. Carbado, "Introduction," in Carbado, 4–9.

48. Michael Eric Dyson, "When You Divide My Body and Soul, Problems Multiply: The Black Church and Sex," in *TRAPS*, 313, 316–17.

15

Beyond Machismo: A Cuban Case Study

MIGUEL A. DE LA TORRE

I am a recovering *macho*, a product of an oppressive society, a society where gender, race and class domination do not exist in isolated compartments, nor are they neatly relegated to uniform categories of repression. They are created in the space where they interact and conflict with each other, in a space I will call *machismo*. The understanding of *machismo* requires a full consideration of sexism, heterosexism, racism, ethnocentrism and classism. All forms of oppression are identical in their attempt to domesticate the Other. The sexist, who sees women playing a lesser productive role than men, transfers to the non-elite male Other effeminate characteristics, placing him in a feminine space for "easy mounting."

This article explores the multidimensional aspects of intra-Hispanic oppression by unmasking the socio-historical construction of *machismo*. Usually disenfranchised groups construct well-defined categories as to who are the perpetrators and the victims of injustices. All too often, we who are Hispanic ethicists tend to identify the oppressive structures of the dominant Eurocentric culture while overlooking repression conducted within our own community. I suggest that within the marginalized space of the Latino/a community there exists intra-structures of oppression along gender, race and class lines, creating the need for an ethical initiative to move beyond what Edward Said terms, "the rhetoric of blame."[1] Specifically, this article will present a paradigm called *machismo*, which explicates intra-Hispanic oppression. The article then employs this paradigm to the Cuban experience by examining intra-Cuban sexism, racism and classism.

THE MACHISMO PARADIGM

To be a man, a *macho*, implies both domination and protection of those under you, specifically women. It becomes the *macho*'s responsibility, his burden, to educate those below his superior standards. Because of my gender, I confess my complicity with sexist social structures, complicity motivated by personal advantage.[2] All things being equal, I prevail over women in the marketplace, in the church community and within our Hispanic community because I am male. It is not my intention to speak for women about their oppression, or to provide them with the necessary pedagogy to achieve liberation. Several, although unfortunately not enough, Latina feminist religious scholars are presenting this voice.[3] My contribution to the discourse must be limited to how I, as a male, as a *macho*, facilitate the oppression of my gender Other.

Because sexism reflects only one aspect of *machismo*, it is appropriate to expand the meaning of this term to include all forms of oppression imposed on those who fail to live up to the manly standards of being a white, elite, Cuban male.[4] *Machismo* is as much about race and class as it is about gender. For Cubans, seriously dealing with our patriarchal structures must be the first stage in the process of dismantling all forms of oppression, providing for the liberation and possible reconciliation of all, including women.

History is forged through one's *cojones* (balls). Women, non-whites and the poor fail to influence history because they lack *cojones*, a gift given to *machos* by the ultimate *Macho*, God. To call a man *lavándole los blumes de la mujer* (one who washes his wife's bloomers) is to question his *machismo*. "*El colmo*" (the ultimate sin) is to be called a "*maricón*" (a derogatory term meaning queer or fag), the antithesis of *machismo*. We, white Cuban elite males, look into Lacan's mirror and recognize ourselves as *machos* through the distancing process of negative self-definition: "I am what I am not." The formation of the subject's ego constructs an illusory self-representation through the negation of *cojones*, now projected upon Others, identified as non-*machos*. Ascribing femininity to the Other forces the construction of female identity to originate with the *macho*. In fact, the feminine Object, in and of itself, is seen as nothing apart from a masculine Subject which provides unifying purpose.

The resulting gaze of the white Cuban elite male inscribes effeminacy upon Others who are not *macho* enough to "make" history, or "provide" for their family, or "resist" their subjugation to the dominant *macho*. Unlike in the United States, sexual identity for Cubans is defined in terms of masculinity not in terms of gender. Women are "the not male." When the gendered Other demonstrates hyper-*macho* qualities, she can be praised for being *macho*. This was the case with both General Maceo, who was black, and his mother,[5] thus both were described as *macho*.

The phallic signifier of *machismo* is located in the *cojones*. For Cubans, *cojones*, not the penis, become our cultural "signifier of signifiers." The Other, if male, may have a penis, but lacks the *cojones* to use it. I conquer, I subdue, I domesticate *por mis cojones* (by my balls). A distinction is made between *cojones,* the male testicles, and *cojones,* the metaphoric signifier. Power and authority exhibit *cojones,* which are in fact derived from social structures, traditions, norms, laws, and customs created by *machos,* who usually are white and rich.

From one perspective, no one has *cojones.* The *macho* lives, always threatened by the possible loss of his *cojones,* while the non-*macho* is forcefully deprived. The potent symbolic power invested in the *cojones* both signals and veils white elite Cuban male socioeconomic power. Constructing those oppressed as feminine allows white Cuban men with *cojones* to assert their privilege by constructing oppressed Others as inhabitants of the castrated realm of the exotic and primitive.[6] Lacking *cojones,* the Other does not exist, except as designated by the desire of the one with *cojones.* Like a benevolent father (*el patrón*), it becomes the duty and responsibility of those with *cojones* to care for, provide for and protect those below. The castrated male (read, race and class Other) occupies a feminine space where his body is symbolically sodomized as prelude to the sodomizing of his mind.

The non-*macho* becomes enslaved by the inferiority engraved upon their flesh by the Cuban ethos. Likewise, the *macho* is also enslaved to his own so-called superiority that flows from his *cojones.* While non-*machos* are forced to flee from their individuality, the *macho* must constantly attempt to live up to a false construction. Both are alienated, both suffer from an obsessive neurotic orientation, and both require liberation from their condition. For Cubans, Gutiérrez's "preferential option for the poor" must be expanded to include a preferential option for those castrated by the *macho,* be they women, homosexuals, Taínos, Africans, Chinese, or the poor.

How did our neurotic state develop? Cuba, unlike other Latin American nations that enslaved the indigenous people, reduced the Taínos to near extinction. To replace this vanishing population, Mayans and Africans were imported as slaves. Later, the Chinese began to take their place. The Cuban concern was the acquisition of cheap labor. Hence, slave merchants did not bother bringing women, contributing to a predominant male society. By the same token, the white overlords were also mostly men, searching for gold and glory. Cuba was a stopping off point to somewhere else. Those passing through were on their way to discover riches on the mainland. Few women accompanied these *conquistadores.* Since the very beginning of Cuban European history, its population lacked sufficient number of women of any color. This absence of women contributed to the creation of an excessively male-oriented society, where weaker males (non-*machos*) occupied "female" spaces. They washed; they cooked; they "entertained."

Cuba was the last Latin American nation to gain its independence from Spain. Rather than having a century of nation building, Cuba spent the 19th century preoccupied with military struggles, contributing to a hyper-*macho* outlook. The physical bravado characterizing a century of bloody struggle for independence fused manhood with nationhood. *Machismo* became ingrained in the

fabric of Cuban culture. Both sides of the Florida Straits proclaim the same message: *Patria* is real man's work.[7] Women, gays and blacks are not *macho* enough
to construct *patria*.[8] Hence Cuba, a predominantly black nation, is ruled by a
predominantly white hierarchy, while in Miami, the Cuban American National
Foundation (CANF) was established by fifty white business*men* organizing to
create a post-Castro Cuba. Exilic Cuban anthropologist Behar describes the
amalgamation of *machismo* with nationhood when she writes:

> In seeking to free Cuba from its position as a colony of the United States, the
> Cuban Revolution hoped to redeem an emasculated nation. Manhood and nation-
> hood, in the figure of the Cuban revolutionary hero, were fused and confused. . . .
> Manhood is an integral part of the counterrevolution too. As Flavio Risech points
> out, "Neither *revolucionario* nor anticommunist *gusano* can be a *maricón*." . . . If
> national identity is primarily a problem of *male* identity, how are Cuban women on
> both sides to write themselves into Cuban history?[9]

With colonization by the United States immediately following "independence" from Spain, Cuba continued in its emasculated status. The long U.S.
military occupation, the Platt Amendment and the transformation of La Habana
into a Western Hemisphere whorehouse for Anglo consumption meant Cubans
lost their manhood, their *machismo*. To regain their *machismo*, Cubans learned
how to imitate their oppressor by enhancing forms of domination over non-
machos, especially women. Those of us who came to this country as infants
or small boys seek now to reinstate our *machismo*. The first generation of the
Exilic-Cuban boy in his teen years experienced both peer and parental pressure
to "prove their manhood." *Machismo* means to be sexually ready for anybody,
anywhere, anytime.[10]

Conquering *la americanita* became an adolescent ritual of *machismo*. Exilic
Cuban boys were encouraged to date the *americanita* in order to prove their
manhood, as long as they remembered to marry *la cubanita*.

This generations of Exilic Cubans who arrived in this country as children were
forced to navigate simultaneously both sexual maturation and cultural adaptation. Both these processes, as author Firmat points out, became interwoven so
that gender and cultural identity became integrated. Thus, cultural preference
merged with sexual preference. In trying to become a mature man in exile,
both regression and assimilation remain constant temptations as I attempt to
construct my identity on the hyphen in Cuban-American.[11] To Firmat's description of the attempt to live on the hyphen, I would add the sexual conquest of
the *americanita*. For as Fanon points out, "When my restless hands caress those
white breasts, they grasp white civilization and dignity and make them mine."[12]
Conquering the *americanita* provided an opportunity for the Exilic *macho* to
converse with the dominant culture from the position of being on top (pun
intended).

To tell a man not to be a *maricón* also means "don't be a coward." Cuban
homophobia differs from homophobia in the United States. We do not fear the
homosexual; rather we hold him in contempt for being a man who chooses not

to prove his manhood. Unlike North Americans, where two men engaged in a sexual act are both called homosexuals, for Cubans only the one that places himself in the "position" of a woman is the *maricón*.[13] Only the one penetrated is labeled *loca* (crazy woman, a term for *maricones*).[14] In fact, the man who is in the dominant position during the sex act, known as *bugarrón*, is able to retain, if not increase, his *machismo*.

While visiting the home of an Exilic Cuban radio commentator (who contributes to the anti-Castro rhetoric common on Miami's airwaves), I noticed a statue proudly displayed on his desk. The statue was of a cigar smoking Fidel Castro on all fours with his pants wrapped around his ankles while a standing Ronald Reagan sodomized him. In the mind of the sculptor and the Cuban men who see the statue, Ronald Reagan is not in any way a homosexual. Quite the contrary, the statue celebrates the *machismo* of Reagan who forces Castro into a non-*macho* position.

Carlos Franqui, director of *Radio Rebelde* and one of Castro's twelve disciples who came down from the mountain in 1959 to serve as editor of the newspaper *Revolución*, describes how *machismo* affects politics. He wrote:

> [The politics of gang warfare in the mid-1940's is] disguised as revolutionary politics. Actually, it was a collective exercise in *machismo*, which is its own ideology. *Machismo* creates its own way of life, one in which everything negative is feminine. As our Mexican friends Octavio Paz and Carlos Fuentes point out, the feminine is screwed beforehand. . . . [*Machismo's*] negative hero is the dictator (one of Batista's motto[es] was "Batista is the Man"), and its positive hero is the rebel. They are at odds in politics, but they both love power. And both despise homosexuality, as if every *macho* had his hidden gay side. . . . The two brands of *machismo*, conservative and rebel, are quite different. The conservatives (generals, soldiers, police) always defend the establishment, while the rebels attack it. Nevertheless, both groups share the same views about morality and culture. They hate popular culture, and all the Indian and black elements in it. Anything that isn't white is no good.[15]

SEXISM

Machismo moves beyond the oppression of women. Although a detailed review of the Cuban patriarchal system would reveal a multitude of examples showing how sexism maintains women's repression, this article will instead examine how the overall conquest of "virgin land" was made possible by the initial conquest of female bodies. Cuban *machismo* and the establishment of *patria* (Motherland) occurred within the zones of imperial and anti-imperial power. Here, land and nationalism are gendered. The land requiring subjection is assigned a female body. Several postcolonial scholars perceive nationhood as resting on this male projection of identity.[16]

The construction of *patria, la Cuba de ayer* or *Cuba Libre,* along patriarchal lines, can be understood as a gender discourse. For Resident Cubans, Fidel Castro serves as the father figure, *el señor*. For Exilic Cubans, the late Mas Canosa was the head of the household, *el patrón*. Below both exists feminine land, needing the masculinity of those who will construct *patria* upon her.

Earlier, the first creation of Cuba required the reduction of women to the status of representational objects.[17] As Mörner suggests, the European conquest of the so-called "New World" began with the literal sexual conquest of the native American woman.[18] Todorov recounts an incident involving Miguel de Cuneo, who participated in Columbus' second journey. Cuneo attempted to seduce an indigenous woman given to him by Columbus. When she resisted, he whipped her and proceeded to rape her.[19] The image of land and woman merge. Another example illustrates how Columbus saw the world. To him, "[The world] is like a very round ball, and on one part of it is placed something like a woman's nipple."[20] The concept of "virgin land" represents the myth of empty land. If land is indeed virgin, then, according McClintock, the indigenous population has no aboriginal territorial claim, allowing for the colonizer "the sexual and military insemination of an interior void."[21]

The first European to gaze upon the naked female body of the indigenous people and the virgin land under their feet was Christopher Columbus.[22] Mason shows Columbus' first reaction was not to the lack of political organization of these islands inhabitants nor to the geographical placing of the island's within the world scheme. Rather, by eroticizing the naked bodies of these inhabitants, visions of Paradise were conjured up, with Columbus receiving the Amerindians' awe and love. Columbus and his men are invited to penetrate this new erotic continent which offered herself without resistance.[23] These naked bodies and "empty" land merge the sexual and the economic preoccupations of the would-be colonizers.[24] Virgin land awaits to be inseminated with man's seed of civilization. A reconstruction and reversal exposing the hidden transcripts of oppression through *machismo*, provides a fundamental step toward dismantling Cuban oppression as manifested on both sides of the Florida Straits. On our way to that task, we must address next the issue of racism.

RACISM

Race is not a biological factor differentiating humans, rather, it is a social construction whose function is the oppression of the Object-Other for the benefit of the Subject. Racism toward the Cuban's Others (Amerindians, Africans, Chinese and any combination thereof) is normalized by the social structures of both Resident and Exilic Cubans. Because domination of a group of people by another is usually conducted by the males of the dominant culture, it becomes crucial to understand the construction of this domination as seen through the eyes of the oppressor. Our patriarchal structure projects unto my "darker" Other the position occupied by women regardless of the Other's gender. For this reason, it is valid to explore Cuban racism as a form of *machismo*.

By examining the Spaniards' domestication of the Taínos (of the Arawakan nation), I will expose the original typology of intra-Cuban oppression. As previously mentioned, the *macho* subdues virgin land, relegating her inhabitants to landlessness. According to Kant, "When America was discovered, . . . it was considered to be without owners since its inhabitants were considered as nothing."[25] The gendering of Taíno men as non-*machos* occurred early in the conquest, and provides a prototype for all subsequent forms of Cuban oppression.

By 1535 Gonzalo Fernández de Oviedo, chronicler of the colonization venture, referred to the Amerindians as sodomites in the Fifth Book of his *Historia General y Natural de las Indias* (General and Natural History of the Indies). There exists no hard evidence about attitudes toward homosexuality among the aborigines, but de Oviedo claims that anal intercourse by men with members of both sexes was considered normal.[26] In a report given to the Council of the Indies by the first bishop of Santa Marta, Dominican friar Tomás Ortiz wrote, "The men from the mainland in the Indies eat human flesh and are more given to sodomy than all generations ever."[27] Juan Suárez de Peralta, a resident of Mexico in the late sixteenth century, describes with obvious distaste, the inverted patriarchal of Amerindian society when he writes:

> The custom [of the Amerindians is] that the women do business and deal with trade and other public offices while the men remain at home and weave and embroider. They [the women] urinate standing while the men do so seated; and they have no reluctance to perform their natural deeds in public.[28]

By the eighteenth century, the supposed prevalence of homosexuality among the Amerindians was assumed. Like other "primitives" of the world, the typical Amerindian was regarded as a homosexual and an onanist, who also practiced cannibalism and bestiality. These sins against nature threatened the institution of the patriarchal family and by extension, the very fabric of civilized society. The supposed effeminacy of the Amerindians was further demonstrated by emphasizing their lack of body hair and pictorially displaying their supposedly small genitals. Simultaneously, the Amerindian woman was portrayed with excessively masculine features and exaggerated sexual traits, justifying the need for *macho* Spaniards to enter the land and restore a proper, phallocentric social order.[29]

By constructing people of the periphery as non-*machos*, one assigns them a function in life: service to the Spaniard *machos*. Colonization becomes a form of sexism, the domestication of the indigenous male Other as woman. Thus, Sepúlveda illustrates the masculine superiority of Spaniards to Amerindians by saying that they relate "as women to men."[30] This feminine space constructed for Amerindians was established through brutality. By linking sodomy to cannibalism and bestiality, the Spaniards justified the treatment of Amerindians, the latter were seen as violators of both divine rule and the natural order of both men and animals. The enslavement of the Amerindian was God's punishment for sins and crimes committed against nature.

Spaniards seeing Taínos in the position of women, waged a ruthless war against *el vicio nefando* (the nefarious sin—a euphemism for sodomy).[31] This crusade was waged with righteous indignation on the part of the colonizers, who had the Amerindians castrated and forced them to eat their own dirt-encrusted *cojones*.[32] So also, conquistador Vasco Núñez de Valboa [Balboa] had forty Amerindians thrown to the dogs on charges of sodomy.[33] Spanish *machismo* entailed contempt and rage toward the non-*macho*, which displayed itself in barbarous acts. Las Casas writes, "[The Spanish soldiers] would test their swords and their *macho* strength on captured Indians and place bets on slicing off heads or cutting of bodies in half with one blow."[34] According to the *licenciado* Gil Gregorio, the only hope for the Amerindian was acquiring civilization by working for the Spaniards so that they could learn how to live "like men."[35] Meanwhile, their not being *machos* allowed the Spaniards to take Amerindian women and daughters by force without respect or consideration for their honor or matrimonial ties.[36]

Cuba's African population also was categorized as feminine. Undergirding the construction of race is the perception that blacks are non-*machos*.[37] Quoting various anthropologists of his time (i.e., Klemm), Fernando Ortiz, the Cuban ethnographer, classified humans into two groups: active or masculine, and passive or feminine. Using morphology, he decided that African skulls reveal feminine characteristics.[38] *Machismo* manifested as racism can be observed in the comments of the nineteenth century Cuban theologian José Augustín Caballero, who wrote, "In the absence of black females with whom to marry, *all* blacks [become] masturbators, sinners and sodomites."[39] Until emancipation, the plantation ratio of males to females was 2:1, with some plantations imbalances reaching 4:1.[40] Usually, black women lived in the cities and towns. Hence, slave quarters, known as *barracónes*, consisted solely of men, creating the reputation of their non-*macho* roles as voiced by Caballero. Skewed sex ratios made black males the targets of the white master who as *bugarrones* could rape them. The wives and children of the male slave were also understood to be the master's playthings.[41]

Paradoxically, while the African man was constructed as a non-*macho*, he was feared for potentially asserting his *machismo*, particularly with white Cuban women. White women who succumbed to the black man, it was thought, were not responsible for their actions because they were bewitched through African black magic.[42] Thus, attraction becomes witchcraft and rape. Likewise, the seductive *negra* (Negress) was held responsible for compromising the virtues of the white men.[43] A popular Cuban saying was "there is no sweet tamarind fruit, nor a virgin mulatto girl." Fanon captured the white Caribbean's sentiments when he wrote:

As for the Negroes, they have tremendous sexual powers. What do you expect, with all the freedom they have in their jungles! They copulate at all times and in all places. They are really genital. They have so many children that they cannot even count them. *Be careful, or they will flood us with little mulattoes. . . .* One is no longer aware of the Negro but only of a penis; the Negro is eclipsed. He is turned into a penis. *He is a penis.* (italics mine).[44]

The African-Cuban may be a walking penis, but a penis that lacks *cojones*. White Cubans projected their own fears and forbidden desires upon the African-Cuban through a fixation with the black penis which threatened white civilization. The black penis is kept separate from power and privilege that come only through one's *cojones*. Casal documents this white Cuban fixation with the black penis in recounting an oral history of blacks being hung on lamp posts by their genitals in the central plazas throughout Cuba during the 1912 massacre of blacks.[45] The massacre was fueled by news reports of so-called black revolt leading to the rape of white women. This peculiar way of "decorating" the lampposts perfectly expressed the sexual mythology created by Cuban white racism.

In this analysis we must also include Asians. Asian laborers were brought to Cuba as "indentured" servants, an alternative to African slavery. Landowners were not necessarily interested in obtaining new slaves. Their concern was to procure domestic workers. Although Coolies were technically "free," their conditions were as horrific, if not worse than slavery.[46] Many died during their long voyage to Cuba, ironically, on the same ships previously used to transport Africans. As in slave-ships, an iron grating kept Coolies separated from the quarterdeck. Cannons were positioned to dominate the decks in the event of a rebellion. A Pacific version of the Middle Passage was thus created. In some instances, almost half the Coolie "cargo" perished in transport.[47]

Cuban structures of white supremacy constructed the Coolie laborer similarly to African slaves. Like Africans, few Chinese women were transported to Cuba. Market demand dictated the need for young men to work the sugar fields, not women. According to an 1861 Cuban census, there were 34,834 Chinese in Cuba; of these, 57 were women. By 1871, out of 40,261 Chinese in Cuba, only 66 were women.[48] As with Africans, the lack of women fostered the construction of the Chinese sexual identity as homosexual. Cuban ethnologist Ortiz credits the Chinese for introducing homosexuality (as well as opium) in Cuba.[49] For Martinez-Alier, the consequence of Chinese rejection by the white and black woman led society to conclude that the Chinese succumbed to "unspeakable vices," a euphemism for sodomy.[50]

The Cuban Asian, African and Amerindian share a sacred bond. These three represent God's "crucified people," victims in the expansion and development of capitalism, who literally bear the sins of the modern world. As a crucified people, seen as the feminine Other by *machos*, they provide an essential soteriological perspective on Cuban history.[51] Sobrino, developing the concept of a crucified people, maintains that God chose those oppressed in history and made them the principal means of salvation, just as God chose the "suffering servant," the crucified Christ, to bring salvation to the world.[52] This theme of solidarity between the crucified God and the suffering of the non-*machos* (in our case the Amerindians, Africans and Asians) leads to atonement for the *macho* perpetrators (the Europeans: Spain and the United States). Through the emancipation of the non-*macho*, crucified people liberate the rest of society.

CLASSISM

The Amerindian, African and Asian were constructed as feminine for the benefit of the *machos*. Similarly, those who were poor, regardless of their whiteness, were also seen as being emasculated. Whatever wealth Cuba produced was accomplished by the sweat, blood and corpses of God's crucified people. If Amerindians, African and Asians represent the oppressed elements of our culture, then our Spanish and Anglo roots represent the oppressive elements. Classism among Cubans can be understood as a manifestation of *machismo* whereby a dialectic is created between the subject (Spaniard and Anglo men) and the object (Amerindian, African, and Asian), consisting of the continuous progressive subordination of the object for the purposes of the subject. Writing of the narrative process by those with *cojones* constructs non-Europeans as a secondary race which needs civilization to be mediated through the paternal white hands of the *macho*.

The *macho* subject sees himself in the mirror of commodity purchasing as one able to provide for family, thus strengthening the patriarchal system. For Exilic Cubans, Cuba's economic difficulties proved Castro's inability to provide. Castro thus forfeits his role as *patrón*, as the head of family. Remembering *la Cuba de ayer* as economically advanced, like the United States, justifies the need to reeducate Resident Cubans in a post-Castro Cuba so as to return to her former glory. Their inability to provide demonstrates the Resident Cubans' lack of manhood. Like children, they require instruction in the ways of freedom and capitalism. The relationship Exilic Cubans hope to reestablish is one where Miami positions itself "on top of" La Habana.

Historically, the highest rung of Cuba's social hierarchy was occupied by whites, divided into a variety of stratified economic classes. Regardless of the degree of whiteness, all enjoyed equal political privileges: namely, the right to own as many slaves as desired, and the right to acquire wealth in any manner whatsoever. The apex consisted of whites born in Spain called *peninsulares*, who dominated the property market. They also dominated the commercial sector and held the majority of colonial, provincial and municipal posts. They were preponderant in the Cuban delegation to the Spanish parliament, and in the military and the clergy. They represented the majority of high court presidents, judges, magistrates, prosecutors, solicitors, clerks, and scribes. More than 80 percent of the *peninsular* population was qualified to vote, compared to 24 percent of the entire Cuban population.[53] The *peninsulares* saw themselves in Lacan's mirror as *machos*, while viewing the white *criollos* (those born on the Island) as effeminate and culturally backward. A frequent *peninsular* charge against the *criollos* was their effeminacy, their non-*macho* position.[54]

Below the *peninsulares* in the social hierarchy were these same white *criollos*. Antagonism between them and the *peninsulares* was checked by a shared racial fear. At the bottom of the white stratum were the *monteros* or *guajiros* who lived in the shadows of the white elite. While their lifestyle economically differed little from the slaves, *peninsulares* and white *criollos* conferred upon them the distinction of being superior to all the non-whites.[55] Valuing their elevation above blacks, they served as vigilantes during "slave revolts," showing intense viciousness in their suppression of blacks.[56]

After the Spanish-American War, a dependency relationship with the U.S. developed. It was, then, on the safe domain of Cuban land where the United States first launched its venture into world imperialism.[57] Maturing as an empire, the U.S. was less interested in acquiring territory than in controlling peripheral economies to obtain financial benefits for the center. A dependency relationship with Cuba, masked by the guise of New World independence, was preferable to incorporating an "effeminate" people into the Union. Theodore Roosevelt and his virile "rough riders" established the myth of United States' masculinity later incarnated in John Wayne and the Marlboro man. Attributing effeminacy to the Cubans justified the economic control of the Cuban periphery. Secretary of War Elihu Root, referring to Cuba, said it best: "It is better to have the favors of a lady with her consent, after judicious courtship, than to ravish her."[58]

On March 16, 1889, an article published in *The Manufacturer* questioned whether the United States should annex Cuba. Developing a case against it, the author writes: "The Cubans are not . . . desirable. Added to the defects of the *paternal* race are *effeminacy* and an aversion to all effort, truly to the extent of illness. They are helpless, lazy, *deficient in morals*, and *incapable by nature* and experience of fulfilling the obligations of citizenship in a great and free republic. Their lack of *virile strength* and self-respect is shown by the apathy with which they have *submitted* to Spanish oppression for so long."[59]

According to the *Manufacturer*, Cuban submission to Spain identified the Cubans as an emasculated people, unworthy of being accepted into the *macho* Union.[60]

The economic result of colonialism was the reduction of *machos* to effeminate positions. The 1959 revolution was an attempt to reclaim our masculinity. Likewise, the exilic experience for those of us who came to the United States was in part the establishment of our *machismo* in terms of North American paradigms, accomplished through the capture of Dade County's political, social, economic and cultural power structures. To my mind, white Cuban men with power and privilege in both resident and exilic communities continue to benefit from repressive social structures built around the concept of *machismo*.

CONCLUSION

When *machos* gaze upon the Other, what do they see? How we "see" them defines our existential selves as *machos*. To "see" implies a position of authority, a privileged point of view. "Seeing" is not an innocent metaphysical phenomenon concerning the transmittal of light waves. It encompasses a mode of thought which radically transforms the object being seen into an object for possession. The white Latino elite *macho* understands who he is when he tells himself who he is not. *Machos* as subject are defined by contrasting themselves with the seen objects: Amerindians, Africans, Asians, women, and the poor. In defining what it means to be a *macho* by emphasizing the differences with our Others, one reflects, established power relations exist which give meaning to those differences.

Specifically, when a *macho* gazes upon one of God's crucified peoples, he perceives a group that is effeminate. When the *macho* looks at himself in Lacan's mirror, he does not see a *maricón*; hence he projects what he is not into his Other, defining himself as a white, civilized *macho*. The power of seeing becomes internalized, naturalized, and legitimized in order to rationalize the dominant culture's position of power. Our task as Hispanic ethicists is to move toward dismantling *machismo*, to go beyond *machismo*, by shattering the illusions created in our hall of mirrors.

NOTES

1. Edward W. Said, *Culture and Imperialism* (New York: Vintage Books, 1994), 14, 96, 228–30.

2. According to Shute, sexism names social structures and systems where the "actions, practices, and use of laws, rules and customs limit certain activities of one sex, but do not limit those same activities of other people of the other sex." See Sara Shute, "Sexist Language and Sexism," *Sexist Language: A Modern Philosophical Analysis*, ed. Mary Vetterling-Braggin (Boston: Littlefield, Adams, and Company, 1981), 27.

3. *Mujerista* Theology and Latina Feminist Theology are a response to the sexism existing within our Hispanic community and to the racial, ethnic, and class prejudice existing within an Anglo feminist community which ignores the fundamental ways white women benefit from the oppression of women of color. These Latina theologies attempt to find a Hispanic community which obliterates those institutions which "generate massive poverty, systematic death, and immense inhumane suffering" so that all, women and men, can find fullness of "life, justice, and liberation." See Maria Pilar Aquino, "Doing Theology from the Perspective of Latin American Women," *We Are a People: Initiatives in Hispanic American Theology*, ed. Roberto S. Goizueta (Minneapolis: Fortress Press, 1992), 90; Ada Maria Isasi-Diaz, *En la Lucha: Elaborating a Mujerista Theology* (Minneapolis: Fortress Press, 1993), 3–4. Absent from the discourse is the privileged position occupied by Exilic Cuban Latinas. Obviously Exilic Cuban women still face discrimination, especially outside of Dade County. But, the existence of an ethnic enclave facilitated Exilic Cuban women in obtaining higher status jobs otherwise unavailable. Recently arriving Latinas often obtain employment characterized as dangerous, low paying, and degrading. This was also the case with Cuban women arriving in the 1960s. Cuban women were able to gain employment faster than their male counterparts, because the market in unskilled jobs preferred women, who could be given lower wages. By 1970, Exilic Cuban women constituted the largest proportionate group of working women in the United States. Their role as wage-earners was more a response to economic survival than a response to the feminist movement for equality (Garcia: 109). Eventually, the establishment of the economic ethnic enclave of Miami shielded more recent arrivals from the predicament still faced by other non-Cuban Latinas. Among some Exilic Cuban women, status and social prestige are measured by the ability to hire *una negrita* (a black girl—regardless of age) or *una india* (a *mestiza*) to come and clean house. Missing from a *mujerista* discourse is how race and class impacts intra-Latina location and oppression.

4. *Machismo* has recently become a popularized term. Although it is used synonymously

with sexism, it originally referred to a celebration of conventional masculinities. The term *machismo*, unlike *machista*, is neither solely associated with the oppression of women, nor solely used in a pejorative sense. *Machismo* described the values associated with being a man, a *macho*. Similarly, the celebration of female attributes is known as *hembrismo*. See Ian Lumsden, *Machos, Maricones, and Gays: Cuba and Homosexuality* (Philadelphia: Temple University Press, 1996), 217. A popular Cuban saying is *"soy tan hembra como tú macho"* (I am as much woman as you are man).

5. Antonio Maceo, Cuba's black general during the Wars for Independence, not only symbolized the hopes of Cuba's blacks, but embodied the *macho* qualities of honor, bravery, patriotism and the best that Cubans can hope to be. His exploits on and off the battlefield served as testimony to his testosterone creating the Cuban compliment *"Como Maceo"* (Like Maceo) said while upwardly cupping one's hand as if to weigh the enormity (of one's *cojones*). Blacks who demonstrate white qualities of *machismo* may receive admiration and praise even while being denied earned positions of power and privilege within Cuban society. Likewise, women who demonstrate *macho* attributes will receive praise for their manliness while being denied positions of responsibility. For example, José Martí, father of Cuban independence, honored Maceo's mother, Mariana Grajales Maceo, for impressive procreation of male patriots while glossing over, if not totally ignoring the efforts of Cuban women of all colors who raised funds, aided refugees, outfitted insurgent forces, attracted Anglo support, fought as *mambisas* (female freedom fighters), and served as spies and couriers. Women in *Cuba Libre* were to serve as a repository of inspiration, beauty, purity and morality lest the unleashed powers of female passion generate the destructive passion of men. For a brief history of Martí's attitudes toward women and their role in *Cuba Libre*. See Nancy A. Hewitt, "Engineering Independence: Las Patriotas of Tampa and the Social Vision of Jose Marti," *Jose Marti in the United States: The Florida Experience*, ed. Louis A. Perez, Jr. (Tempe: Arizona State University Center for Latin American Studies, 1995), 23–32.

6. Elizabeth Grosz, *Jacques Lacan: A Feminist Interpretation* (London: Routledge, 1990), 115–45.

7. Lumsden in *Machos, Maricones, and Gays* quotes Castro as saying, "[Revolutionary Cuba] needed strong men to fight wars, sportsmen, men who had no psychological weakness" (Lumsden: 53–54). Additionally, in a 1965 interview with *El Mundo*, Samuel Feijoo, one of Cuba's most prominent revolutionary intellectuals stated, "No homosexual [represents] the revolution, which is a matter for men, of fists and not of feathers, of courage and not of trembling"(61). Likewise, Exilic Cubans consider *patria* building the task of real men of valor. During an interview with *The Miami Herald*, Miriam Arocena, wife of a convicted Exilic Cuban terrorist responsible for several bombings, told the reporter, "This [her husband's terrorist actions] is a thing for men of valor, not for weaklings like you" (Joan Didion, *Miami* [New York: Simon and Shuster, 1987], 99).

8. Between 1965–68 thousands of artists, intellectuals, hippies, university students, Jehovah Witnesses and homosexuals were abducted by the State Secret Police and interned, without trial, in Military Units for Assistance to Production (U.M.A.P.), reeducation labor camps. Because they were dissidents from the normative point of view, they were constructed as homosexuals as illustrated by the slogan posted at the camp's entrance: "Work will make men of you."

9. Ruth Behar, "Introduction," *Bridges to Cuba*, ed. Ruth Behar (Ann Arbor: University of Michigan Press, 1995), 12.

10. Lumsden in *Machos* (31) cites Mirta Mulhare de la Torre's (no relation to the present author) doctoral dissertation (University of Pittsburgh, 1969) who studied Cuban sexuality wrote: "The dominant mode of behavior for *el macho*, the male, [was] the sexual imperative . . . A man's supercharged sexual physiology [placed] him on the brink of sexual desire at all times and at all places."

11. Gustavo Perez Firmat, *Life on the Hyphen: The Cuban-American Way* (Austin: University of Texas Press, 1994), 41–45.

12. Frantz Fanon, *Black Skin, White Masks*, trans. Charles Lam Markmann (New York: Grove Press, 1967), 63. For Fanon, the fantasy of the colonized man is to occupy the space of power and privilege belonging to the colonizer. McClintock points out that the desire of the colonizer differs between the man and the woman. The white male has the luxury of *seizing* any woman of color, while the white woman who sexually engages the man of color *accepts* him. Instead of seizing, it is giving. See Anne McClintock, *Imperial Leather: Race, Gender, and Sexuality in the Colonial Contest* (New York: Routledge, 1995), 362.

13. For a more detailed discussion on the construction of Cuban homosexuality, see Lourdes Arguelles and B. Ruby Rich, "Homosexuality, Homophobia, and Revolution: Notes Toward an Understanding of the Cuban Lesbian and Gay Male Experience," *Hidden from History: Reclaiming the Gay and Lesbian Past*, ed. By Martin Bauml Duberman, Martha Vicinius and George Chauncey (Markham, Ontario: New American Library, 1989); Henk van de Boogaard and Kathelijine van Kammen, "Cuba: We Cannot Jump over Our Own Shadow," IGA Pink Book, 1985: A *Global View of Lesbian and Gay Oppression and Liberation* (Amsterdam: COC, 1985); Lumsden, *Machos*; and Flavio Risech, "Political and Cultural Cross-Dressing: Negotiating a Second Generation Cuban-American identity," *Bridges to Cuba: Puentes a Cuba*, ed. By Ruth Behar (Ann Arbor: The University of Michigan Press, 1995).

14. Missing from this analysis is the space occupied by lesbians, known by Cubans as *tortilleras* (derogatory term translated as dyke). While *maricones* constitute a "scandal" as men forsaking their manhood, tortilleras are usually ignored due to the overall machismo of the society that grounds its sexuality on the macho's desires, repressing finite sexuality. Tolerance of lesbians is partly due to their unimportance to the macho's construction of sexuality. They simply have no space in the dominant construction. For lesbians, as well as homosexual men, the adage "se dice nada, se hace todo (say nothing, do everything)" remains the accepted closeted norm of the Cuban community.

15. Carlos Franqui, *Family Portrait with Fidel: A Memoir*, trans. Alfred MacAdam (New York: Random House, 1984), 150.

16. Several postcolonialist scholars who analyze the gendering of nationhood and land are Peter Mason, *Deconstructing America: Representations of the Others* (New York: Routledege, 1990); McClintock, *Imperial Leather*; David Spurr, *The Rhetoric of Empire: Colonial Discourse in Journalism, Travel Writing and Imperial Administration* (Durham: Duke University Press, 1993); and Tzvetan Todorov, *The Conquest of America: The Question of the Other*, trans. by Richard Howard (New York: Harper & Row, Publishers, 1984).

17. Spaniards' understanding of racism was unlike the North American which passed laws prohibiting racial mixing. For Spaniards sexual relations were as natural as breathing or eating. Spaniard men took indigenous women as bed-partners, concubines or wives. The children of these unions, claimed by the Spaniards as their own, took their father's name. It is estimated that by 1514, 40 percent of Spanish colonizers had indigenous wives. By 1570, in accordance with the Council of Treat elevation of marriage to a sacrament, the Crown forbade married men from traveling to the Americas for more than six months without their family. This resulted in more single men heading west, stimulating a rise of a miscegenate population. See Magnus Morner, *Race Mixture in the History of Latin America* (Boston: Little, Brown, 1967), 35–52; and Carl Ortwin Sauer, *The Early Spanish Main* (Berkeley: University of California Press, 1966), 199.

18. Morner, *Race Mixture*.

19. Todorov, 48–49.

20. *Ibid.*, 16.

21. McClintock, 30.

22. The entry in his travel diary for Thursday, October 11th reads:

Immediately [the morning of Friday the 12th, after land was sited at 2:00 a.m.] they saw naked people, and the admiral went ashore in the armed boat . . . The admiral called two captains . . . and said they should bear witness and testimony how he, before them all, took possession of the island . . . They [the land's inhabitants] all go naked as their mothers bore them, and the women also . . . they were very well built, with very handsome bodies and very good faces.

See Christopher Columbus, *The Journal of Christopher Columbus*, trans. Cecil Jane (New York: Clarkson N. Potter, Inc., 1960), 22–24.

23. Columbus records indigenous accounts about an island called Matino believed to be entirely peopled by women (See Columbus [January 15, 1493], 150–51). Rather than visiting it, Columbus returns to Spain, possibly indicating that he and his crew have had their fill of native, erotic women.

24. Mason, 170.

25. Immanuel Kant, "Zum ewigen Frieden," *Schriften von 1790–1796 von Immanuel Kant* (Berlin: Bruno Cassirer, 1914), 444; as quoted in Luis N. Rivera Pegan, *A Violent Evangelism: The Political and Religious Conquest of the Americas* (Louisville: Westminster/John Knox Press, 1992), 11.

26. Mason, 56–57.

27. Francisco Lopez de Gomez, "Historia General de las Indias (1552)," vol. 22, *Biblioteca de Autores Espanoles*, ed. Enrique de Vedia (Madrid: Ediciones Atlas, 1946), 155–294; quoted in Pagan, 137.

28. Juan Suarez de Peralta, *Tratado del Descrubrimiento de las Indias* (Mexico, 1589), 5, as quoted in Anthony Pagden, *The Fall of Natural Man: The American Indian and the Origins of Comparative Ethnology* (Cambridge: Cambridge University Press, 1982), 174–76. Pagden also quotes Cieza de León who wrote, "Many of them (as I have been reliably informed) publicly and openly practiced the nefarious sin of sodomy." Also, he quotes Gonzalo Fernández de Oviedo as stating, "[They even wore jewels depicting] the diabolical and nefarious act of sodomy" (174–176).

29. Mason, 67, 173.

30. Rivera Pagan, 135.

31. Sven Loven, *Origins of the Tainan Culture, West Indies*, trans. anonymous (Goteborg: Elanders Bokryckeri Akfiebolag, 1935), 529.

32. Diana Lznaga, "Introduction" to Fernando Ortiz, *Los negros curros* (La Habana: Editorial de Ciencias Sociales, 1986), xviii–xix.

33. Mason, 56.

34. Bartoleme de Las Casas, *History of the Indies*, ed. and trans. Andree Collard (New York: Harper & Row, 1971), 94. Las Casas' accounts of the barbarism inflicted upon the indigenous people lead to the construction of the Black Legend. The Black Legend justified the superiority of Protestantism over Catholicism for Anglos, covering attention from the treatment of the indigenous population of North America. Regardless of how the Black Legend was constructed for Anglo consumption, it cannot be denied that within one lifetime, an entire culture of a people, developed upon the Islands of the Caribbean, was exterminated. Those few Taínos who physically survived were assimilated within the dominant Spanish culture.

35. Pagden, 49.

36. Bartolome de Las Cases, *Historia de las Indias*, in *Two Worlds: The Indian Encounter with the European 1492–1509*, ed. and trans. S. Lyman Tyler (Salt Lake City: University of Utah Press, 1988), 156.

37. In spite of *machismo* positioning the black man as a woman, it must be noted that

within Cuban African culture, sexism also is prevalent. Ibos girls are taught to obey and serve men while boys learn to look down at their mothers. The *machista* ethos of the *abakuá* only allow intercourse if the man is on top and is the only one who is active. See Lumsden, 47, 221–22; Enrique Sosa, *El carabalí* (La Habana: Editorial Letras Cubanas, 1984), 50–51; and Manuel Martínez Casanova and Nery Gómez Abréu, *La sociedad secret abakuá* (Santa Clara: University Central de Las Villas, n.d), 16–17. The *bantú* uses the word "man" to solely apply to the members of their nation. All other Africans are not men. See Fernando Ortiz, *El engano de las razas* (La Habana: Editorial De Ciencias Sociales, 1975), 37.

38. Ortiz, *El engano*, 60, 88.

39. Jose Agustin Caballero y Rodriguez de la Barra, "Exposicion relative al matrimonio entre esclavos y otros asuntos relacionados con la poblacion de la isla, asi como algunos aspectos de la vida sexual de los esclavos," C.M. Morales no. 9 (La Habana: Biblioteca Nacional Jose Marti); quoted in Lumsden, *Machos*, 50. Emphasis added.

40. Franklin W. Knight, *Slave Society in Cuba During the Nineteenth Century* (Madison: The University of Wisconsin Press, 1970), 76–8; and Louis A. Perez, Jr., *Cuba: Between Reform and Revolution* (New York: Oxford University Press, 1988), 87.

41. White Cubans constructed an illness that could only be cured by having sex with a black woman. Esteban Montejo, *The Autobiography of a Runaway Slave*, ed. Miguel Barnet and trans. Jocasta Innes (New York: Pantheon Books, 1968), wrote:

> There was one type of sickness the whites picked up, a sickness of the veins and male organs. It could only be got rid of with black women; if the man who had it slept with a Negress he was cured immediately (42).

42. A case study of this phenomenon is presented by Fernando Ortiz, *Los negros brujos: Apuntes para un estudio de etnologia criminal* (Miami: New House Publishers, 1973), 325–30.

43. Quoting Gunnar Myrdal, *An American Dilemma: The Negro Problem and Modern Democracy* (New York: Harper & Row, 1944), Ortiz shows how the myth of the black man's overly extended penis (when compared to the white man) and the white woman's small clitoris (when compared to the black woman) creates a need for precautions lest the white woman be damaged, as well as spoiled. See Ortiz, *El engano*, 87–88.

44. Fanon, *Black Skin, White Masks*, 157–9, 170. Emphasis added. Fanon continues by asking:

> Is the lynching of the Negro not a sexual revenge? We know how much of sexuality there is in all cruelties, tortures, beatings. One has only to reread a few pages of Marquis de Sade to be easily convinced of the fact. (159)

45. Lourdes Casal, "Race Relations in Contemporary Cuba," *The Cuban Reader: The Making of a Revolutionary Society*, ed. Philip Brenner, William M. LeoGrande, Donna Rich, and Daniel Siegel (New York: Grove Press, 1989), 472.

46. I use the word Coolie to refer to the Chinese laborer because this word best describes their social location of oppression. The word Coolie is composed of two Chinese characters, *coo* and *lie*. *Coo* is defined as "suffering with pain;" *lie* means "laborer." Hence the Coolie is the "laborer who suffers with pain," adequately describing their condition in Cuba.

47. The first shipment of Coolies by Waldrop and Company sailed from Amoy on February 7, 1853 with 803 Chinese and arrived in La Habana with only 480. In 1859, the Spanish frigate *Gravina* embarked with 352 Coolies and arrived with 82. See Duvon Clough Corbitt, *A Study of the Chinese in Cuba, 1847–1947* (Wilmore, KY: Asbury College, 1971), 16, 54. For a graphic documented description of the suffering and humiliation caused by their brutal treatment by "civilized" Cuban, see Ch'ên Lanpin, *Chinese*

Emigration: The Cuba Commission Report of the Commission sent by China to Ascertain the Condition of Chinese Coolies in Cuba, trans by A. MacPherson and A. Huber (Shanghai: The Imperial Maritime Customs Press, 1876); also Rebecca J. Scott, *Slave Emancipation in Cuba: The Transition to Free Labor, 1860–1899* (Princeton: Princeton University Press, 1985) 3–124.

48. Hugh Thomas, *Cuba: The Pursuit of Freedom* (New York: Harper & Row, 1971), 188. By 1942, the Chinese Consulate in Cuba had 18,484 Chinese registered, of which 56 were women. Social and legal regulations forbade African (or white) and Asian intermarriage. See Corbitt, 114–15.

49. According to Fernando Ortiz, in *Los negros brujos*, "The yellow race brought the addiction of opium, its homosexual vices and other refined corruptions of its centuries-old civilization" (19).

50. Martinez-Alier, 79. Early during Castro's regime, China sent over a shipment of "socialist" condoms. *Machos* refused to use them claiming they were "too small," thus contributing to both the myth of the Chinese's small penis and to a national rise in pregnancy. See Carlos Franqui, *Family Portrait with Fidel,* 146.

51. Ignacio Ellacuria, "The Crucified People," *Mysterium Liberationis: Fundamental Concepts of Liberation Theology,* ed. Ignacio Ellacuria and Jon Sobrino and trans. Phillip Berryman and Robert R. Barr (Maryknoll: Orbis Books, 1993), 580–81.

52. Jon Sobrino, *Jesus the Liberator: A Historical-Theological Reading of Jesus of Nazareth,* trans P. Burns and F. McDonagh (Maryknoll: Orbis Books, 1993), 259–60.

53. Knight, *Slave Society in Cuba,* 88–89; James S. and Judith E. Olson, *Cuban Americans: From Trauma to Triumph* (New York: Twayne Publishers, 1995), 13; and Perez, *Cuba,* 135, 152.

54. Robert L. Paquette, *Sugar Is Made with Blood: The Conspiracy of La Escalera and the Conflict between Empires Over Slavery in Cuba* (Middletown, CT: Wesleyan University Press, 1988), 48, 91.

55. The lyrics of a slow rumba sung in Matanzas by slaves after emancipation serve as a hidden-transcript describing the new economic reality for both the ex-slaves and the poor whites. See Rebecca J. Scott, *Slave Emancipation in Cuba: The Transition to Free Labor, 1860–1899* (Princeton: Princeton University Press, 1985), 255.

56. Knight, *Caribbean,* 177; Olson and Olson, 12; and Paquette, 43.

57. Earlier conquests of Texas and Northern Mexico represented the expansionist ideology of extending the United States boundaries and physically possessing and repopulating the new lands. Cuba represented a shift toward imperialism. The late nineteenth century represents a transition in the United States from competitive capitalism to monopoly capitalism. This new stage of capitalism merged with imperialism and found its first expression in Cuba.

58. Louis A. Perez, Jr., *Essays on Cuban History: Historiography and Research* (Gainesville: University Press of Florida, 1995), 39.

59. José Martí, "Manufacturer's Do We Want Cuba?" *Our America by Jose Marti: Writings on Latin America and the Struggle for Cuban Independence,* ed. Philip S. Foner and trans. Elinor Randall, Juan de Onis, and Roslyn Held Foner (New York: The Monthly Review Press, 1977), 229.

60. Martí found it necessary to defend Cuban *machismo.* In "A Vindication of Cuba," *Our America,* he responds:

> Because our half-breeds and city-bred young men are generally of delicate physique, of suave courtesy, and ready words, hiding under the glove that polishes the poem the hand that fells the foe are we to be considered as the *Manufacturer* does consider us an "effeminate" people? . . . These "effeminate" Cubans had once courage enough, in the face of a hostile government, to carry on their left arms for a week the mourning-band for Lincoln (236).

In an interesting pre-Lacanian analysis, Martí accuses the United States of transferring negative characteristics onto Hispanics so as to define the Anglo subject through the negation of the Hispanic Object. In "The Truth About the United States," in *Inside the Monster by Jose Marti: Writings on the United States and American Imperialism*, ed. Philip S. Foner and trans. Elinor Randall, Luis A. Baralt, Juan de Onis, and Roslyn Held Foner (New York: The Monthly Review Press, 1975), Martí writes:

> Those structural qualities which, for their constancy and authority, demonstrate two useful truths to our America: the crude, uneven, and decadent character of the United States, and the continuous existence there of all the violence, discord, immorality, and disorder [are] blamed upon the peoples of Spanish America.

However, Martí is also guilty of seeing the Cuban Other as effeminate. In a May 2, 1895 letter "To the New York Herald," *Our America*, he wrote, "The harsh and jealous Spanish possessions allied 400 years ago against the harsh but effeminate Moor" (429).

Rethinking Sexual Ethics

Marvin M. Ellison
Yoel H. Kahn
Karen Lebacqz
Beverly Wildung Harrison
Rebecca T. Alpert
W. Scott Haldeman

Introduction
to Part 4

Christian conventional wisdom about sex, gender, and power provides a confused and oppressive legacy that begs for critique. As British scholar Karen Armstrong observes, "Sex and gender have long been the Achilles' heel of western Christianity" and, further, "for most of its history, Christianity has had a more negative view of *heterosexual* love than almost any other major faith."[1] For centuries church theologians have intoned that the best sex is "no sex." Sexually active couples were expected to marry, make babies, and then move as quickly as possible beyond youthful passion in order to live together as if celibate Christian brother and sister.[2] Although Protestant theologians flipped the celibacy/marriage dichotomy over onto its head and promoted marriage as a Christian duty, there was still no presumption about marriage as morally or spiritually superior. Because the Reformers were persuaded about the pervasiveness of sin (read: lust), they expressed serious doubts that a consistent lifestyle of celibacy was attainable for very many. In light of this heritage, advocates of traditional family values may fail to appreciate how Christian concern about a sex/sin connection has led to reservations even about marriage.

If the Christian response to sex has long been fear and suspicion, and if the prevailing watchwords are control and restraint, then contemporary Christians must look long and hard to find theological affirmation of erotic pleasure and even longer and harder to find theological interest in *women's* sexual pleasure. At the same time, a move to reconstruct sexual norms and practices is now underway in almost every religious tradition, spurred on by the overlapping communities of feminists and LGBT people of all colors, survivors of abuse including clergy abuse, people with disabilities, and single and divorced people—all of whom seek a sex-positive, justice-centered approach that will empower people to live more freely in their bodies and more compassionately in their relationships and communities.

Marvin Ellison's "Reimagining Good Sex: The Eroticizing of Mutual Respect and Pleasure" examines how many people "find themselves erotically aroused only by dominant/subordinate power relations." If a renewal of sexual ethics, in Christian and other communities, requires unlearning the desire for power as control and equipping one another for "mutual vulnerability and interdependency in all our connections," then what does an ethical eroticism look like? In proposing the outlines of "an ethic that eroticizes justice," Ellison examines four guiding value commitments: honoring the goodness of the body and of diverse bodies, securing bodily self-determination or bodily integrity, mutuality, and fidelity. His argument is that "patriarchal Christianity has it wrong: The erotic is not a hostile, alien force lurking from within to bring us to ruin, but is rather an internal moral guidance system, grounded in our body's responsiveness to respectful, loving touch."

Rabbi Yoel H. Kahn's "Making Love as Making Justice: Towards a New Jewish Ethic of Sexuality" offers a methodology for a liberal Jewish framework for sexual decision making that navigates the conflicting values of the received tradition and the fresh moral insights from contemporary society. After outlining the organizing values of sexuality within rabbinic culture, he contrasts the received paradigm with a modern response whose organizing values, as he notes, reflect "our changed priorities and premises," including the full humanity of women and LGBT persons and "our commitment to the equality, dignity, and autonomy of each person as an individual [which] is unprecedented in our tradition." Two further claims are at play in this essay. First, Kahn contends that it is possible "simultaneously to dissent radically from received teaching while claiming to stand in and even represent the tradition from which it comes." Second, his insistence that "our most intimate relationships should be the place of our primary and greatest expression of covenantal justice" leads to an effort to correct certain distortions within the wider culture, including the excessive focus on personal pleasure, the abuse of erotic and other forms of power, and the skewed focus on genital performance rather than mutual intimacy.

Karen Lebacqz's "Appropriate Vulnerability" makes a case for a renewed Christian ethic of sexuality that does not mandate celibacy in singleness. If the traditional guidance is no longer adequate for singles, Lebacqz insists, "this situation does not mean that anything goes or that the church has nothing to offer by way of a positive ethic for single people." To the contrary, the tradition offers wisdom about the purposes of sexuality, which she argues include not only procreation and loving union, but also appropriate expression of vulnerability. The willingness to be vulnerable in intimate connection is an antidote "to the human sin of wanting to be in control or to have power over another." One of the implications of this emphasis is that any sexual relating that violates appropriate vulnerability is out of bounds, including coerced sex or rape, which is wrong "not only because it violates the vulnerability of the one raped, but also because the rapist guards his own power and refuses to be vulnerable." Another implication is that because sexuality requires vulnerability, it is necessary to explore what Lebacqz calls the "protective structures" necessary for both single and partnered persons, which may well take different forms for the very young and for older persons. Throughout, she insists that "without a good sexual ethic for singles, there cannot be a good sexual ethic for couples either."

Beverly Wildung Harrison addresses "Sexuality and Social Policy" from the perspective that "we need a new understanding of the dialectic between love and justice" insofar as securing personal well-being is dependent upon, and intertwined with, guaranteeing the societal conditions that provide safety, dignity, and a fair share of resources for all community members. Two large dynamics are pushing a reconsideration of sexuality and sexual ethics: (1) emerging social-scientific paradigms about human psychosocial development in the midst of a multiplicity of sexualities, and (2) a global feminist movement that seeks women's full social recognition and rights as persons. Setting social policy priorities with respect to sexuality and gender will also require attention to race and class oppression, or as Harrison puts the matter, we must learn to ask, "How do the matters that are central to my liberation touch the lives of those who are doubly or triply oppressed? We must learn to shape our formulation of sexual justice with this question and these persons in view." After making the case that the most effective social change strategies must aim at both the cultural and legal levels, Harrison analyzes various ways to critique sexual injustice without reinforcing sex-negativity. "What we need," she concludes, "is a deepened and more holistic sense of ourselves that will enable us to grow sexually, to celebrate, and to respect our own sexuality and that of others."

Rebecca T. Alpert takes up the subject of "Guilty Pleasures: When Sex Is Good Because It's Bad" and begins by acknowledging that most religious traditions, including her own tradition of Judaism, regulate sexual behavior, typically by differentiating licit from illicit desires, relationships, and behaviors. Although frequently these regulatory systems have been oppressive, Alpert observes that "they have also had unintended liberating consequences." Because it is likely that such systems will be in place, how might we identify and encourage their positive potential to redefine good sex, especially in her context from a Jewish feminist perspective? Moreover, from a religiously legal perspective, how might we better appreciate and manage the "tension places" insofar as "good sex will always be ethical, but it may also be forbidden"? If problems with regulating sex include the instrumentalizing of sex, gender inequities, and "making sex seem bad, dangerous, and shameful," Alpert notes that a system of control may serve valuable purposes by addressing the power of sexual desire, heightening for some the erotic power of the forbidden, and even educating people about unexpected possibilities. Her conclusion is that "to set up a system that invites transgression teaches people that they can question the values of the societies in which they live, and the results may be dramatic in bringing about the possibility of social change."

W. Scott Haldeman proposes a redefinition, or at least a refining, of fidelity as a relational norm in his essay "A Queer Fidelity: Reinventing Christian Marriage." As a partnered gay man and theologian, Haldeman reflects on what it means to be a "good husband" and suggests that he fails to measure up by conventional standards insofar as he is divorced, lives with another man, and does not equate fidelity with genital sexual exclusivity. In sorting out historical and contemporary theological wisdom about relational integrity, marriage vows, and the refusal to view sex perennially as a "moral problem," Haldeman reclaims the value of fidelity from a queer theological stance by redefining it as radical honesty, deep loyalty, and substantive accountability. His hope is that "there is room for multiple, potentially faithful models" of relational bonding and mutual care and that an invitation to faithfulness in intimate connection may enable "being true both to oneself and to the other in a risky but exhilarating journey."

NOTES

1. Karen Armstrong, "Not So Holy Matrimony," *The Guardian*, June 30, 2003.
2. Mark D. Jordan, *The Ethics of Sex* (Malden, MA: Blackwell Publishers, 2002), esp. chap. 3, "A New Life beyond Sex," 47–75.

16

Reimagining Good Sex: The Eroticizing of Mutual Respect and Pleasure

MARVIN M. ELLISON

For matters moral, I suggest we engage in creative listening, sketch some general directions, and leave the rest up to the good sense of faithful people.

Mary Hunt[1]

The moral problematic about sexuality in this culture is that racist patriarchy annexes body pleasure and attaches it to injustice. Many people find themselves erotically aroused only by dominant/subordinate power relations. They accept these patterns as normative and entirely natural. Progressive people, therefore, in religious communities and elsewhere, have their work cut out for them if they intend to confront this humanly corrupting state of affairs. Eroticizing equality and mutual respect as the normative expectation for all social interaction lies at the heart of challenging every social oppression.

Reversing the workings of a patriarchal culture that eroticizes gender, race, and other injustices will not come easily. Both personal and sociocultural transformations are needed. As Beverly Harrison observes, "the tragedy of our so-called sexual morality is that mutual respect and eroticism are utterly separated in the lives of most people." As if that were not enough, people who "lack a genuine power of eroticism . . . assuage their emptiness by controlling others."[2] Moreover, the eroticization of male gender supremacy allows many men to believe that coercing an intimate partner, whether male or female, feels good. Women are encouraged to believe that being overpowered by a partner is pleasurable or at least tolerable. White supremacy, ableism, and other social dynamics work in conjunction with misogyny to reinforce the cultural link between eroticism and injustice. The powerful presume they are entitled to control others. They feel their entitlement deep in their bones. The less powerful feel obligated to be securely placed under someone else's control. They feel fear and guilt if they venture to cross the line. Inequities of power and status are naturalized as something that feels right to people, close to their skins.

If we fail to see how patriarchal eroticism has electrified injustice and made it titillating, we will not grasp why so many people manage to rest comfortably with oppression, their own and that of others. Why is it that people not only tolerate injustice, but do so with smiles on their faces? Could it be that injustice corrupts at the body level and, therefore, at the core of our personhood? Could injustice not dissipate the human longing for real companionship across a multitude of social differences or numb our social affections altogether? Whenever oppression rubs day and night against the body, people end up not only thinking about but also somatizing racism, sexism, heterosexism, and cultural elitism. These power distortions are felt in, through, and by their bodies. All this affects how they carry their bodies, move their arms and legs, hold their heads, and occupy space in relation to others. People internalize in their bodies, not simply in their psyches, the belief that injustice feels good and safe. Considerable effort will therefore be needed to unlearn our embodied social alienation and, conversely, to appropriate a desire, at a sufficiently deep level, for social relations that are respectful of all people.

The renewal of Christian sexual ethics, in any meaningful sense, requires taking on an extensive project of moral transformation. On the one hand, we must invite people into a process of unlearning the culturally inculcated eroticized desire for power as control. On the other hand, we must teach the value of mutual vulnerability and interdependency in all our connections. Moral education must specifically address what it means to take responsibility for doing what is right and pleasurable with our bodies. For some people, physical touch, including genital touching, will take place primarily or exclusively within a committed relationship. When all goes well, sex enhances an intimacy already established. For others, sex will be an initial avenue for exploring bodily connection with another and for opening up the possibility of further intimacy and friendship.

Accepting sexual touch as a moral resource flies in the face of racist, patriarchal norms. However, mutual pleasuring undertaken with tenderness and respect is a crucial, though widely neglected, component of Christian moral formation. Conventional sexual ethics have not only discouraged such exploration, but have weighed it down with the sternest approbation. The denial of pleasure is characteristic of oppressive systems. Any social order—or religious ethic, for that matter—that discourages people from trusting their feelings, especially their sensuality, or from enjoying their bodies will be experienced as oppressive to the human spirit. Instead of trying to restrain sexual expression through fear, shame, and other social sanctions, we should be enhancing people's interest in and growth toward mature intimacy relations. We need an ethic that appreciates how we become sexually mature persons only through an extended process of exploration and not magically by going through any single life passage (e.g., entering into marriage). We need, but do not yet have, an ethic that would equip us both to enjoy our freedom and to assume our responsibility as sexual beings. We must learn to honor ourselves as lifelong students of erotic discovery, self-awareness, and delight.

The renewal of Christian sexual ethics also requires greater candor about the widening gap between official church teaching about sex and the actual lives of most people. This gap has developed—not as conservatives argue—because people are suddenly less conscientious, but because the conventional religious moral code ("celibacy in singleness, sex only in marriage") is woefully outdated and inadequate. Dissatisfaction with conventional sexual morality is increasing, and for good reason, among young and old, male and female, gay and nongay, married and single persons. No sexual ethic, Christian or otherwise, can claim moral credibility if it is constructed upon human suffering and body alienation.

Our task is nothing less than to break the eroticized link between pleasure and injustice. Rampant fear of erotic power undergirds sexualized oppression against women and against gay, lesbian, and bisexual people of all colors. At the same time, all persons, with or without social power, are diminished because of the cultural disparagement of the body and the refusal to accept mutual pleasure as the norm for all intimate relations.[3] Racist patriarchy promotes eroticized fear as a social control mechanism. People learn to distrust the erotic and identify their sexualities, rather than injustice, as the source of their personal pain and sorrow. A liberating ethic must challenge such confusion and make a decisive break with this sex-negativity, but what sort of ethic would make this break possible? What would it mean to honor the erotic as the spark within and between us that values mutuality? This chapter explores the possibility of an ethical eroticism.

REIMAGINING EROTIC POWER

In contrast to racist patriarchal views that sex is an alien, destructive force that requires heavy restraints, a liberating Christian ethic welcomes sexual energy as an intrinsic, constitutive component of our humanness. Sexuality is our embodied sensuality and capacity for connection. Sexuality is, therefore, more than an isolated segment of our lives. It extends far beyond genital sexual expression. Persons are body-selves. We connect with the world through our senses and through touch. Our sensuality and embodiment as males and females ground our being in the world.

If it is misleading to say that we merely have a body, it is also misleading to suggest that sexuality concerns only one's "private" feelings apart from others and the world. Rather, sexuality is our relational capacity to move beyond ourselves toward others. Living passionately in our bodies, living from the center outward (rather than from external scripts), opens us to vital and at times playful interaction with others. Sexuality is a mode of communication, the giving and receiving of recognition and regard. The erotic desire for knowledge—to know and be known by another—goes far beyond the need of the intellect or the genitals. The whole self becomes engaged. We long for an embodied response from another who confirms our individuality, knows us subject-to-subject, and responds to us as a person fully alive. Sexuality infuses personal and social life with energy for connection and mutual recognition.

Theologian Rebecca Parker, in an essay entitled "Making Love as a Means of Grace," writes that sexuality generates joy in being alive. It also reassures us of our personal power to affect others and, in turn, be affected by them. Most importantly, sexuality releases creative energy, a generative power from within that brings forth a distinctive passion or liveliness. Parker explains, "In this way, again, carnal knowledge saves us rather than damns us." By granting us a sense of ourselves as powerful and present to one another, our sexuality draws us to focus on the joy of creating. Through our embodied capacity for sensuality and pleasure, "the zest for passionate, exuberant, creative living can be tasted and seen and thus restored and sustained."[4]

As sensuous human beings, we know and value the world and therefore become self-directing moral agents only as we feel connected in and through our bodies. As Beverly Harrison contends, "all our relations to others—to God, to neighbor, to cosmos—[are] mediated through our bodies, which are the locus of our perception and knowledge of the world."[5] Patriarchal Christianity fears deep feeling and therefore negates sexuality, but in doing so it also diminishes moral perception and attentiveness in people. "If feeling is damaged or cut off," Harrison explains, "our power to image the world and act into it is destroyed and our rationality is impaired."[6] Moral knowing is rooted in feeling, and we depend upon sensuality to grasp and value the world. When sexuality is feared and evaded, people lack responsiveness and run the risk of becoming out of touch with what causes joy, suffering, and vulnerability, including their own. A people alienated from their bodies are more likely to be content with, and even at home with, pain and oppression.

A liberating ethic affirms, as Valverde suggests, that "where there is strong eroticism, there is power," including the power to claim one's agency as both lover and beloved.[7] Erotic energy is present in all social interaction, but contrary to patriarchal ideology, erotic desire in and of itself is not dangerous. The danger lies in the misuse of this power against another. In a culture in which inequalities of race, gender, and class are eroticized, one person's power becomes the cause of another person's pain and humiliation. Therein lies the real danger.

Eroticizing equality within every social relation would require an equitable redistribution of power and social goods. It would also encourage people to explore friendship and intimacy with appropriate measures of freedom, playfulness, and respect. When two persons are present to each other and recognize each other as fully human, when each can assume the role of the "knower" and the "known," erotic power sharing can generate deep pleasure between them. This kind of lovemaking can fuel a desire to extend right relation throughout other aspects of their lives. Persons thus experience themselves as desirable and lovable, able to combine action and receptivity, feeling and doing. Their body-mediated erotic power is morally good. As Parker notes, when women and, I dare say, men are erotically empowered, we "feel the force of our soul, the reality of our powerful presence in the world, and we feel it with joy."[8]

Erotic joy is typically disparaged as a moral resource. Frequently, "ethics" is taken to mean strict rules without exception that keep people from doing whatever it is they really want to do. People learn that if an activity feels good to them, they probably should not be doing it, at least not without guilt. The forbidden activity varies, but it may be sex, eating desserts, or taking a day off from work. The ethical here is equated with the negative ("Don't do it!") and with duty, acting against one's desires. Pleasure and duty are seen as opposites. Moral minimalism fits neatly with patriarchal antieroticism. It also reinforces the abiding sense of personal inadequacy that plagues so many people in capitalist cultures. People do not trust themselves or their feelings. Patriarchal ethics foster self-hatred.

In contrast, feminist and gay/lesbian/bisexual liberation perspectives are appreciative of materiality, sensuality, and pleasure as ethical guides.[9] If creation, including our humanity, is genuinely good and a source of delight, should we not expect correspondences between what is good and what feels good to us? Would it not be wrong to discount the connection between right conduct and our sense of personal satisfaction, even happiness? A liberation ethic rejects the assumption that delight and pleasure are morally frivolous and fraught with danger.[10] To the contrary, our capacity to take delight in life is an important standard for judging what is worthwhile and useful for ethical living.

Satisfaction should infuse all life activities, not only the explicitly sexual. Audre Lorde, in her essay "Uses of the Erotic: The Erotic as Power," speaks of the erotic as the "nurturer or nursemaid of all our deepest knowledge." When we feel deeply about our life pursuits and the quality of our relationships, we begin to ask that all activities resonate, she writes, "in accordance with that joy which we know ourselves to be capable of." The erotic becomes a source of moral insight, "projected from within each of us, not to settle for the convenient, the shoddy, the conventionally expected, nor the merely safe." Erotic power is our means to say "yes" to life. It insists that actions fit the value of "what is deepest and strongest and richest within each of us."[11]

A feminist and gay liberation ethic challenges the view that eroticism is something merely self-indulgent or a distraction from moral development. Taking the erotic seriously makes us responsible in a new way for using this gift wisely. Centered, self-respecting persons become both responsible to themselves and open to the value of others. Living tenderly into and within our sensuality, we are less likely to become numb to oppression or to ignore our pain or the pain of others. By staying attuned to what feels right to us and by nurturing this awareness in the whole of our lives, we become less willing to tolerate abuse, injustice, and human cruelty. We become more and more desirous of living freely. We therefore also run the risk of becoming a danger to the status quo because of our unwillingness to tolerate abuse and oppression.

Patriarchal Christianity has it wrong: The erotic is not a hostile, alien force lurking from within to bring us to ruin, but is rather an internal moral guidance system, grounded in our body's responsiveness to respectful, loving touch. We have the capacity to comprehend the power of the erotic in our lives and make good choices about its use. We can work through the implications of our feelings, sexual and otherwise. In doing so, we gain confidence in ourselves as thinking, feeling, acting subjects who can respond to life's demands as our own persons, from the inside outward. Contrary to patriarchal voices, therefore, erotic desires are not inherently selfish or antithetical to moral value. Progressive seekers of justice-love can well imagine living by an ethical eroticism that enjoys life's pleasures and at the same time prods us to pursue a more ethical world. The erotic can fuel our passion for justice. It invites us to take ourselves seriously as sexual persons, playfully as erotic equals, and persistently as those who refuse to accept oppression as the way things must be. Defenders of the status quo rightly see erotically empowered people as dangerous and beyond their control.

GUIDING PRINCIPLES
FOR AN ETHICAL EROTICISM

An ethical eroticism operates with four central value commitments: to honor the goodness of the body, of bodily integrity or self-direction, of mutuality, and of fidelity. Each of these contributes to erotic justice within intimate and all other social relations.

To begin with, bodies are good, capable of giving and receiving pleasure. Our bodies deserve respect and care. As Carter Heyward explains, "the body is to be taken with ultimate seriousness. There is nothing higher, nothing more holy."[12] Moreover, sex is good. Sexual touching expresses our moral power to love and care for each other through our bodies. Sensuous touching, sometimes genital and sometimes not, communicates our regard for each other in powerful yet gentle ways.

Bodily integrity or self-direction is a basic moral good. Each person is entitled to choose whether (and how) to relate with his or her body. Body right means freedom from control and manipulation by another, as well as having the power to direct the use of one's body and body space according to context and one's own choices.

Ownership of a person's body and, by extension, of the person's self has been a historic principle of racist patriarchy. The conventional marriage ethic promotes male ownership of women but mystifies its control of women and children by romanticizing family life. Honoring bodily integrity disqualifies, without exception, the right to possess or exploit any person's body space. Another's body is not mine for the taking, nor do I give up my right to my own body either when I consent to have sex with someone or once we have had sex together. Body right requires that we respect each other as persons and, therefore, as whole body-selves. As John Stoltenberg warns, "You may or may not love—but you must always respect. You must respect the integrity of your partner's body. It is not yours for the taking. It belongs to someone real."[13]

Morally sound sexual relations also depend on, and aim for, mutuality. Sex is not doing something to someone else, but is rather a mutual process of being with and feeling with another person. Persons, not mere body parts, meet and touch. An ethical eroticism requires paying attention to the other person as if to oneself. Both parties must show up, and be accounted for, together.

Good touch, it should be emphasized, requires consent. Consent is valid only if each party has the right (and the power) to exit, without penalty, from any interaction. Consent is actualized in relations of mutual respect, in which parties share a common, though rarely an equivalent, vulnerability, that is, a capacity to be affected by the interaction. Mutuality is a dynamic, open-ended process in which each person is empowered to give to, as well as to receive from, the relationship in a fair, nonexploitative manner. In a mutually structured relation, both parties experience themselves as cared for and respected.

Finally, fidelity makes durability, substance, and hope possible within relationships. Fidelity means honoring our commitments, working together to maintain trust, and renegotiating with one's partner as needs, desires, and conditions unfold. Fidelity is dependent on mutual openness and honesty. It is violated by dishonesty, but also by an unwillingness to grow and change as the relationship develops. The precise requirements for fidelity cannot be prescribed in advance or in a legalistic, static fashion, but should be assessed in terms of what best honors the needs of both parties and the integrity of the relationship itself. This is difficult in an erotophobic culture, both fearful of and fixated with erotic power and sexuality. Erotophobia promulgates not only hatred of the body but also deep self-hatred, so we therefore are enculturated not to name our needs forthrightly. Our socialization in a racist patriarchal culture frustrates our desire to be rightly connected, but—wonder of wonders—our imaginations help us envision alternative ways of loving beyond the limited roles the culture has assigned us.

These values undergird an ethic that is sex-affirming and respectful of erotic power as a moral resource. Special controls on sexuality are not necessary, nor do we need fear-based strategies to restrain erotic power. A mature sexual ethic focuses not on what must be prohibited or kept under control, but rather on the quality of relationship, the pattern of respect and care, and how power is distributed and expressed. It also does not lose sight of the fact that the interpersonal is connected to, and dependent upon, the social and cultural matrix in which our lives are embedded. We need an erotic ethic that appreciates how the personal and sociocultural are intertwined, but that also knows how justice makes love more pleasurable and therefore more desirable in all aspects of our lives.

AN ETHIC THAT EROTICIZES JUSTICE

Coming of age in regard to sexuality requires celebrating, not simply tolerating, a rich diversity of sexual relationships that have moral substance. Celibacy and heterosexual marriage are valued insofar as they are freely entered into and enhance people's dignity and well-being, but marriage and celibacy do not exhaust the full range of morally acceptable options. A mature Christian ethic does not restrict sexual activity to marriage alone. Nor does it bless all sex within marriage as morally acceptable. Widespread patterns of coercive sex within marriage, including marital rape, are sufficient reason for discarding highly romanticized notions about the sanctity of the marriage bed.[14] Only those sexual relations, marital and nonmarital, that exhibit mutual respect and genuine care for the partners should be celebrated by the wider community.

The prevailing sexual ideology diminishes human loving, both in scope and beauty, by making heterosexual coupling compulsory. Heterosexual monogamy is regarded as the necessary and "naturalized" arrangement, within a gender hierarchy, for a man and a woman to find their "significant other" who will complement, and therefore complete, their genderized half-identities. Compulsory coupling has several ethically significant consequences. First, if long-term coupling is the only arena for sexual expression, then many people are left entirely out of consideration. Conventional sexual ethics for the most part have paid insufficient attention to the sexuality of single persons.[15] Single persons have been assumed to lack sexual needs altogether or else have been expected to repress their sexuality by remaining celibate, even over the course of a lifetime. On the one hand, then, single persons have been desexualized. On the other hand, they have been oversexualized and viewed with fear and suspicion as potential threats to intact couples.[16]

Second, compulsory coupling also encourages dependency patterns between intimates. As social ethicist Mary Hobgood explains, the idealization of romantic love encourages both men and women to locate that one special person who supposedly can meet all their intimacy needs. This directs them to look outside themselves for fulfillment. "We are thereby taught," Hobgood observes, "to abdicate responsibility for ourselves."[17] Because their "missing half" controls their happiness, people fail to take responsibility for their own happiness or to pursue their own sense of what brings them satisfaction. In addition, compulsory monogamy restricts the range and significance of other friendships. As a couple, people are discouraged from establishing emotionally strong connections outside their twosome. A highly restrictive monogamy ethic, therefore, weakens ties with the larger human community. Couples turn inward and become increasingly isolated from other socially meaningful, emotionally satisfying relationships. An enormous burden is placed on two people, and on them alone, to provide the emotional depth and sociality that only a diverse community can offer.

This marriage ideology fits neatly with, and is reinforced by, the dominant capitalist ethos that patterns all relationships as property relations. In a capitalist patriarchy, men exercise the right of property ownership, especially over female partners. The fiction of a scarcity of love further justifies competition for establishing monopoly control over another person as one's personal "supply." Capitalist ideology also reinforces the prevailing antisexual, erotophobic ideology by positing that the desire for pleasure leads inexorably to narcissistic self-indulgence.

A liberating ethic must insist, quite to the contrary, that viewing our social ties as property relations, in which some seek possession of others, distorts intimacy and blocks real pleasure. Authentic pleasure emerges only as people belong securely to themselves as persons in their own right and as they then relate to others out of strength and personal integrity, rather than from an inner emptiness. A real self can meet another as a real self. As Hobgood comments, "Love, including married love, thrives only as mutual recognition and passionate connection between two distinct selves fully capable of healthy self-love and personal satisfaction in their separate lives."[18]

Sexual ethics traditionally have focused more on the form than on the substance of sexual relations. Conformity to prevailing social expectations about entering marriage (or reentering marriage after divorce) has been the primary criterion for personal maturity and social responsibility. Substantive questions have been downplayed or ignored, especially moral concerns about safety and consent, commitment, and the distribution of power. Similarly, the conventional taboo against same-sex sexual activity has focused on the gender of the sexual partners rather than on the moral quality of their relationship. Following the logic of a patriarchal ethic, people tend to fixate on the question of whether loving, same-sex relations can be morally acceptable. Meanwhile, morally dubious activities, such as rape within "respectable" marriages, escape scrutiny altogether. Conventional sexual ethics have not been sufficiently discriminating.

Patriarchal logic is no substitute for informed ethical judgment. Once we question the normativity of compulsory heterosexuality, it no longer makes sense to validate heterosexual relations merely because they are heterosexual or to discredit same-sex relations because the love expressed is between two women or two men. It no longer makes sense to condemn nonmarital sex simply because it falls outside a particular formal, institutional arrangement. Our ethical sensibilities must be realigned. For too long, the moral problematic has been misnamed, especially in churches, as the "problem" of homosexuality and nonmarital sex. Granted, gay, lesbian, and bisexual persons and sexually active singles enjoy an apparent freedom by establishing their relationships outside the structure of patriarchal marriage. A justice hermeneutic, however, allows us to see that the moral problem does not lie in nonconformity to patriarchal norms of sexuality. Rather, the problem of sexuality is reflected in our society in the large number of loveless, graceless relationships of all kinds, heterosexual and homosexual, marital and nonmarital, and in the splitting off of eroticism from mutuality. The crisis is grounded in the widespread devaluing of women, of gay/lesbian/bisexual people, and of persons in nondominant racial/ethnic communities.

This moral crisis is only made worse by the refusal of religious communities to challenge compulsory heterosexuality, as well as gender, class, and race supremacy. Reaching a new maturity about these matters will require honoring gay men, lesbians, and bisexual persons of all colors in the life and leadership of churches. It will also require public celebration of same-sex relationships, including same-sex marriages, as fully embodying covenantal love between two people. Furthermore, a trustworthy ethic will not seek to control people by fear and guilt, but rather will equip them to make responsible decisions and live gracefully, even in the midst of failure and ambiguity.

By now it should be obvious why neither marriage nor heterosexuality but justice in sexual relationships should be morally normative. A commitment to justice affirms our common decency amid the diversity of human sexualities and honors our shared need for intimacy and affection. As sexual persons, we experience a quite remarkable yearning for communion with others, the natural world, and God. This yearning is at once emotional, cognitive, physical, and spiritual. Sexual passion for connection and communion ennobles our lives. Only by unabashedly reclaiming sex as intrinsic to Christian (and other forms of) spirituality can we begin to recapture a more earthy, sensuous appreciation of how we are created to be justice-lovers, relishing pleasure and mutual affirmation. Staying in touch with our senses, with one another, and with whatever moves us in delight, horror, or curiosity, is an open-ended moral project full of surprises and challenges.

For this reason, it is fitting not to grant special status to heterosexual marriage, but rather to celebrate all sexual relations that deepen intimacy and love. Marriage is valued, but not because it serves as a license for sex or establishes ownership rights over another human being. Rather, egalitarian, justice-bearing marriages offer a framework of accountability and a relatively stable, secure place in which to form durable bonds of mutual trust and devotion. Marriages should deepen friendship beyond, as well as within, the primary relation and avoid fostering patterns of dependency and control.

Some marriages make room for additional sexual partners. Others thrive only by maintaining sexual exclusivity. Although justice requires relational fidelity, the precise requirements of this fidelity cannot be determined in advance. Rather, the concrete "terms of endearment" can be refined only as a particular relationship develops. For some people, the covenant bond will most likely be violated not by satellite friendships or "outside" sexual friendships, but rather by refusals to keep faith and give priority, within a multiplicity of relationships, to the marriage commitment. For all people, fidelity requires an ongoing willingness to respond fairly and forthrightly to the demands of the relationship.

Obviously, what I call justice-bearing marriages require a high degree of moral responsibility, mutual commitment, and willingness to respect the diversity of each partner's needs. Equally, same-sex couples should have the right to participate in and receive community support for an enduring, formalized sexual partnership. For all couples the question becomes: When is their union properly "consummated," and how do they (and others) know that? Sexual activity alone does not mark the establishment of a marriage or an authentic sexual friendship, nor should it. Sex does not "make" a marriage happen. Neither does a religious ceremony nor authentication by the state. Since the church does not make a marriage happen but rather offers a blessing, we need to clarify appropriate criteria for knowing when a marriage actually occurs.

Marriages take place only as persons are wholeheartedly committed to each other as genuine equals and thereby experience mutual respect, care, and affection. At least some divorces signal less an end to a marriage than a public announcement that no genuine marriage had ever taken place. In order to mark the moral significance, therefore, as well as the riskiness, of marriage as a sustained moral commitment, religious communities should be more discriminating about which relationships to bless and when to bless them. At the same time, the blessing of relationships should never become a way to reassert ecclesiastical control or to police people's lives. Rather, public celebrations should highlight the way a faith community honors the moral integrity of its various members and their diverse relationships. As biblical scholar William Countryman notes, "the church would perhaps be better advised not to solemnize marriages at the inception of the relationship itself, but to wait a period of some years before adding its blessing."[19] Then at last religious people might get it right: Neither sexist nor heterosexist unions are "made in heaven."

An ethic of erotic justice celebrates the plurality of friendship and intimacy needs and respects differences within a variety of partnership forms, including heterosexual marriages with and without children, sexual friendships between consenting adults, shared living arrangements, and same-sex unions. It supports persons in exploring their own sexuality with tenderness and joy. It also encourages their respect for the sexualities of others. Appreciation of diversity is essential. Difference rather than uniformity, change rather than stasis, mark human sexuality, as well as our lives more generally—not only among persons and groups, but also within each individual's life. Few of us are the same today as we were in our teen years or in our twenties, forties, or sixties.

Thanks largely to the feminist and gay/lesbian/bisexual liberation movements, fewer people now hold to rigid notions of gender. We are stretching the boundaries of traditional gender roles and challenging patriarchal categories that limit erotic possibility to the narrowly constructed confines of "heterosexuality" and "homosexuality." These labels tell us very little about people's lives or the character of their love. Many people, male and female, have discovered new, often unexpected possibilities beyond such categorical confines. Many women, for example, report the delight of learning how to bring themselves to orgasm, thus shattering for themselves the myth of the frigid, nonorgasmic female who is dependent on the male for sexual gratification. Some heterosexual persons have found themselves erotically attracted to people of the same sex. The lesbian and gay communities include countless people such as myself who have lived formerly (and contentedly) as self-identified heterosexuals. The culture's prevailing gender and sexual categories have never adequately described and in fact have seriously distorted the complex meanings of our lives. These constructs distract people from what genuinely matters.

Living comfortably with change and ambiguity requires maturity and a willingness to delight in difference and novelty. It also requires confidence in our collective ability to make meaningful moral distinctions and responsible choices.

Religious communities should not be policing people's sex lives, but rather educating them about this real world of sexual diversity and expanding their moral imaginations.

A liberating ethic of erotic justice encourages compassion and invites people to learn from failure. Failure is not the end of possibility. People sometimes gain moral insight by failing, making corrections, and moving on. An ethic of grace is not an excuse for irresponsibility. Rather, it welcomes the possibility of new beginnings, of recovering from ill-considered choices or painful experiences, and of retaining a sense of oneself as a responsible person whose task is not to achieve perfection, but to "do the best one can" in light of real limits and sometimes forced options.

A justice ethic recognizes that it is immoral to withhold from people knowledge of their own bodies. Attempts to prevent teenage pregnancy, for example, by prohibiting sexual experimentation or by instilling guilt and shame about sex are both inappropriate and counterproductive to young people's developing moral discernment and decision-making skills. Like adults, teenagers need an ethic of empowerment rather than control. They need access to accurate, reliable information about human sexuality. They need encouragement to explore their own values and needs in a nonjudgmental, supportive environment. They require recognition of their self-worth and ability to make genuinely life-enhancing decisions. Teens must also be credited with the fortitude to deal with the consequences of their choices.

For people of all ages, becoming more responsible about sexuality must include learning how to assert one's own needs while respecting others' body right. It also means sharing insights, skills, and quandaries with others and, above all, being willing to risk being vulnerable and asking for help. Breaking the silences around sex not only dispels myths and misinformation. It encourages us to ask critical questions. It helps us bolster one another and reject unjust cultural norms. It may also empower persons, young and old, to resist abuse and claim their right to safety and bodily integrity.

An ethic of erotic justice from the start rules out relations in which persons are abused, exploited, and violated. People must be empowered to protect themselves from abuse and exploitation, from uninvited touch and coercive sex. Perpetrators of sexual violence and abuse must be held accountable. They must be encouraged to alter their behavior, as well as to make restitution to those they have harmed. At the same time, social structures that breed inequality and violence must be challenged. People also need protection from disease and unintentional pregnancy. In an age when sexually transmitted disease, including HIV infection, is spread epidemically, it is incumbent on all sexually active persons to know their health status and not place themselves or others at risk for infection. Acting "as if" one is HIV-positive and consistently observing safer-sex guidelines is one strategy that allows for a healthy and active sex life and, importantly, keeps the focus on the disease, not the sexual activity, as the appropriate cause for concern.

An adequate sexual ethic does more than insist that no harm be done to others. It strengthens people's well-being and self-respect. Good sex is good because it touches our senses powerfully but also because it enhances our self-worth and deepens our desire to connect more justly with others. The key concerns of this ethic are how power is shared and the quality of caring. Sex is not something one "does to" another person or "has happen" to oneself. Rather sexual intimacy is a mutual process of feeling with, connecting to, and sharing as whole persons. We enhance our sense of self-worth by attending with care to what is happening to the other person as well as to ourselves. In the midst of sexual pleasuring with a partner, we do not "lose" ourselves as much as we relocate ourselves in the in-betweenness of self and other, as we receive and give affection and energy.

Body respect and pleasuring can teach us how wrong it is to regard all self-interest as morally tainted. As lovers and friends, we can be rightly interested in our mutual enjoyment and well-being. Being interested in others does not detract from, but complements, our self-interest, and vice versa. What harms or diminishes another can never be good for me. Positively stated, whatever enhances another's well-being also deepens the quality of my life. In a culture that confuses love with controlling others (or with giving power over to another), religious communities should educate us to trust, deep within our bodies, that we connect with others only to the extent that we stay genuinely present to, and affirming of, ourselves. Self-awareness means monitoring our feelings and, with as much consistency as possible, honoring an obligation to honor ourselves as well as the other person.

An ethic of erotic justice, therefore, does not lower but raises moral expectations. It teaches us to demand for ourselves (and others) what we deserve, namely, to be whole persons to each other and to be deeply, respectfully loved. A gracious, liberating ethic will teach us to claim our right to erotic justice and also to invest in creating a more just and equitable world. In our late-capitalist culture, desire has been commodified to sell goods. In that process of commodification, desire has been narrowly sexualized and privatized, so much so that for many people erotic desire now denotes only desire of a genital sort. More specifically, desire has been truncated to mean taking pleasure in possession. Possessiveness is a primary virtue in a capitalist political economy. Pleasure has become the pleasure of owning consumer goods and status objects, as well as exercising monopoly control over another person as "my man" or "my woman." It is a major challenge to enlarge the meaning of desire to incorporate once again a sense of being free-spirited, full of joy in being alive and "non-possessed," throughout one's life. This expanded notion of desire can be a mighty, though tender, spark from within us, enlivening our desire for a more ethical world. Erotic power can stir us to engage in a full-bodied way in creating justice.

My suspicion is that the pervasive fear of sex and passion, rampant in all patriarchal religious traditions, is deeply implicated in the difficulty many people have in sustaining an interest in, much less a passion for, social justice. By and

large, even liberal Christians either regard patriarchal control as socially necessary or dismiss sexuality as a rather indifferent matter that bears little consequence compared to "larger," more "legitimate" social issues. For many people,
the link between sexuality and justice is muddled at best. By not paying attention to sexual oppression, people fail to grasp how a multiplicity of interconnected social oppressions operate in the small and large places of their lives, in
and on their bodies and the body politic. These injustices diminish human loving. When people are willing to accept power as control in their intimate lives,
they are also likely to acquiesce to other oppressive structures that control them.
They fail to see that sexual oppression is intimately bound up with race, gender,
and class oppression. People fail, therefore, to connect their personal pain with
larger systemic patterns of injustice.

White, middle-strata Christians are deeply hurting but have few clues about
the sources of their suffering. They project their fear and pain onto more vulnerable groups, including feminist women, people of color, and gay/lesbian/
bisexual persons. Out of touch with their own bodies (and feelings), they are
also distanced from the beauty and moral value of other body-selves, especially
among the "culturally despised." They are at a loss about how to reclaim their
personal power and zest for life. Tragically, when people are cut off from genuine community and when their physical and emotional needs are not being adequately met, they tend to become more repressive about sex, more judgmental
about differences, and more unforgiving toward themselves and others. In the
process they become dangerous. They turn their repressed anger and rage on
the very people they ought to be listening to and learning from, the ones most
insistent about the goodness of every body.

MORAL VISION AND PERSONAL COURAGE

A final component of a justice ethic is, therefore, the reclamation of moral
vision and personal courage to step out toward an alternative possibility. Nothing is more important than our capacity to imagine a radically different world.
Such envisioning involves trust. We must trust that we are capable of far more
than greed, violence, and sexual irresponsibility. We can imagine, and commit
ourselves to, the creation of a radical new world in which all belong and no
one's beauty is denied. At the same time, we need a simple yet morally urgent
awareness that not everyone lives and struggles as we do. To imagine the actual
life conditions of other people—whether the other is "other" by gender, sexual
orientation, race, class, culture, age, or physical or mental condition—is indispensable for doing justice. Religious communities serve us well when they forthrightly criticize the "frozen horizon" of present arrangements. They should be
helping to stir in us a more imaginative and more truthful picture of the richly
diverse human community.

Reconstructing Christian sexual ethics requires our moving beyond liberal
presuppositions which privatize love and disconnect justice from personal life. A

social order in which sexism, racism, and economic exploitation are significantly reduced will be a social order in which love has a fairer chance of prospering among the amazing variety of human differences. Men will be better off if they treat women well. Males of all ages will no longer feel required to prove their "manhood" at all costs or falsely claim social superiority in all things. We will be able to rest more comfortably in our own skins as human beings with a full complement of strengths and weaknesses. White-skinned people may learn not to project our fears and anxieties onto darker-skinned peoples, but instead to gauge our humanity by our capacity to make friendships and express genuine solidarity across a wide social diversity. Respect, the valuing of other persons and oneself, is foundational for learning how to eroticize—"turn on" to—relations of equality and fairness, and how to take real delight in other people's company. Where there is mutual respect, admiration, and a desire to equalize relationships, in the bedroom and beyond, we can experience genuine ecstasy down to our toes. When we encounter each other in our differences and manage to express candor, good faith, and trust, we find something beautiful and powerful to our senses. This kind of respectful connecting is erotic, powerful, and good.

Loving well in the midst of cultural crisis means engaging passionately in doing justice, both close to our skins and at a distance. As we gain confidence in our capacity to reorder our relations toward mutual respect and care, it becomes more apparent that we do not need a distinct, separate ethic to regulate sexuality. Erotically empowered people do not need systematized rules and regulations to control and "cover their genitals." In fact, rigid rules and restrictions about sex only perpetuate body alienation and genital fixation. We must not forget that it is racist patriarchy that has posited eroticism as a wayward power requiring special controls to keep things safe and properly ordered. From a feminist and gay liberation perspective, however, what is needed is not a specialized code to regulate sexuality, but rather an adequate life ethic that can incorporate the erotic as an indispensable human power. Such a comprehensive ethic will delight in the incomparable value of people, insist on mutual respect as a basic social norm, and hold people accountable for their actions.

The fact is that we simply do not need a specific ethical code to regulate whether, when, and with whom to touch genitals. Rather, we need a more general, fluid, and dynamic ethic of respectful touching. This ethical approach will value the body's remarkable capacity to communicate powerful meaning, including love and affection, but it will address sexual activity as only one area for such communication between persons. This ethic's primary concern will be strengthening the practices of good touch and ending longstanding patterns of abuse and exploitation, especially of children, older adults, and other socially vulnerable people. Such an ethic will, at long last, allow us to give sex its due as an important, treasured aspect of our lives, but without reinforcing this culture's genital fixation. Sexuality will retain an importance, but not more importance than it deserves. The ethical focus will be on how people learn to negotiate and receive each other at the level of friendship and interpersonal intimacy.

A liberating ethic values the erotic as a resource for enriching life, from its most intimate to its most public aspects, but the notion of pleasure is expanded well beyond erotic stimulation between intimate partners. Pleasure is no longer reduced merely to "private pleasures." People also search for and find genuine satisfaction in nonalienated work, in schools that educate for critical consciousness, in raising children to be in touch with their feelings and self-worth, and in other life pursuits that move body and soul. At home in their bodies, people are more likely to enjoy being in the company of others.

. . . Up to this point I have argued that the contemporary crisis of sexuality is primarily a crisis in heterosexuality, located in the sexist, racist ordering of social relations that legitimate male dominance and female subordination. To speak now more candidly, this moral crisis is primarily a crisis in male sexuality. A racist patriarchal code of compulsory masculinity distorts men's lives, their social connections, and their spirituality whether they are gay, bisexual, or heterosexual.

A contemporary Christian sexual ethic must address this crisis in men's lives at a deep level. How can men of all colors and sexualities embrace erotic justice as a way of life with women, as well as with other men? Blaming men or stigmatizing men is not the answer. Instead we must see in this crisis the opportunity for men in particular to face the radicality of injustice in our daily interactions, including our most intense personal relations. A liberating ethic holds out the hope that by facing the full scope of injustice we can find possibilities for moving forward toward justice and making a truly win-win situation possible among intimates—men and women, men and men, women and women. That possibility depends to a great extent on men's disenchantment with and willingness to unlearn the racist patriarchal ethos of ownership and control. Likewise, it also depends on our desire to learn fairness anew, to negotiate our needs with gentleness and good humor, and to take responsibility as powerful justice-lovers.

NOTES

1. Mary Hunt, "Sexual Ethics: A Lesbian Perspective," *Open Hands* 4:3 (winter 1989): 10.

2. Beverly Wildung Harrison, *Making the Connections: Essays in Feminist Social Ethics*, ed. Carol S. Robb (Boston: Beacon Press, 1985), 148.

3. Christine E. Gudorf, *Body, Sex, and Pleasure: Reconstructing Christian Sexual Ethics* (Cleveland: Pilgrim Press, 1994), esp. ch. 5.

4. Rebecca Parker, "Making Love as a Means of Grace: Women's Reflections," *Open Hands* 3:3 (Winter 1988): 9, 12.

5. Beverly Wildung Harrison, "Human Sexuality and Mutuality," in *Christian Feminism: Visions of a New Humanity*, ed. Judith L. Weidman (San Francisco: Harper & Row, 1984), 148, 147.

6. Harrison, *Making the Connections*, 13.

7. Mariana Valverde, *Sex, Power, and Pleasure* (Toronto: Women's Press, 1985), 43.

8. Parker, "Making Love as a Means of Grace," 12.

9. Karen Lebacqz and Ronald G. Barton point out that feminist and gay liberation epistemologies validate the authenticity of moral insights deriving from inner knowledge,

"feelings," "intuition," and "trusting one's own experience." Trusting feelings, they argue, may have a different meaning and validity depending on whether one is from an oppressed or dominant group. But they also insist that these new epistemologies are not a reversion to subjectivism: "It is not in fact a purely 'subjective' form of knowledge but is a conclusion based on experience and observation and open to the confirmation of other knowers" (166) or, again, "the use of the language of 'feelings' is often a shorthand summary for what are in fact judgments well grounded in data that can be communicated to others" (166–67). *Sex in the Parish* (Louisville, KY: Westminster/John Knox Press, 1991). Also see Mary Field Belenky et al., *Women's Ways of Knowing: The Development of Self, Voice, and Mind* (New York: Basic Books, 1986).

10. James Wm. McClendon, Jr., "Towards an Ethics of Delight," in *Ethics, Religion, and the Good Society: New Directions in a Pluralistic World*, ed. Joseph Runzo (Louisville, Ky.: Westminster John Knox Press, 1992), 53–54.

11. Audre Lorde, "Uses of the Erotic: The Erotic as Power," *Sister Outsider: Essays and Speeches* (Trumansburg, N.Y.: Crossing Press, 1984), 53, 57, 58.

12. Carter Heyward, *Our Passion for Justice: Images of Power, Sexuality, and Liberation* (New York: Pilgrim Press, 1984), 140.

13. John Stoltenberg, *Refusing to Be a Man: Essays on Sex and Justice* (Portland, OR: Breitenbush Books, 1989), 37.

14. Diana E. H. Russell in *Rape in Marriage* (New York: Collier Books, 1982) reports the findings of one survey that 14% of women who had ever been married had been raped by a husband or an ex-husband. Russell argues, "To the extent that this finding may be generalized to the population at large, it suggests that at least one woman out of every seven who has ever been married has been raped by a husband at least once, and sometimes many times over many years" (2). On the accuracy and significance of statistics about rape and other violences against women, children, and some men, see Barbara Chester, "The Statistics about Sexual Violence," in *Sexual Assault and Abuse: A Handbook for Clergy and Religious Professionals*, ed. Mary D. Pellauer, Barbara Chester, and Jane Boyajian (San Francisco: Harper & Row, 1987), 10–16.

15. Karen Lebacqz, "Appropriate Vulnerability: A Sexual Ethics for Singles," in *Sexual Ethics and the Church: A Christian Century Symposium* (Chicago: The Christian Century Foundation, 1989), 18–23.

16. James B. Nelson, *Between Two Gardens: Reflections on Sexuality and Religious Experience* (New York: Pilgrim Press, 1983), esp. chap. 6, "Singleness and the Church," 96–109.

17. Mary E. Hobgood, "Marriage, Market Values, and Social Justice: Toward an Examination of Compulsory Monogamy," in *Redefining Sexual Ethics: A Sourcebook of Essays, Stories, and Poems*, ed. Susan E. Davies and Eleanor H. Haney (Cleveland: Pilgrim Press, 1991), 116.

18. *Ibid.*, 125.

19. William Countryman, *Dirt, Greed, and Sex: Sexual Ethics in the New Testament and Their Implications for Today* (Philadelphia: Fortress Press, 1988), 263.

17

Making Love as
Making Justice:
Towards a New Jewish
Ethic of Sexuality

YOEL H. KAHN

The contemporary question "What does Judaism say about homosexuality?" does not lend itself to a simple answer. In accordance with Jewish tradition, I can best answer this question with another question or two: Which Judaism do you mean—biblical, rabbinic, medieval, pre-modern, or modern? How can ancient sources speak to us about a category of meaning unconceptualized in their language and culture?[1] And if many contemporary Jews do not endorse the historical Jewish condemnation of male homosexual behavior, which, to be sure, is the unequivocal voice of the received tradition, what is our relation to the rest of historical Jewish teaching on human sexuality? How do we describe the logarithm of change that permits us simultaneously to dissent radically from received teaching while claiming to stand in and even represent the tradition from which it comes?

The full exploration of these questions is beyond the scope of this essay. I begin with these questions, though, in order to locate this essay within its larger context. This essay has its roots in an inquiry about Judaism and homosexuality[2] and in turn led to research on what liberal Judaism has had to say about human sexuality in general.[3] Ultimately, this inquiry led to an exploration of the theological self-understanding of how we mediate between the conflicting values of our received religious tradition and the contemporary society, a society of which we are both a part and have helped create. In this essay, a précis of a longer work in process, I shall outline how such a process might proceed by applying a methodology of liberal Jewish decision making to sexuality in general.[4]

The starting place for any Jewish discussion of contemporary standards is historical Jewish teaching, as codified in the *halachah*, traditional Jewish law. Rooted in the Hebrew Bible and formulated in the Talmud, halachah has continued to evolve over the generations. The halachah about human sexuality is expressed in the context of the ancient rabbis' understanding of anthropology and physiology, and reflects their ideas about subjects as varied as authority, "natural law," and revelation as expressed through the Torah. Nonetheless, we can posit five specific organizing values of sexuality within rabbinic culture. Although not always recognized by the rabbis, these organizing values give shape to—and account for much of—the halachah which defines appropriate sexual expression. These five values are: the economy of seed, the procreative purpose of sex, the role of women, *onah* (conjugal duty), and the concern for ritual purity.[5] The application of these values, within the wider context of the rabbinic worldview and its concretization in the halachic system as a whole, generates the rules which regulate when and how sexual relations can occur. These rules are codified as *mitzvot*—sacred obligations. All the individual mitzvot are fulfilled out of the Jew's commitment to the covenant between God and Israel. The proper expression of sexual relations, as codified in the relevant mitzvot, is a significant aspect of a life of holiness in the covenant. We begin with a brief look at these five organizing rabbinic values and how they shaped sexual behavior.

The biblical and rabbinic traditions express abhorrence at the "destruction" of semen. In the ancient Near East, semen was considered a "life force," akin to blood.[6] Apparently, people believed that there was a finite quantity of semen, which could not be wasted. Further, as a "life force" fluid, it had to be properly cared for and disposed of; and only acceptable repository for semen was inside a woman's vagina during intercourse. This concern for the quantity and disposition of seed is the primary basis for the later halachic prohibitions on male masturbation,[7] non-vaginal intercourse and coitus interruptus,[8] and the use of condoms[9] or diaphragms.[10]

Although pleasure and intimacy are known and legitimate aspects of rabbinic sexuality, the halachah has an overwhelming bias towards procreation.[11] Procreation is an affirmative mitzvah for men and, according to Talmudic law, a woman who is barren after ten years can be divorced by her husband.[12]

On the other hand, the halachah permits marriages and sexual relations which are known in advance to be infertile. The symbolic bias towards procreation is reflected in the halachah's permission of sexual intimacy with an infertile woman as long as the particular sexual act would be potentially procreative were the wife not infertile.[13] In general, the halachah only considers sexual acts which are *presumably* procreative licit.[14]

The wife's sexual role is determined in part by her second-class legal status in the halachah. The organizing premise of the halachah on marital relations is that a woman's sexual and reproductive capacities are the property of her husband.[15] Thus, there is a general rabbinic principle that "the husband may do as he pleases" with his wife. This value is in conflict with the rabbinic understanding of women's sexual needs and the husband's conjugal obligation. This conflict is a source of tension throughout the generations.

A husband is obligated to have sexual relations with his wife at regular times. The biblical term *onah* (Exodus 21:10) is understood to mean conjugal rights.

The second-century code the Mishnah specifies the frequency with which onah must be provided; later commentators differ as to whether these times constitute a minimum or maximum requirement. The rabbis expand the mitzvah to encompass the husband's obligation to provide sexual satisfaction to his wife.[16] The man's own sexual pleasure is not recognized by the halachah as a legitimate goal; the ancient rabbis saw men's sexual energy as boundless and in need of "control" while women's is more subdued and therefore must be aroused.[17] The regulation of sexual behavior is extended by some of the ancient rabbis to include approved and discouraged positions.

Finally, according to the halachah, sexual relations are forbidden during times of ritual impurity. A woman is ritually unclean for up to fifteen days of each menstrual cycle,[18] during mourning, and on other days on the personal and communal calendar.

The above organizing values underlie the halachic norms for licit sexuality. Summarizing these values and the behavioral norms they generate, the halachah teaches that sexual relations are licit and sacred when they occur

1. between opposite sex-partners[19]
2. in the context of marriage[20]
3. through vaginal intercourse, preferably in the missionary position
4. at permitted times according to the religious calendar
5. at permitted times during the women's menstrual [cycle]
6. with attention to the women's satisfaction and pleasure[21]
7. with the expectation that the act will be procreative[22]

The above criteria reflect the halachah's specific understanding of sexuality on the micro level, and, on the macro level, are consistent with the entirety of the halachah's worldview. Our modern response properly begins, therefore, with an acknowledgment that our organizing values are different than those of our ancestors, reflecting our changed priorities and premises. These values are grounded in our contemporary understanding of the meaning of God, Torah, and Israel. They emerge out of our ongoing dialogue with God, out of historical Jewish teaching, and out of the lived experience of the Jewish people, men and women, gay and nongay, as the embodiment of contemporary Jewish culture, itself embedded in liberal Western culture. Before turning to the specific question of sexuality, let's first note some of the organizing values of contemporary liberal Judaism and point out how they shape a modern Jewish ethic of sexuality.

The Torah teaches us that each person—as person—is created in the divine image. We first part from previous generations when we place particular emphasis on the ultimate dignity of the person and the individual's autonomy as part of the blessing of being made in the divine image. Accordingly, we explicitly reject Judaism's historical distinction between men and women and insist upon complete equality for all individuals. Second, we lift up the human capacity for relationship as an especially significant aspect of humanity's creation in the divine image. Martin Buber is our primary teacher of this value.

Our sexual lives and sexual relationships should not be separated from the rest of our lives and relationships, but part of a continuum with them. Applying our organizing values of personal dignity, equality, and relationship to the realm of sexuality, we believe that sexuality, at its core, is a yearning for connectedness, intimacy, and relationship. Sexual intimacy, an expression of intimate human meeting, can be a route to and expression of "knowing" another, to borrow from Hosea, "in justice, in truth and in faithfulness."[23] It can therefore be a primary mode of both spirituality—knowing God, as Carter Heyward has taught, and of justice-making—making God known.[24]

Sexual intimacy is one place along an "intimacy continuum," and intimacy is a section of the "relationship continuum." The route to knowing God, says Buber, is through our relationships. If the route to knowing God is through knowing others, then our yearning for another and the seeking after intimacy, connectedness and relationship is a God-seeking act. The experience of knowing another with sexual intimacy can bring us closer to God. Just as our worship can be misdirected and result in idolatry, so can this yearning for intimacy and connection be misdirected in idolatrous ways.[25]

Our commitment to the equality, dignity, and autonomy of each person as an individual is unprecedented in our tradition. We should not be surprised, therefore, that the halachah's categories which strictly regulate permitted and forbidden acts do not satisfy our desire to affirm as much individual autonomy as possible. In general, we turn away from the halachah's concern for the acceptability of discrete acts and instead emphasize the quality of the relationship in which the actions occur. We consider the possibility that any sexual acts—whether previously permitted or forbidden—can be a means to the realization of sanctified human relationship through sexual intimacy. Our most intimate relationships should be the place of our primary and greatest expression of covenantal justice. Our sexual lives are a significant opportunity for, and important place of transformation of the ordinary and instinctual into the sacred.[26] Accordingly, our religious interpretation of sexuality is measured not according to whether acts are permitted or forbidden, nor ritually pure or impure, but whether the relationship as a whole and its specific expression is just or unjust, contributing to or diminishing from holiness.

Sexual relationship can be an expression of and seeking after covenantal relationship. Covenantal commitment is lived out over time and as part of a community. Our sexual relationships, when lived as aspects of covenantal living, are properly respectful of both of these commitments. Accordingly, we must consider the long-term impact and possible consequences of our actions. Made in God's image, we need to consider our own selves. As part of our covenantal relationships, we should be equally concerned for our partners. Covenant living occurs within a community. Responsible sexual expression, therefore, occurs with attention to and respect for the existing commitments of both partners, whether these are commitments to themselves or to others.[27]

How then do we understand received Jewish teaching on sexuality? We reconsider the organizing values—and their consequent embodiment in specific mitzvot in light of our own organizing values and total worldview. We begin with a bias towards affirming historical Jewish practice unless the organizing value or its application conflict with our contemporary organizing values. In order to affirm a primary value, it is sometimes necessary to modify, reinterpret, or even reject a historical value and the mitzvot it generated. Let's return to the five organizing values of the rabbinic teaching on sexuality and consider them in light of our organizing values.

We begin with the ban on spilling seed. The physiological concerns for not wasting semen have been long answered by modern science. We no longer consider ourselves bound by the biblical and rabbinic prohibitions concerning the other life-force fluid, blood; is there any enduring spiritual value in maintaining in some form the ban on wasting semen? We do not think so; in fact, we consider acts which were formerly forbidden on this basis (e.g., masturbation) to be otherwise perfectly acceptable, and, in proper circumstances, even desirable.

Two, if the secondary status of women is a basic premise of the halachah, a central value for Reform Jews is the legal, covenantal, and personal equality of women and men. This emerges from our valuation of every human being as a reflection of the divine image and our internalization of what we value in Western culture. A consequence of this organizing value is our rejection of any aspect of the tradition which discriminates between persons on the basis of gender.[28]

We affirm the traditional value of sexuality as a means of procreation, but we no longer accept procreation as the primary paradigm around which sexuality is organized. Instead, we will propose that covenantal relationship is the paradigm of sexual activity. If procreation is no longer the ontological paradigm, heterosexuality need no longer be the ideal mode of sexual expression.

In the halachic system, responsibility for another's sexual pleasure as a mitzvah is limited to the husband's obligations to his wife. Most halachic authorities hold that a married couple is permitted whatever sexual acts the husband desires regardless of the procreative potential of the act. Combining this traditional norm with our modern commitment to equality between persons, we expand the mitzvah of onah to include obligations of both partners to seek to satisfy the sexual needs of the other. We cannot accept the principle that "a man can do what he wishes" regardless of the woman's desires because it denies the woman's equality and autonomy. We transvalue this rabbinic teaching, and invoking our value of equality and mutuality in relationship, conclude that mutually desired sexual acts between two persons are acceptable, so long as the individual acts and the relationship as a whole meet the ethical criteria for right relationship and right action, as explained below.

The fifth value, the question of ritual purity, is so bound up with other aspects of the rabbinic system of daily life, that a full discussion is beyond the scope of this essay. Let us merely note that we treat the system of ritual purity as another potential route to spirituality whose demand can properly only be taken on by an individual and can no longer be imposed from without.

Earlier, we listed the criteria for licit sexual expression according to the halachah. The comparable list in our system begins in our understanding of sexual expression as a dimension of our covenantal relationship with God, in the context of and contributing to right relation. We believe that this is possible when sexuality is expressed

1. between equals—people who are peers in maturity, independence, and personal and physical power
2. who share mutual respect and affection
3. who assume equal responsibility for the possible consequences of their sexual activity[29]
4. with concern for one another's pleasure
5. with concern for one another's physical and emotional health and wellbeing
6. in the context of open communication and truth telling
7. with respect for one another's body right and bodily integrity
8. in the context of and with attention to each person's existing personal and communal covenantal obligations to others

The above superficially dualistic presentation, between a modern focus on the context and relationship, in contrast to the tradition's emphasis on the specifics and circumstances of actions, distorts the nuances of both systems. Nonetheless we are indeed proposing a radical break with our tradition's teaching.

Up to this point, we have not explicitly spoken about homosexuality. Male homosexual acts are forbidden by explicit biblical command and are condemned as violations of the prohibitions against spilling seed and non-procreative intercourse. In so far as these historical concerns are no longer in force as criteria for heterosexual behavior,[30] the continued application of them as a reason to condemn homosexual acts can only be considered homophobic. We do explicitly reject the biblical prohibition on homosexual acts, applying in its place our contemporary standard of covenant relationship, in which acts and actors are measured not in accordance of who and what they are but how they live.

Some liberal Jewish teachers have cautioned against rejecting traditional values in favor of the prevailing cultural values of the society in which we live. It is appropriate, therefore, to explicitly note some of the ways in which our new Jewish ethic dissents from the prevailing cultural ethos which surrounds us. Although our new ethic is fundamentally a departure of Jewish tradition as seen through the prism of the organizing values of this generation of liberal Jews, it is also a corrective of the culture from which it emerges. We part from the mainstream of American culture in three notable ways: the focus on pleasure, the use of sexuality as an instrument of power, and the genital focus of sexual expression.

American culture treats sexuality primarily as a form of personal pleasure. We consider pleasure desirable, as does the Jewish tradition. However, the excessive focus on personal pleasure and private ego-needs opens the door to the exploitation and abuse of others. Our concern with mutuality excludes a sexual ethic which ends with the self.[31]

The Jewish tradition, through the prophetic tradition, has always been concerned about the abuse of power. By and large, our concern has been with the use and abuse of power in the wider social and political realm. Feminism has taught us to consider the place of power in interpersonal relationships as well. Just sexual relationships cannot occur when sexuality is used as an instrument of control or power. Nor is justice consistent with the use of power or its threat to coerce or force another into sexual intimacy.

Susan Brownmiller argues persuasively that in our culture violence is erotic and passion is associated with having power over another or being overpowered by another.[32] This attitude is supported by the cultural definition of sexual relations as "conquest." Our ethic of sexuality therefore includes the transformation of culture so that mutuality is erotic, personal empowerment is desirable, and passion is linked to both strength and tenderness.[33] The understanding of sexual relations as an act of conquest, along with the historical emphasis on procreation, has led to the focus on genital sexuality. Contemporary cultural images of sexuality, whether in advertising or pornography, gay and straight, continue to equate sexual pleasure with genital contact. In contrast, when sexuality is an instrument of intimacy and relationship, then the total person and the total act will be eroticized. Such sexual expression changes the focus of the act from the goal (orgasm) towards the experience of mutual intimacy.

If, as Buber taught, we come to know God through our I-Thou relationships with others, then our most intimate relationships with others are a unique place for sacred living. The I-Thou relationship demands that we see another not as an object but as a wholistic person in the divine image. Because we are so vulnerable in these private relationships, we are uniquely challenged to practice ethical living and covenant respect in our sexual lives. Through learning to live and act justly in this private sphere, and through the enhancement of our own person which emerges from true relationship, we are strengthened and encouraged to channel passion and action towards justice in wider, more public spheres. The realization of our most intimate yearnings is not a closed circle which in turn leads us back to our partner; rather, the Jewish dialectic of personal and communal obligation turns us outward from the most intimate sphere to return and reengage in the labor of restoring and healing the world.

NOTES

1. Even if we limited our discussion to the contemporary Reform movement, the primary liberal wing of American Judaism, we would immediately discover a vast range of positions.

2. Yoel H. Kahn, "Judaism and Homosexuality: The Traditional/Progressive Debate," *Journal of Homosexuality* 18:3–4 (1989/90), 47–82; this essay appears in a slightly different form in *Homosexuality, the Rabbinate, and Liberal Judaism* (New York, N.Y.: Central Conference of American Rabbis, 1989).

3. The answer is "not much." The paucity of discussion illustrates, in my opinion, the uncomfortableness of the contemporary Jewish community with sexuality and confronting the chasm between the values of the halachah and those of this culture.

4. See Kahn, 1989; Yoel H. Kahn, "The *Kedushah* of Homosexual Relationships," *CCAR Yearbook XCIX* (New York, N.Y.: Central Conference of American Rabbis, 1989), 136–41.

5. The discussion which follows is based in large part on David Feldman's exhaustive research in *Marital Relations, Birth Control and Abortion in Jewish Law* (New York, N.Y.: Schocken, 1974). The conclusions are, of course, my own.

6. In the biblical world, blood and semen both ritually polluted those who came in contact with them. The force of the later rabbinic prohibition was greatly strengthened when the 13th-century mystical book, the *Zohar*, declared the violation of this law "greater than all other transgressions." (*Zohar*, Va'yeshev, 188a). The Zohar's statement was codified in the later codes, including the very influential 16th-century work, the *Shulchan Aruch* (E. H. 23). See Feldman, chap. 6. *passim*, esp. p. 115, n. 37 ff.

7. Talmud, Niddah 13a; Moses Maimonides, *Mishnah Torah*, "Issurei Bi'ah (Laws of Forbidden Intercourse)" 21:18: "*K'ilu harag nefesh.*"

8. See Feldman, 152–54. On non-vaginal intercourse, see 155 ff. and below.

9. See "Hashhatat Zerah," *Encyclopedia talmudit* (Jerusalem, Israel: Talmudic Encyclopedia Institute, 1965) vol. 11, col. 141, n. 179, and Feldman, 229–30.

10. See Feldman, part IV, esp. 227 ff. According to the stringent *poskim* (decisors), the concern for *shefichat zerah* prohibits all non-procreative sexual activity, including intercourse in which the semen is not directly deposited in the vagina. See the responsum of the Ashen, *Teshuvot ha-Rosh*, Klal 33, no. 3, cited in Feldman, 153, and the discussion which follows, esp. 155, n. 60.

11. This principle is articulated in the tannaitic statement "If a man married a woman and remained with her for ten years and she has not yet given birth, he is not allowed to neglect further the duty of procreation." Talmud, *Yevamot* 64a and parallels. See Feldman, 37–45. The rabbis did not require the husband to divorce his wife in practice; see the responsum cited in Feldman, 40, n. 104.

12. Current halachah does not require a man to divorce an infertile wife.

13. What is permitted to a fertile couple is permitted to an infertile couple and what is not permitted a fertile couple is likewise not permitted to an infertile couple. Feldman quotes *Nimmukei Yosef*, the 15th-century commentary to Al-Fasi's code:

> *Intercourse* with a woman incapable at all of childbearing is permissible, and the prohibition of *hashhatat zerah* is not involved so long as the intercourse is in the manner of procreation; for the rabbis have in every case permitted marriage with women too young or too old for childbearing. No prohibition is involved with a barren or sterile woman, except that the mitzvah of procreation is not thus being fulfilled (Feldman, 68; emphasis in original).

14. According to Feldman, 66, it is not particular non-procreative acts but "consciously fruitless marriage" that "so violates the very spirit of Judaism." According to the rabbis, the "natural" sexual act, is intercourse in the missionary position. Some authorities permit "unnatural acts" (woman on top, rear entry, anal intercourse), basing themselves on the talmudic passage: "A man may do with his wife as he will." Feldman, 155, n. 63. See Talmud, Nedarim 20b, Sanhedrin 58b, and Moshe Feinstein, *Igrot Moshe*, E. H., 63–64, cited in Feldman, 165. Feldman comments: "Here we have an example of an

act which, while sanctioned by law, was a source of embarrassment to the many moralists who could not bring themselves to accept so liberal a ruling even in theory. Unnatural positions are prohibited either on the basis of immorality (*Shulchan aruch*, O.H. 240:5), or because they interfere with procreation (E.H. 25:2)." Many *poskim* who were inclined to permit "unnatural acts" on this basis felt constrained by the force of the Zohar's prohibition on *hash-hatat zerah* and its later codification. See *Encyclopedia talmudit*, esp. n. 139, which quotes a later commentator about a permissive ruling: "If he had seen what the Zohar says about the punishment of . . . this [transgression], since it is greater than all of the other transgressions, then he would never have written what he did."

15. The husband [*ba'al*] "acquires" her from her father. This premise begins the mishnaic discussion of marriage: "A woman is acquired in one of three ways . . ." (Mishnah, Ketubot 1:1). The talmudic discussion of this passage explores how marriage is both like and unlike property. See Rachel Biale, *Women and Jewish law* (New York, N.Y.: Schocken, 1984), 46–49. The term *kedushah* in the context of marriage means "set aside" or "reserved" (see Biale, 48; Abraham Ibn-Shoshan, *Ha-Milon he-chadash* (Jerusalem, Israel: Kiryat Sefer, 1979), vol. 6, col. 2292, def. 2). In a divorce, the "setting aside" of the woman is reversed, as she moves from the special status of "reserved for a particular man" ("*mekudeshet li*") to the general "permitted to any man" ("*mooteret le kol adam*"). Adultery therefore is intercourse between a man and another man's wife (Deut. 22:22; Talmud, Kiddushin 80b–81b; Biale, 183–84; Epstein, *Sex laws and customs in Judaism* [New York, N.Y.: Ktav, 1967], 196–99). Rape is considered a crime against property whose penalty was the monetary reimbursement of the value of the raped woman by the rapist to the woman's father (Deut. 21:28–29; Biale, 243).

16. Including, according to Moses Nachmanides, "physical intimacy, appropriate surroundings and regularity." Nachmanides on Ex. 21:11, cited in Biale, 129.

17. Biale, 121–46 *passim*, esp. 137. Biale also discusses the rabbis' understanding of male and female sexual desire, which shaped their norms of acceptable behavior.

18. The biblical basis for the laws of *niddah* is Leviticus 15:19–33. Their application was greatly expanded by the rabbis. A couples' freedom to enjoy sex and physical intimacy together is greatly restricted by the requirements of *niddah*. For a full discussion, see Biale, 147–74.

19. The biblical and rabbinic world has no concept of "homosexuality." Male homosexual behavior is strictly forbidden in Leviticus 18. Lesbianism is also prohibited by the halachah but considered a less severe crime. See Maimonides, "Issurei Bi'ah," 1.14; 21.8, and Biale, 192–94.

20. Intercourse between a man and a woman not forbidden to each other effected a marriage between them; such "marriages" were prohibited by the later authorities.

21. See Feldman, 72–74, and esp. notes 78–82 there.

22. See Feldman, 65–70.

23. Hosea 2:21.

24. Beverly Wildung Harrison, *Making the Connections: Essays in Feminist Social Ethics*, ed. Carol S. Robb (Boston: Beacon, 1985), 149, quoted in Carter C. Heyward, *Touching Our Strength: The Erotic as Power and the Love of God* (San Francisco: Harper and Row, 1989), 55.

25. We consider the exploitation of sexuality and the treatment of people as sexual objects as primary forms of contemporary idolatry. We are aware of the vast potential for evil and abuse in the realm of sexuality and sexual power. While sexuality is not the only or exclusive route to intimacy and connectedness, its special place in the order of human need cannot be ignored or denied.

26. This is our understanding of *kiddushin*—a sanctified relationship.

27. Adultery, therefore, is properly understood as the violation of covenantal trust between two people.

28. See, for example, the rejection of the ceremony for *pidyon ha-ben*, redemption of the first born son, in Simeon J. Maslin, ed., *Gates of Mitzvah* (New York: Central Conference of American Rabbis, 1979), 72, n. 19.

29. I.e., assume mutual responsibility for contraception, safer sex, emotional and material support for abortion, pregnancy, childbirth or offspring.

30. If this were not so, then Jews would practice birth control in accordance with halachic, rather than Western, standards.

31. This is a central theme in Borowitz, *Choosing a Sex Ethic* (New York: Schocken, 1968). We particularly reject the mass cultural portrayal of casual sexual activity without attention or concern for either consequences or continuity.

32. Susan Brownmiller, *Against Our Will: Men, Women, and Rape* (New York: Simon and Schuster, 1975), chap. 4.

33. Carter Heyward and Beverly Harrison in a discussion at "Conference on What Women Theologians Are Thinking," Union Seminary, New York, N.Y., October 1987.

18

Appropriate Vulnerability: A Sexual Ethic for Singles

KAREN LEBACQZ

All of us spend our first years single. Most of us spend our last years single. As adults, many of us are single by circumstance or by deliberate choice. Given these simple facts, it is surprising how little attention and how precious little support the churches have given to singleness (except for the monastic tradition, with its very particular demands and charisms). The scriptural witness on singleness is virtually ignored, despite the fact that Jesus never married and Paul preferred singleness. Throughout history, churches have simply assumed that marriage is the norm for Christians.

Single sexuality, when it is discussed at all, falls under the category of "premarital sex." Churches clearly expect that those who are single will get married and that those who have been married and are now single through divorce or widowhood will simply disappear into the closet until they marry again. The slogan adopted by the United Methodist Church might stand as a summary of the traditional Christian view of sexuality: "celibacy in singleness, fidelity in marriage."

A new ethic for single sexuality is needed, for the tradition that requires celibacy in singleness is not adequate. This situation does not mean that anything goes or that the church has nothing to offer by way of a positive ethic for single people. The task is to thread our way between two views of sexuality: the "old testament" or "thou shalt not" approach exemplified by much of church tradition, and the "new testament" or "thou shalt" approach evident in much of our current culture.

The "old testament" or legalistic approach to single sexuality is well summed up in a delightful limerick by Joseph Fletcher:

There was a young lady named Wilde
Who kept herself quite undefiled
   by thinking of Jesus
   and social diseases
And the fear of having a child.[1]

The "thou shalt not" ethic was characterized by fear—fear of pregnancy and venereal disease—and by a series of "don'ts": don't have sex, don't take pleasure in it (at least, not if you are a woman) and don't talk about it. As the limerick suggests, sexual involvement was regarded as "defiling." "Bad girls" and "good girls" were defined according to their willingness to be sexual or not. There was no discussion of the sexuality of divorced or widowed men and women, and gay men and lesbian women simply stayed in the closet.

With the advent of the so-called "sexual revolution" and the birth-control pill, fear of pregnancy was gone. After the "thou shalt not" of Christian tradition, we encountered the "thou shalt" of contemporary culture. Here, "love" was all that counted. Women were "liberated" and virginity was redefined as "bad." Now people talked about sex all the time, with everyone. Far from being defiling, sexual involvement was regarded as mandatory. Sex was supposed to be pleasurable, and "how-to" manuals abounded. Finally, everyone knew how—but had forgotten why. In short, fear was replaced by pressure—pressure to engage in sex, to do it right, to enjoy it, and to let the world know how much and how well you were doing it.

The result is a clash often internalized into a "Catch 22." In the wonderfully perceptive comic strip *Cathy*, Cathy Guisewite captures the confusion of many. As the almost-but-not-quite-liberated Cathy is getting dressed to go out on a date, she reflects: "I'm wearing the 'heirloom lace' of my grandmother's generation . . . with the conscience of my mother's generation . . . coping with the morals of my generation. . . . No matter what I do tonight, I'm going to offend myself."

Neither the legalistic approach of earlier Christian morality nor the permissive approach of contemporary culture provides a satisfactory sexual ethic for singles. And without a good sexual ethic for singles, there cannot be a good sexual ethic for couples either.

Can we construct a positive, Christian sexual ethic for single people? I think so. Let us begin with Christian tradition, which affirms that sex is a gift from God. It is to be used within the boundaries of God's purposes. As part of God's creation, sex is good. Like all of creation, however, it is tainted by the fall, and therefore becomes distorted by human history. It needs redemption. Such redemption is achieved by using sexuality in accordance with God's purpose and through God's grace.

The two redeeming purposes of sexuality have always been understood as procreation and union. With these purposes in mind, Christian tradition maintained that marriage was the proper context for sex, since it was the proper context for raising children and for achieving a true union. Catholics have tended to stress procreation as the primary purpose while Protestants have stressed union, but both agree on the fundamental purposes of sexual expression.

This tradition has had enormous practical implications for singles. The tradition condemns all genital sexual expression outside of marriage on the assumption that it violates the procreative and unitive purposes of sexuality. Nongenital sexual expression is also suspect, because it is thought to lead inexorably to genital expression. Given such a view of sexuality, it is difficult for single people to claim their sexuality or to develop a positive ethic for that sexuality.

Standards within both Catholic and Protestant traditions have recently loosened, but there has been no fundamental challenge to this basic paradigm. Today, some Catholics and most Protestants accept "preceremonial" sex between responsible and committed adults.[2] Both traditions have moved toward affirming union as primary, while still upholding the importance of procreation. The meaning of the two fundamental purposes has been expanded by replacing the term "procreative" with "creative" and the term "unitive" with "integrative."[3] Thus, there is some acceptance of nonmarital sexual expression, provided it is in the context of deep interpersonal commitment.

But however important such revisions may be, they do not really accept sexuality outside marriage. Single sexuality is still difficult to claim. Neither Catholic nor Protestant tradition provides a totally satisfactory explanation of why sexuality should be fully expressed only in marriage or in a "preceremonial" relationship that will eventuate in marriage. Both traditions still uphold marriage as the ideal, but give no satisfactory reasons for that ideal.

I accept part of the *method* that has led to the traditional interpretation, but wish to offer an additional insight into the nature of sexuality that might provide a fuller appreciation of the ethical context in which sexuality is expressed. I agree with the traditional understanding that sex is a gift from God to be used within the confines of God's purposes. However, I would add to the traditional purposes of union and procreation another God-given purpose of sexuality that I believe opens up a different understanding of human sexuality and of a sexual ethic for singles (as well as couples).

Sexuality has to do with vulnerability. Eros, the desire for another, the passion that accompanies the wish for sexual expression, makes one vulnerable. It creates possibilities for great joy but also for great suffering. To desire another, to feel passion, is to be vulnerable, capable of being wounded.

There is evidence in Scripture for this view of sexuality. Consider the Song of Songs (the "holy of holies"), which displays in glowing detail the immense passion and vulnerability of lovers. This is not married or "preceremonial" sexuality, nor are children the justification for the sexual encounter. It is passion pure and simple. And it is graphic sex. The Stoic fear of passion is not biblical. From the Song of Songs we can recover the importance of sexual desire as part of God's creation.

It is equally important to recover the creation stories in Genesis, which are often the grounds for our interpretation of what God intends human sexuality to be. It is from these stories that we take the phrase "be fruitful and multiply" and turn it into a mandate for procreation. It is from these stories that we hear the deep call for union between sexual partners: "This at last is bone of my bones and flesh of my flesh, . . . and the two shall become one flesh."

Without denying the importance of these phrases and their traditional interpretation, I would stress another passage—one that has been ignored but is crucial for completing the picture. The very last line in the creation story in Genesis 2 reads: "And the man and his wife were both naked, and they felt no shame" (Gen. 2:25). In ancient Hebrew, "nakedness" was a metaphor for vulnerability, and "feeling no shame" was a metaphor for appropriateness.[4] We can therefore retranslate the passage as follows: "And the man and his wife experienced appropriate vulnerability." As the summation and closure of the creation story, the verse tells us that the net result of sexual encounter—the purpose of the creation of man and woman as sexual beings who unite with one another to form "one flesh"—is that there be appropriate vulnerability.

Vulnerability may be the precondition for both union and procreation: without a willingness to be vulnerable, to be exposed, to be wounded, there can be no union. To be "known," as Scripture so often describes the sexual encounter, is to be vulnerable, exposed, open.

Sexuality is therefore a form of vulnerability and is to be valued as such. Sex, eros, passion are antidotes to the human sin of wanting to be in control or to have power over another. "Appropriate vulnerability" may describe the basic intention for human life—which may be experienced in part through the gift of sexuality.

If this is so, then a new approach to sexual ethics follows. If humans are intended to have appropriate vulnerability, then the desire to have power or control over another is a hardening of the heart against vulnerability. When Adam and Eve chose power, they lost their appropriate vulnerability and were set against each other in their sexuality. Loss of vulnerability is paradigmatic of the fall. Jesus shows us the way to redemption by choosing not power but vulnerability and relationship.

The implications for a sexual ethic are profound. Any exercise of sexuality that violates appropriate vulnerability is wrong. This includes violations of the partner's vulnerability and violations of one's own vulnerability. Rape is wrong not only because it violates the vulnerability of the one raped, but also because the rapist guards his own power and refuses to be vulnerable.

Similarly, seduction is wrong, for the seducer guards her or his own vulnerability and uses sex as a weapon to gain power over another. Any sexual encounter that hurts another, so that she or he either guards against vulnerability in the future or is unduly vulnerable in the future, violates the "appropriate vulnerability" which is part of the true meaning and purpose of our God-given sexuality. Prostitution and promiscuity are also generally wrong. In each there tends to be either a shutting down of eros or a form of masochism in which the vulnerability is not equal and therefore not appropriate. Sex is not "just for fun," for play, for physical release, for showing off or for any of the host of other human expressions that are often attached to sexuality. It is for the appropriate expression of vulnerability, and to the extent that that expression is missing, the sexual expression is not proper.

Nothing in what has been said so far suggests that the only appropriate expressions of vulnerability are in marriage. Premarital and postmarital sexuality might express appropriate vulnerability. Gay and lesbian unions, long condemned by the church because of their failure to be procreative, might also express appropriate vulnerability. At the same time, some sexual expressions within marriage might not be an appropriate expression of vulnerability—for example, spousal rape or unloving sexual encounter. We must beware of the deceptions through which we reduce or deny vulnerability in sexuality—both the "swinging singles" image and notions of sexual "duty" in marriage deny appropriate vulnerability.

But what about singleness specifically? Is there any need for a special sexual ethic for single people? Precisely because sexuality involves vulnerability, it needs protective structures. A few years ago, the United Church of Christ proposed a "principle of proportionality" for single sexuality. According to this principle, the level of sexual expression should be commensurate with the level of commitment in the relationship. While I have some problems with this principle, it does have the merit of suggesting that the vulnerability involved in sexual encounter requires protection. The more sexual involvement there is to be, the more there needs to be a context that protects and safeguards that vulnerability. As Stanley Hauerwas puts it, "Genuine love is so capable of destruction that we need a structure to sustain us."[5]

Traditionally, monogamous marriage has been understood to provide that needed context. Whatever the pitfalls and failures of marriage in practice, certainly in theory the commitment of a stable and monogamous marriage provides a supportive context for vulnerable expressions of the self. Marriage at its best ensures that the vulnerability of sexuality is private and that our failures remain protected in a mutually vulnerable and committed relationship.

Singleness carries no such protections. It is an unsafe environment for the expression of vulnerability. No covenant of fidelity ensures that my vulnerability will not lead to my being hurt, foolish, exposed, wounded. In short, in singleness the vulnerability that naturally accompanies sexuality is also coupled with a vulnerability of context. Thus, singleness is a politically more explosive arena for the expression of vulnerability in sex because it lacks the protections of marriage. It heightens vulnerability.

An adequate sexual ethic for singles must therefore attend to what is needed for appropriate vulnerability in sexuality. Attention must be paid to the structural elements in the particular situation that heighten or protect vulnerability. For example, a sexual ethic for singles might take one form for those who are very young and another for those who are older. The protections of age and experience may make it sensible to permit sexual encounter for those who are older and single, while restricting it for the very young. Unequal vulnerability is not appropriate. Therefore, in a culture where men tend to have more power than women and women are more vulnerable to men great care will be needed to provide an adequate context for the expression of sexuality.

We need a theology of vulnerability. Until such a theology is forthcoming we can only struggle toward a proper sexual ethic. Single people will have to explore their own vulnerability to find its appropriate expression in sexuality. Neither the "thou shalt not" of traditional prohibitions nor the "thou shalt" of contemporary culture provides an adequate sexual ethic for singles. "Celibacy in singleness" is not the answer. An appreciation of the link between sexuality and vulnerability is the precondition for an adequate sexual ethic.

NOTES

1. Joseph Fletcher, *Moral Responsibility: Situation Ethics at Work* (Philadelphia: Westminster Press, 1967), 88.

2. Paul Ramsey argues that this is marriage in the moral sense. See his "On Taking Sexual Responsibility Seriously," in *Social Ethics*, ed. Gibson Winter (New York: Harper & Row, 1968), 45ff.

3. See Catholic Theological Society of America, *Human Sexuality: New Directions in American Catholic Thought* (New York: Paulist Press, 1977), 86.

4. On this topic I am indebted to the work of Stephen Breck Reid of Baylor University.

5. Stanley Hauerwas, *A Community of Character: Toward a Constructive Christian Social Ethic* (Notre Dame, Ind.: University of Notre Dame Press, 1981), 181.

19

Sexuality and
Social Policy

BEVERLY WILDUNG HARRISON

In our present society, and far too frequently in our churches as well, persons of very different theological and political persuasions—conservatives, liberals, and radicals—co-conspire to keep in place assumptions about human sexuality, ethics, and social policy that block a much-needed rethinking of how our human capacity for intimacy and love and our aspirations for a just social order coinhere. Taken at face value, this claim may seem incredible. Surely, the conservative who longs for clear and precise normative rules about the rights and wrongs of sexual acts on the one hand and who wishes to keep religion out of social policy or politics on the other appears to have little in common with theological liberals or radicals. After all, the latter usually put concern for the justice of social institutions squarely at the center of their religious commitment and are quite likely to take the position that the ethics of sexuality is merely a personal issue and a matter of relative indifference compared with the "grave" issues of social justice. The fact is, however, that both positions accept a set of assumptions about our human personhood that badly need to be challenged. For both, the personal and the political are sealed off from each other, and the dynamics that make for social and personal well-being are not deeply interconnected. The conventional wisdom that sustains this split is precisely what needs to be challenged, I believe, if we are to rise to a major responsibility in our time: rethinking our understanding of human sexuality to appropriate a sexual ethics deep enough to clarify the relation between our capacity for interpersonal love and our ability to struggle effectually for social justice in our common life.

Without a better grasp of the intimate connection between personal and social well-being, our sexual ethic will simply reinforce a growing trend toward privatism and the churches' withdrawal from social engagement. But equally problematic would be any renewed concern for social justice that is devoid of awareness of how our social passivity is rooted in the dynamics of our inter-personal, primary relationships. The churches are always tempted to avoid altogether the volatile questions of human sexuality, abandoning people in the confused struggle to find more adequate paths to personal fulfillment and human intimacy. What we Christians evade is the connection between our silence on sexuality and our general conventionality toward social relations. Even our pre-sumed "social action" often suffers from lack of creativity and imagination.

That we need a new understanding of the dialectic between love and justice is obvious from the way that both conservative and liberal ideologies within Christianity lead to obvious contradictions in the actions and strategies of their respective proponents. For their part, many Christian social activist liberals are perplexed at a growing political apathy in the churches and seem unable to find ways to mobilize social conscience except through the methods of rhe-torical moralizing, which were the very means deplored as overly individual-istic in the past. At the same time, conservatives who have long cried out for clear-cut standards of right and wrong in personal sexual ethics and who always have insisted that a rigid line be drawn between religion and ethics on the one hand and politics and economics on the other find themselves mobilizing politi-cally to change the direction of social policy to prevent further changes that they deem immoral. So religio-political movements against the defeated Equal Rights Amendment and against legal abortion and the civil rights of homo-sexuals flourish. That many who support these efforts are violating their own deeply held convictions against government interference with or regulation of individual liberty only underscores the inability of established social theory to encompass our lived-world reality.

The complexity of the relation between sexuality and social order becomes clear when we observe how little impact such largely successful political mobi-lization has on our culture's preoccupation with human sexuality. Legislators can gain support by turning back permissive social policies, but our fascination with genital sexuality and explicit sexual themes seems to increase. We even see the emergence of groups, such as the Total Woman Movement, that combine a celebration of heterosexual genital sexual liberation in marriage with a mili-tant reassertion of traditional notions about "woman's place" in home, family, and society. Evidently, the pleasures of genital-sexual eroticism are here to stay, whatever the outcome of social movements aimed at justice for women. This trend is further confirmed by the response of several television networks to com-plaints about gratuitous physical violence during prime-time programming. In a number of cases, detective shows and adventure stories have given way to situ-ation comedies that feature a new and presumably "daring" explicitness about sexuality. Since the television media often know more about our collective tastes and attitudes than we ourselves do, the substitution of the titillations of explicit sex for the presumed excitation of physical violence suggests that we are a long way from any shift back toward more traditional sexual reticence.

The fact is that explicit sexuality is very big business in this nation, and our fascination with the technologies of sex, with sexual therapies, and with the paraphernalia of sexual experimentation is flourishing. Those who cry out for a tightening of sexual standards notwithstanding, "sexual liberation," in its tawdry, commercial guise, will not abate until the profit wanes. The anomaly of our situation can be measured by the way in which sexuality is becoming part of the performance- and achievement-oriented ethic characteristic of a business society. We appear so preoccupied by sexual performance that some commentators wonder whether capacity for sexual pleasure may not be giving way to ennui and boredom. If greater sexual genital expression were, in itself, a panacea for what ails us, we would expect clear evidence that a sense of personal well-being was on the rise in our society. In fact, there is no indication that we are experiencing a reduction in loneliness, isolation, competitiveness, or alienation from community.

In the face of all this, the trivialization of sexuality by those whose concerns are presumably focused on the "more substantive" questions of social justice is understandable. Such people consider preoccupation with sexual concerns and sexual pleasure to be a cause of our social malaise. There has been much loose talk about a "new narcissism," turning to self-preoccupation that presumably threatens our capacity to take the reality of other persons seriously. The problem with much of this sort of social diagnosis is that it does not probe deeply enough to lead to a reintegrated sense of how interpersonal well-being interacts with the wider social realities that shape our experience. The analysis of our presumed narcissism too often confuses "cause" with social "symptom."[1] The almost desperate search for physical pleasure and personal intimacy that pervasively characterizes our culture is much more a symptom of the lack of humanly fulfilling opportunities in work and frustration at depersonalized, bureaucratic institutional patterns that suffuse our life than a cause of our social ills. And the tragedy is that the simple pleasures of sex, while real, are not a sufficiently powerful antidote to the wounds to self-respect we endure elsewhere. Genital sexuality, narrowly conceived, is simply too weak a reed to bear the overloaded expectations that people in our society are encouraged to place on it. What is most needed is an approach to sexuality that aims to be holistic, that sets what we know of ourselves as sexual persons in the broadest possible context of our lives within our existing social order.

SOURCES, PRINCIPLES, AND PRIORITIES
FOR A MORE ADEQUATE ETHICS OF SEXUALITY

The time is ripe for a reappraisal of our understanding of sexuality, ethics, and social policy, in spite of the controversy such reappraisal engenders. There are two salient and appropriate pressures for a reevaluation in contemporary society, and both provide resources for recovering a deeper, holistic understanding of the nature of our sexuality. The first of these pressures derives from the emergence of basic paradigm shifts in social scientific conceptions of the nature of gender difference and "normal" sexuality. What we are discovering today is how little we really have ever understood about ourselves as sexual persons. The new paradigms of psychosocial development make clear that the meaning of our sexuality involves the integration of many levels of biological and social determinants. More and more, we are coming to realize the full range of possible healthy sexual development that characterizes human life. New knowledge per se does not yield new ethical awareness, but the emerging paradigms are themselves more open to humane value questions.[2] These newer scientific perspectives afford us opportunity to appropriate a more adequate sense of human diversity in sexual development and expression. They correlate well with the best insights of our religious and moral tradition about the interrelationship of human freedom and moral responsibility.

However, Christians have as yet been reluctant to embrace an ethic of maturity where sexuality is concerned. In many dimensions of our life as human agents, Christian ethicists have insisted, explicitly, that we must both accept our power as agents and learn to express that power responsibly, without recourse to unexceptional rules. In relation to our actions as sexual beings, however, there remains a lingering fear of affirming any genuine capacity of moral agents to live responsibly apart from largely prohibitive and constricting action guides.[3]

The second pressure and resource for reappraisal of sexual ethics come from the fruit of women's efforts to achieve full social recognition as persons. In our time, it is the women's movement and, more recently, the gay and lesbian liberation movements that have called into question many of the traditional views formerly held to be "scientific." At the deepest level, the insights of contemporary feminism lead to reappropriation of the meaning of our sexuality, which runs counter to the narrow "sexual liberation" fixation on genital sexuality.

What women have discovered, signaled in the phrase "we are our bodies, ourselves," is that in the absence of freedom to understand, control, and direct our own sexuality, our power as self-regulating moral agents does not develop. Numerous feminists have formulated telling critiques of traditional erotic patterns, insisting, for example, that our modern romantic ideals of love between the sexes involve the celebration of dehumanizing seduction and conquest on the male side and feminine passivity and denial of pleasure on the other.[4] A clear break with male myths regarding female sexuality has enabled women to recognize to what extent such myths have been generated to keep women obeisant to the social function of procreation. The religious dictum that the only moral expression of sexuality is that which is at least open to the possibility of procreation has been a source of many women's inability to achieve a self-defining role in relation to their bodies. Many women have denied their own needs for bodily pleasuring as the cost of being "good" women. Conversely, when women have been sexually active or self-initiating, society has defined them as "whores" or "deviants." In the positive reappropriation and appreciation of ourselves as embodied persons, women are regaining the capacity to celebrate our sexuality as inherent in our own embodiedness. But the experience of genuine embodiedness also leads to rejection of the view that sexual pleasure is limited to genital contact or that women's sexuality is passive, mediated exclusively through active relationships with men. The feminist insight is that sexuality is mutual pleasuring in the context of genuine openness and intimacy. That such communication is of "ultimate value" only when it is shaped by procreative potential or procreative intent—the Christian teaching, at least as it applies to women—is simply lingering male supremacist doctrine that reinforces male control of women's self-definition.

The social criticism generated by feminism also has led to a fresh analysis of the way in which sex role patterns in the family operate destructively in relation to women's self-esteem. These sex role expectations have subtly conditioned us, men and women alike, to accept inequities of power and differing capacities for self-direction between men and women in the broader society.[5] It is one thing, however, for groups of women—and, increasingly, for sensitive men—to begin to diagnose the destructive aspects of sex role socialization as they affect the lives of individuals and the broader community; it is another to begin to reverse these powerfully ingrained patterns of traditional gender socialization in society.

The women's movement and the gay and lesbian movements are resources and pressures for change, but they do not provide a simple blueprint that enables us to prioritize issues relating to sexuality and social policy. Insofar as these movements are limited by theory or practice to the reality of white experience or fail to address the dynamics of class, identified priorities will be inadequate. In addition, public knowledge of feminism and gay and lesbian liberation movements is filtered through and conditioned by the mass media that aim to minimize offense to some presumed "general public" and therefore also aim to mute serious systemic criticism. This means that it is mostly the priorities for social policy change that resonate with already existing "public opinion" that are called to our attention. The full implications of a serious feminist social policy are rarely understood in public debate.

The corrective for uncritical acceptance of media-interpreted priorities of these social movements, however, is deeper listening and involvement and a greater effort to respect the principles underlying the specific priorities of all social justice movements. For example, in the women's movement, the principle of bodily self-determination underlies the emphasis on the need for accessible contraception and the availability of legal abortion. The same principle, applied in the context of the existing race and class dynamics of this society, requires equal attention to the abhorrent social practice of developing contraceptive devices through medical experimentation on poor and nonwhite women and the too frequent practice of forced sterilization, especially of poor and nonwhite women.[6] Yet the media focus only on the former issues, leaving concern for the latter, widespread in the women's movement, undiscussed as a serious social evil. The fundamental social attitude toward women—that our competence as moral agents vis-à-vis our bodies and reproductive capacities is not trustworthy—inevitably results in divergent patterns of social control across race and class lines. Many middle-strata white women experience social deprivation only when they insist on self-determination that flies in the face of traditional female roles. They may count on family and community support and personal affirmation if they choose childbearing and function as "good" mothers and homemakers. Only when they resist conformity to these conventional roles does their environment grow hostile or suspicious of them as women. Poor and working-class women, by contrast, suffer more acute deprivation; they have neither easy access to prevention of pregnancy nor support for their exercise of women's "traditional" role. Racism and poverty function as coercive pressures against even traditional fulfillment through procreation.

The point is that the social policy priorities of groups aiming at liberation from the various forms of sexual oppression are adequately liberating only insofar as these priorities are defined by how they touch the lives of persons on both sides of the institutionalized and interstructured patterns of race and class oppression. Andrea Dworkin has put this point forcefully:

> The analysis of sexism . . . articulates clearly what the oppression of women is, how it functions, how it is rooted in psyche and culture. But that analysis is useless unless it is tied to a political consciousness and commitment which will totally redefine community. One cannot be free, never, not ever, in an unfree world, and in the course of redefining family, church, power relations, all the institutions which inhibit and order our lives, there is no way to hold onto privilege and comfort. To attempt to do so is destructive, criminal, and intolerable. . . .
>
> The analysis [of sexism] applies to the life situations of all women, but all women are not necessarily in a state of primary emergency as women. What I mean by this is simple. As a Jew in Nazi Germany, I would be oppressed as a woman, but hunted, slaughtered as a Jew. As a Native American, I would be oppressed as a squaw, but hunted, slaughtered, as a Native American. *The first identity, the one which brings with it as a part of its definition death, is the identity of primary emergency.* This is an important recognition because it relieves us of a serious confusion. The fact, for instance, that many Black women [by no means all] experience primary emergency as Blacks in no way lessens the responsibility of the Black community to assimilate this and other analyses of sexism and to apply it in their own revolutionary work. [Emphasis mine][7]

This same insight must be extended to gay and lesbian analyses and sensibilities. The social priorities of gay men do not always adequately incorporate the needs and sensibilities of lesbians or of black people or the poor. In the churches and in the wider gay movement, white gay men are often those who specify the agenda for change in relation to heterosexism. Setting adequate priorities for just social policy in relation to human sexuality will occur only if we learn to ask, How do the matters that are central to my liberation touch the lives of those who are doubly or triply oppressed? We must learn to shape our formulation of sexual justice with this question and these persons in view. No sexual ethic will be adequate unless it incorporates a full appreciation of the interstructuring of social oppression. For example, economic justice as access to and genuine participation in the production, distribution, and determination of the use of a society's wealth is also a condition of genuine sexual freedom. All distortions of power in society reveal themselves in the inequity of power dynamics in interpersonal life. An adequate normative sexual ethic will be predicated on awareness that where people (men, women, *and* children) are socially powerless, they are vulnerable to irresponsible and inappropriate—that is, nonvoluntary and/or nonmutual—sexual transactions. The goal of a holistic and integrated sexual ethic is to affirm sexual activity that enhances human dignity, that entails self- and other-regarding respect and genuine communication. Such an ethic must challenge actions that degrade, disempower, and reduce oneself's and others' esteem or that aim at control, objectification, or manipulation of another.

The basic theological and moral principles implicit in the feminist and gay liberation movements—the affirmation of the goodness of sexuality as embodiment, the respect for bodily integrity, and the appropriateness of self-direction and noncoercion in expressing sexuality—are constitutive of everyone's human dignity. They are foundational to all claims for human well-being, as fundamental to the eradication of racism and ethnic oppression as to women's and gay men's historic emancipation. As such, they are criteria for a sexual ethic that genuinely affirms personal freedom, community, and responsibility.

DIFFICULTIES OF CONSTRUCTIVE SOCIAL CHANGE IN RELATION TO HUMAN SEXUALITY

Another awareness that must inform our efforts to translate social policy priorities into strategy is a recognition of the difficulty of finding effective loci for social change in this society. Genuine implementation of change in relation to our well-being as sexual persons is difficult to achieve. Liberal social reform efforts tend to focus strategies for change primarily through government, aiming chiefly at legal reform and government administrative change. Neither legal nor administrative reform can be neglected in efforts to implement new policies with respect to gender and sexual justice. But it is important to be clear about the role, and also the limits, of law and procedural reform. Liberals frequently misunderstand the role that law plays in strategies for change. In our society, fundamental legal change (including constitutional change, as, for example, the Equal Rights Amendment) or the achievements of administrative fairness are always as much a response to already partially realized conditions for justice as they are initiators of such change. The initiation of conditions for social justice always begins with social movements. Legislation is important because without it or without administrative fairness, the relevant conditions for sustaining justice will never approximate "normalcy" in the wider society. Reversion to repressive policies is always easier if the requisite legitimations in law and administrative procedure have not been realized.

Nevertheless, it is critical to be aware of the actual dialectic between such legal change and wider social change. Genuine change is always the result of hard-won struggle from below. Some groups and some institutions must begin to shape a liberating praxis within the society before there is sufficient pressure to actualize humane conditions as a legal norm. Theological liberalism has mis-understood this fact, which is why liberal church activism for justice has been so inept. Tragically, liberal Christians who aver that the church should avoid controversy until issues are respectable and who refuse liaisons with social move-ments and activist social policy groups are those who ensure that Christianity will never play an active role in shaping policy development within our society. To "get involved" only when consensus about positive legal change has devel-oped means that such Christians are never influential in the process of change. Social movements are the means whereby any positive change emerges, and the politics of mainstream theological liberals are never engaged enough to interact with such movements.

In sum, double focus on change at the cultural and legal levels offers the best hope for transforming the split between what is presumed to be political or public and what is held to be merely personal or private, a split that reinforces and legitimates our widespread moral schizophrenia and keeps sexual oppres-sion in place. The potential for "radicalizing" people's broader awareness of the importance of social justice by integrating their sensibilities to sexual justice lies precisely here. It is worth emphasizing again that the conventionality of our religion is maintained by our fear of honestly and openly facing issues of human sexuality. If exclusive reliance on the power of government to initiate change is one fallacy of much liberal social strategy, the tendency to overesti-mate the capacity of formal education to transform personal values is another. "Public" education (and, by default, most "private" education as well) is in a weak position to challenge the dominant or established understandings of human sexuality that are transmitted powerfully in our society. "Sex education" in our schools can at most challenge the miasma of misinformation, fear, and prejudice with respect to human sexuality. Furthermore, what actually goes on in the name of "sex education" has some way to go to reach even this minimum standard of effectiveness and moral adequacy. The truth is that our so-called public schools are often rendered educationally ineffectual because of fear of conflict. With respect to sexuality, as at so many other points, this fear often results in an educational strategy that postures a reductionistically "scientific" approach. Sexuality is dealt with from a physiological stance in which human reproductive biology is taught abstractly, in an environment where discussions of values are avoided to evade conflict.[8] The result is a bland conventionality that is more devastatingly effective in reinforcing the status quo than a more explicitly reactionary stance would be.

A strong case can be made that on this issue, at least, the liberal churches (regretfully, by default) have a genuine opportunity to serve the social good by a humane educational approach to human sexuality. Yet because of sexism, that is, the disvaluation of women, and fear of sexuality, the churches are not better equipped than other institutions for this task. Liberal churches, in particular, need a critical perspective on their own past social praxis in relation to public policy. Most of the public utterance of liberal churches vis-à-vis social policy questions has taken the form of voicing support for "the rights of individuals" against state intrusion on those rights. Even the most liberal of our churches have gone only so far as to ground support for sexual liberation in statements that affirm individual civil liberties. Some liberal churches have urged the state to avoid heavy-handed enforcement of sexual morality; they have affirmed women's individual freedom of conscience in seeking access to legal abortion; they have accepted the appropriateness of civil liberties for gay people. Such a posture and such policy positions have been legitimated with reference to a theology that is not substantively social. The bottom line for the liberal churches has been to oppose policies in relation to sexuality that deny status and dignity to the individual within the "public" sphere. These policy positions have helped to reduce pressure from other, more reactionary quarters for more oppressive public policies, but they lack moral vision. We need to recognize that a more adequately social theology would provide a substantive positive political rationale that would go beyond this individualistic bottom line. As it is, liberal Protestant churches have a public policy stance that suggests that it is acceptable for us to be "political" only if and when individual rights have been demonstrably violated. Whether or not the social system itself is just appears, from this perspective, to be a matter of indifference.

The very fact that we resort to such individualistic justifications—supporting individuals' civil rights rather than embracing positive and substantive moral principles rooted in an adequate vision of social justice—bespeaks the disorder of the churches' theological approach to sexual ethics. Because this is so, such defensive, "individual rights" policy stances are ineffectual. They appear to the wider society as hypocritical because they are predicated on a moral double standard that all the world reads (and reads properly) as Christian double-talk. Gay people, we claim, deserve "civil rights," but they do not receive full human affirmation and respect in the churches. Women should have the "civil right" to elect legal abortion, but abortion continues to be viewed as, at best, morally dubious, an evil necessity. The churches have not affirmed people's sexual well-being as basic to their personal dignity. The state is not charged to *support* citizens' sexual well-being but simply to desist from meddling. Because the churches do not embrace theologically the positive, nonfunctional good of human sexuality or affirm the positive principles related to sexual well-being as substantively moral, our "liberal" stance is dismissed as mere accommodation to modern culture. Because we do not accept the mandate to active solidarity with those who are the victims of sexual oppression, our social policy positions appear equivocal. We deny our own best understanding of the inherently theosocial nature of persons and community, and speak instead as individualists whose message to society is that it must adopt a moderate tolerance of human sexual expression, a moderate tolerance that we, within the churches, are not even willing to exemplify in our own community.

There is a long roster of social policy concerns that come into view when we actually embrace a positive, holistic understanding of sexuality. In addition to the policy issues I address here, this roster should include the question of how children and the sexual well-being of the differently abled can be protected and how sexual manipulation of inmates of "total institutions" can be prevented. Here I have limited my discussion to analyzing the way in which an adequate view of human sexuality requires us to take an inclusive view of women's lives and to identify some of the needed social policy concerns affecting men, gay men and lesbians, and families.

As I have already made clear, any identified social policy issue has an economic aspect. Among other things, this means that the matters I address here gain their urgency as social policy questions from the fact that they hold no "priority" in the regular, day-to-day workings of our present political economy. Serious social vulnerability in this society rests on economic marginality; hence, children and older people, all women and gay males, as well as nonskilled males (mostly, though not exclusively, nonwhite) are vulnerable as groups, which also makes them especially susceptible to sexual exploitation, violence, or forms of "benign neglect." Since the capacity to produce income and to accumulate wealth (not to be equated with wages) is *the* measure of personal worth in this society, anyone who does not participate in money-making will also be a priori a victim vulnerable to sexual oppression or to being treated as a nonperson sexually. The elderly or physically handicapped, for example, are frequently characterized as "beyond sexuality" for just this reason. . . .

In keeping with the principles identified earlier, we need always to ask how these policy matters affect persons differently, how the dynamics of class and white supremacy intersect with the social dynamics of human sexuality and gender difference.

CONCLUSION

Many of the thorniest questions of social policy in relation to sexuality will continue to pose dilemmas for morally concerned persons whatever happens in the future. Even if we succeed in deepening our awareness of the connections between personal intimacy patterns and the sociopolitical and economic forces that mold our lives, the constructive shaping of our personal-social relationships is a challenge that does not admit easy solutions. How societies should function, through government, to influence individual behavior is always a difficult question. How and in which ways sexual behavior should be shaped is, perhaps, the hardest question of all.

Efforts to regulate sexual conduct between consenting adults are notoriously difficult and, as I have observed, are fraught with potential for the abuse of state power. Enforcement of laws regulating sexual conduct are more the exception than the rule. The temptation of government authorities to use techniques of police entrapment to catch "sexual offenders" seems inexorable, and the tendency toward corrupt use of public authority in enforcement is strong. This state of affairs is probably inevitable because sexuality involves intimate spaces—where we sleep, dress, and retire for privacy. Given our dominant value patterns, such enforcement will always catch the poor, relatively powerless, socially marginated offenders, while more privileged lawbreakers go free. Conversely, sexual entrapment can always be used against those whose political views are unpopular. Nothing can reduce the tension between those provisional rights to privacy that we all need and initiatives to use law to encourage a positive moral climate regarding sexual conduct because monitoring sexual conduct requires intrusive observation. As a result, our presumptive stance should be that restrictive law needs to be used sparingly where sexuality is involved. In the face of this fact, all of us should exercise caution in looking to government for simple redress of grievances because others' sexual conduct offends our personal moral sensibilities. In spite of considerable social pressure on the churches to demand legal action to curtail "dubious" sexual behavior, we need to exercise critical sensibility and a healthy dose of skepticism as to what such laws actually accomplish.

How a society may best live with this tension between the diverse personal sensibilities of adults and the need for a degree of public order will always be subject to debate. I have already made it clear that we would be well served by considerably "desexualizing" our criminal codes. Morally evil behaviors that are frequently classified as sex offenses—molestation or exploitation of young children, rape, publicly intrusive pandering of sexually explicit or obscene material, and the offensive hawking of sexual devices, including solicitation for prostitution—are wrong, in different degrees, not because they involve genitally explicit activity but because they express morally inappropriate power relations between people—physical and psychic assault or obvious insensitivity to the dignity of another person's rights and capacity for self-direction. The most heinous of these so-called sex crimes are not more "especially wrong" than other acts of violence, unjustified coercion, or manipulation, though in a sex-phobic society "sex crimes" are experienced as especially "dirty" or polluting. These acts are wrong because they involve the harassment or the abuse and degradation of persons who are relatively powerless to resist. Such acts *intend* humiliation or control. Genital or sexual intrusion is perceived as the best way to express contempt or to establish power over another person. Legal changes that desexualize criminal law while strengthening legal sanctions against any bodily harassment or assault toward children or nonconsenting adults might go a long way toward helping us disentangle our fears of sexuality from our fears of being humiliated by other persons through contemptuous physical abuse aimed at the most vulnerable areas of our bodies. No unjustified violence toward another's body, against that person's will, should ever be construed as a sign of positive erotic capacity or mature action. Rather, such actions are usually rooted in fear of closeness and mutuality. They express a need for control and a disordered incapacity for relationship over an appropriate capacity for interdependence. Victims of so-called sex crimes often are more stigmatized than the perpetrators of the crimes because such offenses stereotype victims as sexually "impure." It is time to recognize that those who are recipients of violent "sexual" acts are *not* sexually polluted; they have been victimized by ugly acts of human retribution, evil because of the contempt for persons they express rather than the genital contact they involve.

If acts of coercion and violence involving genitals are "desexualized" and understood as crimes of assault and bodily intrusion, it may be possible to see more clearly why minimal regulation of sexual conduct between consenting adults by the state is desirable, even a positive moral good. If there is any "zone of privacy" that requires, seriously, to be sacrosanct and respected, it is a person's right to bodily integrity. Our body-selves, the zone of body-space we possess by virtue of our being embodied persons, deserve explicit protection from arbitrary interference and unjustified coercion. "Consent" at this level is a condition of having a moral relationship. From a moral point of view, embracing "consent" as a criterion is not to deny a norm or to be merely "permissive." In our most intimate, interpersonal relations, consent or self-direction is a critical condition of human well-being. Space in which it can be expressed is a social good. Those who govern with regard for the conditions of a just society do well to respect this reality. Honoring the decisions regarding sexual expression between consenting adults is not a negative moral norm but a positive moral value. We ought to possess the conditions for nonconstrained expression of intimacy.

We must not be romantic about the quality of sexual communication that characterizes our society. We are sex-preoccupied but neither genuinely sensual nor genuinely pleasure-oriented. Because much that passes for sexual liberation is only a blend of alienated technological consciousness with the most puerile notions of what good male-female eroticism involves—notions, alas, often imitated in same-sex eroticism—we have no reason to celebrate the actual "quality" of the presumed new "sexual liberation" overall. Nevertheless, there are hopeful indications that through "our bodies, ourselves," some of us are learning to ground our capacity for personal fulfillment and for genuine mutuality. The affirmation of our capacity for giving and receiving pleasure and for appropriating our self-worth in and through our bodies has also begun to lead to an important demystification of our sexuality. The ancient idea that sexuality itself is an irrational, alien, even evil power, deeply foreign to our personal integrity and outside the range of our self-direction, is giving way to new integrations of psychosexual identity with socially fulfilling action. The fact that some can now celebrate sexuality as an important, albeit not all-controlling, aspect of selfhood, having learned to value it as a deep mode of communication, is a great step forward. Sexuality involves pleasure and erotic intensity, but it also expresses playfulness, tenderness, and a generalized sense of well-being.

Our culture expresses simultaneously an animalistic affirmation and prim denial of sexuality. We do not yet see clearly that our capacity for caring, for expressing and receiving deep feeling, for reaching out to others is grounded in and through our bodies or not at all. Given this insight, the way is now open for us to affirm genuinely what we have long given lip service to in our theologies—that our sexuality is a gift of God. Positive affirmation of our sensuality leads to the understanding that when we abuse our sexuality, it is not because we have been too free or too permissive or too spontaneous. Rather, it is because our capacity for intimacy and sensual communication has been twisted and distorted by manipulative and nonmutual patterns of relationship. If we cannot tolerate mutually respectful and mutually enhancing erotic communication, if we prefer relational patterns of conquest or subservience, sadism or masochism, or if we are stuck in compulsive, inappropriate, and repetitive patterns of action, it is because we have failed to find the positive power of our own being as sexual persons. If this is so, no repudiation of sexuality, as such, will deliver us. Rather, what we need is a deepened and more holistic sense of ourselves that will enable us to grow sexually, to celebrate, and to respect our own sexuality and that of others. Today no Christian ethics of sexuality can straddle the fence or hedge positive affirmations with qualified Victorian bets of modified prudery. Too many have learned to celebrate the wondrous gift of our created being to want to go back on the discovery.

NOTES

1. I have complained of a related confusion elsewhere. See the discussion in particular of Christopher Lasch's work in Beverly Wildung Harrison, *Making the Connections* (Beacon Press, 1985), 293, n. 7.

2. *Ibid.*, 274, nn. 24–27; 284, n. 4; and 293, n. 5. For a telling critique of empiricist social science, see Liam Hudson, *The Cult of the Fact* (New York: Harper & Row, 1972).

3. "Unexceptional action guides" are, in contemporary moral philosophic parlance, rules or principles that do not admit of conditions or exceptions. Most moral philosophers and Christian ethicists believe that we should treat rules and principles as if they create a presumption for or against acts such that we need to marshal serious reasons if they are not to be honored. Nevertheless, Christian sexual ethics continues to be discussed as if unexceptional rules exist. . . . See Gerard Fourez, *Liberation Ethics* (Philadelphia: Temple University Press, 1982), particularly parts 1 and 2. I share Fourez's assumption that such rigid rules reflect taboo structures and that these are maintained often by the ideology of dominant groups to serve their interests. See also John Lewis, *Marxism and the Open Mind* (Trenton, N.J.: Rutgers University Press, 1957), 211–12.

4. References valuable in discussing sex roles are found throughout the notes of this book, *Making the Connections*, especially those for essays 1, 3, and 7. See also Peter Gabriel Filene, *Him/Her Self Sex Roles in Modern America* (New York: Harcourt Brace Jovanovich, 1974). Also Helen S. Astin, Allison Parelman, and Anne Fischer, *Sex Roles: A Research Bibliography* (Washington, D.C.: Center for Human Services, 1975).

5. Robin Ruth Linden, Darlene R. Pagano, Diana E. H. Russell, and Susan Leigh Star, eds., *Against Sadomasochism: A Radical Feminist Analysis* (East Palo Alto, Calif.: Frog in the Well, 1982); also Pamela Kearon and Barbara Mehrhof, "Rape: An Act of Terror," in *Radical Feminism*, ed. A. Koedt, E. Levine, and A. Rapone (New York: Quadrangle, 1973); Maria Roy, ed., *Battered Women: A Psychosociological Study of Domestic Violence* (New York: Van Nostrand Reinhold, 1977); and Carol Vance, ed., *Pleasure and Danger: Exploring Female Sexuality* (Boston: Routledge & Kegan Paul, 1985).

6. Bonnie Mass, *Population Target* (Toronto: Toronto Women's Press and Latin American Working Group, n.d.); Dr. Helen Rodriguez, "The Social Politics of Technology," *Women's Rights Law Reporter 7*, no. 5 (1983). Also see Beverly Wildung Harrison, *Our Right to Choose: Toward a New Ethic of Abortion* (Boston: Beacon Press, 1983), 272, n. 20; 273, n. 29.

7. Andrea Dworkin, *Woman Hating* (New York: E. P. Dutton, 1974), 22–24.

8. Mary Breasted, *Oh—Sex Education* (New York: New American Library, 1971).

20

Guilty Pleasures: When Sex Is Good Because It's Bad

REBECCA T. ALPERT

Although my formal education ended before the second wave of feminism took hold in the academy, and well before the postmodern era, the insights of both have been crucial to my writing and thinking for many years. One might even say that I learned them, albeit in nascent forms, during my graduate education in religious studies. There, I carefully noted the missing perspectives of women, but I also studied in an interreligious context that made me aware of the multiple perspectives through which the world may be viewed and consequently of how very partial my own truth was. I think I have learned those lessons well. I write only from my own (Jewish and feminist) perspective, and I make every effort to name that perspective and make it clear how particular a viewpoint it is.

These lessons came to me again in the course of working on this project with women from many religious and cultural perspectives. I can write only from my particular context: the privilege of living as a North American Jew at the turn of a new century, influenced by the feminist movement, supported by the presence of a gay and lesbian movement, trained to be a rabbi in a seminary that ordains not only women but gay men and lesbians as well. I thus live under conditions that permit me to write as an autonomous self. Comfortably located in the secular academy, I can afford to challenge the authority of the Jewish community; I can live openly as a lesbian and as a committed Jew and rabbi, inside and outside the community simultaneously. Without the oppression experienced by Jews at other times and places, and by women in many places today, I can both honor and critique my tradition and live with the ambiguity that such a position requires. I preface my work here with the acknowledgment of the privilege of being able to, as a rabbi, "say the darnedest things" as my colleague in the project Suwanna Satha-Anand pointed out. I offer my comments about Judaism at the turn of the century in light of what I learned from my cocontributors and from those about whom they write, many of whom do not live with such privilege.

THE REGULATION OF SEXUALITY

Regulating sexual behavior is a significant dimension of most religious systems, and Judaism is no exception. Throughout its long history, Judaism has defined licit and illicit sexual desires, relationships, and behaviors. Over time, the form and content of what has been permitted and prohibited have changed, but a system of regulation has remained a constant. While some might wish to challenge the need for such a system, I am suggesting that some such system will always be in place, that even in times when regulations have undergone changes, new ones have arisen to take their place. Although these regulations have often been oppressive, they have also had unintended liberating consequences. My goal here is to examine the criteria for the regulation of sexual behavior in Judaism and the consequences in terms of their potential to redefine good sex from a Jewish feminist perspective.

Let me be careful to note that I am not using the terms good (and bad) in relation to ethics, but in relation to law. Sexual ethics are indeed important (as are the ethics of all relationships), but it is my contention that a system of regulation that defines sexual desires and behaviors as permitted or forbidden does not necessarily also define right and wrong. In this context, good sex will always be ethical, but it may also be forbidden.

Of course, I understand that it is inaccurate to make sweeping generalizations about Judaism. Judaism is not by any means a monolithic tradition, and it is an oversimplification to suggest that there is one Judaism. Rather, we are looking at a complex entity whose values vary by historical era and geographic location. Furthermore, Judaism is often defined based on passages from the Talmud, the main text of rabbinic Judaism, compiled and redacted around 500 CE, which itself is a complex document reflecting traditions of several hundred years and of several different communities. The voices of later thinkers and texts, medieval, modern, and contemporary, are often seen only as reflections of that work, while the biblical culture of the Israelites is viewed only as a precursor.

Often, the complexity of the Talmud itself is glossed over. Additionally, feminist insight reminds us that the texts that have been preserved reflect the traditions of the elite group of men whose thought represents only one fragmentary perspective of the world in which the Jews lived. We have no idea of the extent to which the rulings of this elite were taken seriously or put into practice even by the societies in which they lived. What we do know is that portions of those texts, usually taken out of context, are often used to serve some contemporary rhetorical purpose.

Given this complex reality, we must be extremely careful when making generalizations about Judaism's perspective about sex. It is accurate to describe Jewish teachings on sexual desire as complex and ambivalent, containing both positive and negative elements, and changing perspective with time and location.[1]

Still, it is of value to look for strands in Jewish thinking (whether or not they are representative or widespread) that could help us understand how sexuality was regulated in ancient Judaism. My goal is to take into account some of these ancient strands, viewing them through a lens of contemporary feminist thinking about sex in order to create a dialogue between those perspectives, with the hope that what emerges will become one more strand of Jewish thought.

HOW SEX IS REGULATED IN JEWISH TEACHINGS

Connecting Sex, Kinship, and Procreation

Jewish texts generally encourage sexual activity that will result in procreation in a marital relationship. Sexual desire is valued because it drives the reproductive impulse. A rabbinic teaching suggests that it is because of sexual desire that men marry, build houses, and have children.[2] To this end, physical acts of heterosexual sex between people who are obligated to reproduce are encouraged in ancient Jewish texts. Sex acts are broadly permitted within any union that has or had (or even in some cases will have) reproductive potential, which is understood as potential for Jewish continuity. There are traditions that explicitly permit sex in licit relationships which no longer are fertile: sex between infertile wives and husbands, sex with postmenopausal wives, and anal and oral sex within a marital relationship. In the biblical stories of Tamar and Ruth, it is obvious also that laws about sexual boundaries can be transgressed for the sake of procreation. Both of these biblical heroes commit sexual acts to ensure the continuity of the ancestral line—Ruth with a stranger, and Tamar with her father-in-law.

The corollary of this perspective is the prohibition of sexual acts that would in any way interfere with reproduction. One need only examine the biblical ritual for the *sotah*, the wife suspected of adultery, and the rabbinic adumbrations of that text, to see the negative attitudes toward sexuality that might interfere with appropriate procreation.[3] The sotah (and to a lesser extent, the man with whom she is accused of committing adultery) is to be publicly humiliated. Although the sotah ritual was not practiced, certainly after the destruction of the temple, the rabbis' rhetoric about it shows their serious [dis]approbation of sex that counters procreative possibilities.

Sex and Order

Ancient Judaism also regulates sexuality as part of a larger system of creating an orderly universe. Many sexual activities are prohibited as a way to define boundaries between what is permitted and forbidden behavior for a

Jew. What distinguishes these regulations is their arbitrary nature. They fit into the paradigm of "purity and danger" suggested by Mary Douglas. These activities do not necessarily interfere with procreation but are part of a system of containing sexual desire. For the purposes of procreation, sexual desire is understood as useful, but it is still called *yetzer hara*, an evil inclination, and must be controlled and limited.[4] Therefore, activities such as masturbation that might cause someone to be tempted to break the rules are prohibited.[5] Male homosexual behavior is also prohibited.[6] The same logic prohibits sex with people with whom one is not supposed to marry (and therefore procreate), such as certain relatives or non Jews. This system also creates prohibitions of certain sexual activities within the marital context, such as sex during (and in rabbinic Judaism, one week after) a woman's menstrual period or during daylight hours or completely naked.[7]

Regulation by Gender

Sex is regulated differently for men and women. Because the rabbis thought that women were unable to exercise sexual control, rabbinic Judaism mandates that men are obligated to satisfy their wives' sexual desires, described as the obligation of *onah*. The conditions of satisfying that desire are the subject of much debate in ancient sources and by contemporary scholars.[8] Their main goal is to limit women's sexual desire by making sure that it has a regularly moderated outlet.

Men on the other hand must control their sexual desire. Men are understood as having the duty (and the right) to give sexual pleasure, but not to satisfy their own sexual needs. Sexual control places men on a higher spiritual plane than women, as described by Michael Satlow: "For the rabbis, both Palestinian and Babylonian, Jewish piety was linked to self-control. At its (relatively rare) extreme, piety could manifest itself as asceticism. More commonly, however, self-control was exercised through adherence to the law, and above all, through moderation even in legally permitted activities."[9] Manliness is expressed in terms of piety and control. Men were to subdue their powerful sexual desires through adherence to the law and the study of Torah. Women's sexual desires were controlled by men.

Adultery and marriage laws were also different for men and women. For a man, adultery was defined as having sex with another man's wife, tampering with the lineage and possession of another man. The Hebrew Bible is replete with stories of men with multiple wives and concubines. Ashkenazic Jewry did not outlaw polygamy until the year 1000, and it was never officially outlawed by Sephardic Jewry.

The question of homosexuality is also treated differently by gender. Male homosexuality was punishable by death during certain biblical periods (Leviticus 20:13), while female homosexual behavior was considered a minor offense.[10] Male masturbation is discussed at length in the Talmud, while female masturbation is mentioned only once.[11]

Sex and Commitment

Contemporary Jewish thinkers perpetuate these regulations by connecting them to the higher purpose of love and commitment. Orthodox discussions about sex strongly advocate for procreation. But they also explain regulating sex as a way of enhancing love and commitment. Norman Lamm celebrates the restrictions of *niddah*. Lamm suggests (and many Orthodox Jews testify to the fact) that being required to abstain from sexual relations for half the month increases the desire experienced when permitted to engage in sexual encounters and enables couples to prolong the romance of their marriage, thus helping to sustain long-term, committed, monogamous relationships.[12]

Liberal thinkers may disagree with many of the activities that ancient Judaism sought to regulate, but they too construct a system of regulation based on an ethic of relationships that highlights consent and mutuality. Rather than trying to find reasons for the ancient rules, this system creates its own criteria for sexual behavior (love and commitment) and then regulates behavior on that basis. This perspective of Jewish ethics is certainly well grounded in Jewish values about relationships, and the commandment to love your neighbor as yourself.[13] This perspective is supported in ancient Jewish texts where wife beating and rape within marriage were generally viewed negatively.[14] These approaches create a hierarchy that privileges long-term, committed relationships, suggesting that other forms of desire, while valid, are less valued. But they do remove most arbitrary prohibitions, creating room for young people to experiment with sex (provided that they are moving toward commitment), for sex during menstruation, and for the recognition of gay and lesbian relationships.

THE PROBLEMS WITH REGULATING SEX

Regulating sexuality has both positive and negative dimensions. Looking at both dimensions enables us to begin to create new approaches to defining good sex from a Jewish feminist perspective. The various dimensions of sexual regulation in Judaism bring different problems that must be brought to light before we can imagine what benefits a system of regulating sexual desire and behavior might have for the promotion of good sex.

Sex as Instrumental to Other Values

Making sex an instrument to achieve other values like procreation and love is problematic because it does not allow for the possibility that sexual pleasure is a value in its own right. As we have already seen, sex was only acceptable if it was for a higher purpose. In most ancient texts, that higher purpose was procreation. Desire in the service of procreation had few constraints, even when it transgressed other norms.

Linking sex to procreation does not fit in contemporary society. Times have changed, and more sophisticated contraception, the possibilities of adoption, fertility treatments, alternative forms of insemination, and acceptance of the validity of gay and lesbian relationships have severed the automatic connection between sex and reproduction, even in sexual encounters within marriage. Making sexual pleasure instrumental to other values shifts the focus from looking for the meaning and value of sex itself. There is a strong need for the focus to shift from regulation of sexual behavior to the discussion of sexual pleasure.

In contemporary Jewish sexual ethics, the higher purpose of desire is love and commitment. Sex is understood as a vehicle for intimacy and closeness, for the creation of a couple, as a primary value. This has the negative effect of creating hierarchies of sexual behavior, suggesting, for example, that committed monogamous relationships are the most valued, serially monogamous relationships or relationships before marriage less so.[15] But there is not any place to locate a Jewish understanding of desire for its own sake, for the pleasure of sexual and sensual feelings, for touch and for physical release.

Differentiation by Gender

Regulating sex differently for men and women also limits the value of Jewish teachings on sexuality. As sexual power dynamics have changed, it is hard to imagine maintaining the idea that women as a group have less ability to control their sexual desire than men do. Contemporary male scholars of Jewish sexuality like to ask what might have been different if women had the power to write these texts. They urge contemporary feminists to construct a system of sexual desire that is good for women.[16] But these requests miss the point. A reconstructed Jewish feminist view of sexual desire should be based not on defining a new erotic for women, but on the removal of gender as a defining characteristic of desire.

Recent theorists of bisexuality suggest that gender need not be the defining characteristic in choosing a sexual partner.[17] Desire can be constructed around many other issues or pleasures. According to this theory, we are not necessarily attracted to someone because of their gender; we may be more attracted to their eye color, intellect, humor, or height. Sexual desire is not necessarily predicated on the gender of the object of that desire, so we should not assume rigid differentiation according to gender when we are looking at the agent of desire. There is no reason to assume different abilities to control desire, or to create different ways of constructing desire based on gender. So we are left with the idea that men and women have strong sexual desires and that men cannot be viewed as carrying the obligation of controlling women's desires for them. Both men and women need to work at finding a balance between limiting and enhancing sexual desire.

Making Sex Seem Bad, Dangerous, and Shameful

Another difficulty with a system that regulates sexuality based on arbitrary notions of order and chaos is that it connects illicit sexual behavior with shame. The rabbinic exhortations to the sotah are a blatant example of this connection, as are contemporary Orthodox commentaries about male homosexuality.[18] Even contemporary ethical writings tend to devalue sex that is not oriented toward the goal of love and commitment. Sex for pleasure, even autoerotic stimulation, is not examined for its possibility to enhance life. People choosing to be involved in sex for its own sake rarely find support within Jewish circles. People who are not in committed relationships are marked as suspect, or in need of being "fixed up" with someone. The language itself implies discomfort with a person whose sex life is not publicly visible and appropriately regulated.

Such a system is also harmful because it is punitive. In the Hebrew Bible, death is the punishment for many sexual transgressions, including adultery and male homosexuality. Although throughout most of Jewish history corporal punishments were not carried out, sexual transgressors suffered communal approbation and scorn.

This negative valuation of sex for pleasure or without the goal of procreation or commitment forces people to lie and hide their sexual desires. This consequence of the regulation of sexuality is particularly negative, because it additionally compels people to break other important relational values. Jewish practices for regulating sexual behavior are problematic because they differentiate desire by gender and thereby make assumptions about how men and women are; devalue sex for its own sake rather than to achieve some higher goal; make sex appear to be negative and shameful, requiring people without licit relationships to lie and hide; and misuse Jewish texts for the purpose of controlling sexuality.

THE VALUE OF A SYSTEM OF CONTROL

Given these negative dimensions, how can we find value in a system that controls sexuality? Despite the problems inherent in this system, it also provides some advantages and possibilities for good sex.

Acknowledging the Power of Sexual Desire

What is the purpose of a system to control desire? A system based on controlling desire starts from the assumption that desire is overwhelming and chaotic and will disrupt otherwise orderly lives. Forbidding people to act out on sexual desires affirms that sexual desire is dangerous. Acknowledging that everyone has sexual desire, and that desire is a powerful, dangerous, and chaotic force in need of regulation, is helpful within the context of such a system. Sexual desire has the potential to disrupt the order of society, and controls are important in moderating its effects.

Making room for the incredible power of sexual desire is valuable. Sexual desire is irrational and unpredictable. We do not know what creates and stimulates desire within an individual. Love may be gentle and kind, but passion isn't always, nor is it always wise to express or act on it. Recognizing the dangerous dimension of sexual desire can enable people to find creative ways to work with it.

Forbidden Sex

Ironically, a system that seeks arbitrarily to limit and control sexual desire unwittingly enhances the power of sexual desire. The efforts to control desire make it more desirable.

A look at the creation story will help to illustrate. In ancient rabbinic interpretations, this was not a story of forbidden sex. The rabbis assume that Adam and Eve had sexual relations in the garden—to be sure, in the service of procreation. But a Jewish mystical text from the Middle Ages suggests another interpretation: Adam and Eve had sexual relations but did not experience sexual desire until Eve ate from the tree.[19] Eve disrupted the order of creation through her act and brought knowledge to humans. Part of this knowledge was that what is forbidden may be erotic because it is forbidden. This insight may also be apprehended in the Song of Songs, which graphically describes the power of secret love. In her commentary on the Song of Songs, contemporary interpreter Marcia Falk describes the ways in which this text presents lovers in covert, nighttime rendezvous, away from public censure.[20]

Illicit sex is appealing because it is an opportunity to do what is forbidden, to test the rules. The erotic is connected to wildness, chaos, and disorder—just what the rabbinic tradition wishes to tame and make orderly. Part of the appeal of desiring the wrong person at the wrong place or time is precisely that they are wrong, that this desire breaks norms. Let me be careful again to make the point that wrong is not the same as unethical—sex that is bad or wrong can still conform to ethical standards. That is why setting up an arbitrary system of licit and illicit sex is helpful. One can break norms without performing acts that are harmful and still derive the pleasure that attends what is forbidden.

A system that regulates sex encourages people to lie about and hide sex that is not acceptable. While in many instances this is troubling, it is also true that the pleasure of illicit sex is enhanced through secrecy. This is not necessarily a bad thing. Not being able to talk about the sexual encounters you are having may serve to make them more exciting. This is clearly illustrated in the rabbinic text from the *baraita* literature, which suggests that when a man has a strong sexual desire he cannot control he should go to another town, dress in other garments, and fulfill his need, rather than doing so at home or among acquaintances.[21] There was also something quite powerful about "the love that dared not speak its name"—before gay sex became something that could be discussed in public, the closet was sexy, even if oppressive.[22] Gay people developed coded language with which to communicate. The need to be secretive was turned into an erotic of its own.

This kind of guilty pleasure may require no action. There is no need to assume that refraining from acting on these desires diminishes them—the desire itself may suffice to provide sexual pleasure. Forbidding sex in these cases may serve to heighten the desire to experience what we cannot. This kind of desire is guilty pleasure; it can be enjoyed for its own sake but enhanced by its transgressive nature.

Autoerotic sexual desire, having sex with animals, using inanimate objects as stimulation, cross-dressing, or having fantasies about other people when one is involved in a committed relationship that is defined as monogamous are all ways of transgressing the norms of sexuality. Sexual behavior or desire that in most cases harms no one and whose only goal is self-pleasure may be experienced with greater joy and intensity because it is forbidden.

Experiencing desire for the "wrong" person is another form of desire that must be kept to oneself and so is erotic because it is forbidden. This could include an unrequited love or attraction to someone who is married, to someone who would be an unacceptable partner (because of sexual orientation, class, religion, race, age, or familial relationship), or to a total stranger. Sex with the right or wrong person at the wrong place or time enhances erotic pleasure. Those who break the laws of niddah, who begin sexual encounters when time is limited to complete them, who have sex in public places, who visit porn shops or consume erotica on the Internet all indulge in guilty pleasures. While these activities might lend themselves to providing pleasure in any event, that pleasure is enhanced by the illicit nature of the act.

Assuming that forbidden sex is powerful because it is forbidden does not assume that licit sex without limitations cannot also incorporate desire, that forbidden sex cannot also take place within licit relationships, or that sex is automatically wonderful because one has acted on a forbidden desire. But forbidding certain sexual partners or situations can make them seem more attractive. Operating within a system that controls desires may serve ironically to enhance those desires and to contribute to the pleasure one experiences when acting on (or even thinking about) those desires. And it has the potential to challenge the privileged status of licit relationships.

Sex Talk and Sublimation

Talk about prohibiting sex invites discussion of sex and so can be most valuable. There are extensive discussions of licit and illicit sexual behavior in the Hebrew Bible and in rabbinic literature, as well as in later mystical and philosophical literature.[23] As Michel Foucault has suggested, talking about sexual behaviors and their prohibitions can be erotic for some and at the least sexually educational for others.[24] This is an unintended consequence of a system that regulates sexuality.

When sexual desire and behavior is controlled and limited, it may go underground as illustrated earlier, or it may take the form of sublimation. Even the rabbinic ideal of sublimating desire through the study of Torah can be a vehicle to guilty pleasures, albeit unconscious ones. Recent scholars have suggested the homoerotic nature of the house of study for men.[25] The exclusion of women from this site produced an environment presumably devoid of sex, but in fact full of sexual energy, as many same-sex environments tend to be. Furthermore, sexual topics were freely discussed in the houses of study, and these conversations themselves may have stimulated sexual desire. Proceeding from the assumption that sexual desire is not determined by gender, bringing women into the house of study would not necessarily change the environment.

Rabbinic Judaism gave positive reinforcement to men for controlling their sexual desires through the study of Torah. One dimension of this activity of sublimation is to substitute God for the male and the people of Israel for the female erotic partner, such as is often demonstrated in prophetic literature. The Song of Songs, an erotic love poem, was interpreted as an allegory by the ancient rabbis, a description of the relationship between God and Israel, and the literal reading was ignored or denied. The sexual meaning attributed to the chanting of *L'cha dodi* certainly brings erotic energy to that ritual. It is a medieval poem recited every Friday evening in synagogue at the beginning of the Sabbath that uses imagery of marriage to describe the relationship between the people of Israel (groom) and the Sabbath (bride). Rather than eliminating the human dimension of the erotic, sublimation only connects Torah more deeply to eroticism. These allegorical moves are also helpful in creating possibilities for guilty pleasures, for those who are open to interpret them that way.

Employing the strategies of control and sublimation are effective means of dealing with sexual desire. They enable guilty pleasures, while at the same time providing moderating influences on powerful feelings and restricting actions that have the potential to violate ethical standards of relationships. And they connect Torah with the erotic so that the people of the book can also experience ourselves as the people of the body.

BROADER IMPLICATIONS
OF TRANSGRESSIVE SEX

I have argued so far that the option of transgressing these restrictions may produce guilty pleasures, thus enhancing our sexual experiences. But having these experiences may have broader implications. The model of transgression entailed here is a model of resistance to power and to conforming to group norms. If gay men and lesbians had not persisted in transgressing Jewish rhetoric against same-sex relationships, those relationships might still be considered illicit by all of the Jewish community. Transgressing those laws enabled lesbian and gay relationships to be perceived as licit by at least some segments of the Jewish community. The same may be true for other sexual acts and desires that have the potential to be moral, but that are still considered forbidden. To set up a system that invites transgression teaches people that they can question the values of the societies in which they live, and the results may be dramatic in bringing about the possibility of social change.

To begin to think about good sex from a Jewish feminist perspective, we need to understand the power of regulating sex, even if those regulations are enforced only through discursive means. The rhetoric of regulation is problematic because it validates sex only when it is an instrument of procreation or commitment, links sexual differences and capacities to gender, makes sex for its own sake both less valued and shameful, and encourages people to develop secret sex lives. On the other hand, a system of regulation helps us recognize the powerful nature of the erotic and ironically invites transgression, which at the least is seductive and at most transformative. It is a flawed system, but one from which we can benefit if we question it wisely.

NOTES

1. David Biale, *Eros and the Jews: From Biblical Israel to Contemporary America* (Berkeley: University of California Press, 1997), 104.

2. Genesis Rabbah 9.9.

3. Michael Satlow, *Tasting the Dish: Rabbinic Rhetorics of Sexuality*, Brown Judaic Studies 303 (Atlanta, Ga.: Scholars Press, 1995), 173–83.

4. The concept of *yetzer hara* makes clear the rabbinic ambivalence toward sexual desire, which was viewed at best as a necessary evil. See Biale, *Eros and the Jews*, 43–47, for a full explanation of the concept of *yetzer hara*.

5. Satlow (*Tasting the Dish*, 246–61) says the prohibition was not against spilling seed, but against the temptation and disruption it would have caused. Autoeroticism was strictly prohibited, even to the point of forbidding the touching of the penis during urination.

6. Female homoerotic behavior is not included because it is not considered sex and therefore does not disrupt the order of things.

7. B. Niddah 16b, quoted in Satlow, *Tasting the Dish*, 299.

8. On the subject of onah, see Biale, *Eros and the Jews*, 54; Satlow, *Tasting the Dish*, 265.

9. Satlow, *Tasting the Dish*, 320.

10. See Rebecca Alpert, *Like Bread on the Seder Plate: Jewish Lesbians and the Transformation of Tradition* (New York: Columbia University Press, 1997), 29–34.

11. Satlow, *Tasting the Dish*, 264.

12. Norman Lamm, *A Hedge of Roses: Some Jewish Insights into Sex and Marriage* (London: Clarendon Foundation, 1968).

13. See works such as Robert Gordis, *Sex and the Family in Judaism* (New York: Burning Book, 1967); Judith Plaskow, *Standing Again at Sinai: Judaism from a Feminist Perspective* (San Francisco: Harper and Row, 1990); and Eugene Borowitz, *Choosing a Sex Ethic: A Jewish Inquiry* (New York: Schocken, 1969).

14. Daniel Boyarin, *Unheroic Conduct: The Rise of Heterosexuality and the Invention of the Jewish Man* (Berkeley: University of California Press, 1997), 162–68.

15. See Arthur Waskow, *Down-to-Earth Judaism: Food, Money, Sex, and the Rest of Life* (New York: Morrow, 1997).

16. See Biale, *Eros and the Jews*, 225; and Boyarin, *Unheroic Conduct*, 180.

17. Jane Litwoman, "Some Thoughts on Bisexuality," *Lesbian Contradictions*, winter 1990.

18. See Norman Lamm, "Judaism and the Modern Jewish Attitude to Homosexuality," *Encyclopedia Judaica Yearbook* (1974).

19. Quoted in Biale, *Eros and the Jews*, 104.

20. Marcia Falk, *The Song of Songs: A New Translation and Interpretation* (San Francisco: Harper, 1990), 145–47.

21. Quoted in Ephraim E. Urbach, *The Sages: Their Concepts and Beliefs*, trans. Israel Abrahams (Jerusalem: Magnes, 1975), 357.

22. The closet was also regulated by laws that could punish gay people with loss of jobs, family, and housing, and even with death. This is still true in certain settings and detracts from rather than enhances the pleasure of gay sex because it renders it immoral and illegal rather than simply illicit, in the terms we are using here.

23. Biale, *Eros and the Jews.*

24. Michel Foucault, *The History of Sexuality,* vol. 1 (New York: Pantheon, 1978).

25. See Howard Eilberg-Schwartz, *The Savage in Judaism: Excursis in an Anthropology of Israelite Religion and Ancient Judaism* (Bloomington: Indiana University Press, 1990).

21

A Queer Fidelity: Reinventing Christian Marriage

W. SCOTT HALDEMAN

To engage in reflection on Christian marriage is a rather daunting undertaking. Yet it is also a necessary one. The institution and its rites are much controverted in our day. In particular, I have been drawn into the debate by the passage of what has been dubbed the "Inclusive Marriage Resolution" by the 2005 General Conference of the United Church of Christ. With the vote to adopt this resolution, the United Church of Christ became the first US denomination not founded specifically to serve the LGBT community to open the frame of Christian marriage so as to welcome same-sex couples into the "estate of marriage" (i.e., no euphemisms such as "same-sex union" are to be used) with the exact same rite as heterosexual couples.[1] Much hue and cry has ensued as some congregations use this resolution as a reason to leave the denomination or otherwise protest. As a seminary professor at a UCC school, my role as a scholar is to sort through such issues in order to shed light as well as heat on such controversies. And yet the complexity of the history and the attendant theological tensions leave me feeling a bit as Martin Luther must have felt while writing a sermon on the subject in 1522. He puts it this way:

> How I dread preaching on the estate of marriage! I am reluctant to do it because I am afraid if I once get really involved in the subject it will make a lot of work for me and for others. The shameful confusion wrought by the accursed papal law has occasioned so much distress, and the lax authority of both the spiritual and the temporal swords has given rise to so many dreadful abuses and false situations, that I would much prefer neither to look into the matter nor to hear of it. But timidity is no help in an emergency; I must proceed. I must try to instruct poor bewildered consciences, and take up the matter boldly.[2]

While, in my own view, there is plenty of blame to go around, so I rest it not at the Prada-wrapped feet of the newest Vicar of Christ in Rome, dear Benedict the Sixteenth, and his predecessors alone, I do agree that the estate is a mess, that it may be preferable not to look, and yet, as brother Martin concludes, "timidity is surely no help in an emergency, . . . so it is better to proceed with boldness."

For Luther, the "work" involved at least four challenges. First, he sought to dismantle an ecclesial system that designated as illicit many particular relationships—except, of course, for those who were willing to pay a fee and so were granted dispensation. Second, he attempted to overturn the ecclesial ideology that valued celibacy more than domestic life, and that was, in turn, based on misogyny—as if, for men, intimacy with a woman was a "necessary" evil in order to ensure the continuing propagation of the species. Third, he wanted to re-cast prevailing conceptions of the strength of human erotic desires so as to discourage people from making vows they could not keep. And, fourth, he emphasized in new ways the value of mutual care of husband and wife, and the value of married life as Christian vocation and as pleasing to God.

Luther's efforts, like those of all of us who strike out boldly, had unforeseen consequences. The most important of these was the loss for women of the option of vowed religious life, one of the few alternatives to marriage available to them at the time, a way to avoid an institution, which, despite Luther's rhetoric of mutuality, remained unmistakably patriarchal in form.[3] Still, his honesty about human frailty, about the power of our sexual drives, and about the grace of a secure and stable relational life into which such drives could be channeled in order that one might contribute to a productive and faithful household makes this a remarkable pastoral document. Yet his questions are not our own. We contend not so much against a view of marriage as a distant second behind celibacy in terms of the shape of a faithful Christian life, but as the be all and end all of Christian life itself—another ecclesial claim—and one equally as problematic.[4]

Neither does the unmasking of the idolatry of the nuclear family encompass the full gambit of challenges before us. We might also consider important questions, such as: the relationship between love and sex, between sex and procreation, between sex and sin, between faith and sex, between sex and law—and the many social goods and social ills that issue from various perspectives on how these things should be thought about and reinforced by moral precept and legal definition.[5] Or, we could think through the details of wedding ceremonial in historical, theological and ritual perspective to articulate proposals for union services that may be more efficacious.[6] Or, we might reflect upon the various things at stake for both church and society in promoting certain structures of intimate life over others rather than supporting the flourishing of the many and varied shapes of actual families.[7] Or, we could argue about what familial configurations provide adequate security and nurture for children.[8] Or, we could discuss the arbitrariness and injustice of the use of marriage as a gateway of access to significant social privileges.[9] Or, we could trace the relationship between perspectives on marriage and various concepts about the human sex/gender system with competing understandings of the relation between men and women,

women and men, and accounting for all the complexities of gender identity, performance and presentation that are finally being recognized and claimed and considered because of the courage of "trannies" of all kinds.[10] Yes, it does seem that there is much work to be done for me and for Martin—for all of us.

And, in addition to all this, Mark Jordan, in his elegant and complex book, *Blessing Same-Sex Unions: The Perils of Queer Romance and the Confusions of Christian Marriage*, raises still more questions that could occupy us at length, but we must choose among them or never get anywhere.[11] I have settled on one point that sparked my own imagination and fits my self-understanding as a queer theologian. The issue revolves around two observations that Jordan simply notes and yet that seem crucial to productive conversation about same-sex marriage—first, is the conviction, held by many, that it is not possible for two men to form bonds of true fidelity and so gay men do not deserve access to the holy estate of marriage—and, second, that one of the problems we have in engaging this claim is that we tend not to speak frankly about such things, about the sexual practices and parameters that come to shape our relational lives, and about what this means for the sanction of various types of intimacies.[12]

I intend, then, to tell some truth of my own, to allow some light to shine upon the question of a queer fidelity. I am, many of you have no doubt already guessed, less interested in defending gay men as ready and willing to enter into life-long, sexually exclusive, monogamous unions—and so acquiescing to the idolatry of "complementary coupledom" that founds the so-called "traditional family values" claims—than I am in expanding our notions of what fidelity might mean. Because of this, I recognize that this strategy may or may not be the best way to combat my opponents in this debate—I may, in fact, be playing into their hands—but I am willing to take this risk, if, as well, the conversation becomes more honest. I also recognize that my truths may sound to some like an attack on marriage, but I do not intend them as such. Instead I seek only to break silence and provoke others to think with me about the kinds of Christian life we promote as faithful.

We may recall that Jesus said, "the Sabbath is for humankind—not humankind for the Sabbath" to which Juan Segundo added a riff: that "The Sacraments are for the Church and not the Church for the Sacraments."[13] In like attitude, I posit that "Marriage is for humans, not the other way 'round." Or, in other words, that marriage is one arrangement that fosters wholeness for at least some humans, but is, perhaps, not the only faithful one, and, perhaps, in any case, its forms are multiple. For that is really the controversy, isn't it?—that Dobson et al. want to fit people into the box of the so-called "timeless institution" of marriage rather than allowing the marriage box to take shape around the truth of our lives.[14] And how many of us, whether gay, straight, bi-, transgendered, or otherwise, fit—or want to fit—into the box such advocates present to us, since for all its familiarity, it is built on premises that some of us no longer find life-giving? In other words, to put it humorously, how many of us could thrive in homes where one man works as provider, one woman provides constant support and service with a smile, the kids play quietly in the corner and the TVs are on all the time and are tuned to Fox News? Not so many, I suspect.

Of course, if you like this box, by all means set up house in it—but that is different than forcing me, and others, into it—and certainly different than changing the law of the land to allow only one small box to exist and to relegate all of the rest of us to the "Island of Misfit Toys."[15]

I suggest, instead, that we follow lesbian-feminist, poet and essayist, Adrienne Rich, and, paraphrasing her poem, "make of our lives a study . . . [that we] recognize that this may be one of those times when we must take ourselves seriously or die . . . [that we] risk freefall . . . [after] . . . cutting the wires . . . [that held us] . . . to old formularies . . . in [our search for] new language."[16] I, certainly, am committed to take my own life seriously, to take queer lives seriously as sources for queer theologizing, even while recognizing that in speaking the truth I risk rejection by those who would rather not hear. Others have found this approach helpful in the past—I hope it may be again. And so I risk telling uncomfortable truths, being *inappropriate*, as queer folk are so often considered. And, I do so because I believe with Audre Lorde that "your silence will not protect you"[17]—that not speaking, in fact, only adds to the problem, building thicker walls on the closet that may feel safe but, as so many of us have come to recognize, eventually becomes a tomb. This is because relying on easy half-truths, rather than getting to the heart of the matter, we leave in place those structures that define us as deviant and, therefore, as disposable.

And, so, in relation to marriage, here is a first attempt to study my life and get to at least one heart of the matter (as there are several). I trust that while I may offend, beyond scandal there may be further dialogue, space to study one another's lives—not as they should be or as we were told they would be, but as they are in all their messy, perverse beauty—and so we may come to honor one another and find a path towards a peace that is also just—perhaps.

And so, let me posit this claim: I am not a "good" "husband."

What do I mean by this?

First, obviously, I mean that I am something other than "good" in my role as husband—that's the not part. But then "good" needs to be parsed —whose "good"? Ah, here we are. Who gets to decide? The philosophers? The moralists? The churches? The government? My partner? Me? You? As you will see, I am coming to understand "good" in new ways. But I actually don't think I get to decide for myself—that would mean acknowledging those who would call what follows crass and self-serving rationalization are correct. Rather I get simply to lay things out in such a way that you may see and respond—so we can together, perhaps, come to new understandings and define a more truthful ethic—at least that is my hope.

Next, of course, to many, my use of the term "husband" is absurd since I live with a man—to play a bit with the language of the Levitical priests —"as with a woman." Our word, "husband" comes from Old Norse—from "hus" (meaning house) and "bondi" (meaning dweller) and so designates an owner of a house, the head of the household, a conserver and preserver of land and live-stock.[18] Difference, hierarchy and authority are the waters from which this word emerges—a help to many who argue for so-called traditional forms of family, perhaps, but dynamics that raise my suspicions—perhaps yours as well.

It is certainly true that life with another man, especially without either civil or ecclesial sanction or recognition, fits awkwardly in this etymology. For "hus-band" seems to be about preservation and building up of assets (which would include one's wife) and not about love or romance or passion. My "husband" (if I can indulge myself with the term) and I do not own each other's assets—in fact, we must make special arrangements to own things together, to protect the other from financial ruin should something happen to one of us. We have no reason other than love to stay together. And I both mow the lawn and do the dishes—for in our life, assignment of various domestic tasks by gender, so central to our socialization, must be constantly negotiated rather than simply perpetuated. This certainly makes life interesting—but we get ahead of our-selves—the point here is simply that words like "husband" need to be investi-gated and perhaps redefined in debates such as these.

The same is true for the word "good"—at least I hope this is true, because there are at least three ways that, in relation to common understandings of what it means to be a good spouse, I am not good. First, I am divorced. Sec-ond, rather than taking the proverbial plunge into settled stability of the self-sufficient "couple" in this, my second long-term relationship, I have found it necessary to reinvent myself, to practice myself into a new, "gay" identity and so have been reluctant to settle the terms of this "marriage." And, third, and more specifically, I struggle, both conceptually and in practice, with the expectation that committed, intimate relationships require sexual exclusivity. I will reflect on each of these, in turn, in both personal and theological perspective before con-cluding with a brief constructive proposal about a reinvented form of marriage as one shape of a faithful Christian life.

Divorce focuses our attention on biblical authority, and its use in ethical debates. I lived with a woman once—for just over ten years. I held, then, the title "husband" with some familial, social, ecclesial and civil legitimacy. While at least relatively happy for most of those years, the conventions of that life grew constrictive, choking off my life breath. A decision was reached; we divorced and I have taken another. So, at least in terms of the textual record we have—rather than those that we like to make up—in terms of a saying at least directly attributed to Jesus, I am already condemned (Mt. 19:3–9). That the evangeli-cal churches, the same ones that use the Bible to condemn same-sex love as sin and to lead a social movement to outlaw any recognition of families led by adults who happen to have the same genital configuration, have, even if reluctantly, compromised on this point—what, to them, surely must qualify as a direct dominical command—is quite remarkable. Could conversation about this serve as common ground to rethink the ways in which we (both liberals and conservatives) deploy biblical texts in contemporary debates so as to open the conversation about how we should live both as individuals and in relationship? I am not sure, but perhaps it could.

The acceptance of divorce can be seen as a concession to human failure, to human sin—as Jesus characterizes Moses' allowance of divorce—but it also may entail recognition that a single, life-long, monogamous relationship, while a good thing for some, for others hinders rather than encourages their flourishing.[19] It also allows us to begin to recognize the ways in which naming one particular arrangement (such as, one man and one woman) de facto "good" masks much that is not good—domestic violence, emotional abuse, financial exploitation, and the like. That so many of us are not "good" in relation to a norm placed on Jesus' lips challenges us all to consider if what we claim as "good" is really "good for us" or just "for our own good."

Second, I contend we must reconsider the married state as a static arrangement that one enters, once and for all, through the "rite of passage" of the wedding. How many young (and not so young) men and women are counseled, ponderously, to ready themselves to move from the freedom of singleness to the bounds of marriage. For all its supposed benefits, marriage is often characterized as being primarily about discipline, regulation, surrender. Both in personal and theological perspective, I am wondering about the wisdom of such an approach—venerable as it may be.

On the personal side, I met the man with whom I now live very soon after I signed the divorce papers. Too soon, in fact. I was a wreck. The phrase "on the rebound" conveys so little of the jumble of anxieties and exhilarations that spun through my head and heart. Free but lost; lost but free. The image that remains with me is that I was falling—fast, far—and was lucky enough to have someone to catch me. He, too, though quite differently, found me to be, at least, a right person at a right time—for him, a dream deferred, perhaps abandoned, now fulfilled. Yet not all was "happily ever after," not even close. I needed to eat. I took a job 500 miles away, in Nashville, to make a life. Hard times. Yet a chance to make something out of all the broken pieces.

So a few months of dating. A growing certainty of a deep commitment. Yet distance interceded—that long-distance thing.

Alone in a new city I had the opportunity to reinvent myself, to "become" gay, to construct a new self in new modes of gendered behavior, to try out a variety of selves. And, reeling from the ending of a 10-year marriage and all that divorce inflicts and too-soon coupled once more, it was space to be a "bachelor"—as I was certainly not yet ready to be a "husband" of any sort at that point.

One night on one of those many but too-infrequent and so furtive weekends in which my now-partner and I found each other in embrace, I asked him for his understanding of the form of our commitment. Was this the right thing to do? Who knows? I recognize that sometimes vagueness is a good thing—but it is, for me, hard to sustain—I tend to ask such things. In any case, honesty seems a firmer foundation—I asked. "Exclusivity—of course!" came the reply. Not sure what to do with that I said little—"ok" is all I recall.

Wanting to be good, trying to be good, I returned to Nashville, to my life, to my work of self-reinvention.

Needless to say, I wasn't "good"—at least in relation to the terms now expressed.

I wasn't looking for another lover but I was looking for touch, for connection to a variety of kinds of men—a whole new world had just dawned—it seemed to me impossible not to look, not to reach—and, besides, such explorations, such indulgences were things I felt I needed to do to settle in to my new self. Now here I must note that my life probably sounds much more interesting than it was—or is—I certainly did not "hook up" as often as I might have wanted—the point is that I did not meet the expectations set for me—this time not so much by social norms (though they are certainly operative) but the parameters made between another and myself—if, on my part anyway, rather half-heartedly.

Perhaps it was simply a late adolescence, something to move through and grow out of, as I moved from half-hearted to enthusiastic commitment. But the questions that arise for me are why we place so much weight on sexual activity in the making of commitments, and why a commitment is only considered serious when it is exclusive. It could be I needed simply to find out who I was, who I am, who I am becoming so that I could realistically make any commitment at all. But I think something deeper is at issue—an opportunity to reconsider what entails true, wholesome human intimacy. I was coming to know myself as I was coming to know my then boyfriend and as we were coming to define our relationship, a shared future. Reveling in each other's flesh was certainly central to this coming to know, but so were shared meals with many friends, both his and mine, so were conversations both personal and professional, so were all manner of interactions both private and public in which we grew to know that we could depend upon one another, trust one another, envision a path to walk together. These seem central, perhaps universal, aspects of shared life—grounded in strong commitment and pledges of loyalty, honesty, fidelity—but outward-looking, communal, public as much as private—how crucial, then, is sexual exclusivity to such arrangements?

Put in more theological (or ecclesial) terms, I base the Christian vocation in baptism, which, among other things, tempers all claims of kinship, all private relationships by situating them in the midst of communal bonds, membership in the One Body. Those baptized as infants are taken from their parents' arms and thrust under the water. We submit our children to the risk of drowning because we trust in divine care and in order to entrust these young disciples to the community—they belong now to the community, not to us—they belong, as we do, to God. Those baptized as adults give public testimony of their own faith and then submit in the same posture of trust to have their worldly status washed away and become nothing more and nothing less an adopted child of God, a sister or brother or sister/brother to all other members of Christ's church. But, then, when intense love blossoms between individual saints, we focus on these two and we ritualize around their promises to one another and then we send them off to live happily ever after—as if! What irresponsibility, if not lunacy. What if, instead, we constructed practices and rites that offer challenge and support to absolutely everybody in whatever ways they are discerning to live out their baptized life—honoring and supporting those who find themselves suited to a life of intimate bonding with one other, but also honoring and supporting those who remained less singularly attached, and those who adopt children—whether they are happily coupled or simply single generous hearts, and those who have loved and lost, and those who immerse themselves in all variety of webs of intimacy and love.

One central meaning of baptism is that the church should live as if all are equal before God. So, we should stop creating classes of status—the married, the parents, the single, the youth, the old. Instead, all these children belong to all of us, as we belong one to another. Married life can be one honorable and faithful path for some members of the body without being defined as a static institution. For, if God is alive and the Spirit still moves, than any one of us may be called to leave all we know behind and strike out into the wilderness. Marriage has been made by Christians into a fortress of supposed security when the Christian life is better lived as a journey of risk. Even more, are not those who call themselves Christians supposed to be attending to the least of these, offering hospitality to all who knock and to provide food to the hungry, clothing to those dressed in rags, healing touch to ill and injured? Isn't the church and its members meant to embrace the stranger, to be open to new loves? As we engage in these practices, both at church and at home, both as a body and as individuals and families, we may make truer that it has been the claim that the married reflect the love of Christ and church—not as a static hierarchical, pure relationship, but as an open one—moving ever towards the Other, touching with healing touch (Eph. 5:20–33). Marriage, then, as discipleship more generally, is not a relationship of security but a vocation of hospitable loyalty in which honesty is key, in which we do not hide away in the closet of romance but take up a vocation of service in the ways of love—many kinds of love.

Finally, we must contend directly with the matter of sexual exclusivity as the lynchpin of traditional notions of fidelity. Does this sound familiar?

"Can we?"

"Not now."

"Ok, when?"

"I don't know—later."

"Fine!"

"Fine! Whatever."

And so the lovers retire, unfulfilled, at some distance, frustrated.

In traditional language, we are talking now about the issue of the conjugal debt. Paul says that, once married, your body is no longer your own but is controlled by your spouse (1 Cor. 7:1–6). This leads to a number of possible problems—one is abuse—as in when I hit you I am only hurting myself because you belong to me; another is marital rape—as in you have no choice but to let me do what I want; and the third is the less violent but still frustrating problem of depending on one other person to fulfill my need for touch.[20]

Now I know all too well the word "need" is a funny one, slippery at best—it is precisely the proclivity to see one's selfish desires as needs that leads so often to Christian moralists positing structures for the channeling, redirection and repression of desire itself. Such a distrust of desire is precisely how the church added to the celibate ideal a legitimation of conjugal relations as faithful practice—but, at least for many years, only as a lower form of discipleship—as Paul puts it: "It is better to marry than to burn" (1 Cor. 7:9).

One way to read the history of marriage theology is, in fact, as a slow movement towards greater sympathy for erotic desire, towards recognition of purposes for sex beyond procreation—from Paul's "it is better not to marry" to Augustine's three goods of marriage (which were the begetting of children, mutual care between spouses, and the sacramental gift of an indissoluble union)[21] to Luther's elevation of married life above celibacy as the ideal Christian life[22] to more recent acceptance of non-procreative couplings as worthy of honor in which, to use Stephanie Coontz's phrase, "love [has now] conquered marriage."[23] And, this new primacy of the personal feeling of love (as well as the relativization of inequities among the sexes) has, of course, brought us to the point of considering the possible justification of same-sex marriages. Yet, with this movement has also come to focus on the couple as a self-sufficient social unit—forsaking all others, my best friend, my heart. In other words, we have not questioned the basic function of marriage as a form of sexual regulation—that to be a "good" husband is to be content with sex with one other person for the rest of my life.

In recognition of the many arrangements people make—even good Christians—in relation to sexual activity with others besides one's partner and in hopes of reframing our moral evaluation of this, I would suggest that we reconsider what we mean by "fidelity." The word means "to be true"—and what if we took that seriously, if we shifted its import from a norm of exclusivity in the realm of touch to a new norm of self-care and truth-telling. What if our pledge was to take responsibility for our own desires—not dismissing or ignoring our partner, but, if one has more need for physical intimacy than the other, that each can find safe, consensual, non-abusive, enjoyable connections on occasion with others—and, beyond this, we pledge to be loyal—to come home, to answer any question asked, to be accountable not only for acting on our desires but also for the ways our actions may cause pain, for the risks and insecurities that this new arrangement carries with it—to be honest about who we are and what we want and how we are changing and who we are becoming—this seems to me a true form of intimacy, a foundation for a strong yet flexible bond, a fidelity, even if an unfamiliar one.

And, it is crucial to remind ourselves that more familiar arrangements are no less insecure. It seems to me that much thought about Christian marriage has been built precisely on anxiety about our insecurity in relationship—with that anxiety focused, mistakenly in my view, on sex. Despite my attempts to read the sources with an open mind, to see the various claims and hopes of past and present theological constructions, I cannot escape the interpretation that marriage has, for most of church history, been about the regulation of sex, of sexual desire, of eros. Not only has this served to guarantee the failure of many marriages, since some sort of sexual acting out is likely on the part of many, and since such an act is seen as well as the ultimate betrayal and so an irredeemable act of moral failure. Still many marriages survive such indiscretions, as sex with another is recognized not as the central act of betrayal we were told it was but as a symptom of some other problem in the relationship that can then be identified and perhaps overcome.

Could it be that defining sex as the problem makes it the problem rather than it actually being so? I do not mean to dismiss the real feelings of jealousy and hurt, but it is also true that we have been taught to react this way—that our feelings are conditioned as well as "natural." We can, I believe, also practice ourselves into other responses. The question, I suppose, is "why would we?" I would contend, again, that such opening outward is faithful Christian life. That we should live not as two peas in a pod but as companions on the road, two among many, connecting with others who go the same way—towards a life of love and justice.

To see these connections more clearly, we might consider the way marriage has been used to separate groups of people—and keep them separate—and, of course, to keep one group dominant and another subordinate. Through marriage and its policing, some children are designated legitimate, while others are illegitimate. Through marriage and its policing, the white race is kept pure from the black race. Through marriage and its policing, the royals do not mix with commoners and the wealthy, in the phrase of Uncle Max in *The Sound of Music*, get to "keep all that lovely money in the family." Through marriage and its policing, Adam and Eve are given privileges, while Adam and Steve are vulnerable to the whims of kin. Marriage has, in part, been about our fears about not being able to keep things clear. It has too often been much less about love than it has been about control. It is time to admit this—and if we don't like the sound of it—to change it.

In response, an additional question may be raised—well, why do those who do not adopt exclusive commitments deserve the benefits of marriage? Marriage, in such a view, is the mortar that holds securely the bricks of a strong society. Those who participate in such secure arrangements should be rewarded as every member of society benefits from their stability as they keep their vows. Yet, solidity may be unhelpful when it serves more to resist the increase of justice and mercy than to preserve it. If we had a just order then we would want to preserve it— this is true. But we live not in "the new age" but, in Bob Hovda's memorable phrase, in "a cesspool of injustice."[24] The promise of peace with justice is close by, at hand, but, except in glimpses, still eludes our grasp. Fluidity, innovation, protest, struggle—these are the characteristics of those who follow the crucified and risen one, those who seek to build bridges rather than walls.

Just so, such people, those who accept the risk of ongoing negotiation in the context of loyalty may contribute to the shift *from* arrangements where those who accept bounded roles are rewarded to a society that is attentive to every citizen's actual material needs. The real fight, the struggle to be engaged by people of faith, and here I caution those who seek so-called marriage equality, may be less to ensure that loving, stable same-sex couples and their children get social benefits as that all families, all people, are supported and have what they need in terms of health insurance, visitation privileges in hospitals, the distribution of their estate at death and so on. In this way, those who experiment in love may serve the increase of social justice.

The reinvention of Christian marriage, then, involves at least three moves—that I have briefly and inadequately sketched—to reject the idea that God has decreed one arrangement for human society, to de-center marriage in both ecclesial and social structures, and to de-center sex in marriage. The first, one can make the case, is agreed upon by all parties in the American marriage debates—as, if one can allow divorce, one must admit to negotiating biblical norms in the face of human reality and so one must also admit, in the face of sociological data about the variety of forms that families take, that there is room for multiple, potentially faithful models. The second involves re-imagining church not as a haven for the beleaguered, nuclear family but as an alternative family, where one can find rest, where one is honored, where one can hear truth, but where one can also practice sharing food, praying for enemies, forgiving and being forgiven so as to live out in the world with more compassion, humility and hope. The third involves rethinking fidelity—not as repression of desire to maintain security—but as constant, honest communication in the midst of growth and change and difference—being true both to oneself and to the other in a risky but exhilarating journey.

And, so, am I a good husband? You really need to ask my husband, I suppose. But, let me venture that I think I am—but only as I live so as to be worthy of his trust, as I provide care and support, as I communicate as honestly as I can about who I am and who I am becoming, and as I listen deeply to this man that I love—to who he is and who he is becoming, to how who I am becoming affects him—as we take further steps on this adventure called discipleship, trying to model God's profligate love, showing hospitality, joining struggles for justice, embracing the stranger and seeing what may be.

NOTES

1. See http://www.ucc.org/synod/resolutions/gsrev25-7.pdf for the text of the "Equal Marriage Rites for All" resolution and http://www.ucc.org/worship/tnch/ pofmiv.pdf for the proposed rite itself. Both of these pages were accessed 16 June 2006.

2. Martin Luther, *The Estate of Marriage* (trans. Walther I. Brandt, 1522), opening paragraph. Accessed at http://www.warwick.ac.uk/fac/arts/History/teaching/ protref /women/WR0913.htm on 1 June 2006.

3. See Rita Brock, "Marriage Troubles" in Marvin Ellison and Sylvia Thorson-Smith (eds.), *Body and Soul: Rethinking Sexuality as Justice-Love* (Cleveland: Pilgrim Press, 2003), pp. 352–74.

4. See Rosemary Radford Ruether, *Christianity and the Making of the Modern Family: Ruling Ideologies, Diverse Realities* (Boston: Beacon Press, 2000), especially pp. 156–80.

5. To begin thinking about this set of questions, see Janet R. Jakobsen and Ann Pellegrini, *Love the Sin: Sexual Regulation and the Limits of Religious Tolerance* (New York: New York University Press, 2003).

6. To begin thinking about this set of questions, see Mark Searle and Kenneth W. Stevenson, *Documents of the Marriage Liturgy* (New York: Pueblo/Liturgical Press, 1992) (NB: this text is currently out of print); Kenneth W. Stevenson, *To Join Together: The Rite of Marriage* (New York: Pueblo/Liturgical Press, 1987); and Ronald Grimes, *Marrying and Burying* (Boulder, CO: Westview Press, 1985) (NB: this text is currently out of print).

7. To begin thinking about this set of questions, see Saul M. Olyan and Martha Craven Nussbaum, *Sexual Orientation and Human Rights in American Religious Discourse* (New York: Oxford University Press, 1998).

8. To begin thinking about this set of questions, see Don Browning, Bonnie J. Miller-McLemore, Pamela D. Couture, K. Brynolf Lyon, and Robert M. Franklin, *From Culture Wars to Common Ground: Religion and the American Family Debate* (Louisville: Westminster John Knox, 2nd ed, 2000).

9. To begin thinking about this set of questions, see George Chauncey, *Why Marriage? The History Shaping Today's Debate over Gay Equality* (New York: Basic Books, 2004); and Marvin Ellison, *Same-sex Marriage? A Christian Ethical Analysis* (Cleveland: Pilgrim Press, 2004).

10. To begin thinking about this set of questions, see Chrys Ingraham, *White Weddings: Romancing Heterosexuality in Popular Culture* (New York: Routledge, 1999), along with Judith Butler, *Gender Trouble: Feminism and the Subversion of Identity* (New York: Routledge, 10th anniv. edn, 1999).

11. Jordan asks, among other things, whether we need to consider our proclivity to idealize romance—as if any of us live happily ever after in a warm, darkly lit cocoon perpetually intertwined in rapturous embrace (p. 49); whether it is possible to ritualize in ways that are more honest about the ebbs and flows of "eros in time" (pp. 109–10); and how contemporary services of blessing are best constructed in relation to rites of earlier periods, rites of the larger, consumerist culture, and other rites in our lives (pp. 139–55). In relation to the final challenge above, he contends, for example, that we should trace the history of marriage rites—not to return to formularies of old but to tease out the purposes of those rites in their contexts as we develop rites of blessing in our own day for our own purposes. While we might bless a particular same-sex relationship to provide community support to the partners, for instance; we also might perform such a rite to protest the exclusion of such relationship from valuation as honorable—a very different sort of end—perhaps calling for a different sort of rite. *Blessing Same-Sex Unions: The Perils of Queer Romance and the Confusions of Christian Marriage* (Chicago: University of Chicago Press, 2005).

12. Jordan, *Blessing Same-Sex Unions*, pp. 156–59.

13. Jesus' saying is recorded in Mk 2.27; Segundo's phrase appears in his *The Sacraments Today*, vol. 4 of *Theology for Artisans of a New Humanity* (trans. John Drury; Maryknoll, NY: Orbis Books, 1974 [original in Spanish, 1971]), p. 61. See also Tom Driver's discussion of Segundo's work for contemporary sacramental theology in *Liberating Rites: Understanding the Transformative Power of Ritual* (Boulder, CO: Westview Press, 1998), pp. 203–8.

14. I refer to Dr James Dobson, founding president of "Focus on the Family," a major player in the promotion of the so-called traditional family and the discouragement of all other configurations of human intimacy in the current context of early twenty-first century political debates in the US. See his website: www.family.org.

15. The "Island of Misfit Toys" is featured in "Rudolph the Red-Nosed Reindeer," a Christmas special that has aired on television for the last thirty or so years, but the point is to remind us of the threat that campaigns such as the current one to amend the US Constitution to define marriage as between "one man and one woman" pose to the material well-being of many who may lose domestic partner benefits, such as health insurance or the custody of children whether adopted or biological, because the sex/gender of their partner means their familial relationship is not (or no longer) protected.

16. Adrienne Rich, "Transcendental Etude," in *The Dream of a Common Language* (New York: W.W. Norton and Co., 1993 [1978]), pp. 72–77.

17. Audre Lorde, "The Transformation of Silence into Language and Action," in *Sister/Outsider: Essays and Speeches* (Freedom, CA: The Crossing Press, 1984), p. 41.

18. See http://www.etymonline.com/index.php?term=husband (accessed 16 June 2006).

19. Jordan notes that divorce rates, when calculated in relation to, among other things, the increased life expectancy of the average person, have changed much less dramatically than alarmists bewail. He writes: "As people live longer, more of them tend to outlive relationships. Divorce now does what an earlier death used to do." (*Blessing Same-Sex Unions*, p. 185).

20. On the first two sorts of problems that stem from the teaching that one's spouse owns one's body (as well as connections between this teaching and problematics in christological and soteriological doctrinal formulations in Christian tradition), see Rita Nakashima Brock and Rebecca Ann Parker, *Proverbs of Ashes: Violence, Redemptive Suffering, and the Search for What Saves Us* (Boston: Beacon Press, 2001), especially pp. 15–29.

21. Augustine, Bishop of Hippo, "The Good of Marriage," excerpted in Eugene F. Rogers, Jr (ed.), *Theology and Sexuality: Classic and Contemporary Readings* (Oxford: Blackwell, 2002), pp. 71–86.

22. Luther, *Estate of Marriage*, opening paragraph.

23. See, especially, Part 3, "The Love Revolution," in Stephanie Coontz, *Marriage, A History: How Love Conquered Marriage* (London: Penguin Books, 2005).

24. Robert Hovda, "The Vesting of Liturgical Ministers," in John F. Baldovin (ed.), *Robert Hovda: The Amen Corner* (Collegeville, MN: A Pueblo Book, 1994), pp. 213–33 (220).

PART 5

Sexual Health and Bodily Integrity

Elizabeth Stuart
Grace M. Jantzen
Ken Stone
Frances Kissling

Introduction
to Part 5

This section considers further the implications of Christianity's troubling perspectives on sexuality and the body by addressing sexual healing and embodied self-regard in relation to some contested concerns that the church far too often ignores or finds particularly troubling. If the church has found it difficult to deal with matters of sexuality, it has found it even more difficult to address the body issues of persons who have been hypereroticized and thus demonized by the church. In short, the church is often confounded or rendered silent when it comes to the body issues of "bodied people," especially women and gay and lesbian persons. At the same time, the church also struggles with concerns of those persons whose bodies are viewed as "incomplete" or nonprocreative, and who are subsequently deeroticized. The fact that their aged or disabled bodies seemingly prevent them from engaging in "acceptable" intimacy often causes them to be out of the purview of the church's concern or considered theological/ethical "problems." Finally, debate about reproductive health and justice, specifically abortion, continues to embroil the church in passionate political/moral discourse that is often theologically and ethically wanting.

This section opens with Elizabeth Stuart's "Disruptive Bodies: Disability, Embodiment, and Sexuality." Her project is to "centralize the disabled body" as she tries to discern a theo-ethical perspective that recognizes the full humanity of those who are disabled by acknowledging them as fully sexual beings. Stuart adopts a liberationist perspective, yet with a significant twist. Instead of beginning with the experience of the "disabled body" (which has been done), she begins by engaging the Christian tradition itself. Only in engaging the Christian tradition, she argues, will those who are disabled "enter into the consciousness of some Christians." What follows is an illuminating discourse on the way in which disabled bodies are at once "everywhere and nowhere" in the Christian tradition. This essay also carefully delineates some complicated ethical issues that emerge when fully appreciating the disabled body as a sexual body. In the end, Stuart succeeds in "centralizing the disabled body" and thereby exposes the Christian imperative to develop a more affirming theological/ethical perspective when it comes to disabled bodies. After all, Stuart asserts, the "abled body" is only temporary. At some point in time, all persons experience what it means to be a disabled body.

In her "AIDS, Shame, and Suffering," Grace M. Jantzen holds the church accountable for the way in which those suffering with AIDS have been outcasts within society and rejected by various faith communities. She argues that because HIV/AIDS has been overassociated with "homosexuals" and overly defined as a sexual disease, HIV/AIDS sufferers are practically excoriated within Christian faith communities. They become victims of self-righteous anger and blame. They are in our time what lepers were in Jesus' day. Fueling this castigation is the church's theological tradition of fearing sexuality. Jantzen asserts that "the church has much to answer for [in the treatment of HIV/AIDS sufferers] both in its frequent eagerness to be the ringleader of the stone-throwing brigade, and more fundamentally, in its failure to develop a theology of sexuality." Jantzen goes on to note the irony "that a religion named after one who was incarnate love should have so total a vacuum in its theology of embodied desire, and be so frightened of public discourse about sexuality." It is in finding ways to overcome the judgment and fear associated with those living with HIV/AIDS, and thus entering into healing and affirming relationships with them, that Jantzen says the church will "rediscover" the meaning of an incarnate God.

Ken Stone, in "Safer Text: Reading Biblical Laments in the Age of AIDS," changes not just the subject, but also the theological perspective from which we address the concerns of those living with HIV/AIDS. Informed by Michel Foucault's understanding of the relationship between power and knowledge, Stone examines what happens when one regards HIV/AIDS sufferers as subjects of knowledge as opposed to objects of knowledge. They become a source of knowledge not simply about themselves, but also about God. With this understanding, Stone then engages the biblical laments in an "age of AIDS" from the perspective of those who are suffering with such an illness. For him, laments from this perspective allow us to understand not simply the passion and pain being expressed from the one who laments, but especially their theological complaints and hence the "complicity" that God may have in their very suffering.

This section closes with Frances Kissling's "Is There Life After *Roe?* How to Think about the Fetus," which seeks to change the subject from the kind of polarized, either/or stalemate that pro-life and pro-choice groups have been engaged in before and since *Roe.* "The abortion issue is not one in which only rights are at stake," she argues, and any morally serious conversation must speak cogently of competing multiple values, including the value of developing fetal life. She then proceeds to examine moral, legal, and political perspectives in an attempt to articulate a pro-choice perspective that refuses, even inadvertently, to foster a "coarsening of attitude toward fetal life." In the final analysis, Kissling reveals the continued complexity of the abortion debate and thus the need for more considered theological and ethic reflection, a judgment call shared by the many other voices in this volume, including those in the final section addressing current church and societal debates about marriage equality.

22

Disruptive Bodies:
Disability, Embodiment,
and Sexuality

ELIZABETH STUART

The disabled body queers a great deal of the pitch upon which theologies of sexuality and gender have built themselves. For a start, as Jackie Leach Scully has noted, the disabled body casts a shadow over the effort of these theologies to claim embodiment as good. For however true it might be that disability is a social construction, pain and degeneration constitute a different sort of suffering from that created by a society unable or unwilling to embrace the disabled body, and any attempt to theologize positively about them is unconvincing.[1] Having a black skin or gay sexual orientation are not problematic in themselves—the suffering and oppression associated with them is caused by the interpretations of these things by society. Being disabled is to experience a double oppression in the sense that while disability is certainly a social construction and the interpretation of the disabled body by society is oppressive to disabled people, one cannot be liberated from one's own body, and if your body is a site of pain, a liberatory theology of disability will not be enough.

Secondly, the production and maintenance of gender operates differently around the non-disabled and disabled body in contemporary Europe and North America. Feminism has been slow to recognize this fact or reflect upon it. Disabled people are often subject to a process of de-sexing by society. This is perhaps most clearly symbolized in the common sight of signs indicating toilet facilities "Men," "Women," "Disabled." This de-sexing is often worked out in various processes of infantilization to which large numbers of disabled people are subjected, processes which include an assumption of asexuality, the explicit denial of sexual needs in group homes and the dressing of adults in child-like clothes.[2] Disabled men may experience their masculinity in a different way to non-disabled men. If the social construction of masculinity is built upon notions of physical strength and general potency, then disabled men are frequently excluded from it and do not necessarily benefit from the normal privileges of masculinity. Issues of "communication, institutionalization, dependency, insecurity, invasion, assumption and justification"[3] seem to make disabled men and women more vulnerable to abuse, with around 48 per cent of men and women suffering from some sort of sexual abuse.[4] The deaf and those with learning difficulties are particularly vulnerable. This has to be taken into full account in any theologizing around sexuality and disability. Nevertheless, every effort must be made to avoid portraying disabled people as "natural" victims, which is another strategy widely used to disempower people.

Thirdly, a whole cluster of uncomfortable ethical issues surrounding sexuality and disability present themselves over which there is much disagreement among disabled people themselves. Among these issues are the use of sexual surrogates who are paid and specially trained to have sex with disabled people (sexual surrogacy is understood by its advocates to be a type of therapy), the use of prostitutes and pornography, and the part played by care-workers in meeting their clients' sexual needs. These are difficult issues to accommodate in a feminist paradigm which has stressed the ethical primacy of relationships of mutuality and reciprocity. Yet feminist theologies and theologies of sexuality have also generally subscribed to the current Western cultural view that sexual agency is one of the most important and precious elements of mature personhood. When disability is constructed in such a way as to deny disabled people sexual agency or prevent them exercising that agency in ways that the non-disabled take for granted then the feminist ideal becomes problematic.

Lastly, the disabled body does not just represent an exception to the general experience of bodiliness whose epistemology must be found a place within a general theory of embodiment as an exception to the norm. Good health is never a permanent state. The chance of experiencing permanent or temporary disablement (physical or mental) is high and almost an inevitability as a person gets older. The contrast is not between the abled and disabled, but between the temporarily able and the disabled. In truth the human body is only ever temporarily abled, and hence reflection on the disabled body should be central to any theorizing on the body.

In this essay I hope to construct a model for Christian theological reflection upon the body and sexuality which centralizes the disabled body. Unlike other contemporary theologies of disability, however, this essay will not adopt the standard methodology of a liberationist approach by beginning with disabled experience and proceeding to offer theological reflection upon it. This has been done more than adequately by theologians such as Nancy Eiesland and Don Saliers,[5] and in any case I am becoming increasingly convinced that theological reflection upon experience, while being extremely effective in deconstructing dominant models of theological reflection and empowering and providing a voice to those previously excluded from the theological arena, needs to be part of the process of reconstruction, if that reconstruction is to engage and enrich the whole body of Christ. Engagement with the tradition as the primary matrix of authority is necessary because in a real sense the tradition is all Christians have in common, and it constitutes and generates its common language.

Only by starting with the tradition and assuming its primacy will the disabled body ever enter into the consciousness of some Christians. Along with the Radical Orthodox school of theology, I want to claim that the tradition is far richer than either contemporary Protestantism or Catholicism is willing to acknowledge.[6] Also with the Radical Orthodox school and from the Christian tradition, my starting point is the theological concept of participation, which allows for no place where God is not. This not only means that there is no sphere for which theological reflection is inappropriate and that divine illumination is available to any form of knowledge, but also that when talking about bodies, sexuality, and so on, one is appealing to an eternal source for these things. This is not to deny their materiality, but to affirm "that behind this density resides an even greater density—beyond all contrasts of density and lightness (as beyond all contrasts of definition and limitlessness). This is to say that all there is *only* is because it is more than it is."[7]

EVERYWHERE AND NOWHERE? DISABILITY AND THE CHRISTIAN TRADITION

It is one of the paradoxes of the Christian Scriptures and tradition that disabled people are everywhere and nowhere at the same time. The Gospels are populated by disabled people. It is impossible to read more than a few verses without encountering someone with a paralysis, disease or some other physical impairment, and people possessed by unclean spirits. Unlike women or sexual minorities, disabled people are very visible in the Gospels. Yet even as they become visible, they are rendered invisible again by the healing touch of Jesus. The disabled appear to be rendered non-disabled. The focus of the stories is either on the authority of Jesus as healer or on the faith of the person being healed. In both cases the consequences are unfortunate from the perspective of the modern disability rights movement because the first gives the impression that physical and mental "wholeness" are pre-requisites for entrance into the kingdom of God, and the second that such wholeness and any healing necessary to achieve it is dependent upon the faith of the person concerned.[8] In the Hebrew Scriptures the book of Leviticus, in particular, again makes the disabled person very visible because the authors of the book are concerned with the connections between physical state and purity. But

> decisions about physical purity/impurity have a strongly visual basis, and deviations from physical norms may be interpreted as signs of God's displeasure. . . . According to these passages (Leviticus 13–14 and 21.16–24), within the religious community physical imperfection can result in some form of exclusion. The exclusion can range from restrictions in privileged access to divine communion to complete and permanent exclusion from the residential community.[9]

In Leviticus, then, disabled people are often made visible for the purposes of some kind of exclusion, to highlight the wholeness and purity of an able body.

Pre-Enlightenment discussion of the resurrected body also provided some implicit theological reflection upon the disabled body. Pre-modern Christians simply could not imagine a full resurrected life without a body and a body which had some kind of direct continuity with the earthly body.[10] This strong sense of the somatic dimension of personhood was rendered ambiguous, however, by a deep uneasiness with the change and decay of bodily existence. This led to huge amounts of speculation as to the nature of the resurrected body—its gender, height, weight, age, and so on. The overriding consensus seems to have been that the resurrection represented a triumph over the body's orientation towards decay, imperfection, and death, and hence bodies would be raised, repaired and perfected. Certainly by contrast, hell was often conceived as a place of eternal dismemberment, mutilation, and digestion of the body. In this scheme of things the disabled body functions as a reminder of the fallen, even damned body.

Yet this telling of the Christian tradition is only half the story. Within the New Testament, as within a great deal of ancient literature, the disabled body is often constructed in paradoxical terms, as Simon Horne put it, "within inability is striking capability."[11] One of the most common manifestations of this in ancient literature is the blind person who has extraordinary insight. The Gospels pick up on this theme on a number of occasions. The man born blind in John 9 is, as Colleen Grant points out, the only reasonably well rounded disabled character in the Gospels.[12] On the one hand, this is a story about healing as a means of inclusion. James Alison has noted that the means of healing through the use of clay suggests that in this healing Jesus is completing the creation of this man.[13] Indeed Alison maintains that Jesus' practice of healing on the Sabbath can be read as a denial that God's work of creation is complete and that God rests. And this is what is implied in Jesus' reply to "the Jews" in Jn 5:17, "My Father is still working and I am also working." The perfection of his creation allows the blind man to be fully included in the Jewish community. This is symbolized by the fact that after bathing in the pool of Siloam and receiving his sight, he is talked to rather than about. And yet this inclusion is only temporary because "the Jews" cannot cope with the implications of the healing and drive him out. In the middle of the confusion caused to "the Jews" by the healing, the man himself gradually comes to understand who Jesus is and this is really the completion of his humanity. The question which the disciples ask at the beginning of the story, "Who sinned, this man or his parents, that he was born blind?" (Jn 9:2), is used to expose a false understanding of sin. Sin is not some fault that prevents inclusion; sin consists of processes of exclusion and active participation in them; it is not identical with them.

> God has not the slightest difficulty in bringing to a fullness of creation the person who is in some way incomplete and recognizes this. The problem is with those who think they are complete, and that creation is, at least in their case finished,

and for this reason that goodness consists in the maintenance of the established order. . . . The righteous members of the group, thinking that they see, become blind precisely by holding on to the order which they think they have to defend.[14]

What is particularly interesting about this story is that while it has parallels with the ancient tradition of the paradox of the impaired, the parallels are not exact, for the man gains insight after he is cured. His blindness is a symptom of creation not yet complete, but so is the spiritual blindness of the Pharisees. The blind man comes to "see" in both senses of the word; others do not. This story does not romanticize the impairment of blindness, but it does explicitly deconstruct the stubbornly consistent connection between impairment, sin, and exclusion and reconstruct the understanding of sin as exclusion with an explicit connection established between the maintenance of systems of exclusion and a spiritual blindness, blindness to the continuing creative and subversive presence of God in the world. Throughout the Gospels those with physical impairments are portrayed as at least open to, at best audaciously seeking, this presence—in direct contrast to the able bodied who consistently fail to grasp what is going on.

A less radical rendition of the disabled paradox is found in Luke's account of Paul's conversion. Paul is blinded by his encounter with Christ (Acts 9:1–9). Once again we have the juxtaposition of blindness and faith. And once again the restoration of sight is associated with inclusion and the fulfillment of creation, occurring as it does when Paul receives the Holy Spirit and is baptized. In his letters Paul himself positively delights in the paradox of impairment. In 2 Cor. 12:7–10 he asserts that "to keep me from being too elated, a thorn was given me in the flesh, a messenger from Satan to torment me, to keep me from being too elated. Three times I appealed to the Lord about this, that it would leave me, but he said to me, 'My grace is sufficient for you, for power is made perfect in weakness.'" The Greek word translated as "weakness" here, *astheneia*, is associated with illness. Paul uses it in contrast with *dynamis*, translated as "power," also carrying the meaning of "ability" or "capacity." God's ability is fulfilled in incapacity, which is why Paul can boast in his own weakness, incapacity or impairment, whatever that may be, and it is necessary for Paul so to boast in order that "the power of Christ may dwell in me." Horne notes that the word *episkenose*, translated here as "may dwell in me," conjures up images of a tent (*skene*) and an allusion to the tabernacle, the dwelling place of God, which according to Leviticus, is a place from which are excluded priests who suffer from certain illnesses or disabilities (21:16–24).[15] Paul subverts this exclusion: it is in places of weakness, illness, and disability that Christ dwells and the power of God can be most clearly encountered. This subversion of notions of incapacity is part of Paul's wider theology of the cross. The scandal of the cross is that this supreme moment of weakness is the moment of salvation.

The Christ/Messiah saves "in weakness" (2 Cor. 13:4). This subversion is also evident in the emergence from the tomb of the one whom Nancy Eiesland has called "the disabled God."[16] Both Luke and John portray the risen body of Christ as an impaired body. Jesus still bears the marks of his crucifixion. If, as the early Church theologians believed, the resurrected body of Christ recapitulated the fallen bodiliness of Adam and manifested true, perfected humanity, then perfect humanity seems to include an embracing of the contingency of human life and an "unself-pitying, painstaking survival."[17]

> Jesus Christ the disabled God, is not a romanticized notion of "overcomer" God. Instead here is God as survivor. . . . The image of survivor here evoked is that of a simple, unself-pitying, honest body, for whom the limits of power are palpable but not tragic. The disabled God embodies the ability to see clearly the complexity and the "mixed blessing" of life and bodies, without living in despair.[18]

The disabled God reveals the full personhood of disabled people and, therefore, is a crucial symbol and concept in the development of a theology of disability. In the resurrection disabled people are made permanently visible in the image of God. But the subtleties of the resurrection stories should not elude us. The resurrection story is not simply a cheap fairy tale in which everything is all right in the end. It is also more than a story of survival. It is a story of a profound victory which involves both radical continuity and crucial discontinuity. It is a story of victory over death. Jesus who is now alive bears the marks of his death. Death has been resurrected and in the process been neutralized. Death, while a biological inevitability, should no longer have any power over human culture because it is not a theological reality. God does not acknowledge death, it does not disrupt the divine-human relationship, and hence it should not cast its shadow over our lives and relationships. Death does not arrest the process of creation.

The resurrected body of Jesus, while having a direct continuity with the pre-resurrection body, also demonstrates a radical discontinuity expressed in the inability of his friends to recognize him when he first appears to them. It is a body that certainly eats and drinks, but also walks through walls and appears and disappears. What this serves to emphasize is that the body cannot be fully grasped or contained. It is ultimately always a mystery, and there is always more to be revealed. The resurrected body of Jesus participates in the natural and supernatural processes of bodily change and in this process complicates attitudes to the disabled body. On the one hand, with the conquering of death the disabled body is redeemed from the symbolics of death and the absence of the divine. This insight is to be found even in the inhospitable part of the tradition. The second century *Acts of Paul* is clear that the resurrected flesh of all believers bears the marks of suffering, and Gregory of Nyssa reflecting on the death of his sister Macrina was clear that she would bear the scars of a healed tumor in the resurrection, for these scars functioned as identity markers.[19] It is also perceivable in the Levitical commandment "You shall not revile the deaf or put a stumbling block before the blind; you shall fear your God: I am the LORD" (19:14). But this does not rule out the possibilities of a new form of bodiliness in which pain and suffering is absent and the processes of creation continue disrupting all our perceived notions of materiality. Therefore, the beliefs that the resurrection involves some kind of bodily change and that bodies continue to bear the scars of human contingency are not necessarily incompatible. Indeed, they are mysteriously connected.

But, perhaps most importantly, "Jesus Christ, the disabled God, disorders the social-symbolic orders of what it means to be incarnate."[20] It is this theological fact, that the body of Jesus disrupts both the symbolic orders and the material orders which are inextricably bound together, that seems to me to offer the most effective hermeneutical principle with which to interpret the Christian Scripture and tradition on the disabled body. Graham Ward offers a fascinating analysis of how the body of Jesus is displaced in the Gospel accounts of his incarnation, circumcision, and transfiguration, extended in the Eucharist, and transposed in the ascension.[21] This procession of displacement reveals the instability of matter and the symbolics of the material, culminating in the final displacement of the ascension in which the Church becomes the body of Christ: "the body of Jesus Christ, the body of God, is permeable, transcorporeal, transpositional. Within it all other bodies are situated and given their significance. We are all permeable, transcorporeal and transpositional."[22] The Church as the body of Christ (and therefore the paradigmatic human and eschatological community) shares in the unstable body of Christ. The symbolics and social and cultural constructions of the body are rendered profoundly unstable among the baptized, which is why St. Paul could declare to the Galatians that "there is no longer Jew or Greek, there is no longer slave or free, there is no longer male or female; for you are all one in Christ Jesus" (Gal. 3:28).

We cannot, of course, live beyond social and cultural constructions. They are ironically part of the processes of creation as human beings struggle to cooperate with the divine in the bringing of creation to fulfillment. The problem is that the very sense of "lack" that propels us towards God and the activity of creation is also the sense that leads us into the temptation of thinking that our constructions are final and complete. Within the body of Christ all cultural and social constructions are redeemed and given back to us as parodies of their former selves. I do not use parody in the conventional sense of sending up something, but, following Linda Hutcheon, as "an extended repetition with critical difference" which has "a hermeneutical function with both cultural and even ideological implications."[23] Christians operate within culture, which is in the process of being redeemed. It is hard if not impossible to resist the identities our culture gives to us but the Christian is obliged to live out these identities with "critical difference," the difference being shaped by the ecclesial self which is "permeable, transcorporeal and transpositional." This will often involve a deliberate subversion of identity categories. The Christian performance of maleness and femaleness will therefore be strange (and indeed throughout Christian history has often been very strange),[24] but so will be Christian visions of perfection, beauty, and understandings of embodiment and sexuality.

The disabled body, because it participates in the image of the disabled God, functions both as a reminder of the instability of embodiment and is itself caught up in the constant process of unmaking and remaking in which all bodies participate in the body of Christ. Diane DeVries, born without arms and legs, and subjected to all the oppressive attitudes that societal understandings of disability generate, has yet maintained an entirely positive attitude to her body. She has a strong sense of her body as extendable. It does not end with her flesh and bone, but also encompasses her wheelchair. DeVries also experiences fluid boundaries between her own body and those of other people. Her close relationship with her sister enables her to experience things such as dancing and walking through her sister's body. DeVries' sense of the fluidity of her own embodiment echoes something of the fluidity of the body of Christ, and her identification with the Venus di Milo destabilizes notions of perfection and beauty in much the same way as the disabled God does.[25]

Within the Church, then, the disabled body should be valued as one that bears the image of the disabled God and that constantly reminds the body of Christ of the fluidity of all bodies. In other words, the presence of the disabled body is essential to remind the church of the revelation through which it is constituted and which it is called to bear in its own bodiliness. And by "presence" I mean here a real presence, not a marginal presence. It is scandalous that the Eucharist, which is par excellence where Christian identity is produced and performed in a continuous act of breaking open and pouring out of the body of Christ, should often be a place of exclusion or marginalization for disabled people. Often the bread and wine are distributed in such a way that disabled people are not able to participate in the same way as the majority of those present. In this way the disabled body is problematized rather than centralized. Similarly, the exclusion of people with a variety of disabilities from the priesthood and ministry is also a blasphemous denial of the disabled God and the destabilizing of embodiment that takes place in Christ. The celebrant is the one who represents Christ to the people and the people to Christ; it is therefore highly appropriate theologically for that person to be disabled or in some other way (e.g. by being female, gay, or transgendered) to represent the slipperiness of the symbolics of the material order in the body of Christ.

Paul, in his development of the concept of the Church as the body of Christ, explicitly draws attention to the subversion of cultural and social constructions that have to take place in the body of Christ:

> The members of the body that seem to be weaker are indispensable, and those members of the body that we think less honorable we clothe with greater honour, and our less respectable members are treated with greater respect. . . . But God has arranged the body, giving the greater honour to the inferior member, that there may be no dissension within the body, but the members may have the same care for one another. If one member suffers, all suffer together with it, if one member is honored, all rejoice together with it. (1 Cor. 12:22–26)

The body of Christ needs to break itself open to make room at its heart for the disabled body. It is called to parody the world in which the disabled body is marginalized, excluded, problematized, and infantilized.

ARE THEY HAVING SEX? THE DISABLED BODY, SEXUALITY AND THEOLOGY

It is ironic that Paul, in making reference to the "weakest" and "inferior" members in developing his concept of the Church as Christ's body, was probably making allusion to the body's sexual organs. For the Church has not proved itself sensitive to the sexual needs of disabled people. The procreative principle, which though now radically moderated even with the Roman Catholic Church, nevertheless continues to exercise an influence over the cultural constructions of sexuality in the Western world. We can only comfortably imagine sexual activity among the young and those whose bodies measure up to the ideal projected to us constantly. The elderly and the disabled are, therefore, desexualized and in the process the Church avoids dealing with some uncomfortable issues that the sexual disabled body raises.

One of the most notable developments in the Church in the twentieth century has been the gradual embracing of the view that sexuality is an essential part of personhood. Even within the Roman Catholic Church marriage has eclipsed the celibate religious life as the ideal Christian state. On the one hand, this has been a positive movement, recentering the body and sexual relationships within the matrix of Christian discipleship. But in buying into the modern understanding of desire as having its ultimate end, its *telos*, in heterosexual sexual relations, the Church has misplaced the ancient Christian belief that all desire has its *telos* in God. This has important repercussions. The Church finds itself, on the one hand, promoting a sexual relationship as a human good but on the other hand, having implicated itself in the project of modern heterosexual marriage, finds itself relegating those who for whatever reason cannot enter into it to a moral "no man's land" where whatever they do sexually will at best fall short of a God-given ideal, at worst bog them down in a morass of sin.

Even if we were to accept this as a theologically and pastorally justified position, we might then ask what the Church does to encourage disabled people on the path towards marriage? Generally speaking, the Church seems content to let people find each other through the usual social channels and only then steps in to solemnize the relationship. But what if some people cannot find each other through the usual social channels because those social channels are in various ways inaccessible to them? If there is no part of existence in which God is not and through which God cannot work, then it is imperative that the Church should actively work to ensure that such channels are accessible. This will involve the body of Christ concerning itself with accessibility issues in terms of public transport, pubs and clubs, dating agencies, and so on. It will address issues of privacy in residential homes. It will campaign for effective sex education for people with learning difficulties. It will endeavor to participate in the deconstruction of cultural notions of perfection, beauty and attractiveness through attention to its own language, imagery, and liturgical and pastoral practice.

The disabled body challenges the Church to acknowledge its part in promoting what Shakespeare, Gillespie-Sells, and Davies refer to as "fucking ideology," that is, associating "sex" exclusively with penetrative intercourse.[26] This prevailing attitude desexualizes many disabled people in the eyes of society and in their own eyes. The giving and receiving of love through the exchange of physical pleasure is not dependent upon penetrative intercourse or indeed genital contact. As a sexual body called to engage in a parodic critique of cultural constructions, the body of Christ should promote a more diffuse understanding of sexual activity in which the possibilities for the Christian virtues of patience, equality, mutuality, passion, and hospitality can be practiced with perhaps more success than may be allowed by an exclusively penetrative model of sexual activity, bound up as it undoubtedly is with patriarchal constructions of reality.

But as always the Church becomes really unstuck when it has to deal with those who for whatever reason cannot marry. For the maxim of sex within marriage, celibacy without, does not have any integrity in an ecclesial and cultural context in which sexual agency is regarded as being an essential part of adulthood. To say that those who cannot get married, be it because of sexual orientation or life situation, are called to sexual abstinence and when they fail to live up to this calling, they "fall short" or sin, simply does not ring true now that the Church has embraced the modern valorization of sexuality. The current debate on homosexuality within all mainstream Christian denominations is an indication of an implicit awareness at least of this dissonance. Yet that debate is largely and exclusively in official public debate conducted in the context of permanent, stable unions. The Church seems to have little constructive to say to those for whom stable and permanent unions, straight or gay, are an impossibility because of societal attitudes to disability.

Traditionally, one of the ways in which Christians subversively parodied identities and relationships was by the refusal to enter into sexual relations. The refusal to marry or engage in sexual relations embodied the resurrection state (Mt. 22:30) and, therefore, another way of existing and relating that casts a long and critical shadow over contemporary society.[27] For most of Christian history the freely chosen celibate life has been valorized by the Christian community because it provides a consistent critique of society's construction and valorization of sexual relationships. There is an urgent need to restore some of the balance that has been lost in the Church's embrace of modern constructions of sexuality and embodiment at the expense of the single life.

Single people can only successfully be caught up in the Christian project of holy parody if though living the "single" life in fact their experience is of not being single at all. Theologically, in the body of Christ no one is single because all share in the one flesh relationship of Christ with his Church (1 Cor. 6:12–20). All members of the body belong to one another. There should be no loneliness in the body of Christ, no lack of physical affection, companionship, laughter, empathy, and friendship. So to be single in such a context is not to be single at all. Just as to be "male" in the body of Christ should not to be male at all, in the sense that there is a deliberate resistance to societal constructions of masculinity, once again the disabled body functions as a medium of grace in representing alternative constructions of gender. Yet also within the body of Christ the kind of mystical connection that exists between Christ and Church and is replicated in the relationship between members of his body must have some parallels with Diane DeVries' experience of a porous relationship between her own embodiment and that of her sister's, enabling her to "experience through connection what she could not realize independently."[28]

No experience is completely beyond any member of the Church. Just as Christ stands in complete solidarity with humanity and has assumed the totality of human experience, so the Church as his body should be able to bear each other's experience in their bodies, both in terms of feeling the pain of another and in sharing in the joy and pleasure that others embody. Such bearing of each other's bodies within the body of Christ is what makes it possible to speak of the Church "having AIDS" or "being gay" or "being disabled." It is also what makes it possible to speak of the Church as a sexual community in which the single life is an honored model of discipleship. The single life also serves to remind everyone that the end of desire is not heterosexual, or indeed any sexual relationship, but God. This theological fact should act as a brake on the Church's capitulation to the modern valorization of sexual relationships.

The presentation in positive terms of a "single" life is part of the Church's tradition, but it has to be presented as an equally valid way of life to the married, not just a fall back position for those who cannot enter into marriage as it is now. And it has to understand such relationships within the context of the symbolic disordering of the experience of embodiment that Christ's body inaugurates. It is this disordering that creates the possibility of a celibate vocation in the body of Christ, and it is this disordering of gender that makes any discrimination between heterosexual and homosexual relations within the body of Christ nonsensical. Within the body of Christ gender is subverted in such a way as to render moral distinctions based upon gender as void distinctions based upon other forms of embodiment. The Church's own tradition and indeed its head and savior, force it to face the question: is sexual agency an essential part of adult maturity? It must question the pressure that is put upon all people to buy into this myth and at the same time affirm the potential goodness and source of grace of sexual relationships and ensure that all have equal opportunities to enter into such a relationship if they feel so called, while also being aware of and doing all it can to recognize and prevent possibilities for abuse and violence within sexual relationships. This balancing act the Church as a corporate body has yet to achieve, although individuals and groups within it may have had better success in attaining such a balance.

Difficult ethical issues are raised in the contemporary disability rights movement concerning the use of personal assistants or carers for the fulfillment of sexual needs, both with regard to facilitating sexual relationships in terms of positioning and so on and even more controversially in entering into client-carer sexual relationships. In a cultural context in which sexual agency is so highly valued as a signifier of mature personhood, to facilitate a disabled person's work, social life, personal needs but not their sexual relationships seems unjustifiable, provided that the employment rights of the carer or assistant are guarded. Indeed, the involvement of a third party in facilitating sexual activity might serve to remind both Church and society that sexual activity is never simply a private affair—it always has a public dimension and impacts upon other people.

All sexual activity is to some extent facilitated by others in one way or another. A Christian theology grounded in the primacy and normativity of the body of Christ in which members bear one another's bodies and hold the "weakest" members in the highest honour should have no intrinsic difficulty with a third party facilitating a disabled person's sexual activity as long as the dignity of all parties involved is respected. A direct sexual relationship between a carer/assistant and a disabled person is more problematic. Bearing in mind the shocking levels of abuse in the disabled community, the protection of disabled people from abuse must be a priority. There is also the danger of abuse from the other side, as one disabled man, Stuart, notes

> I think personally as a disabled man, I don't like what I see when disabled men exploit female personal assistants, first because of the gender oppression which is reinforced, but also lots of disabled men employ sexual pressure upon their personal assistant to have relationships.[29]

Stuart goes on to argue that such relationships reinforce the idea that it is OK for paid carers and assistants to have sex with disabled people whether they consent or not. If an attraction between the two parties develops, then it should immediately cease to be a working relationship.

Zebedee, on the other hand, argues that "if an able-bodied person wants to masturbate, they do it. In my view, it ought to be taken on by carers if you can't do it yourself."[30] And there are undoubtedly issues here that cannot just be dismissed. Even though the *Catechism of the Catholic Church* describes masturbation as "an intrinsically and gravely disordered action,"[31] there was a marked shift in Christian attitudes to masturbation in the twentieth century, so that even some contemporary Catholic moral theologians acknowledge the grace filled possibilities of masturbation for various groups of people, including the lonely, those who have been abused and need to relearn to love their bodies, for adolescents discovering their bodies for the first time, and for partners isolated from each other for some time.[32] A Church of Scotland report on human sexuality noted the need to acknowledge the sexual needs of the elderly and disabled and that this involves understanding that masturbation often gives comfort and relief and therefore should be dealt with sensitively within an institutional setting.[33]

But what has the Church to say to those who are physically unable to masturbate but still crave the comfort and relief it brings? If it is possible for a person to be employed to act as someone's eyes and hands when they do not have the use of their own, is there anything intrinsically wrong with the use of that person to give sexual relief as long as that person is in full agreement? The issue of masturbation is different from a non-masturbatory social-sexual relationship, for it is purely a matter of physical relief and the carer/assistant is acting purely as an extended limb of the disabled person. Might it be possible for Christians who operate within a concept of the body as unstable and with fluid boundaries, while always maintaining the integrity of individual bodies and seeking to protect them from violence and abuse, to imagine a situation in which one person's hand might act in place of another's?

This situation is markedly different from the issue of sexual surrogacy which causes tensions with the disabled community itself. Presented as a form of therapy rather than prostitution and largely practiced in the Netherlands, people are especially trained and paid to have sexual relations with disabled people. The idea has come in for a great deal of criticism from disabled people themselves for reinforcing the medical (rather than social) understanding of disability and internalized feelings of inadequacy and inferiority.[34] From a theological point of view, the isolation of sexual satisfaction from other bodily needs and desires presents a problem, for the body both individual and corporate is one. Paul's words in 1 Corinthians also need heeding, "Do you not know that your bodies are members of Christ? Should I therefore take the members of Christ and make them members of a prostitute? Never!" (6:15). To unite a body with that of any kind of sex worker in their capacity as a sex worker is to unite that body and Christ with it with the social conditions that usually drive women and men into prostitution and the exploitation and violence that can characterize the sex worker's life. Christ stands alongside prostitutes as he does all exploited persons, but he stands against exploitation. From a theological perspective, another person's body cannot be reduced simply to a tool for self-gratification; all bodies caught up in the mysterious body of the body of Christ are related, and therefore unemotional sex, sex that is detached from relationship, is a counter sign to the body of Christ.

The use of pornography is also a problematic area for many disabled people. Once again some feel that they have a right to purchase and use pornography for sexual gratification because it is the only form of sexual gratification open to them.[35] A theology informed by feminism will be deeply uncomfortable with the use of pornography[36] by anyone because it involves the sexual exploitation of the less powerful by the powerful, the erotic pleasure lying in the playing out of those power relations. The objectification of a person made in the image and likeness of God and, therefore, made for relationship rather than exploitation and objectification is sinful. The disabled body has often been used in this way, and problems caused by fetishism among non-disabled people often hamper the formation of relationships.[37] So the body of Christ will oppose the production, sale and use of pornography by anyone.

Mindful, however, of the marginalization of disabled people and the part the Church has played in creating and reinforcing that marginalization, members of the body of Christ can never simply take away with one hand without giving with another. The Church has in its deposit a whole body of erotic literature, from the Song of Songs through to the writings of the mediaeval mystics, which celebrates sexual desire and activity in a non-exploitative way and as a unitive, hospitable expression of love that is intricately related to the search for God. The celebration of human bodiliness and sexual desire in such a way as to arouse the body and the spirit is a noble part of Christian tradition, and while condemning pornography, the Church should be welcoming and encouraging the creation of erotic texts.

CONCLUSION

Reflection upon the disabled body is essential in any attempt to theologize around sexuality because the disabled body reminds all of us that embodiment (as our ancestors in faith knew well) is always an ambiguous experience even when rid of a dualistic interpretation, and that all bodies, like all aspects of human experience, are in need of redemption in the ongoing project of creation. Yet the symbol of the disabled God also confirms the full humanity of disabled people and their place at the heart of the body of Christ.

Centralizing the disabled body in the body of Christ serves to remind the Church of its call to participate in the continuing creation of the world through parody of the necessarily incomplete and transitory cultural constructions of human identity and the practices that are attached to them. The concept of participation in a "permeable, transcorporeal and transpositional" body, which is something that disabled people may be better able to understand than the temporarily able, offers creative possibilities for the sharing of experience and pleasure as well as pain between disabled and the temporarily able.

The disabled body raises issues around sexuality, somewhat detached from issues of gender, that challenge the Church to face its own compliance with an over-romanticized idealization of heterosexual desire produced by modernity and to engage in a parody-critique not only of modernity's construction of sexuality, but of its own embrace of it.

NOTES

1. Jackie Leach Scully, "When Embodiment Isn't Good," *Theology and Sexuality* 9 (1998), pp. 10–28.

2. Tom Shakespeare, Kath Gillespie-Sells, and Dominic Davies, *The Sexual Politics of Disability: Untold Desires* (London: Cassell, 1996), pp. 49–82.

3. Shakespeare, Gillespie-Sells, and Davies, *The Sexual Politics of Disability*, p. 139.

4. Shakespeare, Gillespie-Sells, and Davies, *The Sexual Politics of Disability*, p. 139.

5. Nancy L. Eiesland, *The Disabled God: Toward a Liberatory Theology of Disability* (Nashville, TN: Abingdon Press, 1994); Nancy L. Eiesland and Don E. Saliers (eds.), *Human Disability and the Service of God: Reassessing Religious Practice* (Nashville, TN: Abingdon Press, 1998).

6. John Milbank, Catherine Pickstock, and Graham Ward, *Radical Orthodoxy: A New Theology* (London: Routledge, 1999), p. 2.

7. Milbank, Pickstock, and Ward, *Radical Orthodoxy*, p. 4.

8. Colleen C. Grant, "Reinterpreting the Healing Narratives," in Eiesland and Saliers (eds.), *Human Disability and the Service of God*, 72–87.

9. Sarah J. Melcher, "Visualising the Perfect Cult: The Priestly Rationale for Exclusion," in Eiesland and Saliers (eds.), *Human Disability and the Service of God*, pp. 55–71 (69).

10. Caroline Walker Bynum, *The Resurrection of the Body in Western Christianity, 200–1336* (New York: Columbia University Press, 1995).

11. Simon Horne, "'Those who are blind see': Some New Testament Uses of Impairment, Inability and Paradox," in Eiesland and Saliers (eds.), *Human Disability and the Service of God*, pp. 88–101 (89).

12. Grant, "Reinterpreting the Healing Narratives," p. 79.

13. James Alison, "The Man Blind from Birth and the Subversion of Sin: Some Questions about Fundamental Morals," *Theology and Sexuality* 7 (1997), 83–102.

14. Alison, "The Man Blind from Birth and the Subversion of Sin," p. 94.

15. Horne, "'Those who are blind see,'" p. 95.

16. Eiesland, *The Disabled God*, pp. 89–105.

17. Eiesland, *The Disabled God*, p. 101.

18. Eiesland, *The Disabled God*, p. 102.

19. Bynum, *The Resurrection of the Body*, pp. 29, 81–86.

20. Eiesland, *The Disabled God*, pp. 103–4.

21. Graham Ward, "Bodies: The Displaced Body of Jesus Christ," in Milbank, Pickstock, and Ward (eds.), *Radical Orthodoxy*, pp. 163–81.

22. Ward, "Bodies: The Displaced Body of Jesus Christ," p. 176.

23. Linda Hutcheon, *A Theory of Parody: The Teaching of Twentieth-Century Art Forms* (New York: Methuen, 1985), pp. 2–7.

24. See my *Spitting at Dragons: Towards a Feminist Theology of Sainthood* (London: Mowbray, 1996).

25. Eiesland, *The Disabled God*, pp. 33–40.

26. Shakespeare, Gillespie-Sells, and Davies, *The Sexual Politics of Disability*, p. 97.

27. Peter Brown, *The Body and Society: Men, Women and Sexual Renunciation in Early Christianity* (London: Faber & Faber; Boston: Columbia University Press, 1988), p. 32.

28. Eiesland, *The Disabled God*, p. 38.

29. Shakespeare, Gillespie-Sells, and Davies, *The Sexual Politics of Disability*, p. 38.

30. Shakespeare, Gillespie-Sells, and Davies, *The Sexual Politics of Disability*, p. 37.

31. *Catechism of the Catholic Church* (London: Geoffrey Chapman, 1994), para. 2352, p. 503.

32. Evelyn Eaton Whitehead and James D. Whitehead, *A Sense of Sexuality: Christian Love and Intimacy* (New York: Crossroad, 1994), pp. 133–37.

33. The Board of Social Responsibility of the Church of Scotland, *Report on Human Sexuality* (Edinburgh: Church of Scotland, 1994), para. 7.1.4.

34. Shakespeare, Gillespie-Sells, and Davies, *The Sexual Politics of Disability*, pp. 131–34.

35. Shakespeare, Gillespie-Sells, and Davies, *The Sexual Politics of Disability*, pp. 122–24.

36. Defining pornography as including "any sexually explicit material (books, magazines, movies, videos, TV shows, telephone services, live sex acts) produced for the purpose of sexual arousal by eroticising violence, power, humiliation, abuse, dominance, degradation, or mistreatment of any person, male or female, and usually produced for monetary profit. Any sexually explicit material that depicts children is pornography." (The Office of the General Assembly, The Presbyterian Church [USA], *Pornography: Far from the Song of Songs* [Louisville, KY, 1988], p. 11).

37. Shakespeare, Gillespie-Sells, and Davies, *The Sexual Politics of Disability*, pp. 124–31.

23

AIDS, Shame, and Suffering

GRACE M. JANTZEN

A man with aids wrote,

> At the age of 28 I wake up every morning to face the very real possibility of my own death.
>
> Whenever I am asked by members of the media or by curious healthy people what we talk about in our group, I am struck by the intractable gulf that exists between the sick and the well: what we talk about is survival.
>
> Mostly we talk about what it feels like to be treated like lepers who are treated as if they are morally, if not literally, contagious.[1]

People with AIDS and HIV are the lepers of modern society. They are looked upon with horror, revulsion and fear. There is fear about any form of contact, from eating together to sharing a communion cup to offering an embrace or a kiss of peace and welcome. Like the lepers in medieval times, people with AIDS and HIV face not only physical revulsion but also moral disapproval, the attitude that their condition is a punishment for sin or that they have brought it upon themselves through sexual activity or drug use that is feared and condemned by the majority. Their human dignity is undervalued and undermined, not least by the church.

Yet the church has had better examples of how lepers should be treated, and it is worth considering one such example as we try to come to a more Christian response to AIDS. According to his biographers, Francis of Assisi was a fastidious young man. He was horrified by poverty and by all forms of suffering, but nothing raised his revulsion so much as leprosy. If he chanced to see a leper while he was out riding, he would dismount, hold his nose, and send a messenger to give some alms. Then one day, at the beginning of his conversion, he came unexpectedly upon a leper on the road. His first impulse was to recoil; then he remembered his desire for discipleship.

> He slipped off his horse and ran to kiss the man. When the leper put out his hand as if to receive some alms, Francis gave him money and a kiss.[2]

This was for Francis a significant turning point in his understanding of Christ. Now that he had identified himself with Christ and with the lepers, in action and not merely in theory, his practical understanding of the incarnation deepened in direct proportion to his active obedience.

> From that time on he clothed himself with a spirit of poverty, a sense of humility and a feeling of intimate devotion. Formerly he used to be horrified not only by close dealing with lepers but by their very sight, even from a distance; but now he rendered humble service to the lepers with human concern and devoted kindness . . . because of Christ crucified, who according to the text of the prophet was despised *as a leper*. He visited their houses frequently, generously distributed alms to them, and with great compassion kissed their hands and their mouths.[3]

It is clear that his biographers do not see this connection as accidental. It was as Francis responded to the invitation to follow Christ in his identification with the lepers that his spiritual vision was enlarged: his love for Christ increased in direct relation to his involvement with the outcasts of his society. Nor do his biographers intend us to see this increased understanding and love as a sort of divine reward for heroic behavior. Rather, it is because Christ really is the one who made himself one with the outcasts that he can be found in solidarity with them. The lepers constituted a concrete opportunity to learn to know and love Christ.[4]

I wish to suggest that as the lepers for St. Francis, so people today with AIDS and HIV offer us the opportunity to rediscover Christ. I am not saying that the church is being offered an opportunity for condescending charity or alms to "victims" while we keep well out of the way and metaphorically hold our noses. I am not even saying only that the AIDS crisis offers the possibility for genuine service, though it certainly does. I am making the much stronger claim that for all the human tragedy of AIDS, like the human tragedy of leprosy, it is also an opportunity to reopen ourselves to people who have the virus, to their love and dignity as well as their suffering and fear, their sexuality and mortality—in short, their humanity—*and our own*. And if the incarnation is about the solidarity of God with humankind, then practical identification with people with AIDS can send us back to reading the New Testament with joyous insight that we didn't have before.

One of the avenues along which we may grow together in a deeper openness to incarnation is by exploring the revulsion and shame associated with AIDS and HIV. Like St. Francis cringing with revulsion from the lepers, our first reaction is often to cringe from those with AIDS. Now, although we need to explore what we do with that revulsion, I would suggest that we should not be too hard on ourselves for having it in the first place. It is an entirely human reaction to recoil from the sight of disease, deformity or pain, or even from the awareness of serious illness where no symptoms are apparent. We are horrified by these things, and we should be. They are horrific. They are not to be romanticized or sentimentalized, and our revulsion to them should not be suppressed, lest we develop calluses around our souls.

Furthermore, encounter with serious disease is a reminder of our own mortality. Again, it would be inhuman not to cringe from death. It may be that we can face it and come to terms with it, but to be unmoved by it is subhuman, not superhuman. When we face our own mortality in the body of another it is right to be appalled, for their sake and our own. The question is not whether we feel fear and revulsion but what we do with it. I have suggested that what we must *not* do is deny those feelings, pretend they are not there, refuse to let the symptoms and suffering of fellow human beings bother us, or repress our fear at their mortality and ours.

Another common way of coping with our feelings of horror is to offer compassion at a distance, as St. Francis did, keeping our own noses carefully covered while sending charity, perhaps very generous charity, by way of a messenger or go-between, but avoiding contact at all costs, lest somehow we be polluted. But what does this accomplish? The recipients of the charity, while perhaps having to accept it out of their necessity, are diminished in their humanity by it, forced to receive condescension, to accept the role of victim. They have to see themselves as people whom no one wishes to touch, people who cause revulsion, people who cannot be received and loved. When one is already suffering and fearful, the burden of such rejection is intolerable. As for us as givers of such charity, we are isolated not only from those who suffer but from our own humanity as well by such refusal to encounter disease and death. We refuse ourselves the opportunity to come to terms with them, and by keeping our distance from those who suffer, distance ourselves also from learning about the dignity and courage, humor and hope available to those who use their illness to discover their meaning and their worth. We deprive ourselves of truth and of love. We deprive ourselves also of God, for God sits with the sufferer against whom we hold our nose.

A further way in which we deal with our feelings of revulsion, especially if we are theologians, is to construct a theory about suffering. Suffering is horrifying: surely a compassionate God must be as horrified as we are? Why then does God continue to permit such suffering, when surely it is within the competence of omnipotence to intervene? These are genuine questions, and it is right that we should ponder deeply the nature of God in the face of suffering. But what can too easily happen is that as we seek for answers to our concerns we turn the whole thing into an intellectual exercise, offering explanation and counter-explanation, theodicy and counter-theodicy, until what may have begun as an effort at understanding human suffering ends as an insulation against it.[5]

Particularly insidious is the sort of theodicy which is so intent on preserving God from all responsibility for suffering that it attributes the responsibility to the sufferer. In some contexts the so-called "free will defense," the theory that all suffering is to be attributed to the free choices of moral agents, reads like a classic exercise in blaming the victim. It is a syndrome only too well known in cases of rape and violence against women: somehow the victim must have asked for it, must be at fault. And it is applied with particular venom to people with HIV and AIDS: they must be deserving of illness because of their sexual practices or drug use or even, in the case of African and Caribbean people with AIDS, because of the race to which they belong. The natural physical revulsion that we feel about suffering and death is turned into a moral revulsion, an imputation to the sufferer of moral failure for which they are being justly punished. By such a strategy it is possible to preserve both our own righteousness and God's, setting ourselves up as with divine authority against the ones "contaminated" through their own fault. . . .

What I wish to do . . . is to draw attention to the connection between fear and blame that is apparent in such a stance. As already noted, we are all afraid of suffering and death; we are also afraid of the unknown and the marginal. Now for many of us sexuality represents something that is deeply unknown and problematical. That is of course not to say that we are not sexually active; but for many of us our sexual impulses and involvements are more complicated than we like to admit. Our society is strongly heterosexist; that is, it sees heterosexuality as the biological and moral norm. In such a society there is an enormous investment in denying, even to ourselves, any homosexual feelings or relationships, and refusing to acknowledge that part of ourselves which is drawn to the same sex. This is true even though it has been widely known for some time that most people are in fact drawn to both sexes to a greater or lesser degree.

Now although AIDS and HIV are by no means restricted to homosexuals, they are popularly so associated in the public mind. This means that when we confront a person with AIDS we are confronted not only by our revulsion at sickness and death but also by our ambivalent sexuality. Many of us find this—especially the combination—deeply threatening. If within ourselves there is repressed discomfort about homosexuality, AIDS is available to become a focus for our fear and uncertainty. As Seymour Kleinberg has said,

> Since the late sixties we have all been living in a society at war, mostly with itself, under dire stress, and the sexual behaviour of gay men has become the radical exponent of tension and disaffection widespread in all adult life. We have come to symbolize every confusion about sexuality in modern history, and thus, we are objects of fascination and abhorrence.[6]

Our societal anxieties emerge as anger against homosexuals, and blame heaped upon those who have AIDS and HIV. The church has much to answer for in this, both in its frequent eagerness to be the ringleader of the stone-throwing brigade, and more fundamentally, in its failure to develop a theology of sexuality. It is deeply ironic that a religion named after one who was incarnate love should have so total a vacuum in its theology of embodied desire, and be so frightened of public discourse about sexuality.

For people who have contracted HIV or AIDS, the effect of all this is invidious, leading all too easily to an internalization of the shame and revulsion which society projects on to them, and eroding their sense of self-worth. Anyone who has a serious illness which may generate painful or difficult-to-manage symptoms is already confronted with bewilderment about her body, fear, physical and mental pain, anger, and often revulsion at the abhorrent symptoms. She may also have to confront not only her own fear and grief but also that of her friends and family as they try to cope with their own reactions, and with a certain level of stigmatization from society. As Dennis Altman has pointed out,

> To be stigmatized because of illness is hardly confined to people with AIDS: anyone suspected of carrying a disease will experience stigma, and it is a stigma that often extends to non-contagious diseases such as cancer and schizophrenia.[7]

But in the case of an illness like cancer, the attitude of society and church is generally sympathetic and supportive: people consider it important to overcome such fear and revulsion as they might feel. Messages of love and encouragement pour in from family, friends and colleagues; at times when morale is low it is possible to ask for support and be confident that such a request will find a sympathetic response. This cannot take away the pain or the fear or even the sense of isolation in the face of possible death, but it does assure the ill person of her worth to those who love her, and of all the care and comfort they can give. It is very common for a person with a life-threatening illness to have periods of anguished questioning: Why me? What have I done to deserve this? But in the case of an illness like cancer it is possible to express such doubt and confusion to a friend or to a visiting minister and to receive assurances that the illness has nothing to do with sin, let alone with God's punishment: that these are natural and normal questions but that they are expressions of understandable rage and bewilderment, not signs that the ill person is particularly sinful or perverse.

People with AIDS and HIV ask these questions too. But because of the fear and suspicion and blame in society and in the church toward drug use and homosexuality, it is by no means a foregone conclusion that they will be offered the care and moral support that someone with some other life-threatening illness can count on. If a person with AIDS asks the vicar, "Why me? What have I done to deserve this?" she or he may well get, not comfort, but a list of accusations probably coupled with an invitation to repent. At a time when vulnerability is highest and morale is lowest, self-esteem is further eroded by the opprobrium heaped upon them even by well-meaning individuals, let alone by attitudes of society percolated through the media. A person who is ill and frightened needs a lot of hugs: who will hug a person with AIDS?[8]

Even at the level of medical care major differences can arise. A person with cancer can rest assured of skilled and sympathetic medical attention and does not need to add to her fears and grief about death any worry about whether appropriate funeral arrangements can be made. But for a person with AIDS it is always possible that some of the medical staff will be hostile; and there are still many undertakers who refuse their services. As well as the anxiety which such attitudes generate for the person with AIDS, there is inevitably a strong reinforcement of self-revulsion and shame.

By no means all people with AIDS and HIV are homosexual, but for those who are, such undermining of self-worth strikes at a very vulnerable point. All of us who are lesbian or gay have had the task of coming to terms with our sexuality in an oppressively heterosexist society, and for many of us it has not been easy. If we are Christians it has probably been more painful rather than less, as the church has reinforced the attitude that respectability is to be accorded only to heterosexual marriages or to total celibacy. We have all been aware of how our families and friends and colleagues would prefer us to keep silent: as long as we do not confront them with the fact of our homosexual choices they will pretend that we are "normal" and accord us respectability.

Yet we know too that respectability based on silence and pretence is bought at the expense of our self-esteem. Of course our sexuality is not the only or even necessarily the most important thing about us, any more than skin color is the only or even the most important thing about blacks; but if this is the focus of denigrating attitudes, whether sexist or racist, then it must be affirmed with pride over and over again, partly to do what we can to change such attitudes, and partly to keep ourselves from colluding with the silence that offers respectability at the price of betrayal of a fundamental aspect of our identity. If this is hard for a person in a heterosexual marriage to understand, they might try to imagine what it would be like for them if they were placed in a situation where they could be accepted and esteemed only if they pretended that their spouse and children did not exist, or that their relationship with them was only casual.

For many of us, the decision to be open about being lesbian or gay has been costly even while also being enormously liberating and joyful. Attitudes of the unacceptability of homosexuality have been so internalized that even though we have begun to find our voice and our dignity and our pride it does not take much to tip us back into feeling vulnerable and insecure, uncertain of our value. Self-questioning and shame are easily induced.[9]

Accordingly, when a homosexual person contracts AIDS or HIV, and is faced with the revulsion and opprobrium of society and the church, how can they help but find in themselves feelings of shame and guilt about their sexuality? How can they not feel angry with themselves and their lovers, horrified at what is happening, as if they are to blame and are being punished not only for their acts but for their very being? How can anyone not in their position begin to grasp the level of courage required to face their illness with dignity and without self-loathing?

When we try, however inadequately, to imagine ourselves in their position we can see how enormously important it is that the church should be able to offer resources of dignity and support, not attitudes of shame. Like St. Francis, the church needs to stop holding its holy nose and take the men and women with AIDS and HIV into its arms and learn from them to see Christ. If the Gospels are about anything, they are about God coming alongside us, not identifying with the self-righteous, but giving dignity and esteem and support to those who were the outcasts of society by eating and drinking with them, touching them, being their friend. One thing that Jesus did not do was to reinforce internalized shame: what he did was to set people free to see their worth in his eyes and in God's.

In a Psalm which the church has regularly taken as descriptive of Christ, one of the qualities calling forth awe is his readiness to be alongside a sufferer:

> For he has not despised or abhorred
>   the affliction of the afflicted;
> and he has not hid his face from him,
>   but has heard, when he cried to him.
>
> (Psalm 22:24, RSV)

The Hebrew word translated "abhorred" is *shiqef*: it means "to shrink from, to detest or abominate." It is used of the loathing that someone might have for filth, or for the detestation for idols that was to be engendered in the Israelites.[10] Such abhorrence would have been as familiar to those with leprosy in Jesus' time as it is to people with AIDS today: people would shrink from them, seeing them as filth and probably as wicked, coupling their fear and revulsion with moral rectitude.

We need to hear it plainly: *such an attitude is not God's attitude.* It is not God's attitude even if it is widely held in society. It is not God's attitude even if it is held by many who profess to speak in God's name. In Jesus we are shown that God does not detest or shrink from the affliction of the afflicted, but comes alongside in tenderness and brotherhood.

Such coming alongside is enormously important for the recovery of dignity. As Arnold Isenberg has pointed out, shame can only be healed by replacing it with self-worth. Such healing is to be contrasted with two inadequate efforts to deal with shame. The first of these is "forgetfulness": that is, trying to pretend that the cause of shame is not there by thinking about other things, while still leaving intact the external and internal value judgments on which the feelings of shame feed. The other is "consolation," in which the shame is not forgotten, but substitutes or compensations are suggested as though somehow if there are other good things about the person then the shameful things don't matter. Neither of these really resolves the shame; they only push it away, making it even harder to deal with. The only way in which it can be resolved is not by resorting to either pretence or substitutes, but by confronting the value judgment from which the shame originates.[11]

This is precisely what Jesus did. The society of his time shrank from and abhorred its outcasts, seeing them as sinners punished by God. Jesus counted them his friends, ate meals with them, spent time with them, thus reversing the value judgment that they were not of worth. It is also what St. Francis did. He overcame his revulsion and his condescending charity by embracing the lepers, facing his own initial value judgment with the human reality of the sufferer. It is important to notice that he did not stop feeling revulsion first and then went and embraced the leper. He went and embraced the leper, and the love that he gave and received melted the revulsion away.

And this is what Christians are invited to do in response to people with AIDS and HIV. We need to confront our own value judgments which generate shame and fear with the loving acceptance of Christ. If we open ourselves to love people with AIDS and to receive love from them we will find that we can let go of our projections of shame and revulsion. As we spend time together we can find our attitudes being healed and our being alongside one another opening us to the presence of Christ. We may be challenged to be more in touch with our own sexuality and our mortality by women and men who have much to teach us about both. Who knows, we may even lose some of our self-righteousness!

Yet it would not be true to say that Jesus never expresses shame of anyone. In the Gospel of Mark there is a poignant sequence of events, Jesus performs miracles, multiplies loaves and fishes, heals a blind man. Then he asks his disciples who they say that he is, and Peter answers, "You are the Christ." But when he begins to teach them what that means, how being Christ means being on behalf of those who are seen as sinners and accepting the consequence of the cross and its shame, the disciples cannot handle it at all: Peter begins to rebuke him. The disciples wanted a Christ of power and invulnerability; Jesus offered them a totally different perspective. He taught them (and us) something about what following him means: it means taking up one's cross, doing in our own lives what Jesus did in his, giving our love and if necessary our reputations and our lives in being alongside those who suffer, just as Jesus was alongside them. And as Jesus concluded this teaching, for the only time in the Gospels Jesus speaks of shame: not shame at a sinner or a sufferer or an outcast, but shame at the pretended followers of his who disown the cross and the solidarity with human shame and suffering it represents.

> For whoever is ashamed of me and of my words, . . . of them will the Son of man also be ashamed, when he comes in the glory of his Father with the holy angels.
>
> (Mark 8:38; par. Luke 9:26)

Jesus projects no shame on those who suffer, not even when by the standards of his society they are sinful. But he expresses deep shame of those of us who affirm him as Christ, call ourselves after his name, and yet refuse to follow him in a vocation of being alongside. This, not suffering or the rejection it attracts, is shameful, abhorrent to God, contrary to Jesus, and contrary to our own souls as followers of his. And from the shame of God, who will deliver us?

NOTES

1. Michael Callen quoted in F. and M. Siegal, *AIDS: The Medical Mystery* (New York: Grove Press, 1983), 182–83.

2. Bonaventure, *The Life of St. Francis*, I.5, in Ewart Cousins, ed., *Bonaventure,*

Classics of Western Spirituality (London: SPCK, 1978), from Thomas of Celano, *Second Life*, 9.

3. Bonaventure, I.6; Thomas of Celano, I.17 and II.9.

4. See Leonardo Boff, *Saint Francis: A Model for Human Liberation* (London: SCM Press, 1981), 23–28.

5. For an investigation of the insulating effects of theodicy, see Ken Surin, *Theology and the Problem of Evil* (Oxford: Basil Blackwell Publisher, 1986).

6. Seymour Kleinberg, "Dreadful Night," in *Christopher Street #76*, 1983.

7. Dennis Altman, *AIDS and the New Puritanism* (London: Pluto Press, 1986), 59.

8. See *ibid.*, 25.

9. For further discussion of the relationship between societal attitudes and shame, and its distinction from guilt, see John Rawls, *A Theory of Justice* (Cambridge, Mass.: Harvard University Press, 1971), 442–46.

10. Nahum 3:6; Zech. 9:7; Deut. 7:26.

11. "Natural Pride and Natural Shame," in *Explaining Emotions*, ed. Amelie Rorty (Berkeley, Calif.: University of California Press, 1980), 368.

24

Safer Text: Reading Biblical Laments in the Age of AIDS

KEN STONE

In a recent theological response to AIDS, J. Michael Clark has cast doubt on the value of biblical interpretation for lesbians, gay men, and persons affected by the AIDS crisis.[1] Attempting to account for what he calls his "scripture-phobia," Clark points out that "the Bible has been used, over and over again. . . . as the ideological justification not only for excluding gay men and lesbians, but also for blaming the victims in the AIDS health crisis. . . ."[2] Religious responses to AIDS are, of course, diverse,[3] but the problem that Clark points to is real. It is not difficult to think of biblical passages which state or imply that disaster and distress are divine responses to sinful activities formerly carried out by those who suffer. Thus, the Bible—which is already used to justify discrimination against lesbians, gay men, bisexuals and transgendered folk—can also serve as a powerful rhetorical weapon for those who interpret the HIV virus as a sign of perversity.

One way of dealing with this problem is, certainly, to refuse to read the Bible, and Clark has good reasons for being inclined toward this solution. Yet such a refusal also runs the risk of remystifying the Bible and fails to engage with contemporary trends in biblical scholarship that have opened up space for the development of a range of non-traditional reading strategies.[4] Thus, I would like to consider the possibility that certain lament psalms can be read in a manner that will encourage resistance to the attitudes toward AIDS that rightly trouble Clark. The immediate context for such a consideration lies in my own interest in the contemporary "queering" of the biblical texts, of the religious traditions that claim to be based on those texts, and of the conventions that structure the reception of those texts. Such a project may sound dubious to some readers, and particularly in relation to the book of Psalms, for among the biblical books, Psalms appears on the surface to be one of those least useful for attempts at (to borrow a phrase) "queering the canon."[5] But as Biddy Martin notes, "queerness is not always where we expect to find it."[6] Hence, it would be unwise to make hasty assumptions about the incompatibility of biblical laments and queer activism in the age of AIDS.

The term "queer" is a contested one, however, and its use requires theoretical specification. My understanding of "queer" is indebted to a recent work by David M. Halperin which suggests that Foucault's discursive and constructionist view of sexuality enables a radical sexual politics.[7] Foucault, as is well known, questioned the assumption that sexual identity pre-exists relations of power; and Halperin, following Foucault and subsequent work in queer theory, argues that "the heterosexual/homosexual binarism is itself a homophobic production."[8] This argument has been controversial even among self-identified gay scholars, some of whom worry that Foucault's thesis undermines the foundation on which a gay politics could be constructed.[9] It is true that Foucault's work casts doubt on particular assumptions about the homosexual subject underlying certain discourses of sexual liberation. Halperin, however, argues that Foucault's thesis is an attempt to call into question forms of power that claim to reveal the truth about homosexuality by making homosexuality an object of knowledge. Such claims simultaneously allow heterosexuality to be constituted as a category of identity and assumed as an unproblematic norm. In the light of Foucault's work, Halperin construes antihomophobic struggles as attempts "to *reverse the discursive positioning* of homosexuality and heterosexuality: to shift heterosexuality from the position of a universal subject of discourse to an object of interrogation and critique, and to shift homosexuality from the position of an object of power/ knowledge to a position of legitimate subjective agency—from the status of that which is spoken about while remaining silent to the status of that which speaks."[10]

Halperin, therefore, does not discuss homosexuality in terms of a substantive definition but, rather, in terms of a discursive position in a network of power/ knowledge relations: "The aim . . . is to treat homosexuality as a position from which one *can* know, to treat it as a legitimate *condition* of knowledge. Homosexuality . . . is not something to be got right but an eccentric positionality to be exploited and explored: a potentially privileged site for the criticism and analysis of cultural discourse."[11] Rather than understanding homosexual desire as the deep truth of one's identity, and rather than insisting that a stable homosexual identity exists across time and space waiting only to be freed from repression, those who are marginalized because of sexual practice can engage in what Halperin, building upon Foucault's late work on the practices of the self as spiritual exercises, calls "an ongoing process of self-constitution and self-transformation."[12]

Halperin refers to this process as "queer politics."[13] For "queer," according to Halperin, "acquires its meaning from its oppositional relation to the norm. Queer is by definition *whatever* is at odds with the normal, the legitimate, the dominant."[14] Queer subjectivity and agency are not precisely coterminous with homosexual object-choice, then, and cannot simply be assumed to exist if an individual self-identifies as lesbian, gay, or bisexual. Such self-identification may

offer an opportunity for queer subjectivity, but a political movement "is genuinely *queer* insofar as it is broadly oppositional."[15] Thus, for Halperin the key
term of a queer politics is not liberation but *resistance*. A queer politics does
not acquire its shape from any assumed essence of homosexuality waiting to be
liberated, but rather from the concrete process of resisting structures of power
and knowledge.

There are a number of ways in which Halperin's positional and oppositional
notion of "queer" might be used to reshape practices of biblical interpretation.
For example, it might call into question the tactical value of endless debates
about (to quote the title of one brisk-selling text) "What the Bible *Really* Says
about Homosexuality."[16] While many such books are written to counter hegemonic interpretations of the Bible, it is clear that "homosexuality" remains in
this formulation an object of biblical discourse and an object of the discourse
of biblical interpretation, even when seen as an object whose status needs to
be reassessed. What sorts of interpretations might result if homosexuality functioned instead, in line with Halperin's suggestion, as a "legitimate condition of
knowledge" *about* the Bible?

But Halperin's notion of "queer" may also create a theoretical framework
in which it becomes possible to respond to Clark's concern about the ways in
which the Bible is used to "blame the victims" of the AIDS crisis. Halperin
himself argues that a close link exists between queer politics and certain types of
AIDS activism. After all, AIDS activism is not equivalent to gay identity politics;
and, as Simon Watney among others has noted, AIDS activism generates political identities that did not precede the AIDS crisis and that continue to evolve,
often in unexpected ways.[17] Queer subjects of AIDS activism emerge from resistance to the practice of reducing persons with AIDS to objects of authoritative
discourses—including, I would suggest, the discourse of biblical interpretation.

Clark, too, is worried about situations in which persons with AIDS are
treated as objects of authoritative discourses. More specifically, Clark recognizes
that individuals use the Bible to speak about persons with AIDS or about persons infected with, at risk for, or thought to be at risk for, HIV. In the readings
that most trouble Clark, such persons are objects of speech, and their distress is
focalized by someone other than the sufferer.[18] In view of Halperin's discussion,
attempts might be made to reverse the discursive positioning that structures
such readings, focusing not on biblical texts that speak *about* the person who
suffers, but rather on texts in which suffering is focalized by a speaking subject
that is, itself, a suffering subject. Such a change of focus already hints at the possible value of re-reading biblical laments, for a defining feature of the laments
is their articulation by a speaking subject characterized by some sort of distress.

The potential importance of analyzing ancient texts in relation to the appearance therein of a suffering subject has been highlighted by Judith Perkins, who
points out that the attitudes toward suffering found in much early Christian literature are strikingly different from the attitudes found in certain Greco-Roman
texts. In Perkins's view, the emphasis in the latter group of texts on self-mastery,

and the corresponding lack of emphasis on material conditions and the body, produce a sort of "ideological veil" that functions to "mask" the realities of a world characterized by suffering.[19] Many early Christian texts, on the other hand, emphasize and even glorify suffering. While the rhetoric of such texts has sometimes been dismissed as pathological, Perkins argues that the early Christian texts participate in the discursive construction of a new form of social subject, a subject characterized by a frank recognition and valorization of physical suffering rather than a denial of its importance.

Two initial observations might be made about the biblical laments in the light of Perkins's discussion. First, the laments also affirm the crucial significance of human suffering. By offering a discursive position from which this suffering can be acknowledged, affirmed, and articulated, the biblical laments, like the early Christian texts studied by Perkins, present an alternative to any discourse that would attempt to deny the importance of such suffering.

Yet there is also a striking difference between the texts analyzed by Perkins, on the one hand, and the biblical laments, on the other. For if the early martyr texts glorify suffering, interpreting it as a means with which one might achieve imitation of, and union with, the divine, the laments make the quite different claim that *suffering needs to be alleviated*. While the early Christian texts respond to suffering by giving it a positive justification, many of the laments respond to suffering with *resistance*. The laments do not generally acquiesce to suffering, do not in most cases try to give it a positive interpretation. Rather, they complain about it; and this complaint offers readers a subject-position from which an end to suffering and distress can be actively pursued.

In spite of the frequent appearance of such complaints in the laments, the precise nature of the calamity in question can be difficult to identify and seems in any case not to be the same from lament to lament. Some of the laments do include references to physical suffering, a fact that catches one's eye in the age of AIDS; but it can be difficult to decide whether the physical symptoms are meant to be understood literally or figuratively. More often the distress in question is related to some social situation, in the sense that enemies contribute to, or are responsible for, both individual and collective suffering. Indeed, references to physical symptoms are often embedded in complaints about social or interpersonal conflict, making any absolute distinction between them impossible in cases like Ps. 22:12–18:

> Many bulls encircle me, strong bulls of Bashan surround me;
> they open wide their mouths at me, like a ravening and roaring lion.
> I am poured out like water, and all my bones are out of joint;
> my heart is like wax; it is melted within my breast;
> my mouth is dried up like a potsherd, and my tongue sticks to my jaws. . . .
> For dogs are all around me; a company of evildoers encircles me.
> My hands and feet have shriveled; I can count all my bones.
> They stare and gloat over me;
> They divide my clothes among themselves, and for my clothing they
> cast lots.[20]

Another example of this blending of physical and social distress occurs in Ps. 31:9–13:

> Be gracious to me, O God, for I am in distress;
> my eye wastes away from grief, my soul and body also.
> For my life is spent with sorrow, and my years with sighing;
> my strength fails because of my misery, and my bones waste away.
> I am the scorn of all my adversaries, a horror to my neighbors,
> an object of dread to my acquaintances; those who see me in the street flee from me.
> I have passed out of mind like one who is dead; I have become like a broken vessel.
> For I hear the whispering of many—terror all around!—
> as they scheme together against me, as they plot to take my life.

Like much contemporary AIDS activism, then, these laments recontextualize individual physical distress in relation to social and interpersonal practices. Moreover, such practices are not located solely at the level of the nation or of the community, as is clear from the references to neighbors and acquaintances. Indeed, the appearance of both macroconflicts and microconflicts contributes to the potential value of the laments for a counter-reading in the age of AIDS. Persons living with HIV/AIDS are unfortunately well acquainted with the fact that suffering can be exacerbated at both societal and interpersonal levels, and for that reason may resonate with a text like Ps. 55:12–14, 20–21:

> It is not enemies who taunt me—I could bear that;
> It is not adversaries who deal insolently with me—I could hide from them.
> But it is you, my equal, my companion, my familiar friend,
> With whom I kept pleasant company;
>   We walked in the house of God with the throng. . . .
> My companion laid hands on a friend and violated a covenant with me
> with speech smoother than butter, but with a heart set on war;
> with words that were softer than oil, but in fact were drawn swords.

In various ways, then, the discursive construction of a suffering subject in the laments is linked to the construction of an opponent. This fact may trouble some readers, particularly when it involves calls for vengeance. Such calls do appear in certain laments and can be articulated in extremely brutal language, as in Psalm 137. Yet it is important to remember that the opponents in the laments are nearly always a cause of, or contributor to, the suffering of the speaker. Thus, complaints about opponents and enemies in the laments parallel complaints that appear in the rhetoric of AIDS activism. For one characteristic of such activism that is frequently remarked upon, by friend and foe alike, is the way in which it is willing to confront those thought to be responsible for prolonging or exacerbating the AIDS crisis. Politicians, clergy persons, bureaucrats, scientists, social workers, physicians and media professionals have all been subjected publicly to the anger and frustration of AIDS activists. Indeed, even a less obviously political response to AIDS, such as the AIDS Quilt, while denigrated in some quarters for its lack of militancy, has been interpreted by certain commentators as participating in the symbolic "construction of an enemy."[21] Once suffering is seen to have social and interpersonal causes, it should not be surprising that a discourse in which the suffering subject sees and speaks should articulate anger at human opponents. The AIDS activist will therefore understand all too well the plea of the psalmist that "as they hoped to have my life, so repay them for their crime" (Ps. 56:6b–7a).

Yet the anger articulated in the laments is not directed solely at human opponents. A number of laments also accuse God of being implicated in the speaker's suffering. In some cases this accusation has to do with God's failure to respond to or alleviate distress, as is true, for example, of Ps. 13:1–2:

> How long, O God? Will you forget me forever?
>   How long will you hide your face from me?
> How long must I bear pain in my soul, and have sorrow in my heart all day long?
> How long shall my enemy be exalted over me?

In other cases the accusation is more severe: God has not only forgotten or turned away from the speaker, but is actively involved in the speaker's suffering. Indeed, certain laments such as Psalm 44 and Psalm 88 actually *combine* the two sorts of accusation: God is said to be both turning away from the one who suffers and an active cause of the suffering in question.

Some readers may wonder just how useful this gesture of accusation can be in the context of the AIDS crisis. Does not such language reek of traditional theism, a mode of theology whose relevance for the age of AIDS has been rejected by a number of gay theologians?[22] Is it not true that this mode of language will be dismissed by many of those who live with AIDS or HIV as hopelessly anachronistic or simply unintelligible? And if readers *do* subscribe to some version of traditional theism, are not the potential problems even more severe? Most of us, after all, would be hesitant to encourage persons living with AIDS or HIV to read biblical texts if such readings resulted in the search for some sort of *deus ex machina*.

These issues are serious ones, and they raise questions about theological language that cannot be explored adequately here. But there are several reasons why, in my estimation, such questions should not lead us to dismiss too quickly the potential value of reading biblical laments in the age of AIDS. In the first place, this willingness to confront God directly and to accuse God of some sort of complicity in one's suffering helps to constitute part of the radicality of the laments, and part of their attraction for religious social critics. Walter Brueggemann, for one, has long argued that such complaints against God can be interpreted, at least in part, as complaints against an unjust social order that uses religious language for legitimation.[23] In addition, to the extent that the complaints against God acknowledge that suffering can be caused by forces other than human beings, these complaints give readers a precedent for recognizing a tragic dimension to human existence without falling into complacency about suffering. Such a tragic consciousness is important with respect to AIDS, for there is a sense in which the AIDS crisis cannot be reduced to human social evil even if it is exacerbated by such evil.[24]

But perhaps most importantly, the willingness of the laments to accuse God of complicity in human suffering underscores the unacceptability of such suffering in an uncompromising and astonishing fashion, calling into question any theological discourse that is willing to construct a comforting God while refusing to confront the difficult question of evil.[25] Borrowing Perry LeFevre's formulation that "prayer is a matter of desire," we might say that these particular prayers reflect and produce a desire for an end to pain that is even stronger than the desire for a coherent and comfortable theological system.[26]

This insistence upon the need to take human pain seriously does not lead, however, to a sense of absolute despair. After all, it has long been argued that the cries of distress found in the laments need to be understood in relation to the cries of praise that are also found there, cries of praise which indicate a belief in the possibility that suffering can be brought to an end.[27] Indeed, biblical scholars have often been so quick to move from lament to praise that a few readers have asked, with some justification, whether the language of suffering in the laments has truly been heard.[28]

This is a very important question, and the total lack of anything like praise at the end of Psalm 88, while admittedly an exception rather than the rule, ought to caution any reader from believing that lament is inevitably subordinated to praise in the biblical texts. In the present context, however, where my reading lenses have been deliberately chosen in relation to the AIDS crisis, I am inclined to interpret the fact that some sort of praise or affirmation does appear in most of the laments as a recognition of the importance of hope. For as Walt Odets has recently noted, survival in the age of AIDS requires a difficult psychological balancing act, a refusal to submit to the alternatives of denial on the one side or hopelessness on the other. So, for example, Odets points out that both denial and despair can lead an uninfected individual to put himself or herself at risk for HIV infection. In the opinion of Odets, it is crucial that gay men in particular be able to acknowledge the seriousness of the present situation while also imagining alternatives to it.[29] Thus, the presence in most of the laments of both a radical recognition of pain and suffering *and* a willingness to hope that things can be otherwise contributes to the potential value of the laments for readers affected by the AIDS epidemic.

It would nevertheless be foolish to pretend that all of the laments are equally useful for a queer counter-reading in the age of AIDS. For those laments which involve repentance often imply or state explicitly that suffering is primarily a result of the misdeeds of the sufferer; and the reading of such texts could easily contribute not only to "blaming the victims," as Clark puts it, but also to an internalization of that blame by those who suffer. Consider, for example, the potential effects on those who live with AIDS of a psalm such as Ps. 38:3–5:

There is no soundness in my flesh because of your indignation;
there is no health in my bones because of my sin.
For my iniquities have gone over my head;
    they weigh like a burden too heavy for me.
My wounds grow foul and fester because of my foolishness.

It is not difficult to imagine ways in which readings of laments such as Psalm 38 might contribute to the very problem that motivated this essay. I would not for that reason conclude that texts which do blame suffering on the sufferer ought *never* to be read. For one of Halperin's arguments, in his elaboration of a queer politics, is that the precise shape of queer resistance cannot be predicted, but can only be determined strategically in relation to some context. It is thus impossible to rule out, *a priori*, the possibility of a given text ever being taken up in an oppositional fashion. My response to Psalm 38 is relative to the context with which I have framed this . . . [essay]—a context in which, as Clark recognizes, those living with HIV are in constant danger of being told, or of themselves believing, that HIV infection represents punishment for iniquity. In that context, such a psalm must be approached with great caution.

Indeed, I should note in conclusion that a debate is currently raging among gay men, especially in the United States, about the extent to which gay men have themselves been guilty of causing or furthering the AIDS crisis. Some of those engaged in the debate wish simply to encourage a healthy sense of responsibility and self-preservation among gay men, and this desire is of course to be commended. Others, however, go much further, agreeing with the author of one recent article in the gay press when he appeals to nature to support his claim that "we brought AIDS upon ourselves. . . ."[30] This rhetoric strikes me as being similar, in certain respects, to the rhetoric of laments such as Psalm 38. In both instances of speech—that articulated in Psalm 38, and that articulated in the gay press—the speaker understands a present situation of distress to be the result of improper behavior. The one who suffers, and who now wishes such suffering to be brought to an end, believes himself or herself to have caused the suffering in the first place.

I for one agree that gay men need to be vigilant with respect to modes of HIV transmission and related health issues. However, I also continue to be surprised by the frequency with which AIDS is interpreted as a sign for the dubious nature of gay male sex as such, even among certain gay men. Ultimately, I believe that this interpretation still has to be resisted. To the extent that a reading of biblical laments fosters resistance in the face of claims that those who suffer deserve their suffering, a reading of the laments can be encouraged and practiced, individually and collectively, by those affected by the AIDS crisis. To the extent, however, that the structure of certain laments does make them useful for the interpretations that trouble Clark, then the potential risks involved in reading such texts need to be recognized. Indeed, just as queer resistance to AIDS refuses to reject gay sex as such, but responds to potential health risks by developing practices of safer sex, so also such resistance needs to focus, not on a wholesale rejection of the admittedly dangerous practice of biblical interpretation, but rather on the queer development of safer texts and safer readings.

NOTES

1. An earlier version of this paper was read at a session of the Theory, Reading, and the Bible Section at the 1997 Society of Biblical Literature meeting. I wish to thank Horace Griffin for comments on that paper.

2. J. Michael Clark, *Defying the Darkness: Gay Theology in the Shadows* (Cleveland: Pilgrim Press, 1997), p. 10.

3. Cf. Mark R. Kowalewski, "Religious Constructions of the AIDS Crisis," in Gary David Comstock and Susan E. Henking (eds.), *Que(e)rying Religion: A Critical Anthology* (New York: Continuum, 1997), pp. 366–71; J. Gordon Melton (ed.), *The Churches Speak on AIDS* (Detroit: Gale Research, 1989).

4. For a helpful discussion of such trends, see the Bible and Culture Collective, *The Postmodern Bible* (New Haven: Yale University Press, 1995).

5. Ann Pellegrini, "There's No Place Like Home? Lesbian Studies and the Classics," in Linda Garber (ed.), *Tilting the Tower: Lesbians Teaching Queer Subjects* (New York: Routledge, 1994), p. 73.

6. Biddy Martin, *Femininity Played Straight: The Significance of Being Lesbian* (New York: Routledge, 1996), p. 14.

7. For Foucault's account, see Michel Foucault, *The History of Sexuality. I. An Introduction* (trans. Robert Hurley; New York: Random House, 1978). For an influential constructionist account of sexuality developed in dialogue with Foucault, see Halperin's earlier *One Hundred Years of Homosexuality and Other Essays on Greek Love* (New York: Routledge, 1990). For a positive theological reception of Foucault's work on sexuality, see Mark Vernon, "Following Foucault: The Strategies of Sexuality and the Struggle to be Different," *Theology & Sexuality* 5 (1996), pp. 76–96.

8. David M. Halperin, *Saint Foucault: Towards a Gay Hagiography* (Cambridge, MA: Harvard University Press, 1995), p. 44.

9. See, e.g., Richard Mohr, *Gay Ideas: Outing and Other Controversies* (Boston: Beacon Press, 1992), pp. 221–60.

10. Halperin, *Saint Foucault*, p. 57, emphasis mine.

11. Halperin, *Saint Foucault*, pp. 60–61. Halperin's term "eccentric positionality" is derived in part from the fine article by Teresa de Lauretis, "Eccentric Subjects: Feminist Theory and Historical Consciousness," *Feminist Studies* 16.1 (Spring 1990), pp.115–50.

12. Halperin, *Saint Foucault*, p. 122. For the late work of Foucault, which is increasingly receiving the attention it deserves, see his *The Use of Pleasure* (trans. Robert Hurley; New York: Random House, 1985); idem, *The Care of the Self* (trans. Robert Hurley; New York: Random House, 1986); and Paul Rabinow (ed.), *Ethics: Subjectivity and Truth: The Essential Works of Foucault 1954–1984* (New York: The New Press, 1997), I, pp. 87–319. The term "spiritual exercises" is borrowed by Foucault and Halperin from Pierre Hadot, *Philosophy as a Way of Life* (ed. with an introduction by Arnold Davidson, trans. Michael Chase; Cambridge, MA: Basil Blackwell, 1995). Cf. my own comments on Foucault's late work in "Biblical Interpretation as a Technology of the Self: Gay Men and the Ethics of Reading," in D.N. Fewell and G.A. Phillips (eds.), *Bible and Ethics of Reading* (Semeia, 77; Atlanta: Scholars Press, 1997), pp. 139–55.

13. Halperin, *Saint Foucault*, p. 122.

14. Halperin, *Saint Foucault*, p. 62.

15. Halperin, *Saint Foucault*, p. 63, emphasis in original.

16. Daniel A. Helminiak, *What the Bible Really Says about Homosexuality* (San Francisco: Alamo Square Press, 1994), emphasis in original. While the structure of Helminiak's title conveniently makes my point, the structure of his argument is typical of a substantial portion of the literature on the Bible and homosexuality.

17. Simon Watney, "Practices of Freedom: 'Citizenship' and the Politics of Identity in the Age of AIDS," in his *Practices of Freedom: Selected Writings on HIV/AIDS* (Durham: Duke University Press, 1994), pp. 148–59. Cf. Martin P. Levine, Peter M. Nardi and John H. Gagnon (eds.), *In Changing Times: Gay Men and Lesbians Encounter HIV/AIDS* (Chicago: University of Chicago Press, 1997).

18. For the literary theory, relating speech and focalization to subject/object positions, on which I am relying for this formulation, see Mieke Bal, *Narratology: Introduction to the Theory of Narrative* (trans. Christine van Boheemen; Toronto: University of Toronto Press, 1985); idem, *On Storytelling: Essays in Narratology* (ed. David Jobling; Sonoma, CA: Polebridge Press, 1991), esp. pp. 73–108,146–70.

19. Judith Perkins, *The Suffering Self: Pain and Narrative Representation in the Early Christian Era* (New York: Routledge, 1995), p. 84. Thanks to Wil Brant for calling this important text to my attention.

20. All translations are taken from *The New Testament and Psalms: An Inclusive Version* (New York: Oxford University Press, 1995).

21. Marita Sturken, "Conversations with the Dead: Bearing Witness in the AIDS Memorial Quilt," *Socialist Review* 92.2 (1992), p. 77. On the political dimensions of the AIDS Quilt, see also Douglas Crimp, "Mourning and Militancy," *October* 51 (1989), pp. 3–18; Peter S. Hawkins, "Naming Names: The Art of Memory and the NAMES Project AIDS Quilt," *Critical Inquiry* 19 (Summer 1993), pp. 752–79; Michael P. Brown, *RePlacing Citizenship: AIDS Activism and Radical Democracy* (New York: Guilford Press, 1997), pp. 155–83.

22. Thus, Ronald Long and J. Michael Clark both reject the relevance of traditional theism in the age of AIDS in spite of the fact that they agree about little else. See their *AIDS, God, and Faith: Continuing the Dialogue on Constructing Gay Theology* (Las Colinas: Monument Press, 1992).

23. See, e.g., Walter Brueggemann, *The Psalms and the Life of Faith* (Minneapolis: Fortress Press, 1995), pp. 104–107 and passim.

24. As Clark, for example, recognizes in *Defying the Darkness*, pp. 39–41. On the importance of recapturing a "tragic" dimension in theological responses to suffering, see Wendy Farley, *Tragic Vision and Divine Compassion: A Contemporary Theodicy* (Louisville, KY: Westminster/John Knox Press, 1990); Kathleen M. Sands, *Escape from Paradise: Evil and Tragedy in Feminist Theology* (Minneapolis: Fortress Press, 1994). Cf. F.W. Dobbs-Allsopp, "Tragedy, Tradition, and Theology in the Book of Lamentations," *JSOT* 74 (June 1997), pp. 29–60.

25. This is also one of the strengths of David Blumenthal's use of the Psalms in his *Facing the Abusing God: A Theology of Protest* (Louisville, KY: Westminster/John Knox Press, 1993). While I find Blumenthal's work fascinating, I am ultimately more sympathetic to the position articulated by two dialogue partners whose critical questions are incorporated by Blumenthal, than I am to what I understand to be Blumenthal's own position.

26. Perry LeFevre, *Radical Prayer: Contemporary Interpretations* (Chicago: Exploration Press, 1982), 20. LeFevre's formulation occurs in a discussion of Dorothee Soelle's approach to prayer. For a discussion of the laments in the context of other biblical prayers, see Patrick D. Miller, *They Cried to the Lord: The Form and Theology of Biblical Prayer* (Minneapolis: Fortress Press, 1994), pp. 55–134.

27. See, e.g., Tod Linafelt, "Margins of Lamentations: Or, The Unbearable Whiteness of Reading," in Timothy K. Beal and David M. Gunn (eds.), *Reading Bibles, Writing Bodies: Identity and the Book* (New York: Routledge, 1997), pp. 220–21.

28. A well-known example of a work that insists upon understanding lament in relation to praise is Claus Westermann, *Praise and Lament in the Psalms* (trans. Keith R. Crim and Richard N. Soulen; Atlanta: John Knox Press, 1981).

29. Walt Odets, *In the Shadow of the Epidemic: Being HIV-Negative in the Age of AIDS* (Durham: Duke University Press, 1995), pp. 204–79, passim.

30. Larry Kramer, "Sex and Sensibility," *The Advocate* 734 (27 May 1997), p. 59.

25

Is There Life after Roe? How to Think about the Fetus

FRANCES KISSLING

In the thirty years since *Roe v. Wade* ushered in a new paradigm in the legal understanding of the right to choose abortion, there has been little about the issue that has not been said—and said time and time again. Supporters of choice have argued that it is important to recognize women as autonomous persons with the moral capacity and moral right to decide whether a pregnancy will be aborted or brought to term. We have enhanced our core argument with references to broader values, such as religious freedom, opposition to government intervention in our personal lives, and the right to medical privacy. The most powerful of prochoice messages has been the multi-faceted question, "Who Decides?" which highlights both women's rights and keeping government out of the bedroom without ever mentioning either. Inherent in our focus on women's rights has been our belief that fetal life does not attain, at any point in pregnancy, a value that is equivalent to that of born persons, most specifically women, infants, or children who are most often cited in discussions of abortion. Our belief about what value fetal life may possess is not yet well articulated, and prochoice supporters are not of one mind on this question. Neither, it should be noted, are the world's religions, ethicists, or theologians of one mind on this matter.

Those who are opposed to legal abortion seem more certain and monolithic on the question of the value of fetal life. Their core message has been simple: fetal life at all stages of development has an inviolable right to life. Fetuses are, they claim, the most vulnerable persons among us, and our humanity requires that we protect them from destruction by intentional abortion. This position did not resonate with most Americans at the time *Roe* was decided and still has little support. At the time *Roe* was decided, public opinion largely favored legal abortion, and people spent little if any time thinking about the fetus. It was, after all, the mid-1970s, and we were in the midst of a sexual and reproductive revolution brought on by the discovery of the pill and an increasing acceptance of women's rights. The tragedy of women dying or suffering serious health consequences following illegal abortion was front and center. Added to this was the strong desire, felt by many couples, to have fewer children, which was seen as central to achieving the working class dream of owning your own home, sending your kids to a good college, and having more meaningful and better paid work.

For both supporters and opponents of abortion rights, single focus positions have presented some difficulties. Supporters of abortion rights are pushed to the limits on abortions later in pregnancy and on the question of the extent to which abortion can be regulated if not restricted. Those who oppose abortion rights have struggled with the logical conclusion of the claim that there is no distinction in fetal value at any stage in pregnancy and have ended up opposing abortion in tragic cases, such as after rape and for very young women who have been victims of incest. Consistency (and here the phrase, "A foolish consistency is the hobgoblin of little minds," comes to my mind) has meant that they have had to oppose embryonic stem cell research that could contribute to saving lives and emergency contraception for women who have been raped on the slight chance that a conception may have already taken place.

After a number of failed attempts to overturn *Roe* outright, opponents of abortion developed a long term incremental legislative strategy designed as much to win the hearts and minds of moderate supporters of abortion rights as to change the law itself. They aimed to chip away at access to abortion services for groups perceived to be powerless and unpopular, such as poor women and adolescents. In the case of poor women, they claimed they did not want their tax dollars to pay for a service they considered immoral. In the case of adolescents, they asserted that no adolescent should be treated without the consent of her parents. However, their major goal was to convince people that fetuses are indeed persons. In recent years, antichoice activists have poured resources into ensuring that the law treats fetuses as persons and highlighting scientific advances in fetal medicine. In spite of the antiabortion movement's incremental strategy, its leaders are clear that their ultimate goal is an absolute ban on all abortions except those needed as immediate life saving measures. This obstinate insistence on an absolute legal ban is the major obstacle to what might have been the development of an abortion praxis that combined respect for the fundamental right of women to choose abortion with an ethical discourse that included the exploration of how other values might also be respected, including the value of developing human life.

Instead, those committed to the right to choose have felt forced to defend what appears to be an absolute right to abortion that brooks no consideration of other values—legal or moral. This often means a reluctance even to consider whether or not fetal life has value, or an attempt to define that value or to see how it can be promoted without restricting access to legal abortion. As the fetus has become more visible through both antiabortion efforts and advances in fetal medicine, this stance has become less satisfying as either a moral framework or a message strategy responding to the concerns of many Americans who are generally both supportive of and uncomfortable with legal abortion.

RIGHTS AND VALUES

I believe women have a basic human right to decide what to do about a pregnancy. Other well-established human rights concepts bolster this argument, including bodily integrity, the right to health, the right to practice one's religion (or not), and the right to be free from religious laws in modern democratic societies. Despite the assertions of some very intelligent prolifers[1] that the abortion issue is a question of the human rights of the fetus, the human rights community is moving steadily towards recognizing a woman's right to choose and there is no countervailing view in this community that even considers the question of whether or not fetuses are rights-bearing entities.

But the abortion issue is not one in which only rights are at stake. There are at least three central values that need to be part of the public conversation about abortion and, as appropriate, influence behavior, if not law. They are:

  i) The human right of women to decide whether or not to continue a pregnancy.
 ii) A respect for human life that takes the form of what Daniel Callahan called more than 30 years ago a moral presumption in favor of life.
iii) A commitment to ensure that provisions which permit the taking of life (whether it be fetal, animal, or plant) not coarsen the overall fabric of society and our attitudes toward each other, as well as toward developing human life.

First, and I would say primary, is our obligation to respect in law and social thought the right of women to bodily autonomy. Generally speaking, nobody should be forced to carry a pregnancy to term without their consent. I am revolted by the thought that a law banning most or all abortions would, if it were to be more than a rhetorical exercise, require an enforcement mechanism that actively forces women to continue pregnancies that they believe to be antithetical to their needs or identities. But the right to choose abortion is not absolute, and in practice and law even those of us most ardently prochoice do not demand absolutism. The law clearly does not recognize that the right is so fundamental that it requires the government to provide abortion services routinely for free. The first restriction of *Roe* was the court decision that freed the federal government from the obligation to provide funding for abortions for women dependent on the government for their medical care. Medical ethics, on the other hand, demands that a patient who arrives at a health service at death's door must be treated even if he or she has no money. Our clinics turn away some women who cannot afford abortions. We insist on full payment in advance, sometimes delaying an abortion until the pregnancy is further advanced and carries a greater risk of complications.

Many accept that post-viability abortions can be denied unless the woman's life is at risk, the fetus has a condition that is truly incompatible with life, or there is a serious health risk to the woman. We are thus prepared to "force," or at least not to facilitate, an abortion at eight months for a woman who is, for example, abandoned by her partner and no longer wishes to have a child. But, with those limits acknowledged, we believe a good society will make it possible for women who do not want to be pregnant to get safe, dignified, and compassionate abortion services. It will also do everything it can to help women and men prevent pregnancies if they do not want to have children. This is not necessarily out of respect for the fetus, but out of respect for women. The act of taking life in abortion is defensible and can have positive results, but in and of itself is not a moral good. We should do everything we can to enable people to live lives that affirm human beings and other forms of life that are not harmful to our world. One colleague who reviewed this article noted that the term "right to life" and its unrelenting and vague formulation obscures the fact that some life is dangerous and does not deserve to be respected. Cancer cells are a form of life, as are viruses like polio and HIV/AIDS. Should they be respected?

VALUING FETAL LIFE

This brings us to the second value of a good society: respect for life, including fetal life. Why should we allow this value to be owned by those opposed to abortion? Are we not capable of walking and chewing gum at the same time; of valuing life and respecting women's rights? Have we not ceded too much territory to antiabortionists by not articulating the value of fetal life? In an important op-ed in the *New York Times*, author William Saletan claimed that "supporters of abortion rights . . . still don't know how to articulate the value of unborn human life." Saletan makes a good point, but he does not pursue it and offers no suggestions for how we could articulate this value.

Such an effort will take a lot of work and involve exposing deep differences among supporters of choice regarding our views on the inherent value of fetal life on its own terms and in relation to women's rights. An interesting thought exercise might help to clarify what prochoice (and antiabortion) leaders believe about fetal value. Imagine a world in which it was possible to remove fetuses prior to viability from women's bodies and allow them to develop in a nonuterine environment. Perhaps they could be implanted in men or other women who want them; perhaps they could develop in a specially equipped nursery. In this world, medicine is so far advanced that this could be accomplished painlessly and without risking the health of either the woman or the fetus. Of course, this is at present largely a fantasy and by that time we would have found the ideal, risk-free, and failure-free contraceptive, but let's pretend.

What are the first five concerns and reactions that come to your mind? Is one of them the fact that this would mean fetuses need not die? My own experience in presenting this option to both advocates and opponents of abortion is that the fetus's life is rarely a consideration. Among the most interesting reactions of those who are prochoice is a concern that some women might find the continued existence of the fetus painful for them or that women have a right to ensure that their genetic material does not enter the world. Abortion in this sense becomes the guarantee of a dead fetus, if desired, rather than the removal of the fetus from an unwilling host, the woman. To even offer women such an option is, some think, cruel. For some the right to choose abortion seems to include the right to be protected from thinking about the fetus and from any pain that might result from others talking about the fetus in value-laden terms. In this construct, it is hard to identify any value fetal life might have.

This level of sensitivity to protecting women from their feelings takes other forms. For example, some prochoice advocates have objected to public discussion of abortion that includes concern for the number of abortions that occur in the U.S. or has as its goal reducing the number of abortions. Some bristled at President Clinton's formula that abortion should be "safe, legal and rare." If abortion is justifiable, why should it be rare? Even the suggestion that abortion is a moral matter, as well as a legal one, has caused concern that such a statement might make women feel guilty. Words like "baby" are avoided, not just because they are inaccurate, but because they are loaded.

In a society where women have long been victims of moral discourse, these concerns are somewhat understandable, but they do not contribute much towards convincing people that when prochoice people say they value fetal life, it is more than lip service.

The reaction of antiabortionists to the idea that a fetus could be removed from the body of an unwilling woman is as troubling. Again, one rarely hears cries of joy that fetal lives would be saved. The focus also is on the woman. But here, the view that women are, by their nature, made for childbearing dominates. Women have an obligation to continue pregnancies, to suffer the consequences of their sexuality. It is unnatural to even think that fetuses could become healthy and happy people if they did not spend nine months in the womb of a woman. One is led to believe that, for those opposed to abortion, it is not saving fetuses that matters, but preserving a social construct in which women breed.

THINKING ABOUT MESSAGES

Thought exercises, however, have their limits and there is much that could be done to balance women's rights with an expression of fetal value without resorting to science fiction. A first step might be a conversation among prochoice leaders that explored what we think about the value of fetal life. You cannot talk cogently about things you have not thought about or discussed. And not thinking leads to mistakes. At times there is a kind of prochoice triumphalism in operation. Abortion is a serious matter; it is a woman's right, and no woman needs to apologize for making this decision. On the other hand, no woman needs to brag about her choice, and the decision of one prochoice organization to sell T-shirts announcing, "I had an abortion" was in poor taste and diminished the seriousness of the act of abortion.

A second step might include care not to confuse legal arguments with moral messages. Too often the legal arguments that win in a court of law are the very arguments that lose in the court of public opinion. Antiabortion legislators have played on this tendency by introducing legislation that appears unrelated to abortion, but "protects" the fetus. The most emotionally charged legislation was the Unborn Victims of Violence Act, which introduced an extra penalty for anyone convicted of harming a fetus during the commission of certain federal crimes (separate from penalties related to the injury or death of the pregnant woman). It gave separate legal status to a fertilized egg, embryo, or fetus even if the woman did not know she was pregnant. Crafted in the wake of the death of Laci and Conner Peterson, the legislation captured people's sympathy. Prochoice responses that focused on the fact that the legislation was not needed or that argued that it was a back door attempt to eviscerate the right to abortion made us seem heartless. As difficult as it may be, this may have been one piece of legislation we could have tolerated. In the war of ideas, not every hill is worth climbing.

Up to now, the conventional wisdom in the prochoice movement has been that talking about fetal life is counterproductive. In the polarized climate created by absolutists opposed to legal abortion, a siege mentality has developed. Prochoice advocates fear that any discussion of fetal value will strengthen the claim that if the fetus has value, abortion must be prohibited in all or most circumstances.

An interesting example of the way in which some opponents of legal abortion are taking a different approach (which may make prochoice people more comfortable talking about this question) is the current debate in Great Britain about reducing the time limit for abortion from 24 weeks to 20. The impetus for this comes from a minority view on the prochoice side, including Sir David Steel, who introduced prochoice legislation in the parliament in 1966. Some in the prolife movement think that the best thing they can do is to sit it out, suggesting that the bishops should not intervene and that the more absolutist antiabortion groups should permit this conversation to go on among prochoice people. Perhaps, they speculate, if not threatened by the notion that any restrictive change in abortion laws is part of an antichoice campaign to make all abortions illegal, some moderate change might happen. In citing this example, I am not suggesting that it would be a good thing to reduce the time limit on abortions in Britain, nor do I want to overstate the extent of a prochoice discussion on the matter. Within the organized British prochoice movement, there is little if any support for such a move and much distress that some who are prochoice would even consider it. But it does represent an attempt by some who are prochoice to address new information about potential fetal capacity that does not automatically reject thinking about these issues as "antiabortion propaganda."

In addition to the fear that acknowledging fetal life as valuable would lead to making abortion illegal is the reality that the ethical discussion about when the fetus becomes a person (whether theological, legal, sociological, or medical) seems abstract to most people. In theology, the question has traditionally focused on when is it most likely that God gives the developing fetus a soul, a discourse pretty much abandoned by both traditional and innovative theologians; in sociology, most often the capacity for relationships is central—when can one say a meaningful relationship exists between the fetus and society; in medicine, the weight is on viability and on the physical and mental capacity of the fetus—when could it survive outside the womb, when is there higher brain development. Fascinating speculation, but similar to arguments over the number of angels that could dance on a pinhead. The precise moment when the fetus becomes a person is less important than a simple acknowledgement that whatever category of human life the fetus is, it nonetheless has value; it is not nothing.

In this context the various *ad hoc* remarks of Senator John Kerry are interesting, if flawed. Kerry has said that he "opposes abortion, personally. I don't like abortion. I believe life does begin at conception." When later pressed on this he said, "Within weeks, you look and see the development of it, but that's not a person yet, and it's certainly not what somebody, in my judgment, ought to have the government of the United States intervening in." Kerry's statements reflect what most people think. Personhood is a code word for extent of value, not a fine scientific fact. What those who favor abortion rights are saying is that whatever value fetal life has—from none to much—it is not the moral equivalent of those of us who have been born. In fact, prochoicers argue, there are a number of values greater than the fetus that justify answering the "Who Decides?" question strongly in favor of the woman.

However, once one moves away from the narrow question of when the fetus becomes a person to the more meaningful question of what value does the fetus have and when that value emerges, it becomes difficult to develop an ethical formula for assigning value and asserting the obligations that flow from that value. There is a wide range of respectable opinion on these questions and few hard and fast conclusions.

AN URGENT TASK

But the need to offer some answers from a prochoice perspective is both morally and politically urgent. Those opposed to abortion have moved aggressively for laws that depend on the recognition of the fetus as a person, as a rights-bearing entity. At the same time, there are scientific advances that affect the way we think about the fetus and, indeed, make it more present among us. For some, these realities lead to a greater connection to fetal life; perhaps not as a person, but as part of the continuum of what we are, of humanity. Examples include 3-D and 4-D pictures of fetuses in utero that appear to be awake, asleep, walking, yawning—engaging in activities that are related to human identity—and the few, very few, very premature babies who struggle and appear to have a great determination to live. Even the reality that pre-embryos used to create stem cells that may ultimately save the lives of thousands makes the embryo more human and more valuable—it can give, as well as receive, even at a stage of development that bears little resemblance to even fetal life. Of course, there is an element of my ode to the embryo that is poetic and romantic, even anthropomorphic, as the embryo does not consciously "give." It is instead useful, but nonetheless that usefulness is a positive quality that should not be feared, but appreciated.

The fetus is, indeed, a wondrous part of our humanity. We are drawn to it as part of the ongoing mystery of who we are. Do we not question our own value, why we are here, what we contribute, and what we take from the world? There is, of course, a danger in over-romanticizing fetal life or in defining its value primarily in relation to ourselves. For an infertile couple who deeply want a child, someone else's fetus is very precious and potentially their child. For a woman who has been raped, that fetus may well be seen as a monster. The relation of value to wantedness is complex and at times troubling. Antiabortionists have countered the "Every child a wanted child" message by pointing out that if wantedness is what gives us value and a right to life, then who among the unwanted will be the next to be declared disposable—the sick, the disabled, the poor or the unemployed?

TOO HARD?

Such concerns should not be quickly dismissed. I am deeply struck by the number of thoughtful, progressive people who have been turned off to the pro-choice movement by the lack of adequate and clear expressions of respect for fetal life, people who are themselves grappling with the conflict between upholding women's rights and the right to conscience and respecting the value of nascent human life. A recent article by John Garvey in *Commonweal* put it well. Struggling with his inability to cast a vote for George Bush for all the usual liberal reasons and his distaste for what he saw as Kerry's—and by extension the prochoice movement's—inability to acknowledge one iota of value in fetal life, he said: "Our attitude toward life at this stage has much to say about what we believe about humanity as a whole: this is where we all come from, and at no point does it mean nothing." Garvey suggests that perhaps there has been a "hardening of the heart" resulting from the prochoice position.

The John Garveys of the world have a point. They are not the enemies of choice. They occupy the middle ground that we seek to convince that being prochoice is morally sound, and they sometimes express the wisdom that flows from those who can see different sides in a moral dilemma.

Garvey's comments are suggestive of the last of the three values I believe must be included in an ethical prochoice perspective: avoiding a coarsening of humanity that can result from the taking of life. Prochoice advocates may bristle at such a claim. We see ourselves as deeply compassionate and good people who are working hard to alleviate women's pain and to create a world in which children are wanted and loved. How could anyone suggest that our sensibilities could become coarsened by exposure to the taking of fetal life that is currently a necessary component of abortion?

And, while little research has been done on this question, it and history point to no coarsening of respect for persons as a result of legal abortion. Those countries with long-standing liberal abortion laws have been among the most supportive of life. Japan, for example, widely uses abortion as a method of birth control. Yet the respect the Japanese show for the elderly is great and their love of children renowned. While abortion is common in Japan, there are rituals of respect for both aborted and miscarried fetuses that express value. The Scandinavian countries have liberal abortion laws and some of the most people-friendly social policies in the world. There is more evidence that denying women the right to choose abortion leads to a coarsening of attitudes toward children than permitting it does. In Ceacesceau's Romania, abortion was strictly forbidden and women's pregnancies monitored closely to prevent abortion. The resulting massive abandonment of children is well known. Likewise, studies of what happens to children born after their mothers were denied abortion in the former Czechoslovakia and several Scandinavian countries show that these children have a significantly higher rate of crime, mental illness, and problems in school.[2]

For me, a more troubling question is whether or not regular exposure to the taking of life in abortion or the defense of a right to choose abortion would, if not addressed, lead to a coarsening of attitude toward fetal life. The inability of prochoice leaders to give any specific examples of ways in which respect for fetal life can be demonstrated or to express any doubt about any aspect of abortion suggests that such a hardening of the heart is possible. This concern or possibility does not lead me to say that abortion should become illegal, more restricted, or more stigmatized. It does lead me to believe that we would do well as prochoice people to present abortion as a complex issue that involves loss—and to be saddened by that loss at the same time as we affirm and support women's decisions to end pregnancies. Is there not a way to simply say, "Yes, it is sad, unfortunate, tragic (or whatever word you are comfortable with) that this life could not come to fruition. It is sad that we live in a world where there is so little social and economic support for families that many women have no choice but to end pregnancies. It is sad that so many women do not have access to contraception. It is sad that this fetus was not healthy enough to survive, and it was good that this woman had the right to make this choice for herself and her family, to avoid suffering, and to act on her values and her sense of what her life should be."

Are there not ways to affirm and protect the right to choose abortion while actively promoting policies which would actually enhance reflection and good decision making and supporting voluntary mechanisms for nonjudgmental reflection and alternatives to abortion? For example, should we not combine our support for the right of adolescent girls to decide to have an abortion with greater efforts to involve their parents, including seeking funding for counseling for teens facing the abortion decision and their parents as an alternative to mandatory parental consent and notification laws? Surely we agree that young women aged 13, 14, 15, and even older need their parents at this time? And, surely, our response to date, which implies that only teens who are at risk from their parents choose not to tell them, rings hollow in the ears of most parents who know that their kids are loath to tell them where they are going on Saturday afternoon, let alone that they are pregnant? The youngest of teens should not have to face an abortion or any medical procedure alone. This is not just about rights; it is a matter of health, safety and compassion.

RESPONDING TO ANTICHOICE LEGISLATION

There are many examples of ways in which those of us who are prochoice could have better responded to unreasonable legislative initiatives by those who are antiabortion, but two are at the top of my list: how we dealt with legislation regarding so-called "partial-birth" abortion and how we should deal with upcoming legislation on the provision of fetal anesthesia in abortions after 20 weeks' gestation.

It has long been a strategy of those opposed to legal abortion to concentrate on second- and third-trimester abortions, in spite of the fact that few abortions occur in the third trimester and a very small number in the second trimester. According to the latest figures available, 88 percent of abortions are performed in the first trimester (up to 12 weeks), just over 10 percent are performed between 13 and 20 weeks, two percent after 20 weeks and only 0.08% in the third trimester (after 24 weeks). Among those who do not believe that fetuses are persons from the moment of conception (and the "moment" of conception is a dubious concept), there is a commonsense insight that fetal life gains in value as it develops capacity and physical structure and the ability to survive outside a woman's body. There is a sense that more significant moral justification is necessary for abortions later in pregnancy at the same time as one might hold that those justifications need not be subject to law.

If only, antiabortion leaders say, people knew what happens in an abortion they would turn against abortion with revulsion. Thus, some 10 years ago, legislation was introduced to ban a procedure known medically as intact dilation and extraction, except in cases where the woman's life was at risk. It is not easy to isolate this procedure from a continuum of abortion techniques used after about 15 weeks of pregnancy, and the legislation fails to do so, creating a serious obstacle to its implementation. Nonetheless, all methods of abortion along this continuum are grim, as frankly are all late-term abortion procedures. There is nothing aesthetically attractive about the abortion of fully formed, relatively well-developed fetuses, and there is equally nothing simple and painless about the situations women face that lead them to seek abortions later in gestation.

There is much blame to be placed at the door of antiabortionists who sought this legislation. In fact, they showed little interest in crafting a bill that would be constitutionally accepted and thus save fetal life. Instead they opted to use the bill as an educational tool—a crass attempt to bombard society with gruesome visual images. The legislation was also dishonest. It tried to use a method of abortion as a surrogate for a desire to ban ultimately all abortions and immediately all post-first trimester abortions. Moreover, had it contained an exception allowing the continuum of procedures to be performed if a woman's health was at risk, it might even have passed constitutional muster and effectively, if tragically, banned many medically indicated abortions, particularly those performed primarily due to serious damage to fetuses that made it likely or certain that they would not survive birth or a short painful life.

Responding to such traps is not easy for those who are prochoice, but our movement, as is often the case, did an excellent job in the courts pointing out the legal and constitutional flaws of the legislation. We failed miserably, however, to touch on the broader unrest about abortion itself that the procedure raised in the minds of many. The movement, some felt, has gone too far when it defends such gruesome procedures. I am convinced that the negative reaction, for example, of some Catholic leaders to Senator Kerry's candidacy to the presidency was based on his opposition to banning this procedure. In the absence of any other way for prochoice legislators to express a concern about abortion, this bill and others like it became the only way people might have come to believe that prochoice does not mean proabortion. It is as if we demand that our political supporters mask moral concern and merely uphold legal rights because we fear that the expression of any sadness for the loss of fetal life that is part of abortion will be interpreted as weakness. I believe that the exact opposite is true. The prochoice movement will be far more trusted if it openly acknowledges that the abortion decision involves weighing multiple values and that one of those values is fetal life. These acknowledgements must be made at the same time and with the same vigor that bad legislation is criticized and fought.

In the world in which I move, people who support legal abortion do not believe that discussing the morality of abortion is an act of treachery. They do not believe that to suggest that some abortions may happen for less than admirable reasons and to question some behaviors that lead to abortions is antiwoman or antiabortion. In this world people are waiting for some sign that prochoice advocates are not proabortion and are sensitive to the values that are in conflict when abortion is considered or performed. And the lack of concern for fetal life and the gruesome nature of late term abortion procedures in our response to the "partial-birth" abortion debate has pushed some potential supporters over the edge. Is there nothing, they ask, that concerns prochoice people about abortion?

The intact dilation and extraction debate has about run its course. Prochoice forces have won the legal argument again and again, as we should. The most recent attempt at legislation will most likely be ruled unconstitutional. But the question remains whether we emerge from that debate having won any hearts and minds. Who looks extreme in the strategic tug of war between prochoice and antiabortion forces—in which characterizing the other side as extremists is a key, if less than admirable goal?

A NEW FRONTIER

A new opportunity is emerging. Legislation has been introduced by the most extreme antichoice members of Congress to require doctors to inform women seeking abortions after 20 weeks that the fetus may feel pain and offering fetal anesthesia. The bill includes a mandated script that doctors must read to women seeking abortions and specific written consent forms they must sign. The wording of the script doctors are required to use is cruel. It is not completely accurate, is highly judgmental, and completely negates the basic principles of good patient care, in which a health professional needs the freedom to decide how best to convey important information to patients. However much compassion its sponsors believe they are expressing for the fetus, they are totally insensitive to how to care for women at a very difficult moment.

More important than this specific bill is the underlying issue of whether or not fetuses feel pain during abortion and what that possibility requires of us. Should our approach to the bill be an immediate assumption that it must be defeated or a reflection on what is the right thing to do if there is a possibility that the fetus feels pain? Since the subject of fetal pain has been written about in medical journals for some time, should the prochoice movement have considered this matter before the bill was introduced? Such a review of the science might have suggested a standard of care that would have made legislation moot. Those in the community involved in providing abortion services would have weighed the evidence in consultation with ethicists, fetal surgeons, anesthesiologists, gynecologists, and women. If there were reliable evidence suggesting the possibility that fetuses might feel pain, a protocol would have been developed. Standard medical practice for abortion at that stage of pregnancy when fetal pain was a possibility would subsequently include either routine use of fetal anesthesia or the offer of anesthesia when requested by the woman, following sensitive and careful counseling about the possibility that the fetus might feel pain.

The optional route would be preferred if there was any indication that fetal anesthesia posed a significant risk to the woman. At present, there is little information about what additional risks such anesthesia might present to the pregnant woman. Concerns that the additional cost of anesthesia would raise the cost of abortion beyond the means of some women, while serious, would be seen as a problem to be solved. Treating the fetus humanely during the termination of its life would be seen as an important human value—more important than the extra cost factor. One might even go so far as to seek prochoice legislation that would offer reimbursement for anesthesia costs, possible through CHIP (the federal Children's Health Insurance Program) that since 2002 has covered fetal health. If such protocols were established by groups like Planned Parenthood and the National Abortion Federation, as well as the American College of Obstetricians and Gynecologists, the need for federal or state legislation mandating such services would be largely eliminated, and if antiabortionists proceeded, it would be enormously positive for the prochoice community to be able to say that we have thought about and solved this problem ourselves in conformity with the highest medical and ethical standards.

Should the fetal pain legislation move forward, as appears to be the case, what would a response look like that combined respect for a woman's right to choose, a compassionate and respectful attitude toward fetal life, and a desire to ensure that our society does not approach life callously? What message would we want to send to the public?

First, this is one more opportunity to assure the public that we do value fetal life. We are concerned about the possibility that fetuses may feel pain and are committed to ensuring that abortion services are delivered in a way that respects a woman's right to choose and provides her with all available information about the abortion procedure and its risks. To the extent possible, abortion should be a humane and compassionate procedure and although it involves the termination of fetal life, we approach that termination with respect and compassion. Thus, we would recommend that those who provide abortion provide the option of fetal anesthesia.

After clearly establishing that value, we could and should address the legislation itself. While the desire to ensure that no unnecessary suffering is experienced by women or fetuses in abortion is a noble one, this specific piece of legislation is insensitive to women's health and well being. The extent of intervention into the private relationships between doctor and patient exceeds the boundaries of medical ethics. Further, legislation in this area is unnecessary given the commitment of the profession and advocates to anesthesia. If the proposed legislation is to go forward, it needs serious amendment.

At present we do not know whether the fetus experiences pain, and there are even differences of opinion about the definition of pain. Funding for further objective scientific research that could answer these questions should be provided to the National Institutes for Health.

While the science at this stage is inconclusive, there are scientists who consider fetal pain possible who are reputable and not motivated by politics. A law that would mandate that anesthesia be made available on an optional basis should thus focus on the principal barrier to its provision, cost. The bill must allocate funds to cover the costs of the additional personnel, equipment, and medical supplies needed to provide this service. Beyond requiring that women be informed of the availability of anesthesia and give informed consent for its use, no specific wording should be mandated either verbally or in writing. Doctors should be allowed to exercise their judgment regarding what words best express the medical facts and how that information is best conveyed to women at a difficult time. Compassion for women is as important as compassion for fetuses. The title and language of the bill should be non-polemical and avoid loaded terminology. While there is a reasonable argument to be made that medical practice should not be the subject of legislation, this argument has limits. It is also true that health is an appropriate matter of legislation and as long as medical privacy and the right of doctors to make medical decisions in the interests of their patients is preserved, we want laws that protect public health. Medical practice is complex and best regulated by professional associations and accrediting agencies, but it is not completely beyond the scope of law.

Such an approach and message would signal a new era in prochoice advocacy—one that combines a commitment to laws that affirm and enhance the right of each woman to decide whether to have an abortion or bear and raise a child, with an expressed commitment to human values that include respect for life, recognition of fetal life as valuable, and a concern for fostering a society in which all life is valued.

HONORING LAW AND MORALITY

It has long been a truism of the abortion debate that those who are prochoice have rights and those who are against legal abortion have morality; that those who support abortion rights concentrate on women and those opposed focus on the fetus. After 30 years of legal abortion and a debate that shows no signs of ending and has no clear winner—is it not time to try and combine rights and morality, to consider both women and developing human life? Ultimately, abortion is not a political question, and politics will not end the enormous conflict over abortion. Abortion is a profoundly moral question, and any movement that fails to grapple with and respect all the values at stake in crafting a social policy about abortion will be inadequate in its effort to win the support of the majority of Americans.

NOTES

1. A word about terminology. Any thoughtful article on abortion runs afoul of what to call opponents and proponents of legal abortion. Generally I try to use the more specific terms "those who support" or "those who oppose" legal abortion. Occasionally it seems fair to describe some groups and individuals as prolife if their position is broader and includes opposition to war and capital punishment, as well as supporting social and political measures that enable people to lead healthy and productive lives. At the same time, I am convinced that few opponents of legal abortion are truly motivated by a deep respect for fetal life. If they were, they would, as Randall Terry, the founder of Operation Rescue said many years ago, "Act as if abortion were murder." The example of the Catholic bishops is most illuminating. I would expect that if bishops really believed that abortion was murder, they would individually and collectively make far more sacrifices

to ensure that abortions did not happen. While the bishops provide very little detailed information about their expenditures, it is clear that the amount of money spent on preventing abortions is very little. The bishops claim that abortion is the greatest moral issue of our time, that Catholics cannot vote for candidates who are prochoice, and that prochoice Catholic legislators are committing a grave sin by supporting legal abortion. This is a weak rhetorical response to "murder." How can any bishop or parish priest justify spending one penny on anything discretionary rather than on helping the many women who would continue their pregnancies if they had the resources to bear and raise a child? No dinners, no business class plane tickets, no vacations, no flowers on the altar as long as one penny is needed to prevent abortions. The same standard should be applied to the lay Catholics speaking out against abortion. Few of them are doing anything other than attacking prochoice Catholic politicians and supporting the Republican Party. Nothing short of austerity and sacrifice is called for if you believe that abortion is the greatest evil facing humanity.

2. See, for example, Henry P. David et al., eds., *Born Unwanted: Developmental Effects of Denied Abortion* (Springer Publishing Company, 1988).

PART 6

Marriage Equality: A Test Case for the Church

Kelly Brown Douglas
Daniel C. Maguire
Marvin M. Ellison
Dale B. Martin

Introduction
to Part 6

The first edition of this book concluded with a section titled "Sexual Orientation: A Test Case for the Church." In their introductory comments, editors James B. Nelson and Sandra P. Longfellow wrote: "Not since the slavery debates of the mid-nineteenth century has the church been engaged by such a troublesome, heated, and divisive ecclesiastical issue as sexual orientation. Homosexuality is *the* scare issue in the churches."[1]

Today there is greater awareness that the landscape of human sexualities is "unsettled and unsettling terrain" and much more diverse, fluid, and difficult to navigate than perhaps first imagined. Language about sexuality has changed insofar as the "T" (transsexuality) and the "I" (intersexuality) have been added to the "G" (gay) and the "L" (lesbian) to denote more varieties of human identity alongside heterosexuality. Others add "Q" (queer and/or questioning), "A" (asexual and/or allies), and other letters out of appreciation for the complexity of human sexualities and the importance of self-naming, as noted in Part 3.

In addition to the effort to push beyond the hetero-homo binary, another change since the first edition of this book has been the steady movement within various religious traditions to incorporate LGBTQ persons as full members with equal rights and responsibilities, including authorization for spiritual leadership. A Welcoming Church movement has gained momentum in many Protestant denominations, within some Jewish traditions, and among progressive Catholics as well as Unitarian Universalists.[2] Therefore, the test case pressed upon the church is no longer the inclusion of nonheterosexual persons ("Let us in"), even though that battle is still being waged. The cutting edge of the debate has shifted to the critique and reconstruction of religious assumptions, norms, and symbols (reordering "the rules of the game") that have naturalized compulsory heterosexuality (the assertion that everyone is and should be heterosexual) and legitimated heteronormativity (the presumption that heterosexuality is the exclusive norm for human life and loving). Moving beyond heterosexism requires, first, embracing the rich diversity of human sexualities as morally good ways to be human and, second, refocusing ethical attention on conduct (how one acts in relation to self and others) rather than on identity or status.

In light of these shifts, the emerging test case for the church has become marriage equality. Is same-sex love morally equivalent to different-sex love? Should same-sex couples be free to marry, both civilly and religiously? What is the role of the state and the church in promoting family values, especially if some families are gay and lesbian?

Already considerable evidence is available to show that a societal, as well as ecclesiastical, debate about marriage and marriage equality is heating up. By August of 2009, thirty-one states had enacted restrictive laws and ten states had passed constitutional bans to prohibit marriage between two men or two women. At the same time, five states had granted gays and lesbians the freedom to enter into civil marriage: Connecticut, Iowa, Massachusetts, New Hampshire, and Vermont. Other states recognized domestic partnerships and civil unions as marriage-like arrangements.[3]

Another clue is to follow the money. During the 2008 election season, proponents and opponents of California's Proposition 8 spent in excess of $75 million in order to secure or deny the right to marry for same-sex couples, which the California Supreme Court had authorized in May of that year. The measure narrowly passed, thereby preventing civil marriages in the future for same-sex couples in that state, but the California court also later upheld the marriages of the 18,000 same-sex couples who were legally married between May 15 and November 4, 2008.

Yet another indicator that a contentious debate is underway is the clash of diverse, even irreconcilable viewpoints. Marriage traditionalists regard marriage as an exclusively heterosexual institution and fear that any redefinition will undermine the meaning and integrity of the institution. In contrast, marriage advocates, including gay social critic Andrew Sullivan, argue that "including homosexuals within marriage, after all, would be a means of conferring the highest form of social approval imaginable."[4] Moreover, Sullivan proposes, "Gay marriage is not a radical step; it is a profoundly humanizing, traditionalizing step."[5] A third voice in the marriage debate is that of marriage critics. Gay social historian John D'Emilio, in an article titled "The Marriage Fight Is Setting Us Back," argues that "the campaign for same-sex marriage has been an unmitigated disaster. "As a movement," D'Emilio writes, "haven't we been pushing to further de-center and de-institutionalize marriage? Once upon a time we did."[6]

Our purpose in Part 6, as it was in the first edition, is not to settle this issue, but more modestly "to focus on the issues and assumptions that *underlie* much of the current debate."[7] We begin with Kelly Douglas's essay "Contested

Marriage/Loving Relationality," in which she analyzes how the debate about same-sex marriage may be illumined by examining the contested unions of black men and women within U.S. history. Chattel slavery refused to acknowledge that black people share the human capacity to love and sustain intimate associations and, accordingly, denied them the freedom to marry. Enslaved blacks resisted their oppression by continuing to form loving intimate relationships and even entering into marriages, which for the most part were illicit. In light of the courage of an oppressed people to love against the odds, Douglas writes: "Just as enslaved marriages were a contested reality within a white racist society defined by a slavocracy, so too are same-sex unions a contested reality in a heterosexist society defined by white hetero-patriarchy." Her conclusion is provocative: "The church must come to the theological place of realizing that there may be same-sex unions that are more deserving of sacred affirmation than certain female-male unions. However, in order for the church to achieve this level of theological clarity, it must first acknowledge the inherent theological problem of its prevalent view toward sexuality."

Daniel Maguire takes up the challenge by providing "A Catholic Defense of Same-Sex Marriage." The desire for loving relationality is not an exclusively heterosexual desire, but rather a human desire that same-gender loving persons share. As Maguire argues, "The desire to bond lovingly and sexually with persons of the same sex or of the opposite sex is a fact of life, a fact of God's creation, and we have no right to call it unholy. . . . To do so, in fact, is a sin." At the same time, Maguire is aware that some might grant the possibility of same-sex unions, but not recognize them as "really marriage," so he offers this revised theological definition of marriage: "the unique and special form of committed friendship between sexually attracted persons." Because he is persuaded that both same-sex couples, no less than different-sex couples, can meet these requirements, he concludes that "we have no right to say that marriage, with all of its advantages and beauty, is a reward for being heterosexual."

Marvin Ellison's "Marriage in a New Key" begins by noting that "no monolithic or fixed Christian tradition exists." Instead, there is a plurality of dynamic, often conflicting Christianities that are deeply divided over sexuality, economics, and other concerns. To illustrate the split over sexuality and sexual justice within Christianity (and other religions), often characterized in terms of a traditionalist-progressive dichotomy, his essay contrasts the divergent stances of the conservative Southern Baptist Convention and the liberal United Church of Christ with respect to same-sex marriage. Traditionalists, he argues, are not seeking to preserve marriage, but rather a certain (patriarchal) model of marriage and, by extension, other social relations structured on the basis of presumed natural hierarchies of power and control (male over female, white over nonwhite, rich over poor, native-born over immigrant, and Christian over non-Christian). In contrast, the United Church of Christ in 2005 became the first mainline Christian denomination to give official support for same-sex marriage. For this liberal church movement, marriage equality signals two things: equality for the partners *within* marriage and equal access *to* marriage by same-sex couples. The change agenda for a truly progressive Christianity, he suggests, is to educate and equip persons as advocates for a comprehensive social justice that includes sexual and gender justice as indispensable components.

New Testament scholar Dale Martin provides the concluding essay in this section and challenges both proponents and opponents of same-sex marriage to exercise caution when claiming that the Bible, especially the New Testament, and Christian tradition support marriage and family values. "Contrary to most contemporary opinion," Martin argues, "there are many more resources in Christian Scripture and tradition to *criticize* the modern family than to promote it." In reviewing the Gospels, the Pauline and pseudo-Pauline Letters, early church theologians including Jerome and Augustine, and the Puritan Revolution, he reaches this conclusion: "Though the Christianity of the vast sweep of history from the church fathers until the Reformation did not go so far as to condemn marriage outright, it consistently assigned an inferior position to marriage and to those Christians who married. The 'higher calling' was most often understood to be avoidance of marriage, certainly in much of the New Testament and for almost all of late ancient Christianity." Ironically, North American Christianity, especially evangelical Protestantism, has "reversed the traditional valuations of Christianity" when it comes to sex, marriage, and family. Martin thus argues, "When modern gay and lesbian Christians urge the recognition of same-sex marriages in churches, they are actually asking for a change much less radical than that already accomplished by the Reformers and the Puritans, who completely reversed doctrines and ethics of 1,500 years of Christian tradition and made the married state not only equal to singleness but superior to it."

As Martin and the other authors in this section attest, the test case of marriage equality is an opportunity to reflect, once again, on the sources, norms, and authority for Christian theology and ethics and, most important, consider what the demands of justice-love require. As Nelson and Longfellow put the matter in this book's first edition, by wrestling deeply with this issue, "the church might gain more theological faithfulness and ethical integrity in other issues as well."[8]

NOTES

1. James B. Nelson and Sandra P. Longfellow, "Introduction to Part 5," in *Sexuality and the Sacred: Sources for Theological Reflection*, ed. James B. Nelson and Sandra P. Longfellow (Louisville, KY: Westminster/John Knox Press, 1994), 357.

2. See the Religious Institute for Sexual Morality, Justice, and Healing and its Open Letter to Religious Leaders on Sexual and Gender Diversity at its Web site, www.religiousinstitute.org.

3. For a national map and more discussion of state laws about same-sex relationships, see the Web site of the National Gay and Lesbian Task Force at www.thetaskforce.org.

4. Andrew Sullivan, *Virtually Normal: An Argument about Homosexuality* (New York: Vintage Books, 1996), xx.

5. Ibid., 185.

6. John D'Emilio, "The Marriage Fight Is Setting Us Back," *The Gay and Lesbian Review* (November–December 2006).

7. Nelson and Longfellow, "Introduction to Part 5," 357.

8. Ibid., 360.

26

Contested Marriage/ Loving Rationality

KELLY BROWN DOUGLAS

"Why does the slave ever love?"[1] This was the question asked by Linda Brent almost one hundred fifty years ago. Miss Brent was a young black woman, perhaps not yet twenty, when she fell in love for the first time. The gentleman that she loved "with all the ardor of a young girl's first love"[2] was a young carpenter from the neighborhood whom she had known since childhood. Eventually, a childhood friendship grew into a mutual attraction that led to the young man proposing marriage to Miss Brent. This proposal, however, did not bring joy. Instead, it caused much consternation. Miss Brent recalled, "But when I reflected that I was a slave, and that the laws gave no sanction to the marriage of such, my heart sank within me."[3] Linda Brent was well aware that not only would the authority of the laws prevent her from marrying, but so too would the authority of her master. She, like most enslaved persons in antebellum America, needed her master's permission to form any type of marriage union, regardless of whether or not that union would be accepted as valid within the laws of the state. Brent knew, however, that her master would not permit the one who was his property, and for whom he lusted, to marry. And so it was that Linda Brent's "love-dream" ended with a proposal.

The fate of Linda Brent's "love-dream" was, in some respects, typical for those black men and women who were deemed the legal property of another. For various reasons, marriage was not a viable option for the black enslaved. As "chattel" they had no rights as human beings, of which marriage was one. In addition, many slaveholders viewed marriage as a threat to the slavocracy's re-productivity. It was thought to interfere with the enslaved's ability to be good breeders. Moreover, the idea of enslaved marriages certainly ran counter to the white supremacist ideology that undergirded the slavocracy. This racist ideology projected black women and men as hypersexualized beasts controlled by lust (i.e., the sexual urgings of their genitalia) and thus, with no capacity to engage in loving (i.e., reasoned), intimate relationships. The sentiments of the "Father of Democracy" and slaveholder, Thomas Jefferson, well reflect the judgments of white supremacy in regard to black women and men. Jefferson wrote:

> [Black men] are more ardent after their females; but love seems with them to be more an eager desire, than a tender delicate mixture of sentiment and sensation. . . . In general their existence appears to participate more of sensation than reflection.[4]

In general, marriage was a contested reality for enslaved men and women within antebellum America. It was simply not a right granted to a brutally marginalized, hypersexualized people. It is in this regard that Linda Brent's story of love is typical.

Yet, in other respects Miss Brent's story is atypical. Linda Brent gave up on her dream of sharing any form of married life with the man she loved. She thus ended the relationship, ostensibly to protect him as well as herself from her master's vile wrath. Many other black women and men, however, defied the fact of their contested marriages and married anyway. They contrived ceremonies to honor the sacred validity of their loving relationships. Some ceremonies were as simple as jumping over a broom. One enslaved black man, Joe Rawls, remembers enslaved weddings this way:

> Well, dey jis' lay de broom down, 'n' dem what's gwine ter git marry' walks out 'n' stest ober dat broom bofe togedder, 'n' de ole mass, he say, "I now pronounce you man n'n' wife'," 'n' den dey was marry'. Dat was all dey was t' it—no ce'mony, no license, no nothin', jis' marryin'.[5]

Other ceremonies were more elaborate, performed by black or white preachers of their master's choosing, and followed by a banquet given by the master and mistress. One enslaved black woman, Tempie Durham, described her wedding day this way:

> *When I growed up, I married Exter Durham. . . . We had a big weddin'. We was married on de front po'ch of de big house. Marse George killed a shoat, an' Mis' Betsy had Geogianna, de cook, to bake a big weddin' cake, all iced up white as snow wid a bride an' groom standin' in de middle holdin' han's. De table was set out in de yard under de trees, an' you ain't never seed de like of eats. . . . Dat was some weddin'. I had on a white dress, white shoes, an' long white gloves dat come to my elbows, an' Mis' Betsy done made me a weddin' veil out of a white net window curtain. When she played de weddin' ma'ch on de piano, me an' Exter ma'ched down de walk an' up on de po'ch to de alter Mis' Betsy doen fixed.*
>
> *Uncle Edmond Kirby married us. He was de [black] preacher dat preached at de plantation church. . . . Marse George got to have his little fun. He say, "Come on Exter, you an' Tempie got to jump over de broomstick backwards. You got to do dat to see which one gwine be boss of your househol'. . . . Marse George*

hold de broom 'bout a foot high off de floor. De one dat jump over it backwards an' never touch de handle gwine boss de house, an' if bofe of dem jump over without touchin' it, dey ain't gwine be no bossin dey just' gwine be' genial.[6]

Even if, as seen in the testimony above, the master did permit his chattel to marry, such permission did not imply that the master respected the marriage union. The exigencies of the slavocracy prevailed over the commitment of marriage. In other words, the married couple still remained chattel. Thus, the master retained the right, and usually exercised it, to use the husband and wife as breeders, or to sell them away from one another. But again, despite the contempt shown for their marriages, enslaved black women and men continued to marry. For them, the marriage ceremony—whatever it may have been—was not about their master's approval or respect but rather the mutual affirmation of a loving, committed relationship. And most significantly, the sanctity of their relationship was far more significant than the legality of their union. Essentially, enslaved women and men were more concerned with divine approval of their loving relationships than with lawful recognition. To them their relationship was what mattered. It was the relationship which they struggled to maintain against all odds that was for them sacred in the eyes of God. This brings us to the focus of this essay.

The marriage unions between enslaved black women and men are not the focus of this discussion. Black enslaved marriages reflect a rich and complex social/cultural/historical reality that demands more thorough attention than can be given in this short essay. However, these marriages, in light of their contested state, do provide insight for the topic at hand: how the church should respond—liturgically or otherwise—to same-sex unions.[7] Just as enslaved marriages were a contested reality within a white racist society defined by a slavocracy, so too are same-sex unions a contested reality in a heterosexist society defined by white hetero-patriarchy. The question becomes, what role, if any, should churches play in recognizing same-sex unions? It is in answering this question that the reality of enslaved marriages becomes helpful. Before going further, however, it is necessary to clarify the limits of this discussion.

In this essay I do not pretend to provide a definitive answer to the question of same-sex unions/marriages. This piece rather reflects my preliminary thoughts as I move toward a fuller understanding of the role and responsibility of the church in admitting or acknowledging these same-sex "marriages." This essay thus serves as a prolegomenon for further theological reflection on this issue. With that said, let us now explore what it is that enslaved marriages suggest to us as we reflect on the church and same-sex marriages.

THE IMAGO DEI: LOVING RELATIONALITY

Black people's tenacity to be "married" despite the obstacles imposed by the rule of slavery, witnessed not primarily to their need to conform to white cultural/social conventions, but rather to their desire to affirm before God and community the sanctity of intimate relationship. At stake for the enslaved, as earlier mentioned, was not so much the propriety of their marriages, as the sacredness of their intimate relationships. It is in this regard, that enslaved marriage suggests the theological foundation for discerning the church's response to same-sex marriages—*loving relationality.*

Any appreciation for what it means for human beings to be created in the image of God and thereby to reflect that image must begin with the imperative to engage in loving relationality with one another. The Genesis creation narrative puts it thus: "So God created humankind in [God's] image, in the image of God [God] created them; male and female [God] created them" (Genesis 1:27).[8] What is made clear in this creation account is that human beings are not meant to live in solitary existence, but to live relationally. In this regard, the emphasis is not on the biological creation of male and female but on the existential creation of human relationship. Essentially, made clear in the creation of male and female is that the fullness of one's humanity is to be found in relationship. The model for this relationship is God's very Self as attested to by the claim that humans are *imago Dei.* Thus, human relationships are to reflect a God who is *trinitas.*

Despite the patriarchally sexist manner in which the Trinitarian doctrine has been traditionally expressed (Father, Son, and Holy Spirit), this doctrine avows a God who is internally and eternally relational. God in God-Self, the Godhead, is in a relationship of mutuality and reciprocity as redeemer, creator, and sustainer. Again, the affirmation that human beings are *imago Dei* is a call for men and women to reflect in their lives God's internal/eternal life of Trinitarian relationality. For Christians, the most complete expression of such a life is Jesus Christ. Jesus not only signifies God reaching out to humanity in loving relationship, but He also perfectly embodies what it means to reflect the image of God. As revealed in Jesus' compassionate solidarity with the poor, marginalized, and outcast in his own time, it means nothing less than enjoying loving relationality, that is, relationships of mutuality and reciprocity, with others.

The reality of enslaved "marriages" suggests the value that enslaved women and men placed upon intimate loving relationality. And in so doing, these marriages point toward the mandate inherent in human creation to live in loving relationality. This mandate has important implications for the church in relation to same-sex marriages. In order to appreciate these implications, however, we must also examine the matter of human sexuality. The contested marriages of the enslaved again provide us with insight.

HUMAN SEXUALITY

First, it is important to note the understanding of human sexuality that guides this discussion. Sexuality refers to that which makes human relationships possible. It is considered, as ethicist James Nelson says, "a sign, a symbol, and a means of [the human call] to communication and communion."[9] Sexuality thus allows human beings to enter into loving relationships. It drives human relationality. In this regard, sexuality is not primarily about gender, or genitalia; rather it is about that which propels human beings into relationship, especially intimate relationship. In essence, sexuality is the vehicle through which human beings are able to live out the meaning of being created in the image of God. Unfortunately, black sexuality has not always been regarded with such sacred respect.

Sexualized Humanity

As seen in Thomas Jefferson's comments [above], the sexuality of black men and women was impugned. As part of its dehumanizing efforts, white culture (that culture which protects and sustains white supremacist notions and practices such as slavery) has historically depicted black women and men as hypersexual, lustful, passionate beings governed by their genitalia. White cultural rhetoric projects black men as rapacious predators—"mandingo bucks"—and black women as promiscuous seductresses—"Jezebels." This sexualized caricature provided sufficient justification for the enslavement of black people. It also vindicated the inhumane demands of slavery, such as forced breeding. In effect, enslaved humanity was a sexualized humanity. This meant that who black men and women were as human beings was defined according to their sexuality. Concomitantly, their sexuality was itself essentialized according to genitalia. To repeat, they were regarded as hypersexualized beasts driven by lustful desires.

White cultural eroticization of black people attests to French philosopher Michel Foucault's apt analysis of the relationship between sexuality and power. "How is it that in a society like ours," Foucault asks, "sexuality is not simply a means of reproducing the species, the family, and the individual? Not simply a means to obtain pleasure and enjoyment?"[10] Foucault answers that this occurs because sexuality is integral to power. It is the axis where the human body and reproduction come together. Power is exerted over people through careful manipulation of their bodies, their perceptions of their bodies, and their reproductive capacities.

Foucault most significantly notes the role of sexuality in maintaining power, especially inequitable power. He argues that sexuality provides a method for making distinctions between classes and groups of people. To question or malign the sexuality of another invariably reinforces one's claim to superiority as it implies another group's inferiority. An attack upon a people's sexuality then provides for oppressive control, marginalization, and discrimination of that people. This is what occurred in relation to the black enslaved. Overall, white cultural sexualization of them allowed for their bodies to be exploited in ways that benefited the slavocracy at the same time that it provided ideological grounds for contesting their marriages. Essentially, enslaved men and women were objectified just as their sexuality was essentialized. They were viewed as either objects of lust or objects for breeding. They were not seen as contributors to loving relationality. This fact of enslaved existence is also suggestive of the church's response to same-sex marriage.

Unfortunately, an influential Christian tradition advances a view of sexuality that corresponds with oppressing power's manipulation of human sexuality and thereby allows for social and political, if not ecclesial, marginalization of various people. Let us now examine this tradition before finally offering theological reflections concerning the church and same-sex marriages.

Platonized Christianity

Shaped by the intellectual climate of the Greco-Roman world of which they were a part, early Christian thinkers and apologists integrated into their Christians theologies the accepted philosophies of contemporary Hellenistic culture. In so doing, they introduced into mainstream Christian thought platonic and stoic views toward the body and sexuality. The platonic belief in the perfect immaterial world (the world of reason/spirit/soul) and the imperfect material world (the world of passion/flesh/body) became a part of a significant strand of Christian thinking. The stoic regard for reason and disregard for passion was also integrated into Christianity. As this body-devaluing ideology was appropriated by influential Christian interpreters, platonized Christianity developed.[11]

Platonized Christianity invariably places the body in an antagonistic relationship with the soul. The soul is divinized while the body is demonized. The soul is revered as the key to salvation. The body is condemned as a source of sin. The locus of bodily sin is human passion, that is, sexual pleasure/lust. This "sacred" disdain for the sexual body pervades the Christian theological tradition, especially as it has given way to a definite sexual ethic. The Apostle Paul is perhaps the earliest representative of this body-denouncing tradition and corresponding sexual ethic.

Consumed with a belief in the imminent end of the world and informed by his platonized understanding of Christianity, Paul viewed sex as an impediment to salvation. He made clear that unrestrained sexual activity, that is sexual pleasure, was immoral and a sin against the very body. He encouraged faithful Christians to "flee from sexual immorality" while admonishing them that "he who sins sexually sins against his own body" (I Corinthians 6:18).[12] While he urged his followers to remain unmarried and celibate, he conceded that if they could not refrain from sexual activity they should marry, "for it is better to marry than to burn with passion" (I Corinthians 7:9). Some 300 years later, Paul's views were taken up by one who would have perhaps the greatest impact upon Western theological thought, Augustine of Hippo.

Troubled by his own uncontrollable sexual urges, Augustine eventually heeded Paul's words to "make no provision for the flesh, to fulfill the lusts thereof" (Romans 13:14). Consonant with (if not exaggerating) Pauline sexual attitudes, Augustine developed a theology that unambiguously pronounced sex as sin. Sexual desire was considered nothing less than diabolical and a reflection of sinful nature. The only moral reason to engage in sex was for procreative purposes. Augustine put it plainly:

> Now surely any friend of wisdom and holy joys who lives a married life but knows, in the words of the Apostle's warning, "how to possess his bodily instrument in holiness and honour, not in the sickness of desire . . ." surely such a man would prefer, if possible, to beget children without lust of this kind. For then the parts created for this task would be servants of his mind, even in their function of procreation. . . .[13]

To reiterate, Augustine was the major conduit for *platonized* Christianity into Western theological thought. In fact, some have suggested that "Augustine has fixed a certain reading of Paul for generations of later readers," thus allowing for his own Augustinian platonized imprint on Christian sexual morality to be virtually unsurpassed.[14] In this regard, he has influenced both Catholic and Protestant traditions; and in so doing he helped firmly to establish within these traditions a platonized sexual ethic.

Platonized Christianity advocates a dualistic sexual ethic. That is, it suggests only two ways in which to engage sexual activity, one tolerable, not inherently sinful and the other intolerable, sin. Procreative use is tolerably good; non-procreative use is intolerably evil. Characteristic of platonized Christianity, a third possibility is not offered. A platonized sexual ethic does not allow for sexual activity to be an expression of an intimate, that is, loving relationship. For all intents and purposes, platonized Christianity severs intimate sexuality from loving relationality. Platonized Christianity essentially objectifies sexuality in a manner commensurate with oppressive power's objectification of certain human beings. Again, within a platonized framework, sexuality is rendered an object of either procreation or lust. Sexuality is not granted the theological space to be a vehicle for or expression of loving relationality. In this regard, it is easy to see how a platonized Christian tradition was able to provide shelter for the dehumanization of black people along with the accompanying vile treatment of their bodies. For ironically, such a theology of sexuality is better suited to accommodate the use of black people as breeders (as their expression of sexuality was for procreative purposes), than it is to affirm their loving relationality and hence provide theological legitimacy to their marriages. Indeed, as we will soon see, platonized Christianity with its concomitant sexual ethic, most certainly contributes to the marginalized reality of nonheterosexual persons within the church and hence for ecclesiastical resistance to their "married" unions.

To review, the reality of contested enslaved marriages points to two key factors which must be taken into account in any discussion of the church's response to same-sex marriages: the challenge of the imago Dei for humans to engage in loving relationality, and the correspondence between unscrupulous power's manipulation of human sexuality and the platonized sexual ethic of a prevailing Christian tradition. Let us explore the implications of both of these factors as they involve the church's response to same-sex marriages.

CONCLUDING THOUGHTS

What the church must first affirm is what many enslaved men and women apparently understood: the sacredness of loving relationality. The theological imperative of human creation is not for men and women to conform categorically to social/historical contrivances of marriage, but for them to adhere to what it means to be imago Dei. Given this theological imperative, the church has a fundamental obligation to nurture, sustain, and affirm loving relationality. That is, the church must encourage and provide a protected space for those relationships that mirror the mutuality and reciprocity of a trinitarian God. At theological issue is not the biological/gendered form of a committed intimate union, but instead the relational character of that union. In this regard, the church faces at least a twofold challenge.

The church is principally challenged to open itself to recognizing the sanctity of same-sex loving relationality and thus, to affirming theologically, liturgically, and pastorally the inviolability of same-sex unions. The church is also compelled to be theologically scrupulous in its sanction of various heterosexual unions. Again, at stake is not the union's gendered form, but its relational character. The point of the matter is that the church must come to the theological place of realizing that there may be same-sex unions that are more deserving of sacred affirmation than certain female-male unions. However, in order for the church to achieve this level of theological clarity, it must first acknowledge the inherent theological problem of its prevalent view toward sexuality.

Inasmuch as the prevailing theology of the Christian tradition is a platonized theology that naturally projects an essentialized/dualistic view of sexuality, then this tradition virtually suborns the oppression of sexualized people, such as non-heterosexual persons. For, characteristic of socially marginalized groups, non-heterosexual men and women are a sexualized people. That is, they are routinely objectified according to their sexuality, which of course has already been essentialized in respect to genital activity. In short, nonheterosexuals are wrongly defined primarily in relation to their presumed sexual practices. Consequent to being characterized as a people categorically engaged in nonprocreative sexual activity, nonheterosexual persons are at best deemed sinners in need of redemption (i.e., conversion from a nonheterosexual lifestyle) or at worst considered ungodly. In either case, platonized Christianity readily sustains social, political, and ecclesiastical discrimination of gay, lesbian, and other nonheterosexual persons. Specifically, the sexualized caricature of these persons colludes with a platonized sexual ethic in such a way virtually to invite a sacrosanct derision and disparagement of them. And to be sure, this insidious collusion contests the very notion of church support for same-sex marriages.

To the extent that marriage is seen as a privileged context for procreative sexuality, then it is absolutely off-limits to nonheterosexual people. For, non-heterosexuals are considered incapable of engaging in procreative sexuality and are thereby seen as embodiments of lustful sexuality. Problematic to such an exclusionary privileging of marriage is not only the hetero-patriarchal notion of marriage that it implies (similar to the white patriarchal notion of marriage that precluded enslaved marriages) but most especially the approach to sexuality that this exclusion projects, an approach fostered by platonized theology.

As I stated earlier, platonized theology severs the tie between sexuality and loving relationship. A practical consequence of this severance is church repudiation of same-sex marriages. A theological consequence is the church's betrayal of its obligation to provide for relationships that mirror a trinitarian God. It is thus essential for the church to disavow a platonized sexual ethic, and correspondingly to assert a sexual ethic that affirms sexual intimacy as an expression of loving relationality. Such a sexual ethic allows for sacred validation of same-sex marriages at the same time that it signifies the integrity of the church's commitment to provide protected space for relationships that reflect the internal/eternal relationality of a trinitarian God. Essentially, the church must adopt a theological view of sexuality that allows it to be a more reliable steward of loving relationality.

In the end, the question of Linda Brent some one hundred fifty years ago, "Why does the slave ever love?" is prescient. For it is more than just a rhetorical lament about the contested reality of slave marriage; it is most significantly a bold affirmation of those who dared to love, regardless. And as such, it is a challenge to the church to be a place that embraces the love of all those who dare to love.

NOTES

1. Harriet Jacobs, *Incidents in the Life of a Slave Girl: Written by Herself* with an introduction by Jean Fagan Yellin (Cambridge, MA: Harvard University Press, 1987), 37. It should be noted that Jacobs wrote under the pseudonym Linda Brent.

2. *Incidents in the Life*, 37.

3. *Incidents in the Life*, 37.

4. Thomas Jefferson, "Notes on the State of Virginia," in *The Life and Selected Writing of Thomas Jefferson,* edited with an introduction by Adrienne Koch and William Peden (New York: The Modern Library, 1998), 239.

5. Joe Rawls, testimony in *Bullwhip Days: The Slaves Remember*, edited by James Mellon (New York: Avon Books, 1988), 146.

6. Tempie Durham, *Bullwhip Days*, 146–147.

7. In this article the church refers to the Christian ecclesiastical in general. The underlying assumption is that the issue of same-sex unions is of concern for the Christian church universal, even as responses to this issue may vary within particular church communities. What I offer here is not a response to any particular Christian church tradition, but a response to the challenge of same-sex unions faced by the wider church in general.

8. Translation taken from New Revised Standard Version of the Bible (NSRV).

9. James B. Nelson, *Embodiment: An Approach to Sexuality and Christian Theology* (Minneapolis: Augsburg Publishing House, 1978), 17.

10. Foucault quoted in James Miller, *The Passion of Michel Foucault* (New York: Doubleday/Anchor Books, 1993), 293.

11. This particular discussion of platonized Christianity draws upon my discussions of this in other places, most notably in "The Black Church and Homosexuality: The Black and White of It" in *Union Seminary Quarterly Review* 57, nos. 1, 2 (2003), 32–45.

12. Pauline scripture reflects the New English Bible translation.

13. Augustine, *City of God* (London: Penguin Classic, 1972), Book XIV, ch. 16, p. 577.

14. Mark D. Jordan, *The Ethics of Sex* (Blackwell Publishing, 2002), 109.

27

A Catholic Defense
of Same-Sex
Marriage

DANIEL C. MAGUIRE

The Catholic Church is beginning to rediscover what it once knew: that not all persons are heterosexual, that many people are homosexual, and that this is just fine. In the past, the church accepted homosexuality more openly and even had liturgies to celebrate same-sex unions.[1] There was recognition that different sexual orientations are clearly part of God's plan for creation. Some people are heterosexual, and some are homosexual. This is the way God made us, and we have no right to criticize God.

Wherever the human race is found, we find persons of differing sexual orientations. (We find the same thing in God's animal kingdom.) Human history shows that some humans have same-sex attractions and unions, and others have opposite-sex attractions and unions. The desire to bond lovingly and sexually with persons of the same-sex or of the opposite sex is a fact of life, a fact of God's creation, and we have no right to call it unholy. As the Acts of the Apostles says in the Bible, we have no right to declare unclean anything that God has made (Acts 10:15). To do so, in fact, is a sin.

Obviously, not all Catholics have heard this message. Prejudice against homosexual persons is common. Theologians call this the sin of heterosexism, a sin like racism, anti-Semitism, and sexism. These are sins that condemn people for being what they are, not for what these people do. These sins of prejudice are cruel sins that condemn people, no matter how good these people are. If people are not white or are not male or are not heterosexual, they are condemned, even if they are saints. This is what racism, sexism, and heterosexism do. If homosexual persons live out their reality and enter into beautiful, same-sex relationships full of love and commitment and fidelity, we condemn them. Even if their unions are more successful, more lasting, and more exemplary than some heterosexual unions, we still condemn them. Surely that is unjust.

Years ago, the Catholic theologian Father Andre Guindon wrote: "Christian communities should begin to receive homosexuals in their midst as full-fledged brothers and sisters and as those to whom God also offers his love."[2] Catholic theologian Mary Hunt asks: "What could possibly be wrong with loving, mutual, safe, consensual, community-building sexual relationships between committed male or female partners?"[3]

But, are same-sex unions really marriage?

All the religions of the world give marriage a very high place. Marriage can be defined as the unique and special form of committed friendship between sexually attracted persons. This definition does not say that the persons have to be heterosexually attracted. Persons attracted to a person of their same-sex can still be married. Marriage is a supreme human good involving exclusive, committed, enduring, generous, and faithful love, and this kind of love is not something that only heterosexuals can achieve. In fact, some heterosexuals are not very good at it. As theologian Mary Hunt points out, "In fact, heterosexual marriages end in divorce as often as in death."[4] Friendship and love and commitment are human virtues, and gay and lesbian persons are human and fully capable of a healthy human committed love in marriage. We have no moral right to declare marriage off limits to persons whom God has made gay. We have no right to say that marriage, with all of its advantages and beauty, is a reward for being heterosexual.

Dr. Hunt also points out how unfair it would be to say that heterosexual Catholics have seven sacraments, but homosexual Catholics only have six if marriage is denied them. Who could imagine God creating people who are gay and then denying them the right to express their sincere and honest love in the holy sacrament of matrimony!

But what of the objections to same-sex unions?

St. Thomas Aquinas always said that it is important to know the objections to any teaching that you accept. When you face those objections, you can come to know your own position better.

OBJECTION #1: THE BIBLE SAYS ALL HOMOSEXUAL ACTIVITY IS EVIL AND SINFUL

First of all, this is true. There are objections to same-sex unions in the Bible. However, many things in the Bible simply describe how people lived when the Bible was written. Not everything that the Bible tells us is something we could or should do today. For example, the Bible (Leviticus 25:44–46) tells us that we may buy and own slaves, "use them permanently," and will them to our children when we die! In the past, people who did not know how to interpret the Bible used these texts to justify slavery in Latin America and in North America. They did not know that sometimes the Bible is telling you what people used to do, not what people should do today. Sometimes the Bible gives you a lot of bad examples of how terrible people can be. The Bible treated slavery as a fact of life and talks about "a man who sells his daughter into slavery" (Exodus 21:7). Surely we would not want to do that today!

The Bible also forbids eating shellfish (Leviticus 11:9–10), but we do not feel we should obey that today.

The Bible also says that wives should obey their husbands as if their husbands were God (Ephesians 5:22–24) and that wives should be "subjects to their husbands in everything." This made women slaves to their husbands, and for a long time people justified male control of women by using these Bible texts. The Church then learned that these texts described the way life was lived at that time, but did not prescribe that we should live that way. They found better ideals in the same Bible and used them to correct these texts. Thus, interpreters of the Bible went to Galatians 3:28 and there found the liberating ideal that "all persons [male and female] are one person in Christ Jesus," and that therefore no hostile divisions should be made between male and female, with neither one dominating the other.

When we come to the biblical texts on homosexuality, we see right away that we could never treat them as rules for our day. The book of Leviticus says that anyone who has sex with someone of the same-sex "shall be put to death: their blood shall be on their own heads" (20:13). St. Paul in the Epistle to the Romans condemns homosexual relationships and lists persons who do such things among those who "deserve to die" (1:26–32).

The Catholic Church today condemns capital punishment, and even conservative Catholics and other Christians who condemn all homosexual relationships do not call for the death penalty for gays and lesbians.

Obviously, there are many moral questions that are not answered in the Bible. Homosexuality is one of them. What Catholic and other Christian and Jewish scholars do is to take the main principles of justice, compassion, respect, and love for persons as God created (both heterosexuals and homosexuals are created in God's image) and apply these principles to today's moral issues, such as homosexuality and same-sex marriage. That is why Catholic and other Christian and Jewish theologians defend same-sex marriages today. They say that denying all homosexual persons the expression of their sexuality is unjust and sinful.

Do all Catholics and other Christians agree on same-sex marriage? No. Just as some Christians see all war as immoral and become pacifists, some others say there can be a "just war." Christians, including Catholics, have learned to live with these differences and to respect one another and live together anyhow. Catholics are now beginning to practice the same tolerance regarding homosexuality.

OBJECTION #2: THE CATHOLIC HIERARCHY CONDEMNS ALL HOMOSEXUAL SEX

That is true. When Cardinal Ratzinger, now Pope Benedict XVI, was head of the Congregation for the Doctrine of the Faith, he issued a teaching that said:

"Respect for homosexual persons cannot lead in any way to approval of homosexual behavior or to legal recognition of homosexual unions."[5] Undoubtedly that is still the position of the pope. The question is how Catholics should evaluate the pope's position.

The Church consists of more than the pope and the bishops. In Catholicism there are three sources of truth (or three "magisteria"): the hierarchy, the theologians, and the wisdom and experience of the laity (called in Latin *sensus fidelium*). In Catholic history, each of these sources of truth has at times been right, and each of them has at times been wrong. So, for example, for many centuries the bishops, popes, and theologians taught that it was a mortal sin to take any interest on a loan, even one half of one percent interest. After a while, the laity, through their own experience with lending money, decided that a little interest was reasonable and fair to compensate the lender. Too much interest was wrong, but a little interest as payment for the use of your money was reasonable and moral. In other words, the laity disagreed with the hierarchy and the theologians, and the laity was right. A hundred years after the laity made a decision on interest and acted on it, some theologians said they agreed; a hundred years later, the Vatican also decided that the laity was right. The Vatican even went on to open a bank and charge interest.

At other times in history, the hierarchy and theologians taught that slavery was moral and that anti-Semitism was not a sin. Obviously, they were wrong, and they eventually were corrected.

Something like that is now going on regarding homosexuality. Many Catholic theologians agree now with Protestant and Jewish theologians that same-sex unions can be moral, healthy, and holy.[6] Many Catholic people are living in same-sex unions and adopting children and still practicing their Catholic faith. Many priests realize this and welcome these couples to Communion at Mass and even have private liturgical celebrations of their unions. Bishop Walter Sullivan of Richmond, Virginia, even wrote a welcoming introduction to a book of essays by various Catholic theologians, some of whom defended the right of sacramental marriage for same-sex couples.[7]

Obviously, then, Catholic teaching is in transition on this subject and Catholics are free to let their consciences decide either for or against same-sex marriages. Both views—for or against homosexual marriage—are at home in the Catholic world, and neither one of them can be called more orthodox or more official or more Catholic than the other.

Is the pope then wrong? I would join many other Catholic theologians in saying that he is definitely wrong, and he will be corrected some day by one of his successors and by the rest of the church as previous popes who permitted slavery, etc., were corrected. This is the way of the church. After all, Pope Benedict also teaches that a spouse whose partner is HIV-positive is still not permitted to use a condom for protection. This is obviously wrong, and some bishops have even come out and said so. Almost all Catholic theologians say the pope is wrong on that point.

There is a clear distinction to be made between "Vatican theology" and "Catholic theology." As in the above example, Vatican theology says a spouse cannot use condoms for protection from an HIV-positive partner! Catholic theology, including the theologians and the *sensus fidelium*, the wisdom of the laity, does not hold that strange and damaging view.

In an old Catholic teaching called *Probabilism* we find the answer for Catholics. When there is a debate on a moral issue (in this case same-sex unions), where there are good reasons and good authorities on both sides of the debate, Catholics are free to make up their own minds.[8]

This means that Catholic same-sex couples are perfectly free to practice their Catholic faith, receive the sacraments, and never feel that God forbids their union—or that their faithful, sexual union is anything but holy.

The view that homosexual people are condemned to involuntary celibacy for life is as cruel as it is absurd. Jesus said of celibacy: "Let those accept it who can" (Matthew 19:12). Voluntary celibacy for a good cause is something some can do, but it is seen as a special talent, a special gift that not all have. The Vatican council called it "a precious gift of divine grace which the Father gives to some persons," but not to all.[9] Abstaining from all sexual activity is seen by the Council as something "unique."[10] You cannot demand from all homosexual people that which is "unique."

St. Paul recognizes the same thing when he says "it is better to marry than to burn" (1 Corinthians 7:9). What kind of gospel "good news" would it be to tell all gay persons that their only choice is to burn?

OBJECTION # 3: HOMOSEXUALITY IS A MENTAL ILLNESS

Some psychiatrists in the past did think homosexuality was an illness. That is no longer the case, and it is an insult to homosexual people to keep repeating that old and outmoded theory. Studies of gay couples indicate that they tend "to appear as well adjusted as heterosexuals, or occasionally, even more so."[11]

OBJECTION # 4: CHILDREN WILL BE DAMAGED UNLESS THEY GROW UP IN A HOME WITH A MOTHER AND A FATHER

This is not true. Psychologist Charlotte Patterson, among many others, has done extensive research on children of lesbian and gay parents. Her conclusion is that this does not present problems and does not lead to any higher rates of homosexual children.[12] Theologian Mary Hunt writes: "Many lesbian and gay families have adopted children, welcoming them with love and affection, reasoning that a child's life with one parent or two parents of the same-sex is far better than languishing in an institution or, worse, dying from neglect."[13]

OBJECTION #5: HOMOSEXUALITY IS UNNATURAL BECAUSE IT IS NEVER FOUND IN ANIMALS

This is untrue. In his extensive study, *Biological Exuberance: Animal Homosexuality and National Diversity*, biologist Bruce Bagemihl shows that homosexuality is part of our evolutionary heritage as primates. He reports that more than 450 species regularly engage in a wide range of same-sex activities ranging from copulation to long-term bonding.[14]

CONCLUSION

Homosexuality is not a sin. Heterosexism—prejudice against people who are homosexual—is a sin. It is a serious sin because it violates justice, truth, and love. It also distorts the true meaning of sex and thus also harms everyone, including heterosexuals.

It's what you do with your homosexuality or your heterosexuality that determines morality. Homosexuality, like heterosexuality, is morally neutral. As Catholic philosophers Daniel Dombrowski and Robert Deltete from the Jesuit Seattle University say, "Homosexual sexual relations [like heterosexual sexual relations] can be moral or they can be immoral."[15] Moral theologian Christina Traina says that "the ultimate fruitfulness and durability of any union—heterosexual or homosexual—have everything to do with faith, friendship, generosity, community support, sexual and verbal affection and the hard work that goes into mutual formation of a working partnership."[16]

Sexuality is a gift to be cherished. We have no right to deny it to those whom God has made gay. As theologian Kelly Brown Douglas says, we have to create "a church and community where non-heterosexual persons are able to love themselves and those whom they choose to love without social, political or ecclesiastical penalty," so that they may enjoy life and enjoy sex with gratitude that life is so full of goodness and enriching variety.[17]

NOTES

1. John Boswell, *Same-Sex Unions in Premodern Europe* (New York: Vintage Books, 1995). Boswell writes that in the same-sex ceremonies, we see the two persons of the same-sex "standing together at the altar with their right hands joined (the traditional symbol of marriage), being blessed by the priest, sharing Communion, and holding a banquet for family and friends afterward. . . Same-sex unions were thus neither a threat to nor a replacement of heterosexual marriage," 191.

2. Andre Guindon, *The Sexual Language: An Essay in Moral Theology* (Ottawa: University of Ottawa Press, 1977), 370.

3. Mary Hunt, "Eradicating the Sin of Heterosexism," forthcoming in *Heterosexism: Roots and Cures in World Religions*, ed. Daniel C. Maguire.

4. Ibid.

5. Congregation for the Doctrine of the Faith, "Considerations Regarding Proposals to Give Legal Recognition to Unions between Homosexual Persons," June 3, 2003.

6. See Robert Nugent, ed., *Challenge to Love: Catholic Views of Homosexuality* (New York: Crossroad, 1983); Daniel C. Maguire, "Catholic Ethics in the Post-Infallible Church," in *The Moral Revolution: A Christian Humanist Vision* (San Francisco: Harper & Row, 1986).

7. See *Challenge to Love: Catholic Views of Homosexuality.*

8. On Probabilism and homosexual marriage, see Daniel C. Maguire, "The Morality of Homosexual Marriage," in *The Moral Revolution*, 98–102.

9. See Walter M. Abbott, ed., *The Documents of Vatican II* (New York: Herder and Herder, 1966), 71, in the "Dogmatic Constitution on the Church."

10. Ibid., 71–72.

11. Alan P. Bell and Martin S. Weinberg, *Homosexualities: A Study of Diversity among Men and Women* (New York: Simon & Schuster, 1978), 208. See also Isaiah Crawford and Brian D. Zamboni, "Informing the Debate on Homosexuality: The Behavioral Science and the Church," in Patricia Beattie Jung and Joseph Andrew Coray, eds., *Sexual Diversity and Catholicism: Toward the Development of Moral Theology* (Collegeville, Minn.: The Liturgical Press, 2001), 216–51.

12. See "Lesbian and Gay Parenting: A Resource for Psychologists," http://www.apa.org/pi/parent.hyml Accessed August 15, 2005.

13. Mary Hunt, "Eradicating the Sin of Heterosexism."

14. Bruce Bagemihl, *Biological Exuberance: Animal Homosexuality and Natural Diversity* (New York: St. Martin's Press, 1999).

15. Daniel A. Dombrowski and Robert Deltete, *A Brief, Liberal, Catholic Defense of Abortion* (Urbana and Chicago: University of Illinois Press, 2000), 86.

16. See Christina L.H. Traina, "Papal Ideals, Marital Realities: One View from the Ground," in *Sexual Diversity and Catholicism: Toward the Development of Moral Theology*, ed. Patricia Beattie Jung and Joseph Andrew Coray (Collegeville, Minn.: The Liturgical Press, 2001), 269–88.

17. Kelly Brown Douglas, "Heterosexism/Homophobia and the Black Church Community," in Daniel C. Maguire, ed., *Heterosexism: Roots and Cures in World Religions*, forthcoming.

28

*Marriage in
a New Key*

MARVIN M. ELLISON

A shift of perspective is not unfamiliar in Christian history; it is called conversion.

Robert McAfee Brown[1]

To date religion has played a pivotal role in the North American debate about same-sex marriage, but in a manner that has intensified rather than helped resolve this controversy. Given the Christian Right's fixation on homosexuality and aggressive "traditional values" campaign,[2] it is not surprising that appeals to religious belief and the Bible are frequently cited as grounds for resisting changes in civil law and religious practice that would accommodate non-heterosexual couples and their families. At the same time, not all religious authorities and traditions condemn homosexuality or reject same-sex marriage. Because advocates for marriage equality include leaders and activists within a wide range of faith traditions,[3] it would be a mistake to consign religion to the forces of reaction. It would also be politically counterproductive because opportunities might be overlooked for entering into alliances with progressive religionists, thereby further impeding efforts to reorder social, economic, and cultural conditions so that all persons may experience security and justice, including those who identify as gay, lesbian, bisexual, and transgender.

In analyzing the conflict about marriage policies and practices within North Atlantic, white Reformed Protestantism, the tradition within which I stand, I find good news in Daniel Maguire's observation that "from the beginning, there has never been just one Christianity."[4] No monolithic or fixed Christian tradition exists. Instead, there is a plurality of dynamic, often conflicting Christianities that are deeply divided over sexuality, economic justice, and other concerns. Religion should, therefore, be approached with care and discernment as a complex, ideologically divided force that either promotes justice or legitimates injustice.

This religion divide is vividly illustrated by the wildly divergent responses to the 2003 election of V. Gene Robinson as the Episcopal bishop of New Hampshire. The controversy has been sparked by the fact that Bishop Robinson is not only a divorced father of two adult children, but also an "out," that is, a self-respecting and publicly self-identifying gay man who lives openly with his male life-partner. Christian traditionalists are distressed that a church body would fail to underscore the incompatibility of Christian identity with what they rhetorically invoke as "the gay lifestyle," much less give explicit approval to what they regard as blatant immorality. They are equally alarmed by the heightened visibility of families headed by same-sex couples, the legalization of same-sex marriage in other countries (Canada, Belgium, the Netherlands, and Spain), as well as in parts of the United States (civil marriage in Massachusetts, civil unions in Vermont and Connecticut), and the movement within various religious traditions to bless same-sex partnerships.[5] They contend that homosexuality is intrinsically sinful, that homo-sex threatens personal health and social well-being, that only monogamous heterosexual marriage is biblically authorized, and that the marital family, the cornerstone of society and Western civilization, is undermined whenever church or state adopts a neutral stance toward non-normative sexualities and "endorses" non-traditional families. In contrast, Christian progressives welcome non-heterosexuals into the life and leadership of the church and support their full civil, human, and ecclesiastical rights, including the freedom to marry. They also press for a reformation of Christian theology and sexual ethics in light of the biblical mandate to pursue justice for those marginalized and oppressed in every community and context.[6]

This split over sexuality and sexual justice within Christianity and other religious traditions[7] has been characterized in terms of a traditionalist-progressive dichotomy. In *Christianity and the Making of the Modern Family*, historian and theologian Rosemary Ruether proposes that "no reconciliation is possible" between the two sides of this religious divide because "their outlooks are based on irreconcilably different presuppositions."[8] Christian fundamentalists, operating with an absolutist worldview "of fixed certainties that support patriarchal hierarchy, militarism, and free-market capitalism" regard gay sex as morally objectionable "regardless of how loving or how committed is the relationship in which it takes place."[9] In contrast, Christian progressives acknowledge and show regard for a range of human sexualities, place the pursuit of an egalitarian justice at the heart of the moral-spiritual life, and, as Ruether notes, "have accepted the diversity of cultures and religious perspectives" as rich assets for community life rather than threats to religious identity or problems that require fixing.

Because those of us who are progressive Christians increasingly find that we have more in common—in terms of shared faith and values—with our liberal counterparts in other denominations and traditions than we have with our conservative co-religionists, a massive realignment is taking place within the religious landscape. This realignment, which Ruether describes as a "new ecumenism," seeks to link the progressive wings of various denominations so that, among other things, they might more effectively pursue justice making throughout the social order.[10]

While the distinction between traditionalist and progressive is commonplace in popular discourse and may be useful for grassroots organizing, the dichotomy can be overdrawn and misleading. In particular, framing the debate between only these two poles does not readily draw attention to the limitations of a centrist notion of justice as equal opportunity or equal access. In my judgment, progressives need a richer, more comprehensive notion of justice that emphasizes the restructuring of social power and reconstruction of moral norms, in this case norms regulating sexuality and sexual difference. Otherwise, liberals seeking the inclusion of the disenfranchised may leave unaltered the norms and power dynamics that create the divisive, exclusionary practices in the first place.

To make a case for a broader notion of sexual justice for grounding religious responses to sexual difference, I begin by comparing church resolutions on same-sex marriage from the Southern Baptist Convention and the United Church of Christ. After drawing the contrast, I suggest that while progressive commitments in favor of marriage equality move in the right direction by validating same-sex love, actualizing a comprehensive justice requires more. In order to dismantle entrenched social patterns of privilege and exclusion, progressives must stop privileging not only heterosexuality, but marriage, as well. The *marital* family must be de-centered in order to give recognition and support to a diversity of family and relational options. In rethinking marriage in a postmodern key, I conclude by considering a set of challenges to the liberal Christian marriage paradigm and offer a constructive proposal for moving toward sexual and relational justice. Shifting in this direction resonates well, I argue, with a Reformed Protestant affirmation of justice in intimate, as well as wider, social relations. It may also allow us to appreciate that while heterosexuality and marriage are vocations to be undertaken by those with these particular gifts, they are not divinely willed or naturally mandated obligations to be expected of all. Making this shift may foster the awareness that the moral evil of which Christians are called to repent is not "the sin of homosexuality," but rather its own sex-negativity, the idolatry of heterosexual supremacy, and the refusal to enter into community as co-equals with the sexualized Other.

MARRIAGE TRADITIONALISTS: THE VIEW FROM ABOVE

Opponents of same-sex marriage, idealizing a nineteenth-century middle-class (and typically white) nuclear family as the Christian norm, argue against extending the right to marry to same-sex couples because of what they believe about marriage and about homosexuality. A Southern Baptist Convention statement on sexuality defines marriage as an exclusively heterosexual institution, the union of "one man, and one woman, for life."[11] In 1998 the SBC amended its "Baptist Faith and Message" by adding a section on "The Family," which notes three purposes for marriage: to provide a framework for intimate companionship between a husband and wife, to control sex by channeling sexuality "according to biblical standards," and to provide "the means for procreation of the human race."[12] Because the presumption is no longer unassailable that marriage requires gender difference to be valid, the SBC has offered additional reasons for opposing same-sex marriage by declaring that homosexuality is "not a 'valid alternative lifestyle,'" but rather, biblically speaking, a sin.[13] According to this viewpoint, for the church to grant religious affirmation or the state to offer legal standing to same-sex unions would be to "sanction immorality." In a 1996 resolution opposing the legalizing of same-sex unions in Hawaii, the SBC elaborated on its objections by describing homoerotic relationships as "always a gross abomination . . . in all circumstances, without exception," as "pathological," and as "always sinful, impure, degrading, shameful, unnatural, indecent, and perverted." Leaving no doubt about its opposition to marriage equality, the SBC concludes by stating that the movement to legalize same-sex unions "is and must be completely and thoroughly wicked."[14]

These opponents of same-sex marriage claim to speak from the center of Christian life and culture. As the SBC puts it, the church must protect the integrity of the Christian tradition, and, therefore, marriage should be defended as a divinely mandated "order of creation" and "therefore first and foremost [as] a divine institution (Mat. 19:6) and only secondarily a cultural and civil institution."[15] However, in claiming the authority to speak for all, these Christians speak not from the center, but "from above," from a position of social power and privilege, and they intend to deploy their power in order to forestall changes they fear will erode their cultural dominance.[16]

In opposing same-sex marriage, these traditionalists are not seeking to preserve marriage, but rather a certain model of marriage (patriarchal marriage) and, by extension, a certain model of social relations organized in terms of presumably natural hierarchies of power and control. Although affirming that husband and wife are "of equal worth before God," the SBC describes marriage as an unequal power relation in which the two parties have different roles and expectations. The husband must be the leader; he is to "provide for, to protect, and to lead his family." A wife is expected "to submit herself graciously" to her husband "as the church willingly submits to the headship of Christ."[17] This hierarchical marriage paradigm is defended as natural, "pre-political," and divinely mandated, presumably for the benefit of all the parties affected, including the broader social order.

As historian Mark Jordan observes, traditionalists seek to enshrine a definition of marriage as "always and only" one man and one woman by invoking the Judeo-Christian tradition as its chief warrant, but "of course, they are plainly wrong." Polygamy was a sanctioned practice among the Hebrew patriarchs, and Augustine, Aquinas, and the Protestant Reformers all wrestled with the question of holiness and non-monogamy, including how the New Testament's affirmation of "new life in the Spirit" and an inclusive Christian love seem to justify polyamorous affiliations. "The most urgent challenge for Christian marital theology," Jordan argues, "has been to prevent the universality of the agapic [love] feast from reaching erotic relationships—how to prevent agapic community from enactment as erotic community. Christianity," he proposes, "is latent polyamory."[18]

The heterosexual marriage paradigm that the SBC and other traditionalists seek to reinforce as the only legally (and religiously) recognized household pattern resonates with, and gains cultural weight from, modernist assumptions about gender, sexuality, and family. A prevailing sexological paradigm emphasizes biological factors ("anatomy is destiny"), views sexuality as naturally determined and unchanging, and operates within a binary sex/gender schema, in which biological or anatomical sex is presumed, first, to give rise to "proper" masculine or feminine gender identity and social roles, then to generate "normal" heterosexual desires and interest in the "opposite sex," and finally to lead steadily to procreation in the context of marriage. The notions that there are two (and only two) naturally complementary sexes, that "opposites attract," that sexuality is primarily procreative, and that homosexuality signals deviance from the heterosexual norm are unquestioned assumptions among traditionalists.

The prevailing cultural sex/gender paradigm seems commonsensical to conservative Christians because it fits with and helps reinforce two familiar and problematic dynamics within the Christian tradition: first, a devaluing of body and deep ambivalence, if not outright negativity, toward sexuality, passion, and women; and second, a patriarchal bias that legitimates male control of women's lives, including their reproductive and other labor. Because sex has long been viewed with suspicion as a dangerous energy that threatens to overwhelm and disrupt established order, marriage has been latched onto as the appropriate "safe container" for keeping this energy within check, in particular by allowing male control of wives and daughters and for the orderly transmission of property, including children. In this framework, marriage is as much, if not more about gender hierarchy, gender control, and the regulation of sex and property as it is about love and affection.

According to the logic of patriarchal Christianity, moral order is equated with sexism, white racial supremacy, class elitism, and so forth. In order to maintain good order, all must play their proper roles and, in this instance, fulfill the obligations of compulsory heterosexual monogamy. Failure to conform to patriarchal norms and role expectations place individuals and communities in jeopardy, including risking, as the SBC points out, "God's swift judgment."[19] Given their fear of social anarchy and invocation of divine wrath, traditionalists have become deeply agitated by efforts to "normalize" gay people and grant legitimacy to same-sex partnerships and families, precisely because homosexuality is lifted up as the preeminent example of willful departure from "traditional values." By upending the sex/gender rules, same-sex marriage threatens to disrupt and dismantle not only "the" family, but also the entire social edifice constructed on the basis of the heterosexual (and racist, masculinist) social contract.

ADVOCATES FOR EQUALITY: TRANSFORMING A PATRIARCHAL, SEX-NEGATIVE CHRISTIAN PARADIGM

On July 4, 2005, the United Church of Christ became the first mainline Christian denomination to give official support for same-sex marriage by adopting a resolution at its General Synod that affirms "equal marriage rights for couples regardless of gender." In keeping with its longstanding advocacy for justice and social equality, including advocacy for lesbian, gay, bisexual, and transgender persons, the UCC has identified the marriage exclusion as yet another form of discrimination which violates the principle of equal protection under the law. However, this denomination's stance in favor of marriage equality is rooted more fundamentally in theological and biblical affirmations. "The message of the Gospel," its resolution reads, "is the lens through which the whole of scripture is to be interpreted," and it is a message that "always bends toward inclusion."[20]

In recognition of the fact that marriage is a changing, ever evolving institution and, therefore, subject to greater humanization or dehumanization, the UCC emphasizes its commitment to marriage as a covenant of equals and contends that the biblical call to justice and compassion "provides the mandate for marriage equality" (1–2). Justice, a value to be embodied in interpersonal relationships as well as institutional structures, should seek the elimination of "marginalization for reasons of race, gender, sexual orientation or economic status" (2) and work to create the conditions for social equality. From this justice perspective, the mandate to pursue marriage equality expresses two interrelated notions of equality. First, marriage is defined as a covenantal relationship based on the "full humanity of each partner, lived out in mutual care and respect for one another" (1). The UCC is, therefore, affirming equality of partnership within marriage. Second, equality refers to an affirmation of the full humanity of persons with differing sexual orientations. "We also recognize and affirm that all humans are made in the image and likeness of God," the marriage pronouncement states, "including people of all sexual orientations." The key implication is that, "as created in God's image and gifted by God with human sexuality, all people have the right to lead lives that express love, justice, mutuality, commitment, consent, and pleasure" (2). Equality in this second sense means equal access to marriage, including the moral freedom of same-sex couples to marry, legally and religiously, as well as the freedom not to marry.

Importantly, the UCC statement affirms marriage, but also acknowledges that there are other ways that responsible people live and love. In fact, there are "many biblical models for blessed relationships beyond one man and one woman." Marriage is not the only place in which people "can live fully the gift of love in responsible, faithful, just, committed, covenantal relationships." To underscore this point, the resolution states that "indeed, scripture neither commends a single marriage model nor commands all to marry, but rather calls for love and justice in all relationships" (2). In keeping with these commitments, the UCC calls upon its congregations to adopt marriage policies and rituals that do not discriminate against same-sex couples and asks its membership to "prayerfully consider and support" local, state, and national legislation that grants "equal marriage rights to couples regardless of gender," and to work against legislation, including constitutional amendments, that would deny civil marriage rights to gay and lesbian couples (5).

The strength of the United Church of Christ resolution is its refusal to privilege heterosexual coupling. Same-sex and different-sex partnerships are affirmed as covenantal relationships having comparable worth. Such covenants should be regarded equally within the church and be eligible to receive equal benefits and protection under civil law. At the same time, by calling for full equality between marriage partners, the UCC statement challenges the legacy of patriarchal Christian marriage in which the spiritual equality of spouses has been asserted, but men have remained in charge and enjoyed advantages of unequal power and status. Finally, the UCC position paper makes room for covenantal relationships outside the institution of marriage. While doing so, it encourages a single ethical standard for all intimate (and other) relationships: that relationships are ethical only when they are loving, just, and based on mutual respect and care for all persons.

The UCC affirmation of marriage equality moves in the right direction, first, by de-centering heterosexuality and making room for sexual diversity (in this case, gay and lesbian couples in committed, covenantal relationships), and, second, by de-centering marriage insofar as this resolution approaches marriage as a valued, though not exclusive, place for organizing intimate life. Other options have integrity. There are those who love and express their love sexually, but do not marry. The church's justice-and-love standard sets an expectation for egalitarian intimate relationships whether these are marital or not.

These emphases are important correctives to the sex-negativity and marriage exclusivism that characterizes the Southern Baptist Convention's approach. Traditionalists espouse the notion that the only acceptable sexual expression is heterosexual, marital, and procreative. Those abiding by this standard are given permission to police others and keep them under control. According to conventional Christian mores, respectable people marry and restrain their sexuality by "settling down," thereby establishing themselves as responsible adults. In this schema, sexually active singles and especially gay men and lesbians are defined as "out of control" because they live and love outside the marriage zone. Gayness has become cultural code-language for a generalized immorality that signals both social immaturity and sexual laxity, all because gayness departs from compulsory heterosexuality and because gay sex is neither marital nor procreatively driven and, therefore, not properly constrained.

Given what Gayle Rubin has described as the "dangerously crazy" attitudes about sexuality that typically emerge during times of heightened social and cultural stress,[21] some advocates of same-sex marriage choose to dodge the sex question and avoid dealing forthrightly with the sexual ethics question, including what makes sex ethical or blessed. Instead, they have tried to make a case for equal marriage rights by downplaying sex and "mainstreaming" gay men and lesbians by de-sexualizing homosexuality. Their message is that gayness should be viewed as a non-threatening difference similar to left-handedness or eye color. Moreover, they insist that same-sex couples are not interested in altering the institution of marriage, but only in joining the ranks of the "happily conjoined," thereby reinforcing rather than upsetting the status quo.

Downplaying sexual difference and sanitizing gay sex are efforts to reduce the threat that gay identity and culture pose to dominant norms. According to this strategy, safety and access to basic rights, including the right to marry, depend on making "queerness" invisible. In the process, the prevailing norm of compulsory heterosexuality goes unchallenged. The moral problem is mystified, once more, as the "problem" of homosexuality (or of gender and sexual non-conformity), and the debate centers on whether a minoritized group of outsiders can ever qualify for access to the majority-insiders' privileges through assimilation or by hiding difference and becoming "like them." Defined this way, the solution to injustice is for gay men and lesbians to conform, to the degree possible, to heterosexist values and practices.

William Eskridge, a gay legal scholar, in defending the legal right to marry for same-sex couples, buttresses his case by putting forward sex-negative and homophobic arguments. His book, subtitled "From Sexual Liberty to Civilized Commitment," proposes that in the midst of an AIDS pandemic, gay men, especially the "more sexually venturesome," are "in need of civilizing." His argument for extending marriage rights to same-sex couples is that "same-sex marriage could be a particularly useful commitment device for gay and bisexual men."[22] If marriage were the normative expectation among gay men, he suggests, gay male cruising and experimentation with multiple anonymous sex partners would give way "to a more lesbian-like interest in commitment. Since 1981 and probably earlier, gays were civilizing themselves," he continues. "Part of our self-civilization has been an insistence on the right to marry."[23]

To argue that marriage is necessary as a social control mechanism to tame men's sexuality only reinforces the sex-negativity that is so much in evidence among Christian and other social conservatives. To argue, as Eskridge does, that "same-sex marriage civilizes gay men by making them more like lesbians" presumes, first of all, that women are not interested in sex or sexual pleasure, but concerned only with intimacy and making relational commitments.[24] Moreover, marriage's purpose becomes sexual discipline and control, this time of gay men. In the process, sexual fundamentalism is not critiqued with its sex-negative control ethic and presumption that only marital heterosexuality is morally sound.

In seeking to legitimate the extension of marriage eligibility to same-sex couples, some advocates adopt a problematic strategy of "containing" eroticism, including homoeroticism, within marriage. An alternative, more risky, but in the long term more effective strategy, one which the UCC resolution begins to map out, is to launch a non-apologetic defense of healthy eroticism, inclusive of gay sex; to spell out a principled critique of heterosexist norms and values; and to reformulate a sexual ethic no longer based on either the heterosexual or marital assumption.

A *non-reconstructed* Christian tradition will hardly be helpful in moving toward sexual and relational justice. The conventional Christian approach is not sex positive. Rather, it promulgates a fear-based, reactive, and restrictive moral code aimed at restraining sex within rigidly defined marital boundaries. However, the prevailing Christian code—celibacy for singles, sex only in marriage—is no longer adequate, if it ever was, for at least three reasons. First, this code is fear-based, punitive, and aimed at control rather than empowerment of persons. Second, the Christian marriage ethic has not been sufficiently discerning of the varieties of responsible sexuality. Third, it has not been sufficiently discriminating in naming the ethical violations of persons even within marriage. A reframing of Christian ethics is needed that realistically addresses the diversity of human sexualities while focusing not on the "sin of sex," but on the use and misuse of power and on enhancing the dignity of persons and the moral quality of their interaction. What matters is not the sex or gender expression of the partners or their marital status, but whether the relationship exhibits mutual respect and care, a fair sharing of power and pleasure, ongoing efforts to maintain health and prevent transmission of disease, and, in those cases where it applies, avoiding unintended pregnancy. This justice-centered ethical framework also gives pride of place to the mutual giving-and-receiving of pleasure as a moral resource for enhancing intimate communication.

REVISING PUBLIC POLICY BY BREAKING
THE MARRIAGE MONOPOLY

If the strength of the UCC statement is its conception of marriage as a *human* rather than exclusively heterosexual institution and its movement toward revising Christian sexual ethics, its weakness is its failure to address more critically the role of the state with respect to marital (and other) families. Civil marriage always involves a third party in addition to the couple: the state with its considerable powers not only to grant privileges and material benefits, but also to enforce its notion of sexual morality and public order. A state-sponsored marriage system not only distributes material benefits to some and withholds them from others; it also dispenses cultural legitimation by authorizing some relationships but not others.

Breaking the state-sanctioned marriage monopoly may require several different strategies. One strategy would be to disconnect civil marriage from a wide range of legal rights and economic benefits that the state currently distributes exclusively on the basis of marital status. Instead, those benefits, including social security and access to health care, would be made available to persons on the basis of their citizenship status or membership in the community. If basic rights were guaranteed regardless of marital status, people would be less likely to marry solely or primarily for reasons of economic security. They would also be less likely to stay within unsatisfactory partnerships. Individual freedom, as well as personal dignity and well-being, would be enhanced.

A second strategy would be for the state to disestablish the *marital* family as the singular state-sanctioned associational pattern. The state should instead be neutral toward the diverse family and intimacy patterns that people create to meet their relational needs. Disestablishment of civil marriage would also mean the disestablishment of heterosexuality as the normative sexuality in much the same way that the disestablishment of a state-church has encouraged religious pluralism to flourish.[25] This would mean, among other things, that the state would no longer seek to regulate sexual affiliations between consenting adults. The one exception would be laws and procedures for protecting vulnerable adults and children from violence, harassment, exploitation, and abuse.

Along these lines, legal scholar Martha Fineman favors replacing the marital family, with its core sexual (and reproductive) affiliation, with what she calls the caretaking family with its core relationships of dependency and care, such as parents' care of children and adults caring for ill or aging family members.[26] Abolishing civil marriage as a state-subsidized institution would not mean abolishing marriage or family. Family is not coterminous with marriage. As many LGBT families demonstrate, non-married persons are able to bond together successfully and fulfill basic family functions. Fineman writes, "We do not need *legal* marriage to accomplish many societal objectives," such as nurturing children, caring for dependent adults, and sustaining domestic partners economically. By no longer privileging the *marital* family above other families, it would be possible to "transfer the social and economic subsidies and privilege that marriage now receives" and distribute these communal resources more equitably to what she identifies as "a new family core connection—that of the caretaker-dependent."[27] The state's constructive role would be to guarantee the social and economic conditions so that all families will have adequate resources and the tools necessary to raise children and do the other functions that society depends upon for the well being of its members and for its own future.

Even if marriage no longer conveyed a legal status, the institution would retain importance as a cultural institution because of its symbolic and expressive power. However, if marriage were no longer privileged and regulated by the power of the state, then a couple's decision to marry (or not) would be determined on other grounds, most likely on the basis of their desire to have their covenant witnessed, celebrated, and supported by their faith community if they belong to a religious tradition. At the same time, civil marriage would no longer serve as the exclusive conduit for distributing state-conferred benefits and protections. Instead, distribution would be made on the basis of the needs of caretaker-dependent family units, some of which would certainly be marital families, but not all. All families would be treated equally, and justice would be enhanced across social and cultural differences.

CONTINUING THE REFORMATION

Protestant Christianity, born as a reform movement in the sixteenth century, is in need of further reformation in keeping with what theologian Robert McAfee Brown calls the adaptable "spirit of Protestantism." Protestantism is a tradition that, at its best, understands itself as "reformed but always to be reforming."[28] The reformation needed this time concerns sexual difference and sexual ethics because this tradition has fostered sexual injustice. Its relational ethic has been constructed on the basis of heterosexual exclusivism, the presumption that the only acceptable sexual expression is heterosexual, marital, and procreative. Countering religiously sanctioned sexual oppression requires critiquing the prevailing heterosexist sex/gender paradigm and developing an ethical paradigm that respects a diversity of human sexualities and places the focus not on identity, but on conduct and the character of relationships.

In this regard, my conviction is that the theo-ethical conversation must be redirected away from a preoccupation with the gender (and gender roles) of persons in partnership and toward an emphasis on the character of the relationship. Moreover, rather than promoting marriage per se, the church should promote only egalitarian marriages, in which the parties are each honored and protected as persons in their own right, share power and resources in a mutual give-and-take, and are committed over the long haul not only to their mutual well-being, but also to building up of the common good. In other words, the church's educational and pastoral focus should be on helping people, regardless of gender, to figure out—and live out—a genuinely holy and blessed relationship.

No one should be naïve about the difficulty of eradicating sex and gender oppression or about how deep the ideological divide runs within religious traditions about these matters. Feminist philosopher Mary Daly noted some years ago that the very categories that frame the debate, namely heterosexuality and homosexuality, are patriarchal classifications and that they mystify rather than clarify what makes genuinely life-enhancing relationships possible. "In a nonsexist society," Daly has argued, "the categories of homosexuality and heterosexuality would be unimportant."[29] However, because we live "between the times," we must stretch our moral imaginations to envision what a non-sexist, non-heterosexist church and society would look like, along with how to shape an inclusive, woman-friendly, and gay-affirming model of Christian marriage.

What is abundantly clear is that for religionists, the affirmation of the full humanity of gay persons, along with advocacy for securing their human rights, marks a dividing line between progressives and those who would bifurcate the human community according to sexual difference and grant heterosexuality a privileged status. Arguments against same-sex marriage pivot on the disapproval of gay sex and the denial that same-sex love is morally comparable to hetero-sexual love. Viewing heterosexuality and homosexuality as binary opposites reinforces heterosexual supremacy and gives credence to the notion that het-erosexuality alone is an authentic basis upon which to develop intimate relations and family life.

In contrast, once the patriarchal construction of male supremacy and female inferiority is discredited, and once marriage is valued primarily as a protective, stabilizing context for intimacy and ongoing care between partners, then justi-fications for excluding same-sex couples and keeping marriage a "heterosexu-als only" club melt away. When the assumptions of "gender complementarity" (coded language for male superiority, female inferiority) and of "opposites attracting" no longer hold, it becomes possible to affirm the goodness of a variety of sexual and social relations based on mutual respect and care. In addi-tion, a progressive Christian ethic honors eroticism, both gay and non-gay, as a divinely gifted source of power and energy—of zest for life—that suffuses not only sexual activity, but life pursuits more broadly. Humans in their sexual and social diversity share a remarkably similar desire (and capacity) for intimate connection, communication, and communion with other persons, the earth, and God. While this does not mean that either marriage or sex is necessary for human fulfillment, it does mean that it is wrong, arbitrary, and cruel to exclude an entire class of persons from these routes to intimacy and shared pleasure.

As the battle rages within Protestant Christianity about granting the freedom to marry to same-sex couples, it is necessary to make a compelling religious case for marriage equality.[30] In doing so, advocates have certain Protestant emphases and commitments upon which to draw: first, the primacy of the unitive rather than procreative purpose of marriage; second, the defining of marriage as a covenantal relationship between co-equals; and, third, the moral obligation to deepen respect for the personhood of women and LGBT persons, as well as to protect their human rights.

Although extending the freedom to marry to same-sex couples would be good, in my judgment it would be an ambiguous good. Positively speaking, marriage equality rightly affirms that gay and lesbian people share the human capacity to enter into and sustain loving, morally principled intimate relation-ships. Accordingly, they too merit full religious and legal standing. Nega-tively speaking, same-sex marriage may only reinforce compulsory coupling, a dynamic that Protestant Christianity has helped fuel by expecting all (at least able-bodied, nominally heterosexual) adults to marry. As ethicist Beverly W. Harrison observes, "The Reformers, none more passionately than Calvin, embraced marriage almost as a duty." In fact, marriage had to be compelled within a patriarchal religious system because "if men must marry women, whom they view as deficient in humanity, the external role of 'duty' necessarily must be invoked."[31] Because of its marriage exclusivism, Protestant Christianity has not only condoned women's second-class status in the family and beyond, but also consistently failed to celebrate other ways in which people make families and engage in meaningful intimate association.

From a progressive religious perspective, the trouble with marriage lies far beyond the exclusion of same-sex couples although this, too, is an injustice that must be corrected. There is a larger problematic: how the Christian tradition has fostered fear of sexuality, legitimated male control of women's lives, promulgated compulsory (patriarchal) marriage, and castigated non-conformists as particularly sinful. This *non-reformed* Christian marriage paradigm has caused great damage, first, by reinforcing gender oppression and legitimating male authority and control over women; second, by making alternatives to sexist (and heterosexist) relationships seem unimaginable; and, third, by demonizing sexual nonconformists as "enemies of God" whose bodies and lives could be excoriated with impunity.[32]

In contrast, a progressive Christianity, in promoting sexual justice as an indispensable component of a more comprehensive social justice, advances a larger change agenda than the freedom to marry for gay men and lesbian women or even the restructuring of marriage on egalitarian terms, as necessary and important as these changes would be. Relational justice also requires a positive revaluation of sexuality, including appreciation for the goodness of gay sex; the dismantling of the prevailing sex/gender paradigm that privileges heterosexuality; and conscientious efforts to provide the social, economic, and cultural/religious conditions so that all persons, whether partnered or not and whether heterosexual or not, may flourish and be honored within their communities, including their faith communities.

The church's educational and pastoral responsibilities, along with its justice advocacy, require an expansive moral vision along these lines. In addition, greater candor is needed about how much contemporary Christian moral wisdom about sexuality, marriage, and family stands forthrightly in *discontinuity* with the received tradition. Progressive Christians must insist that good sex is not necessarily procreative, but should be mutually pleasurable for the partners and ethically principled. So, too, good marriages are not male dominant, but rather exhibit flexibility about gender roles, power sharing, and ongoing negotiation so that the well-being and integrity of each person is enhanced. Finally, good families do not fit a single pattern, but rather take a variety of forms, including marital families, those headed by single parents, blended families, and families of choice.

Even these post-modern affirmations, however, when viewed through a Christian justice-love lens, resonate quite deeply with the central vocational commitment that resides at the heart of the Christian moral life: the double commandment to love God and neighbor as self. Supporting the freedom of same-sex couples to marry is grounded in a commitment to learn, together, how to live more gracefully with difference, including sexual difference, in an increasingly multicultural, religiously pluralistic society. In doing so, the church may find itself shifting—undergoing conversion is not too strong a word—to be able to stand more solidly within, and add its blessing to, the long-term historical movement toward a comprehensive social justice that delights in the equal status of marriage (and other intimate) partners, shows full regard for the humanity of non-heterosexual persons, and gives abundant thanks to God for wherever holy love is found.

NOTES

1. Robert McAfee Brown, *Theology in a New Key: Responding to Liberation Themes* (Philadelphia, PA: The Westminster Press, 1978), 51.

2. See Suzanne Pharr, *In the Time of the Right: Reflections on Liberation* (Berkeley, CA: Chardon Press, 1996); and Susan Brooks Thistlethwaite, "Enemy Mine: Why the Religious Right Needs Homophobia," *Chicago Theological Seminary Register* 91:3 (2001), 33–40.

3. For a progressive interfaith statement in support of marriage equality, see the 2004 "Open Letter to Religious Leaders on Marriage Equality" on the website of the Religious Institute for Sexual Morality, Justice, and Healing (*www.religiousinstitute.org*). For suggestions on how religious leaders can promote marriage equality, see the Action Kit prepared by the Freedom to Marry Project (*www.freedomtomarry.org/take_action.asp*).

4. Daniel C. Maguire, *A Moral Creed for All Christians* (Minneapolis, MN: Fortress Press, 2005), 216.

5. The Central Conference of American Rabbis (Reform Judaism), the Ecumenical Catholic Church, Ohalah, Alliance for Jewish Renewal, and the Reconstructionist Rabbinical Association have endorsed their clergy performing commitment ceremonies for same-sex couples. In addition, the United Church of Christ, the United Church of Canada, the American Baptist Churches, the Christian Church (Disciples of Christ), and various Religious Society of Friends (Quaker) meetings leave it to their clergy, congregations, or local governing bodies to decide whether to perform same-sex unions. The Presbyterian Church (U.S.A.) and the Episcopal Church in the United States of America allow clergy to bless same-sex unions if these unions are not called marriages.

6. Two journals in religious studies have addressed religious perspectives on same-sex marriage. For a "sample" debate between progressives and traditionalists, see *Philosophia Christi* 7:1 (2005) with an exchange of point-counterpoint presentations about same-sex marriage by Marvin M. Ellison ("Should the Traditional Understanding of Marriage as the One-Flesh Union of a Man and a Woman Be Abandoned?"), Francis J. Beckwith ("Legal Neutrality and Same-Sex Marriage"), Ronald E. Long ("In Support of Same-Sex Marriage"), and J. Budziszewski ("The Illusion of Gay Marriage"). In particular, see the responses to the presentations, including Ellison's "Heterosexism Is the Moral Scandal: A Response to Francis J. Beckwith" and Long's "Of Argument and Aesthetic Distaste: A Response to J. Budziszewski." In contrast, for a feminist roundtable discussion on same-sex marriage, see the *Journal of Feminist Studies in Religion* 20:2 (fall 2004) with essays by Mary E. Hunt, Marvin M. Ellison, Emilie M. Townes, Patrick S. Cheng, Martha Ackelsberg and Judith Plaskow, and Angela Bauer-Levesque.

7. See *Body and Soul: Rethinking Sexuality as Justice-Love*, ed. Marvin M. Ellison and Sylvia Thorson-Smith (Cleveland: The Pilgrim Press, 2003); Janet R. Jakobsen and Ann Pellegrini, *Love the Sin: Sexual Regulation and the Limits of Religious Tolerance* (New York: New York University Press, 2003); Patricia Beattie Jung and Ralph F. Smith, *Heterosexism: An Ethical Challenge* (Albany: State University of New York Press, 1993); *Sex and Religion*, ed. Christel Manning and Phil Zuckerman (Belmont, CA: Thomson Wadsworth, 2005); and *Homosexuality and World Religions*, ed. Arlene Swidler (Valley Forge, PA: Trinity Press International, 1993).

8. Rosemary Radford Ruether, *Christianity and the Making of the Modern Family* (Boston: Beacon Press, 2000), 224.

9. Ibid., 223, 173.

10. Ibid., 224.

11. Southern Baptist Convention, "Sexuality," available at www.sbc.net.

12. SBC, "The Baptist Faith and Message," XVIII. The Family, available at www.sbc.net.

13. SBC, "Sexuality."

14. SBC Resolution on Homosexual Marriage (June 1996), available at *www.sbc.net/resolutions*.

15. SBC, "Resolution on Homosexual Marriage," 2.

16. On this, see Beverly Wildung Harrison, "Agendas for a New Theological Ethic," in *Churches in Struggle: Liberation Theologies and Social Change in North America*, ed. William K. Tabb (New York: Monthly Review Press, 1986), 89–98. Also, Susan Brooks Thistlethwaite, "Enemy Mine: Why the Religious Right Needs Homophobia," *Chicago Theological Seminary Register* 91:3 (2001) (The Castaneda Addresses 1998–2001: Confronting Homophobia in Bible and Theology), 33–40.

17. SBC, "The Family," in "The Baptist Faith and Message," para. XVIII.

18. Jordan, *Blessing Same-Sex Unions: The Perils of Queer Romance and the Confusions of Christian Marriage* (Chicago, IL: The University of Chicago Press, 2005), 165.

19. SBC Resolution on Homosexual Marriage, 3.

20. United Church of Christ Synod 25 (2005), "In Support of Equal Marriage Rights for All," 2, available at *www.ucc.org*. Subsequent page references are to this document.

21. Gayle S. Rubin, "Thinking Sex: Notes for a Radical Theory of the Politics of Sexuality," in *The Lesbian and Gay Studies Reader*, ed. Henry Abelove, Michele Aina Barale, and David M. Halperin (New York: Routledge and Kegan Paul, 1993), 3–4.

22. William N. Eskridge, Jr., *The Case for Same-Sex Marriage: From Sexual Liberty to Civilized Commitment* (New York: The Free Press, 1996), 9.

23. *Ibid.*, 58.

24. *Ibid.*, 84.

25. See Nancy F. Cott, *Public Vows: A History of Marriage and the Nation* (Cambridge, MA: Harvard University Press, 2000).

26. Martha A. Fineman, *The Autonomy Myth: A Theory of Dependency* (New York: The Free Press, 2004), 132.

27. *Ibid.*, 152.

28. Robert McAfee Brown, *The Spirit of Protestantism* (New York: Oxford University Press, 1965), esp. chapter 4, "The Spirit of Protestantism," pp. 40–50.

29. Mary Daly, *Beyond God the Father: Toward a Philosophy of Women's Liberation* (Boston: Beacon Press, 1963), 126.

30. For progressive yet divergent perspectives, see Marvin M. Ellison, *Same-Sex Marriage? A Christian Ethical Analysis* (Cleveland, OH: The Pilgrim Press, 2004); Mark D. Jordan, *Blessing Same-Sex Unions: The Perils of Queer Romance and the Confusions of Christian Marriage* (Chicago, IL: The University of Chicago Press, 2005); and David G. Myers and Letha Dawson Scanzoni, *What God Has Joined Together? A Christian Case for Gay Marriage* (New York: HarperCollins Publishers, 2005).

31. Beverly Wildung Harrison, *Justice in the Making: Feminist Social Ethics*, ed. Elizabeth M. Bounds et al. (Louisville, KY: Westminster John Knox Press, 2004), 55.

32. Kelly Brown Douglas, using the term "platonized Christianity" to describe the dualistic distortions that have plagued western Christianity, analyzes how an oppressive Christian tradition, in demonizing sexuality, has entered into alliance with state power to punish non-normative people as "sexual deviants" and, therefore, enemies of God. See her *What's Faith Got to Do With It? Black Bodies/Christian Souls* (Maryknoll, NY: Orbis Books, 2005), esp. Part I.

29

*Familiar Idolatry
and the Christian Case
against Marriage*

DALE B. MARTIN

Contemporary Christianity in the United States—whether Protestant or Catholic, liberal or conservative—has so closely aligned the basic message of Christianity with the family and "traditional family values" that it is currently in a state of idolatry.[1] Increasingly, whether they are religious or not, people in America tend to equate Christianity with the family and "family values." It is not just that gay and lesbian people have largely left their churches; single people in general often feel out of place in churches. And other people in non-"traditional" family structures—whether divorced, cohabiting, or in partial nuclear families—tend to be much less active in churches. The reason is that American churches have so identified themselves with the modern, heterosexual, nuclear family that people without such families feel less at home in most churches.[2] The religious term for the identification of anything but God at the center of Christian faith is idolatry. And the idolatry of contemporary American Christianity is the familiar idolatry of the church's current focus on the family.

Not only is contemporary Christianity idolatrous in its focus on the family and marriage; it is also hypocritical. It either explicitly states or assumes that its current values are the obvious expression of Christian scripture and tradition. Though most Christians *assume* that the current centrality of marriage and family represents a long tradition in Christianity, it is actually only about 150 years old. One could even make the argument that the current focus on the heterosexual *nuclear* family dates back only to the 1950s.[3] In this chapter, I pass over the long tradition of Christianity, though it also provides little support for the modern family. Rather, I here concentrate mainly on the New Testament and the writings of the early church. Contrary to most contemporary opinion—Christian as well as non-Christian—there are many more resources in Christian scripture and tradition to *criticize* the modern family than to promote it.

THE HISTORICAL JESUS

Jesus of Nazareth was not a family man. Though we could debate the construction of the historical Jesus—and all "historical Jesuses" are in fact hypothetical constructions based on the flimsiest of evidence—according to all our available evidence, Jesus never married. This *could* have been an accident of history. It wasn't unusual for men in the ancient world to put off marriage, if they married at all, until their thirties. If Jesus was about 30 years old when he began his ministry, as suggested by some traditions (deriving from Luke 3:23), he could have been unmarried just because he hadn't gotten around to it. But there are other indications that he rejected marriage and family ties and taught his disciples to do likewise. Whatever the historical Jesus taught about sex, about which we have no real evidence, his message apparently included a severe critique of the traditional family, including marriage.

One of the sayings of the Gospels that must be historical is Jesus' response when told that his mother and brothers (and sisters according to one source [a textual variant at Mark 3:32]) wanted to see him. Jesus answers, "Who is my mother and who are my brothers? . . . Whoever does the will of God, that one is my brother and sister and mother" (Mark 3:34–35; cf. Matt. 12:46–50; Luke 8:19–21). Jesus refused to identify with his traditional family and instead substituted for it the eschatological community that shared his vision of a new, divinely constituted family.

Indeed, all our Gospels present Jesus as creating and living within an alternative to the household: an itinerant group of men and women unrelated to one another by blood or marriage, most of whom had also apparently separated from their families. Jesus called his disciples away from their households. Although perhaps teaching that the commandment to honor one's parents should still be obeyed (the evidence is either nonexistent or inconclusive), he told one man not even to bury his father—a teaching that would have been perceived as an incredible and offensive affront to family values in ancient Palestine (Luke 9:59–60; Matt. 8:21–22).[4] In another saying, as passed on by Luke, Jesus says, "If anyone comes to me and does not despise [or hate: *miseó*] his own father and mother and wife and children and brothers and sisters, and yes, his own life, he is not able to be my disciple" (Luke 14:26). Most modern Christians prefer to remember the saying in its Matthean version, where in place of "despise" or "hate," the author has Jesus say merely that one must not "love more" one's family than Jesus (Matt. 10:37). But the Lukan use of "hate" has support from the *Gospel of Thomas* 55, which may well be an independent witness to an early tradition. And it is more likely, many scholars believe, that the Lukan form better reflects an earlier, Aramaic source.[5] Moreover, Matthew would more likely have altered a "Q" saying to the less offensive "love more" in order to make Jesus' teaching fit his own high regard for the law of Moses.[6] Thus, the more radical version passed on by Luke and *Thomas* has the stronger claim to authenticity. A clearer indication that the historical Jesus taught the rejection of the traditional family can scarcely be demanded.

But doesn't Jesus' teaching about divorce, as contained mainly in Mark 10:6–12 and Matthew 19:4–9, imply the support of marriage? Here Jesus forbids divorce even though the law of Moses had allowed it. Wouldn't this imply that Jesus, if the saying is historical, supported marriage and the traditional family at least to the extent that the law did? Not really. After all, Matthew includes Jesus' forbidding of divorce but then follows it up with his saying about those who have "made themselves eunuchs for the sake of the kingdom of God" (Matt. 19:12). The saying is admittedly difficult to interpret and may not be historical—it is found only in Matthew, after all—but its most likely meaning is that the avoidance of procreation and marriage is preferable. The combination of the sayings is evidence that a writer could be opposed to divorce without advocating marriage and family. That possibility is upheld by almost all the church fathers, who almost without exception coupled a severe critique of marriage, in some cases all but forbidding it for truly pious Christians, with an even stronger prohibition of divorce.[7] Even if Jesus did forbid divorce, therefore, that cannot be taken as evidence that he advocated marriage.

What was the meaning, though, of Jesus' rejection of marriage and the family for himself and his disciples? One clue comes from his saying about the resurrection and marriage. Jesus says, "In the resurrection of the dead, people neither marry nor are married, but they are as angels in heaven" (Mark 12:26; Matt. 22:30). Thus far the saying as in Mark and Matthew. Luke, perhaps realizing that the saying was too cryptic, expands it, having Jesus explain it this way, "For they [that is, the resurrected dead] are no longer able to die, for they are equal to the angels and are sons of God, being sons of the resurrection" (Luke 20:36). Luke's version may be epexegetical, but it probably does correctly portray the basic meaning of the saying about angels. A common understanding among ancient Jews and Christians was that angels are androgynous or perhaps completely male. They needn't, in any case, reproduce themselves the way human beings do because they are not subject to death. The understanding throughout much of the ancient world was that marriage was for the purposes of legitimate and controlled procreation, which was necessary only because of the fact of death. Marriage, therefore, was completely implicated in the dreaded cycle of sex, birth, death, and decay, followed by more sex, birth, death, and decay. As John Chrysostom put it many years later, "Where there is death, there is marriage" (*On Virginity* 14.6). In the resurrection, Jesus taught, that cycle will have been broken. Marriage will be obsolete and even offensive in the kingdom of God. Jesus' rejection of the traditional family and his creation of an alternative community signaled the imminent, or perhaps incipient, inbreaking of the kingdom of God.

All our evidence pointing to the historical Jesus, therefore, indicates that he not only avoided marriage and family himself, but also taught people to forsake those institutions and enter into an alternative, eschatological society.

The household was part of the world order he was challenging. It, along with other institutions of power, would be destroyed with the coming kingdom. The household, moreover, represented traditional authority, which he was challenging at every turn. The household was implicated in the cycle of death. Indeed, the household, as the site of procreation, birth, and burial, was the very technology of life *and death* in the ancient world. For the historical Jesus, the rejection of marriage and the family was as necessary as the proclamation of the resurrection and the eternal kingdom of God.

THE GOSPEL OF LUKE
AND THE ACTS OF THE APOSTLES

Different Christians in the early church took these early Jesus traditions in different directions. We've already seen that Matthew toned down Jesus' anti-familial teachings somewhat, apparently uncomfortable with having Jesus speak of "hating" one's family. As we will see, later Christians actually turned the gospel around so that it supported rather than challenged the traditional household. Still other Christians carried on the anti-familial tendencies of the historical Jesus. The author of the Gospel of Luke and the Acts of the Apostles laces his entire narrative with the theme.

First, we should note how he himself may have edited the saying I've already quoted about "hating" one's family. Only Luke includes "wives and children" in the list of those a disciple is supposed to "despise." Although Thomas also uses the word "hate" or "despise," Thomas's account agrees with Matthew in *not* including wives in the list. It is possible, therefore, that Luke added "wives and children" to a list of family members he found in Q. This suggestion is supported by an analysis of the rest of the Gospel.

There occur a few small details special to Luke's Gospel that tip his hand about his stance on the traditional family. Only Luke contains Jesus' teaching that people should *not* invite their friends and family to a dinner they host, but that they should instead invite the poor, outcasts, those who cannot return the favor (14:12–14). A few sentences later, in the parable of the great banquet, only Luke has a character decline the invitation because he is about to be married (14:20), an excuse not found in Matthew's version.[8]

Other details in the early portions of Luke's Gospel, details usually overlooked, can also suddenly appear significant when seen in a larger context of Luke's critical stance toward the traditional family. Luke portrays the birth of Jesus, for example, as a very "public" event, not at all a "family affair." And toward the close of that narrative, Luke ominously adds that Mary "pondered in her heart" all that had happened (2:19). The next ominous foreshadowing concerning Mary occurs just a few verses later, when Simeon prophesies that a sword will pierce Mary's soul (2:35). And then again only a few verses later things become more explicit. At the age of twelve, Jesus in the Temple, though "obedient" to his parents (2:51), clearly expresses his ultimate independence from his fleshly family. He names God as his "father" and his "business" as God's "business" (2:41–51). The Greek here—*en tois tou patros mou*—could refer to the "matters" or "business" of the father (so the KJV?), the "household" of the father (and thus the RSV?), or even the "people" of the father (if taken to be masculine).[9] In any case, the contrast between Jesus' traditional family and the household of God is here early highlighted. Mary's soul is already being pierced.

The author of Luke-Acts then constructs his narrative to emphasize this contrast between the community of Jesus and the traditional family. In Luke 8:1–3, we are informed about Jesus' entourage, which includes the twelve male disciples, Mary Magdalene, Joanna, Susanna, and "many other" women. Jesus' "household" now consists of twelve men and several women, none of whom is mentioned as traveling with a spouse or family. It is no surprise, therefore, when a few verses later Jesus gets explicit about his substitution of this new community for his traditional family (8:19–21). Those who travel with him, not the nuclear family of his birth, are his family. In the next chapter Jesus tells the young man to forget burying his father and to follow Jesus instead (9:59–62), which is followed a few verses later by a description of the intimacy of Jesus with his true father: "Everything has been given to me by my father. No one knows who the son is except the father, and who the father is except the son and whomever the son chooses to reveal it to" (10:22). The contrast is thus made between the disruption Jesus brings to "normal" father-son relations and the intimacy of Jesus' own relation to his heavenly father.

Even clearer contrasts occur in the narrative of Acts. At the beginning of the book, for instance, the communal life of the disciples in Jerusalem is described (Acts 2:42–47). They meet in the Temple and in different houses all together. They share belongings and common meals. They hold all things in common (*eichon apanta koina*, 2:44). To make sure we get the point, the author rehearses the account two chapters later. He says that the disciples were all happily united; no one claimed any private property, but they rather held all things in common; whoever owned land or houses (think "households") sold them and delivered the proceeds to the whole group, to be administered by the apostles, who gave to each according to need. Joseph, an apparently single man called "Barnabas" by the apostles, is cited as a particular example: he sold a field and gave the entire proceeds to the community (4:32–37).[10]

Immediately and in direct contrast to this description of communal life, the author introduces the negative countertype: the married couple Ananias and Sapphira, to this point the only married couple mentioned in Acts.[11] In fact, they are the only married couple explicitly mentioned in Acts apart from Prisca and Aquila, who are themselves anything but the "normal," traditional married couple.[12] Note how the actions of Ananias and Sapphira are described (5:1–11). They are Christians with their own private possessions. But instead of doing as the others have done, they sell their possessions and bring only a portion of the proceeds to the church. Twice in the text, the author emphasizes that the two *conspire together* to deceive the church and avoid the communalism of the others (5:2, 9). As usual, the author of Acts presents Satan as the instigator of actions opposite those demanded in the kingdom of God, and also as usual, the actor on the side of the church is the Holy Spirit, to whom, Peter says, the couple has actually lied (5:3).[13] When Ananias and Sapphira die, we are told that they are carried out and buried by "young men," a detail repeated twice that is hard to explain, but may represent the "new" thing happening in this eschatological community of the future (the Greek word for "young men" builds on the Greek word that may also be translated "new"; 5:6, 10; cf. 2:17). Finally, the text emphasizes that the couple is buried together, the wife "right by her husband" (*pros ton andra autēs*, 5:10), together now in death as they were together in their conspiratorial marriage that sought its own interests before the communal interests of the spirit-led church.[14] Then, at the end of the story about the married couple, the narrative returns our vision once again to the (non-household) community, telling us that "great fear fell on the whole church and on all those who heard about these events" (5:11).

I think it cannot be an accident that a married couple, one of only two named in the book of Acts, serves as the negative countertype to the nonhousehold, eschatological community of the first part of the book, a community clearly foreshadowing and representing the coming community of God that will replace the traditional family for good. The solidarity of the married couple represents the old, self-serving order of the traditional family and familial solidarity, with its concerns for economic stability, inheritance, and continuity, in contrast to the new, young, growing, communal, eschatological household, whose procreation is a miraculous gift of the spirit and whose survival is assured by common solidarity and the gifts of God, a household of brothers and sisters rather than husbands and wives, fathers and mothers. Or to use another early and fundamental social metaphor for the church, the traditional couple is opposed to the *ekklēsia*, the "town gathering," the new polity of the gathered people of God that outgrows, transcends, and ultimately rejects the traditional family.

More such examples of the Christian critique of marriage and the family from Luke and Acts could be given, but I will mention only one. It has not often been noted that there is no explicit condemnation of divorce in Luke, though there is in both Matthew and Mark. Luke, unlike Matthew, does not appropriate the material from Mark 10:2–12, in which Jesus explicitly prohibits divorce. The only place where the subject comes up explicitly in Luke is in his quotation of a Q saying, but its precise wording should be analyzed carefully. According to Luke's wording, Jesus said, "Everyone who divorces his wife and marries another commits adultery, and any woman who has been divorced from her husband and marries another commits adultery" (Luke 16:18; compare Matt. 5:32; 19:9). According to most interpretations, this is read as a prohibition of *both* divorce *and* remarriage. But that, I argue, is to read the Lukan passage under the influence of the explicit prohibitions of divorce in Mark and Matthew. Luke's statement could easily be read as a prohibition only of the *combination of divorce with remarriage*. And that is the way I think it must be read. After all, we have already seen that Jesus in Luke, in contrast to the accounts in Matthew and Mark, *urges* his disciples to "hate" their wives. In Luke, Jesus demands that his disciples give up wives and children as well as their other family members in order to follow him. If Luke had Jesus forbid divorce or separation (and we must remember that for most people in the ancient world there was no real difference between divorce and separation)[15] while at the same time implying that his disciples must leave behind their wives, he would be caught in an obvious contradiction. But there is no contradiction if we assume that what Luke believed Jesus was prohibiting here was not divorce, but remarriage after divorce. This would also explain why he would *not* want to reproduce Mark 10:2–12 in his Gospel. Thus, Luke leaves out of his Gospel any prohibition of divorce; he has Jesus allow divorce but forbid remarriage. This fits perfectly with the other indications in Luke and Acts that the author took marriage and the traditional family to have been not just "relativized," but actually rejected by the gospel. Luke presents the church as replacing, not supporting, marriage and the family.[16]

THE REVELATION OF JOHN

Luke is not the only New Testament author who dreams of an eschatological community in which marriage and the traditional family are replaced by other social formations. The Revelation of John offers a similar vision, though it is also different in significant ways. The most obvious difference lies in the place assigned to women in the two different texts. Whereas the Christian community in Luke-Acts includes women, sometimes even in central roles, John imagines an exclusively male community, a kingdom of male priests and prophets who have "not been defiled by women" (14:4). There is no room in Revelation for actual, human women or for "normal" marriage and family.

John's world is ruled by God, the Pantocrator, the ruler of all, a designation for the Emperor appropriated by Christians for God. Jesus is also the "ruler of the kings of the earth" (1:5), another imperial title. John and his fellow Christians themselves constitute "the kingdom" (1:6). For John, Christians are priests serving God in the kingdom-empire ruled by God and Christ. John's universe is populated mainly by males. In his vision, he meets twenty-four male elders, four male beasts (4:4–7), two male prophets (11:3ff), and Michael, a male angel who leads an army of apparently male angels (12:7–9). John and his fellow Christians play several different roles in his universe: they are most often designated as fellow-slaves with the angels and brothers of one another, but they are also priests, prophets, and even kings (see 20:6). This is an entirely male community: God is father and Jesus is the eldest son, who is also repeatedly portrayed as a huge, vicious, violent, bloody, horned Lamb. The other members of the household are all brothers and fellow slaves—an all male household.

The first time we encounter a female figure in Revelation is with the appearance of Jezebel, the false prophet who seduces Jesus' "slaves" in the church at Thyat-ira (2:20). She is depicted as an adulteress and is promised a violent end along with those who have had sex with her, that is, those led astray by her from the strict ascetic Christianity advocated by John. There are only two or three other female figures in Revelation, according to how one counts. The starring role is played by Babylon, the great Whore, Rome, who spreads her legs for any king who wants her (Rev. 18:3, 9). The other two female figures are the woman who gives birth to the male child in Revelation 12 and the Bride of the Lamb, who appears at the end of the book, but some have speculated that these two figures perhaps overlap in the confusing and fluid symbolism of the Apocalypse. At any rate, they are completely passive figures; they are acted upon but scarcely act. The woman of chapter 12 gives birth to a male child (apparently representing Jesus as the Messiah: 12:5), is persecuted by the dragon, and is eventually saved by being put out of the way in "her place" prepared by God for her in the desert (12:13). Unlike her male child, who is snatched up to sit with the male God on the heavenly throne, she apparently doesn't get to go to heaven but spends the rest of the book in "her place" in the desert.

The last female character of Revelation is, of course, the Bride. She is prepared by the father God to marry his son the Horned Lamb (19:7). She is clothed in pure, clean linen, in contrast to the filth and blood and gore of the Whore; in fact, her clothing is actually *composed of* the "righteous deeds of the saints," that is, John and his fellow brother-slaves (19:8). At the end of the vision, we discover that she is the New Jerusalem (21:2, 10), which is of course populated by the male, servile household of God, including the twelve male apostles of the Lamb (21:14) and the twelve tribes of the *sons* of Israel (21:12). Thus, although the Horned Lamb marries a female figure, her body and clothing are actually composed of male deeds and bodies, the population of the divine household, the eschatological city, the finally victorious kingdom and empire.

We see here that although actual *sexual intercourse* is *supposed* to be absent from the eschatological community, desire and the erotic, especially the erotic of the eye, is everywhere.[17] First, there is the voluptuous though gruesome seduc-tiveness of Jezebel and the Whore—both of whom are depicted as promiscuous and dangerous. But John and his slave-brothers have resisted that seduction. And they have certainly resisted the seduction of normal marriage and family. They have, remember, "not been defiled, or polluted, by women" (14:1–5). The seduction they have apparently not been able to avoid is a certain erotic of homo-social male-bonding that pervades the vision. We have the image more than once in Revelation of God the father and Jesus the Horned Lamb, both sitting on the heavenly throne. Jesus also makes this promise to John, "The one who is victorious I will give to sit with me on my throne, as I was victorious and sat with my father on his throne" (3:21; see also 12:5). It is hard to avoid the image, once we actually picture it, of a bunch of men scrambling all over one another and sitting on one another's laps on a huge throne in the sky; perhaps God the father is on bottom, then the Horned Lamb on his lap, and then John and all his slave-brothers on their laps. Furthermore, it is curious that although there is a marriage in Revelation between a male and a female, the female's body and clothing are, as we saw, made up of male bodies. John and his brothers, in the person of the Bride herself, actually in the end *do* get to marry the Horned Lamb.

It is as if, for the author of the Apocalypse, there is no room for "normal" marriage and family in his world. The enemy, Rome, is not a "wife" but a whore who has slept around with every important man in the known world. Jesus is the bridegroom who is about to wed his bride. Christians are slave brothers who serve in the great household of God and have no contact with women. In fact, they must not do so since they constitute themselves the body of the bride of the Horned Lamb. They keep themselves pure (and John is obsessed with dirt, filth, and cleanliness, as well as with sex),[18] so they can be properly clean for their nuptial copulation with the Horned Lamb. How, in this universe, could Christians find a place for "normal" marriage and family?

In very different ways, therefore, Luke and John the Seer both envisioned Christian community as displacing marriage and family and replacing them with new eschatological social formations. And they may, in fact, have been inspired, as we have seen, by the teachings of Jesus himself. I now turn attention, though, to an obvious source for early Christian thinking about marriage and family: Paul and Paulinism.

THE APOSTLE PAUL

I have dealt at length with Paul's own position on sex and marriage elsewhere, so let me briefly summarize those findings here.[19] As we can see from 1 Corinthians 7, Paul was no proponent of marriage or the traditional family. He preferred that all Christians follow his example and remain unmarried. But he believed that some Christians, perhaps even most Christians, would be too weak to avoid the dangers of desire without sexual activity in marriage. So he allowed Christians to be married, in fact encouraged them to be married, if they were too weak to avoid desire otherwise. Note, however, that Paul never gives any indication that he believed marriage was the proper arena for the *expression* of sexual desire. Rather, his language makes it clear, I have argued, that he viewed marriage as the vehicle for the *avoidance* of desire. According to Paul, Christians do not *express* desire by means of marital sex; they *preclude* it. "It is better to marry than to burn" (1 Cor. 7:9). Since "burning" is a reference to sexual passion and desire, and Paul does not say that it is permissible to "burn" just a little, to "simmer," Paul's statement means that he viewed sex within marriage as the technique that would allow Christians to avoid the experience of sexual desire—ironically, from our perspective, through sexual intercourse performed within marriage but devoid of desire.

This interpretation is borne out by a careful examination of what Paul says in 1 Thessalonians 4:3–8. Paul tells the newly converted brothers in the church in Thessalonica (for whatever reason, he addresses only men) that each of them should "possess" or "control" his "thing" or "vessel," probably referring either to their genitalia or their wives, "in holiness and honor, not in the passion of desire like the Gentiles who do not know God" (4:4–5). Sexual passion, for Paul, is something that these Christian men should no longer experience; it is part of the Gentile world they have left behind. Marriage is the arena in which they should be able to have sex but avoid desire.

Whether or not one accepts my admittedly controversial interpretations of these passages, it must be admitted that Paul clearly preferred celibacy to marriage for Christians. He had no interest in the "propagation of the species," making babies, or raising families. He cannot be enlisted as a supporter, certainly in the romantic, modern sense, of marriage and family.

THE "PRO-FAMILY" PAUL

But of course, he has been so enlisted, not least by his disciples and probably not long after his death. The letter to the Colossians, which I take to be pseudonymous, does not actively promote the family, but it does assume it in the so-called "household code" proposed to maintain hierarchy and order in the household (3:18–4:1). Wives are told to submit to their husbands "as is fitting in the Lord"; husbands are told to love their wives and not treat them bitterly. Children are told to obey their parents in everything "for this is pleasing in the Lord"; fathers are told not to provoke their children or render them despondent. In the only admonition that exceeds a couple of phrases, slaves are then addressed with a full paragraph. Basically, they are told to serve their masters as if they were serving Christ, and that any misbehavior on their part will be severely punished not only by their earthly masters, but even, it is implied, by Christ himself. Then, in a return to the short phrase, masters are told to treat their slaves equitably, realizing that slave-owners themselves have a heavenly master.

Here in the name of Paul, the hierarchy of the ancient patriarchal household is reinforced in a way it never was in the authentic letters of Paul. True, Paul never advocated the abolition of slavery or the true equality of women, but his letters contain nothing really like this.[20] The position of this writer is nonetheless understandable. In the ancient world, if you were going to encourage marriage and the traditional household at all, you did so by placing the household in the structure of the universe, in a descending hierarchy with God on top, then male heads-of-households, then wives, then children, then slaves. The disproportionate attention given here to keeping slaves obedient and submissive works to make their slavery even more secure by inscribing it into their hearts and minds and into their relation even to God and Christ. When early Christian authors encourage marriage and family, without fail they do so by reinforcing the patriarchal ideology of their society.

The author of Ephesians, writing later and also in Paul's name, elaborates the household code from Colossians. The author of Ephesians, though, makes the male, patriarchal ideology even more insidious by conflating the superior male's role with that of God and Christ in relation to the church. As Christ is head of the church, so the man is head of the woman; as the church is submitted to Christ, so wives must submit to husbands and women to men in everything (5:21–24). Perhaps it should be noted that the Greek terms here for husband and wife are those also for man and woman. We in English have to decide how we will translate them, but we should not forget that the husband-wife hierarchy is but an instance of the universal male-female and man-woman hierarchy. The Greek ambiguity (are we talking about just husbands and wives or all men and women?) nicely preserves the universal ideological "truth" that enforces the household-gender hierarchy.

In the next few verses, the role of the husband is expanded, but significantly the comparison of the husband to Christ ends up allowing Christ and his activity to take over the context: "Husbands, love your wives, just as Christ loved the church and handed himself over for her, in order that he might make her holy, cleaning (her) by the washing of water of the utterance, in order that he may present to himself the glorified church, not having any stain or wrinkle or any such thing, but in order that she might be holy and blameless" (5:25–27). Note how the gendering of dirt is introduced. The gender duality makes the male the active agent: the male brings holiness, cleanness, blamelessness, glory, and spotlessness to the profane, dirty, stained, wrinkled, guilty, *female* principle.

Furthermore, the superior male agent is the *only* active agent. Besides "cleaning up" their wives, husbands also feed them, warm them, nourish them, as they do their own bodies. Women, on the other hand, don't do much of anything for their husbands except obey and fear them (5:33). Likewise next with the relationship of children to parents. Children are told simply to obey and honor their parents, but fathers (not the parents in general, note) are to nourish, educate, and admonish their children (6:1–4). Women and children are not told to "love" their husbands and fathers, just to obey, honor, and fear them. And they provide nothing for their men, but are themselves provided for. As in all ancient patronal ideology, the superior is the benefactor, the one who supplies the lack experienced by the inferior, whether of cleanliness, holiness, or nourishment. The patriarchal ideology of the ancient world becomes more pronounced and explicit the more the traditional household is encouraged.

This trajectory becomes simply more explicit and pronounced in the later Paulinism of the Pastoral Epistles. The author of 1 and 2 Timothy and Titus (not Paul, but a Christian writing in his name many years later) goes to greater lengths to reinforce and encourage the presence of the ancient family in the church and the structuring of the ancient church itself to resemble the hierarchical household and state. Early in 1 Timothy, for instance, the readers are instructed to pray for "kings and all in authority" (1 Tim. 2:2). (It is hard to imagine John making any such statement in his Apocalypse, just as it is hard to imagine him encouraging marriage and household economy as this author does.) In the Pastorals, women are not even allowed to pray or speak; they must learn "in silence and all submission" (2:11). They may teach younger women, but they are to have no authority over men whatsoever (2:12). This is justified because of their implication in the deception and sin of Eve. Their main role is as childbearers, through which they may be saved if they behave themselves properly (2:15).

Not only is the patriarchal household strengthened within the church; the church itself—no longer a "town meeting"—is forced into the mold of the patriarchal household (3:5). Thus women without husbands become a particular problem for this author. The author, anxious to allow neither young nor old women to escape the confines of the household, urges that the younger women be encouraged to find themselves husbands. For the older women, for whom that would not usually be a practicable solution in the ancient world, the author must figure out some way to insert them into the household of the church. They cannot be allowed to be independent or outside patriarchal authority. They therefore are inscribed in roles within the church family under the authority of its male leaders (5:3–16). It goes without saying that slaves in these letters are similarly dealt with: they are told not to expect any relief from Christianity for their servitude (6:1–2).

The familial hijacking of the apostle Paul, therefore, began early in Christianity. Paul was made to support marriage and the traditional family. But not surprisingly, that meant that Paul became a stronger proponent of social, cosmic, and ecclesiastical patriarchy and hierarchy than he had been in his authentic letters. In the ancient world, to promote marriage and the family necessarily meant to promote patriarchal ideology. And Paul was put to service to that end.

THE "ANTI-FAMILY" PAUL

If the canonical disciples of Paul worked to enlist the apostle in their pro-family agenda, other followers of Paul in the ancient church made him their spokesman for an anti-familial Christian message, a message that eventually proved to be more powerful and dominant in the Christianity of late antiquity than the pro-family version. One of the most popular of ancient ascetic tracts was a short document known to modern scholars as *The Acts of Paul and Thecla*.

The story of Thecla recounted in the document is fascinating for the way it appropriates many of the elements of the Greek romantic novel in order to promote a Christian ascetic message. Ancient Greek novels are highly eroticized and romanticized narratives in which two young people struggle throughout the long narrative to consummate their love. The characters are usually separated at the beginning of the story and seek to be reunited. They are placed in all sorts of tragic and traumatic situations of love and danger. They cry about their fate, weep, mourn. Though their virtue is continually assaulted, they are usually able to remain loyal to one another, and they are eventually reunited and married. The ancient novels actually worked to teach quite conservative notions about the value and eternity of marriage and the traditional, elite Greek household.[21]

The Acts of Paul and Thecla plays on these themes and disrupts them at the same time. The heroine, Thecla, is an upper-class woman who becomes enamored by the ascetic message of the apostle Paul, which teaches young people and women to keep themselves absolute virgins, to avoid sex entirely, to reject marriage, to devote themselves to complete and pure celibacy. According to Paul in this text, the only way to keep the flesh pure and experience the resurrection and eternal life is to remain virginal and celibate. Thecla's attraction to Paul and his message is narrated in the tones of the desire and passion of the novels: her desire for Paul is provoked simply by hearing his voice or seeing him teaching (§7); like a love-struck heroine, she wastes away when apart from him and is "taken captive" by him (§§8–9); she experiences her love for Paul like a disease (§10). When she is finally allowed to come into his presence, she kisses his fetters and rolls herself around in the dust where he had earlier been sitting (§§18, 20). Throughout the narrative, moreover, the exceptional beauty of Thecla is emphasized; she is even repeatedly portrayed as naked and exposed to the voyeuristic public and authorities (§§33, 34). The emphasis throughout the narrative on the absolute necessity of celibacy is surpassed only by the story's highly charged eroticism. Thus, though the Christianity presented by the text is one of complete sexual renunciation, it is scantily clothed in the obviously erotic rhetoric of the ancient romantic novel.

The ultimate "enemy" of the narrative is the household. Over and over again, the story sets up a conflict between the male heads-of-households—*patres familiae*—along with the male political authorities, on the one hand, and the vast majority of the women, on the other. When Thecla is arrested or condemned to torture, it is the women of the city who pray for her, beg for her release, and bemoan her fate. But interestingly, the wives are not the only ones who side with Thecla against their own husbands. They are joined by the "young men and women" of the towns and cities. And in one scene of torture, a lioness, meant to attack Thecla, ends up siding with her. The lioness attacks the male lion and eventually gives her own life in battle against the *male* beasts in order to save Thecla. Conflict in the story pits male heads-of-households against all other potential members of households—women, girls, and young men—on the other side with Thecla. The men understand perfectly what is at issue: they themselves insist that if Christianity and Thecla succeed, that will mean the destruction of their households (§§10, 15–16).[22]

In the end, Thecla triumphs. She baptizes herself (in a huge vat of killer seals, which are all miraculously killed by a lightning bolt before they can eat Thecla); she promises to cut her hair like a man's; she dresses herself like a man. At the end of the story, she is given a fortune by a rich widow so that she (and her mother!) can become independent and self-supporting. Thecla no longer needs a man even for financial support. Totally freed from the family and household, financially and spiritually independent, she leaves even Paul, becomes an apostle *like* Paul, and goes off to spread the Christian message of the destruction of the ancient household and to establish alternative communities of erotic Christian ascetics. Traditional marriage is rejected in favor of erotic asceticism.

The Acts of Paul and Thecla appropriates the authority of the apostle Paul to promote a woman-centered, though admittedly androgynous, form of ascetic Christianity set up in direct opposition to the male-dominated, traditional hierarchical household as promoted by other early Christian documents, such as the Pastoral Epistles. Though it must be admitted that Thecla plays the really starring role in the narrative, Paul also becomes here a radical opponent of the family. The story seems to recognize what we had surmised when reading the pseudepigraphical Pauline texts: if you want to challenge the male-dominated authority structures of ancient culture, you must reject marriage and the family.

THE JOVINIAN CONTROVERSY

Though there were some early voices, such as the author of 1 and 2 Timothy and Titus examined above, who promoted ancient "family values," the opposite point of view, which valued celibacy over marriage, gradually became the more dominant position in late ancient Christianity, at least among the church's leaders and as portrayed in its writings. As J. N. D. Kelly has put it:

> From the second century onwards a widening stream of such [ascetic] essays [he is here referring first to Jerome's Letter 22, really a treatise denigrating marriage and advising celibacy] had been published by Christian writers. . . . They all draw on a common fund of ideas and expound, though with widely differing nuances, what is essentially the same doctrine. This is that marriage is, on the most favorable interpretation, a poor second best; virginity is the original state willed by God, and sexual intercourse came in only after the Fall. The underlying presuppositions are that the sexual act is intrinsically defiling, and that indulgence in it creates a barrier between the soul and God. If one is married, it is better to abstain from intercourse; a second marriage betokens regrettable carnal weakness.[23]

By the late fourth century, it was difficult to find a church leader with a different opinion.[24]

Difficult, but not impossible. In fact, the issue came to a head in a controversy centered around a Roman Christian named Jovinian, who, sometime around 390, began teaching, not the *superiority* of the married state, but that those who married and had sex were no worse in the eyes of God than virgins or celibates. Jovinian based his argument on a "high" view of baptism. He taught that all baptized Christians were and would continue to be of equal spiritual and moral status whether they were married, widowed, or virgin. Christians who fast are not superior to those who eat with thankfulness. And at the last judgment, all Christians who have preserved their baptism faithfully will receive equal reward regardless of whether they have been ascetics or not.[25]

Jovinian was quickly and firmly condemned. In probably 393, the bishop of Rome, Pope Siricius, called a synod that promptly rejected Jovinian's views and excommunicated Jovinian and eight of his associates. Siricius announced the excommunication in a letter to Italian bishops, in which he called Jovinian and his friends "the authors of a new heresy and blasphemy." They were, he says, "wounding Catholics, perverting the continence of the Old and New Testaments, interpreting it in a diabolical sense; by their seductive and deceitful speech they have begun to destroy no small number of Christians and to make them allies of their own insanity."[26] David Hunter has noted the historical significance of the letter: "Siricius's letter marked the first time in the history of Christianity that the superiority of celibacy over marriage was officially defined as doctrine, and conversely, that its denial was labeled as 'heresy.'" Though the sentiment had long been held by at least the vocal leadership of Christianity, it had not before been explicitly affirmed as the only permissible Christian view. "Siricius's letter, therefore, marked a distinctive hardening of boundaries in the later fourth century, the moment at which a previously implicit Christian consensus about marriage and celibacy reached a consequential degree of explicitness"—by means, that is, of an explicit statement declaring the inferiority of marriage as doctrine.[27]

In the wake of the condemnation, Jovinian and his friends betook themselves to Milan, but the famous and powerful bishop there, Saint Ambrose, also convened a synod of his own and confirmed both the condemnation of Jovinian's views and the excommunication. Both the pope and one of the most respected of the church fathers had condemned as "heresy" the opinion that the married state could be held to be of equal virtue with celibacy.

The most vocal opponent of Jovinian, however, was Jerome, one of the most prolific and famous of early church fathers and biblical interpreters, who wrote a fairly long treatise refuting Jovinian's claims point by point and besmirching his reputation. Never one to rise above personal invective and misrepresentation, Jerome exaggerates Jovinian's arguments and claims that Jovinian had disparaged celibacy, for which there is absolutely no evidence. Jovinian had simply argued that celibacy was not a *superior* state when compared to marriage.[28] Jerome's main concern is to maintain hierarchy of virtue and reward. He ranks virginity highest, followed by marriage, with fornication ranking below both. Elsewhere, he ranks virginity highest, followed by widowhood, and then marriage. Or he can combine widows and those who avoid sex even though married, and place them above sexually active wives, but below virgins.[29]

Jerome *claims* that he is not condemning marriage or sex completely (e.g., *Against Jovinian* 1.3). When he is careful, he writes that "the Church does not condemn marriage but makes it subordinate."[30] But Jerome gets carried away in his disgust for sex and marriage, and many of his readers, ancient and modern, have felt that Jerome does in fact come very close to condemning marriage. Jerome argues that sex is permissible *only* for procreation (*Against Jovinian* 1.20). He argues that since abstaining from sex with one's wife "honors" her, having sex with her is equivalent to "shaming" her (1.7). Throughout, he portrays any kind of sexual activity, even that in marriage, as impure and polluting to the participants: *all* sexual intercourse is "unclean" (1.20). Finally,

Jerome also (though he had apparently not by this time heard about the official condemnations of Siricius and Ambrose) calls Jovinian's view of the equality of marriage and virginity "heresy" (2.37).

Saint Augustine somewhat later also came out with publications against Jovinian's view of the "equality" of marriage. Augustine felt Jerome had gone too far, making sex and marriage sound not only "second best" but even sinful. Augustine seems to have altered his views about sex and marriage at different stages of his life. Generally, at any rate, Augustine ended up advocating that marriage was indeed a "good" and that sexual intercourse within marriage should not be condemned if done under the right conditions and with proper attitudes. The main purpose of sex is to produce children, and so sex within marriage should be indulged only for purposes of procreation. Thus, couples should not indulge if the woman is already pregnant.[31] Yet against Jovinian, Augustine affirms the superiority of celibacy: "For this reason it is a good to marry, since it is a good to beget children, to be the mother of a family; but it is better not to marry, since it is better for human society itself not to have need of marriage."[32] Augustine's position would be the one to become *the* view of the church until the Reformation and the beginnings of modernity.

This debate should not be simply ignored as "ancient history." Jovinian's view—and remember that he was advocating simply the *equality* of marriage, not its superiority—was declared heretical by a pope and three of the most honored church "fathers" and saints: Ambrose, Jerome, and Augustine. Whereas Jovinian seems to have been motivated by notions of equality that remarkably resemble modern Christian sensibilities, the "orthodox" Christian leaders were all concerned to maintain strict hierarchies both in this life and in the life to come, hierarchies of virtue and reward in which perpetual virginity occupied the highest position, with celibacy, then abstinence in marriage, then sexual activity in marriage occupying positions of virtue in a descending grade. That was the view that was considered the Christian view for most of Christian history. It is highly ironic that promoters of modern Christian "family values" and the centrality of marriage and family for Christianity portray themselves as the supporters of Christian tradition. In fact, they would be considered heretics by the "orthodox" Church Fathers.

THE PURITAN REVOLUTION

The long history of the "orthodox" position on marriage and family came under challenge beginning in the sixteenth century and reached a new height with the writings of Anglicans and especially Puritans in the seventeenth century. Some precursors to the Protestant Reformation had already challenged the critical view of marriage and sex of the previous centuries. "Humanist" scholars began proclaiming the superiority of the married state to celibacy. Erasmus may have been influenced by his contact with English humanists in his writing of *Encomium Matrimonii*, in which he praised the married state in comparison to celibacy. The Council of Trent, however, condemned Erasmus's views, and *Encomium Matrimonii* was placed on the index of prohibited books in 1547.[33]

Though the movement was encouraged by the Reformers Luther and Calvin, it was in England, no doubt due to the English Reformation and the abolition there of monasteries and the allowance of clerical marriage, that a change of doctrine became increasingly popular. As Lawrence Stone explains, "The medieval Catholic ideal of chastity, as a legal obligation for priests, monks and nuns and as an ideal for all members of the community to aspire to, was replaced by the ideal of conjugal affection. The married state now became the ethical norm for the virtuous Christian. . . ."[34] The very notion of what constituted a proper Christian churchman changed. In the words of Christopher Hill, "The monasteries, nunneries, friaries and chantries disappeared, and the priest, set apart by his celibacy and mediating the sacraments of the universal Church, yielded place to the parson as good family man."[35]

We must recognize that this was not simply a "reform" of previous corrupt practices or a "purifying" of the Church along the lines of acknowledged orthodoxy. It was, rather, a radical *reversal* or *overturning* of previous Christian teaching about the superiority of celibacy over sex and the family.[36] And it was happening among Puritans and Anglicans alike. The theme of "holy matrimony" pervaded Protestant sermons throughout the sixteenth century.[37] Puritans increasingly took the concept further, and it is not difficult to see why: especially after the Restoration of the monarchy and the re-"Establishment" of the Church of England in 1660, Puritans were forced to rely on "separated" churches, and these were constructed as voluntary associations of "pure" and "holy" households. For the Puritans, the separated church made up of pious households replaced the "parish" as the true locus for religious observation.[38]

The seventeenth century saw the publication of many books of advice for the householder, informing him how to arrange and manage his family in a productive and pious manner. But they also sounded the new note of approval for marriage and sex, and explicitly valued marriage over celibacy. William Perkins, at the beginning of the 1600s, provided readers with his sage recommendations on the subject "Of Christian Oeconomie, or Household Government," and though he sounds reserved about marriage compared to the unrestrained encomia of our own day, he insists that it is the superior state: "Mariage of it selfe is a thing indifferent, and the kingdome of God stands no more in it then [sic] in meates and drinkes; and yet it is a state in it selfe, farre more excellent, then the condition of single life."[39] Puritans in the New World read these manuals and wrote their own. They repeatedly insist that God had ordained marriage for everyone and that sex in marriage was essential.[40]

As we have seen, a few early Christian writers, most notably the author of 1 and 2 Timothy and Titus, offered the household as model for the structure of the church. Puritan authors, in a sense, reversed the direction of influence: in work after work of the sixteenth and seventeenth centuries, they admonish their readers to make their home into "a little church." It is as if the household comes to replace the church as the primary locus of religious activity, certainly as the primary ideological model for piety and observance. The male head of the household assumes the role of priest or pastor. In a commentary on the conversion of the jailor's household in Acts 16:34, Thomas Taylor preached, "Let every Master of Family see to what he is called; namely, to make his house a little Church, to instruct every one of his Family in the feare of God, to containe every one of them under holy discipline, to pray with them, and for them: that there may be a draught or Modell of a Church in his House."[41] In a regularly recurring theme of the entire period, authors told their readers, here in the words of William Gouge in the early seventeenth century, ". . . a family is a little Church, and a little commonwealth."[42] It is not surprising, therefore, that the period, according to Levin Schücking, saw the development of home Bible study as a Protestant invention emphasized even more by Puritans. In fact, the era saw the rise of the "Family Bible" in homes.[43]

Lest this portrait sound too much like the "family" of our own day, we should emphasize that we are speaking here not of the modern, private, nuclear family but of the "household." Though the nuclear family certainly became more visible in this period, perhaps sociologically as well as ideologically, and it may even be true that most Puritans experienced household as predominantly nuclear (that is, it may be that many households *did* include only husband, wife, and immediate children), the kind of household that we see in literary remains of the period, including legal records and the like, was not *presented* mostly as the nuclear family. These advice books, for instance, always have large sections on how to deal with one's servants, sounding as if they *assumed* their presence in any "normal" household. The ideal Puritan household in New England included apprentices and servants, who would live with the family, and sometimes children from other homes who had been "sent out" to live with another family for any number of reasons. Moreover, New England colonies and communities were officially and legally constructed as collections of households, not individuals. Therefore, the authorities made repeated attempts in some locales to keep single adults from living alone or together outside a "normal" household. Single adults, even males, were forced to live within other existing family units. There were, therefore, all sorts of experiments attempting to incorporate "all stray bachelors and maids under the discipline of a real family governor."[44]

Furthermore, there was no expectation in New England communities that the family was "private" or immune from governmental interference or "social engineering." Modern conservatives might argue that "it doesn't take a village to raise a child; it takes a *family*." But their Puritan forefathers were ready to interfere when they felt that a householder was not fulfilling his role properly. The "state," therefore, was in control over who would be a householder and who not, and over their behavior. In the early and mid-1600s, if a householder was not behaving as the governing authorities felt he should, they could disband his household, take away his children and servants, parcel them out to other households, and force him to become a member of another household himself.[45] The Puritan household was a far cry from the nuclear family free from governmental interference so central to modern conservative romance.

The Puritan family was also firmly patriarchal. New England communities did have laws limiting the rights of husbands and providing protection for wives and children. Communities, according to recent studies, did sometimes side with women against their husbands. Some scholars have argued that Puritan women experienced better situations than women of previous eras in Europe. Yet the Puritan household was staunchly hierarchical, with the "master" firmly in charge, at least ideologically.[46] No modern notion of egalitarianism in marriage made its way into the Puritan family. Rather, it is as if what we saw to be the case in early Christianity was true also in Puritanism: the more the family is emphasized, the more patriarchy and hierarchy are strengthened.[47]

Modern Christians, if they paused long enough to look at the actual history rather than their American romanticizing of it, should think twice before calling on their Puritan "forefathers" to support their own ideology of the family. First, they must admit that the Puritan revolution was, by the standards of earlier Christianity, "heresy." When modern gay and lesbian Christians urge the recognition of same-sex marriages in churches, they are actually asking for a change much less radical than that already accomplished by the Reformers and the Puritans, who completely reversed doctrines and ethics of 1500 years of Christian tradition and made the married state not only equal to singleness but superior to it. In comparison, simply evaluating gay and lesbian relationships on a par with those of their heterosexual neighbors is a modest innovation. Second, modern advocates of "traditional family values" should admit that their notion of the (usually) egalitarian, private, nuclear family is *not* a true continuation of the Reformation or Puritan household after all. The irony, or rather hypocrisy, of modern appeals to "tradition" or the "religious heritage" of American "forefathers" to support the modern notion of family should be obvious.

THE CHRISTIAN LEGACY OF THE FAMILY

There were certainly voices in ancient Christianity, as throughout its history, that have *interpreted* the gospel to support and promote traditional family values—of the *ancient household*. But I would argue that the vast majority of the resources of scripture and Christian tradition until the modern period lend themselves much more readily to a critique of marriage and the family than to advocacy of them. Though the Christianity of the vast sweep of history from the church fathers until the Reformation did not go so far as to condemn marriage outright, it consistently assigned an inferior position to marriage and to those Christians who married. The "higher calling" was most often understood to be the avoidance of marriage, certainly in much of the New Testament and for almost all of late ancient Christianity.

It is thus ironic, though not really surprising, that American Christianity, especially Protestantism, has reversed the traditional valuations of Christianity.

Coupled with the obscene emphasis on patriotism and nationalism, the emphasis on the family in American Christianity and popular culture approaches idolatry. "Family values" are practically the only values, along with perhaps nationalism, that seem universally recognized as "Christian values" in American popular culture, including most churches.

One of this chapter's goals is to highlight how wrong modern Christians are when they claim that their own ideology, and idolatry, of the family is simply "the biblical" or "the traditional" position. If they were true to the historical meaning of the texts and the tradition, they would have to admit that their high valuation of marriage and the family runs *counter* to the teachings of Jesus, authors of the Gospels, Paul, other biblical writers, as well as most of the church "fathers," popes, and saints. Furthermore, their own promotion of marriage and their adoration of the family run counter to the longer tradition of Christianity, at least of "orthodox" Christianity, and represent a rather radical and recent innovation in Christian doctrine and ethics. It is simply misleading, perhaps hypocritical, to say that modern family values are simply "the biblical" or "the Christian" view. In fact, there are more resources in scripture and tradition to *critique* marriage and the family than to support it.

Another goal of this chapter, therefore, is to point out the many texts available to queer Christians that may be used to criticize the modern idolatry of marriage and family. Though I support to some extent the extension of state recognition of same-sex unions on a par with heterosexual marriage—gay and lesbian couples should have all the rights and privileges recognized by the state for heterosexuals—I am deeply ambivalent about pursuing same-sex marriage as a solution to the injustices of homophobia. I believe that both the state and the church should get out of the marriage business.

There are many excellent reasons why people in general and Christians in particular should *not* want to give the state the power to recognize and regulate marriage. When we give the state the right to legitimize one kind of sexual relationship or social formation, we automatically give it the right to render all other relations illegitimate.[48] Surely, the church should never cede its own prerogatives to the state—especially a state as bloodstained and beholden to the interests of the powerful as ours is. But *all* people should realize this: when you marry, you give power to the state over your sexual relations, your person, the most intimate details of your life and body. To agree to marriage is to agree that the modern, violent, bureaucratic state has the right to control your life in its most intimate realms, public and private, personal and sexual, individual and collective. Not to put too fine a point on it, marriage cedes your genitals to the government.

The modern emphasis on marriage and the nuclear family, moreover, fools people into thinking that the modern family can do what it cannot do. The modern family simply cannot bear the weight placed on it; it cannot deliver all the goods demanded of it, whether social, economic, emotional, or psychological. Conservatives and liberals who focus on the family, therefore, are allowing the state to shirk its own responsibilities.[49] They are attempting to push off onto the fragile modern family the responsibilities that only the state in the modern world can really bear: for universal child care and education, health care, care for the elderly and disadvantaged. The state should get out of the marriage business and get to the tasks that are its true responsibilities: caring for its citizens.

But I believe the church should also get out of the marriage business. Marriage is an exclusive and exclusionary technology for control.[50] Modern churches legitimate one kind of social and intimate bonding and therefore declare illegitimate all others. *This* relationship is good—in fact, "divine." All others are bad or at best inferior.

This exclusionary technique can be seen also in the connection of marriage to procreation. Though the stigma and shame associated with births "out of wedlock" have gradually diminished, they are still present—as is proven by the fact that cohabiting couples so often decide to marry when they become or decide to become expectant parents. Marriage legitimates childbirth. But it necessarily therefore declares other births illegitimate. Why should the church want to allow *any* of its children to be thought "illegitimate"? *Our* cry, rather, should be "No bastard children!" Bastard children are not created by the absence of marriage, but by marriage itself. Marriage makes bastards by making the category possible. For these and many other reasons we could give, both the state and the church should get out of the marriage business.

Yet queer Christians need not stop with the simply negative task of critiquing marriage and the family. Another goal of this essay is to provoke contemporary Christians into thinking about different ways of reading Christian scripture and tradition. Queer Christians (whose queerness may manifest itself in all sorts of unexpected ways) should use their imaginations to allow scripture and tradition to inspire new visions of Christian community free from the constraints of the modern, heterosexual, nuclear family. We could imagine traveling bands of erotic followers of Jesus, or spirit-filled "town meetings" sharing things in common, or lively communities of men or women living together, or lively communities of men *and* women living together. We could imagine "households" of new construction, representing in their own adventuresome lives together hopes for new communities of the future. Eschatological communities. Communities in which single people are not second class citizens, in which there are no "bastards," in which sexual orientation does not in itself stigmatize, in which varieties of households are nurtured. Alternative models to the traditional family are ready to hand in rich Christian scripture and tradition.

The texts of scripture and tradition I have analyzed bring both problems and possibilities. Some of them offer alternative visions of human community, but at the price of an asceticism that renders desire and sex shameful or even sinful, a course we must also reject. Others are built on ideologies that despise the body or women. There will be no resource in Christianity or any other tradition, however, that is not to some extent problematic. All human models are tainted. There are no clean words. But these resources may also be used for retraining our imaginations both to see the inherent evils in the modern idolatry of marriage and family and to develop visions of alternative, eschatological, forward-looking communities. Rather than looking to scripture and tradition to justify the recognition of same-sex unions and marriage, we should attempt to recover and revise resources from a forgotten Christianity vouchsafed to us in scripture and premodern traditions: the long and valuable history of the Christian case against marriage.

NOTES

1. Rodney Clapp notes that the church may be called "the last great stronghold of family idolatry"; see *Families at the Crossroads: Beyond Traditional and Modern Options* (Downers Grove, Illinois: Intervarsity, 1993), 12; see also Janet Fishburn, *Confronting the Idolatry of Family: A New Vision for the Household of God* (Nashville: Abingdon, 1991), esp. 107. The idolatry of the family can be seen by a careful analysis of one study that argues that "the healthy family as we know it today would not exist but for the profound influence of religion, especially Christianity, through the ages" (Anthony J. Guerra, *Family Matters: The Role of Christianity in the Formation of the Western Family* [St. Paul: Paragon House, 2002], xi). Guerra states that the most important factor promoting the "healthy family" is religion (xxi–xxiii). He also insists that no one religion "has a monopoly" on the value he attributes to religion in general to promote and protect "family values" (xii–xiii). Since there is no belief or doctrine that *all* "religions" hold in common (not even monotheism or the belief in "God" at all), the *only* thing all "religions" must hold in common (in Guerra's construction) is the promotion of the family. But that is what Guerra is highlighting as the fundamental value of Christianity. Unwittingly perhaps, Guerra has substituted "family values" for all other doctrines, beliefs, and practices as *the* central aspect of Christianity of any importance. The theological word for that is "idolatry." (Incidentally, the "healthy family" for Guerra is only the modern, nuclear family consisting of a heterosexual couple, only once married, and their immediate children; see pp. xii–xiii, xiv, xvi, xvii.)

2. See Kathy Rudy, *Sex and the Church: Gender, Homosexuality, and the Transformation of Christian Ethics* (Boston: Beacon, 1997), 119.

3. On the novelty and *aberration* of the 1950's ideal family when compared to most of human history and most cultures, see Stephanie Coontz, *The Way We Never Were: American Families and the Nostalgia Trap* (New York: Basic Books, 1992), 25–29.

4. Byron R. McCane, "'Let the Dead Bury Their Own Dead': Secondary Burial and Matt. 8:21–22," *Harvard Theological Review* 83 (1990): 31–43.

5. T. W. Manson, *The Sayings of Jesus* (Grand Rapids: Eerdmans, 1957), 131; François Bovon, *L'Évangile selon Saint Luc (9,51–14,35)* (Geneva: Labor et Fides, 1996), 471.

6. "Q," from the German word *Quelle*, which means "source," is the designation given to a hypothetical document many scholars *believe* was used by both Matthew and Luke in the writing of their own Gospels. If they both used it, it obviously would represent a source earlier than their own texts.

7. Elizabeth A. Clark, *Reading Renunciation: Asceticism and Scripture in Early Christianity* (Princeton: Princeton University Press, 1999), 242–250.

8. Or that of Thomas in the precise sense. Thomas has a man excuse himself in order to arrange the wedding of someone else (*Gospel of Thomas* 64).

9. François Bovon, *Luke: A Commentary on the Gospel of Luke 1:1–9:50* (Minnesota: Fortress, 2002), 1.114.

10. I take it that Barnabas is not married because no wife or family is ever mentioned for him, he travels around with Paul, likewise unmarried, without a family, and he is mentioned in this capacity by Paul in 1 Corinthians 9:6. Though the precise verse in which

Barnabas is mentioned refers to working for a living rather than living off contributions from the churches, the context also includes "traveling around with a sister-wife" as had Peter and other apostles. I take it that Paul then includes Barnabas with himself as someone who has not taken advantage of that "right."

11. Commentators generally note that Barnabas serves as a positive example and Ananias and Sapphira as negative examples of the communalism expected of early Christians in Acts. See, e.g., C. K. Barrett, *A Critical and Exegetical Commentary on the Acts of the Apostles* (Edinburgh: T. and T. Clark, 1994), 2.257–271; Joseph A. Fitzmyer, *The Acts of the Apostles* (New York: Doubleday, 1964), 315.

12. They aren't "normal" for several reasons. They have no children, nor a "stable" household, but rather are themselves fairly itinerant; Prisca (or Priscilla, as in Acts) is often mentioned first, implying higher status for her, at least for the author, than her husband; their "household" is permeable enough to include Paul in it at times. Paul moves in with them, works with them, and relocates with them. Their relationship, in any case, cannot be made into a "nuclear family," and neither does it look like the traditional extended family of antiquity.

13. For the activities of Satan in Luke-Acts, see Susan R. Garrett, *The Demise of the Devil: Magic and the Demonic in Luke's Writings* (Minneapolis: Fortress, 1989).

14. The "togetherness" of Ananias and Sapphira "violated the togetherness of the Christian community" (Ben Witherington III, *The Acts of the Apostles: A Socio-Rhetorical Commentary* [Grand Rapids: Eerdmans, 1998], 218). Ananias and Sapphira represent a "counter-community . . . over against the spirit-community that shares its possessions" (Luke Timothy Johnson, *The Acts of the Apostles*, Sacra Pagina Series, vol. 5 [Collegeville, Minnesota: Liturgical Press, 1992], 87; see also 89).

15. For most people in the Greco-Roman world, separation *meant* divorce, even legally. According to Roman family law, which may not have even applied to non-Roman Christians and Jews, divorce was effected simply by one of the partners "willing" to be no longer married. Abandonment was almost always sufficient for divorce. Moreover, without marriage laws to regulate the daily lives of most inhabitants of the Greco-Roman world (Roman family law applied only to Roman citizens), "divorce" would have most normally been effected simply by "separation."

16. I take the language of "relativization" mainly from Stephen C. Barton, *Discipleship and Family Ties in Mark and Matthew* (Cambridge: Cambridge University Press, 1994), passim. Though Barton is dealing with Mark and Matthew rather than Luke, I believe he, even for those contexts, is too eager to downplay any possible "anti-familial" message in the texts. Referring to Mark 10:1–31, for instance, he claims, "Nevertheless, it should be pointed out that this material reflects no animosity to family and household *per se*, something we had cause to observe in relation to earlier pericopae, as well. Instead, their significance is made relative to cross-bearing discipleship for the sake of Jesus and the gospel" (107; see also 122). It is hard to evaluate such a claim, which is repeated several times in one form or another in Barton's study, because Barton never really explains what "animosity" means or what "*per se*" covers. Certainly it would be stretching the evidence to say that it shows that Jesus had some *personal, psychological hatred* ("animosity") to the family *in the abstract* ("*per se*"). But it is just as unlikely that the texts make *only* the point—similar to modern Christian piety—that Jesus and the gospel are to demand "relatively" more loyalty than one's household. Rather, the statements teach the replacement of the traditional household by the eschatological community of God initiated by Jesus. There is nothing "psychological" or "abstract" going on here; it is rather a radical challenge of the "normal family" by the kingdom of God.

17. Tina Pippin, *Death and Desire: The Rhetoric of Gender in the Apocalypse of John* (Louisville: Westminster/John Knox, 1992), 57–86.

18. References to pollution: 14:1–5; filth or dirt: 22:11; "abomination" (*bdelygma = delyssō*, meaning "rot" or "stink"; 21:8, 27); see also 7:14; 16:13; 17:4; 18:2; 19:2.

One can also discern the obsession by noting the many references to fire and sulphur, i.e. "purifying" substances.

19. See Dale B. Martin, *The Corinthian Body* (New Haven and London: Yale University Press, 1995); and "Paul Without Passion" in Dale B. Martin, *Sex and the Single Savior: Gender and Sexuality in Biblical Interpretation* (Louisville, KY: Westminster John Knox Press, 2006), 65–76.

20. I have elsewhere shown that modern attempts to read Paul as a "gender egalitarian" do not stand up to scrutiny, though such claims do continue to be made, presumably by those wishing to "save" Paul from his fairly obvious, and natural for his time, hierarchical view of gender. See, e.g., Martin, *The Corinthian Body*, 230–233; and the essay "The Queer History of Galatians 3:28: No Male and Female" in Martin, *Sex and the Single Savior*, 77–90. Contrast James D. G. Dunn, "The Household Rules in the New Testament," in *The Family in Theological Perspective*, ed. Stephen C. Barton, 43–63 (Edinburgh: T. and T. Clark, 1996), 55.

21. See R. P. Reardon, *Collected Ancient Greek Novels* (Berkeley: University of California Press, 1989); Judith Perkins, *The Suffering Self: Pain and Representation in the Early Christian Era* (London and New York: Routledge, 1995), 44–76.

22. See Andrew S. Jacobs, "A Family Affair: Marriage, Class, and Ethics in the Apocryphal Acts of the Apostles," *Journal of Early Christian Studies* 7 (1999): 105–138.

23. J. N. D. Kelly, *Jerome: His Life, Writings, and Controversies* (New York: Harper and Row, 1975), 102.

24. David Hunter provides a collection of early church writings on marriage: David G. Hunter, ed., *Marriage in the Early Church* (Minneapolis: Fortress, 1992). It is telling that though Hunter clearly attempted to balance out the "negative" views with the few available "positive" views of marriage, the book is rather thin. There just aren't enough "positive" views in early Christianity to balance out the "negative" ones.

25. For brief introductions to the controversy, see Kelly, *Jerome*, 181–182; Peter Brown, *The Body and Society: Men, Women and Sexual Renunciation in Early Christianity* (London: Faber and Faber, 1989), 359–362. For the original texts: Wilhelm Haller, ed., *Iovinianus: Die Fragmente seiner Schriften, die Quellen zu seiner Geschichte, sein Leben und seine Lehre* (Leipzig: J. C. Hinrich, 1897). The best and most up-to-date research on the Jovinian controversy is contained in articles by David G. Hunter; see esp. "Resistance to the Virginal Ideal in Late-Fourth-Century Rome: The Case of Jovinian," *Theological Studies* 48 (1987): 45–64; "Helvidius, Jovinian, and the Virginity of Mary in Late Fourth-Century Rome," *Journal for Early Christian Studies* 1 (1993): 47–71; and "Rereading the Jovinianist Controversy: Asceticism and Clerical Authority in Late Ancient Christianity," *Journal of Medieval and Early Modern Studies* 33 (2003): 453–470; reprinted in *The Cultural Turn in Late Ancient Studies: Gender, Asceticism, and Historiography*, Dale B. Martin and Patricia Cox Miller, eds. (Durham: Duke University Press, 2005). John Gavin Nolan's earlier study (see *Jerome and Jovinian* [Washington: The Catholic University of America Press, 1956], an abstract of his Catholic University dissertation) is too biased towards Jerome and against Jovinian to be reliable. Nolan often takes Jerome's obvious exaggeration and misrepresentation at face value—with regard, for instance, to Jovinian's alleged lack of education.

26. These translations are from Hunter, "Rereading the Jovinianist Controversy," 453; for the Latin, see Siricius, *Epistolae* 7.4–6 (Corpus Scriptorum Ecclesiasticorum Latinorum 82/3:301).

27. Hunter, "Rereading the Jovinianist Controversy," 453.

28. Hunter, "Resistance to the Virginal Ideal."

29. Jerome, *Against Jovinian*, 1.7; 2.35; and 1.33, respectively.

30. *Against Jovinian* 1.40; trans. W. H. Fremantle, with G. Lewis and W. G. Martley, *The Principal Works of St. Jerome*, Nicene and Post-Nicene Fathers, 2d ser. (Grand Rapids: Eerdmans, 1979), vol. 6.

31. See, e.g., *The Good of Marriage* 6. For the English of this as well as other excerpts from Augustine's relevant writings, and including an excellent introduction, see Elizabeth A. Clark, *St. Augustine on Marriage and Sexuality* (Washington, D. C.: The Catholic University of America Press, 1996). See also Elizabeth A. Clark, "'Adam's Only Companion': Augustine and the Early Christian Debate on Marriage," *Recherches Augustiniennes* 21 (1986): 139–162; Philip Lyndon Reynolds, *Marriage in the Western Church: The Christianization of Marriage During the Patristic and Early Medieval Periods* (Leiden: Brill, 1994), 259.

32. Augustine, *The Good of Marriage* ch. 9; trans. Clark, *St. Augustine on Marriage and Sexuality*, p. 51.

33. Edmund Leites, *The Puritan Conscience and Modern Sexuality* (New Haven and London: Yale University Press, 1986), 80–83.

34. Lawrence Stone, *The Family, Sex and Marriage in England 1500–1800* (London: Weidenfeld and Nicolson, 1977), 135.

35. Christopher Hill, *Society and Puritanism in Pre-Revolutionary England* (New York: Schocken Books, 1964), 453.

36. Anthony J. Guerra, *Family Matters*, 30.

37. Stone, *Family*, 136.

38. See Stone, *Family*, 141.

39. William Perkins, *Works* (Cambridge: Cantrell Legge, 1618), 3.671. Perkins goes on to say that had the Fall not occurred, the single life should have no place in the world at all, but because of the exigencies of existence after the Fall, *some* people, no doubt only a few, may do better to remain single *if* they "have the gift of continence."

40. Edmund S. Morgan, "The Puritans and Sex," in *The American Family in Social-Historical Perspective*, 2d ed., Michael Gordon, ed., 363–373 (New York: St. Martin's, 1978), see esp. 364, 371.

41. Thomas Taylor, *Works* (London: Printed by T.R. & E.M. for J. Bartlet the elder and J. Bartlet the younger, 1653), 190.

42. William Gouge, *Of Domesticall Duties: Eight Treatises* (London: John Haviland, 1622), 18.

43. Levin L. Schücking, *The Puritan Family: A Social Study from the Literary Sources*, 2d ed. (New York: Schocken Books, 1969), 65–66.

44. Edmund S. Morgan, *The Puritan Family: Essays on Religion and Domestic Relations in Seventeenth-Century New England* (Boston: Boston Public Library, 1944), 85.

45. Morgan, *Puritan Family*, 86–89; Guerra, *Family Matters*, 43.

46. Morgan, *Puritan Family*, 9–14; Schücking, *Puritan Family*, 67; Hill, *Society and Puritanism*, 458–462.

47. For other Christian ethical critiques of the Puritan family model, see Lisa Sowle Cahill, *Family: A Christian Social Perspective* (Minneapolis: Fortress, 2000), 51.

48. Much of my point here is dependent on Michael Warner, *The Trouble With Normal: Sex, Politics, and the Ethics of Queer Life* (New York: Free Press, 1999).

49. The focus on the family is ultimately *antisocial*. It is politically quietistic, opposed to social reform, and "tolerant of economic injustice." The "private family" is therefore socially *irresponsible*. See Coontz, *The Way We Never Were*, 97–98. Or as Jessie Bernard has put it, "Marriage is a cheap way for society at large to take care of a lot of difficult people. We force individuals—a wife or a husband—to take care of them on a one-to-one basis" (*The Future of Marriage* [New Haven: Yale University Press, 1982], 161); quoted and affirmed by Brian W. Grant, *The Social Structure of Christian Families: A Historical Perspective* (St. Louis: Chalice, 2000), 147.

50. Even an author intent on affirming the normativity of marriage for Christians (though she does suggest that it should be now balanced with "a favourable account of celibacy") admits that "the 'Christian family' makes plenty of people feel excluded, not strengthened" (Helen Oppenheimer, *Marriage* [London: Mowbray, 1990], 87, 110).

Acknowledgments

These pages constitute a continuation of the copyright page. Grateful acknowledgment is made to the following for permission to quote from copyrighted material:

Chapter 1. Carter Heyward, "Notes on Historical Grounding: Beyond Sexual Essentialism," in *Touching Our Strength: The Erotic as Power and the Love of God* (San Francisco: Harper & Row, 1989). Copyright © 1989 by Carter Heyward. Used by permission of the author.

Chapter 2. Judith Plaskow, "Setting the Problem, Laying the Ground," from *Standing Again at Sinai: Judaism from a Feminist Perspective*, by Judith Plaskow, 1–24. Copyright © 1990 by Judith Plaskow. Reprinted by permission of HarperCollins Publishers.

Chapter 3. Christian Scharen, "Experiencing the Body: Sexuality and Conflict in American Lutheranism," *Union Seminary Quarterly Review* 57:1–2 (2003): 94–109." Used by permission of the Union Seminary Quarterly Review.

Chapter 5. "Uses of the Erotic: The Erotic as Power," © the Estate of Audre Lorde, excerpted from *Sister Outsider*, by Audre Lorde, published by the Crossing Press (1984) and reprinted herewith by permission of the Charlotte Sheedy Literary Agency, Inc.

Chapter 6. Katie G. Cannon, "Sexing Black Women: Liberation from the Prisonhouse of Anatomical Authority," in *Loving the Body*, ed. Anthony B. Pinn and Dwight N. Hopkins, published 2007 by Palgrave Macmillan. Reproduced with permission of Palgrave Macmillan.

Chapter 7. James B. Nelson. "Where Are We? Seven Sinful Problems and Seven Virtuous Possibilities," in *Body Theology* (Louisville, KY: Westminster John Knox Press, 1992), 29–40. Reprinted with permission of Westminster John Knox Press.

Chapter 9. Kwok Pui-Lan, "Touching the Taboo: On the Sexuality of Jesus." Copyright © Kwok Pui-Lan, 2009. Used by permission of the author.

Chapter 10. Christine E. Gudorf, "The Erosion of Sexual Dimorphism: Challenges to Religion and Religious Ethics," *Journal of the American Academy of Religion* 69, no. 4 (December 2001): 863–91. Reprinted by permission of Oxford University Press.

Chapter 11. Beverly Wildung Harrison and Carter Heyward, "Pain and Pleasure: Avoiding the Confusions of Christian Tradition in Feminist Theory," in *Christianity, Patriarchy, and Abuse: A Feminist Critique,* ed. Joanne Carlson Brown and Carole R. Bohn (New York: The Pilgrim Press, 1989), 148–73. Reprinted with permission of The Pilgrim Press.

Chapter 12. Mary E. Hunt, "Lovingly Lesbian: Toward a Feminist Theology of Friendship," in *A Challenge to Love: Gay and Lesbian Catholics in the Church,* ed. Robert Nugent (New York: Crossroad, 1983), 135–55. Reprinted by permission of the author.

Chapter 13. Laurel Schneider, "What If It Is a Choice? Some Implications of the Homosexuality Debates for Theology," *Chicago Theological Seminary Register* 91, no. 3 (2001): 23–32. Used by permission of the Chicago Theological Seminary Register.

Chapter 14. Dwight N. Hopkins, "The Construction of the Black Male Body: Eroticism and Religion, " in Anthony B. Pinn and Dwight N. Hopkins, *Loving the Body,* published 2007 by Palgrave Macmillan. Reproduced with permission of Palgrave Macmillan.

Chapter 15. Miguel A. De La Torre, "Beyond Machismo," *Journal of the Society of Christian Ethics* 19 (St. Cloud, MN: Georgetown University Press, 1999): 213–33. Reprinted with permission of the *Journal of the Society of Christian Ethics.*

Chapter 16. Marvin M. Ellison, "Reimagining Good Sex: The Eroticizing of Mutual Respect and Pleasure," in *Erotic Justice: A Liberating Ethic of Sexuality* (Louisville, KY: Westminster John Knox Press, 1996), 76–93. Reprinted with permission of Westminster John Knox Press.

Chapter 17. Yoel H. Kahn, "Making Love as Making Justice: Towards a New Jewish Ethic of Sexuality," in *Gay Affirmative Ethics,* ed. L. Stemmler and J. Michael Clark (Las Colinas, TX: Monument Press, 1993). Used by permission of the author.

Chapter 18. Karen Lebacqz, "Appropriate Vulnerability: A Sexual Ethic for Singles." Copyright © 1987 by the *Christian Century.* Reprinted by permission from the May 6, 1987, issue of the *Christian Century.*

Chapter 19. Beverly Wildung Harrison, "Sexuality and Social Policy," in *Making the Connections,* by Beverly Wildung Harrison. Copyright © 1985 by Beverly Wildung Harrison and Carol S. Robb. Reprinted by permission of Beacon Press.

Chapter 20. Rebecca T. Alpert, "Guilty Pleasures: When Sex Is Good Because It's Bad," in *Good Sex: Feminist Perspectives from the World's Religions.*

Copyright © 2001 by Rutgers, the State University. Reprinted by permission of Rutgers University Press.

Chapter 21. W. Scott Haldeman, "A Queer Fidelity: Reinventing Christian Marriage," *Journal of Theology and Sexuality* 13, no. 2 (2007): 137–52. Copyright © Equinox Publishing Ltd., 2007. Used by permission of Equinox Publishing Ltd.

Chapter 22. Elizabeth Stuart, "Disruptive Bodies: Disability, Embodiment, and Sexuality," in *The Good News of the Body: Sexual Theology and Feminism*, ed. Lisa Isherwood (New York: New York University Press, 2000), 166–84. Used by permission of the author.

Chapter 23. Grace Jantzen, "AIDS, Shame, and Suffering," in *Embracing the Chaos*, ed. James Woodward (London: SPCK, 1991), 22–31. Reprinted by permission of SPCK.

Chapter 24. Ken Stone, "Safer Text: Reading Biblical Laments in the Age of AIDS," *Theology and Sexuality* 10 (March 1999): 16–27. Copyright © Equinox Publishing Ltd., 1999. Used by permission of Equinox Publishing Ltd.

Chapter 25. Frances Kissling, "Is There Life after *Roe*? How to Think about the Fetus," *Conscience* (Winter 2004–05). Reprinted with permission of Catholics for Choice.

Chapter 26. Kelly Brown Douglas, "Contested Marriage/Loving Relationality," *Liturgy* 20, no. 3 (2005): 51–59. Copyright © 2005 The Liturgical Conference, Inc. All rights reserved. Used by permission.

Chapter 28. Marvin M. Ellison, "Marriage in a New Key," in *Defending Same-Sex Marriage: Our Family Values; Same-Sex Marriage and Religion*, vol. 2, ed. Traci C. West (Westport, CT: Praeger Perspectives, 2007), 163–76. Copyright © 2007 by Traci C. West. Reproduced with permission of ABC-CLIO, LLC.

Chapter 29. Dale B. Martin, "Familiar Idolatry and the Christian Case against Marriage," in *Authorizing Marriage?* ed. Mark D. Jordan (Princeton: Princeton University Press, 2006). Reprinted by permission of Princeton University Press.